Artificial Crime Analysis Systems:
Using Computer Simulations and Geographic Information Systems

Lin Liu
University of Cincinnati, USA

John Eck
University of Cincinnati, USA

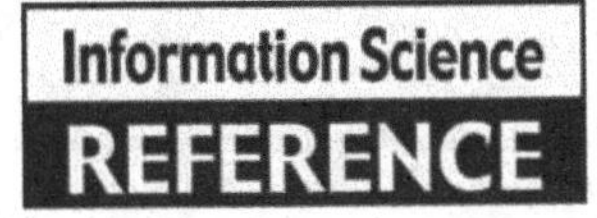

INFORMATION SCIENCE REFERENCE
Hershey · New York

Acquisitions Editor:	Kristin Klinger
Development Editor:	Kristin Roth
Assistant Development Editor:	Meg Stocking
Editiorial Assistant:	Jessica Thompson
Senior Managing Editor:	Jennifer Neidig
Managing Editor:	Sara Reed
Copy Editor:	Erin Meyer
Typesetter:	Jamie Snavely
Cover Design:	Lisa Tosheff
Printed at:	Yurchak Printing Inc.

Published in the United States of America by
Information Science Reference (an imprint of IGI Global)
701 E. Chocolate Avenue, Suite 200
Hershey PA 17033
Tel: 717-533-8845
Fax: 717-533-8661
E-mail: cust@igi-global.com
Web site: http://www.igi-global.com

and in the United Kingdom by
Information Science Reference (an imprint of IGI Global)
3 Henrietta Street
Covent Garden
London WC2E 8LU
Tel: 44 20 7240 0856
Fax: 44 20 7379 0609
Web site: http://www.eurospanonline.com

Library of Congress Cataloging-in-Publication Data

Artificial crime analysis systems : using computer simulations and geographic information systems / Lin Liu & John Eck, editors.

p. cm.

Summary: "This book discusses leading research on the use of computer simulation of crime patterns to reveal hidden processes of urban crimes, taking an interdisciplinary approach by combining criminology, computer simulation, and geographic information systems into one comprehensive resource"--Provided by publisher.

Includes bibliographical references and index.

ISBN-13: 978-1-59904-591-7 (hardcover)

ISBN-13: 978-1-59904-593-1 (ebook)

1. Crime analysis--Data processing. 2. Criminology--Computer network resources. 3. Digital mapping. 4. Information storage and retrieval systems--Law enforcement. 5. Geographic information systems. I. Liu, Lin. II. Eck, John.

HV7936.C88A77 2008

364.0285--dc22

2007024488

British Cataloguing in Publication Data
A Cataloguing in Publication record for this book is available from the British Library.

Table of Contents

Section IV
Criminal Justice Operation Simulations

Section V
Conclusion

Detailed Table of Contents

This chapter outlines how simulation methods might be used to make valid causal inferences in the social sciences, specifically the study of crime. We argue that significant threats to validity exist for simulation studies and that, if researchers do not actively take measures to minimize these, much of the promise of simulation will not come to pass. Further, we nominate replication as a general method to facilitate the generation of valid findings. It is anticipated, with the burgeoning interest in simulation methods in criminology, that simulation studies will be published in sufficient detail that allows researcher scrutiny and replication, with a view to developing a cumulative body of scientific knowledge.

This chapter considers whether it is worthwhile and useful to enrich agent based spatial simulation studies in criminology with a real geographical background, such as the map of a real city? Using modern GIS tools, such an enterprise is in principle quite feasible, but we argue that in many cases this course is not only not producing more interesting results, but in fact may well be detrimental for the real reason of doing criminal simulation studies, which is understanding the underlying rules. The argument is first outlined in general, and then illustrated in the context of a given example of the ThESE perceptual deterrence simulation model (Van Baal, 2004), a model that actually is using a simple checkerboard as its spatial backcloth.

Crime is a multidimensional complex and dynamic activity. In order to understand its nature one has to comprehend not only its spatio-temporal dimensions but also the nature of crime, the victim-offender relationship, and role of guardians and history of similar previous incidents. This is a formidable task due to the limitations of present visualization methods. Both for the police department and criminal justice researcher the need to visualize a vast amount of data is a pre-requisite to the task of dealing with the crime phenomenon. This chapter presents an interactive visualization intended to present the viewer with an accurate and intuitive view of the criminal activity in a cityscape. The technique employs many different visualization elements, which taken together presents a useful methodology that can be used to visualize many of the associated factors of crime. The chapter also presents the software technique and discusses points for future investigation.

This chapter introduces the use of geographic information systems simulations and visualizations in urban landuse changes as a means of studying spatial pattern of crime incidents. Through literature reviews the chapter provides a survey of different simulation tools and techniques that have been used in landuse planning. It also provides an overview of the models available for examining landuse changes in the context of planning processes. It argues that three-dimensional simulations of urban landuse change scenarios encourage public participation in the decision making process. The author hopes that the chapter would be useful for criminologists unfamiliar with landuse scenario simulation models and techniques. Furthermore, the chapter suggests how the crime analysts could utilize the available landuse simulation models and tools in analyzing existing crime patterns or predicting future patterns in an urban setting.

This chapter presents results for the first large-scale analysis of street crime rates that utilizes accurate on-street pedestrian population estimates. Pedestrian counts were generated at the street segment level for an area in central London (UK) using a modeling process that utilized key indicators of pedestrian movement and sample observations. Geocoded street crime positioned on street segments then allowed for street crime rates to be calculated for the entire central London study area's street network. These street crime rate measures were then compared against street crime volume patterns (e.g., hotspot maps of street crime density) and street crime rate statistics and maps that were generated from using the residential population as the denominator. The research demonstrates the utility of pedestrian modeling for generating better and more realistic measures for street crime rates, suggesting that if the residential population is used as a denominator for local level street crime analysis it may only misinform and mislead the interpretation and understanding of on-street crime risk to pedestrians. The research also highlights the importance of crime rate analysis for understanding and explaining crime patterns, and suggests that with accurate analysis of crime rates, policing, and crime prevention initiatives can be improved.

This chapter summarizes fundamental models for microscopic simulation (such as vehicle generation model and car-following model) and other critical models (such as lane-choice model, lane-changing model, and route-choice model). Most of the critical models introduced in this chapter reflect the latest research results by the author. The primary purpose of this chapter is to provide fundamentals for better understanding of the travel behaviors that are modeled for traffic simulations. To facilitate the applications of traffic simulation models, several key elements for applying state-of-the-art computer traffic simulation tools are summarized. They include the procedure for building models, model calibration and validation. Further more, techniques for collecting vehicle trajectory data, critical elements used for model calibration and validation, are also introduced.

This chapter introduces the concepts of cellular automata (CA) which have been increasingly used for simulating urban dynamics. Simulation and prediction of urban evolution can provide the useful inputs to crime models. However, calibration of urban cellular automata is crucial for simulating realistic cities. Simulation of multiple land use changes using CA is difficult because numerous spatial variables and parameters have to be utilized. The incorporation of neural networks with CA can alleviate the calibration problems. This chapter illustrates how complex land use dynamics can be simulated by the integration of CA and neural networks.

This study proposes methods for space-time diffusion measures and a simulation on crime analyses. A spatial pattern of crimes is a constantly changing and ongoing process. However, prior research on spatial crime analysis has focused primarily on identifying fixed spatial patterns, and has neglected temporal aspects. As a result, the literature has difficulty in explaining the formation and development of such spatial crime patterns. This study investigates both spatial and temporal aspects of crime occurrences, particularly on the space-time diffusion process by using the temporal extensions of local spatial autocorrelation measures. In addition, space-time diffusion simulation is applied based on Hagerstrand's diffusion

offender agents, target agents and crime places for crime pattern simulation purposes. This is a theory-driven system, in which the processes that generate crime events are explicitly modeled. The simulated crime patterns are shown to have similar properties as seen in reported crime patterns.

It is widely recognized that the spatio-temporal components of human behavior strongly influence where and when people converge in space and time. Routine activity theory (Cohen, & Felson 1979) ties the frequency of convergence to crime rates. This chapter builds on an earlier agent-based model (Groff, in press-a) by drawing on geographic theory to develop two additional versions of the model in which the agents have more fully developed activity schedules. A series of experiments are conducted which compare the spatial pattern of street robbery events from the original version of the model to the two new versions and to the empirical distribution of street robberies in Seattle, WA. The findings indicate temporally and spatially defined activity spaces have a significant impact on the spatial pattern of crime events produced by the model. The version with spatio-temporal activity spaces produces patterns most like the empirical distribution of street robberies.

Pattern and Routine Activities theories suggest that through a combination of decisions and innate understandings of environmental cues, likely offenders are able to separate good criminal opportunities from bad risks. The nature of this process is highly structured and allows researchers to anticipate likely concentrations for a variety of regular, daily activities, including criminal offences. This chapter sets out to model and test these theoretical principles. Mastermind represents an interdisciplinary research project in Computational Criminology jointly managed by ICURS and the Software Technology Lab at Simon Fraser University. Using abstract state machines (ASM) formalism in combination with a multi-agent based modeling paradigm, we devise a formal framework for semantic modeling and systematic integration of the theories for crime analysis and understanding crime patterns. We focus on crime in urban areas and model spatial and temporal aspects of crime potentially involving multiple offenders and multiple targets Mastermind is used in a hypothetical analysis of motor vehicle theft.

This chapter presents an innovative approach to the study of the journey to residential burglary. We demonstrate a simulation model that is built upon the integration of cellular automaton (CA) and multi-agent system (MAS). The model utilizes both social disorganization (SD) and routine activity (RA) theories to predict locations of residential burglary targets. The model simulates an offender as an intelligent agent of MAS that interacts with the target and place automata of CA. The likelihood of a residential burglary is modeled as a function of offender's motivation, target desirability and place guardianship, which in turn are determined by the offender's individual characteristics often used by RA and the target and place's neighborhood properties frequently utilized in SD. The model was initialized and parameterized using "real" crime data from Dallas, Texas Police Department. Results under two different weighting scenarios was obtained and compared with the actual distribution of offense locations, revealing the flexibility of model in its capability to assessing the influence of the two theories in burglary crime simulation. In closing we propose possible modifications that could be made to the model in the future.

Experience in the domain of criminology has shown that the spatial distribution of some types of crimes in urban centers follows Zipf's Law in which most of the crime events are concentrated in a few places while other places have few crimes. Moreover, the temporal distribution of these crime events follows an exponential law. In order to reproduce and better understand the nuances of such crime distribution profile, we introduce in this chapter a novel multi-agent-based crime simulation model that is directly inspired by the swarm intelligence paradigm. In this model, criminals are regarded as agents endowed with the capability to pursue self-organizing behavior by considering their individual (local) activities as well as the influence of other criminals pertaining to their social networks. Through controlled experiments with the simulation model, we could indeed observe that self-organization phenomena (i.e., criminal behavior toward crime) emerge as the result of both individual and social learning factors. As expected, our experiments reveal that the spatial distribution of crime occurrences achieved with the simulation model provides a good approximation of the real-crime data distribution. A detailed analysis of the social aspect is also conducted here as this factor is shown to be instrumental for the accurate reproduction of the spatial pattern of crime occurrences.

This chapter shows that white-collar crime can be approached using an agent-based model. Fraud in public delivery programs often involves several entities that are loosely interrelated and interact dynamically. However, the crime literature has not paid sufficient attention to these characteristics, thus providing limited utility for public managers. This chapter frames a public delivery program as a complex system. The patterns of fraud in such a system are simulated using an agent-based model called FraudSim. We demonstrate that FraudSim closely replicates the statistical and spatial patterns of fraud and provides a framework for future work in this area.

Section IV
Criminal Justice Operation Simulations

Patrolling in a nonrandom, but focused manner is an important activity in law enforcement. The use of geographic information systems, the emerging real-time data sets (spatial and non-spatial) and the ability via global positioning systems to identify locations of patrol units provide the environment to discuss the concept and requirements of an intelligent patrol routing system. This intelligent patrol routing system will combine available data utilizing map algebra and a data structure known as a Voronoi diagram to create a real-time updatable raster surface over the patrolling area to identify destination locations and routes for all patrol units. This information system will allow all patrol units to function "in concert" under a coordinated plan, and make good use of limited patrolling resources, and provide the means of evaluating current patrol strategies. This chapter discusses the algorithmic foundations, implications, requirements, and simulation of a GIS based Intelligent Patrol Routing System.

This chapter describes an agent-based model called SimDrugPolicing that explores the relative impact of three law enforcement strategies—standard patrol, hotspot policing and problem-oriented policing—on an archetypal street-based illicit drug market. Using data from Melbourne (Australia), we simulate the relative effectiveness of these different drug law enforcement approaches. We examine the complex interactions between users, dealers, wholesalers, outreach workers and police to examine the relative effectiveness of the three drug law enforcement strategies, analyzing several outcome indicators such as the number of committed crimes, dealers' and users' cash, overdoses, and fatal overdoses. Our results show that problem-oriented policing is the most effective approach to disrupting street level drug markets in a simulated urban environment.

Criminal justice systems are complex. They are composed of several major subsystems, including the police, courts and corrections, which are in turn composed of many minor sub-systems. Predicting the response of a criminal justice system to change is often difficult. Mathematical modeling and computer simulation can serve as powerful tools for understanding and anticipating the behavior of a criminal justice system when something does change. The focus of this chapter is on three different approaches

Preface
An Overview of Crime Simulation

Lin Liu
University of Cincinnati, USA

John Eck
University of Cincinnati, USA

Artificial crime analysis and crime simulation is an emerging research area that has the potential of revealing hidden processes behind urban crime patterns and criminal justice system operations. This book takes an interdisciplinary approach, combining criminology, computer simulation, and geographic information systems to examine how crime patterns form and what can be done to prevent crime.

In the last decade there has been a phenomenal growth in interest in crime pattern analysis. Geographic information systems (GIS) are now widely used in urban police agencies throughout industrial nations. With this, scholarly interest in understanding crime patterns has grown considerably. The central problem of empirical crime analysis, both applied and academic, is that many of the underlying processes that give rise to crime patterns are not visible, and so are not well understood. To address this problem, a number of crime researchers have drawn from the experience of other disciplines to create virtual cityscapes to model artificial crime patterns within a computing environment. This new and exciting area has no guiding text or repository of experience. This book seeks to fill this need, and thus accelerate the rapid growth in this area.

BACKGROUND

Artificial crime analysis and crime simulation is an up-and-coming research area that was started about six years ago by a relatively small group of environmental criminologists and geographers. It aims to study mechanisms that generate individual crime events and give rise to crime patterns by operationalizing criminology theories in a GIS-based computing environment. This new interdisciplinary research field typically involves criminology (especially environmental criminology), geography (especially GIS), and computer science (especially agent-based modeling and simulation).

The collaboration between the Department of Geography and the Criminal Justice Division at the University of Cincinnati represents one of the leading efforts in initiating the research in this area. Liang (2001) constructed the first crime pattern simulation for his dissertation, supervised by Liu and Eck, and publicly presented his analysis at the UCGIS Summer Assembly in 2001 (Liang, Liu, & Eck, 2001).

His simulation implements aspects of routine activity theory with two types of agents: store robbers and store managers. Managers are immobile, but update their protection based on tension of robberies transmitted using cellular automata. Robbers move randomly around a street grid representing a small area of Cincinnati and decide to rob a store based on a comparison of their capabilities with the store's protection level. The resulting pattern of robberies looks surprisingly similar to the actual pattern of robberies in the same geographic area (Liu, et al., 2005).

Following this simulation Wang (2005) developed a simulation of street robberies, also under Liu and Eck's supervision. In Wang's simulation both the targets of crimes (pedestrians) and the offenders are mobile. Pedestrian agents assess the costs of distance and crime risk in choosing their routes. Offender agents choose their routes by assessing the availability of pedestrians. Routine activity theory, crime pattern theory, and rational choice perspectives inform the construction of this simulation. Agent based modeling is used to orchestrate agent mobility and cellular automata to communicate crime risk. The latest work is presented in a chapter by Wang, Liu, and Eck in this volume.

Another leading effort in developing artificial crime analysis is centered at Simon Fraser University, where collaborations between Patricia Brantingham and Paul Brantingham's group at the School of Criminology and Uwe Glässer's group at the School of Computer Science have produced very useful simulations of crime patterns (Brantingham, & Brantingham, 2004; Brantingham, Glässer, et al., 2005). Their latest works are presented in two chapters in this volume.

The objectives of these efforts are to simulate the micro-level decision processes that give rise to patterns of crime. In artificial crime analysis, researchers model criminological theories of micro-level behavior in computer environments to determine if these theories can produce patterns that mimic observable macro-level patterns in the real world. Specifically, researchers want to determine whether the actions of individual agents (i.e., offenders, targets, handlers, guardians, managers, and others) are sufficient to give rise to the crime patterns we detect in empirical investigations. The theoretical bases of many crime simulation models are routine activity, rational choice, and crime pattern theories.

Offenders and targets are modeled as individual agents. These agents are intelligent and adaptable in their behavior and spatial movement; they make decisions based on forms of bounded rationality. They learn from past offending and victimization experience, and adjust their future behavior accordingly. For example, target agents move along street as part of their routine activities. The exact travel path they take is influenced by network proximity and crime risk. As new crime events change the spatial distribution of risk, target agents adjust their path using a heuristic reinforcement learning algorithm. At the same time, offenders seek opportunities and adjust their spatial movement based on the reward/penalty of their past experience.

The prototype systems developed in these early efforts have been used as virtual laboratories to uncover the interplay of multiple criminology theories. Analysis of simulated data reveals plausible crime patterns and helps generate hypotheses. It is widely accepted that the distributions of criminal behavior among offenders are highly skewed—a few offenders commit most of the crimes. Research has also shown that a relatively few victims are involved in a far larger proportion of crimes, and that a few places where crimes take place are responsible for a very large proportion of all crimes. In fact, most crime related data appears to follow a power-law distribution. The prototype systems are able to replicate these power-law distributions, and to simulate spatial crime patterns that resemble those observed in empirical studies.

The models are also used to examine possible future crime patterns based on different policing and crime prevention strategies. They have the potential of providing insight for testing applied theories of crime prevention, teaching students and practitioners, carrying out what-if analysis of proposed prevention programs prior to implementation, and assisting in the evaluation of implemented crime prevention measures.

Despite these initial successes with crime pattern simulations, there are still many challenges ahead. Due to the non-linear nature of crime simulation models and the large number of parameters, calibration of the model is extremely difficult. Although the models can be adjusted to match simulated patterns to real crime patterns that may advance understanding of how to calibrate and validate simulation of complex spatial systems, the calibration method is far from satisfactory. Part of the problem is that simulated crimes with no measurement error are compared to police records of actual crimes that contain massive amounts of measurement error. One challenge is to model the measurement error process in the simulation such that two forms of patterns can be produced: patterns based on error free artificial crimes, and patterns on artificial crimes measured with substantial error.

So far, the models are mostly theory driven and need verification. The simulation models can be productively expanded in a number of ways: incorporating police and other agents; improving the detail of street configurations and the built environment; incorporating accurate information on the number, value, and spatial distribution of crime targets; and modifying the basic simulation to address a wider variety of violent and non-violent crimes. To accomplish these challenging goals, there is a need to draw experience and knowledge from simulation studies in other disciplines such as GIS, computer science, engineering, and transportation.

To help meet these challenges, this book has attracted contributions from criminologists, geographers, computer scientists, urban planners, transportation planners and engineers. The authors of these chapters confront a wide variety of issues concerning artificial crime analysis: validation and calibration, crime specificity, the types of background (substrates) upon which the agents act, and a host of other topics. When we first envisioned this volume, we expected to receive a few manuscripts. We were pleasantly surprised by the number and diversity of the submissions. This speaks to the rapid growth and high interest in artificial crime analysis. It is our hope that this book stimulates more interdisciplinary collaborations and accelerates interest in artificial crime analysis and crime simulation.

THE STRUCTURE OF THIS BOOK

We have divided the chapters in this book into five parts based on their topics and themes. Though this division is helpful, most chapters speak to themes in more than one part. Section I focuses on general principles, methods, and controversies; Section II examines the simulation of the background environment and explanatory variables, such as streets networks, target distributions, and spatial-temporal autocorrelation; Section III, the largest part of the book, consists of eight chapters presenting state-of-the-art simulations of crime events and crime patterns; Section IV showcases recent developments in the simulation of criminal justice agencies and systems; The final section consists of a single chapter summarizing the current state of crime simulation research—both internally and in comparison to more traditional forms of criminological research—and providing theoretical frameworks for future research. The following sections describe each of these parts in detail.

Section I – The Role of Simulation in Crime Research. The four chapters in Section I address critical topics in using simulation to understand crime patterns and criminal justice processes.

In Chapter I, *The Need for Systematic Replication and Tests of Validity in Simulation*, Michael Townsley and Shane Johnson examine the potential role simulation methods in making valid causal inferences in the study of crime. They contend that only validated models can be used to make such inferences. They discuss a variety of issues related to the validity of simulation models and conclude that replication is a general method to validate simulation models and facilitate the generation of valid findings. Validation is a topic picked up by a number of the authors of other chapters.

Henk Elffers and Pieter Van Baal, in Chapter II, *Spatial Backcloth Is Not That Important in Agent Based Simulation Research: an Illustration from Simulating Perceptual Deterrence*, take on a controversial topic—the level of detail needed in the geographic environment in order to generate useful results. They claim that the use of real geographic backgrounds in simulations is not only unnecessary but is detrimental to the understanding of underlying processes that generate crimes. The conceptual discussions are followed by an illustration of a perceptual deterrence simulation. As can be seen in the chapters that follow, there is no general agreement on this important issue. Some authors share the view of Elffers and Van Baal, but others seem to disagree. This critical and controversial issue is examined in detail in the concluding chapter.

In Chapter III, *Visualization of Criminal Activity in an Urban Population*, Alex Breuer, Joshua J. Hursey, Tonya Stroman, and Arvind Verma present an interactive visualization that provides an accurate and intuitive view of the criminal activity in a cityscape. Their approach is based on a set of linked displays, each representing a particular aspect of urban crime. The implementation of their visualization system is coupled with ArcGIS, one of the most widely used GIS software packages.

Md Mahbubur R. Meenar provides a survey of simulation and visualization for landuse planning in Chapter IV, *GIS-Based Simulation and Visualization of Urban Landuse Change*. Meenar argues that urban landuse is a vital backcloth for the study of crime, therefore crime simulation should benefit from many of the techniques used in studying landuse change.

Section II – Streets, Networks, and Crime Distribution. The second section of this book focuses on conditions that might influence crime patterns. In particular, its chapters look at ways simulation can be used to model target distribution, methods for simulating traffic flow, the influence of urban landuse changes on crime, and how one might model spatio-temporal autocorrelation.

In Chapter V, *Modeling Pedestrian Movement to Measure On-Street Crime Risk*, Spencer Chainey and Jake Desyllas study street crime rates based on accurate on-street pedestrian population estimates. Street segment level pedestrian counts are modeled from key indicators of pedestrian movement and sample observations. The result of their analysis suggests that the crime rates derived from their approach are more accurate than the ones using residential population as the denominator.

Just as street robberies are closely associated with pedestrian flows, vehicle related crimes are influenced by street level traffic flows. Heng Wei presents a comprehensive review of micro-level traffic simulations in Chapter VI, *Core Models for State-of-the-Art Microscopic Traffic Simulation and Key Elements for Applications*. This chapter summarizes microscopic simulation models such as vehicle generation and car-following models, as well as other important models such as lane-choice, lane-changing, and route-choice models. Wei also examines model calibration and validation, two of the most critical issues in traffic simulation.

Urban dynamics can influence crime. In Chapter VII, *Simulating Urban Dynamics Using Cellular Automata*, Xia Li applies cellular automata (CA) to simulate urban dynamics. He argues that forecasts of urban changes provide useful inputs to crime models. One of the challenges in simulating realistic urban growth is the calibration of urban cellular automata. To overcome this difficulty, Li incorporates neural networks to CA to improve model calibration.

Chapter VIII, *Space-Time Measures of Crime Diffusion,* by Youngho Kim, introduces space-time diffusion measures for crime simulation. As the spatial pattern of crime changes in time, it important to investigate both spatial and temporal processes that lead to crime. Kim examines the spatial and temporal aspects of crime by extending local spatial autocorrelation measures to the temporal dimension.

Section III – Crime Event and Pattern Simulations. This section presents eight studies of creating crime simulations. The authors use a variety of approaches to a number of different types of crime, showing that there is no single method of artificial crime analysis and that many different crimes can be simulated.

In Chapter IX, *Synthesis over Analysis: towards an Ontology for Volume Crime Simulation*, Daniel J. Birks, Susan Donkin, and Melanie Wellsmith examine the use of agent-based modeling as a tool for criminologists. They argue that this type of models has the potential to help examine, test, validate, and refine criminological theories. By way of illustration, they present two proto-type systems—one for robbery and another for domestic burglary—using agent-based modeling.

In Chapter X, *Offender Mobility and Crime Pattern Formation from First Principles*, Jeffrey Brantingham and George Tita develop a series of elegant mathematical and agent-based models to examine the relationship between basic movement decisions of offenders and emergent crime patterns. They show that it is possible for crime patterns to arise solely from different movement strategies deployed by offenders. This chapter also nicely illustrates a major point made by Elffers and Van Baal: that much can be learned by keeping the simulation very simple.

To investigate the interaction of robbers and targets, Xuguang Wang, Lin Liu, and John Eck display a multi-agent based simulation system (named SPACES) in Chapter XI, *Crime Simulation Using GIS and Artificial Intelligent Agents*. Their approach is based on the integration of agent-based modeling and cellular automata. The targets visit a set of activity nodes as part of their routines, while offenders seek opportunities. The movement of both agents along streets is guided by a reinforcement learning mechanism. A simulated tension surface mimics the propagation of the fear of crime in space and time. The agents interact in a small neighborhood area of Cincinnati. The results suggest that SPACES is capable of generating crime patterns that are similar to those found by empirical investigation.

In Chapter XII, *Characterizing the Spatio-Temporal Aspects of Routine Activities and the Geographic Distribution of Street Robbery*, Elizabeth Groff examines how the spatial patterns of simulated street robberies vary as she experiments with different methods for operationalizing routine activities of the agents. The movement and the awareness spaces of agents are set by agents' routine activity schedules. An application of this model to the City of Seattle generates spatial patterns that are consistent to empirical crime data.

A team led by Patricia L. Brantingham presents their interdisciplinary research in Chapter XIII, *Mastermind: Computational Modeling and Simulation of Spatiotemporal Aspects of Crime in Urban Environments*. They use abstract state machines (ASM) formalism and multi-agent based modeling to devise a formal semantic modeling framework for crime simulation and analysis. Their prototype system, named Mastermind, is capable of modeling the movement of offenders in an abstracted real street network. It is demonstrated in a hypothetical analysis of motor vehicle theft.

In Chapter XIV, *The Simulation of the Journey to Residential Burglary*, Karen L. Hayslett-McCall's team simulates the journey to residential burglary. They build their simulation on two foundations: social disorganization and routine activity theories. Their simulation model integrates cellular automaton and multi-agent system. With the initialization and parameterization using real crime data from Dallas Police Department, the model is capable of generating plausible spatial patterns.

Inspired by the swarm intelligence paradigm, Vasco Furtado's team introduces a multi-agent-based crime simulation model in Chapter XV, *Simulating Crime against Properties Using Swarm Intelligence and Social Networks*. They model criminals as agents who interact in their social networks. Their behavior is influenced by both individual and social learning factors. Results from simulation experiments reveal the impact of social networking in producing plausible spatial patterns of crime.

The final chapter of Section III deals with white-collar crime. In Chapter XVI, *FraudSim: Simulating Fraud in a Public Delivery Program*, Yushim Kim and Ningchuan Xiao develop an agent-based model (named FraudSim) to simulate fraud in public delivery programs. In their model, recipients of a public delivery program exchange government issued vouchers for food at participating vendors. Both recipients and vendors are modeled as agents. Results from experiments demonstrate that FraudSim is capable of closely replicating the statistical and spatial patterns of fraud. The simulation shows how crime simulations can be expanded beyond modeling street crimes.

Table 1 compares and summarizes the eight simulations by the following characteristics. We can see that these eight chapters use a variety of approaches, but we can also see some commonalities.

- **Continuity:** Is the modeled process continuous or discrete process? Most continuous processes require the use of differential equations. Discrete processes rely on computer algorithms, instead of mathematical equations. Agent-based models are discrete.
- **Environment:** Is the model based on a real environment or an artificial environment? Can a real environment such as a street network be used as an input to the simulation?
- **Foundation:** Is the model theory driven or data driven? Theory driven models tend to be process based, while data driven models are mostly pattern based. It is possible to combine their two approaches in a single simulation.
- **Substrate:** A substrate is a network that connects agents, allows them to communicate or move, and upon which patterns form. A substrate can be spatial such as street networks, aspatial such social networks, or a combination of the two.
- **Movement:** Are agents stationary or mobile in the simulation? Agents can move randomly in space, or move with intelligence through learning and adaptation.
- **Probabilistic:** Is the simulated process deterministic or stochastic? A deterministic model generates the same results every time, while a stochastic model generates slightly different results every time due to a random process built in the model.

Table 1. The characteristics of the simulations in Section III

Chapter**	**Continuity* (continuous/ discrete)**	**Environment* (artificial/ real)**	**Foundation* (data/ theory)**	**Substrate* (spatial/ aspatial)**	**Movement* (mobile/ stationary)**	**Probabilistic* (deterministic/ stochastic)**	**Scale (micro/ macro)**
9	discrete	both	theory	spatial	mobile	stochastic	micro & macro
10	discrete	artificial	theory	spatial	mobile	stochastic	micro
11	discrete	real	theory	spatial	mobile	stochastic	micro
12	discrete	real	theory & data	spatial	mobile	stochastic	micro & macro
13	discrete	in between	theory	spatial	mobile	stochastic	micro
14	discrete	real	theory & data	spatial	mobile	stochastic	micro & macro
15	discrete	artificial	theory	mostly aspatial	mobile, but limited	stochastic	micro & macro
16	discrete	artificial	theory & data	spatial	mobile, but limited	stochastic	micro & macro

**Simulation characteristics adapted from Liu (2007).*
*** Chapter IX - Birks, Donkin, and Wellsmith; X - Brantingham and Tita; XI - Wang, Liu, and Eck; XII – Groff; XIII - Brantingham, et. al.; XIV - Hayslett-McCall, et. al.; XV - Furtadọ, et. al.; XVI - Kim and Xiao*

- **Scale:** Is crime modeled at the person and place level (micro) or at some aggregate level, such as population or neighborhood (macro). Micro level simulations rely on local knowledge, while macro level simulations make use of global knowledge.

These characteristics are addressed in more detail in Chapter XX, *Varieties of Artificial Crime Analysis: Purpose, Structure, and Evidence in Crime Simulations.*

Section IV – Criminal Justice Operation Simulations. Simulating crime patterns is only one application of artificial crime analysis. Computers can also be used to simulate how agencies and systems of agencies behave. There is a longer history of such simulations (reviewed in Chapter XIX) compared to crime pattern simulations, but recent developments in computer software and hardware has renewed interest in this area.

In Chapter XVII, *Development of an Intelligent Patrol Routing System Using GIS and Computer Simulations*, Joseph Szakas and his team use GIS and Global Positioning Systems to facilitate smart patrol routing for a police department. A Voronoi diagram layer is generated at a given point of time, with each Voronoi polygon representing the service area of the patrol unit in the polygon. Armed with this information, all patrol units can coordinate with each other to make better use of limited patrolling resources.

In Chapter XVIII, *Drug Law Enforcement in an Agent-Based Model: Simulating the Disruption to Street-Level Drug Markets*, Anne Dray's team presents an agent-based model, called SimDrugPolicing, to compare and analyze three law enforcement strategies –standard patrol, hotspot policing and problem-oriented policing—on a street-based illicit drug market in Melbourne, Australia. Users, dealers, wholesalers, and outreach workers are modeled as agents, and their properties and behaviors are defined by a panel of interdisciplinary experts. In addition to examining the relative effectiveness of the three drug law enforcement strategies, the chapter analyzes outcome indicators such as the number of committed crimes, dealers' and users' cash, overdoses, and fatal overdoses. The simulated results suggest that the problem-oriented policing strategy is the most effective approach to disrupting street level drug markets.

In Chapter XIX, *Using Varieties of Simulation Modeling for Criminal Justice System*, a team led by Azadeh Alimadad introduces three different approaches to modeling and simulating criminal justice systems: process modeling, discrete event simulation, and system dynamics. Complex criminal justice systems—including police, courts, and corrections—are inherently difficult to model. The chapter takes advantage of recent advances in these modeling techniques and applies them to simulate the British Columbia criminal justice system by exploring different types of "what-if" scenarios. These simulations facilitate the evaluation and test of various policy proposals prior to implementation.

Section V – Conclusion. This section consists of a single chapter. It draws general conclusions from the literature and the chapters in this volume. Chapter XX, *Varieties of Artificial Crime Analysis: Purpose, Structure, and Evidence in Crime Simulations,* summarizes the approaches presented in the book, contrasts simulation methods to other research methods, and look at the process and prospects of simulation methods for the study of crime and related phenomena. It addresses six questions:

1. What are the purposes of artificial crime analysis?
2. What are the characteristics of crime simulations?
3. How does artificial crime analysis compare to other research methods?
4. When should simulations be used?

5. Who should construct simulations?
6. What is the future of artificial crime analysis?

CONCLUSION

Artificial crime analysis is an exciting new development in the study of crime and prevention. In a relatively short period of time researchers from around the globe have found a variety of ways of simulating different forms of crime, as well as criminal justice processes. As illustrated by the backgrounds of the members of the authoring teams, artificial crime analysis is multidisciplinary. Because no single discipline owns artificial crime analysis we should expect substantial progress in this area from the resulting interplay of ideas. But members of different disciplines have different ways of conversing and this can often create barriers to communication. We hope that this first book on the topic will help break down some of these barriers by showing what can be accomplished and by pointing to some of the exciting problems ahead.

REFERENCES

Brantingham, P. J., & Brantingham P. L. (2004). Computer simulation as a tool for environmental criminologists. *Security Journal, 17*, 21-30.

Brantingham, P. L., Glässer, U., Kinney, B., Singh, K., & Vajihollahi, M. (2005). A computational model for simulating spatial aspects of crime in urban environments. In *Proceedings of 2005 IEEE International Conference on Systems, Man, and Cybernetics, Hawaii,* (pp. 3667- 3674).

Liang, J. (2001). *Simulating crimes and crime patterns using cellular automata and GIS.* Unpublished doctoral dissertation, Department of Geography, University of Cincinnati.

Liang, J., Liu, L., & Eck, J. (2001). *Simulating crimes and crime patterns using cellular automata and GIS. Presentation to the 2001 UCGIS Summer Assembly.* Buffalo, New York. Retrieved September 5, 2007, from http://www.ucgis.org/f2oppor.html

Liu, L. (2007, January 29- February 2). The role of street network in crime analysis and simulation. In *Proceedings of Crime Hot Spots: Behavioral, Computational and Mathematical Models.* Institute for Pure and Applied Mathematics, University of California, Los Angeles.

Liu, L., Wang, X., Eck, J., & Liang, J. (2005). Simulating crime events and crime patterns in a RA/CA Model. In F. Wang (Ed.), *Geographic information systems and crime analysis* (pp. 198-213). Reading, PA: Idea Publishing.

Wang, X. (2005). *Spatial adaptive crime event simulation with the RA/CA/ABM computational laboratory.* Unpublished doctoral dissertation. Department of Geography, University of Cincinnati.

Section I
The Role of Simulation in Crime Research

Chapter I
The Need for Systematic Replication and Tests of Validity in Simulation[1]

Michael Townsley
University College London, UK

Shane Johnson
University College London, UK

ABSTRACT

This chapter outlines how simulation methods might be used to make valid causal inferences in the social sciences, specifically the study of crime. We argue that significant threats to validity exist for simulation studies and that, if researchers do not actively take measures to minimize these, much of the promise of simulation will not come to pass. Further, we nominate replication as a general method to facilitate the generation of valid findings. It is anticipated, with the burgeoning interest in simulation methods in criminology, that simulation studies will be published in sufficient detail that allows researcher scrutiny and replication, with a view to developing a cumulative body of scientific knowledge.

INTRODUCTION

Scientific approaches to understanding phenomena are distinguished from other methods by an obsession with validation. In academia this usually amounts to peers attempting to replicate or falsify results to examine the validity of published findings. For successful replications, modifications may be introduced to test the limits of context and to identify exceptions. Once sufficient replications have been conducted (and disseminated) the observation becomes "established lore" in the field, or where replication is not forthcoming, or further research challenges the established convention, theories are revised (and sometimes reinvented) and the cycle begins again.

While the scientific method relies on an iterative cycle of hypothesis generation, testing and modification, academic disciplines advance under two conditions: (a) when its theories are falsifiable; and (b) when research findings are replicable. These are arguably easier to achieve when true experiments are possible. That is, where the effect of X on Y can be tested by manipulating X while observing the effect on Y, and those who do and do not receive the manipulation can be randomly selected.

In general, the social sciences have suffered, in some ways, due to an inability to conduct experiments in an absolutely controlled environment. Putative causal variables are not easily manipulable; "natural" experiments are rare; and field experiments expensive or ethically dubious. Ethnographic research is valuable but open to problems of memory distortion and impression management. However, recent technological advances have made simulation techniques[2] (i.e., *in silico*), particularly agent based methods for which interacting actors (pseudo victims, offenders, or guardians) with heterogeneous characteristics or propensities can be observed across a variety of settings, a viable social science analogue to traditional experimental designs. This presents previously unimagined opportunities for social scientists, but also introduces a number of complications.

As exciting as the potential for simulation-as-method is, serious methodological issues will arise as the popularity of simulation grows. The chief concern of this chapter is to explore the ways in which simulation studies and their findings could be described as valid. If we truly believe in the benefits of *in silico* experimentation, just like any other well established research method, effort must be committed to ensuring the approach is valid, or at least to establish its strengths and weaknesses. In setting out our position, we treat simulations as *in silico* experiments. It follows, we argue, that establishing the validity of *in silico* experiments will be very similar to the means through which this is achieved for experimental and quasi-experimental studies.

The rest of this chapter is organized around the validity typology conceived by Donald Campbell (1957), which has been built upon by others (Campbell & Stanley, 1963; Cook & Campbell, 1979; Shadish, Cook, & Campbell, 2002) and on which at least two generations of social scientists have cut their methodological teeth. There exist criticisms of definition and completeness of this typology, nevertheless we are satisfied that it covers the most germane and prevalent validation issues related to causal inference in social science.

ARE COMPUTER SIMULATION TECHNIQUES JUST A FAD?

Underpinning this chapter is a provocative contention: computer simulation, as a methodology, has the potential to be no more than a fad. As evidence, consider the characteristics of fads. Aguirre, Quarantelli, and Mendoza (1998) distil their attributes by claiming that fads are *novel*, in that the practice is a new behavior or has no history; and are *perceived as odd* with respect to extant cultural norms[3]. Computer simulation techniques certainly share these traits. It is only due to Moore's Law[4] and the declining cost of computer processing that these simulation approaches are now possible. The concept of creating an artificial world as detailed and nuanced as imaginable in which entities interact according to defined rules and produce patterns that are often unanticipated *is* odd.

Further, Richiardi, Leombruni, Sonnessa, and Saam (2006) lament that despite the increase in agent-based research over the last 15 years there has not been a corresponding penetration on social science journals. In Economics they estimate that less than 0.03% of articles published in the 20 most influential economic journals feature computer simulation as a methodology. Similar levels of representation were reported for Sociology.

Simulation methods, as many other chapters in this volume attest, hold great promise for social scientists. Our crude attempt to observe and quantify slippery or vague concepts (e.g., fear of crime) has been one of the primary reasons that progress in social science is glacial in speed. This operationalization problem is only compounded in Criminology where Law, Sociology and Psychology intersect. By operationalizing certain concepts *in silico*, studies that would be unethical or prohibitively expensive become potentially viable. In effect, any researcher with a computer can, by creating a system with interacting actors and defined modes of interaction, play puppet master with endless configurations of infinite factors and sample sizes constrained only by processing power and imagination.

How Disciplines Progress

From an epistemological perspective, scientific knowledge develops under two general conditions: when theories are testable (Popper, 1972) and generalizable (Cronbach, Ambron, Dornbusch, Hess, Hornik, Phillips, Walker & Weiner, 1980; Cronbach, 1982). For a range of reasons these conditions have been relatively rare in criminology.

Moss and Edmonds (2005) claim that the natural sciences have historically prioritized evidence over theory and that observations contradicting theory eventually force a revision. In comparison the social sciences have been constrained by prior theory and are starved of direct evidence of the phenomena under study. This is usually because the variables of interest are conceptual (e.g., fear, desire) and so problems with measurement are commonplace. They go on to state more explicitly that "[i]t is a characteristic of the natural sciences that a great emphasis is given to developing new methods of measurement (as compared to the development of abstract theory" (3.2). This is not the case for social science.

Thus, simulation techniques may provide much needed experimental methods for social scientists to conduct the kinds of studies that are not feasible in the real world due to reasons of finance, measurement/logistics issues, ethical concerns, or where the observation of "subjects" may bias experimental outcomes (for an excellent example see Jung, 1971). Where the concepts to be studied may be formally (explicitly) expressed (e.g., the propensity to offend, awareness spaces), different actors within a simulation may be allocated different characteristics and their interactions with each other and their simulated environment perfectly observed. The results of the interactions between agents with heterogeneous characteristics (e.g., propensities to be victims, offenders and guardians) are perhaps of most interest and it is measurement of the results of such convergence that simulation so easily permits.

Repeat After me: "Repetition is the key"

To summarize, while criminology has developed slowly due to an inability to conduct highly controlled experiments and to measure causal factors accurately, simulation techniques offer a potential solution, or at the very least a complimentary methodology to those extant. Simulation holds considerable promise because it provides social scientists with an analogue to a petri dish. The challenge becomes how to best design and interpret simulation studies such that valid causal inferences can be drawn.

If simulations offer the benefits of experiments in terms of causal inference, it follows that they should conform to the rigorous standards of experiments as well. Arguably the easiest way this might be achieved is to determine whether, in the language of Donald Campbell and colleagues, plausible threats to validity exist for an individual study. Even well conducted experiments need to be replicated if their findings are to be held up beyond the local context in which they were initially conducted.

In the next section we consider a variety of threats to the validity of inferences that might be drawn from the application of *in silico* methods and propose a strategy for their minimization which principally relies on replication and collaboration with other researchers. We discuss the threats to validity that need to be addressed namely construct, internal, external, statistical conclusion and ecological validity, focusing on the particular and unique concerns with respect to this kind of experimentation.

Replicating to Maximize in Silico Construct Validity

Construct validity can be measured by the disconnect between our definition of a construct and the property used to quantify it. For instance, if crime is the construct of interest then its measurement will be stymied by reporting/recording practices, the presence of a suitable denominator to calculate a rate, and so on. *In silico* methods introduce a number of additional construct validation issues which need to be considered, but before so doing, let us consider construct validation in the real world in more detail.

In their general theory of crime, Gottfredson and Hirschi (1990) proposed that criminal activity might be thought of as the interaction between two primary constructs. One concerns the opportunities to which the individual is exposed, whereas the other refers to their self-control; the extent to which a person is "vulnerable to the temptations of the moment" (Gottfredson & Hirschi, 1990). A question which emerges with respect to the testing of this particular theory is whether the approaches used to measure self control actually do so. One such approach is the self-report questionnaire. Participants are asked to rate the extent to which they agree with a series of statements using a Likert scale. In the scale devised by Gramsick, Tittle, Bursik, and Arneklev (1993) examples of the items used include "I often act on the spur of the moment without stopping to think" (one of four items designed to measure impulsivity) and "Sometimes I like to take risks just for the fun of it" (one of four items designed to assess risk seeking). Gramsick's et al. (1993) study provided evidence in line with Gottfredson and Hirschi's theory, but subsequent research (Longshore, Turner, & Stein, 1996) suggested that this was subject to qualifications. Most relevant here was the finding that the identified factor structure used as a measure of self control appeared to be valid for male participants, but not so much for females, and in particular for those women with a criminal history. Thus, the particular construction of the measure used was not necessarily universal, and the Longshore et al. (1996) findings thus serve to illustrate how replication can help to test the limits of validity.

Another more pedestrian example is the meaning of the spatial distribution of drug seizures by police. Patterns observed from this distribution may reflect patterns of drug selling, drug use or police activity (because police tend to find drugs wherever they look). One would need to proceed carefully when making causal inferences about the spatial morphology of the problem when using a variable that feasibly represents a number of activities.

The difference between the real world and the rendering of a simulated environment can cause serious difficulties in causal inference. Generally speaking, statisticians who model data collected in the real world strive for parsimony so that a model or system is created that it is a rough approximation of reality. If it is too detailed, or too similar to the real world then the model loses its pragmatic value, and rather than testing theories the research does little more than enumerate what happens under a specific and limited set of conditions. Similarly the goal of simulation is the construction of an environment at a level of resolution fit for purpose—neither more nor less accurate. Thus, the researcher must select the variables that comprise a parsimonious, but sufficiently complete, representation (the simulated setting) of the real world.

In the real word, humans have an infinite number of characteristics: hair color, height, eye color, eye shape, skin color, temperament, interest in art, weight, age, income, IQ, fitness level, ability to delay gratification, waist size, number of delinquent peers, father's occupation, number of fillings, highest score on Pac-man, and so on. Some of these are important in determining (say) propensity to offend, others are less so and some presumably have no influence. However, the observed impact of interventions or experimental conditions in the real world is due to myriad factors, even if some of these are not measured and recorded. Thus, the real world calculus that determines human behavior may contain a very large number of inputs.

In a simulated environment the corresponding calculus is limited to the complexity and interrelatedness of the formalisms prescribed to the settings and experimental units by the researcher. Unmeasured factors can to some extent be taken into account by including a stochastic element in the decision making processes of the agents, but the question exists as to whether this can adequately model those processes that cannot be otherwise factored in. Thus, while an observed impact of experimental manipulation may be logically valid because it is the product of a subset of potential influencing variables included, its theoretical validity will be weaker because the results cannot entirely emulate real world processes. The extent of the difference (between real and simulated world) will be due to the degree of parsimony achieved in the simulated environment and the degree of influence those factors excluded from the simulated environment have over the variable of interest.

How might these problems be overcome? It is clear that construct validity's influence on general causal inference is sufficiently large to warrant considerable deliberation and reflection on the part of the researcher. Although this point is self evident, the danger of not doing so cannot be overstated. From an *in silico* perspective, construct definition and development are intrinsic and fundamental components of the experimental design and should be regarded as the foundations of the simulated environment. A lack of attention to this area is akin to building a house on sand.

Another route to maximizing *in silico* construct validity is through replication by allowing other researchers to develop formalisms for a given construct in distinct ways. If constructs that are conceptually similar but formalized differently by different researchers generate similar experimental effects, there is a greater chance that valid causal inferences will be drawn. Likewise if a construct generates very different experimental effects across a constellation of formalisms, then efforts to unpick these contradictions need to take place. Moreover, replications may introduce additional constructs thought to be intervening or suppressor variables. These variations immediately generate a host of questions: is the contradiction purely a result of different formalisms? Perhaps the addition of new constructs in some replicates reveals spurious associations? Or the experimental effect is the result of a chain of intervening factors, again only fully contained in some replicates?

The possible culprits for inconsistent experimental effects are potentially numerous. Part of the reason for this is the complexity created when even a small number of variables are examined for their interrelatedness. Given that causal inference is not straightforward, replication seems the best candidate to interrogate the interrelatedness of explanatory factors and contextual variables. This point underpins the importance of a clear articulation of constructs and formalism construction.

A further approach is to manipulate the parameters of a particular formalism in such a way that it is believed to no longer represent the construct of interest. Under such conditions, different results should be observed across the range of parameters used. Where they are not, further iterations in the experimentation process will be required.

Construct validity issues are more onerous for *in silico* experiments because not only do constructs need to be understood and explicitly articulated (like every other methodology), but also formalisms have to be carefully constructed which will dictate how these constructs operate and interact. Assumptions need to be checked and clearly described for others to assess.

Replicating to Maximise in Silico Internal Validity

Internal validity concerns the extent to which observed differences can be attributed to an experimental manipulation, and thus requires the consideration of competing explanations for an observed effect. In computer science nomenclature this is verification. In principle this should be the easiest type of validity to maximize for *in silico* experimentation. The simulated environment offers the experimenter a sterile setting in which entities adhere strictly to whatever heuristics they are assigned and within selected parameter bounds. Competing explanations should be completely controllable and the influence of confounding variables minimized.

While *in silico* experimentation offers considerable power and control to the experimenter, additional considerations arise due to the methodology. In an experiment in the real world the calculus behind stimuli (S) and response (R) will operate under virtually all conditions. We denote this f(S) = R[5]. Importantly, for the vast majority of human beings this function operates continuously. That is, when placed in a particular situation an individual will evaluate many factors (immediate situational factors, intermediate dispositional factors and apparently inconsequential factors) and compute what action(s) will either maximize reward or minimize risk. Whether the response is irrational, from the perspective of a detached observer, is not important (see Cornish & Clarke, 1986). The key point is that in the real world the response is only a product of the stimuli.

Under *in silico* conditions, however, the calculus needs to be explicitly formalized; for instance, every time an agent encounters an opportunity to offend it needs to determine whether the risks exceed the benefits, say.

With respect to internal validity we are not here concerned with the accuracy of *in silico* formalisms—that is the remit of construct validity—but rather their conceptual fidelity. Plainly speaking, the issue is the extent to which the relationship between stimuli and response (f(S) = R) is the result of any particular configuration of formalizations implemented and to what degree the mapping between S and R is affected by the simulation architecture or nuances in the programming language selected. If f(S + other programming features) = R then we cannot be confident that the experimental effect is due to the formalisms or some other influence. To illustrate, consider a study in which male and female subjects are asked to jump as high as they can. No differences between groups (other than gender) are apparent, and so the only variables considered are the height that each participant can jump and their gender. Against the experimenters' expectation, on average the females jump higher than the males. Unbeknown to the experimenters, the females are wearing special bouncy shoes whereas the males are not. In this deliberately silly example, where the constructs of gender and height are perfectly defined and observed, the observed gender difference is a product of actual group difference and a systematic difference between groups that was not considered (wearing of bouncy socks).

What might make up other programming features? These may include coding errors[6], inadvertently inherited features of subroutines available in software formulations, or other features of the environment used to create the experimental system which the individual researcher may overlook in the scrutiny of their model. Apart from coding errors, none of these threats to *in silico* internal validity will be exposed without replication or external scrutiny. This is important to consider, given that verification bias is arguably a particular risk in research where development of the simulation can take a considerable amount of time.

Formalisms in real world experiments are unlikely to behave deterministically across all units of analysis, being influenced by (for example) cognitive malfunction, bias or measurement error. Nevertheless, the objective of such experiments is to establish generalizable mechanisms that emerge with sufficient consistency to suggest regularity. Where confounding/competing/alternative explanations for emergent patterns are unlikely, and similar patterns emerge across a range of contexts, this provides support for the articulated theory. However, the fact that competing explanations for patterns that emerge within *in silico* experiments could be systemic features of the experimental system used means that they cannot be ignored and that sufficient attention should be given to their identification and investigation.

Edmonds and Hales (2003) provide an illuminating example of the point. They took a published simulation (Riolo, Cohen, & Axelrod, 2001) and developed and tested two independent replications. There was agreement between the two replications but not with the published findings of the original simulation! They comment, "the process revealed a host of minor bugs and ill-defined implementation issues in simulations that otherwise appeared to be working well and according to their specification" (1.5).

The final internal validation issue relates to the logical fallacy of the circular argument, where an assumption is used to prove itself. This might arise where the outcome of a study is not emergent but rather presupposed by virtue of being included in the assumptions of the experiment. An example is given by Chalmers' (1999) description of a high school science experiment:

> [my] pupils were required to conduct an experiment along the following lines. The aim was to measure the deflection of a current-carrying coil suspended between the poles of a horseshoe magnet and free to rotate about an axis perpendicular to the line joining the poles of the magnet. The coil formed part of the circuit containing a battery to supply a current, an ammeter to measure the current and a variable resistance to it possible to adjust the strength of the current. The aim was to note the deflection of the magnet corresponding to various values of the current in the circuit as registered by the ammeter. The experiment was to be deemed a success for those pupils who got a nice straight-line graph when they plotted deflection against current, revealing the proportionality of the two. I remember being disconcerted by this experiment, although, perhaps wisely, I did not transmit my worry to my pupils. My worry stemmed from the fact that I knew what was inside the ammeter. What was inside was a coil suspended between the poles of a magnet in such a way that it was deflected by a current through the coil causing a needle to move on the visible and evenly calibrated scale of the ammeter. In this experiment, then, the proportionality of deflection to current was already presupposed when the reading of the ammeter was taken as a measure of the current. What was taken to be supported by the experiment was already presupposed in it, and there was indeed a circularity. (p38-9)

Logical circularities can be avoided by careful interrogation of the formalisms that underpin the simulated environment so that the assumptions used to develop the system are not related to those theories being tested. This is a condition of any sound experiment. In the example above, the strength of the current needs to be measured in a way different to the deflection of a coil[7].

In silico experiments run a high risk of inadvertently generating emergent behavior because the characteristics and dynamics of the system are directly formalized by the experimenter. If agents make decisions by weighing risk and reward, then of course the study will support a rational choice perspective. *Thus, simulations should always include presupposed emergence as a rival hypothesis by default.* The original researcher through critical examination can examine this but this, as the Edmonds and Hales (2003) study illustrates, is perhaps most reliably achieved through systematic scrutiny and replication by others.

Replicating to Maximize in Silico External Validity

External validity is the degree to which the findings in a local setting, containing a single set of sampling units, are applicable to the population of sampling units as well as other settings. Traditionally replication is the default means of maximizing external validity, so it should be no surprise that we envisage considerable benefit in replicating *in silico* experiments.

The key benefit to replication is that the extent to which context influences outcomes may be estimated. A criminological example is the Minneapolis Domestic Violence Experiment (Sherman & Berk, 1984) where a randomized control trial implemented in one US state suggested that a mandatory arrest policy for domestic violence offenders lowered recidivism. However, this result was not observed in projects that implemented the same approach in other states (Sherman, 1992), suggesting a more complicated causal relationship than the first experiment claimed (see Tilley, 2000).

For the purposes of this chapter, we take it as given that readers do not need convincing that repeated implementations of an *in silico* experiment involving changes to sampling units and/or settings would offer evidence that findings are generalizable. However, to make the point transparent we refer to the chapter by Birks, Donkin and Wellsmith in this volume. They describe an agent-based model of criminal activity simulation by formalizing a number of components of a simulated environment in an incremental fashion with a view to incorporating further theoretical perspectives and settings. It is these future modifications which will demonstrate the generalizability of observed behavior. Thus the entire modular development of their model was, among other things, chosen to make the barriers to external validity as low as possible.

The extensions listed are different types of agents (such as guardians), different types of crime, additional and more complex agent behavior, evolutionary decision making by agents and more refined environmental information. Birks et al (in press) acknowledge the import of generalizability when they comment that "[t]he scope of such work is vast…it is important for developers to possess a roadmap of future extensions to follow" (XX). We concur but are skeptical that true generalizability will be established without relying on the wider community of scholars to actively test for this.

Other ways that external *in silico* validity may be maximized through replication is by observing the experimental effect across different simulation techniques (agent-based, microsimulation, cellular automata), programming languages, or operating systems. For example, Klüver and Stoica (2003) test no less than four algorithmically different simulation models for a given problem and found quite high levels of agreement between the models compared (a series of experiments were conducted and not all models were appropriate for each step) and concluded the observed equivalence was the result of methodological and theoretical consistency in the model construction.

Replicating to Maximize in Silico Statistical Conclusion Validity

Part of the appeal of agent-based simulation is that while the rules followed by each agent may be simple the emergent properties (the aggregate patterns generated) need not be. Moreover, because such models *are* stochastic, one run of the simulation will produce different results to another. This variation and unpredictability presents a potential challenge to establishing statistical conclusion validity—the extent to which results observed may be considered reliable—in simulation research.

To illustrate, consider simple random walks. These may be generated for a variety of purposes, but the simulation of time-series data is illustrative. In this context, the data generating process works by assigning the value of a particular variable at time *t* as the sum of the same variable at time *t-1* plus a random number. Such processes can easily provide the impression of a trend in data where the reality is that none exists. Two realizations of such a model are shown in Figure 1, both with identical initial conditions. The stochastic element for both is a random variable with mean of zero and standard deviation of 25. Two things are worthy of note. Both realizations generate time-series patterns that resemble those frequently seen in crime data, although the precise trends differ considerably for the two examples and second, the range of values for the two simulations vary considerably. Despite their differences the two distributions were produced using the same (random) data generating process. Nevertheless, we suspect (and have found) that if presented with either graph and asked to explain the patterns, researchers would be able to provide what they consider as reasonable hypotheses for the data generating process, and that these would exclude chance variation.

For the purposes of theory testing and falsification, the identification (or lack) of regularity that deviates from chance expectation is vital. Fortunately, much like data collected in the real world, simulations generate data that can be analyzed using traditional inferential statistical methods (e.g., analysis of variance or correlation). Thus, when conducting simulation research it is important to perform the relevant statistical tests to see if the results vary in such a way as to provide support for (or against) the ostensible theory of interest. Determining that the results are unlikely to be due to a chance process is, of course, essential given that a stochastic process will be built into the model. Failing to do so in any study represents a threat to conclusion validity.

For simulation research there are at least two types of analysis required. The first to show that

Figure 1. Examples of a time series generated using only a random walk data generating process with identical initial values

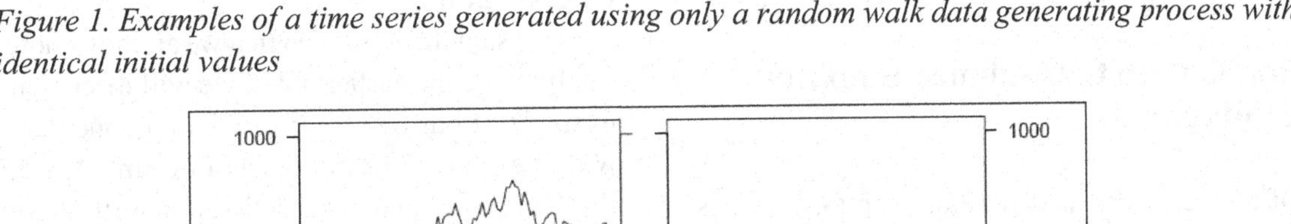
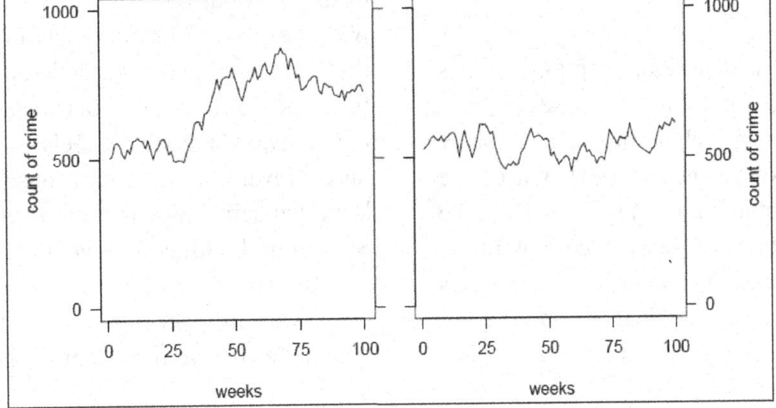

any observed relations between variables deviate from chance expectation, otherwise known as null hypothesis testing. Second, that observed relations are systematic across runs of the simulation; finding hypothesized results for one run of a simulation would not be particularly convincing. Thus, assessing statistical conclusion validity involves a form of replication for which researchers will be required to run the simulation many times. Across different runs of the simulation the same parameter settings should be used but the random number generator should be reseeded each time. In the example shown in Figure 1, further realizations of this model (say 99) would reveal that the process is purely random. Looking at the results of one simulation run would not. When rerunning statistical analyses of the data generated, some variation in coefficient effect sizes across simulations is to be expected but for reliable results the general conclusions should typically (say 95% of the time) align.

It was beyond the scope of this chapter to give statistical conclusion validity anything more than a brief treatment and so we refer the interested reader to Shadish et al. (2002). The aim of this section was instead to highlight the need to conduct robust statistical analyses and to note that a different kind of replication (i.e. within-model) is central to the establishment of statistical conclusion validity in simulation research.

Replication to Maximize Empirical Validity

Of course, even if all of the aforementioned issues can be addressed, research which uses simulation-as-method is unlikely to be taken seriously unless the models developed can be shown to have some degree of empirical validity. That is, for the findings to be embraced by a wider community of researchers, the emergent properties of the models need to be shown to resemble those observed in the real world to some extent at least.

As illustrated by Chalmers' example, the use of different metrics may lead to different inferences being drawn. Consequently, one salient factor that will influence the extent to which the empirical validity of models can be estimated is our knowledge and enumeration of real world phenomena. The more we know the more thoroughly we can test our models. We thus argue that in parallel with the development of simulation methodology, a concerted effort is required to better identify the range of phenomena that the models should be able to demonstrate. The obvious point is that few academics would be convinced by a simulation experiment for which little data were available with which to compare the results of the model.

A more detailed understanding of patterns of crime should therefore perhaps be a priority, as should the testing of the external validity of patterns identified. Demonstrating that the emergent properties of simulations resemble those observed in a single study may achieve little in the way of theory development if the likely ubiquity of the phenomena replicated is unknown. Exposition of the factors, environmental or otherwise, that may influence real world phenomena is also desirable so that the parameters of a model may be manipulated to examine the concordance of findings in and out of the microchip across a range of settings.

That said there is much that we already know. To illustrate the earlier point, we will discuss an example of our own recent research concerned with the space-time clustering of crime. We do this for two reasons: first, to disseminate the basic findings to a community of researchers who may not be aware of them. We feel that this is particularly relevant as the patterns observed are of the kind that some models should seek to generate. Second, to highlight the fact that what we think is quite basic knowledge about how patterns of crime vary in space and time, and the statistical techniques required to identify them, have only recently been discussed within the criminological literature. This raises the question of what else that in hindsight may seem obvious, do we not yet know or lack the statistical tools to identify?

Research consistently demonstrates that crime is spatially concentrated, forming hotspots and hotdots of crime (Pease, 1998). A range of studies, conducted across a variety of countries have shown that crime is not uniformly distributed in space, and that at a micro level of resolution some victims experience a much greater risk of victimization than others (Pease, 1998). With respect to temporal signatures, as noted by Felson and Poulson (2003) crime also clusters in this dimension, with different types of crime having different rhythms (their periodicity) as well as tempos (their rate of occurrence). Considering repetition against the same victim, for burglary, a distinct time course also emerges, with most events occurring shortly after an antecedent (e.g., Townsley, Homel, & Chaseling, 2000). Repeats also appear to occur at a similar time of day to earlier victimizations (Sagovsky & Johnson, 2007).

More recently, using epidemiological techniques for testing disease contagion, research conducted by the authors (e.g. Johnson et al., 2007; Johnson & Bowers, 2004; Townsley, Homel, & Chaeling, 2003) has shown that the risk of burglary clusters in space and time. Following a victimization at one home, those nearby experience an elevated risk of victimization, which decays as time elapses. Some of the patterns are quite distinct, showing that for Merseyside (UK) such communication of risk is greatest to homes on the same side of the street (Bowers & Johnson, 2005), and that in Beenleigh (Australia) neighborhood composition with respect to housing homogeneity influences the patterns observed (Townsley et al., 2003).

Where robust or at least established empirical findings are available this provides a pattern of findings against which to test simulation models. Stylized facts of this kind need not relate to the exact numerical values as observed in empirical research (such as how many homes are expected to be repeatedly victimized). Instead, it is perhaps more useful to consider expected distributions of events such as those discussed above with respect to space-time clustering, or power-law distributions (e.g., Newman, 2005) for repeat victimization (for an example, see the chapter by Liu et al. in this volume).

As discussed, a variety of factors may influence the outcome or realization of a particular simulation model. One central factor yet to be discussed is how researchers determine the various parameter values used in a simulation. Where the explanation of offender and victim activity is the goal of simulation, such parameters may include (heterogeneous) lambda values (rates of offending) for individual offenders, or the propensity of all agents to commit crime, act as guardians or become victims of it. Different approaches are possible, but perhaps the most intuitive is to calibrate the parameters of the simulation inductively using existing empirical data concerned with offenders and victims[8]. Challenges arise where insufficient data are available, as will be the case for at least some parameters in a model concerned with crime, or where different parameter values are suggested by the results of different empirical studies. In these cases, researchers will need to be clear about their assumptions and ideally sensitivity analyses will be employed to establish how the results of the model vary for differences in initial conditions. Running separate models for all permutations of parameter settings is likely to be beyond the scope of most research and so a Monte Carlo approach to sampling from all possible permutations (or the range of values suggested by empirical data or theory) is sensible (Werker & Brenner, 2004). Where variations in the outputs of the model occur for different realizations of parameter settings, commonalities in those models that generate patterns most approximate to empirical findings should be examined to determine their theoretical value (see Werker & Brenner, 2004).

A final issue concerns the degree to which data collected in the real world are fit for purpose with respect to pattern recognition. In the example provided above, the data analyzed—crimes committed at residential addresses—have accurate data concerned with the location of the crimes committed. For other types of crime, such as robbery, this is unlikely to always be the case. Moreover, it is well acknowledged that crime sometimes goes unreported, with under-reporting varying by crime type, meaning that research findings may sometimes be based on biased samples. Thus, the question arises as to whether simulation models should only be developed for those crimes for which we have the most complete understanding and for which the data available have suitable reliability to facilitate their analysis. This remains, at this stage, an open question.

On the one hand the benefits of simulation methods allow us to study crime phenomena that is unlikely to be observed and studied by any other means. This however yields the problem of how to validate these findings (especially in light of surprising emergent behavior). On the other, if empirical validity is a prerequisite for simulation studies, research agendas may be directed by what is measurable rather than what is of most theoretical or practical importance. The situation is, we feel, akin to the relationship between pure and applied mathematics. While pure mathematics is theoretical and serves no apparent practical benefit, given sufficient time applications for real world problems may emerge (e.g., number theory and encryption). Thus, simulations of crime phenomena where empirical validity is not possible may be of value if, in the future, an application emerges or empirical evidence exists.

Replicating to Increase Ecological Validity

Although not discussed by Campbell and colleagues, a further type of validity we consider is that of *ecological validity*. More often a particular concern in the field of psychology, this form of validity concerns the extent to which experimental laboratory conditions reflect those of the real world. The concern is that where experimental conditions vary systematically from those typical in the real world, these differences may affect the results in ways that would render the outcome of the experiment of little value outside of the laboratory.

To take an example from cognitive psychology, consider studies of human memory in which participants are asked to learn lists of words (during an initial encoding phase) and to then remember these some time later. As Neisser (1978) questioned, to what extent do such studies tell us anything about memory in the real world (the ultimate aim of such research)? The problem is that people are tested under contrived settings that bear little resemblance to those of reality. For example, rarely are those things that we would like to remember in everyday life presented to us on a sheet of paper, rarely are they just lists of words, and rarely are we asked to recall them (say) twenty minutes later free of distraction. The demands of the task fail to reflect those of everyday cognition. In response to this problem, many studies of human memory have been designed to more closely approximate real-world conditions and the results of such studies often differ from those of their more sterile equivalents (for examples, see Cohen, 1996). Given the explicitly artificial nature of simulation research, one might wonder why this type of validity is relevant here. Two examples should hopefully illustrate the point.

To begin, we will discuss two studies that examined game theory, implementing the same type of cooperation problem in ways that differed only subtly but that produced radically different results. In the first study, Nowak and May (1992) implemented a spatial variant of the prisoner's dilemma. Using a computer simulation, players located in a two-dimensional lattice interact with their neighbors, selecting either to cooperate or defect. Following each interaction, players receive points determined by their interactions (defectors who interact with cooperators receive the highest score). Depending on the points awarded, each player will leave the game, remain in their own cell, and/or possibly take over a cell previously inhabited by another player. Nowak and May (1992) showed that using a deterministic model in which the agents have no memory and always adopt the same strategy the simulation quickly (after about 55 runs) produces a stable population of those who cooperate (around 32%) and those who do not.

Results of this kind have important implications for theories of the evolution of cooperative behavior and how this might be influenced by spatial structures. However, Huberman and Glance (1993) challenged the way in which the model was implemented, suggesting that it lacked ecological validity. Specifically, they highlighted the fact that all players in the Nowak and May (1992) simulation were updated simultaneously, whereas in the real world such synchronicity is unlikely. To examine the effect of manipulating this element of the simulation, they implemented the same model using both synchronous and asynchronous updating. Results consistent with those of Nowak and May (1992) were observed for the synchronous model, but where asynchronous updating was used, after about 100 iterations of the model no "cooperators" remained. In this case, varying the simulation in a way that introduced a more ecologically valid process led to very different conclusions being drawn.

A further example concerns spatial mobility. Consider a cellular automata model of offender behavior in which simple rules are used to explore the spatial distribution of offences committed (for examples see Groff, 2007; Lui et al., chapter in this book). Offender agents could either be placed on a lattice over which they can move freely between neighboring cells, or on one for which movement might be constrained by a rendering of the street network, defined using a contiguity matrix. One measure of the empirical validity of this model may be the extent to which crime clusters spatially, a pattern which appears ubiquitous for analyses of recorded crime data (e.g. Block, Dabdoub, & Fregly, 1995; Ratcliffe & McCullagh, 1998; Sherman, Gartin, & Buerger, 1989). One issue here is that in the real world offender spatial targeting decisions are influenced by the distribution of opportunities, and for on-street crimes in particular, the distribution of the street network. Failing to take account of this influence in a model is likely to affect the results. In particular, spatial clustering will inevitably be greater for a model where offending opportunities are spatially clustered (i.e., where crimes only can take place in those cells of the lattice that represent road segments) than where they are not. Thus, failing to take account of spatial constraints that affect offender movement or where they might offend may lead to errors of causal inference in such modeling exercises.

The purpose of this section was not to suggest that simulation models should seek to approximate reality. Rather, the aim was to encourage researchers to consider carefully those factors that might realistically influence the behaviors they seek to simulate. The Huberman and Glance (1993) study elegantly illustrates how subtle manipulations of a system can generate very different results even where a deterministic model is employed. These findings do, of course, also have relevance to our earlier discussion of internal validity and illustrate the need for researchers to systematically vary parameters of interest (and where relevant the structure of the code) to examine the influence of so doing.

CONCLUDING EXPECTATIONS

This chapter was written in the spirit of identifying some of the potential stumbling blocks that may reduce the acceptance of simulation as methodology, and to discuss some of the potential solutions to these issues. The discussion focused on a variety of different types of validity, some of which are common to most forms of research, but some of which are specific to simulation methodology or represent variations of existing issues. If these (and other) factors can be addressed then research that uses a simulation approach has considerable potential for the field of criminology. We argued that the most direct route to achieving this is through scrutiny by other researchers; in practice this will largely be via replication as this is the route through which much of mainstream science attempts to build a body of knowledge.

Despite offering what we believe is a robust solution to the "simulation-is-fad" possibility, it has not escaped our understanding that systematic *in silico* replication will be easier said than done. Axtell, Axelrod, Epstein, and Cohen (1996) describe an attempt to align two different models of the same social behavior. While not a replication, they describe the factors which made elements of this similar task either straightforward and difficult[9]. Even so, without replication, the findings arising from simulation studies, like any other, will enjoy scant influence or penetration in the field. Axtell et al. (1996) said it best: "[a]nd what is the alternative to confronting these difficulties, to look away and rest our theorizing on unverified assumptions of equivalence?" (p134)

Replication is not just a problem restricted to computer science methods applied to social problems. In a widely read piece, Ioannidis (2005) argues that most research findings are false and persuasively demonstrates this by modeling the post-study probability that a finding is true. There are a number of conditions which make this more likely, one of which is the number of studies on the same question. In a follow up, Moonesinghe, Khoury, and Janssens (2007) extended Ioannidis' model to include the impact of replications. Holding other variables constant they demonstrated the probability of a research finding being true increases dramatically for every replication showing the same result. The solution, Ioannidis claims, is more effort by researchers to scrutinize others' findings. This would expose inadvertent bias, poor design and spurious findings.

FUTURE RESEARCH DIRECTIONS

The potential for crime simulation is feasibly tremendous. We have argued that unless researchers take an active role in minimizing threats to validity this potential will not come to fruition. Some obligations lie with researchers being critical of their own (and not just others) work and investing time and effort into construct and model development; but these comments apply to any methodology.

The novel emphasis (but one that we hoped will be repeated elsewhere) of this chapter is that replication is a route to validation. Replication is rarely conducted in simulation studies, yet is the cornerstone of cumulative science (Axelrod, 1997). Will this change? We predict "yes" for a very basic reason. As increasing numbers social scientists are conducting *in silico* experiments the impetus to replicate previous work will increase. This is natural as domain experts have a selfish desire to build a body of knowledge in their field. The temptation to test previously untestable theories will surely be too great for a sizable group of researchers to resist.

Of course, efforts to replicate studies probably need some coordination, similar in nature to the efforts of the Campbell Collaboration. In fact, a form of *systematic replication* needs to be defined which sets out the requirements for replication. This will probably focus on sets of replications, each testing specific components of causal inferences. As such, systematic replications will probably not be possible without the collaboration of teams of researchers.

As a final point, in writing this chapter, the authors often struggled with vocabulary. Putting aside our inadequate grasp of the English language *per-se*, difficulties were met (for example) when trying to translate familiar phrases from the social science nomenclature to express a simulation analogue. In the introduction to this chapter we quoted others who have suggested that academic disciplines progress under two conditions, we would like to revise this by suggesting that they progress under three. The third is that progression is facilitated by common understanding. Thus, effort is required to develop an agreed vocabulary and shared understanding of concepts. Moreover, and perhaps more saliently for simulation than other forms of research, if replications of other people's work are to be possible, investigators will need to specify precisely how their models are implemented and the assumptions they make. Whilst reportage of the methods and procedures used is essential for any research methodology, it should be obvious that the degree of information required for the replication of simulation models requires considerably more detail than a typical Psychology or Criminology study. Doing so may not be possible in journal articles but the relevant documentation should be made freely available in some format, and stored, for example, on the author's personal website (see Axelrod, 1997).

REFERENCES

Aguirre, B. E., Quarantelli, E. L., & Mendoza, J. L. (1998). The collective behavior of fads: The characteristics, effects, and career of streaking. *American Sociological Review, 53*, 569-584.

Axelrod, R. (1997). *Advancing the art of simulation in the social sciences.* In R. Conte, R. Hegselmann, & P. Terna (Eds.), *Simulating social phenomena.* Lecture Notes in Economics and Mathematical Systems. Berlin: Springer-Verlag.

Axtell, R., Axelrod, R., Epstein, J. M., & Cohen, M. D. (1996). Aligning simulation models: A case study and results. *Computational and Mathematical Organization Theory, 1*(2), 123-141.

Block, C. R., Dabdoub, M., & Fregly, S. (1995). *Crime analysis through computer mapping.* Washington, DC: Police Executive Research Forum.

Bowers, K. J., & Johnson, S. D. (2005). Domestic burglary repeats and space-time clusters: The dimensions of risk. *European Journal of Criminology, 2*(1), 67-92.

Campbell, D. T. (1957). Factors relevant to the validity of experiments in social settings. *Psychological Bulletin, 54*, 297-312

Campbell, D. T., & Stanley, J. C. (1963). *Experimental and quasi-experimental designs for research.* Chicago: Rand-McNally.

Chalmers, A. F. (1999). *What is this thing called Science?* (3rd ed). Maidenhead, UK: Open University Press.

Cook, T. D., & Campbell, D. T. (1979). *Quasi-experimentation: Design and analysis issues for field settings.* Chicago: Rand-McNally.

Cohen, G. (1996). *Memory in the real world.* (2nd ed). Hove: Psychology Press.

Cornish, D., & Clarke, R.V.G. (Eds.) (1986). *The reasoning criminal.* New York: Springer-Verlag.

Cronbach, L. J., Ambron, S. R., Dornbusch, S. M., Hess, R. D., Hornik, R. C., Phillips, D. C., Walker, D. F., & Weiner, S. S. (1980). *Toward reform of program evaluation.* San Francisco: Jossey-Bass.

Cronbach, L. J. (1982). *Designing evaluations of educational and social program.* San Francisco: Jossey-Bass.

Edmonds, B., & Hales, D. (2003). Replication, replication and replication: Some hard lessons from model alignment. *Journal of Artificial Societies and Social Simulation,* 6(4). Retrieved August 22, 2007, from http://jasss.soc.surrey.ac.uk/6/4/11.html

Felson, M., & Poulson, E. (2003). Simple indicators of crime by time of day. *International Journal of Forecasting, 19*, 595-601.

Gottfredson, M. R., & Hirschi, T. (1990). *A general theory of crime*. Stanford: Stanford University Press.

Grasmick, H. G., Tittle, C. R., Bursik, R. J., & Arneklev, B. J. (1993). Testing the core empirical implications of Gottfredson and Hirschi's general theory of crime. *Journal of Research in Crime and Delinquency, 30*(1), 5-29.

Groff, E. (2007). Simulation for theory testing and experimentation: An example using routine activity theory and street robbery. *Journal of Quantitative Criminology, 23*(2), 75-103.

Huberman, B.A., & Glance, N. (1993). Evolutionary games and computer simulation. *Proceedings of the National Academy of Sciences, 90*, 7716-7718.

Ioannidis, J. P. A. (2005). Why most published research findings are false. *PLoS Medicine, 2*(8), 696-701.

Johnson, S. D., & Bowers, K. J. (2004). The burglary as clue to the future: The beginnings of prospective hot-spotting. *European Journal of Criminology, 1*(2), 237-255.

Johnson, S. D., Bernasco, W., Bowers, K. J., Elffers, H., Ratcliffe, J., Rengert, G., & Townsley, M. T. (2007). Space-time patterns of risk: A cross national assessment of residential burglary victimization. *Journal of Quantitative Criminology, 32*(3), 201-219.

Jung, J. (1971). *The experimenters dilemma*. New York: Harper Row.

Kelling, G. L., Pate, T., Dieckman, D., & Brown, C. (1974). *The Kansas City preventive patrol experiment: A summary report*. Washington, DC: Police Foundation.

Klüver, J., & Stoica, C. (2003). Simulations of group dynamics with different models. *Journal of Artificial Societies and Social Simulation, 6*(4). Retrieved August 22, 2007, from http://jasss.soc.surrey.ac.uk/6/4/8.html

Longshore, D., Turner, S., & Stein, J. A. (1996). Self-control in a criminal sample: An examination of construct validity. *Criminology, 34*(2), 209-228.

Moss, S., & Edmonds, B. (2005). Towards good social science. *Journal of Artificial Societies and Social Simulation, 8*(4). Retrieved August 22, 2007, from <http://jasss.soc.surrey.ac.uk/8/4/13.html

Moonesinghe, R., Khoury, M. J., & Janssens, A. C. J. W. (2007). Most published research findings are false—But a little replication goes a long way. *PLoS Medicine, 4*(2), 218-221.

Neisser, U. (1978). Memory: What are the important questions? In M. M. Gruneberg, P. E., Morris, & R. N. Sykes (Eds.), *Practical aspects of memory*. London: Academic Press.

Newman, M. E. J. (2005). Power laws, Pareto distributions and Zipf's law. *Contemporary Physics, 46*(5), 323-351.

Nowak, M. A., & May, R. (1992). Evolutionary games and spatial chaos. *Nature, 359*, 826-829.

Pawson, R., & Tilley, N. (1997). *Realistic evaluation*. London: Sage.

Pease, K. (1998). *Repeat victimisation: Taking stock*. Crime Detection and Prevention Series Paper 90. London: Home Office.

Popper, K. R. (1972). *The logic of scientific discovery*. London: Hutchinson.

Ratcliffe, J., & McCullagh, M. (1998). The perception of crime hot spots: A spatial study in nottingham, U.K. In N. LaVigne, & J. Wartell (Eds.), *Crime mapping case studies: Successes in the field.* Washington, DC: Police Executive Research Forum.

Richiardi, M., Leombruni, R., Sonnessa, M., & Saam, N. (2006). A common protocol for agent-based social simulation. *Journal of Artificial Societies and Social Simulation, 9*(1). Retrieved August 22, 2007, from http://jasss.soc.surrey.ac.uk/9/1/15.html

Riolo, R. L., Cohen, M. D., & Axelrod, R (2001). Evolution of cooperation without reciprocity. *Nature, 411*, 441-443.

Sagovsky, A., & Johnson, S. D. (in press). When does repeat victimisation occur? *Australian and New Zealand Journal of Criminology.*

Shadish, W. R., Cook, T. D., & Campbell, D. T. (2002). *Experimental and quasi-experimental designs for generalised causal inference.* New York: Houghton Mifflin Company.

Sherman, L. W., & Berk, R. A (1984). The specific deterrent effects of arrest for domestic assault. *American Sociological Review, 49*(2), 261-272.

Sherman, L. (1992). *Policing domestic violence.* New York: Free Press.

Sherman, L., Gartin, P., & Buerger, M. (1989). Hot spots of predatory crime: Routine activities and the criminology of place. *Criminology, 27*(1), 27-55.

Tilley, N. (2000). Experimentation and criminal justice policies in the united kingdom. *Crime & Delinquency, 46*(2), 194-213.

Townsley, M., Homel, R., & Chaseling, J. (2000). Repeat burglary victimisation: Spatial and temporal patterns. *Australian and New Zealand Journal of Criminology, 33*(1), 37-63.

Townsley, M., Homel, R., & Chaseling, J. (2003). Infectious burglaries: A test of the near repeat hypothesis. *British Journal of Criminology, 43*(3), 615-633.

Werker, C., & Brenner, T. (2004). Empirical calibration of simulation models (Papers on economics and evolution No. 0410). Jena: Max Planck Institute of Economics.

ENDNOTES

1 The authors would like to acknowledge the two anonymous reviewers who provided very insightful comments on a draft version of this chapter.

2 To be clear, for this chapter our definition of "simulation" is any technique widely understood as such excluding resampling methods. A non-exhaustive list would include microsimulation, agent-based models, cellular automata, genetic algorithms, system dynamics models.

3 These authors set out other two other characteristics, but these (to our eyes) seem irrelevant or incorrect with respect to fads so are not listed.

4 The observation by Intel cofounder Gordon Moore that the density of transistors on a computer chip will double every two years. The 'law' was coined by computer scientist Carver Mead.

5 This function will never be observed, but the scientific task is to reveal aspects of the computation.

6 Gilbert and Troitzsch (2005) state that "[e]xperience shows that it is almost impossible to create simulations that are initially free of bugs" (p. 212). Moreover, as Murphy's law states, "anything that can go wrong, will go wrong", and numerous errors can go undetected in a computer program.

7 An example of circularity closer to criminology is that of the justification of racial profiling based on high detection or clearance rates among certain ethnic groups. If there are such high rates within certain

groups, this warrants greater levels of police scrutiny of members of that group. Greater levels of scrutiny are bound to result in high detection rates, and so on.

8 One should avoid any tautology in so doing.

9 As simulation methods become mature, they suggest the task should become easier.

Chapter II
Realistic Spatial Backcloth is not that Important in Agent Based Simulation:
An Illustration from Simulating Perceptual Deterrence

Henk Elffers
Netherlands Institute for the Study of Crime and Law Enforcement NSCR, and Vrije Universiteit Amsterdam, The Netherlands

Pieter Van Baal
National Institute for Public Health and the Environment RIVM, The Netherlands

ABSTRACT

This chapter considers whether it is worthwhile and useful to enrich agent based spatial simulation studies in criminology with a real geographical background, such as the map of a real city? Using modern GIS tools, such an enterprise is in principle quite feasible, but we argue that in many cases this course is not only not producing more interesting results, but in fact may well be detrimental for the real reason of doing criminal simulation studies, which is understanding the underlying rules. The argument is first outlined in general, and then illustrated in the context of a given example of the ThESE perceptual deterrence simulation model (Van Baal, 2004), a model that actually is using a simple checkerboard as its spatial backcloth.

INTRODUCTION[1]

In this chapter we reflect about the status of the use of detailed geographical context within agent based simulation work. We challenge the idea that such simulation studies are making much progress by means of importing real life geography, and make a plea for being content with very modest artificial spatial backgrounds instead. The argument is largely based on rethinking our position after having finished a project in perceptual deterrence simulation (Van Baal, 2004). We asked ourselves, is the natural next step in the research program to implement a real life geographical background? Pondering that question, we realized that the scientific status as well as the aims of simulation work is sometimes rather unclear. Reviewing a number of recent simulation studies in criminology, we realized that many simulation projects restrict themselves to just developing a simulation environment and illustrating eloquently how well it works. Often these efforts do not lead to a concise research program in which the built simulation environment is exploited. The "lean back and think again"-modus of the present chapter dictates its character a bit: we refrain from discussing and criticizing individual simulation work, because these individual projects often produce impressive results. However, on a more abstract level, we feel a need to think about where all this ingenious work is leading to. In a sense, most simulation programs seem to breed a dayfly. What we urgently need is a better exploitation of the promising simulation environments that are already out there. It is our conviction that simulation work would gain most from exploiting existing simulation models in depth, instead of making new ones. Importing ever fancier geographical detail into existing or new simulations does not seem the wisest option here.

WHAT IS AGENT-BASED SIMULATION ALL ABOUT?

The agent based simulation approach in behavioral research can be seen as a relentless pursuing of the wish to find answers to "*what if*"—questions. What happens *if* "acts" ("behavior") of a number of "agents" are fully governed by certain "law like processes"? These law-like processes specify completely which specific act an agent will perform, in a given situation in which that actor finds itself ("state of the actor"). Usually these law like processes are specified by means of a decision rule in the form of a mathematical formula—possibly, but not necessarily with probabilistic elements—that tells us what act will be performed by that actor, given his situation, a situation that often is characterized by the availability of other actors, themselves governed by equal or different law like processes. Moreover, the environment may be changing according to a related law like process as well. We constrain our discussion here to agent-based models with fixed rules, not mentioning adaptive models in which during simulation the rules may change (under the influence of higher order rules for adapting), such as learning models, neural network models.

Simple problems of this type, with not too many actors, not too many different situations, and not too complex law like processes, sometimes can be analytically solved through mathematical analysis. For instance, current probability theory is powerful enough to predict what will happen with a gambler possessing a given amount of money, who plays roulette against the bank, and has as strategy to set an equal amount of money each round on the outcome "red".

However, simulation becomes indispensable as soon as the complexity of the problem defies our mathematical skills, for example what is happening when 30 gamblers play roulette, all with a different start capital and different (though fully specified) gambling strategies. It may be that the outcome is after all probabilistically determined, but the necessary analysis to find that outcome is too difficult as yet. A well-known characteristic that increases complexity considerably is when the various agents are located in geographical space. The old maxim "*processes occurring in two-dimensional space are four times as difficult to understand*" comes to mind. Simulation may be used then to observe *what* happens *if* those agents are governed by those analysis-defying rules. As such simulation may be seen as continuation of analytical mathematical work with other means.

Notice that, as a nonempirical enterprise, simulation work, in first instance, has no need for empirical data to test models. It is all about understanding models, not so much about whether these models could be true in reality. Of course, seen from a long-term perspective, simulation work may well lead to an understanding of rules detailed enough to make it possible to derive predictions about what should be the case in a real world. These predictions can then, in a later phase, be subjected to formal empirical testing.

In our view, a simulation study proper is aiming at, and limited to, the better understanding of rules, and is a theoretical exercise. Notice that there are no validity concerns in simulation work of this type, because there is no direct link between what happens in the simulation and what happens in the real world. The only criterion for a simulation researcher is that the whole set-up is interesting and promises to increase the understanding of what is embodied in the law like rules. If the researcher is not interested in the interplay of exactly these law-like rules, the researcher should not bother to do this simulation. Of course, a good reason for being interested in this particular set of law like rules may well be that the researcher indeed entertains the idea that these rules will be close to what happens to real life agents. But whether that is true or not, is not affecting the simulation work at all.

Notice that we are reserving the term "simulation" here as referring to contexts where artificial actors artificially act in an artificial environment. As such we distinguish the term from another current usage, when real subjects are brought into an artificial (i.e., simulated) environment, in order to observe their behavior. That type of work uses an experimental approach and is indeed empirical, hence reliability and validity problems crop up as important issues. An example of simulation work in that latter tradition is Robben (1991), cf. also Webley, Robben, Elffers, and Hessing (1991).

SPATIAL BACKGROUND IN CRIMINOLOGICAL SIMULATIONS

In simulation work in a criminological context, agents are often meant to be models of offenders and guardians, who live in a situation characterized by the availability of targets of various attraction value to the offenders, targets that may or may not be supervised by the guardians. Such targets may indeed be located in space. The law-like rules are about modeling the decision of offenders in choosing targets, taking stock of the presence or absence of guardians. A rather common idea in the community of simulation researchers, in criminology as well as elsewhere, seems to be that a good simulation is one that mimics reality as closely as possible. Agents, in that approach, should be as much like agents in the real world, for example agents that model offenders should have as many characteristics equal to human offenders as is possible, and as real offenders live in the real world, it is often thought that it is important to build a simulation environment that is close to the real world as well, entailing that the details about the geographical location of targets are seen as essential parts of a good and interesting simulation model.

That idea is certainly shared by criminologists from outside the simulation community, that is, if they take at all notice of the work of simulation researchers. It is the experience of the authors when presenting simulation work that time and again audiences react by challenging the real world correspondence of the model presented, often in a positive way by suggesting improvements to a lacking correspondence. Not surprisingly then, much effort is directed by simulation researchers to building a "real background" for the simulation process being studied, for example by using the street network of real cities as backcloth.

Of course, simulation problems that essentially need a fixed real life geographical background do exist. As an example, if we like to find the optimal location of police stations in a given city, and approach that problem by simulation methods, we should use the geography of that particular city. In such cases, however, the study is not aiming at understanding the consequences of the rules, rules that are not challenged as such. It is about figuring out the particular outcome of the rules in a given geographical context. Researchers who study such a problem do not care about the rules; they do care about the resulting spatial pattern. As such, this is not a theoretical but an applied exercise.

We certainly do not challenge that also theoretically flavored work using real geography may be of great interest, but we like to make the point here that sometimes too much effort of simulators goes to this "background" work, while the essence of simulation work is rather independent of it. As analyzed previously, the real world correspondence is not the kernel of a simulation model; therefore lack of correspondence is not a priori a great problem. A simulation model aims at understanding how rules interact, about seeing through the complex consequences of many interacting rules. Even when these rules have spatial aspects, it does not follow that the important issues at stake, that is what consequences we do not understand well enough at any given moment, are particularly located in the spatial part of a model. In many cases other parts of the law like rules suggest many unsolved problems already, problems that may well be more fundamental than the space related question.

Take for example somebody who studies the influence of police presence on location choice in an agent based model starts modeling possible offender agents, police officer agents, and target agents, giving all these agents characteristics that govern their model behavior, for example that make the officer and offender agents move around a space filled with possible targets, and react on each others presence. The kernel of such a simulation study is the investigation of how the chosen model of decision rules—about reaction on other agents and on the attraction of targets—governs the behavior of the agents, and how rules mutually influence each other. It is about understanding the consequences of the law like processes for behavior choice. In fact, such a model claims that for *every geographical background* the interaction of would-be offenders and guardians is being governed by those rules.

This implies, however, that studying the effects of these rules can be done, if at all, in every geographical environment whatsoever, so there is no particular reason to chose an environment that exists in the real world. Or even worse, using a given real life geography may well restrain the scope of the simulation work. If, for instance, it turns out that target density may be an important aspect of the dynamics of the decision rules, it seems wise to experiment (i.e., run the simulation model) with various densities, hence the link with the fixed density of a real geographical background should be severed.

A model concentrating on interaction between localized agents should be performing well in every environment, and can, therefore, perfectly be executed in a rather artificial environment, as long as all relevant environmental characteristics that are addressed in the model decision rules are present. This means that in many cases agents moving around over a checkerboard can teach us just as much about the rules modeled as agents moving around over a map of, say, Amsterdam. And probably, it is much easier experimenting with simple rules (simple backcloth) than with complex ones, indeed that is the whole rationale behind using simulation. We are afraid that in many cases too much effort goes to sophisticatedly modeling a real environmental background, using geographical information systems, downloading real data on the various variables that characterize the geographically units. Perhaps, study of the basic rules of how agents interact will sometimes even be hampered by the immense complexity of the realistic background. If simulation can contribute to our understanding, it is by studying the already complex consequences of interaction of agents under very simple rules. Simulation is most useful under the simplest circumstances, and importing complex environmental characteristics may not be a very good idea.

Researchers using real life geographical backgrounds quote two reasons for indeed using them. The first is that nowadays geographical information systems (GIS), completed with associated databases on many socio-economic details of the units of analysis, are commonly available, and therefore importing the geography is rather easy. In this way, they challenge our statement that they spoil much time by working at the geographical backcloth. We have, of course, to admit, that there is some truth in that argument. Making such a simulation environment is less difficult than it used to be. But even so, the constraints intrinsically imported by using that background are still there: using the simulation for understanding the interaction of rules is still threatened by the complexity of real life backcloth.

The second argument is that a simulation being dynamically depicted on a colored real map of a really existing city is much more helpful in getting your point through to an audience. That argument is in fact admitting that the backcloth of a simulation is just a selling point, just like the packing material of any consumer good, which, essentially, has nothing to do with the kernel of the product. If we could agree on that point, we would be very happy.

THE SIMULATION PROGRAM THESE FOR RESEARCHING PERCEPTUAL DETERRENCE

We will illustrate our plea for minimizing real geography by treating elements from a study in perceptual deterrence of Van Baal (2004). He developed a simulation framework, called *ThESE* (*The Erasmus Simulation Environment*) which examines agents whose perception of deterrence levels are dynamically changing, by incorporating information about what is happening to their neighbors when they transgress or comply to rules. The concept of neighbors introduces a geography into the model. But it is really a very simple geography.

We will first briefly introduce *ThESE*, than present some of Van Baal's results, and finally discuss the role of geography in this work. We will then discuss whether a more sophisticated form of geography would enhance the usefulness of the work.

The Structure of the ThESE simulation Model

ThESE works with agents ("citizens") that are living on the cells of a checkerboard (× in Box 1), and whose neighbors are the agents living on adjacent cells ("n" in Box 1), as well as on the cells two steps away (*"n"*), at least in one variant of the model. The agents repeatedly have to decide to transgress a rule or comply with it. Transgressing a rule undetected gives a positive outcome, but transgressing it and being caught by the authorities (who audit a sample of all citizens every round) leads to a negative outcome, on behalf of being fined. Compliance is neutral. Agents' perceptions of deterrence levels are dynamically changing, by incorporating information about what is happening to their neighbors when they transgress rules.

The theoretical framework behind ThESE views noncompliance as committed intentionally, because the citizen preferred to transgress

Box 1.

n	*n*	*n*	*n*	*n*
n	n	n	n	*n*
n	n	×	n	*n*
n	n	n	n	*n*
n	*n*	*n*	*n*	*n*

rather than to comply with a rule, knowing the possible consequences of the behavior. The rule governing the choice of citizens is completely deterministic, and whether the citizen transgresses or not is solely a function of perceptions of various parameters. Having said this, it does not mean that citizens are rational in the Von Neumann-Morgenstern tradition. With regard to decision making, concerning noncriminal issues, laboratory experiments (Kahneman & Tversky, 1979) and field evidence (Camerer, 2000; Thaler, 1985) indicate that people violate the axioms of expected utility theory not only substantially but also systematically. Criminological research (e.g., Cornish & Clarke, 1986) also indicates that, although criminals may make elementary cost/benefits calculations, they probably do not adhere to the axioms of the standard economic model.

More descriptive models of criminal decision would therefore fall in the category of bounded rational decision-making (Simon, 1982). Citizens in *ThESE* behave in a bounded rational way because of the following

- Citizens do not know the actual level of law-enforcement, and although they make efforts to learn the actual level of law-enforcement, they do not optimize their search efforts and do not update their initial beliefs about the law-enforcement level in a perfectly rational manner.
- Citizens do not optimize over the entire lifespan, they only do what is best for them in the current period, so their behavior is short-sighted.

All citizens repeatedly face a choice between complying, and transgressing a rule. After all citizens have made their choice, the law-enforcement agency has the possibility to audit a percentage of the citizens. If a citizen is audited and caught transgressing a rule, the citizen does not profit from rule transgression and receives a legal sanction instead. One period t consists of a decision round in which all citizens decide whether to comply or transgress, and an audit procedure.

The pay-off of compliance equals zero. Individual differences that could influence the pay-off of transgression (such as personal feelings of guilt, shame, and embarrassment) are captured in differences in the pay-off for citizen c of transgression X_c that may differ over citizens. Citizens who anticipate feelings of guilt and shame after rule transgression attach a lower pay-off to transgression than citizens who do not anticipate feelings of guilt. Some citizens attach a higher pay-off to transgression than others do, but these differences are fixed throughout a simulation run. Therefore, the pay-offs have been standardized so that the pay-off of compliance equals zero and the pay-off of transgression equals X_c.

If a citizen transgresses, the pay-off depends on whether the citizen is audited or not by the law-enforcement agency: if a citizen is not audited the citizen receives the pay-off of transgression $X_{c,}$ (X_c>0). If a citizen is audited then does not receive the pay-off of transgression $X_{c,}$ but a legal sanction L is deducted. Thus, the choice between compliance and transgression is a choice between a risky prospect (with a positive pay-off if one is not audited: X_c >0, and a negative pay-off if one is audited: $-L$, and a riskless prospect with a pay-off of zero. Strictly speaking, if one looks at the pay-off structure, it is modeled such that the benefits of transgression are contingent upon detection, so that apprehension entails the confiscation of benefits. However, making the assumption that the benefits are not contingent upon detection would not alter the basic simulation model and its predictions. This means that the pay-off structure is a metaphor for transgressions such as drunk driving or vandalism whose benefits are not contingent upon detection, and for transgressions such as property crime and robberies in which apprehension often entails the confiscation of benefits.

The decision function in the *ThESE* model is not a probabilistic function, it is completely deterministic so that all citizens will transgress with probability one if they expect it to pay off, and refrain from it with probability one when they expect it not to pay off. Let $d_{c,t}$ indicate whether citizen *c* complies in period *t* or transgresses in period *t*. Citizens break the rules only if the expected pay-off of transgressing a rule is higher than the expected pay-off of compliance:

$$d_{c,t} = \begin{cases} \textit{transgress} & \text{iff } (1 - p_{c,t}) * X_c - p_{c,t} * L > 0 \\ \textit{comply} & \text{otherwise} \end{cases} \quad (1)$$

$d_{c,t}$ = decision of citizen c in period t

$p_{c,t}$ = *the assessment of the audit probability P of citizen c in period t*

$0 \leq p_{c,t} \leq 1$

X_c = *pay-off of transgression for citizen c* $\quad X_c > 0$

L = *legal sanction* $\quad L > 0$

In Van Baal (2004) an extension of the model is introduced as well, in which also informal sanctions are catered for. We do not treat this variant here.

The expected pay-off of transgression of all citizens denotes the expectation associated with their own assessment of the audit probability $p_{c,t}$, and should not be confused with the expectation associated with the "true" probability distribution of the actual audit process *P*. From equation (1) it can be seen that all citizens in the simulation model eventually will commit crimes if their assessment of the audit probability is below a certain threshold (all people become motivated when tempted enough). This threshold is termed the *break-even probability* (denoted $BEP_{c,t}$). This break-even probability can be written as a function of the pay-off of transgression and the size of the legal sanction.

$$BEP_c = X_c / (L + X_c) \quad (2)$$

$BEP_{c,t}$ = break-even probability of citizen c in period t

From equation (2), one sees that a severe legal sanction cause a decrease in $BEP_{c,t}$. Self-imposed costs that could decrease the pay-off of transgression (such as personal feelings of guilt, shame, and embarrassment) result in a lower pay-off of transgression (lower X_c) and therefore a lower $BEP_{c,t}$. Using (2) the decision function can be rewritten:

$$d_{c,t} = \begin{cases} \textit{transgress} & \text{iff } p_{c,t} < BEP_{c,t} \\ \textit{comply} & \text{otherwise} \end{cases} \quad (3)$$

If citizens have a lower assessment of the audit probability than the break-even probability they will transgress, otherwise they will comply. Citizens with a higher *BEP* transgress more easily than citizens with a lower *BEP*. Thus, citizens who attach a higher pay-off to transgression will transgress more easily. To assume in the simulation model that individual differences will result in differences in the value they attach to transgression, is in fact equivalent to assuming that individual differences will cause some citizens to take more risk than others do.

In the model, the expected pay-off of transgression depends on a citizen's assessment of the audit probability. The changing assessment of the audit probability can cause individual behavior to change from transgression to compliance or vice versa. The higher the assessment, the lower the expected pay-off of transgression. Van Baal chooses for this way of formulating the transgression rule on the basis of perceptual deterrence literature, in which the assessment of the audit probability often is called the perceived certainty of punishment. Since a citizen's assessment of the audit probability in the simulation model depends not only on his own experiences but also on that of other citizens' experiences, we prefer to use the term *assessment of the audit probability* instead of *perceived certainty of punishment.*

Longitudinal studies indicate that an individual's perception of the certainty of punishment changes over time (Minor & Harry, 1982; Paternoster, Saltzman, Waldo, & Chiricos, 1983a, 1983b; Piliavin, Gartner, Thornton, & Matsueda, 1986). Although research on the formation of sanction perceptions is scarce (Nagin, 1998), evidence suggests that perceptions of the certainty of punishment are influenced by personal experiences and personal experiences of acquaintances (Parker & Grasmick, 1979). These acquaintances are termed "significant others" and are part of a citizen's social network. The idea that sanction perceptions determine behavior and are influenced by experiences of others and oneself was also acknowledged by the late sixteenth century Dutch writer Coornhert, as is illustrated by the following citation:

> *...because when lazy good-for-nothing persons become acquainted with real criminals, they will observe that their number is large and that very few are punished, in view of the fact that they are seldom captured and imprisoned [...]. Therefore, they come to expect that if they also go out robbing and stealing they too will escape punishment. As a result these types unconcernedly start to commit crimes as well, with the idea that this will enable them to lead a life of idleness and luxury.* (Coornhert, 1587; translated from the Dutch original by Laraine Visser-Isles)

In *ThESE* individual perceptions of the certainty of punishment are modeled through an assessment of the audit probability that each citizen has and updates if the citizen gets new information about the current audit probability. In the initialization of a simulation run, all citizens receive an initial assessment of the audit probability. From then on, citizens adapt their assessment of the audit probability by comparing their assessment of the audit probability with an observed audit rate: after each auditing procedure all citizens communicate with their neighboring citizens about their outcomes and update their assessment of the audit probability by comparing their assessment with the number of transgressors (*B*) who were audited (*A*) in their social network. If their assessment is lower than the observed audit rate they will adjust their assessment upward, if it is higher they will adjust their assessment downward:

$$p_{c,t} = \begin{cases} p_{c,t-1} + s_c * \left(\left(A/B \right)_{c,t-1} - p_{c,t-1} \right) & \text{if } B_{c,t-1} > 0 \\ p_{c,t-1} \quad \text{otherwise} \end{cases} \tag{4}$$

$p_{c,t}$ = assessment of the audit probability P of citizen c in period t

$0 \leq p_{c,t} \leq 1$

s_c = *assessment adaptation parameter of citizen c* $0 \leq s_c \leq 1$

$B_{c,t-1}$ = number of citizens who transgress in the social network of citizen c in period t-1

$A_{c,t-1}$ = number of citizens who transgress and are audited in the social network of citizen c in period t-1

Thus, the assessment of the audit probability of citizen *c* in period *t* ($p_{c,t}$) depends on his assessment of the audit probability in period *t*–1 ($p_{c,t-1}$), and the audit rate he observed in period *t*–1 ($(A/B)_{c,t-1}$). The random audit procedure and the number of committed offences in their social network are the dynamically determined quantities that influence individual assessments of the audit probability. Equation (4) illustrates that citizens who are part of social networks where more crimes are committed have more information (high value of *B*) to base their assessment on, and that citizens who are part of social networks where no crimes are committed (B equals zero) do not update their assessment. The more compliers in a citizen's neighborhood the less information a citizen has to update this assessment.

The *assessment adaptation* parameter is s_c. This parameter captures to what extent citizens adjust their assessment of the audit probability after observing the audit rate in their social network. The higher the value of s_c, the faster the pace with which citizens adjust their assessment towards their latest observed audit rate, that is more weight is given to recent empirical evidence. The assessment adaptation parameter is closely related to the concept of impulsivity, which is considered a major determinant of criminal behavior (Gottfredson, & Hirschi, 1990; Wilson, & Herrnstein, 1985). A higher value of s_c means that a citizen's action is more guided by recent experiences and events than by older experiences and events. Citizens with a higher value of s_c react more heavily to recent experiences and can therefore be seen as more impulsive. In an "artificial" society created by the simulation model citizens can have different values for s_c. In the initialization of a simulation run values of s_c can be distributed over the population of citizens according to various distribution functions.

In the audit procedure, a fixed percentage of all citizens who transgress are audited, regardless of how they behaved in previous periods. Thus, the expected audit probability (denoted P) for citizens who transgress is fixed throughout a simulation run. The way this is modeled in *ThESE* is that in every period a fixed percentage of all citizens is audited. Citizens who have complied do not know that they have been audited, but citizens who have transgressed know that they have been audited since they will be fined. Thus, the law-enforcement agency makes no errors, in the sense that if they audit they see every case of noncompliance, and they never misclassify a case of compliance or transgression.

SOME RESULTS OF USING THESE: THE INFORMATION EFFECT

Van Baal (2004) investigates meticulously the petering out of initial conditions in runs with his simulation model, and he shows how to diagnose whether a society (a 50 by 50 checkerboard) is in a steady state, having a society-wide steady state average dynamical compliance-rate. He executes a number of studies with various parameter combinations, concentrating on how differences in individual parameters result in differences in aggregated characteristics of the whole society, especially the steady state compliance rate. For details we refer to the original book. We characterize his work as that he was able to prove that the actually chosen law like processes that govern the citizens' behavior (i.e., formulae (1) to (4)) produce certain results, results not all being foreseen. He analyzed among others the effect of audit probabilities, sanction severity and of the distribution over citizens of the adaptation parameter s_c (impulsivity).

We will here only treat one of the findings of these exercises, the so-called *information effect.* A higher audit probability will result in a lower over-all noncompliance rate. A lower noncompliance rate in its turn means that most citizens have only a few or perhaps even no neighbors that transgresses. And if only a few neighbors transgress, even less of them will be audited. This then results in that such citizens get not much information about the current audit rate. In the analysis below it is argued how this will affect the compliance levels. We show it here in some detail, because we believe that this is a good example how a mix of analytical reasoning and observing simulation results is helpful, and the true contribution of simulation. The treatment here is closely following Van Baal's original discussion.

If the number of offences committed in a social network is fixed for every citizen during a simulation one can assume that after some periods the distribution of assessments is approximately stable. It can be shown (Van Baal, 2004: appendix B) that this distribution is independent of the size of the legal sanction, and has a mean that equals the real audit probability. The shape of this distribution depends on the number of committed offences, the assessment adaptation parameter, and the audit probability. Figure 1 displays two hypothetical distributions of assessments in a given period *t*. Assuming that the audit probability equals *P1* and the break-even probability equals *BEP*, the area marked with the diagonal lines is the fraction of citizens that comply this decision round since they have a higher assessment of the audit probability than *BEP*.

Let us compare two audit probabilities *P1* and *P2*. A shift from *P1* to *P2* corresponds to a shift to the right of (approximately) the entire distribution and since *BEP* stays constant this will result in a higher level of compliance. This direct effect of an increase in the audit probability on the level of compliance is depicted in Figure 1. If the audit probability would be increased from *P1* to *P2* the level of compliance would become 100% in the following simulation period, since all assessments will be higher than *BEP* in that case. Thus, an increase in the audit probability will probably result in an increase in the level of compliance (if the level of compliance is not already 100%). However, an increase in the audit probability also has an indirect effect on the level of compliance: more compliance means that on average fewer offences are committed in a social network so that citizens have on average less information on which to base their assessments. This affects the shape of the distribution of assessments and results in more variance in the distribution of assessments. This can affect the level of compliance. The indirect effect that increases in the controllable factors have on the level of compliance by their impact on the number of committed offences on which citizens base their assessments of the audit probability is termed the *information effect.*

A hypothetical scenario of the information effect is depicted in Figure 2. An increase in the audit probability from *P1* to *P2* shifts the distribution of assessments to the right but the variance in the distribution also increases, so the distribution of assessments becomes flatter and has longer tails. Since the distribution of assessments has longer tails the level of compliance in Figure 2 does not equal 100%, as was the case in Figure 1. In Figure 2 the area pointed at by the arrow indicates that some citizens have an assessment of the audit probability that is lower than *BEP*. Thus, less information as a result of a higher audit probability results in more variance in the distribution of assessments, which in this scenario weakens the deterrent effect of increases in the audit probability. Since less information results in less compliance the information effect in this case is considered negative.

Figure 1. Direct effect of increases in the audit probability on the level of compliance

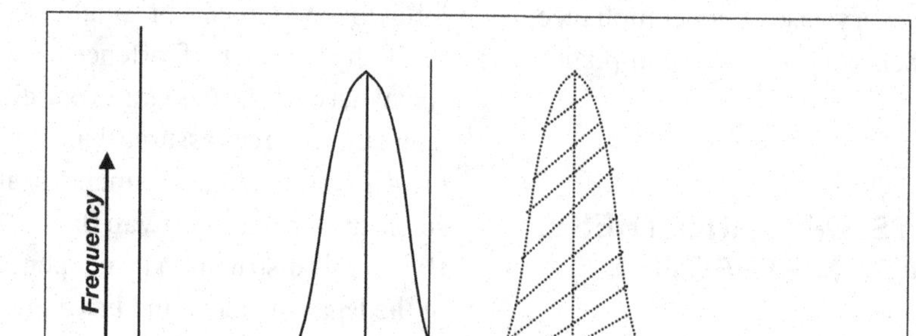

Figure 2. Information effect due to increases in the audit probability

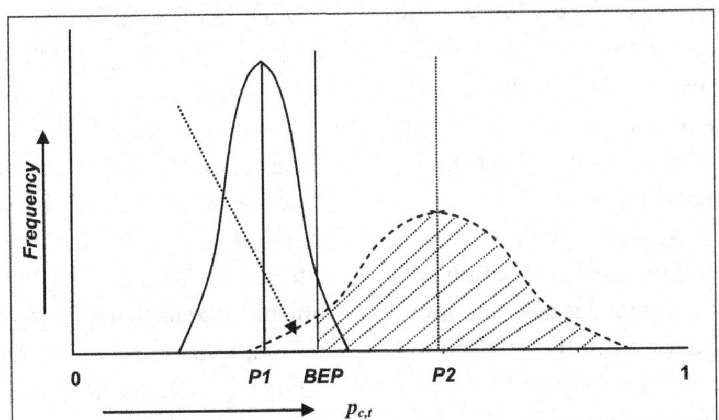

In Figure 2, the depicted distributions are such that the information effect is negative, that is the indirect result of changing parameters, as outlined above, is *less* compliance. However, this is a purely hypothetical scenario; it could be the case that even under the assumption that the number of committed offences is fixed, an increase in the audit probability will cause a positive information effect. The size and sign of the information effect depend on the exact shape of the distribution of assessments of the audit probability and *BEP*.

Assuming that the pay-off citizens attach to transgression of all citizens is the same, an increase in the size of the legal sanction results in the same amount of decrease in the *BEP* of all citizens. Figure 3 shows what would happen to the level of compliance if the size of the legal sanction were increased. Assuming that *BEP*=*BEP*1 and that the distribution of assessment is indicated with the straight line in Figure 3, an increase in the legal sanction that causes *BEP*1 to shift to *BEP*2 results in less compliance. The level of compliance in a

Figure 3. Information effect due to increases in the legal sanction

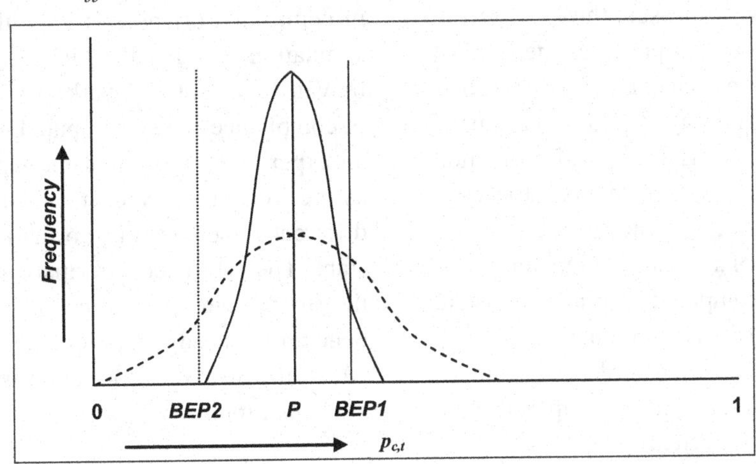

simulation period after such a change would be 100% since all assessments are now higher than *BEP1*. However, more compliance also means less committed crimes, so that citizens have on average less information on which to base their assessments. This will also cause an information effect, which is depicted in Figure 3. In Figure 3 the distribution of assessments indicated with the dotted line is based on less information and therefore in flatter and has longer tails and more variance, hence a larger part of the distribution falls below the break-even probability. If the legal sanction causes a decrease from *BEP*1 to *BEP*2 the information effect is negative and weakens the deterrent effect of an increase in the legal sanction.

The shape of the distribution is critical for the sign and the size of the information effect and all this reasoning depends on the assumption that the number of committed offences is fixed in every social network throughout a simulation run. In the simulation runs, the number of committed offences is a dynamically determined quantity and therefore the interactions may cause different relations at the macro level. It is not possible to predict the size and sign of the (or if there even will be an) information effect if the number of committed offences is a dynamically determined quantity, since in this case the shape of the distribution of assessments is not known. Even if there is an information effect in a simulation run, the problem arises how to measure this?

The simulation model produces the level of compliance in each period of a simulation run as output, and there is no way of telling what part of the level of compliance is due to the information effect and what part is not. To do this, the steady-state level of compliance, which may contain an information effect of a particular combination of factors has to be compared with a steady-state level of compliance that does not contain an information effect. In other words, a benchmark steady-state level of compliance to measure the information effect is needed.

It is possible to calculate a benchmark steady-state level of compliance in the simulation model by keeping the level of information constant for all citizens. The way this is modeled in *ThESE* is that in this case all citizens know whether they have been audited or not, and citizens who comply face the same audit probability as citizens who transgress. Citizens who have complied and are audited are not punished, but will tell their neighboring citizens that they have been audited. Each period, citizens therefore receive the maximum amount of information about the audit probability. Thus, dependent on the size of social network, each period citizens receive information about the audit probability from 9 or 25 citizens. This has the same effect on individual assessments as assuming that the number of offences is fixed at 9 or 25 for all citizens for a particular combination of factors. The steady-state level of compliance based on maximum information is termed the *benchmark steady-state level of compliance.* This allows for a formal definition of the *information effect* as the steady-state level of compliance based on a dynamically determined number of committed offences, minus the benchmark steady-state level of compliance based on a maximum level of information that is fixed throughout a simulation run.

So, the information effect equals the change in the steady-state level of compliance that cannot be explained under the assumption that the number of committed offences is fixed throughout one simulation run. In all experiments carried out in Van Baal (2004)'s work, a benchmark level of compliance is also computed by carrying out an experiment with the same input parameters as specified in the experimental design with one difference: the level of information is held constant. The estimated information effect is then the steady-state level of compliance minus the benchmark steady-state level of compliance in which the level of information is held constant at its maximum.

Van Baal goes on showing that indeed a negative information effect occurs in most of his simulation runs, that the resulting effect size is not only dependent on the steady-state level of compliance but also on social network size (Figure 4). With this last conclusion we have reached the point where we can resume our discussion about the importance of geography in the *ThESE* simulation.

CONCLUSION: THE ROLE OF GEOGRAPHY IN THESE RESULTS

The *ThESE* simulation models perception of deterrence by letting all agents look at their neighbors, where they observe how many of the neighbors do not comply and are caught or not. In a sense this represents a minimal geography, only using the concept of adjacency, and the underlying geography is the simple one of a checkerboard. (Van Baal (2004) sees his model as representing social networks, instead of spatial networks, in the sense that he likes to apply his results also to agents whose neighbors are not necessarily physical neighbors, but have a social connection only. For the present discussion we pass this extension of the results, however). Indeed, the result on the information effect outlined above shows that geography matters: in the *ThESE* variant in which agents experience only the first ring of checkerboard cells around them as neighbors, the information effect is different from what we observe when agents also consider the second ring of cells as their neighbors.

Figure 4. Information effect as function of compliance-rate

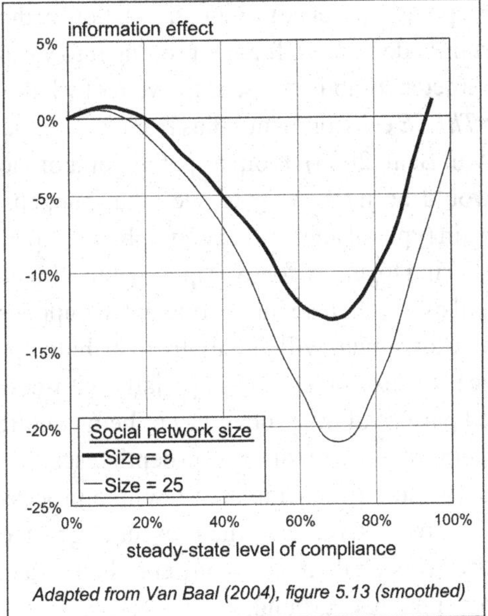

Adapted from Van Baal (2004), figure 5.13 (smoothed)

Let us ponder about whether it would be useful to augment ThESE with a "real" geography. That would mean that we would look to agents that live in a certain dwelling, and count as their neighbors, people living in the dwellings next door, or above and below them, or, alternatively, people living within a certain radius around an agent's own home. With present day GIS systems, it is in principle very well possible to register which dwellings around every home can count as neighbors under such definitions. In a real city, the density of housing, and the particular arrangement of houses in streets and lanes, as well as the housing type (e.g., high rise buildings vs. detached dwellings) would influence the number of neighbors, in the sense that not all agents have the same number of neighbors any more. As we have already seen that the size of network is important, at least in the case of the information effect (and for a number of other application as well, as Van Baal has shown) it is sure that such a real life background would change the outcomes of a simulation run, compared to the checkerboard.

Though it is in principle possible to adapt *ThESE* to this real backcloth, we challenge that we would learn a lot more from that. First of all, there is no reason to believe that real citizens look to all of their neighbors with the same intensity. It may well be that they know better the compliance behavior of some of those neighbors then that of others. So introducing a better geography will not necessarily introduce a better model of what a real citizen perceives. And neither should it, for we are not presenting simulation work as producing a model of real citizens. The point here is that we do not propose *ThESE* as a model of what happens in that real city at all, we use it as a metaphor for society in general, not as proposed snapshot of a given society.

The second drawback of using a real geography is that it becomes immensely difficult to sort out whether any given result is due to the interaction of the perceptual deterrence process as such, or due to the underlying geography. For example, when we would observe that the information effect has a certain value in, say, Amsterdam, how could we ascribe that to either perception processes as modeled in formula (1) to (4), or to the special neighborhood structure that the city of Amsterdam has? While the idea may be that enhancing the model with a "more real" backcloth will improve its usefulness, we contrarily run the risk of destroying the power of simulation research, which is being able to sort out, by careful comparison of simulation results at various parameter choices, how various elements in our law like processes are responsible for the results, how they interact with each other, and what unexpected effects show up. The only way in which real geography can be helpful here is when we run models with different geographical backcloth, such as comparing results for a simulation on the map of Amsterdam with an equal one on the map of Cincinnati. But even then, it will be difficult to get a clear and comprehensive picture of what exactly are the differences between the spatial structures of Amsterdam and Cincinnati, and which of these differences is responsible, in what interaction with the other rules of the simulation, for what results. Real geography simply is too complex to assist in simulation research of this type.

It rather may be hypothesized that progress in this type of simulation work must be sought in a different direction, viz. in the systematic variation of various parameters and various mechanisms in the underlying model. That certainly will be a long and tedious process. Interpreting results of systematically exercising through variants of the model may well result in identifying which of the assumptions are not tenable at all, as well as giving insight in what assumptions and parameters are more robust than others. Such a process should be undertaken in a systematic and comprehensive way, varying elements in the model first one-at-a-time, subsequently in combinations. Adding a real geography is dangerous in this respect, as it changes too many aspects of a simulation simultaneously and in an uncontrollable way. In fact, the simulation researcher may well not be aware which assumptions and parameters in the model are relaxed, altered or strengthened by introducing a real spatial backcloth. As such, adding geography does not provide any useful purpose, and may in fact retard understanding, or even give misleading results that are tied to the geography, without being recognized as such.

FUTURE RESEARCH DIRECTIONS

Our conclusion is that a better understanding of perceptual deterrence through simulation methods certainly demands a further probing into various parameter combinations, in the vein of what—in the *ThESE* environment—has been done already in Van Baal (2004). From a spatial point of view, it would be interesting to see what happens if certain types of agents are geographically spoken clustering together, for example agents with high impulsivity. Or, also interesting, what happens if law enforcement will unequally distributed over space, for example with a spatially auto-correlated pattern of the probability of being audited. It seems to us that that such in-depth research for understanding the simulated law like processes will be more fruitful in the present "light geography" version than in any one enriched by a real geographic background.

We notice that the previous argument, though developed in the context of Van Baal's deterrence simulation, seems *mutatis mutandis* to be valid for quite some more simulations. Our general conclusion is that future work on criminological simulation would do well in concentrating on a further exploitation of simulation models already present, and not spend too much time on augmenting simulations with a real life geographical background.

REFERENCES

Camerer, C. F. (2000). Prospect theory in the wild: Evidence from the field. In D. Kahneman, & A. Tversky (Eds.), *Choices, values and frames.* Cambridge: Cambridge University Press.

Coornhert, D.Vzn. (1587). *Boeventucht* [*Disciplining villains*]. Amsterdam: Harmen Muller.

Cornish, D. B., & Clarke, R. V. (Eds.) (1986). *The reasoning criminal: Rational choice perspectives on offending.* New York: Springer.

Gottfredson, M. R., & Hirschi, T. (1990). *A general theory of crime.* Stanford, CA: Stanford University Press.

Kahneman, D., & Tversky, A. (1979). Prospect theory: An analysis of decision under risk. *Econometrica, 47,* 263-291.

Minor, W., & Harry, J. (1982). Deterrent and experimental effects in perceptual deterrence research: A replication and extension. *Journal of Research in Crime and Delinquency, 19,* 190-203.

Nagin, D. S. (1998). Criminal deterrence research at the outset of the twenty-first century. In M. Tonry (Ed.), *Crime and justice: A review of research* (Vol. 23). Chicago: University of Chicago Press.

Parker, J., & Grasmick, H. G. (1979). Linking actual and perceived certainty of punishment. *Criminology, 17,* 366-379.

Paternoster, R., Saltzman, L. E., Waldo, G. P. & Chiricos, G. (1983a). Estimating perceptual stability and deterrent effects: The role of perceived legal punishment in the inhibition of criminal involvement. *Journal of Criminal Law and Criminology, 74,* 270-297.

Paternoster R., Saltzman, L. E., Waldo, G. P. & Chiricos, G. (1983b). Perceived risk and social control: Do sanctions really deter? *Law & Society Review 17,* 457-479.

Piliavin, I., Gartner, R., Thornton, G., & Matsueda, L. M. (1986). Crime, deterrence and rational choice. *American Sociological Review, 51,* 101-119.

Robben, H. S. J. (1991). *A behavioral simulation and documented behavior approach to income tax evasion.* Deventer: Kluwer.

Simon, H. (1982). *Models of bounded rationality.* Cambridge: MIT Press.

Thaler, R. (1985). Mental accounting and consumer choice. *Marketing Science, 4,* 199-214.

Van Baal, P. (2004) *Computer simulations of criminal deterrence. From public policy to local interaction to individual behaviour.* Den Haag: Boom Juridische uitgevers.

Webley, P., Robben, H. S. J., Elffers, H., & Hessing, D. J. (1991) *Tax evasion: An experimental approach.* European Monographs on Social Psychology, Cambridge: Cambridge University Press.

Wilson, J. Q., & Herrnstein, R. J. (1985). *Crime and human nature.* New York: Simon and Schuster.

ADDITIONAL READING

An, L., Linderman, M, Qi, J., Shortridge, A., & Liu, J. (2005). Exploring complexity in a human-environment system: An agent-based spatial model for multidisciplinary and multiscale integration.

Annals Association of American Geographers, 95(1), 54-79.

Axelrod, R. (2006). Advancing the art of simulation in the social sciences. In J-P., Rennard (Ed.), *Handbook of research on nature inspired computing for economy and management*. Hershey, PA: Idea Group.

Bonabeau, E., Dorigo, M., & Theraulaz, G. (1999). *Swarm intelligence: From natural to artificial systems.* New York: Oxford University Press.

Bosse, T. Jonker, C. M., & Treur, J. (2004). Representational content and the reciprocal interplay of agent and environment. In *Proceedings of the Third International Joint Conference on Autonomous Agents and Multiagent Systems* (Vol. 3), 1408-1409. Washington, D.C.: IEEE.

Bosse, T., & Treur, J. Formal interpretation of a multi-agent society as a single agent. *Journal of Artificial Societies and Social Simulation, 9*(2).

Brantingham, P. L., & Brantingham, P. J. (2004). Computer simulation as a tool for environmental criminologists. *Security Journal, 17*(1), 21-30.

Cornelissen, F., Jonker, C. M., & Treur, J. (2003). Compositional verification of knowledge-based task models and problem-solving methods. *Knowledge and Information Systems, 5*(3), 337-367.

Dibble, C. (2006). Computational laboratories for spatial agent-based models. In L. Tesfatsion, K. L. Judd (Eds.), *Handbook of computational economics, Vol. 2: Agent-based computational economics* (Vol. 2). Amsterdam: Elsevier.

Groff, E. R. (2007). Simulation for theory testing and experimentation: An example using routine activity theory and street robbery. *Journal of Quantitative Criminology, 23,* 75-103.

Liu, L., Wang, X., Eck, J., Liang, J. (2005). Simulating crime events and crime patterns in RA/CA model. In F. Wang (Ed.), *Geographic information systems and crime analysis* (pp. 197-213). Singapore: Idea Group.

Van Baal, P. H. M., Feenstra, T. L., Hoogenveen, R. T., De Wit, G. A., & Brouwer, W. B. F. (2006). Unrelated medical care in life years gained and the cost utility of primary prevention: in search of a 'perfect' cost-utility ratio. *Health Economics, 16*(4), 421-433.

Van Baal, P. H. M., Hoogenveen, R. T., De Wit, G. A., & Boshuizen, H. C. (2006). Estimating health-adjusted life expectancy conditional on risk factors: Results for smoking and obesity. *Population Health Metrics, 4,* 14.

ENDNOTE

1 Many discussions about simulation issues with colleagues helped in forming our ideas, we especially like to mention discussions with Michael Townsley (Jill Dando Institute, London), as well as the comments on the previous version of the paper by reviewers, editors and by Wim Bernasco (NSCR, Leiden).

Chapter III
Visualization of Criminal Activity in an Urban Population

Alex Breuer
Indiana University-Bloomington, USA

Joshua J. Hursey
Indiana University-Bloomington, USA

Tonya Stroman
Indiana University-Bloomington, USA

Arvind Verma
Indiana University-Bloomington, USA

ABSTRACT

Crime is a multidimensional, complex, and dynamic activity. In order to understand its nature one has to comprehend not only its spatio-temporal dimensions, but also the nature of crime, the victim-offender relationship, role of guardians and history of similar previous incidents. This is a formidable task due to the limitations of present visualization methods. Both for the police department and criminal justice researcher the need to visualize a vast amount of data is a prerequisite to the task of dealing with the crime phenomenon. This chapter presents an interactive visualization intended to present the viewer with an accurate and intuitive view of the criminal activity in a cityscape. The technique employs many different visualization elements, which taken together presents a useful methodology that can be used to visualize many of the associated factors of crime. The chapter also presents the software technique and discusses points for future investigation.

INTRODUCTION

Crime mapping is now an acknowledged tool for criminal justice practitioners. Its utility has been suggested in supporting problem solving and community policing efforts improving law enforcement and criminal justice operations to apprehending and convicting offenders (LaVigne

& Wartell, 1998). Crime mapping has also led to some powerful investigative techniques such as "geographical profiling" (Rossmo, 1995) to track serial offenders and understand the movement patterns of offenders. The utility of crime maps in analyzing crime data (Hirschfield & Bowers, 2001; Law & Haining, 2004), in understanding neighborhood ethnic composition (Brimicombe, 2001), in analyzing drug markets (Voltz, 1999), in examining homicide hot spots (Adams, 2001), repeat victimization (Ratcliffe & McCullagh, 1998) and in police management (Walsh & Vito, 2004) have all been demonstrated unambiguously. However, crime-mapping applications have generally been confined to a limited number of dimensions; in particular, the spatial dimensions (Block, Dabdoub, & Fregly, 1995; O'Kane, Fisher, & Green, 1994; Weisburd & McEwen, 1997).

Brantingham and Brantingham (1981) suggest that there are four dimensions that constitute a criminal event: the law which defines the act to be criminal; the motivated offender; the victim or the target and the coming together of all three at a geographical convergence. Further, that crime is facilitated by the environment surrounding a criminal event that takes place against the backdrop of awareness space of the motivated offender. Obviously, the convergence that takes place at the geographical location is itself facilitated by several factors. For example, "routine activities" brings the victim and offender in close proximity in the absence of guardianship at a specific place (Cohen & Felson 1979). Similarly, the nature of "hot spot" (Sherman & Buerger 1989) that makes the place criminogenic and the situational factors (Clarke, 1993) which provide opportunities for the criminal event to occur also play an important role in facilitating crime at a particular spot. Despite this multidimensional nature of criminal activities visualization techniques have largely remained confined to a limited number of dimensions. Commonly, crime maps use street networks and colored symbols to depict the nature of criminal incidents. By adding orthogonal images and surrounding landmarks, mappers are able to add more information to the visualization. However, these methods are unable to depict and incorporate simultaneously other factors and dimensions of crime thus reducing the utility of visualization.

Since a criminal event is an interconnected incident of several dimensions, investigators and analysts need more information than the simple geographical location of the incident. The ability to solve crimes and develop preventive methods is dependent upon the capability of answering the six W's about the criminal incident: Where and when did it take place, what is the nature of incident, who has done it to whom, and why. Thus, it is not only necessary to know where the crime took place, the spatial coordinates, street address and neighborhood information but also the time period, victim-offender characteristics, relation to previous and neighboring incidents as well as knowledge of police response. This knowledge is best acquired and transmitted through some form of visualization technique and consequently crime mapping is a necessary tool for investigators.

Two-dimensional maps have been used to describe crime since 1830. Due to the inherently geospatial nature of the data, crime visualization borrows heavily from cartographic design, and most designs are based in a geospatial substrate. Current approaches to geospatial crime visualization have successfully addressed the problems of representing crime density information with techniques from cartography utilizing chloropleth maps, graduated symbol maps and topographical maps. However, the temporal dimension of crime in most analyses is neglected in favor of the spatial dimensions. One reason is the inherent difficulty of visualizing space and time together. The approaches to representing temporal data in a geospatial substrate are not as well developed as the former techniques.

One current approach is to represent crime data in an artificial 3-D perspective, in which the third dimension represents time. This approach suffers from the problems of projecting a 3-D model into a 2-D projection, such as occlusion and distortion of data. Two dimensional computer screens and paper copies make it impossible to display more than the three spatial dimensions. Therefore, another method attempted by the researchers is to display the data through creative use of colors and symbols that add more information about the nature of crime incidents (Bonneau, Ertl, & Nielson 2006). Another method is to use a series of separate map windows where the incidents are shown over different periods of time. Such a technique is limited since it is difficult to comprehend information from separate windows and fails to provide comprehensive information that accrues from viewing space and time together.

More advanced computational methods such as virtual reality modeling language (VRML) have been used to add temporal information to the spatial dimension in an interactive manner (Lodha, & Verma 1999). However, this demonstration has suffered from two limitations: the project was not directly geared towards the development of spatio-temporal dimensions but more concerned with enhancing the ability of the investigators to visualize the crime data in a new manner. Second, it did not develop a system of visualization that could easily be adopted by investigators. That is, criminal justice practitioners could realize the capabilities of VRML but had no way of knowing how to adopt it to their own problems and data sets. Nevertheless, packing greater and greater information is difficult if not impossible with the techniques mentioned above. In order to deal with these problems we develop and present another technique that enables several dimensions of the information to be visualized simultaneously by the researcher. Recently, Brantingham and Brantingham (2004) have suggested computer simulation as a new tool for understanding the crime phenomenon, a technique that forms the raison d'teur for this book.

Our objective is to transform the large, complex and detailed dataset that is available about crime incidents, and present it in a visually appropriate and nonoverwhelming manner. We believe such visualizations will enable crime analysts to easily interpret the data and find patterns for solving the crimes. It will also enable police officers to find historical hotspots of crime, and tract crime trends for a specified area. Accordingly, in this chapter, as an illustration we set out to visualize the following dimensions of the criminal incidents:

- Crime rate and density in a specific area.
- Number of arrests made for a specific crime.
- Trend of a type of crime of a given time range.
- Top 5 or 10 most dominant crime types.
- Locations of dense criminal activity.
- Location of significant landmarks (e.g., police stations, fire departments, hospitals, and schools) in relation to areas of crime.

The visualization technique is based upon "multiple window system" where the crime data is divided into its constituent parts that are viewed in an overlapping manner. This enables the viewer to obtain all or any part of the information in an easy to comprehend manner. The technique was developed to provide the ability to transition between viewing the data representation for a specific location and the whole city. This suggests the need for a zoom and pan feature for map interactions; provide the ability to zoom into the data, eventually presenting the exact statistical data for a specific crime; and representing significant landmarks prominently on the map. This establishes a common reference system, and easy correlation between incident response resources and crime incidents. We also incorporated the capability to represent the trend of a type of crime for some time period. This is used to determine if an area is becoming safer or not. Further, our interest was to represent the most dominant types of crime, and their relation to each other for a specific area.

Data and Its Transformation

We used the data provided by the Indianapolis police department representing selected criminal incidents in Indianapolis between Jan. 1, 2000 to Dec. 31, 2000. For each criminal incident, the dataset provided: street address, geographic information system (GIS) coordinates, timestamp (date & time), and criminal code reference. The data, numbering roughly 33,000 records, was brought into the ArcGIS 9.1 software where using the street address, we were able to map the criminal incident to a specific location on the map. We used census tracks to define a spatial grouping for the crimes. Using this as a reference, we can focus the zoom in on a specific census track in the map. Once focused on a specific area, we can represent the density and rate of crime in that area at a higher resolution. The GIS software also allows us to access the locations of various landmarks such as the location of police stations, fire stations, hospitals, and schools. In addition to these landmarks, we also represented primary streets, and landmarks of significant note. These landmarks help orient the viewer when presented with the map at different scales.

Timestamp

By using the timestamp, we can group crimes into temporal categories. We incorporated the facility to let the viewer determine the granularity of the categories. For example, if the viewer requests a single year of data, then the categories may be represented by month. If they request a single day, then the categories may be represented by hour. By restricting the time range, the viewer also limits the amount of data that needs to be processed, since we need not process data outside the specified time range.

Crime Code

The crime code classification allows us to group crimes together into a hierarchy of categories. For this dataset we were able to represent the following primary categories: Assault, Burglary, Homicide, Larceny, Rape, Robbery, and Vehicle Theft. Each primary category has one or more subcategories. By representing crime in a hierarchical manner we could present the viewer with an overall view of the crime density or rate in an area, and then allow them to focus their attention on a specific type of crime. We aggregate the crime data into these seven categories because these are the major crimes represented in the data set provided. Exploring alternative aggregation categorizations is left for future work

Visualization

The objective of the visualization was to represent the spatiality of, trends in, and correlations between crimes, while always preserving a common reference system. From our data analysis we were able to extract the visualizations and incorporate the facility to provide a viewer the desired information in an appropriate and nonoverwhelming manner. Each of these visualizations was represented in a distinct overlapping window that ensured the information was available if desired.

Spatial Representation

We began with a 2-D geographic map of Indianapolis generated with GIS software which overlays the landmarks (noted earlier) onto the visual field. This map allows for a common reference system for the viewer. To this map we added a hillshade representation of the crime data.

The hillshade representation expresses the density (or rate) of criminal incidents in a specific area in relation to adjacent areas, over the entire time range specified. The color representation ranges from high crime density in red (darker in the black and white figure) to low crime density in green (lighter in the black and white figure). The shading adds depth to the 2-D image without tilting the map into the 3-D plane. Areas of higher

Figure 1. Spatial representation

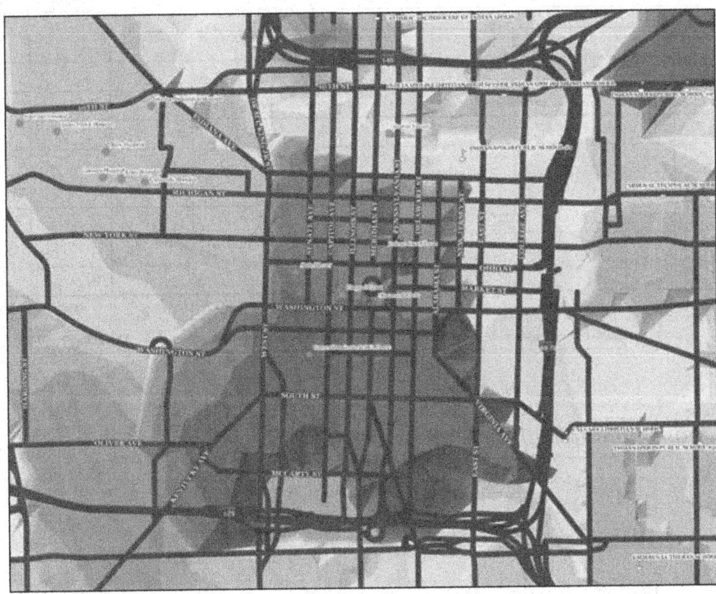

elevation correlate to areas of high crime density. The city map is then overlaid on the hillshade representation, which allows the landmarks to stand-out more prominently without being obfusticated by the hillshading. For each zoomed view, this spatial representation is recreated for the zoomed area. The zoomed area is then overlaid upon the full map of the city, emanating from the center of the mouse click. This allows the viewer to move between views of the entire city, and associate the current view with a region of the city.

Treemap Visualization Technique

In our visualization, we sought to preserve the hierarchical nature of the crime code classification system. By using a treemap visualization technique (Shneiderman, 1992) we were able to preserve the hierarchy and allow the viewer to zoom into the data by clicking on the primary categories.

If a user clicks on a primary category then they are presented with another window, on top of the previous, that presents the subcategories for that category in a treemap format. The user is able to ascend the hierarchy by clicking on the treemap window under the current window. The color-coding matches the color-coding selected by the user. By allowing the user to define the color-coding used in the visualization they can more readily identify those crime categories that they are most concerned with, and identify them with a color that is significant to the viewer.

Temporal Representation

We explored many different techniques for expressing trends in crime for a given area. The most obvious of which, is the line graph that provides the crime trend for a specific time period.

Apart from the line we wanted to explore a different representation that might assist the viewer in identifying trends more readily. One option we created was a crime clock where the trend is presented radially. The advantage with this representation is that for the daily period of time it has a familiar look and is more comprehensible. The clock visualization is shown in Figure 4.

Figure 2. Temporal line graph

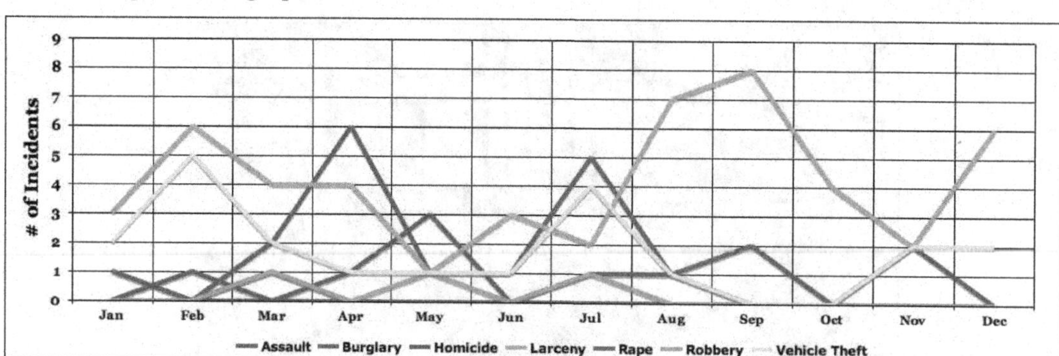

Figure 3. Crime relationship treemap

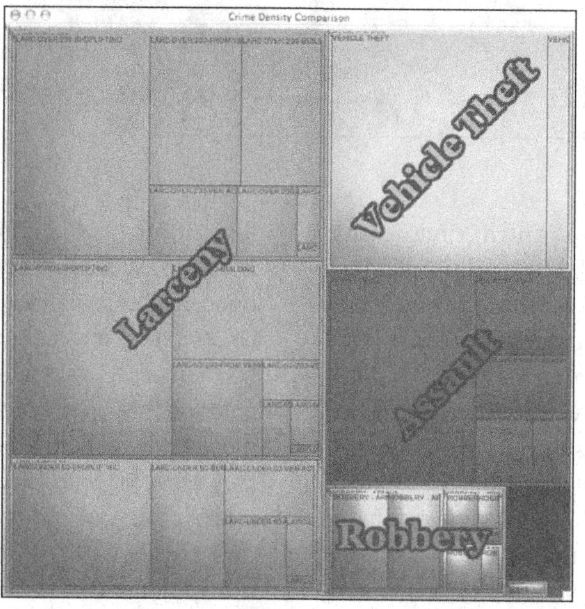

Each slice of the clock represents a time segment in which crimes are aggregated. The number of incidents for the time segment is in red so as to stand out, and each time segment is labeled appropriately. By placing the color-coded name for the category in the middle of the clock, we allow for the viewer to easily identify the current category in view. The shading of the time segments is meant to visually indicate the progression of time around the circle in a clock-wise manner. For each category, there is one clock for visualization. In order to depict all of the clock visualizations at the same time, we employ a fisheye distortion technique (Bederson, 2000). This allows the viewer to bring into focus one-clock visualization at a time, and the others become pushed to the periphery.

Combination of Visual Elements

When all of the visual elements are taken together, we produce an interactive visual environment in

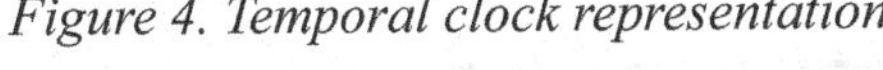

Figure 4. Temporal clock representation

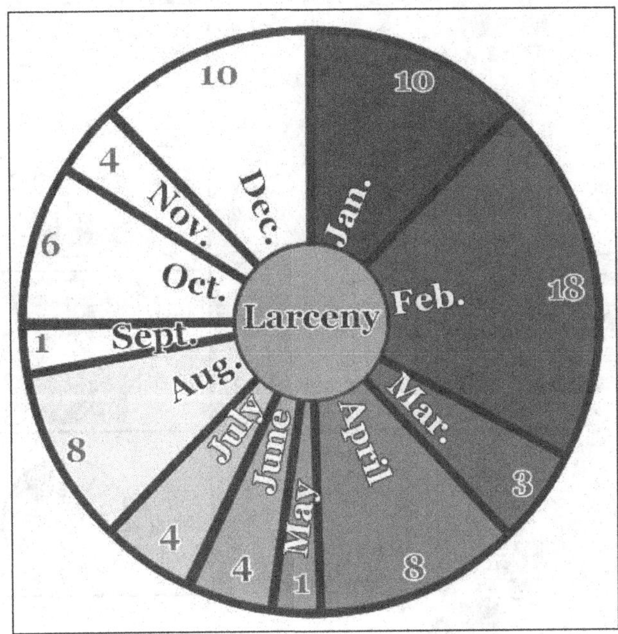

which the viewer can explore the criminal incident dataset. Each visual element depicts the relationship between the density, or rate of criminal activity to time, space, or each other. A snapshot of the visualization can be seen in Figure 5.

Technical Specifications

Programming Tools

The following tools and programming languages were utilized in developing the visualization[1]:

- ArcGIS Software (ArcSDE API)
- Java, Perl, C/C++ Programming Languages
- Relational Database (e.g, Oracle, PostgreSQL)
- An interactive visualization environment (e.g., Open GL, Processing (Fry and Reas))

Pipeline

The visualization is accumulated in a pipelined manner, developing the data and visual representations as it progresses from the raw data to the final rendering. The individual stages allow for distinct re-execution based on user-guided input possibly minimizing the amount of data to be recomputed for the desired visualization. In addition, by allowing the user to interact with earlier stages in the pipeline the software can effectively generate a more customized visualization.

There are four main stages: Raw Data, Data Table Transformations, Visual Mapping, and View Transformations.

Raw Data

This is the raw data representation. The data is saved in a relational database, and is accessed using standard SQL queries. ArcGIS uses this

Figure 5. Visualization snapshot

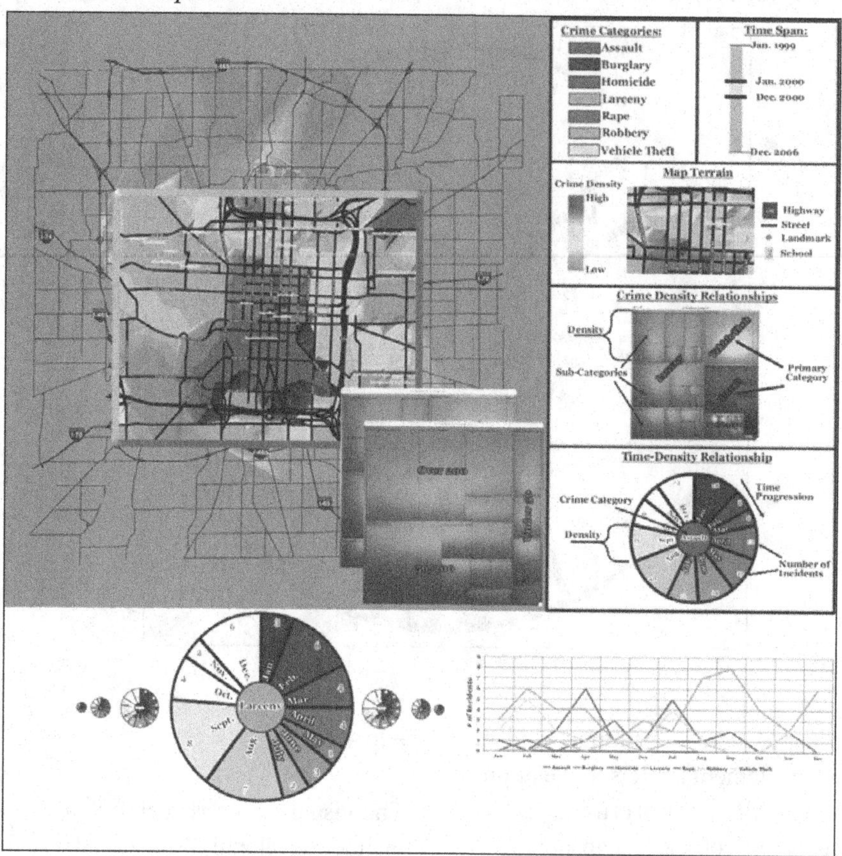

Figure 6. Visualization pipeline

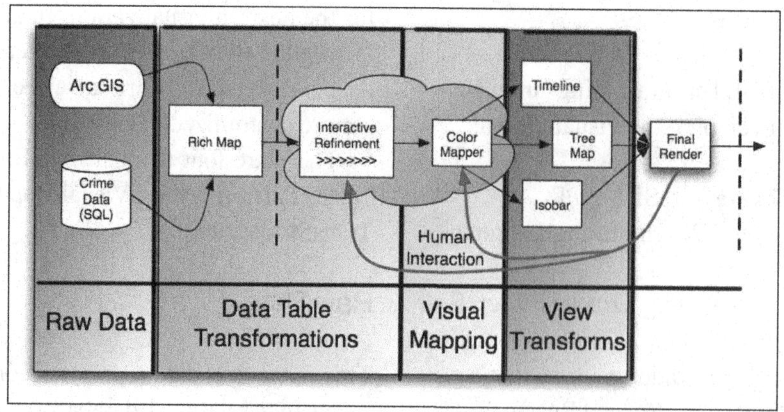

database to aggregate the data when rendering the spatial representation. The combination of ArcGIS and the relational database generate a map with associated metadata from the database. The development of the *Rich Map* is the first aggregation of data, which contains all of the data represented by both the ArcGIS and database systems. This *Rich Map* can be saved to a database, as to alleviate the need for ArcGIS in the pipeline.

Data Table Transformations

In this section of the pipeline, the system is attempting to refine the data set based upon the parameters set the by user and their interactions with the system. For example, the user will select a time range over which they wish to view the data set. The *Interactive Refinement* stage will reduce the *Rich Map* to a subset of the data included in this range. Similarly this stage would also reduce the *Rich Map* to just the data that is currently in zoom. This is all to prepare just the subset of the data that the user is concerned with for the visual elements to work with at a later stage in the pipeline. This is the first stage where the user has influence upon the data that is displayed.

Visual Mapping

This takes the constrained *Rich Map* of data, and imposes a color mapping upon it in the *Color Mapper* component. The *Color Mapper* component takes the user defined color-to-crime mapping and adds it to the *Rich Map*. This is then all of the information that the different visual elements need to produce their respective visual elements.

View Transforms

This is where each individual visual element is able to act upon the reduced and enhanced *Rich Map* dataset. For this visualization this stage includes the visual elements: *Timeline*, or the temporal representations; *Treemap*, or the crime relationship representation; and *Isobar*, which is the spatial representation. These are described in more detail in the subsequent section. Each visual element module produced one or more images for the *Rich Map* that they were presented with, which represents the user requested dataset.

Final Render

Once all of the visual elements have been produced, they are all combined together with the base map and legend to produce the final rendering of the image, which is presented to the user. As the user interacts with the final rendering of the image they have influence upon the pipeline. The stage at which they influence is the stage at which the pipeline must restart from. For example, if the user changes the color-coding, then the pipeline is re-executed from the *Visual Mapping* stage, as the *Data Table Transformations* stage is not directly affected by this interaction. An example of a final rendering is shown in Figure 6.

Spatial Representation

There are several choices for algorithms to interpolate a function over a nonlinear surface defined by discrete measurements. For example, one could use polynomial splines, Levenberg-Marquardt, or Delaunay triangulation (Okabe, Boots, & Sugihara 1992). Since the surface need not be differentiable, Delaunay triangulation is an appealing choice due to its simplicity relative to the other options, and that it is included in popular GIS tools. In order to draw the temporal crime map, it is necessary to have geospatial crime density information. Although this could be accomplished by imposing an arbitrary grid over the map, and computing crime density based on those cells, such a grid is inherently arbitrary. In is important to use more natural boundaries for the crime density data to have meaning. Furthermore, it is important to have an appropriate level of granularity, so the geospatial subdivisions must not be too large or small. For computing crime density, we used crimes per police precinct for the crime topology, and census tracts for other experimental maps. We observed that the police precinct divisions produced appropriate density information, which was more granular than the census tracts, although this may not necessarily hold generally.

The ArcGIS tools provide all the database functionality to produce the static features of the maps we used for our design proof. Indeed, one could automate the map generation process using the ArcSDE programming API. Most data processing steps only require simple database operations; the only GIS specific data processing operations are spatial joins and geocoding. ArcGIS also offers creation of triangulated irregular networks for crime topology synthesis. In coloring the crime topology, we found that color categories were best assigned by Jenk's natural breaks, which ArcGIS supports. Finally, ArcGIS can rasterize map information, which would allow another program to associate points on the map with database entries for interactive tree and temporal map drawing. An example of a spatial representation is shown in Figure 1.

Crime Relationship Representation

For this visual element we used a treemap that was generated with a popular library written in Java (HCIL, Treemap Project). The treemap can be zoomed in as the user clicks on the different primary nodes in the tree. The labeling is something that needs to be improved in the library, to produce the visualization needed for this interactive visualization. As the user zooms into the treemap by clicking on primary nodes, another treemap should be overlaid upon the parent as to represent a stack hierarchy, allowing the user to return to a previous, higher view of the tree. If the user hovers their mouse over a node in the treemap it will popup with a small "tooltip"-like window showing the specific data for that node, and it's children. This is a feature currently built into the library.

Representation Themes

All of the temporal representations were presented close together in the final rendering, as to directly correlate them to each other. The line graph representation was developed in Microsoft Excel, but could also be produced with other graphics packages such as GNUplot. The actual number associated with the density or rate of crime was presented at the edge of the interior of the image in red, as to standout in the image. The textual representation of the time slice was placed near the interior of the graphic. The interior circle was associated with the color-coded crime and name of the crime for quick identification. The time slices were ordered in a clock-wise manner and their background shading in degrading gradients of grey, as to express the clock-wise ordering of the information. One such clock was presented for each crime category in the dataset.

By producing one temporal clock for each crime category in the dataset, the system produced more clocks that can be easily displayed on the final rendering. Therefore, we used a fisheye menu technique that can allow the user to focus upon one clock, and move the other clocks into the periphery of the menu. We also provided an interactive legend that could explain all of the different visual elements. We also provided interactive buttons to allow the user to dynamically restrict the time range explored, and color-coding of crimes in the final rendering. Preliminary user studies indicated that the clock representation was a useful representation.

CONCLUSION

The work does not stop with the final rendering. The user needs to be able to interact with the data to properly explore the face of crime in the city. If the visual element distorts the data in any way, the user will interpret inaccurate data, and be lead to make improper correlations from the visualization. Thus, while developing this application we attempted to make sure that the user is able to intuitively interact with each of the visual elements and that the visual elements accurately represent the data that they are acting upon.

The advantage of using this visualization technique is the ability to create multiple overlapping windows for depicting the different dimensions of crime. Apart from the spatio-temporal dimensions, information about the nature of crime, victim-offender characteristics, neighborhood, previous incidents, and police action can all be displayed in separate windows for the viewer. As the fisheye visual suggests the windows could be made to hide behind other windows so that the viewer can focus upon the needed information. The facility to add colors and symbols of choice, of selecting time and spatial cone of resolution further adds capabilities of adding more information to the incident and area under study. Since the required computer programming is not too challenging, most researchers can easily adopt the technique.

A further area of research is to embed this technique with the VRML for panning into the area for a variety of images. VRML has been shown to present space and time together in an interactive manner. The capability of zooming into the area and viewing the image from a variety of angles is a special feature of VRML. By incorporating the two techniques the visualization becomes dynamic and extremely versatile in displaying almost all the features of criminal incidents.

FUTURE RESEARCH DIRECTIONS

Visualization is a young field, barely 20 years old, yet it is fast emerging as a powerful tool of analysis for criminal justice. The US Department of Homeland Security has pressed for its applications in intelligence analysis, emergency response and disaster prevention, and border security. A recent symposium on visualization (Ribarsky, 2006) explored topics such as visual thinking, medical diagnosis applications, the promise and challenges in the new field of visual analytics, and the prospects for automating graphic design. Visualization is providing insight into new frontiers by the growing association of physical scientists, artists, engineers, managers, and social scientists. Interestingly, new techniques in visualization are taking more complex tasks that involve exploratory and diagnostic processes. These in turn are encouraging researchers to consider the whole perceptual and cognitive ranges that can test bold hypothesis and build new realms of knowledge.

For example, a new development called Sense-making is a framework for modeling and understanding visual analyses that lead to decisions, starting with evidence gathering, leading to hypothesis building, and ending with presentation for action (Card, Mackinlay, & Shneiderman 1999). This is likely to have significant importance for criminal justice where decisions ranging from patrol deployment to narrowing down the list of suspects are going to benefit from this process. Another promising concept is that of knowledge building where the researcher deals directly with knowledge artifacts rather than data artifacts that may enable the creation of visualizations of much higher value. Yet another application helps police in detecting transportation of dangerous substances. A simulation program designed to track the illicit trade in fissile and nonfissile radiological material well enough to predict who is building the next nuclear weapon and where they are doing it. This program uses cluster analysis algorithm to evaluate traffic patterns and routes in which thefts, seizures, and destinations of materials were reported. This program was tested on the AQ Khan network which was linked to the illicit proliferation of nuclear technical knowledge. Cluster analyses linked data of common-place, time, and material and the data established the validity of the program. The program is being used for understanding transportation of drugs and smuggled goods (York, 2007).

The RAND Corporation is using simulation to train police officers in firearms tactics and firearms discharge review procedures, and examine reflexive or "contagious" shooting issues. Simulation is also being used to understand the impact of natural disasters and test police as well as emergency team responses. TARAS, a private corporation has developed simulation techniques to investigate and reconstruct accidents involving police and other emergency vehicles (Perlman, 2006). The company also helps in issues involving work zone traffic control; roadway signing and vehicle crush damage analysis. An interesting application is the concept of "near match of DNA" (Cook, 2006). At present, investigators look for perfect match to identify the suspect. However, if there is only a near match, the researchers suggest, that person is likely to be a sibling, parent, or child of the suspect, providing detectives with a lead. This could help in identifying a relative that could provide the crucial break to focus upon the likely suspect. This familial searching could be an effective tool for police investigators. The computer simulation suggested that this procedure would increase the number of times DNA would point to the right person by almost 40%.

In our presentation we utilized the TreeMap visualization technique for matter of convenience and visual appeal. However, the tree-map is a two-dimensional visualization technique for displaying *large* amounts of hierarchically structured information. An alternative technique is that of Cone-Tree which is a three-dimensional representation of hierarchical information. The hierarchy is presented in 3-D to maximize effective use of available screen space and enable visualization of the whole structure. Reconfigurable disc trees (RDT) is a further extension or improvement to the cone tree approach. RDT has key information associated with each cone: a reference point and an apex point. Different tree shapes can be created by changing the distance between the parent node, reference point, apex node, and center point of a cone base. By varying these distances, the cone can be flattened out and become a disc, thus making more effective use of screen space. With this feature, more nodes can be visualized before visual clutter sets in. Accordingly, application of these techniques is likely to enhance the quality and power of visualization and would be worth pursuing. We also used the Jenskins natural method to classify the data points. It is well known that there are many other choices for classification; all give something different from the other methods. The choice is subjective but worth exploring with different data sets to determine which provides the best form of visualization.

There are additional areas that we propose for a similar crime data set:

- Consider implementation of the full interactive environment for the crime data.
- Define and complete more rigorous user studies for each visualization elements effectiveness.
- Explore alternative techniques for aggregate data-set categorization.
- Evaluate different spatial aggregation units as alternative to the census track version we used. This may improve effectiveness for small neighborhood visualizations.
- Assess the level of visual error and trust expressed by this visualization environment.
- Explore alternative applications of this visualization technique to different kinds of criminal activity (e.g., visualization of social criminal network evolution).

In this chapter we have restricted ourselves to static visualization techniques. However, to adequately incorporate the dimension of time into the visualization of space, and to take advantage of the rapidly expanding field of visualization and more powerful methods of computation dynamic animation, simulation and visualization approaches are likely to be more effective and futuristic. For example, XD3, an established ISO standard for real-time 3-D computer graphics features useful extensions to VRML, such as the ability to encode the scene using XML syntax and enhanced application programmer interfaces (APIs). This and similar emerging technologies will be the next frontier in visualizing crime.

REFERENCES

Adams, T. M. (2001). *Historical homicide hot spots: The case of three cities.* Ann Arbor, MI: UMI.

Bederson, B. B. (2000). Fisheye menus. In *Proceedings of the 13th Annual ACM Symposium on User interface Software and Technology,* San Diego, California (pp. 217-225) ACM Press. Retrieved August 24, 2007, from http://doi.acm.org/10.1145/354401.354782

Block, C. R., Dabdoub, M., & Fregly, S. (Eds.) (1995). *Crime analysis through computer mapping* (pp. 15-32). Washington, D.C.: Police Executive Research Forum..

Bonneau, G-P., Ertl, T., & Nielson, G. M. (Eds.) (2006). *Scientific visualization: The visual extraction of knowledge from data.* Berlin: Springer.

Brantingham, P. J., & Brantingham, P. L. (1981). *Environmental criminology.* Beverley Hills, CA: Sage.

Brantingham, P. L., & Brantingham, P. J. (2004). Computer simulation as a tool for environmental criminologists. *Security Journal, 17*(1), 21-30.

Brimicombe, A. J., Ralphs, M. P., & Sampson, A. (2001). An analysis of the role of neighborhood ethnic composition in the geographical distribution of racially motivated incidents. *British Journal of Criminology, 41*(2), 293-308.

Card, S. (2006). *Using vision to think.* Paper presented at Symposium on the Future of Visualization. Charlotte Visualization Center, Charlotte, NC. Retrieved August 24, 2007, from http://www.viscenter.uncc.edu/symposium06/

Cook, G. (2006). *Near match of DNA could lead police to more suspects.* Globe.

Chattoe, E., & Hamill, H. (2005). It's not who you know—It's what you know about people you don't know that counts: Extending the analysis of crime groups as social networks. *British Journal of Criminology, 45*(6), 860-876.

Chen, H., Miranda, R., & Zeng, D. D. (2003). *Intelligence and security informatics: First NSF/NIJ Symposium,* ISI 2003 (Vol. 2665) Tucson, AZ.

Clarke, R. V. (1993). *Crime prevention studies.* Monsey: NY: Criminal Justice Press.

Cohen, L. E., & Felson, M. (1979). Social change and crime rate trends: A routine activity approach. *American Sociological Review, 44,* 588-608.

Fry, B., & Reas, C. *Processing* 1.0 (BETA). Retrieved August 24, 2007, from http://processing.org/

Hirschfield, A., & Bowers, K. J. (2001). The development of a social, demographic and land use profiler for areas of high crime. *British Journal of Criminology, 37*(1), 103-120.

LaVigne, N. G., Wartell, J. (1998). *Crime mapping case studies: Successes in the field.* Washington, D.C.: Police Executive Research Forum.

Law, J., & Haining, R. (2004). A Bayesian approach to modeling binary data: The case of high-intensity crime areas. *Geographical Analysis, 36*(3), 187-216.

Lodha, S., & Verma, A. (1999). Animations of crime map using virtual reality modeling language. *Western Criminology Review.* Retrieved August 24, 2007, from http://wcr.sonoma.edu/v1n2/lodha.html

Oatley, G. C., & Ewart, B. W. (2003). Crimes analysis software: "Pins in maps," clustering and Bayes net prediction. *Expert Systems with Applications, 25*(4), 569-588.

Okabe, A., Boots, B., & Sugihara, K. (1992). *Spatial tessellations: Concepts and applications of Voronoi diagrams.* New York: Wiley & Sons.

O'Kane, J. B., Fisher, R. M., & Green, L. (1994). Mapping campus crime. *Security Journal, 5*(3), 172-180.

Perlman, D. (2006, March 29). Scientists recreate action of '06 quake: Detailed depiction of temblor's severity. *San Francisco Chronicle.*

Ratcliffe, J. H., & McCullagh, M. J. (1998). Identifying repeat victimization with GIS. *British Journal of Criminology, 38*(4), 651-662.

Ribarsky, W. (2006). *Symposium on the future of visualization.*, Charlotte, NC: Charlotte Visualization Center. Retrieved August 24, 2007, from http://www.viscenter.uncc.edu/symposium06/

Rossmo, K. (1995). *Geographic profiling: Target patterns of serial murderers.* Unpublished doctoral thesis. Burnaby: Simon Fraser University

Sherman, L. W., & Buerger, M. E. (1989). Hot spots of predatory crime: Routine activities and the criminology of place. *Criminology, 27*(1), 27-55.

Shneiderman, B. (1992, January). Tree visualization with tree-maps: 2-d space-filling approach. *ACM Transactions on Graphics, 11*(1), 92-99. Retrieved August 24, 2007, from http://doi.acm.org/10.1145/102377.115768

Treemap Project. *HCIL*, University of Maryland. Retrieved August 24, 2007, from http://www.cs.umd.edu/hcil/treemap/

Voltz, D. (1999). *Mapping illicit drug markets.* Brisbane, Australia: Queensland Police Service.

Walsh, W. F., & Vito, G. F. (2004). The meaning of COMSTAT: Meaning and response. *Journal of Contemporary Criminal Justice, 20*(1), 51-69.

Weisburd, D., & McEwen, T. (Eds.) (1997). *Crime mapping and crime prevention.* Monsey, NY: Criminal Justice Press.

York, D. (2007). *Sandia computer simulation monitors traffic in contraband nuclear material.* Retrieved August 24, 2007, from http://www.sciencedaily.com/releases/2007/01/070117134034.htm

ADDITIONAL READINGS

Badler, N. I., & Webster, R. W. (1998). SIGgraph VRML 3D Conetree. *ACM SIGgraph Computer Graphics, 32*(3), 43-44.

Baeza-Yates, R., & Ribeiro-Neto, B. (1999). *Modern information retrieval.* Addison Wesley.

Brown, J. R., Jern, M., Vince, J., & Earnshaw, R. A. (1995). *Visualization: Using computer graphics to explore data and present information.* John Wiley & Sons.

Card, S. K., Mackinlay, J. D., & Shneiderman, B. (1999). *Readings in information visualization: Using vision to think.* Morgan Kaufmann Publishers Inc.

Furnas, G. W. (1986). *Generalized fisheye views.* In *Proceedings of the SIGCHI Conference on Human Factors in Computing Systems CHI '86* (pp. 16-23). New York: ACM Press.

Harris, R. L. (2000). *Information graphics: A comprehensive illustrated reference.* Oxford University Press.

Johnson, G., Ebert, D., Hansen, C., Kirk, D., Mark, B., & Pfister, H. (2004). *The future visualization platform visualization.* IEEE, *10*(15), 569-571.

Krygier, J., & Wood, D. (2005). *Making maps: A visual guide to map design for GIS*. The Guilford Press.

Kuniavsky, M. (2003). *Observing the user experience: A practitioner's guide to user research*. Morgan Kaufmann Publisher.

MacEachren, A. M. (2004). *How maps work: Representation, visualization, and design*. The Guilford Press.

Mayhew, D. J. (1999). *The usability engineering lifecycle*. Morgan Kaufmann Publisher.

Ormsby, T., Napoleon, E., Burke, R., Groessl, C., & Feaster, L. (2001). *Getting to know ArcGIS desktop*. Esri Press.

Skupin, A. (2000). *From metaphor to method: Cartographic perspectives on information visualization*. In *Proceedings of the IEEE Symposium on Information Vizualization 2000*. INFOVIS. IEEE.

Shreiner, D., Woo, M., Neider, J., & Davis, T. (2005). *OpenGL programming guide* (5th ed). Addison-Wesley.

Tufte, E. R. (1997). *Visual explanations*. Graphics Press.

Tufte, E. R. (1990). *Envisioning information*. Graphics Press.

Tufte, E. R. (1986). *The visual display of quantitative information*. Graphics Press.

Ware, C. (1999). *Information visualization: Perception for design*. Morgan Kaufmann Publishers.

Ware, C., Chi, E.H., & Gossweiler, R. (2000). *CHI 2000: Visual perception and data visualization, Tutorial Notes*. Retrieved August 25, 2007, from http://www-users.cs.umn.edu/%7Eechi/tutorial/perception2000

Wiegers, K. (1999). *Software requirements*. Microsoft Press.

ENDNOTE

1 Due to the sensitive nature of the data set, the dataset and associated source code cannot be released publicly, but is available upon request and approval.

Chapter IV
GIS-Based Simulation and Visualization of Urban Landuse Change

Md Mahbubur R. Meenar
Temple University, USA

ABSTRACT

This chapter introduces the use of geographic information systems simulations and visualizations in urban landuse changes as a means of studying spatial pattern of crime incidents. Through literature reviews the chapter provides a survey of different simulation tools and techniques that have been used in landuse planning. It also provides an overview of the models available for examining landuse changes in the context of planning processes. It argues that three-dimensional simulations of urban landuse change scenarios encourage public participation in the decision making process. The author hopes that the chapter would be useful for criminologists unfamiliar with landuse scenario simulation models and techniques. Furthermore, the chapter suggests how the crime analysts could utilize the available landuse simulation models and tools in analyzing existing crime patterns or predicting future patterns in an urban setting.

INTRODUCTION

Landuse is considered as one type of physical variable behind any crime incidence. Research has shown that the physical characteristics of urban neighborhoods influence crime patterns and particular landuses, such as bars and liquor stores, may attract more crime in their vicinity (Block & Block 1995; Byrne 1986; Greenberg 1986; Loukaitou-Sideris, Liggett, & Iseki, 2002;). This chapter introduces the techniques, methods, and models available for simulating urban landuse changes over time in two and three dimensional (2-D or 3-D) geographic information systems

(GIS) based environment to the criminologists unfamiliar with such models.

The application of GIS based simulation and visualization in the filed of urban and regional planning is a growing one. This chapter focuses on issues related to urban landuse changes over the time. Simulating urban landuse change is a complex problem, as the process requires interdisciplinary communication among planning professionals, technicians, citizens, and stakeholders. Today's GIS software allows the users to visualize 2-D or 3-D virtual simulations of future landuse scenarios with the capability of creating still images and video clips for presentation purposes.

It is the visual representation of any proposed landuse changes—not only numerical output—that attracts the general citizen to get involved in the planning process. Technologically improved and user friendly visualization techniques of urban simulations have always encouraged people to participate in the decision making process.

The use of GIS and other geospatial technologies can play an important role in building trust among planners, policy makers, and citizens. When planners and policy makers make decisions on future development pattern of any community or a subdivision, the use of advanced visualization techniques can overcome the trust issues, especially in disadvantageous communities, which are traditionally the least informed or consulted but the most detrimentally impacted group.

This chapter will discuss some GIS-based methodology and software used for developing and visualizing 2-D or 3-D simulations in the context of urban landuse changes in the United States. It will start discussion on landuse planning, specifically on how the landuse pattern changes over the time and how it affects the spatial distribution of crime pattern. The next section discusses the development process of GIS simulations and scenarios, followed by another section on the creation process of 3-D GIS visualization. Finally some issues and future trends will be discussed with remarks on how these simulation methods could become useful to the criminologists.

BACKGROUND

Change of Urban Landuse Over the Time

Land is a finite resource for most human activities, including settlement, agriculture, communication, and recreation. Land transformation is considered as one of the most important fields of human induced environmental transformation (Wolman & Fournier, 1987). According to Wegener (2005), "the distribution of landuses, such as residential, industrial, or commercial, over the urban area determines the locations of human *activities*, such as living, working, shopping, education, or leisure" (p. 206). However, landuse pattern is constrained by topography, soil type, or vegetation, and landuse-change decisions are frequently driven by property rights, politics, changing demographics, technological advancements, mobility, and market forces of any particular community.

In the United States, the landuse pattern of a community often is a result of the zoning ordinance. Zoning acts as a planning instrument to limit densities, floor-area ratios, or unwanted development; whereas landuse regulations separate the land uses, limiting mixing of residential with commercial or industrial uses (Cullingworth & Caves, 2003; Levine, Inam, & Torng, 2005). Subdivision regulation is another type of landuse tool, which controls the division of larger parcels into smaller ones for sale or redevelopment.

Landuse and zoning regulations vary from region to region or municipality to municipality. For example, the Delaware Valley Regional Planning Commission consists of five counties of Pennsylvania and four counties of New Jersey. This regional planning commission develops digital landuse data based on digital ortho-photography after every five years. Same landuse categories are followed in all of the municipalities inside this region. However, zoning codes are municipality specific. The townships, boroughs, or cities in this region have their own zoning codes.

Landuse patterns change over time for various reasons. Land, being a basic factor of production, always has been tightly coupled with economic growth. The growth of urban built environment can be classified either as expansion or compaction (denser development). Although the expansion of urban areas is still associated with population growth in developing nations, it is rather associated with a more mobile population who demand greater living space and lower densities in the developed countries (Batty & Xie, 2005).

Planners, driven by local objectives and overall community and regional goals, play a key role in the process of predicting future landuse changes by preparing long-term development or preservation plans for the community (Cullingworth & Caves, 2003). Depending on the jurisdiction, a property owner or a planning commission also may propose a zoning amendment in order to allow a more intensive use of any particular area. GIS visualization can help simulating possible scenarios of the outcome of such "upzoning" which can help residents and local officials make decisions about any particular amendment.

Social and Environmental Impacts of Landuse Change

The changes in landuse generate many socio-environmental issues at local, regional, or even broader scale. Cullingworth and Caves (2003) have explained how changes in zoning ordinance may change the physical and environmental character of a particular area. Any kind of upzoning may enhance a particular property and make it more profitable. However, such changes in property use may invite unwelcome neighbors which eventually arouse a fall in property values in that neighborhood. Upzoning also can change physical characteristics of that neighborhood.

One of the leading issues in landuse planning is growth management. The landuse growth pattern is different at different parts of the world. While the developing nations are struggling with the rapidity of growth of the major cities, sprawl has become a problem of urban growth in Europe and North America. Urban or suburban sprawl has been considered as the cause of many social ills, including deterioration of older communities, racial segregation, inadequate job access to poor people, and consumption of farmland and wooded land. Growth management or smart growth is the opposite concept of urban sprawl. According to American Planning Association (2002), "Compact, transit accessible, pedestrian-oriented, mixed use development patterns and land reuse epitomize the application of the principles of smart growth" (p. 2).

Driven by the revolution in transportation technology, rise in personal wealth, and high dependence on the automobile and highway construction, the contemporary land development pattern in the developed nations has loosened ties to the central cities. Considering suburbanization as the predominant form of new growth, this trend follows the outward extension of new development into prime agricultural land, forests, wooded land, or other environmentally sensitive areas (Batty & Xie, 2005; Cervero, 2003; Cullingworth & Caves, 2003; Galstar, Hanson, Ratcliffe, Wolman, Coleman, & Freihage, 2001; Walker, 2004). Some environmental impacts of landuse change from a forest to a residential development may include an increase in the release of greenhouse gases, loss of biodiversity, and sedimentation of lakes and streams (Walker, 2004).

Many communities throughout the United States have been restrictive to such sprawling pattern in order to channel urban growth in desirable directions and manage and preserve their open spaces, green fields, wooded lands, biodiversity, and overall quality of life. Over the last decade planners, economists, and sociologists have been using GIS and other spatial-analytical techniques to understand and analyze this phenomenon.

Influence of Landuse Planning on Crime Pattern

When criminologists analyze the spatial pattern of crime, they tend to ask one common question—where the crime is happening. Is it inside or outside of the building? Is it on the street intersection? What is the landuse type—park, commercial, or rail station? The contextual knowledge of natural and built environment is essential for the proper visual inspection of a crime pattern (Hermann & Maroko, 2006). Many times, crime incidents are related to the landuse pattern of any particular area, such as railway stations, liquor store, or an area with no night activity.

According to Clarke and Eck (2005), built environment is an important criterion in the classification scheme that addresses a crime problem. The authors have specified 11 distinct types of built environment such as residential, recreational, offices, retail, industrial, agricultural, education, human services, public ways, transport, and open/transitional. Most of these classifications are known as landuse classifications in municipalities throughout the United States.

Every landuse category is distinct in their physical or social characteristics. Certain types of crime can be associated with certain types of landuse. For example, areas with vacant lots, schools, parks, ATM machines, and dilapidated houses may attract youth and gang-related crime (Perkins, Meeks, & Taylor, 1992). A study in the city of Buffalo shows that the incidents of larceny are higher surrounding the middle or high school campuses (Taylor, 2001). Another study at Bronx, New York demonstrates that the highest frequency of auto theft is recorded in commercial parking garages located within close proximity to a busy shopping plaza (Hermann & Maroko, 2006). Again, the research of Loukaitou-Sideris, et al. (2002) has shown how the rate of transit crime is highly correlated to the landuse type of the surrounding neighborhoods of the transit stations.

Some crime incidents are influenced by planned landuse changes. For example, a newly developed regional shopping area may create increased theft opportunities, including shoplifting in the stores, thefts from vehicles in the parking areas, and thefts of vehicles in the area. However, much serious crime could be the result of unplanned changes, particularly the deteriorating neighborhoods resulting from the outflow of economic activities.

Landuse information can also be useful to the law enforcement agencies. Among much other information, the zoning and landuse information of a crime scene and its immediate surrounding area can help law enforcement agencies plan and react to a crime incidence more effectively.

Landuse simulation and its relationship to crime incidents can provide useful insight to the city planning agencies. Once the hot spot areas are located in a city map, the city planning authority may consider rezoning or changing the landuse pattern of those areas.

Forecasting Future Landuse Pattern

As an essential part of their profession, landuse planners envision and forecast alternate future landuse and activity patterns in order to change the status quo (Landis, 2001). Market forces can support alternative landuse development forms, which allow the residents to forge a closer link between their preferences for transportation and landuse environments as well as their actual choices (Levine, Inam, & Torng, 2005). Assessing, forecasting, and evaluating future landuse change is a difficult set of tasks; and those should be performed by a better scientific knowledge of the physical extent, character, and consequences of land transformation (Turner & Meyer, 1994).

A typical landuse planning process requires planners understand, define, and analyze current issues, forecast future development patterns, and propose plans based on available information (Putman & Chan, 2001). According to Landis (2001), planners usually approach this task in two ways—a predominant or traditional approach and an analytical approach. The traditional approach foresees a future landuse outcome and then prioritizes present-day policies required to achieve that outcome. The analytical approach simulates alternate present-day policies and compares their effects.

In recent decades, planning has become more participatory. Planners encourage public participation in planning commission meetings or city council debates for their explorations, predictions, knowledge building, decisions, and actions (Cullingworth & Caves, 2003; Langendorf, 2001). However, in order to participate in the decision making process in a meaningful way, the citizens need to understand the information they have been provided by planners or the public agencies (Cullingworth & Caves, 2003). Virtual simulations of any proposed landuse change encourage citizens to review any proposed design and suggest alternative ideas.

DEVELOPING GIS SIMULATIONS AND SCENARIOS FOR LAND USE CHANGE

Spatial Modeling and Urban Landuse Models

A spatial model represents one or more processes that may occur in the real world. According to Goodchild (2005), "a model is a computer program that takes a digital representation of one or more aspects of the real world and transforms them to create a new representation" (p. 2).

Spatial models are used to identify needs, make forecasts, build scenarios, and measure effects. Spatial models can be either static or dynamic. A static model uses indicators that combine various inputs to create a useful output (i.e., impacts, sensitivities, and vulnerabilities) at a particular time period. A dynamic model modifies some aspects of the earth's surface through time, quantifies impacts into the future, and assesses alternative scenarios (Goodchild, 2005). Among many well-developed applications of spatial analysis and modeling, the urban landuse models will be discussed in this section.

Urban landuse and transportation models were conceptualized in the 1950's and expanded and continued to be developed and applied since the 1960's (Putman & Chan, 2001). An urban landuse simulation model includes modeling of landuse, transportation, population, housing, water quality and quantity, air quality, and ecological integrity (Hopkins, Kaza, & Pallathucheril, 2005).

The urban landuse model can be termed as a dynamic process model, which uses computer programs to represent or simulate activities of the real world, and predict the impact of landuse regulations and socio-economic conditions on suburban sprawl. Such a model can predict or forecast the future development scenarios of any community or a region based on existing development conditions, development trends and restrictions, and population/job growth trend. These models can be either rule-driven or demand-driven. Rule-driven models simulate urban growth as a series of algorithms (rules) without statistical calibration on previous landuse change in a region or community. In demand-driven models, population and employment forecasts are converted to demand for different types and densities of urban land. Demand-driven models usually offer more interactions between citizens and decision makers and are more commonly used in the urban planning field.

Any urban development simulation model is constructed from a set of elements, including, activities, flows, facilities, investments, rights, and regulations (Hopkins, 1999). A scenario, which may include a number of runs of different models addressing different aspects of a set of proposed actions, consists of elements such as investments and regulations (Hopkins, 1999). The users need to understand these elements in order to run the models and generate the scenarios. Hopkins (2005, 1999) has explained these elements in detail. Actors can be individuals (including firms and developers) or collective (including voluntary groups and governments). Activities are the things that the actors do and flows are the trips the actors generate. Facilities are capital stocks, such as buildings, roads, and services. Rights specify the available actions for different types of actors. Investments change the facilities and regulations change the rights.

Cellular automata (CA), for example, is a widely used tool for urban development modeling, landuse simulation, and landuse/landcover change modeling (Torrens, 2003). This model represents the earth surface as an equally distributed same size square cells and determines whether a particular cell will be developed or not, based on various criteria, such as slope, water bodies or other restricted areas, and proximity to transportation and other services (Batty, 2005a; Goodchild, 2005; Longley & Batty, 2003; Torrens, 2003). The three earliest attempts of this model simulated urban growth in metropolitan regions, medium-size towns, and suburban areas (Batty & Xie, 2005). Another example is the landuse change (LUC) model, where networks and interactions do not explicitly appear and the "transitions between cells or zones, regular or irregular, can be implemented using map algebras of various kinds" (Batty, 2005a, p. 50).

Use of GIS in Urban Landuse Models

A typical planning process has four main stages: data gathering, data analysis, policy-making, and implementation (Kelly & Becker, 2000). GIS can be used in all of these four stages of any planning process, especially in tracking and forecasting landuse changes. Landuse change generates environmental, economical, and social processes, which are inherently spatial in their nature and cannot be fully understood without their spatial dimensions.

GIS, as a system, was not developed originally for the use of planning professionals. Later on, planners found the ability of GIS in spatial data management, analysis, and visualization very effective for their professional field. GIS is used as an effective decision making tool because of its ability to calculate population change, development impacts, and resource protection needs.

However, plan preparation and evaluation, which are the basic tasks of planners, cannot be done only with GIS, as those also require integrated computer-based models and advance visualization techniques (Klosterman, 1999). Static modeling and the calculation of indicators are classic GIS applications; and their power has been even enhanced recently by the graphic interfaces that allow user interaction to the modeling through a point-and-click environment (Goodchild, 2005). In addition, GIS can be also "used for dynamic modeling through a process of iteration, in which standard GIS functions are used to transform the system at each time step, and the output of one time step becomes the input for the next" (Goodchild, 2005, p. 12).

"GIS-based spatial analysis and modeling is critical in helping us describe, explain, and predict patterns and processes on the surface of the earth" (Maguire, Batty, & Goodchild, 2005, p. 446). GIS effectively has been used in defining sprawl and predicting landuse changes by using a number of indicators to understand effective or ineffective local landuse measures for directing residential growth (Hasse, 2004). Over the last fifty years "a consensus has been emerged that generally models should be predictive in structure but nested or embedded within a wider process of control or planning. These wider process can be expressed as metamodels, within which predictive models are used to explore alternative futures, that is, to pose what if questions" (Batty, 2005b, p. 147).

Since the 1960's there has been enormous progress in software engineering, mathematics, and the science of spatial analysis and modeling (Maguire, 2005; Maguire, et al, 2005). Although very few of the urban landuse models developed in this early stage have been integrated with GIS, some GIS-based models have been emerged during the last 15 years. However, many urban growth models up to the early 1990's were based on administrative data units (i.e., census tract or municipality boundary) and used GIS to integrate this kind of data with land suitability data (Batty & Xie, 2005). The new generation of GIS-based models can simulate temporal decisions concerning land development at a finer scale, and display how cities grow or change dynamically from the bottom up according to different decision rules (Batty & Xie, 2005).

In this age, spatial analysis and modeling software does not have to be custom built for any particular project; it can be developed within a GIS framework. GIS is now considered as an effective platform for spatial modeling for a number of reasons: (1) it is an excellent environment for spatial variation; (2) it provides numerous tools, such as projection change, data conversion, resampling, and management, for acquiring and pre-processing data for use in modeling; (3) it provides tools for rendering, querying, and analyzing model results and their accuracies; (4) its object-oriented models can represent events, flows, and other classes of information, and thus can handle time more effectively than before; and (5) its ability to become even more powerful when coupled with an extensive toolkit of methods of simulation (Goodchild, 2005).

Planning Support Systems and What If Scenarios

In this age, planning projects usually are more successful when they engage more public participation. Access to the latest information and technology only can make this process more focused as well as transparent. Planning support systems (PSS), spatial decision support systems (SDSS), or Urban Simulation Models are integrated systems of computer-based methods and models, which can support core-planning functions and engage public participation in this process. The PSS database "must store both the logic of plans—how plans work—and the processes of urban development—what plans are about" (Hopkins et al., 2005, p.173).

Although conceptualized several decades ago, PSS or other similar systems have become popular among urban and regional planners, policy analysts, advocacy groups, and citizens since 1990's. Some of the reasons include increased capability of computer processing, ability to store and handle spatial data in the GIS environment, and better availability of spatial data. Today's GIS-based PSS can foster clearer perception, improve interpretation, and interrogate complex spatial data (Lloyd, Haklay, Thurstain-Goodwin, & Tobon, 2003; Tobon & Haklay, 2003).

Since planning and politics sometimes have an uneasy relationship, planners have to prove or rationalize their decisions on different locational alternatives through analytical methods (Yeh, 2005; Waddell, 2001). PSS, which is built on GIS and related technologies (spreadsheets, models, and databases), provides tools, models, and information necessary for planning (Yeh, 2005). Using a PSS the planners are able to analyze and predict future landuse patterns, generate computer simulations, and visualize alternative development scenarios—in two and three dimensions. The detail framework of locational models and a GIS-based PSS can be found in Harris (1989), Harris and Batty (1993), and Putnam and Chan (2001).

Changes in landuse patterns in any community or a region over a long period of time usually have consequences in term of environment, ecology, and economy. The PSS enables communities to visualize and interactively analyze their future landuse scenarios under multiple circumstances and conditions and thus helps making critical policy decisions. The system helps "communities shift land-use decision from regulatory processes to performance-based strategies, and they can make the community decision-making process more proactive and less reactive." (Hudson-Smith & Evans, 2003, p. 50).

Planners try to model several what if scenarios of future landuse changes, because they cannot predict the likelihood of different scenarios. A scenario may go wrong, no matter how accurate the data and model are. Once the scenario outputs are available, GIS can visualize each scenario for any particular time period as a simple snapshot in raster format without considering any moving objects (Goodchild, 2005).

The PSS is built on various elements of planning with a broad range of applications. However, this section only discusses urban development simulation models and scenarios. All of the following different types of models and conceptual frameworks add dynamics to GIS and offer a broad range of choices to the users.

The integration of PSS and GIS was started in the 1990's. One such application is metropolitan integrated landuse system (METROPILUS) PSS, developed by Stephen Putman of University of Pennsylvania and Shih-Liang Chan of National Chung-Hsin University, Taiwan. The application uses Microsoft Excel and ArcView GIS software (ESRI) and its scripting language Avenue™. It was also linked to the modified versions of employment allocation model (EMPAL) and disaggregate residential allocation model (DRAM), two landuse models developed by Putman in the 1980's. DRAM locates households and EMPAL locates employers and employees. Using METROPILUS, the planners can get descriptive information of existing or potential problems; forecast output information; analyze and compare different policies and their impacts; and perform spatial queries (Putman & Chan, 2001).

The dynamic urban evolutionary model (DUEM) was developed to generate future landuse scenarios in three different scales: neighborhood, district, and region. The model, which was loosely coupled with GIS, generated five distinct landuse changes: housing, industry, commerce, vacant, and transport (Batty & Xie, 2005).

Sometimes landuse modeling is integrated with transportation modeling, which allows a wider range of policy analysis and a longer-term projection. TRANUS is such an integrated modeling system and is applicable in any scale. The detail description of this system and its advantages over the transportation-only modeling systems can be found in Barra (2001). Developed by Modelistica, TRANUS consists of three modules: the landuse and the transportation modules simulate the probable effects of applying particular landuse and transportation policies; and the evaluation module compares the social, economic, financial, and environmental effects of an alternative scenario with an existing one (Barra, 2001; Evans & Steadman, 2003). The Centre for Advanced Spatial Analysis (CASA) of University College London has developed TRANUS GIS Module, which is able to transfer TRANUS files to a fully customized GIS interface, such as ArcGIS.

Another integrated landuse and transportation model is planning and research of policies for landuse and transport for increasing urban sustainability (PROPOLIS). The objective of this model is to research, develop, and test integrated policies, tools, and comprehensive assessment methodologies in order to demonstrate the sustainable long-term strategies in European cities (Evans & Steadman, 2003). Developed by the University College London and many European partners, this model uses a set of indicators to anticipate the long run (20 years or more) landuse effects on the social, economical, and environmental components of sustainability (Evans & Steadman, 2003).

In the 1990's, the University of California at Berkeley developed the California urban futures (CUF) family of urban simulation models, which includes three GIS-based regional simulation models: CUF I, CUF II, and California urban and biodiversity analysis model (CURBA). The

CUF models can predict locational growth pattern across a 20-year projection period (Simpson, 2001). CUF I incorporates "land developers and homebuilders as central actors in determining the pattern, locations, and density of new development;" CUF II incorporates competitive site bidding between landuses as well as redevelopment activities; and CURBA deals with habitat consumption and quality (Landis, 2001). Details of these models will be found in Landis (2001, 1995).

Another landuse model, UrbanSim, has been developed by several states and the federal government, and is used by many metropolitan planning agencies. This model can create mutually consistent transportation, landuse, and air quality plans with a strong link to urban economics and transportation modeling. This object-oriented model is based on behavioral approach for simulating the land development process and is primarily designed for Web distribution in the public domain (Waddell, 2001). Some of the key features of this model are as follows: (1) it simulates urban development based on the location choices of the households, businesses, and developers as a dynamic process over time and space; (2) it accounts for land, structures, and occupants; (3) it simulates land market as the interaction of demand and supply; and (4) it uses parcel level data to addresses both new development and redevelopment (Waddell, 2001).

Using GIS and other geospatial technologies in the public participation process have many advantages. Technical capabilities and skills can engage public interests and enhance the interaction between public and planning options by making modifications immediately possible (Craig, Harris, & Weiner, 2002).

Criterion's INDEX, an ESRI's ArcGIS-based system, is widely used software that is based on a set of over 85 indicators from regional to neighborhood level. Planning practitioners and community stakeholders can use these indicators to benchmark existing conditions and assess current policies of a community; and then evaluate and monitor the incremental impact of alternate policies over the years (Allen, 2001; Criterion Planners Web site, 2006). Some examples of indicators are block size, developed acres per capita, single family or multi-family dwelling density, transit proximity, water consumption, pedestrian safety, bicycle network connectivity, and access to bus stops or grocery stores. While other PSSs, such as TRANUS or UrbanSim, can perform dynamic analysis, INDEX is suitable for static time scale applications (Allen, 2001).

Richard Klosterman of What If Inc. has developed the GIS-based landuse simulation software *What if?*, which is compatible with ESRI ArcGIS products and any other GIS software that can read shape files (What If Web site, 2006). The model is inspired by the design concept of the CUF 1 model and developed from Microsoft Visual Basic and ESRI's MapObject software. *What if?* consists of three major components: (1) Suitability—considers the supply of land; (2) Growth—considers the demand for land; and (3) Allocation—considers supply and demand by allocating the projected demand to the most suitable locations to project future landuse patterns (Klosterman, 1999). It also analyzes the possible impacts of alternate landuse policies and associated population and employment trends (Klosterman, 1999). The *What if?* scenarios are based on some underlying assumptions, which can be easily modified to see their impacts on the model results and to compare the assumptions as well as the scenarios. This feature is extremely helpful to visualize alternative landuse or zoning change scenarios.

The Orton Family Foundation's CommunityViz is another ArcGIS-based decision support system which adds interactive tools and a decision-making framework to ArcGIS and gives powerful tools for geographic analysis and visualization (CommunityViz Web site, 2006). Using this system, planners and stakeholders can visualize, analyze, and communicate about geographic decisions, in an interactive, 3-D, and real-time environment. They can test and evaluate the implications or impacts of any design proposal at various scales. The two main components of CommunityViz are Scenario 360 (for interactive analysis) and Site Builder 3-D (for visualization). One popular application of the software is buildout, which allows the users to calculate and visualize how many new buildings could be built in a community based on existing landuse regulations. CommunityViz suitability application enables users to perform interactive site suitability studies, with the ability to change the input layer's weights and influence levels in real time.

A sample application of GIS-based PSS will be presented here. Using CommunityViz and ESRI ArcView software, the Center for Sustainable Communities (CSC) of Temple University has developed three primary scenarios for Milford Township, a rural area on an urban fringe in Pennsylvania. These scenarios are: (1) development with no control (development permitted in floodplains, wetlands, agricultural soils, and woodlands); (2) preservation with no control (development prohibited in these areas); and (3) development and preservation with growth management (high density development permitted in most suitable areas, low density development in moderately suitable areas, and no development in highly unsuitable areas). The third scenario proved to be the most desirable one, as it allocated more population than the second scenario but preserved more open space and prime agricultural areas (Meenar, Bari, & Sherry, 2004).

VISUALIZING LANDUSE CHANGE SCENARIOS

GIS-Based Visualization

Visualization, or more particularly—geovisualization, is as much an art as a science, which is used for the exploration, transformation, representation, recreation, communication, and explanation of large or complex geographical datasets (Berke, Godschalk, Kaiser, & Rodriguez, 2006; Tobon & Haklay, 2003; Tufte, 1997). According to Batty (2005a), "The visual domain has become one of the most important ways of communicating spatial problems to a wide range of interests, particularly where the phenomena in question can be represented in digital form" (p. 42). Visualization can overcome racial and social obstacles; reduce the potential for confusion; and cross cultural, disciplinary, and language divides more easily than words (Al-Kodmany, 2002; Langendorf, 2001).

3-D GIS-based visualization should be applied before a particular plan is drafted or adopted in order to engage public participation and debate. Once the planners and policy makers forecast the future landuse scenarios of any community with the help of active public participation, they would like to visualize the scenarios and compare them. They may want to walk through or fly over the virtual spaces, using either software or an interactive Web site.

GIS-based visualization thus has become a common practice among planning professionals for creating and understanding landuse simulations. The technology allows the users to interact with environments and situations before these are implemented in the real world (Al-Kodmany, 2002). Since 3-D GIS visualization can represent complex geospatial data in a user-friendly way, it can reduce confusions and increase the trust between the planners and the citizens or stakeholders. In fact, there is no alternative way to effectively display the complex urban systems and structures and their relationships to environmental features (Longley & Batty, 2003; Simpson, 2001;). For example, the e-book *City Sites*, with 150,000 words, 150-plus images, and 200 Web pages, was developed to demonstrate how new multimedia technologies could enhance conventional scholarly understandings of urban culture (Balshaw, 2003).

Box 1.Data elements of 3-D scenarios

Surface: DEM, TIN, or contour
Background Image: Ortho-photo, Satellite Image
Natural Features: Rivers, creeks, water bodies, forests
Structure: Buildings, utility poles
Landscaping Features: Benches, sidewalk, trees, fountains
People
Transportation: Car, bicycles, roads, rail tracks
Land Features: Landuse, zoning

In recent years the quality and interfaces of visualization and simulation have expanded because of the increase in computer processing speed and data storage capacity; increase in sophistication of 3-D GIS and computer aided design (CAD); and decrease in cost of high-end machines (Batty, 2005a; Hudson-Smith & Evans, 2003; Simpson, 2001). With the production of user-friendly software such as SketchUp and Google Earth, even new users can create 3-D scenes more easily within a short period of time. The availability of high resolution satellite imagery or ortho-photographs help creating more realistic virtual simulations.

3-D Visualization Elements

3-D Digital Model

3-D digital models can be built in many formats. They can be solid mass models; solid models with textures; solid models with wrapped images; detail models with basic architectural features; and detail models with all architectural features. Based on the focus of a project, its budget and total running time, the users select the model they would prefer. Software like MultiGen's ModelBuilder 3D, Google's SketchUp, Graphicsoft's ArchiCAD, AutoDesk's 3D Studio Max, Map 3D, Maya, and Visual Nature Studio can provide a powerful environment to create 3-D models with various levels of difficulties.

The use of digital images and the ability to manipulate them can help any 3-D model achieve a high degree of realism that works well for a non-expert audience (Al-Kodmany, 2002). Software such as SketchUp can apply or drape digital images as textures to the facades of simple geometric models (prismatic blocks or mass models).

The process of creating such photo-realistic models in SketchUp is illustrative. At first, digital images of structures have to be collected from the study area. Once a digital library is developed, images need to be edited using image processing software, such as Adobe Photoshop. Digital images are generally captured from ground-level photography that often gets obscured by trees, cars, or other features (Batty et al., 2001). Editing may include cropping the images according to the outlines of the building facades; correcting the brightness and contrast; and stretching and skewing, if necessary. Jepson, Liggett, and Friedman (2001) have mentioned that this is the most time consuming task in the whole process.

In SketchUp, the mass models can be built with their specific spatial references. For doing so, a GIS file (shape file or raster) with spatial reference (ideally ortho-photo) has to be imported to SketchUp before the buildings or other models are created. When the models are saved, the coordinate information is also saved. In MultiGen, models can be saved only in a geographic coordinate system (GCS) and later can be transferred to a different coordinate system. MultiGen creates 3-D models in .flt format, SketchUp in .skp format, 3D Studio in .3ds format, and Morfit in .wrl format.

ESRI's ArcGIS 3D Analyst extension can create models from line, point, or polygon shape files and can be extruded according to the height. The software also has a built-in library of more than 500 3-D models of different objects, including buildings, trees, cars, and street furniture, and can be directly used in a 3-D scene. ArcGIS recognizes 3-D models created from other software, including 3D ModelBuilder, SketchUp, and 3D Studio. AutoDesk AutoCAD provides an environment to create more detailed and standard 3-D models in .dxf format. AutoCAD files can be transferred to 3D ModelBuilder and then digital textures can be applied to those models.

3-D Simulation and Virtual Urban Areas

GIS-based urban simulations can be an essential part of public participatory planning. Depending on the type or scope of any project, such simulations can be operated at any scale—from local to regional, and can be highly interactive, engaging people to participate instead of being just viewers (Al-Kodmany, 2002).

Recent advancements in remote sensing and aerial photography technologies offer new ways to deliver high-resolution digital elevation models (DEM) and to collect 3-D information of real world features. Digital Photgrammetry is a technology that obtains spatial measurements from ortho-photographs. The Remote Sensing Research and Development Team of the National Geodetic Survey has developed an airborne technology called light detection and ranging (LiDAR), which is used in conjunction with the global positioning system (GPS). Many communities use LiDAR to generate rapid 3-D mapping that includes block models of cities. LiDAR is "based upon camera systems that use a pulsed laser device to record the distance from the camera to each point in the image." (Batty et al., 2001). The ground-based sensors of this technology are suitable for large scale architectural surveys; and the airborne sensors are suitable for small-scale surveys.

In many cities and regions, virtual 3-D databases and customized simulations have been generated for the whole or for specific areas, and made available to citizens through interactive Web sites. Virtual cities usually have realistic 3-D models of buildings, people, cars, streets, trees, and other city elements that offer users to flyover or walk through the streets and visualize any proposed development with the context of the existing scenario.

For example, the University of Toronto created one model for the City of Ottawa; the University of California Los Angeles (UCLA) has created one for downtown Los Angeles; the CASA of University College of London has created one for the City of London; the Tokyo CAD Center has constructed 1:1000 scale models of Tokyo, Manhattan, Yokohama, and Shanghai; Zenrin has fully functional 3-D GIS models for about 300 major cities of Japan; the Environmental Simulation Center (ESC) of New School of Social Research has developed 3-D GIS models for parts of Manhattan and other cities; the CASA and Petrie Museum of Egyptian Archeology have created prehistoric Egypt; and the urban data solutions (UDS) has created GIS and CAD-based 3-D models for many cities, including Manhattan, Washington D.C., and Chicago.

The UCLA visual simulation system, developed by the urban simulation team of UCLA, uses a C/C+ programming interface with a high-performance rendering library in a 3-D software toolkit (Jepson et al., 2001). This system was used to develop a virtual 3-D application of three 300 square mile area of the Los Angeles basin, where high-resolution street level models were inserted into a digital terrain model (DTM) (Jepson et al., 2001). The system was also used to display the *before* and *after* views of proposed developments.

Web-based visualization technology, such as virtual reality markup/modeling language (VRML), can be used to create virtual cities. For example, the firm Planet 9 Studios (www.planet9.com) has developed over 45 "off the shelf" virtual city models and a robust viewing/tools environment called eScene™. These are based on highest quality urban simulation data and visualization tools (Planet9 Studio Web site, 2006).

3-D Animations

According to Langendorf (2001): "Animation creates the illusion of incremental change through the presentation of still images at the rate of 24 to 30 frames per second." (p. 321). This change is applicable to any element that has a visual effect, including the shape, color, transparency, structure, and texture of objects; lighting and light source position; camera position, orientation, and focus; and rendering technique (Langendorf, 2001).

A number of software packages, including ArcGIS 3D Analyst, 3D Scene, and CommunityViz are able to simulate 3-D user interfaces that allow the users to drive-through or fly-over any simulated scene. Such packages have the capability to create animations of future landuse scenarios and save those as movie files. Animation of landuse scenarios may include simulation of physical reality, such as walk-through or flyover; and simulation of changing daytime, season, or even shadow pattern. For example, a flyover or birds-eye view can constructively convey information on urban building masses, street pattern, impervious surfaces, and open space ratio. In order to engage effective public participation, animations of virtual built environments can be published in interactive Web sites.

LANDUSE SIMULATION MODELS AND CRIME ANALYSIS: THE CONNECTION

GIS technology offers full potential to provide invaluable insight into criminal dynamics. Using spatial analysis techniques, the criminologists can study crime patterns, hot spots, and trends. According to ESRI Web site, "the ability to integrate crime data with other spatial datasets (such as land parcel data; demographics; and location of facilities such as schools, hospitals, and liquor shops) can help in better deployment of resources and proactive community policing." (ESRI, 2007) Using landuse as one of the key layers in a GIS-based crime analysis can be helpful in determining the spatial relationship of crime incidents.

Among many types of analyses, a crime analyst performs the following services that are related to landuse planning to a certain extent: (1) analyzing existing crime patterns and trends and (2) forecasting future occurrences in crime series so that the law enforcement agencies can attempt to apprehend the offenders.

As it is discussed before, crime pattern may change with the landuse pattern. When criminologists forecast spatial pattern of crime incidents they need to understand the possible future landuse condition of a neighborhood. Simulating GIS-based future landuse scenarios can help crime analysts in forecasting possible crime incidence patterns.

3-D visualization of urban land areas helps analyzing crime pattern and apprehending the criminals. For example, night-time 3-D simulations can generate shadow patterns of downtown high rise buildings in order to identify or prioritize the dark and unsafe locations. 3-D simulation can also help analyzing the visibility of the downtown area. It can demonstrate whether some activities in a certain location are visible from other well-lit locations or streets. Another example of utilizing 3-D simulation is the noise pattern analysis. Noise pattern depends on many factors, including topography, building position, and building height. It is useful to find out whether the victims can be heard from the hot spot areas to the nearby major streets or areas with more public activities. 3-D simulations also help identifying the escape routes of the criminals in locations with multi-level transportation options, such as a central station with accessibility to a metro network, ground level bus network, above the ground rail network, and even an airport.

ISSUES

Here are some of the issues faced by the industry as well as local/regional governments, which simulate and visualize 3-D landuse scenarios.

Coupling Landuse Models with GIS

Although the use of PSS was initially limited to only specialized users, since the 2000's a good number of software, complimented by planning theories and mathematical models, have been fully integrated to GIS and are now available to many users at affordable prices. However, many of the spatial models are loosely coupled with GIS, where GIS is not deeply embedded with the models, but is used for data storage, analysis, and visualization only (Maguire et al., 2005). The advancement in the research of multidimensional space-time modeling in GIS will add another dimension in landuse modeling as well.

Data Quality and Data Processing Efficiency

Over time, the analytical and 3-D visualization capabilities of GIS have been increased. However, the GIS-based simulation and visualization rely heavily on the availability and quality of input datasets. The time and efficiency required to process data and refresh simulations are also critical issues. Although we have seen significant improvements in computer industry in the last few decades, there are still limitations in creating and handling massive datasets that are needed for computer simulations. Many landuse simulation software packages require datasets with extensive details that are not easy to create and maintain by many local and regional governments. Acquiring and working with high resolution satellite imagery and GPS devices also have budget and security related issues. Most of the time, the users have to compromise with the limited amount of high quality and reliable data resources.

Limitations of Models

Most of the future simulation or scenario creation process models consider some assumptions. Some of these assumptions might turn into their limitations. One such assumption is that the number of existing buildings, their conditions, and their locations will be the same in future. However, in reality, buildings get older and some buildings may even become dilapidated over time. Also, a single unit building may be converted to double or triple units.

Public Participation

One of the main reasons for using 3-D visualization in planning practice is to encourage public participation. However, it is hard to get the public involved in the decision making process all the time. Technology can help planners dissimilate information to the public through community Web sites and thus get their comments even before any formal discussion. Unfortunately, Internet speed and bandwidth limitations sometimes place barriers to such Web postings. Moreover, even if the planners could engage enough the public participation, sometime it becomes difficult to allow the participants to design and alter any representation (Al-Kodmany, 2002).

3-D GIS visualization has some negative aspects as well. Sometimes, a simulated scene may provide either too much or too little detail. If a simulation lacks the minimum details, the public may not always estimate or predict the full picture. Again, if there are too many details and aesthetics in the simulated environment, people tend to believe that the reality would be exactly like the simulation, which is often untrue and could be misleading.

User Specific Issues

One of the main users of landuse simulation software is local government. Very often municipalities do not have enough financial and technical support to acquire and use such software and update the input data sets.

For multimunicipal or regional forecasting, handling zoning data is a big issue. Although landuse codes are usually similar for a region (given the fact that the data is created by regional planning agencies), zoning codes are different for different municipalities. That is why multimunicipal simulation will require aggregation and interpretation of varieties of zoning codes.

Another issue that users face is related to the choice of a good model. Some models are appropriate for larger scale and some are for smaller scale. To reflect the complex planning process in future landuse simulation processes, a combination of multiple models may be useful to serve the purposes or objectives of a range of people, including planners, policy makers, citizens, and professionals.

CONCLUSION

Landuse-planning needs to be supported by technical data and analysis. Technology helps planners and public officials make better decisions about future landuse changes and the public understanding of the rationale for those decisions. GIS-based simulations of urban landuse change not only include the visual representation but also the numerical assessment and analysis of planning decisions. Specifically, the GIS-based modeling systems can project landuse changes into the future, construct multiple future development scenarios, visualize future conditions in 2-D or 3-D, and evaluate these alternative options, both in local and regional scales. All of these may play significant role in spatial crime analysis.

Many communities and regional agencies throughout the United States are using a number of landuse models, especially the GIS-based PSS, to predict their future landuse scenarios. The advancement in computer hardware and software technology, better availability of updated and accurate data, and improved methods of visualization and user interaction can be considered as the key factors for such wide-range applications of GIS-based PSS. The public is becoming more active in the planning process with the help of aesthetically enhanced 3-D visualization of future scenarios.

However, the industry has some limitations, including the integration of landuse models with GIS, data accuracy, technology affordability, and citizen engagement and perception. The industry and users need to overcome these issues and better train local staff and citizens in using these models and software so that they could participate more interactively in the landuse planning decision-making processes.

FUTURE RESEARCH DIRECTIONS

The future of landuse simulation and visualization techniques relies on the advancement in GIS industry, wired and wireless network industry, and public participation process. GIS is no longer considered only as a tool to transform data into information; it is now more directly associated with spatial knowledge acquisition (Longley & Batty, 2003). According to Longley, et al. (2003), the future development in landuse simulation technique will focus on more advanced interaction of 3-D GIS and other forms of multimedia based on virtual reality systems.

During the last decade, users have experienced rapid evolution in the capacity of computer hardware and the sophistication of computer software that has expedited computer simulation and visualization process. This trend will be seen in future as well.

The technological advancements and availability in the data collection and creation process will definitely increase the potential for creating more useful data with affordable budgets and minimum manpower, and eventually help improve the simulation and visualization of future landuse scenarios with less time and high accuracy level.

Since the level of photo-realism in 3-D simulation depends on the data storage capability and data processing speed of computers, the future of GIS-based simulation will largely depend on the availability and affordability of state-of-the-art computer processors. Internet speed and Web site bandwidth limitations need to be overcome to more easily share the landuse simulation results through the Internet, and receive comments from many residents who are unable to attend public meetings.

According to the criminologists, the difficulty landuse change modeling faces with regards to crime is the challenge of providing credible transfer functions that show how changes increase or decrease important forms of crime. Future research should address this particular aspect of crime analysis.

REFERENCES

Al-Kodmany, K. (2002). Visualization tools and methods in community planning: From freehand sketches to virtual reality. *Journal of Planning Literature, 17*(2), 189-211.

Allen, E. (2001). INDEX: Software for community indicators. In R. Brail & R. Klosterman (Eds.), *Planning support systems: Integrating geographic information systems, models, and visualization tools* (pp. 229-261). Redlands, CA: ESRI Press.

American Planning Association. (2002). *Policy guide on smart growth.* Retrieved August 26, 2007, from http://www.planning.org/policyguides/pdf/SmartGrowth.pdf

Balshaw, M. (2003). Digital cities: Multimedia research and American urban studies. *Journal of Urban History, 29*(4), 421-436.

Barra, T. D. (2001). Integrated landuse and transport modeling: The Tranus experience. In R. Brail & R. Klosterman (Eds.), *Planning support systems: Integrating geographic information systems, models, and visualization tools* (pp. 129-156). Redlands, CA: ESRI Press.

Batty, M. (2005a). Approaches to modeling in GIS: Spatial representation and temporal dynamics. In D. J. Maguire, M. Batty, & M. Goodchild (Eds.), *GIS, Spatial analysis, and modeling* (pp. 41-65). Redlands, CA: ESRI Press.

Batty, M. (2005b). Introduction to Chapter 3: Socioeconomic applications. In D. J. Maguire, M. Batty, & M. Goodchild (Eds.), *GIS, Spatial analysis, and modeling* (pp. 147-149). Redlands, CA: ESRI Press.

Batty, M., & Xie, Y. (2005). Urban growth using cellular automata models. In D. J. Maguire, M. Batty, & M. Goodchild (Eds.), *GIS, Spatial analysis, and modeling* (pp. 151-172). Redlands, CA: ESRI Press.

Batty, M. et al. (2001). Visualizing the city: Communicating urban design to planners and decision makers. In R. Brail, & R. Klosterman (Eds.), *Planning support systems: Integrating geographic information systems, models, and visualization tools* (pp. 405-443). Redlands, CA: ESRI Press.

Berke, P. R., Godschalk, D. R., Kaiser, E. J., & Rodriguez, D. A. (2006). *Urban landuse planning.* Chicago: University of Illinois Press.

Block, R. L., & Block, C. R. (1995). Space, place, and crime: Hot spot areas and hot places of liquor-related crime. In J. Eck & D. Weisburd (Eds.), *Crime and place.* Monsey, NY: Willow Tree.

Byrne, J. (1986). Cities, citizens, and crime: The ecological/nonecological debate reconsidered. In J. Byrne, & R. J. Sampson (Eds.), *The social ecology of crime* (pp. 77-101). New York: Springer-Verlag.

Cervero, R. (2003). Road expansion, urban growth, and induced travel. *Journal of American Planning Association, 69*(2), 145-163.

Clarke, R. V., & Eck, J. E. (2005). *Crime analysis for problem solvers in 660 small steps.* Washington, DC: Office of Community Oriented Policing Services, U.S. Department of Justice.

CommunityViz Web site. (2006). *Community viz products.* Retrieved August 26, 2007, from http://www.communityviz.com

Craig, W., Harris, T., & Weiner, D. (2002). *Community participation and geographical information systems*. London: Taylor and Francis.

Criterion planners Web site. (2006). Retrieved August 26, 2007, from http://www.crit.com

Cullingworth, B., & Caves, R. W. (2003). *Planning in the USA: Policies, issues and processes*. London: Routledge (Taylor & Francis Group).

ESRI Web site. (2007). Retrieved August 26, 2007, from http://www.esri.com

Evans, S., & Steadman, P. (2003). Interfacing land-use transport models with GIS: The Inverness model. In P. Longley, & M. Batty (Eds.), *Advanced spatial analysis: The CASA book of GIS* (pp. 289-307). Redlands, CA: ESRI Press.

Galster, G., Hanson, R., Ratcliffe, M. R., Wolman, H., Coleman, S., & Freihage, J. (2001). Wrestling sprawl to the ground: Defining and measuring an elusive concept. *Housing Policy Debate, 12*(4), 681-717.

Goodchild, M. (2005). GIS, spatial analysis, and modeling overview. In D. J. Maguire, M. Batty, & M. Goodchild (Eds.), *GIS, Spatial analysis, and modeling* (pp. 1-17). Redlands, CA: ESRI Press.

Greenberg, S. (1986). Fear and its relationship to crime, neighborhood deterioration, and informal social control. In J. Byrne, & R. J. Sampson (Eds.), *The social ecology of crime* (pp. 47-62). New York: Springer-Verlag.

Harris, B. (1989). Beyond geographic information systems: Computers and the planning professional. *Journal of American Planning Association, 55*, 85-92.

Harris, B., & Batty, M. (1993). Locational models, geographic information and planning support systems. *Journal of Planning Education and Research, 12*, 184-198.

Hermann, C., & Maroko, A. (2006). Crime pattern analysis: Exploring Bronx auto thefts using GIS. In J. Maantay, & J. Ziegler (Eds.), *GIS for the urban environment* (pp. 408-413). Redlands, CA: ESRI Press.

Hasse, J. (2004). A geospatial approach to measuring new development tracts for characteristics of sprawl. *Landscape Journal: Design, Planning and Management of the Land, 23*(1), 52-67.

Hopkins, L. D., Kaza, N., & Pallathucheril, V. G. (2005). A data model to represent plans and regulations in urban simulation models. In D. J. Maguire, M. Batty, & M. Goodchild (Eds.), *GIS, Spatial analysis, and modeling* (pp. 173-201). Redlands, CA: ESRI Press.

Hopkins, L. D. (1999). Structure of a planning support system for urban development. *Environment and Planning B: Planning and Design, 26*, 81-98.

Hudson-Smith, A., & Evans, S. (2003). Virtual cities: From CAD to 3-D GIS. In P. Longley, & M. Batty (Eds.), *Advanced spatial analysis: The CASA book of GIS* (pp. 41-60). Redlands, CA: ESRI Press.

Jepson, W. H., Liggett, R. S., & Friedman, S. (2001). An integrated environment for urban simulation. In R. Brail, & R. Klosterman (Eds.), *Planning support systems: Integrating geographic information systems, models, and visualization tools* (pp. 387-404). Redlands, CA: ESRI Press.

Kelly, E. D., & Becker, B. (2000). *Community planning: An introduction to the comprehensive plan*. Washington, D.C.: Island Press.

Klosterman, R. E. (1999). The what-if? Collaborative planning support system. *Environment and Planning B: Planning and Design, 26*, 393-408.

Landis, J. D. (1995). Imagining land use futures: Applying the California urban futures model. *Journal of American Planning Association, 61*(4), 438-457.

Landis, J. D. (2001). CUF, CUR II, and CURBA: A family of spatially explicit urban growth and land-use policy simulation models. In R. Brail, & R. Klosterman (Eds.), *Planning support systems: Integrating geographic information systems, models, and visualization tools* (pp. 157-200). Redlands, CA: ESRI Press.

Langendorf, R. (2001). Computer-aided visualization: possibilities for urban design, planning, and management. In R. Brail, & R. Klosterman (Eds.), *Planning support systems: Integrating geographic information systems, models, and visualization tools* (pp. 309-359). Redlands, CA: ESRI Press.

Levine, J., Inam, A., & Torng, G. (2005). A choice-based rationale for land use and transportation alternatives: Evidence from Boston and Atlanta. *Journal of Planning Education and Research, 24*, 317-330.

Lloyd, D., Haklay, M., Thurstain-Goodwin, M., & Tobon, C. (2003). Visualizing spatial structure in urban data. In P. Longley, & M. Batty (Eds.), *Advanced spatial analysis: The CASA book of GIS* (pp. 267-288). Redlands, CA: ESRI Press.

Longley, P. A., & Batty, M. (Eds.) (2003). Advances spatial analysis: Extending GIS. *Advanced spatial analysis: The CASA book of GIS* (pp. 1-17). Redlands, CA: ESRI Press.

Loukaitou-Sideris, A., Liggett, R., & Iseki, H. (2002). The geography of transit crime: Documentation and evaluation of crime incidence on and around the green line stations in Los Angeles. *Journal of Planning Education and Research, 22*,135-151.

Maguire, D. J. (2005). Towards a GIS platform for spatial analysis and modeling. In D. J. Maguire, M. Batty, & M. Goodchild, (Eds.), *GIS, Spatial analysis, and modeling* (pp. 19-39). Redlands, CA: ESRI Press.

Maguire, D. J., Batty, M., & Goodchild, M. F. (Eds.) (2005). GIS, spatial analysis and modeling: Current status and future prospects. *GIS, Spatial analysis, and modeling* (pp. 445-455). Redlands, CA: ESRI Press.

Meenar, M., Bari, A., & Sherry, J. (2004, August). *Growth management plan for Milford Township, PA: Suitability analysis and buildout scenarios.* Paper presented at the meeting of the ESRI International User Conference, San Diego, CA.

Perkins, D., Meeks, J., & Taylor, R. (1992). The physical environment of street blocks and resident perceptions of crime and disorder: Implications for theory and measurement. *Journal of Environmental Psychology, 12*, 21-34.

Planet9 Studios Web site. (2006). Retrieved August 26, 2007, from http://www.planet9.com

Putman, S., & Chan, S. (2001). The METROPILUS planning support system: Urban models and GIS. In R. Brail, & R. Klosterman (Eds.), *Planning support systems: Integrating geographic information systems, models, and visualization tools* (pp. 99-128). Redlands, CA: ESRI Press.

Simpson, D. M. (2001). Virtual reality and urban simulation in planning: A literature review and topical bibliography. *Journal of Planning Literature, 15*(3), 359-376.

Taylor, H. H. (2001). *The health status of the near east side community and neighborhood conditions.* Buffalo, NY: State University of New York at Buffalo, Center for Urban Studies.

Tobon, C., & Haklay, M. (2003). Human-computer interaction and usability evaluation in GIScience. In P. Longley, & M. Batty (Eds.), *Advanced spatial analysis: The CASA book of GIS* (pp. 391-406). Redlands, CA: ESRI Press.

Torrens, P. M. (2003). Automata-based models of urban systems. In P. Longley, & M. Batty (Eds.), *Advanced spatial analysis: The CASA book of GIS* (pp. 61-79). Redlands, CA: ESRI Press.

Tufte, E. R. (1997). *Visual explanations: Images and quantities, evidence and narrative*. Cheshire, UK: Graphic Press.

Turner, B. L., & Meyer, W. B. (1994). *Changes in land use and land cover: A global perspective*. New York: Cambridge University Press.

Waddell, P. (2001). Between politics and planning: UrbanSim as a decision-support system for metropolitan planning. In R. Brail, & R. Klosterman (Eds.), *Planning support systems: Integrating geographic information systems, models, and visualization tools* (pp. 201-228). Redlands, CA: ESRI Press.

Walker, R. (2004). Theorizing land-cover and land-use change: The case of tropical deforestation. *International Regional Science Review, 27*(3), 247–270.

Wegener, M. (2005). Urban land-use transportation models. In R. Brail, & R. Klosterman (Eds.), *Planning support systems: Integrating geographic information systems, models, and visualization tools* (pp. 203-220). Redlands, CA: ESRI Press.

What If Web site. (2006). Retrieved August 26, 2007, from http://www.what-if-pss.com

Wolman, M. G., & Fournier, F. G. A. (Eds.) (1987). *Land transformation in agriculture*. Chichester, UK: John Wiley and Sons.

Yeh, A. G. (2005). The integration of case-based reasoning and GIS in a planning support system. In D. J. Maguire, M. Batty, & M. Goodchild (Eds.), *GIS, Spatial analysis, and modeling* (pp. 289-314). Redlands, CA: ESRI Press.

ADDITIONAL READING

Al-Kodmany, K. (2000). Extending geographic information systems to meet neighborhood planning needs. *URISA Journal, 12*(3).

Boba, R. (2005). *Crime analysis and crime mapping*. Thousand Oaks, CA: Sage Publications, Inc.

Brantingham, P. J., & Brantingham, P. L. (1995). Criminality of place: Crime generators and crime attractors. *European Journal of Criminal Policy and Research, 3*, 5-26.

Chainey, S., & Ratcliffe, J. (2005). *GIS and Crime Mapping*. West Sussex, UK: John Wiley & Sons Ltd.

Colquhoun, I. (2004). *Design out crime: Creating safe and sustainable communities*. Burlington, MA: Elsevier.

Goldsmith, V., McGuire, P. G., Mollenkoph, J. H., & Ross, T. A. (Eds.) (2000). *Analyzing crime patterns: Frontier of practice*. Thousand Oaks, CA: Sage Publications, Inc.

Harries, K. (1999). *Mapping crime: Principle and practice*. Washington, D.C.: U.S. Department of Justice.

Harris, B., & Batty, M. (1993). Locational models, geographic information, and planning support systems. *Journal of Planning Education and Research, 12*, 184-98.

Hirschfield, A., & Bowers, K. (2001). *Mapping and analyzing crime data: Lessons from research and practice*. London: Taylor & Francis.

LaGrange, T. C. (1999). The impact of neighborhoods, schools and malls on the spatial distribution of property damage. *Journal of Research in Crime and Delinquency, 36*, 393-422.

Leipnik, M. R., & Albert, D. P. (2003). *GIS in law enforcement: Implementation issues and case studies*. London: Taylor & Francis.

Lersch, K. M. (2004). *Space, time, and crime*. Drham, NC: Carolina Academic Press.

Meenar, M., & Ambrus, A. (2006). Three dimensional models encourage public participation. *ArcUser, 9*(2), 34-37.

Murray, C. (1995). The physical environment. In J. Q. Wilson, & J. Petersilia (Eds.), *Crime* (pp. 349-361). San Francisco: Institute for Contemporary Studies.

Verburg, P. H., Soepboer, W., Veldkamp, A., Limpiada, R., Espaldon, V., & Sharifah Mastura, S. A. (2002). Modeling the spatial dynamics of regional land use: The CLUE-S model. *Environmental Management, 30*(3), 391-405.

Wang, F. (2005). *Geographic information systems and crime analysis.* Hershey, PA: Idea Group Inc.

Weisburd, D., & McEwen, T. (1998). *Crime mapping & crime prevention.* Monsey, NY: Willow Tree Press, Inc.

Section II
Streets, Networks, and Crime Distribution

Chapter V
Modelling Pedestrian Movement to Measure On-Street Crime Risk

Spencer Chainey
UCL Jill Dando Institute of Crime Science, UK

Jake Desyllas
Intelligent Space Partnership, UK

ABSTRACT

This chapter presents results for the first large-scale analysis of street crime rates that utilizes accurate on-street pedestrian population estimates. Pedestrian counts were generated at the street segment level for an area in central London (UK) using a modeling process that utilized key indicators of pedestrian movement and sample observations. Geocoded street crime positioned on street segments then allowed for street crime rates to be calculated for the entire central London study area's street network. These street crime rate measures were then compared against street crime volume patterns (e.g., hotspot maps of street crime density) and street crime rate statistics and maps that were generated from using the residential population as the denominator. The research demonstrates the utility of pedestrian modeling for generating better and more realistic measures for street crime rates, suggesting that if the residential population is used as a denominator for local level street crime analysis it may only misinform and mislead the interpretation and understanding of on- to pedestrians. The research also highlights the importance of crime rate analysis for understanding and explaining crime patterns, and suggests that with accurate analysis of crime rates, policing, and crime prevention initiatives can be improved.

INTRODUCTION

Measures and approaches for analysing patterns of street crime (i.e., robbery from the person and thefts from persons) are typically performed using volume statistics presented in tables and graphs, and as hotspot maps to identify the volumetric density patterns of street crime. With the proliferation of geographical information systems (GIS) into police and crime reduction agencies, hotspot analysis is seen as a crucial first step in developing intelligence to help identify and explain crime problems (Chainey & Ratcliffe, 2005; Eck, Chainey, Cameron, Leitner, & Wilson, 2005; Home Office, 2005). This analysis can then help inform the focused targeting of patrol and crime reduction resources to specific areas to help tackle the identified crime issues.

Hotspot maps certainly have a purpose, but can hide the relative levels of risk from being a victim of crime that people may experience. For example, hotspot maps show areas where crime is high but may purely be a product of the volume of people that frequent (or targets that exist in) the areas of high crime concentration. Geographic analysis that considers the spatial distribution of crime rates can provide added value to hotspot maps by considering some underlying population. This type of analysis may also make it easier to identify certain underlying causes of crime by classifying differences between hotspots (Clarke & Eck, 2003).

The analysis of crime rates alongside crime volume is regularly applied to burglary patterns (for examples see Chainey & Ratcliffe, 2005; Harries, 1999; Home Office, 2001a). Hotspot maps showing high concentrations of burglary may only reveal where there is a large amount of housing stock, hence the calculation of burglary rates against the underlying distribution of housing stock can provide an added dimension to the geographical analysis of burglary patterns by revealing where residents are at most risk of being a victim of this type of crime. Burglary rate maps are straight-forward to construct because most developed countries possess census data at fine geographic resolution that describe the number of residential households in each census geographic unit, although, the choice and source of other denominators for other crime types is not as straight-forward (Chainey & Ratcliffe, 2005).

Rate maps and statistics calculated for crime rates for other crime types often make use of the resident population. For example, in England and Wales, published crime statistics include crime rates for vehicle crime and robbery to the person by using the resident population as a denominator. As a general-purpose measure to compare differences between areas it does have utility, however, in some cases it can greatly mislead (Chainey & Ratcliffe, 2005). Table 1 lists UK Home Office published robbery statistics for April 2002 to March 2003 for a sample of seven police force command areas (Home Office, 2003). The table also shows that the average robbery rate in England and Wales was 2.1 crimes per 1000 population per annum.

Table 1 demonstrates the large variation in robbery rates between areas in England and Wales. This can partly be explained due to the genuine differences in robbery between these areas. For example, inner city areas such as Lambeth in central London do tend to experience more problems with robbery than a provincial town such as Stratford-upon-Avon. These differences being explained due to the different socioeconomic and demographic characteristics between the two areas. There is though a large variation in the resident population between these six areas. The robbery rate statistics suggest that the likelihood of being a victim of robbery in the City of London is three times that of Newcastle, but half of that when compared to the neighbouring London borough of Lambeth. This may be useful as a general relative measure between areas, but may also be inherently inaccurate, as it does not consider the daytime population that frequent these areas. For example, the City of London is the financial centre of the UK, with land use mainly consisting of offices. Many thousands of people travel into the area each day for work, but very few people live in this area of central London. Similarly, the London Borough of Westminster is a centre for business, education, shopping, and tourism, and attracts over one million visitors each day.

The impression given by crime statistics in this form is that the areas of Lambeth, Westminster, and the City of London are some of the most unsafe areas in the country for robbery crimes committed against persons on the street. For all the areas shown in Table 1 the robbery rate only considers the residential population and does not take into account how the levels of daytime population may influence the robbery levels experienced between areas. For example, the City of London witnessed only 45 robberies between April 2002 and March 2003 whereas Birmingham experienced 5,976 robberies. The impression given by the crime rate statistics is that Birmingham is marginally safer than the City of London.

Table 1 highlights the exaggerated effect that resident population may have as a denominator for calculating crime rates. This denominator offers some utility for comparisons between large areas, but could particularly exaggerate and mislead the identification of crime problems when considered at finer levels of geographic resolution (e.g., census blocks and census output areas).

The problems with applying inappropriate denominators for calculating and interpreting crime patterns were highlighted by Clarke and Mayhew (1998). While their analysis was on vehicle crime, the principles of applying suitable denominators to calculate crime rates are applicable to all crime types. The British Crime Survey suggests that two-thirds of vehicle thefts occur when a vehicle is parked in the vicinity of the owners' home (half of this crime occurring when the car is parked on the street rather than a driveway or garage) and 17% occurs in public car parks. In Clarke and Mayhew's research they used exposure (the time the car was parked at a particular location) as the denominator revealing that the risk of a car being stolen from a public car park was actually over four times that of the risk of the vehicle being stolen while parked on the street outside the owner's home. This research was fundamental in identifying the differences between types of localities in risks to being a victim of crime and demonstrated that although car parks may not necessarily appear as hotspots on a crime density map, the risk of having a vehicle stolen from a car park is much higher than any other locality. The impact of this research was the call for specific crime prevention initiatives to be targeted to these high-risk areas. The similar problem of inappropriate use of denominators for street crime may also mean that certain patterns are hidden in the data, and opportunities are being missed to think more considerately about effective crime prevention for tackling street crime.

Table 1. Robbery rates in eight police command unit areas in England and Wales, shown with the average rate for England and Wales and each area's resident population. Source: Home Office, 2003.

Police force area	Robbery rate per 1000 population per annum	Resident population
Birmingham	6.1	976000
City of London	6.3	7200
Lambeth	15.1	267000
Manchester	12	393000
Newcastle-upon-Tyne	1.8	260000
Stratford-upon-Avon	0.2	112000
Westminster	9.6	182000
England and Wales	2.1	52 million

THE MEASURE AND ANALYSIS OF STREET CRIME

Street crime is usually only analyzed at the local municipal and neighborhood level by exploring patterns in its volume. Attempts that are made to analyze street crime rates use resident population statistics. These figures can have little bearing on daytime street population, particularly in city centres and areas where there are shopping malls and entertainment centres where street crime tends to be most highly concentrated (Home Office, 2001b). If resident population values are used as denominators in these areas then it is likely that the rate will be highly exaggerated and misleads the interpretation of crime patterns. Similarly, in areas where the volume of street crime could be low, the street crime rate could be underestimated, as the area is a locale of high resident population.

Street crime volume statistics and hotspot density maps do have their purpose. They can be used as important tools for helping target resources to relatively small geographic areas where they could have a positive impact in reducing crime. However, volume analysis may miss two important features that can aid intelligence development. Firstly it could fail to identify those places where pedestrians on the street are at most risk of being a victim of street crime. Instead, resources may only be targeted to those places where the numbers are high, but the chances of someone being a victim could be relatively low. Secondly, analysis of crime rate patterns provides an important dimension to explaining why crime may persist in certain places. By identifying areas where the crime rate is high can be more useful in revealing the underlying causes to the crime, rather than identifying the problem as a product of the volume of people that frequent that location. For example, analysis of crime density patterns and crime rates could distinguish between areas acting as a crime generator or a crime attractor (Brantingham & Brantingham, 1995; Clarke & Eck, 2003).

Accurate analysis of street crime rates requires measurement of the on-street population. This type of measure has been utilized for better understanding crime rates in shopping malls (Brantingham & Brantingham, 1995) and for analysis of populations available to stop and search (MVA, 2000), but has yet to be applied in larger scale studies. The on-street population measure would also need to be geographically precise because large differences in pedestrian traffic can exist within very short distances (Duxburry & Desyllas, 2000, 2001). Developments in pedestrian modeling make it possible for accurate estimates of the on-street population to be calibrated, for specific time periods, and at fine levels of geographic resolution. With the use of street crime data that can similarly be geocoded to these same high levels of precision it is possible to analyze geographic patterns of street crime rate.

AIMS OF THIS RESEARCH

This research had five main aims. First it aims to demonstrate how on-street pedestrian volumes can be generated using pedestrian modeling, and secondly how data derived from the model can be linked with crime data, in a large-scale study area, to compare patterns of. The third and fourth targets were to investigate if geographic patterns of were different to street crime volume patterns (i.e., hotspots), and if maps generated using the resident population as a denominator were different to patterns revealed in rate maps generated using on-street population values. Finally, the research aimed to generate better information for understanding street crime, proving if there was value in street crime rate analysis alongside analysis of volumetric patterns.

STUDY AREA AND DATA

Study Area

The study area for this research was within the London Borough of Westminster in central London (see Figure 1). The area includes busy pedestrian areas such as Oxford Street, Soho, Piccadilly, Trafalgar Square, Leicester Square, Parliament Square and Covent Garden, and 19 London Underground stations. It also includes residential areas such as Pimlico and Westminster.

This study area was selected because extensive pedestrian modeling had already been performed in the area for the purposes of monitoring changes in pedestrian levels resulting from the introduction of the central London congestion charging zone (CCZ)—the CCZ was introduced in February 2002 and aims to reduce traffic congestion by requiring drivers to pay a daily fee if they drive into the zone. It is also an area that experiences high levels of street crime, but attracts many millions of visitors for work, education, shopping, and tourism—within the study area are several major attractions such as Buckingham Palace, Nelson's Column, Big Ben, 10 Downing Street, the Houses of Parliament and Westminster Abbey. The study area is referred to as the "West End study area" throughout this chapter.

Crime Data

Street crime data for the period January 2003 to December 2003 was sourced from the Metropolitan Police via the Westminster Crime and Disorder Reduction Partnership. Street crime was defined as robbery from the person of personal property and theft from the person. Robbery involves some form of violence or the threat of violence, while theft from the person involves property being stolen from the person without the person being violently attacked or threatened with violence. It may though include some degree of force being applied, for example, the struggle for a bag that

Figure 1. The West End study area in Central London

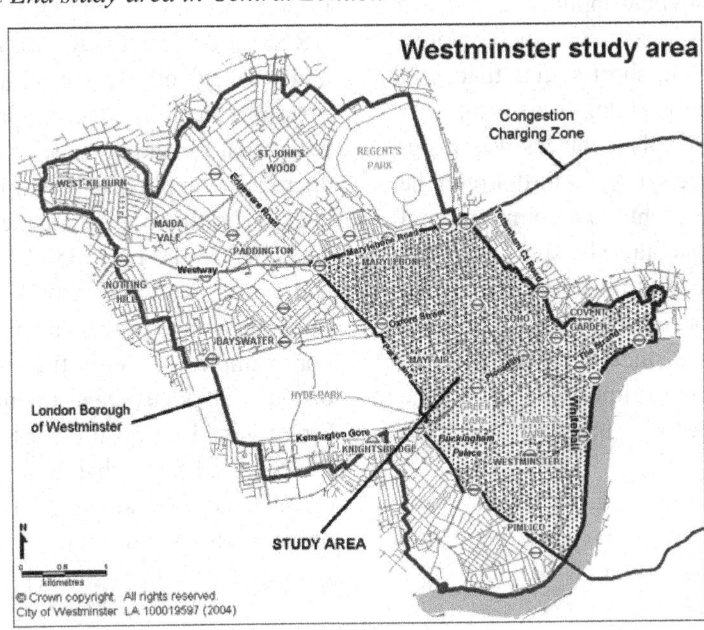

has been snatched by the offender from the victim. It does not include pick pocketing.

The street crime data was geocoded by Westminster Crime and Disorder Reduction Partnership. Precise geocoding of street crime data can present more of a challenge compared to other types of crime because of the ambiguous entry of location information that can be recorded in a street crime record. For example, if a person was robbed on Oxford Street in central London they may not know if it happened outside number 5 Oxford Street or number 105 Oxford Street. Oxford Street is nearly 2 kilometres in length, so difficulties will result in pinpointing the crime location if only "Oxford Street, London" is the location entry in the crime record. Data input can include an organization name (e.g., Selfridges) or "location text" entry (e.g., "junction with Regent's Street") that can be manipulated and used to precisely geocode the crime record (Chainey & Ratcliffe, 2005). However, nearly 20% of records may remain where the only address or location entry in the crime record is the street name. This may result in these crimes being positioned to the centroid or some other "common" location on the street. For short streets this does not cause a problem for most analytical applications. Indeed for this study, as the spatial resolution of interest was the street segment, short streets that were not dissected by street junctions means that this geocoding problem for these places was insignificant. For long streets (e.g., Oxford Street) the positioning of crime events to a common point can result in creating a "false hotspot".

A function that the Westminster CDRP's geocoding software performs is one that successfully handles the problem of uncertainty in precisely determining where the crime took place. The function works in the following way:

- It identifies those crime events that have been successfully and precisely geocoded on the street in question.
- The location of these precise records determines the weights for positioning the affected records. The greater the number of incidents that have been precisely located to a position on the street the greater the weight and draw to that location for points that require this calculated positioning.
- The weighting function also includes an element of random distribution along the street so that no particular location can overly dominate.
- The function is then applied to the affected records, grid coordinates are determined, and this calculated position is recorded in the record's audit code so it can be identified from those that did not require this treatment (Chainey & Ratcliffe, 2005).

The geocoded street crime data were then validated by the researchers conducting this study. This was performed using a methodology for geocoding accuracy analysis as reported in Chainey and Ratcliffe (2005, p 61-63). This revealed the street crime data to be more than 95% accurate and fit for purpose for this research.

Geocoding of crime records in the UK most often makes use of the Ordnance Survey ADDRESS-POINT dataset. This address list can be added to with other points of interest and nonaddressable locations (e.g., public lavatories, parks, car parks) for the purposes of geocoding. This approach is applied in Westminster. However, it does mean that a street crime is most typically geocoded to the position of the building of the address or location where the offence occurred, rather than on the street and outside of a premise. For example, a robbery that may have occurred outside Selfridges Department Store on Oxford Street would be positioned to the ADDRESS-POINT seed point that is geographically referenced to a point at the approximate centre of the building. A process has to be applied to this geocoded data to position it on the street segment where the crime occurred. This process is explained in a following section.

Pedestrian Data

As part of a study into the impact of the central London congestion charging zone (CCZ), Transport for London (TfL) and the Central London Partnership commissioned Intelligent Space to develop a pedestrian model of the total walking volumes for each segment of the street network in central London. The model was calibrated using geographic information on key indicators that influence pedestrian movement with observed pedestrian flow data from 107 sample locations. The model has been tested and validated independently by Transport for London, who has approved its accuracy in generating on-street pedestrian estimates. The model estimated flow values for 25 square kilometres of street length and over 7,500 street segments. A description of the pedestrian modeling method is provided in a following section.

The origins of the pedestrian model were for comparing changes in pedestrian movement as a result of the introduction of the CCZ. The CCZ only applies between the hours of 07.00 and 19.00. Therefore a limitation of the model was that it had only been calibrated to generate estimates of pedestrian movement between these hours (we refer to this period as "daytime" hours from this point forward).

Figure 2 shows the output of the model for each street in the West End study area. A thematic range was used to indicate those areas of high pedestrian flows, from areas with low flows. These are also shown with photographs for each thematic class to help visualize the level of pedestrian traffic experienced on the street.

Crime and Pedestrian Features of the Study Area

The West End area of London within Westminster provides an ideal study area for exploring patterns of on s. Published statistics on street crime levels in Westminster often appear to exaggerate the actual on street risk as these statistics are calculated against the relatively small resident population that lives in this area, and not the millions of

Figure 2. Modeled daytime pedestrian counts per street segment in the West End of London, shown thematically with a photographic representation of the on-street population. Source: Chainey and Desyllas (2004).

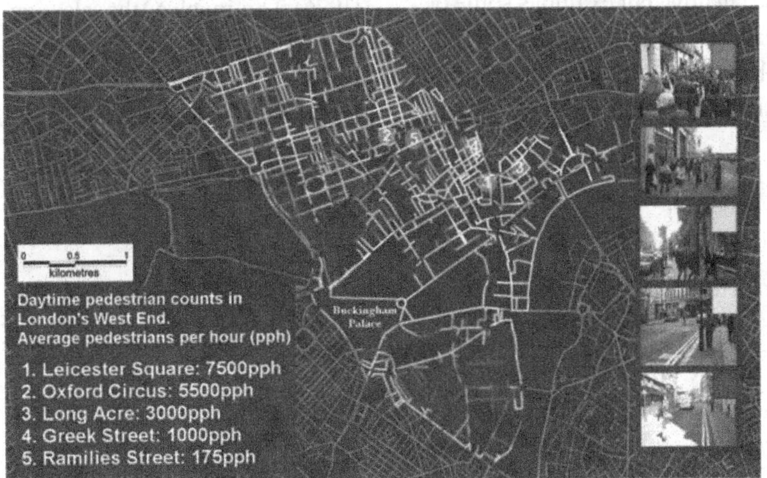

tourists, shoppers, and commuters that visit or pass through the area.

Table 2 lists the volume of robbery and theft from the person in the study area for the period January 2003 to December 2003. As the West End study area's pedestrian model was calibrated for observing daytime pedestrian movement it was only possible to consider street crime events that had occurred during this same daytime period. However, this did not influence the aims that were originally set out in the research, the main focus being to prove the concept of a large scale study of investigating patterns, and comparing it against hotspot density patterns and crime rates generated using the resident population as a denominator. Table 2 lists the sample of crime data that was available for daytime hours that could be linked to street segments, from which street crime rates could be calculated.

The West End study area contains some of the highest flows within Central London and the core of the pedestrian movement network. For example, the average pedestrian daytime population per year (ppa) on Oxford Street was 33 million—the arterial route that runs from East to West through Oxford Circus (see Figure 2). One of the key characteristics of pedestrian flows is the large difference in the volume of flows on streets within close proximity of each other. This is exhibited in the study area where there is a great diversity in levels of pedestrian flow. For example, some of the side streets leading off Oxford Street have an estimated 0.7 Million ppa—these streets joining directly onto sections of Oxford Street with a ppa of 25 Million.

METHODOLOGY

Pedestrian Modeling

Pedestrian modeling uses a flexible and testable framework of multiple regression analysis whereby key indicators that influence pedestrian movement are calibrated against observed flows from the study area. This modeling process is shown in Figure 3. The modeling process allows for continuous retrials for new areas or new policy levers, and independent validation by users of the model outputs—in Figure 3 the validation of the central London pedestrian model was performed by Transport for London (TfL). With every extension of the model, the importance of all factors can be retested to ensure an optimal balance between specific site accuracy and the wider application of the model design.

Observation Samples

Three studies were conducted in the central London study area to collect sample observation data. Two of the studies were conducted between 08:00 and 19:00, with the third taking place between 12:00 to 18:00. The dates of each study were March 2000, July 2001 and August 1999. The methodology adopted to collect observation samples was similar to that of Benham and Patel (1976). This involved the selection of "study zones" that were representative areas for capturing the variations in pedestrian traffic in the study area. Pedestrian flows were sampled for each street in these study zones.

Table 2. Street crime in the West End study area (January 2003 – December 2003)

	Number of crimes	Number of crimes during daytime hours
Robbery	487	125
Theft from the person	651	277
Total - street crime	1138	402

Figure 3. The pedestrian modeling process (Source: Chainey & Desyllas, 2004)

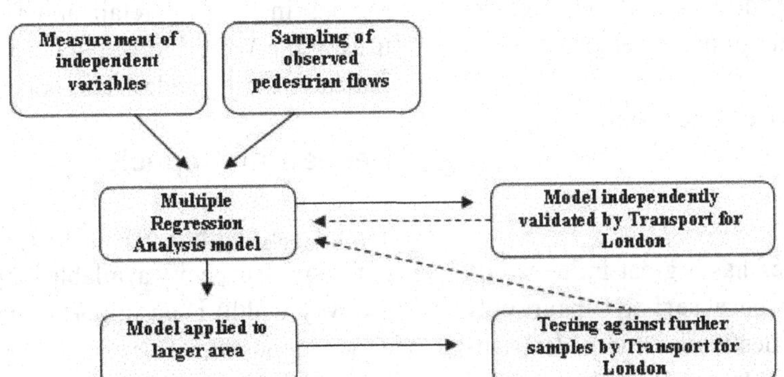

Observation points were located on both pavements at the mid point of each street segment. These pavement midpoints were then organized into circuits for observers to carry out sampling. This involved each observer walking a circuit, taking pedestrian flow counts at each pavement midpoint for five minutes, so that each mid-point was covered once for each hour of the survey. If the observer finished a circuit before the end of the hour they would return to the circuit starting point and wait until the end of the hour before commencing the next count. Flow rates per hour for each street segment in the study zones could be derived by multiplying the five-minute counts by 12. The sampling and gathering of pedestrian counts can also be performed by utilizing automated counting technologies such as passive infrared, or by performing observations using street closed circuit television cameras (UTMC, 2000).

A key characteristic of sample data that the model has to capture is the variations in counts that may result with direction: there were street junctions in the study area that experienced flows averaging over 3,000 people per hour on one street and zero people per hour on the perpendicular street. This natural fine scale anisotropic character of pedestrian movement network can be masked by aggregating the data and presents issues associated with "ecological fallacy" (Robinson, 1950). For this reason, the modeling was performed at the street segment level, meaning that the unit of the model was the flow along any street, including both pavements if the street was not pedestrianised. No attempt was made to average flows in any other way, such as along a line of sight (Hillier, Penn, Hanson, Grajewski, & Xu, 1993).

Another key characteristic of observed movement the model was required to replicate was the uneven distribution of flows, with a small number of streets exhibiting very large higher flows compared to most others. Pedestrian flows are logarithmically distributed (Duxburry & Desyllas, 2000, 2001). The pedestrian model therefore has to be able to identify the primacy of these key streets in order to represent the pattern of pedestrian movement successfully.

The sample size observation sites for the pedestrian model was 231 street segments. These observations were not just for the streets with the West End study area, but the central London area that the pedestrian model was originally calibrated for.

Statistical tests were then used to determine the key indicators that significantly impact pedestrian flows within urban landscapes. The key indicators that were identified were

- The pattern of land use
- The accessibility of public transport facilities

- The capacity of pavements or footways
- The visibility or "desire lines" for movement within the layout of the street grid

Each indicator is explained next.

Land Use

The mix of land uses has a great influence on pedestrian movement because short trips are only possible where local destinations for pedestrians are available. This was demonstrated in several of the first pedestrian models developed in the 1970's following the tradition of land use transportation models by Lowry and McLughlin (Willumsen & Ortuzar, 1994) and large scale urban models of the 1960's (Lee, 1973). Pushkarev and Zupan (1975), and Benham and Patel (1976) also demonstrated a strong correlation between independent land use variables and pedestrian movement, resulting in this indicator as being an input variable that would be tested for its suitability in a modern central London pedestrian model.

The pattern of land use in central London was analyzed for the pedestrian model in order to test the influence that different building use had as a "trip generator" for pedestrian flows. Statistical tests from this analysis showed that the key land uses which influenced the pattern of pedestrian movement were retail, food, and drinking establishments. This partly relates to the importance of shopping and leisure trips within overall pedestrian movement—these generate 24% of overall movement within the UK, whereas commuting account for up 16% of trips.

The fact that a shop, restaurant, bar, or pub may exist on a street can be inconsequential if the pedestrian cannot see this form of land use. A separate model was therefore generated to analyze how many premises of this type a pedestrian would be able to see as they walked around the central London street network. This output revealed a large number of highly visible shops and food/drink establishments were clustered in certain places in the West End study area. The regions in view of retail and food/drink land uses in the West End were put forward as a key indicator for the pedestrian model.

Pedestrian Capacity

The infrastructure provision for walking (in terms of the space capacity available for pedestrians or footway width) is an important factor as it can either support flows or discourage walking. The influence of footway capacity on pedestrian flows has been well established since Fruin formalized the level of service (LOS) concept for walkways (Fruin, 1971), showing that reduced capacity leads to congestion and thereby reduced flows. Previous pedestrian modeling studies such as Pushkarev and Zupan (1975) found walkway area to be a significant independent variable. Capacity is important because low quality pavements of inadequate width are an active deterrent to walking.

The capacity of central London's streets was analyzed using a computer program to calculate the average total pavement width of each street segment. This was possible due to the rich base mapping data that is available in Great Britain that is produced by the ordnance survey—Britain's national mapping agency.

Street Configuration

Street configuration (the urban design or layout of streets) has an important influence on pedestrian flows. Street systems are complex and irregular, and pedestrians have to navigate through these networks in order to go anywhere. Pedestrians are sensitive to the complexity of routes and tend to choose simple, more direct options for most trips over complicated, indirect routes (Hillier, 1996). This means that the urban design of an area can have an important effect on supporting or hindering pedestrian movement. The layout of streets can either provide clear, simple routes that are easy to use for pedestrians or it can provide more complex, confusing routes which are much harder to use.

Street configuration was measured by calculating lines of site from every location across the West End study area. This revealed how certain streets offer very clear pedestrian visibility in comparison to others within the dense labyrinthine street network of parts of central London where visibility is poor.

Access to Public Transport

Transport facilities are a key factor in pedestrian flows because pedestrian movement is limited to short trips and so other modes are critical to generating pedestrian activity within an area. There are over 8.6 million trips on the public transport network of London each day (Transport for London, 2003), most forming part of a multimodal trip that includes walking.

Within the study area of central London, the importance of transport for pedestrian movement is underlined by the majority of daytime pedestrian space users within central London who arrive into the area using mechanized transport of some form. The pedestrian mode is often the first and last stage of the overall trip, so pedestrian movement in the study area often originates from the last point of mechanized transport. As transport nodes are important in delivering pedestrians to the area that they will walk in, the pattern of the flows at the local level is influenced by how walkers distribute away from and towards these nodes. Those streets offering clear distribution channels around transport nodes will be more heavily used than those that do not lead towards transport facilities.

It is possible to capture these differences at a large scale, for local areas, using a computer model. For the central London pedestrian model a measure of accessibility to London underground stations within the street network was developed using visibility graph analysis. The output from this model was a calculation of the path complexity from each sample point to the nearest Underground station entrance.

Model Testing

Standard quality control procedures were used in the statistical modeling, such as checking the frequency distributions of each of the variables to ensure that all logarithmic distributions were transformed, checking that all coefficient signs were as expected and testing for autocorrelation of independent variables. Stepwise regression was used to confirm that the four key indicators had a statistically significant influence on observed pedestrian movement. A linear regression of the expected number of pedestrians (calibrated from the model) was performed against observed flows, and this produced an r^2 of 0.82. This is a far higher correlation than any of the previous published urban pedestrian models; Benham and Patel's (1976) correlation of 0.764 was the closest, but with a much smaller sample of 20 cases. The published correlations of the Pushkarev and Zupan (1975) and Hillier, et al. (1993) studies were 0.61 and 0.55 respectively.

Multiple regression analysis of the key indicators revealed that visibility in the central London study areas was the most important variable. This suggested that given that pedestrian trips in central London tend to be short, visibility could be the most appropriate spatial measure of the street network for capturing the aggregation of short journeys. Another assumption would be that simpler routes tend to use the more visible spaces and pedestrians economise on route complexity, not distance. Visibility may also be considered as the most direct aid to wayfinding, especially as pedestrians have imperfect knowledge of the street network, with pedestrians choosing the most obvious routes, which are also the most visible.

The pedestrian model was then independently verified by TfL and a program of testing against additional observation data was carried out. This included a recalibration of the model using the values from two areas to estimate the pedestrian levels for a third area that was not included in the original models calibration. When the estimated values were compared to the new third area in central London it produced an r^2 of 0.74. This demonstrated that the model held up well to scrutiny against data that was not used to calibrate the model.

Linking Crime Data to Pedestrian Flows

Geocoded crime data were linked to pedestrian flow data by following a dual-combinational approach of assigning the crime to its relevant street segment. This was performed in a GIS using a database of street segments. The process involved referencing the street name that was listed in the crime record against the street name recorded in the street segment database, and positioning the crime on the nearest adjacent street segment as long as the street names between the two files matched. This process was particularly important for locations near junctions or where a street crime was geographically positioned at some distance from the street it occurred on (e.g., this occurred for some large buildings where the ADDRESS-POINT seed was several metres from the street where the crime occurred and on occasion was more adjacent to a different street). Validation of this process assured the linking of crime data to street segments had been performed accurately.

Calculating Street Crime Density and Street Crime Rates

Street crime density maps were generated using kernel density estimation (see Eck et al., 2005; Chainey & Ratcliffe, 2005 for more details on this technique). These maps were generated in MapInfo professional using default settings in Hotspot detective (Ratcliffe, 2004).

Rate measures can be calculated by comparing a numerator (i.e., crime) against a denominator (i.e., population) and presented as normalized value (e.g., the number of crimes per 1,000 population). Resident population is commonly used to generate street crime rates. 2001 Census data on resident population for geographic output areas (OAs) was sourced from the UK's online Neighbourhood Statistics Service and linked to geographic polygons of OAs in MapInfo GIS. A count of the number of street crimes in each OA was calculated in MapInfo from which a street crime rate (crimes per 1,000 population) for each OA was calculated. These street crime rate patterns at the OA level were then mapped.

Street crime data that had been linked to street segments was aggregated to form a count of crimes per street segment. These values were then calculated as a street crime rate against the daytime pedestrian population for each street segment and were mapped.

Street Crime in the West End Study Area

For the period January 2003 to December 2003, 1,138 street crimes were recorded in the West End study area. The street crime rate per 1,000 populations for daytime hours in the study area was 9.9 per 1,000 population per annum. This rate was calculated using a 2001 Census derived population of 40756 residents. Table 3 shows

Table 3. Street crime rates (per 1000 population per annum) in the West End study area between January 2003 - December 2003

	Rate (per 1000 population per annum)
Robbery	3.1
Theft from the person	6.8
Street crime rate	9.9

rates for robbery and theft from the person for the daytime period.

Figure 4 shows the pattern of street crime across the study area during daytime hours. This shows that the major robbery density hotspot areas (4a) were in Soho and in pockets along Oxford Street that were centred around Tottenham Court Road, Oxford Circus, and Bond Street Underground stations. The rate map (4b), drawn using Census Output Areas, suggests that the area between Piccadilly and Oxford Street, and the eastern section of Oxford Street were the highest risk areas. The OAs with the highest rates were greater than 45 per 1000 population per annum, with street crime peaking in an OA with a rate of 58.8 per 1000 population per annum.

Figure 4c shows theft of the person hotspots (during daytime hours) in the study area. Hotspots were apparent along the middle section of Oxford Street around Oxford Circus, the area near Marble Arch at the west end of Oxford Street, the area extending from Piccadilly and across Leicester Square and into Covent Garden, and the area due north of Piccadilly in Soho. The rate map (4d) suggests the area between Piccadilly and Oxford Circus (and to the west of Regent Street) as one the most vulnerable areas for this type of street crime, along with the area surrounding Leicester

Figure 4. Street crime in the West End study area: (a) robbery hotspots, (b) robbery rates by Output Areas, (c) theft from the person hotspots, (d) theft from the person rates by Output Areas

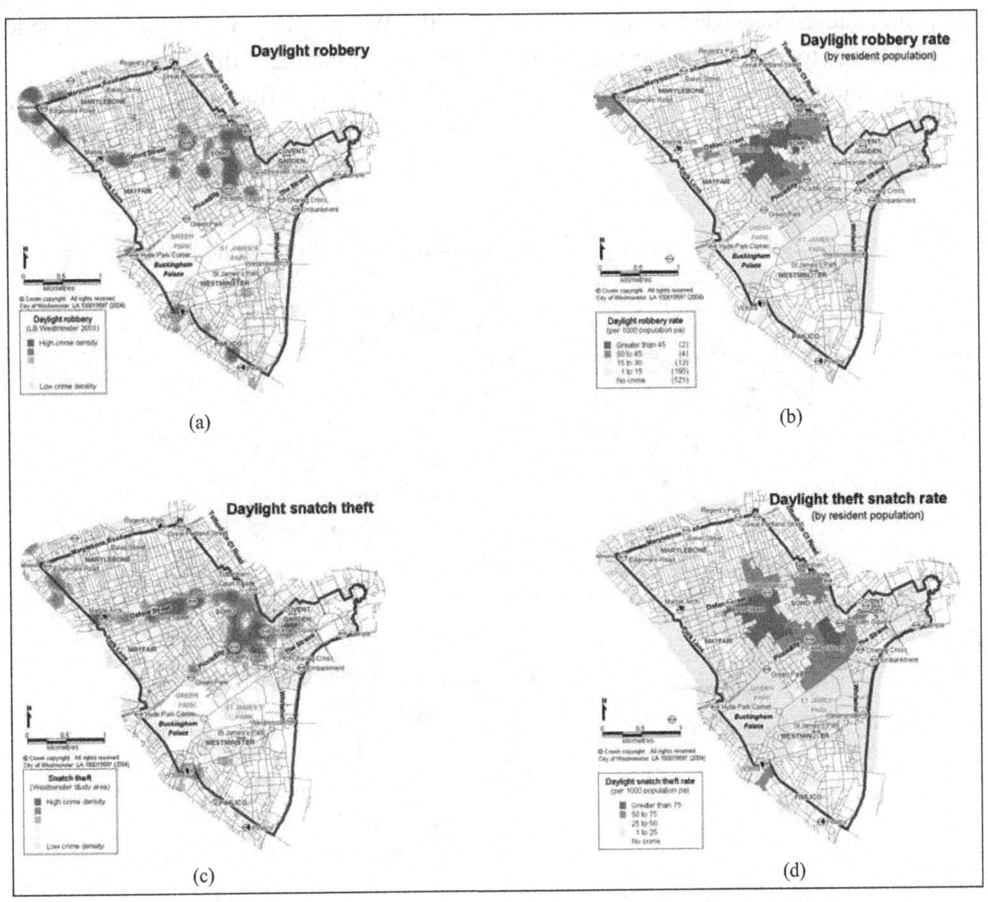

Square. These areas recorded rates that were greater than 75 thefts per 1,000 population per annum, with the worst OA surrounding Oxford Circus, recording a rate of 133.7 thefts from the person per 1,000 population per annum. This could be interpreted as over 1 in 10 residents in the area being a victim of thefts from the person.

PEDESTRIAN

Street crime rates were calculated for each street segment using the modeled pedestrian counts as the denominator. The first most striking finding was how significant the difference was between street crime rates calculated with on-street populations and street crime rates calculated using the resident population. The street crime rates in the areas that recorded the highest levels, using resident population, exceeded 45 per 1000 population per annum for robbery and 75 per 1000 population per annum for theft from the person.

Using pedestrian counts as the denominator for calculating, the areas with the highest street crime rates recorded levels of:

- **Robbery:** 0.0019 per 1000 pedestrians per annum
- **Theft from the person:** 0.0051 per 1000 pedestrians per annum

In comparison to the rates reported using the resident population the difference in magnitude is extremely significant. The pedestrian risk statistics for robbery equate to requiring 500,000 people to walk along the highest risk segment of street in the West End study area before a pedestrian becomes a victim of this crime. Similarly, these calculations suggest that it requires 200,000 people to walk along the segment of street with the highest calculated rate of theft from the person in the West End study area before a pedestrian becomes a victim of this crime.

As well as differences in magnitude, there are also significant differences in the geographic

Figure 5. Robbery rate patterns in the West End study area derived from modeled pedestrian counts

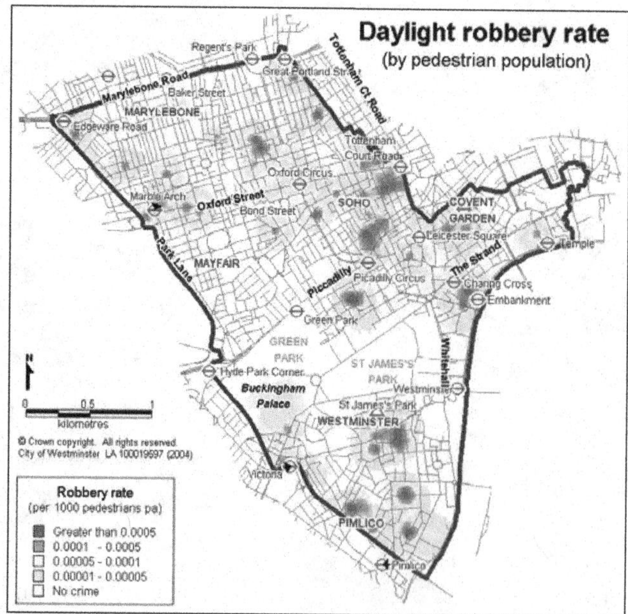

pattern of street crime rates when resident populations and on-street populations (as denominators to street crime) are compared. Figure 5 shows geographic patterns of robbery rates derived from modeled pedestrian counts. This reveals different areas with the highest on-street risk of street crime to pedestrians in comparison to the rate map shown in Figure 4b. This demonstrates that the attention drawn to the robbery rates in areas along Oxford Street, to the west of Regents Street and north of Piccadilly into Soho appear to mislead when the residential population was used as the denominator. Certain areas in Soho do remain as high-risk areas, but other areas in the north and south of the study area are revealed that had not appeared previously as exhibiting high robbery rates.

Figure 6 shows the geographic patterns of theft from the person crime rates derived from modeled pedestrian counts. The different patterns shown by this rate map in comparison to the residential population derived rate map are again significant. The central section of Oxford Street, the area west of Regents Street and Leicester Square were the areas where street crime rates appeared to be highest in the resident population based rate maps. In comparison, the street crime rate map derived from pedestrian counts exhibited many other areas as the worst affected areas for pedestrians suffering from this type of crime. These areas include the area immediately south of Tottenham Court Road Underground Station and into Soho (e.g., an area known as Soho Square), Covent Garden, and small pockets situated to the north of Oxford Street, the area to the south of Charing Cross Underground station, the top of The Mall (north of St. James's Park), and the area between Victoria Station and Buckingham Palace. Neither Leicester Square, the central section of Oxford Street, nor the area to the west of Regent Street showed up as areas of high risk to this type of crime.

These results suggest that the rates calculated for street crime that use the resident population as a denominator offer very little in helping identify

Figure 6. Theft from the person crime patterns in the West End study area derived from modeled pedestrian counts

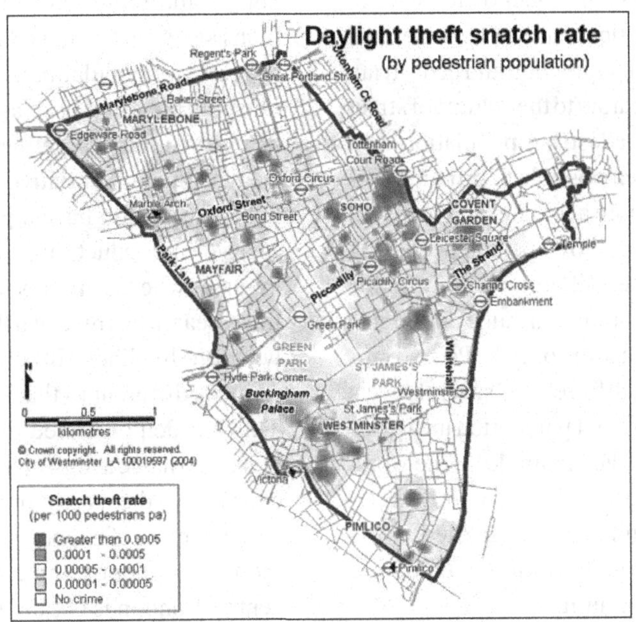

and understand relative patterns of street crime risk, and only confuse and misinform. Instead, street crime rates calculated using street segment modeled pedestrian counts offer a more reliable basis for identifying and interpreting patterns of risk for this type of crime.

DISCUSSION

This research was the first ever study that used a large-scale pedestrian model to generate precise street crime rates. In many ways the research has served as a proof of concept exercise to demonstrate how the use of modeled pedestrian count data can act as an accurate denominator for understanding measures and patterns of . In this section we discuss the results in terms of the street crime rate statistics that are generated as a result of using pedestrian counts as the denominator to street crime volume and geographic patterns of street crime rates, and the application of these measures.

Street Crime Rate Statistics

This research has shown the clear differences in street crime rate statistics that can be generated from using the resident population and pedestrian population as denominators to the volume of street crime. By using the pedestrian population as a denominator it has been possible to produce new statistics that offer a more accurate (and realistic) measure of the likelihood of a person becoming a victim of street crime. We argue that from this research the resident population value does nothing but misinform measures of risk. Pedestrian-based measures were different by several levels of magnitude to the resident population measures that are routinely used. For example, in the worst affected street crime areas the was not 133 per 1,000 population per annum (as suggested by using resident population data), but was 0.005 per 1,000 population per annum.

Reassuring the public about the actual levels of crime is an agenda that many national and state governments are active to promote to help better address the public's fears, worries and perceptions of crime. To do this it requires the appropriate presentation of statistical facts that can truly reflect the very rare chance of someone becoming a victim of street crime. Policing and Crime and Disorder Reduction Partnership activity in Westminster is very much focused towards reducing street crime and the fear that this crime can present, and by using measures that describe that in its worst areas it takes half a million pedestrian journeys along this street before a member of the public may become a victim of robbery can only help to reassure those that are resident or that visit Westminster of the likely risks and the rarity of being a victim of a robbery or having an item stolen from them.

Street Crime Rate Geographic Patterns

This research has shown the clear degree of difference between the geographic patterns of street crime rates generated from modeled pedestrian counts and those generated for hotspot density maps and street crime rate maps generated using the resident population at the OA level. Volume hotspots are often used as the only geographical analysis tool for targeting police operations and crime reduction initiatives on street crime. These hotspot maps do have a purpose as they help to focus crime reduction and policing initiatives to the areas where crime does concentrate. However, this research has revealed that there are other areas where the likelihood of being a victim from a street crime is different to that of the volume hotspots. This has demonstrated that several of the areas that experience a high volume of crime often only exist due to the large number of pedestrians (and larger number of opportunities) that travel through these areas. For example, an area well-known in central London is Oxford Circus. The street segment to the east of Oxford Circus, outside a large shop called Top Shop is a theft from the person hotspot (there were 8 thefts at this location in 2003) and therefore very often receives targeted police attention and is covered by closed circuit television (CCTV) surveillance. However, in any one daylight hour over 5,000 people on average walk this section of street. It therefore requires 2,500,000 pedestrian journeys along this section of street before a member of the public may become a victim of this type of crime.

Other streets in the study area experienced low volumes of street crime, but their pedestrian traffic was also observed as being relatively low. Calculation of the number of street crimes against pedestrian levels for these areas revealed several of these streets to experience high levels of street crime rate. Yet, because they did not appear in volume hotspot statistics they were places that typically receive very little, if any, policing or crime reduction attention. Other areas were identified where the volume of crime was high and the rate was also high, but their attention for targeted policing and for crime reduction was most often considered with the same solution that was used for the high volume, low risk areas.

Areas that have a street crime problem may require different treatment due to differences in the reasons why crime occurs at these locations. In the analysis of street crime hotspots, each hotspot is often assumed to display similar qualities that explain why crime concentrates at these places. More considered analysis that can classify each hotspot in terms of the spatial differences in volumes and rates can help to unpack why crime may persist at these particular places.

Hotspots can be broadly classified into three types; crime generators, crime attractors, and crime enablers (Brantingham & Brantingham, 1995; Clarke & Eck, 2003). Each can be typified by differences in the volume of crime and the crime rates that each experience (see Table 4). For example, crime generators are places that appear on hotspot maps due to the high numbers of crime that are experienced at these types of locations. However, they are also places where the relative crime rate is low, due to the large numbers of targets and opportunities that are a product of these types of areas. For example, a crime hotspot at a busy shopping centre can be classified as a crime generator. Other areas that appear on a density map as hotspots could also be crime generators, but some, where the crime rate is also high can be classified as crime attractors—these areas tending to be places where specific crime opportunities exist (e.g., places where people can by drugs) or where offenders know there to be a good reputation for committing crime of a certain type at these places (e.g., robbery that may occur late at night around the vicinity of bars and nightclubs). Further analysis of a crime rate map may also reveal places that exist as crime enablers—places where the volume of crime is low but where the rate is high. For example, these could be places where there is an environmental or situational lack of control, and little regulation of behavior—such as a pavilion in the middle of a park, a public lavatory, or a bus shelter, which is prone to repeated incidents of vandalism and criminal damage. The number of crimes committed against these targets may be relatively low, but their isolation can make them particularly vulnerable to criminal activity.

Examples of these three definitional differences between types of hotspots can be seen in the study area when comparing Figures 5 and Figure 4:

- **Crime generator:** Oxford Circus, where the volume of robbery is high but the relative rate is low.
- **Crime attractor:** The area immediately north of Piccadilly Circus and into Soho where the volume of robbery is high and the relative rate is also high.
- **Crime enabler:** An example of this type of hotspot can be seen in figure 5 in the area immediately south of Piccadilly Circus

Table 4. Classifications of hotspots, determined by differences in the volume of crime and the rates that each experience. Adapted from Clarke and Eck (2003).

	Number of crimes	Rate
Crime generators (e.g., shopping centres)	HIGH	LOW
Crime attractors (e.g., areas around bars)	HIGH	HIGH
Crime enabler (e.g., park pavilion)	LOW	HIGH

where the relative robbery rate is high, but the volume of crime (as shown in Figure 4) is low.

Classifying hotspots in this way helps to diagnose differences between them. Analysis of crime rates alongside analysis of volumetric patterns is therefore important in intelligence development for helping to understand and explain why crime may persist at particular locations. To address these issues it therefore calls for different types of police and crime prevention responses, rather than a single response that is considered as appropriate for each location. For example, a targeted police presence may help address one type of hotspot, but in others an effective and sustained reduction of crime may require a situational crime prevention measure to address the problems.

Spatial and Temporal Analysis of Street Crime Rates Using Pedestrian Modeling

This research has concentrated on the use of pedestrian modeling for analyzing spatial patterns of street crime rates, with the model's output being limited to pedestrian movement during daytime hours. Time also plays an important role in crime analysis, and pedestrian traffic varies across geographical space over time. Extending the pedestrian model to cover night-time hours would be an obvious next step, allowing for a complete 24 hour picture of street crime to be analyzed. The pedestrian model could also be calibrated to be precise to hours in the day, therefore providing the opportunity to explore in spatial and temporal terms. As the use of pedestrian modeling is considered by a larger audience, including police and crime reduction professionals, it is hoped that extending the model to cover these times will be possible.

CONCLUSION

This research has used a pioneering approach for modeling on-street pedestrian movements in central London. The pedestrian model combines variables that influence pedestrian movement (such as land use, pavement width capacity, and on-street natural surveillance) with samples of on-street pedestrian counts collected at strategic points within the study area to generate accurate and precise measures for pedestrian movement. These pedestrian measures have then been used to calculate street crime rates at the street segment level to determine how these rates compare and differ to hotspot density maps and street crime rate maps generated using the residential population (at the census output area level) as a denominator.

The research has found the following:

- The difference in measures of street crime risk between using resident population and pedestrian population as denominators were significant. For example, in the worst areas for street crime that was 133 per 1,000 population per annum when the resident population was used as a denominator, and was 0.005 per 1,000 population per annum when the on-street pedestrian count estimate was used. The research has therefore produced new statistics that offer a more accurate (and realistic) measure of the likelihood of a person becoming a victim of street crime, and argue that the resident population value does nothing but misinform measures of risk

- The degree in difference between the geographic patterns was also significant. Volume hotspots are often used as the only mapping analysis tool to target efforts for street crime. These hotspot maps do have a purpose as they help to focus crime reduction and policing initiatives to the areas where crime does concentrate. However, this research has revealed that there are other areas where the likelihood of being a victim from a street crime is different to that of the volume hotspots, and that the high crime volume areas often only emerge due to the large number of pedestrians that travel through these areas. Other streets in the study area experienced lower volumes of crime, but their pedestrian traffic was also relatively low. Street crime rate measures for these areas were higher than several of the crime volume hotspot areas, yet because they did not appear in volume hotspot statistics they typically receive very little attention for targeted policing or crime prevention. Other areas were identified as both high volume and high-risk areas, but their attention from policing and for crime reduction was typically treated with the same solution that was used for the high volume, low risk areas.

This research provides a starting agenda for discussing improvements to street crime reduction initiatives that consider not only crime volume but also risk to pedestrians—by starting with a measure and a map of the real risk faced by people on foot, stakeholders can begin to target initiatives for risk reduction. The significance in the results generated from this study call for the need for further work that explores the risk generators in high crime rate areas, and how attention to these will help support sustainable crime reduction programmes in street crime and improvements to pedestrian personal safety.

FUTURE RESEARCH DIRECTIONS

Pedestrian modeling in London has been designed to allow for other variables to be included once they become available and prove to contribute to further improvements. The most promising variable to include would be a measure of urban density, with previous research showing that there is a clear, log-linear negative relationship between urban density and private transport energy use per capita (Newman & Kenworthy 1999). This suggests that higher urban densities result in higher pedestrian flows. A weakness with the existing model is that it is best suited to urban rather than suburban areas, but the inclusion of an urban density measure may help improve its flexibility. The current model is also not sensitive to estimating temporal changes in pedestrian volume over a 24-hour period. Research has commenced though that is adapting the pedestrian model to be sensitive to pedestrian volume differences by modeling these volumes for each one-hour interval.

The creation of the pedestrian model used in this research was for the particular purpose of monitoring pedestrian changes as a result of the introduction of London's congestion charging zone. London is therefore fairly unique in its requirement, hence why many other areas in the UK have yet to be treated to similar modeling. However, this is slowly changing as planners and transport providers begin to better recognise the important role that walking has as a mode of transport, and thus commission models similar to that carried out in London. Indeed, spaces in the cities of Melbourne (Australia), High Wycombe (UK), Kingston upon Thames (UK), Duisburg (Germany) and Boston (USA) have already been treated to pedestrian modeling. Interest from this street crime research has also stimulated the requirement to better consider on-street pedestrian populations in the analysis of crime and has already resulted in another similar study into violent crime Haringey (UK).

Most importantly though, this research has highlighted the need to consider pedestrian volumes for helping to qualify and define crime hotspots. While not all areas may be in the position to commission a pedestrian model, simply visiting the crime study area during different times of the day will help to put into context the drivers behind crime that has been committed.

REFERENCES

Benham, J., Patel, B. (1976). A method for estimating pedestrian volume in a central business district. *Transportation Research Record, 629*, 22-26.

Brantingham, & Brantingham (1995). Criminality and place: Crime generators and crime attractors. *European Journal on Criminal Policy and Research, 3*, 3.

Chainey, S. P., & Desyllas, J. (2004). Measuring, identifying and analysing . In *Proceedings at the 2004 UK National Crime Mapping Conference, University of London, London.* Retrieved August 28, 2007, from www.jdi.ucl.ac.uk/news_events/conferences/index.php

Chainey, S. P., & Ratcliffe, J. H (2005). *GIS and crime mapping.* London: Wiley.

Clarke, R. V., & Eck, J. (2003). *Become a problem-solving crime analyst in 55 small steps.* London: Jill Dando Institute, University College. Retrieved August 28, 2007, from http://www.jdi.ucl.ac.uk/publications/other_publications/55steps

Clarke, R. V., & Mayhew, P. (1998). Preventing crime in parking lots: What we know and what we need to know. In M. Felson, & R. B. Peiser (Eds.), *Reducing crime through real estate development and management.* Urban Land Institute.

Duxbury, E., & Desyllas, J. (2000). *St. Giles circus: Report on current patterns of pedestrian movement and accidents.* London: Intelligent Space Partnership.

Duxbury, E., & Desyllas, J. (2001). *Shoreditch triangle pedestrian movement and safety report.* London: Intelligent Space Partnership.

Eck, J. E., Chainey, S. P., Cameron, J. G., Leitner, M., & Wilson, R. E. (2005). *Mapping crime: Understanding hot spots.* USA: National Institute of Justice. Retrieved August 28, 2007, from www.ojp.usdoj.gov/nij

Fruin, J. (1971.) *Pedestrian and planning design.* Alabama: Elevator World Inc.

Harries, K. (1999). *Mapping crime: Principle and practice.* United States National Institute of Justice. Retrieved August 28, 2007, from http://www.ojp.usdoj.gov/nij/maps/pubs.html

Hillier, B. (1996). *Space is the machine.* Cambridge University Press.

Hillier, B., Penn, A., Hanson, J., Grajewski, T., & Xu, J. (1993). Natural movement: Or configuration and attraction in urban pedestrian movement. *Environment and Planning B: Planning and Design, 20*, 29-66.

Home Office (2005). *Crime mapping: Improving performance, a good practice guide for front line officers.* London: Home Office. Retrieved August 28, 2007, from http://www.jdi.ucl.ac.uk/downloads/publications/other_publications/crime_mapping_guide.pdf

Home Office (2003). *Crime in England and Wales: April 2002 to March 2003*. London: Home Office. Retrieved August 28, 2007, from www.homeoffice.gov.uk

Home Office (2001a). *Crime reduction toolkit: Focus area and hotspots. Crime reduction unit.* Retrieved August 28, 2007, from www.crimereduction.gov.uk/toolkits/fa00.htm

Home Office (2001b). *Crime reduction toolkit: Street crime and robbery. Crime reduction unit.* Retrieved August 28. 2007, from www.crimereduction.gov.uk/toolkits/sc00.htm

Lee, D. B. (1973). Requiem for large-scale models. *Journal of the American Institute of Planners, 39*, 163-178.

MVA (2000). *Profiling the populations available for stops and searches.* Police Research Series Paper 131. London: Home Office.

Newman, P., & Kenworthy, J. (1999). *Sustainability and cities, Overcoming automobile dependance.* Island Press.

Pushkarev, B., & Zupan, J. (1975). Urban space for pedestrians. Cambridge: MIT Press.

Ratcliffe, J. (2004). *HotSpot detective for mapInfo Helpfile* (Version 2.0).

Robinson, W. S. (1950). Ecological correlations and the behavior of individuals. *American Sociological Review, 15*(3), 351-357.

Transport for London (2003). *Analysis of the transport programme to support the draft London plan.* Technical Report. Transport for London.

UTMC (2000). *Review of current and future data requirements and detector technologies and the implications for UTMC.* Urban Traffic Management and Contol, Deliverable 2. Retrieved August 28, 2007, from http://www.utmc.gov.uk/research/index.htm

Willumsen, L. G., & Ortúzar, J. de D. (1994). *Modeling transport.* Sussex, England: John Wiley and Sons Ltd.

ADDITIONAL READING

The references that are listed provide many valuable starting points for further reading. In particular we identify to the reader the Brantingham and Brantingham article that discusses the different definitions of hotspots (and why rates are important for understanding crime) and the MVA UK Home Office publication that makes many important points about why it is important to understand on-street pedestrian levels in policing.

The papers listed below provide useful further reading in the background to pedestrian modeling, and further information on the pedestrian model that was calibrated for central London;

Desyllas, J., Duxbury, E., Ward, J., & Smith, A. (2003). *Pedestrian demand modeling of large cities.* Centre for Advanced Spatial Analysis, University College London. Working Paper Series 62. Retrieved August 28, 2007, from http://www.intelligentspace.com/

Desyllas, J., & Duxbury, E. (2004). *Pedestrian modeling of central London.* Intelligent Space paper written for Transport for London. Retrieved August 28, 2007, from http://www.intelligentspace.com/

Chapter VI
Core Models for State-of-the-Art Microscopic Traffic Simulation and Key Elements for Applications

Heng Wei
University of Cincinnati, USA

ABSTRACT

This chapter summarizes fundamental models for microscopic simulation (such as vehicle generation model and car-following model) and other critical models (such as lane-choice model, lane-changing model, and route-choice model). Most of the critical models introduced in this chapter reflect the latest research results by the author. The primary purpose of this chapter is to provide fundamentals for better understanding of the travel behaviors that are modeled for traffic simulations. To facilitate the applications of traffic simulation models, several key elements for applying state-of-the-art computer traffic simulation tools are summarized. They include the procedure for building models, model calibration and validation. Further more, techniques for collecting vehicle trajectory data, critical elements used for model calibration and validation, are also introduced.

INTRODUCTION

Crime preventive measures somehow influence several elements of transport behavior, such as the choice of the number of trips, the destination and the mode of transportation. For example, increased crime offense rates likely lead to decreasing of trips as a consequence of crime-related reputation of an area. The choices of transportation modes, routes, and destinations may also be influenced by the crime rates of an area. Quantitative relationships between criminal behaviors, criminal opportunities, and transportation environments may provide insight into how to design better crime prevention strategies. Among the factors constituting the transportation environments, travel behaviors over the transportation network play a key role in representing operations of the transportation systems. Microscopic simulation modeling is a significant approach to provide understandings of traffic characteristics and travel behaviors as required by the analysis of on-street crime preventive measures.

Microscopic traffic simulation models are computer models that "mimic" the movements of individual vehicles traveling around a roadway network and effect of traffic control operations. The simulation models are composed of multiple travel behavior models, such as car-following and lane-changing models, gap acceptance rules, signal control operation schemes, and so forth. Those models are coded into computer algorithms which are then embedded within a computer software system. The integration of those models enables simulating vehicle-by-vehicle based traffic by updating position, speed, acceleration, lane position, and other state variables on time steps, as the vehicles interact with traffic signals, signs, other vehicles, and roadway geometrics. The time steps are usually designed on a second or smaller time interval basis in order to implement a more accurate behavioral analysis.

Microscopic simulation models aim at providing a representation of actual driver behaviors and network performance. They are therefore viewed as an effective tool for analyzing a wide variety of dynamical problems which are not amenable to study by other means. The purpose of this chapter is to introduce major microscopic simulation models that are viewed as the core of simulation modeling and key elements for simulation application in traffic and safety operations. The chapter is organized as follows: (1) core microscopic traffic simulation models, (2) procedure for building models, (3) techniques for vehicle trajectory data collection, (4) calibration and validation of applying advanced microscopic simulation software, (5) summary and conclusions, and (6) future research directions.

CORE MICROSCOPIC TRAFFIC SIMULATION MODELS

This section presents fundamentals of core models for microscopic traffic simulation modeling, including vehicle generation model, car-following model, lane-choice model, lane-changing model, and route-choice model.

Vehicle Generation Model

A vehicle generation model addresses methods for creating vehicles to enter a simulated network which is assumed "empty" at the beginning of a simulation run. While numerous methods in terms of computer programs have been developed to generate random numbers, these numbers only "appear" to be random, sometimes called "*pseudo-random*" numbers (Lieberman & Rathi, 2000). Departing time models attempt to represent a pattern of how travelers choose a time to hit the road based on their daily travel decisions on the experience gathered from repetitively traveling through the transportation network (Ettema, Tamminga, & Timmermans, 2003).

Random variants in traffic simulation are used to generate a stream of vehicles. According to headway distribution based on specified volumes, vehicles are generated at origin points, usually at the periphery of the analysis network, that is, the shifted negative exponential distribution will yield the following expression (Lieberman & Rathi, 2000).

$$h = (H - h_{min})(-\ln(1-R)) + H - h_{min} \qquad (1)$$

Where,

h = Headway, seconds;

H = Mean headway = $3600/V$, where V is the specified traffic volume, vph;

h_{min} = Specified minimum headway; and

R = Random number in the range (0 to 1.0), obtained from a pseudo-random number generator.

Ettema, et al. (2003) proposed a micro-simulation approach in which individuals base their consecutive departure time decisions on a mental model. The mental model is the outcome of a continuous process of perception updating according to reinforcement learning principles, based on a more general theoretical framework proposed by Arentze and Timmermans (2003). In this model system, individual decision makers decide about departure time for a routine trip, such as commuting, on consecutive days. Their decision making is based on a mental model of traffic conditions, specifying the mean and variance of travel time for various departure times. This mental model is updated once new experiences become available.

It is assumed that when choosing a departure time, travelers desire an arrival time to be as closer and prior to the preferred arrival time (PAT). The PAT is associated with the work start time or other scheduled time. Based on Small's (1982) study, the utility of a trip departing at t, that is, U_t, can then be specified by the following equation.

$$U_t = \beta_1 \times T_t + \beta_2 \times SDE + \beta_3 \times SDL + \beta_4 \times L \tag{2}$$

Where,

T_t = travel time when departing at time t;

SDE = early schedule delay;

SDL = late schedule delay;

$\beta_1, \beta_2, \beta_3, \beta_4$ = Parameters; and

L = Variable indicating late arrival.

The schedule delay is the amount of time one arrives before or after the preferred arrival time *PAT, that is,*

$$SDE(t, T_t, PAT) = \max((PAT - t - T_t), 0) \tag{3}$$

$$SDL(t, T_t, PAT) = \max((t + T_t - PAT), 0) \tag{4}$$

L is a dichotomous variable indicating late arrival, representing the discomfort of late arrival irrespective of the amount of delay. L is calculated by the following equation,

$$L = \begin{cases} 0 & \text{if } t + Tt < PAT \\ 1 & \text{if } t + Tt < PAT \end{cases} \tag{5}$$

In reality, however, in an individual's perception of the travel time T_t is not a constant value but a stochastic variable which can be defined by μ_t and σ_t, provided following normal distribution. The perceived probability distribution forms an expected utility for a trip departing at t, specified as, (see equation (6)).

Where, $f(T_t)$ = normally distributed with $N(\mu_t, \sigma_t)$.

In the expected utility, individuals account for uncertainty in travel time by weighting each outcome by its probability. An error term is associated with each expected utility EU_t. The model described by equation (6) was applied using parameter values reported by Small (May, 1990) as follows:

Equation 6.

$$EU_t = \int_{T_{\min}}^{T_{\max}} \{\beta_1 T_t + \beta_2 SDE(t, T_t, PAT) + \beta_3 (t, T_t, PAT) + \beta_4 L(t, T_t, PAT)\} f(T_t) d(T_t)$$

$\beta_1(T_t) =$ -0.106 (1/min)

$\beta_2(SDE) =$ -0.065 (1/min)

$\beta_3(SDL) =$ -0.254 (1/min)

$\beta_4(L) =$ -0.58 (1/min)

Car-Following Model

One of driving tasks concerned in microscopic simulation models is to keep appropriate spacing to the immediate front vehicle for a single vehicle on a single lane. A car-following depicts speed-acceleration-spacing relationships of a vehicle following another where there is no passing, in a given time interval based on the action of the front vehicle at a time step. Car following is a relatively simple task compared to the totality of tasks required for vehicle control (Rothery, 2000). However, it is a task that is commonly practiced on dual or multiple lane roadways when passing becomes difficult or when traffic is restrained to a single lane. Car following is a driving task that has been of direct or indirect interest since the early development of the automobile.

Reuschel and Pipes (May, 1990) firstly developed car-following models in the early 1950's. Pipers' model followed the rules suggested in the California Motor Vehicle Code, "A good rule for following another vehicle at a safe distance is to allow yourself at least the length of a car between your vehicle and the vehicle ahead for every ten miles per hour of speed at which you are traveling." The car-following theories developed by researchers associated with the General Motors group were much more extensive. Comprehensive field experiments were conducted and the mathematical bridge between microscopic and macroscopic theories of traffic flow was discovered. The development of car-following models has experienced multiple generations of endeavors by the research team, and all of the models take the following form:

$$\textit{Speed response} = \textit{function (sensitivity, stimuli)} \tag{7}$$

The speed difference of the two vehicles $\dot{x}_n(t) - \dot{x}_{n+1}(t)$ is termed as the *stimuli*, which could be positive, negative, or zero. The speed response could then be an acceleration, deceleration, or keep constant speed. α is defined as *sensitivity term* which is associated with spacing between vehicles. The numerical values for the *sensitivity term* could be measured as an inverse function of the distance headway *d*, i.e.,

$$\alpha = \frac{\alpha_0}{d} = \frac{\alpha_0}{x_n(t) - x_{n+1}(t)} \tag{8}$$

Where, α_0 is constant representing a linear curve sloping between the *sensitivity term* and inverse of the distance headway. Parameter of distance headway exponent *l* and the parameter of speed exponent *m* are used to define a general form of the car-following model as shown in the following equation:

$$\ddot{x}_{n+1}(t + \Delta t) = \frac{\alpha_{l,m}[\dot{x}_{n+1}(t + \Delta t)]^m}{[x_n(t) - x_{n+1}(t)]^l}[\dot{x}_n(t) - \dot{x}_{n+1}(t)] \tag{9}$$

Where,

$n =$ Ahead vehicle

$n + 1 =$ Following vehicle

$x_n =$ Position of the ahead vehicle (ft)

$x_{n+1} =$ Position of the following vehicle (ft)

$\dot{x}_n =$ Speed of the ahead vehicle (ft/sec)

$\dot{x}_{n+1} =$ Speed of the following vehicle (ft/sec)

$\ddot{x}_{n+1} =$ Acceleration (deceleration) rate of the following vehicle (ft/sec^2)

$t =$ At time t

$t + \Delta t =$ Δtime after t time

$l =$ Parameter of distance headway exponent

$m =$ Parameter of speed exponent

$\alpha_{l,m} =$ Sensitivity parameter at l and m

In the equation, various scenarios could be distinguished by *m* and *l* exponents. When *l* =

0 and m = 0, the α = [0.17, 0.74] (1/sec) while the reaction time Δt =[1.0, 2.2]. When l = 1 and m = 0, the parameter values of α and Δt were resulted from field experiments at three testing sites, namely, General Motors test track, Holland Tunnel, and Lincoln Tunnel. $(\alpha, \Delta t)$ = (1.5, 40.3) at General Motors test track; $(\alpha, \Delta t)$ =(1.4, 26.8) at Holland Tunnel; and $(\alpha, \Delta t)$ =(1.2, 29.8) at Lincoln Tunnel. It should be aware that α is measured in different units. For example, it is measured with the unit of 1/sec when l = 0 and m = 0; ft/sec when l = 1 and m = 0.

Lane-Choice Model

Lane-choice model addresses a new concept for urban street microscopic simulation. The term "lane-choice" is referred to a driver's initial lane choice as maneuvering a right or left turning into a multilane urban street segment, as shown in Figure 1. Generally, driving guidance from driving handbook typically stipulates that drivers should choose the closest lane (Wei, Lee, Li, & Li, 2002). For example, if making a right turn in a four-lane highway, it is suggested for drivers to

Figure 1. Histogram of lane-choice data over a two-way street

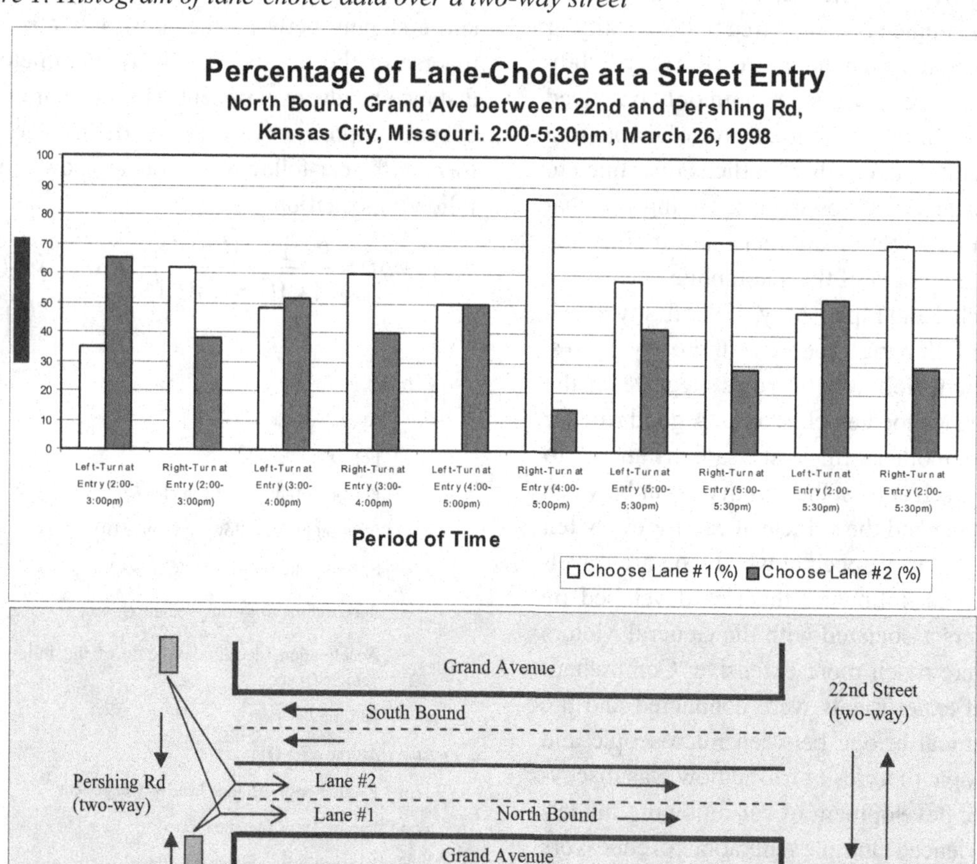

make a tight turn into the right lane of the cross street. For a left turn, enter the cross street to the right of the centerline. If a driver follows this guidance, the lane-choice behavior is regarded as a regular or normal behavior; otherwise, as an "irregular" or "abnormal" behavior. As building a model to simulate lane-based routes, the lane choice issue would grow at the rules how to select a lane when a vehicle is turning into an immediate next street segment from a left or right turning lane at a signalized intersection. It was used to assume that the driver selects a lane strictly following driving handbook.

Wei, Meyer, Feng, and Lee (2002) conducted a study based on field observations. In this study, eight urban streets in Kansas City, Missouri, were selected as videotaped observation sites. Figure 1 exhibits an example of statistical analysis of the observations (Wei et al., 2002). Hourly statistical frequencies of choosing the closest lane and the farther lane at Grand Avenue between 22nd and Pershing Road (north bound traffic) are present. The result indicates that such an "irregular" lane-choice is a frequently occurring phenomenon. It was found out that a driver's initial lane choice is actually related to the driver's route plan. The choice is most likely beneficial to the driver's travel maneuvers at downstream intersections. In other words, drivers have common intentions to choose the "target lane" as they are turning into a segment from an intersection. The *target lane* is defined as the intended destination lane in which the driver needs not to make a lane change before making a turn at the immediate next intersection. In case of entering a segment from a right turn at an intersection, that is, the farther lane (e.g., lane #2 in Figure 1) is the *target lane* if the driver intends to make a left turn at next intersection. On the other hand, the closest lane (e.g., Lane #1) is the *target lane* if the driver intends to make a right turn at the next intersection.

Probabilities of various types of lane-choices are derived from statistical analysis of the observed data. Probabilities associated with different lane-choice alternatives are defined as follows:

$$P(\text{target lane} / \xi = 1) = \frac{V_{R1R} + V_{R2L} + V_{L1R} + V_{L2L}}{\sum_i (V_{RiR} + V_{RiL} + V_{LiR} + V_{LiL})} \tag{10}$$

$$P(\text{non-target lane} / \xi = 1) = 1 - P(\text{target lane}) \tag{11}$$

$$P(\text{farther lane} / \xi = 0) = \frac{V_{R2S} + V_{L1S}}{\sum_i (V_{RiS} + V_{LiS})} \tag{12}$$

$$P(\text{close lane} / \xi = 0) = 1 - P(\text{farther lane}) \tag{13}$$

Where,

$\xi =$ Index that represents a vehicle's intended maneuver at the next intersection; 0 = go straight; 1 = either right turn or left turn;

$V_{RiR} =$ Number of vehicles entering lane #*i* from right-turn entry and turning right at the exit; *i* = 1, 2, ..., n;

$V_{RiL} =$ Number of vehicles entering lane #*i* from right-turn entry and turning left at the exit; *i* = 1, 2, ..., n;

$V_{RiS} =$ Number of vehicles entering lane #i from right-turn entry and going straight at the exit; *i* = 1, 2, ..., n;

$V_{LiR} =$ Number of vehicles entering lane #*i* from left-turn entry and turning right at the exit; *i* = 1, 2, ..., n;

$V_{LiL} =$ Number of vehicles entering lane #*i* from left-turn entry and turning left at the exit; *i* = 1, 2, ..., n;

$V_{LiS} =$ Number of vehicles entering lane #i from left-turn entry and going straight at the exit; *i* = 1, 2, ..., n.

Table 1 summarizes results of statistical analysis of observations conducted in Kansas City, Missouri (Wei et al., 2002). The results indicate that the sampling percentage of choosing the *target lane* ranges from 97% to 100% while choosing the *non-target* lane under 3%. It is apparent that the probability of choosing a *target lane* is very high in reality. Accordingly, it is reasonable to assume that if a driver intends to make a turn at the next intersection, the initially chosen lane is the *target lane*.

Results also show that the ratio of the percentages of choosing the farther lane over choosing the closest lane ranges from 31%:69% to 85%:15%. The fact that so many drivers chose the farther lane can be reasonably explained by the drivers' intentions of seeking the correct lane to minimize the number of lane changes that would be needed during the remaining journey. This kind of lane-choice behavior may be regarded a "preemptive" behavior to be in the target lane in advance.

Lane-Changing Model

The lane-changing behavior is an important component that has a significant impact on the characteristics of traffic flow. With the increas-

Table 1. Summary of sampling percentage of various lane choices (%)

(March 26, 1998, Grand Avenue between 22nd and Pershing Road, Kansas City, Missouri)				
Time	2:00 - 3:00 PM	3:00 - 4:00 PM	4:00 - 5:00 PM	5:00 - 5:30 PM
Target lane Choice	100	97	98	100
Non-target Lane Choice	0	3	2	0
Closest Lane Choice	69	55	62	51
Farther Lane Choice	31	46	38	48
(June 3, 1998, North Bound, Grand Avenue between 13th and 14th, Kansas City, Missouri)				
Time	2:30 - 4:30 PM	3:30 - 4:30 PM	4:30 - 5:30 PM	5:30 - 6:30 PM
Target lane Choice	100	100	100	100
Non-target Lane Choice	0	0	0	00
Closest Lane Choice	51	29	15	16
Farther Lane Choice	48	71	85	84
(June 3, 1998, South Bound, Grand Avenue between 13th and 14th, Kansas City, Missouri)				
Time	2:30 - 4:30 PM	3:30 - 4:30 PM	4:30 - 5:30 PM	5:30 - 6:30 PM
Target lane Choice	100	100	100	100
Non-target Lane Choice	0	0	0	0
Closest Lane Choice	57	48	48	61
Farther Lane Choice	43	52	52	39
(June 3, 1998, 13th St. between Broadway and Washington, Kansas City, Missouri)				
Time	8:30 - 9:30 PM		9:30 - 10:30 PM	
Target lane Choice	100		97	
Non-target Lane Choice	0		3	
Closest Lane Choice	52		52	
Farther Lane Choice	48		48	
(October 30, 1998, 12th St. between Wyandotte and Central, Kansas City, Missouri)				
Time	1:00 - 2:00 PM		2:00 - 3:00 PM	
Target lane Choice	100		100	
Non-target Lane Choice	0		00	
Closest Lane Choice	49		56	
Farther Lane Choice	51		44	

ing popularity of microscopic traffic simulation tools, a number of lane-changing models have been proposed and implemented in various simulators in recent years. Most lane-changing models classify lane changes as either mandatory or discretionary. For clarity of the description of concepts used in lane-changing models, Figure 2 illustrates the definitions of various vehicles involved in a lane-changing maneuver.

For freeway users, two types of lane changes are widely acknowledged as mandatory lane change and discretionary lane change. Drivers consider mandatory lane changes when they must move away from their current lanes to follow their paths, avoid a lane blockage, or comply with lane use regulations. In any of these cases, drivers will change to the nearest acceptable lane (Toledo, Choudhry, & Ben-Akiva, 2005). Drivers pursue discretionary lane changes when they perceive that driving conditions in an adjacent lane are better. The evaluation of the current and adjacent lanes is based on variables such as the traffic speeds and densities in these lanes, the positions and speeds of vehicles that surround the subject vehicle (or called target vehicle), and presence of heavy vehicles. Drivers who decide to change to an adjacent lane evaluate whether the available gap in traffic in this lane can be used to complete the lane change or not.

Toledo, et al. (2005) explained the lane-changing model with two choice models: target lane choice model and gap acceptance model. The target lane choice model is defined as the following:

$$P(TL_{\text{int}} = i * \upsilon_n) = \frac{\exp(V_{\text{int}}^{TL} * \upsilon_n)}{\sum_{j \in TL} \exp(V_{\text{int}}^{TL} * \upsilon_n)}$$

$$\forall i \in TL \{\text{lane 1, lane 2, ...lane n}\} \qquad (14)$$

Where,

V_{int}^{TL} = Utility of lane i as a target lane (TL) to driver n at time t, i.e., $V_{\text{int}}^{TL} = \beta_i^{TL} X_{\text{int}}^{TL} + \alpha_i^{TL} \upsilon_n + \varepsilon_{\text{int}}^{TL}$, $\forall i \in TL \{\text{lane 1, lane 2, ...lane n}\}$

X_{int}^{TL} = Vector of explanatory variables that affect the utility of lane I

β_i^{TL} = Corresponding vector of parameters

α_i^{TL} = Parameter of υ_n

υ_n = Individual-specific latent variable assumed to follow some distribution in the population

$\varepsilon_{\text{int}}^{TL}$ = Random term associated with the target lane utilities

The choice of the target lane dictates the change direction. If the current lane is also the target lane, no change is needed. Otherwise, the change will be in the direction from the current lane to the target lane. The gap acceptance model determines a driver's choice whether the available gap in the adjacent lane in the change direction can be used to complete the lane change or not. An available gap is acceptable if it is greater than the critical gap. Critical gaps are assumed to fol-

Figure 2. Definition of vehicles affecting lane-changing behavior

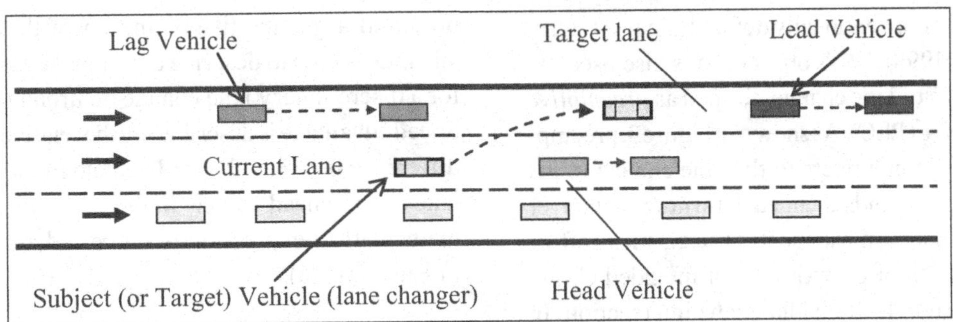

low lognormal distributions to ensure that they always nonnegative (Toledo et al., 2005):

$$\ln(G_{nt}^{gd,cr}) = \beta^{gT} X_{nt}^{gd} + \alpha^{g} \upsilon_{n} + \varepsilon_{nt}^{gd} \qquad (15)$$

$$g \in \{\text{lead, lag}\},\ d \in \{\text{right, left}\}$$

Where,

$G_{nt}^{gd,cr}$ = Critical gap g in the direction of change d (m)

X_{nt}^{gd} = Vector of explanatory variables

β^{gT} = Corresponding vector of parameters

ε_{nt}^{gd} = Random term, where $\varepsilon_{nt}^{gd} \in \sim N(0, \sigma_{g}^{2})$

α^{g} = Parameter of the driver specific random term υ_{n}.

To date, most available models deal with lane changing behavior on freeways. The lane-changing behavior over the urban street networks has not been studied extensively. Additionally, most available models are based upon either theoretical analysis or limited spot observations. This is likely due to the difficulty of getting simple and clean vehicle trajectory data appropriate for studying lane-changing behavior. Wei (1999) developed a video-capture-based method and a computer software tool, vehicle video-capture data collector (VEVID) to help extract traffic related data from a digitized video. Availability of this tool enables the field observations and study of vehicle–based travel behaviors, as well as simulation modeling with use of empirical data.

There are lots of reasons for drivers to change lanes during their travel journeys on urban streets. In addition to mandatory and discretionary lane-changes as conventionally defined (Zhang, Owen, & Clark, 1998), Wei's observations disclosed the third types of lane change, termed as *preemptive lane change* (PLC). As shown in Figure 3, preemptive lane change refers to the lane change to get in a lane that leads to an easy turning maneuver at a downstream intersection (e.g., turn left or right, get out of the exit lane of intended closed lane), but not the immediate next intersection. In other words, the primary purpose of such a lane change is to get in the correct lane in advance to follow the planned path. Wei's observations indicate that 461 of total 994 lane-changing samples fall into the category of preemptive lane change (Wei, Meyer, Lee, & Feng, 2000). The preemptive lane changing samples were analyzed based on different traffic conditions when lane changes occurred, as shown in Figure 3.

Wei characterized lane-changing behaviors on an urban street network with three key components (Wei et al., 2000): (1) a lane-changing decision model, (2) a lane-changing condition model, and (3) a lane-changing maneuver model. Drivers' decisions to change lanes depend on rout plans, the current lane type (i.e., the relationship between the current lane and the driver's planned route), and traffic conditions in the current and adjacent lanes. A lane-changing condition model is the description of acceptable conditions for different types of lane changes. A lane-changing maneuver model describes the subject vehicle's speed and duration when a certain type of a lane change is executed. The lane-changing decision model could be established in a heuristic structure, as shown in Figure 4.

Discretionary lane change refers to a lane change executed to pass a slower moving vehicle ahead. A driver expects a lane change whenever he or she thinks the speed of the vehicle ahead in the current lane is intolerable while acceptable gaps in the target lane are available. Gipps (2001) proposed the concept of speed advantage to identify a motivation of a (discretionary) lane change, and Wei (Wei, Meyer et al., 2000) proposed a quantitative definition of the speed advantage (SA) to describe decisional conditions for a discretionary lane change on urban streets. Speed advantage is described by the relative speed difference between the lead vehicle in the target lane and the head vehicle in the current lane. Its mathematical expression is suggested as shown in equation (16).

$$SA = \frac{V_{LD} - V_{FT}}{V_{LD}} \quad (16)$$

Where,

SA = Speed advantage compared to an adjacent lane; 0 if $V_{LD} \leq V_{FT}$

V_{LD} = The lead vehicle's speed in an adjacent lane, ft/s or mph

V_{FT} = The front vehicle's speed, ft/s or mph

Using the SA variable, the probability of motivating a lane change incurring from a speed disturbance by the front vehicle can be estimated by the following equations, which are derived via regression analysis from accumulative curves of observed SA values using the data observed in Kansas City, Missouri (Wei et al., 2000):

For two-way streets:

$$P(SA) = (0.010 - 0.3175SA + 3.682SA^2 - 2.376SA^3) \times 100\% \quad (17)$$

For one-way street:

$$P(SA) = (0.008 + 0.443SA + 0.541SA^2) \times 100\% \quad (18)$$

Where P(SA) = probability of generating a motivation to change to the speed-advantaged lane in correspondence to a value of SA. The correlation coefficient R^2 value for equations (17) and (18) is 0.9915 and 0.9836, respectively. For example, if the front vehicle reduces its speed to 30 mph while the adjacent lane's speed remains at 50 mph, 31.8% of followers would possibly change

Figure 3. Illustrations of observed typical cases of preemptive lane changes

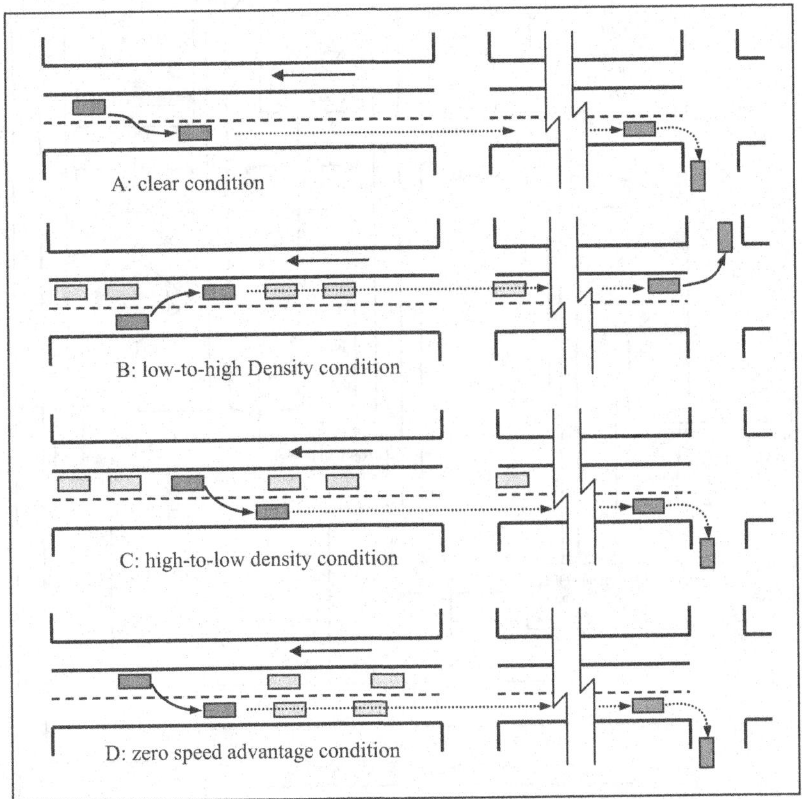

to the adjacent lane in a two-way street. Similarly, 27.2% of followers do so in a one-way street.

Both the gap between the lead (in the adjacent lane) vehicle and the subject vehicle (termed as "lead gap") and the gap between the subject vehicle and the lag vehicle that is in the adjacent lane (termed as "lag gap") are major factors affecting the driver's lane-changing decisions. The minimum acceptable gaps are greatly dependent upon the speed of the subject vehicle and the lag vehicle. It is hence assumed that the minimum acceptable lead gap for a lane-changing decision could be expressed as a function of the subject vehicle's speed and the lag gap as a function of the lag vehicle's speed.

Figure 5 visualizes the distribution of the observed lead gaps versus the subject vehicle's speeds and the lag gaps versus the lag vehicle's speeds. It presents the concerned gap and speed values at the moment as the maneuver of a lane

Figure 4. Lane-changing hierarchy

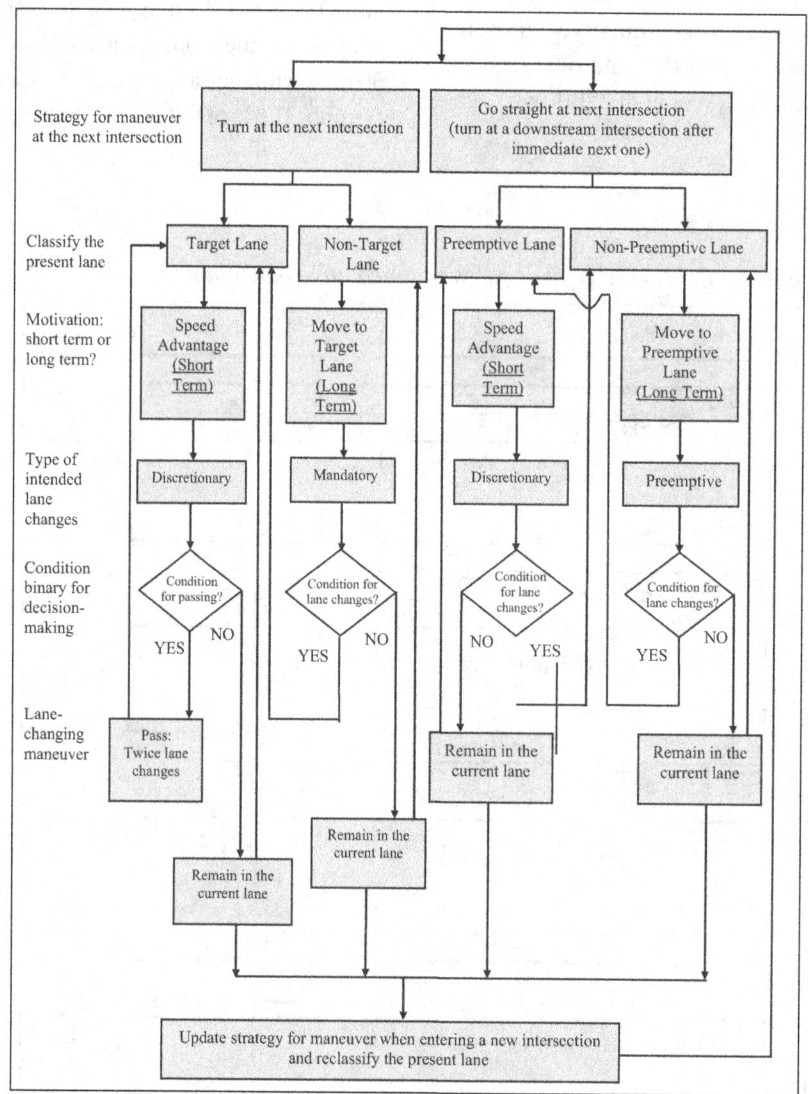

change is started. Comparisons between the observed gap values and the recommended minimum safe gaps (minimum safety braking distances plus reacting distances at varied speeds) recommended in *Kansas Driving Handbook* (1996) are also presented in Figure 6.

It is seen from Figure 5 that a portion of the sampling drivers, who perform discretionary lane changes as a reaction to a speed disturbance, actually accepts smaller gaps than the handbook-recommended values. Drivers accepting gaps greater than or equal to the handbook-recommended values are viewed as conservative drivers; otherwise as regular drivers. The critical acceptable gaps are modeled using a curve representing the lower boundary of the observed data, as shown by the lowest curve in Figure 5. The minimum acceptable gap conditions to execute a discretionary lane change can be described in equation (19).

k in V_k denotes either the subject vehicle or the lag vehicle. As estimating the minimum lead gap, V_k is the speed of the subject vehicle; V_k is the speed of the lag vehicle as to estimate the minimum lag gap. Tao Wei, Wang, & Sisiopiku (2005) and Wei, et al. (2000) findings from vehicle trajectory data (Wei, 1999) indicate that 90% of observed discretionary lane changes happen before the lane-changers' speeds are actually affected by the speed disturbance from the front vehicles. A driver who is potentially trapped in the car-following speed disturbance tends to switch onto an adjacent lane before reducing its speed. The 90% probability is on the observation basis. In summary, a driver tends to consider a discretionary lane change only when the following two conditions exist: (1) The driver perceives that the speed of the head vehicle is less than his or her desired speed; (2) The driver perceives that

Equation 19.

$$\text{Minimum Lead/Lag Gap (m)} = \begin{cases} 0.3336(2.2237V_k(m/s))^{1.6398} & \text{(conservative drivers)} \\ 7.979e^{0.1244V_k(m/s)} & \text{(regular drivers)} \end{cases}$$

Figure 5. Acceptable gap conditions in the adjacent lane for lane-changing decision-making

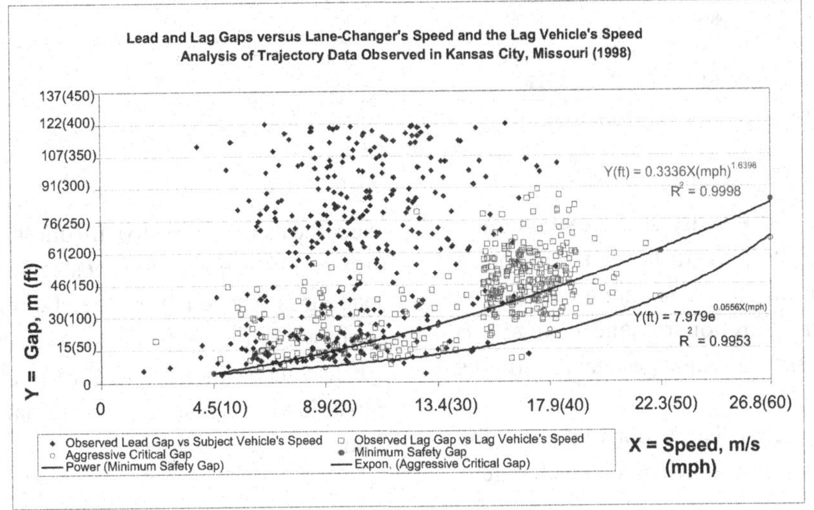

*Figure 6. Observed spacing between pairs of vehicles at control action times**

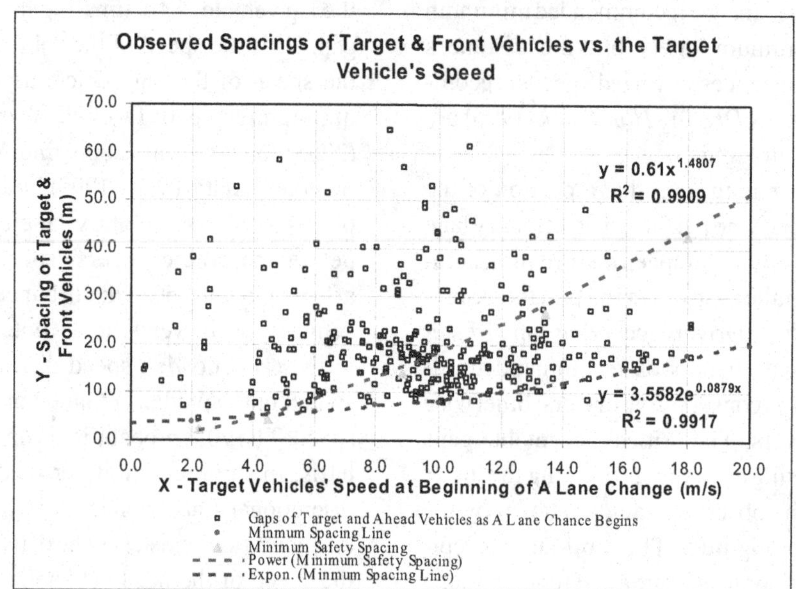

* *Control Action Time δ in this figure represents the time as the follower begins a lane change as a response to the speed disturbance (slowdown) by the front vehicle*

Table 2. Observed maximum accelerations for 10-mph increments in urban streets Data Source: Vehicle trajectory data observed in Kansas City, Missouri, 1998 (Wei, 1999)

Type					
Starting Speed	0 - 15 ft/s (0 - 10 mph)	15 - 29 ft/s (10 - 20 mph)	29 - 44 ft/s (20 -30 mph)	44 - 59 ft/s (30 - 40 mph)	59 - 73 ft/s (40 - 50 mph)
Two-way	+11.2 -8.8	+12.0 -15.6	+10.4 -11.0	+8.4 -10.5	+7.8
One-way	+8.9 -6.9	+10.8 -12.7	+11.0 -11.2	+6.9 -12.6	+6.3

he could remain or increase speed by changing to another lane. It is worth being noted that a driver's motivation for a lane change, including mandatory and discretionary lane changes, is determined by the lane-change decision model (Wei et al., 2000).

Figure 6 shows the distribution of the spacing between pairs of vehicles when a lane change is executed as a reaction to car-following speed disturbance. The equation for estimating minimum spacing is derived from the statistical analysis, as shown in Figure 6. Those minimum spacings are also recommended as thresholds control for car-following scenarios, as summarized in Table 2 and described below.

Minimum disturbance-effecting spacing vs. speed V:

$$S_{\min}(m) = \begin{cases} 3.5582e^{0.0879V(m/s)} & (Regular\ Driver) \\ 0.61V(m/s)^{1.4807} & (Conservative\ Driver) \end{cases} \quad (20)$$

A lane-changing vehicle may accelerate or decelerate when manipulating a lane-changing maneuver so as to keep a safe headway to the lead vehicle and/or to the lag vehicle (in the adjacent lane). Acceleration varies with the individual speeds of the lane changer and the lead vehicle, as well as the differences between them. Table 2 gives observed maximum acceleration or deceleration values for each 10-mph increment for determining thresholds of acceleration as simulating a lane-changing maneuver.

Wei's observations also indicate that lane-changing duration has little coherent relationship with speeds of over 10 ft/sec (3 m/s). For discretionary lane change, the average duration of lane changing ranges from 2.33 seconds to 2.51 seconds with standard deviations from 0.56 to 0.93 seconds. Therefore, 2.3 ~ 2.5 seconds may be recommended as an average duration of a lane change.

Route-Choice Model

Conventionally a route-choice model is to determine the routes in a concerned transportation network, which is used in traffic assignment models to allocate the traffic onto the simulated roadway network. Rout-choice modeling is typically divided into a two-stage process (Ben-Akiva et al.,, 2004): the generation of a choice set of alternative routes and the choice of routes among the alternatives in the choice set. A well-known, simplest method for generation of alternative routes is K-shortest path algorithm, which generates the first "k" shortest paths for a given-destination pair. Ben-Akiva, Ramming, and Bkhor (2004) developed the *labeling* approach that exploits the availability of multiple link (i.e., roadway segment in a network) attributes, such as travel time, distance and functional class to formulate different "generalized cost" functions that produce alternative routes. The criteria, such as minimum time or distance, or maximum use of expressways, may be used to label the alternative routes.

Several types of route choice models have been recently developed. Most of these models represent modifications or generations of the logit structure, such as C-Logit (Cascetta, Nuzzolo, Russo, & Vitetta, 1996), path-size logit (PSL) (Ben-Akiva & Bierlaire, 1999), cross-nested logit (CNL) (Vovsha, 1997), and so forth. These models are members of the generalized extreme value (GEV) family of models developed by McFadden (Vovsha, 1997). The advent of intelligent transportation systems (ITS) has renewed the interest in modeling the effects of traffic information system on route choice behavior. Advanced traveler information systems (ATIS) are expected to have significant impacts on individual driver behaviors through disseminating routing information onto drivers. Using ATIS, accurate, real-time information about the characteristics of the travel environment can be provided to travelers before their departures and while they are en route. The goal is to alter travel behavior in such a way as to improve the individual driver's efficiency and the overall characteristics of the travel environment, resulting in accessibility gains for all drivers (Vaugh, Kitamura, & Jovanis, 1995). For example, the benefits of ATIS in reducing congestion and the potential of large savings in travel time and fuel consumption are based on real-time diversions of traffic from main facilities (e.g., the Interstate system) to lower-class roads (e.g., arterials and the local street system). The effectiveness of ATIS depends on drivers' reactions to information provided, which is affected greatly by the degree of information's accuracy. Consequently, the assumptions about real-life route choice behavior in dynamic traffic assignment have received increasing attention recently. One study (Kaysi, Ben-Akiva, & Palma, 1995) indicates that using shortest path guidance is likely to fail if the guidance strategy ignores the impact of drivers' reactions to information.

Mahmassani and Tong's investigation (1986) indicates that commuters' route choices are usually based on perceived delay, the difference between actual arrival time and preferred arrival time, called *tolerable schedule delay*. This implies that drivers do not switch to another route that is predicted to have minimum travel cost if the estimated delay falls into the range they can tolerate, called *indifference band of route delay* (IBRD). This is especially true for urban commuters. Iida, Akiyama and Uchida's experiment disclosed an interesting attribute of route choice behavior. Drivers may consider other drivers' behaviors when choosing routes. They believe that when all travelers are given access to the same network information, and if some of them react to it, those staying on the current route may benefit from other drivers' leaving. These drivers are usually those who are very familiar with the routes based on their driving history. Polydoroulou, Ben-Akiva and Kaysi's survey (1994) shows that about 75% of the sample drivers are very familiar with at least two different routes to work and around 50% are strongly willing to try new routes to avoid traffic delays. From another survey sample of drivers, they also found that 63% of them rarely or never change their planned route, while 16% often make such a change. 37% of drivers indicated that they often listen to radio traffic reports, and 27% usually follow the recommendations. Only 25% think that radio traffic reports are reliable, whereas 22% consider them irrelevant. Among the drivers who listen to radio traffic reports, 20% often change their routes after listening, whereas 50% completely ignore traffic reports when they are different from their own observations.

In a vehicle-based microscopic simulation system that considers the impact of traveler information on traffic assignment, it is necessary to build a routing choice model that predicts route-change behavior as a function of available information. The IBTD criterion may be used to both objectively evaluate the potential impact of ATIS on route choice, so that vehicle-based microscopic simulation systems may provide higher accuracy of traffic information by better simulating route choice behavior. Wei, Meyer, & Lee (2001) presents a structure of a route choice model based on insight from his study of observed travel behaviors (e.g., lane-choice and lane changing behaviors). A fuzzy set is used to reflect different effects of an *indifference band of route delay* on driver tendency to change routes. Fuzzy sets are also used to model driver response to traveler information with respect to the tendency to change routes.

In this section, the C-Logit Model and the Logit Kernel to route choice situation are briefly presented. A route choice model using *indifference band of trip delay* is then described.

Logit Model and the Logit Kernel Formulation

The C-logit model is formulated as the following equation (Cascetta et al., 1996):

$$P(i \mid C_n) = \frac{e^{V_{in} - CF_{in}}}{\sum_{j \in C_n} e^{V_{in} - CF_{in}}} \qquad (21)$$

Where,

V_{in} = the utility of path i for person n;

C_n = the path-set for person n; and

CF_{in} = the commonality factor of path i for person n.

The commonality factor of path i, CF_{in}, is used to measure the degree of a person's similarity of path i between an origin and destination in a network. It can be specified as the following expression (Cascetta et al., 1996; Cascetta & Papola, 2001):

$$CF_{in} = \beta_0 \ln \sum_{j \in C_n} \left(\frac{L_{ij}}{\sqrt{L_i L_j}} \right)^{\gamma} \qquad (22)$$

or

$$CF_{in} = \beta_0 \ln \sum_{j \in C_n, j \neq i} \left(\frac{L_{ij}}{\sqrt{L_i L_j}} \right) \left(\frac{L_i - L_{ij}}{L_j - L_j} \right) \qquad (23)$$

Where,

L_{ij} = the length of links common to path *i* and path *j*

L_i, L_j = overall lengths of path *i* and path *j*, respectively

B_0, γ_j = parameters to be calibrated

The general form of the factor analytic logit kernel model is proposed by Ben-Akiva, et al. (2004):

$$U = \beta^T X + F\xi + \nu \qquad (24)$$

Where,

U = $(J \times 1)$ vector of utility

β = $(K \times 1)$vector of unknown parameters

X = $(J \times K)$ corresponding vector of parameters

F = $(J \times M)$ factor loadings matrix

ξ = $(M \times 1)$ vector of m multivariate distributed latent factors

Route Choice in a Lane-Vehicle-Based Simulation Process

A lane-vehicle-based simulation process describes a vehicle's position during its journey in an urban street network (Wei et al., 2000). To clarify the relationship between route choice and other travel behaviors, primary simulated states are defined as follows and illustrated in Figure 7.

- **Origin state:** Defines the original location of a simulated vehicle (where it enters the simulated network), the departure time, and the destination. The vehicle enters the street network at the nearest intersection to the original location.
- **Entering state:** Defines the intended route from the origin to the destination at the time of departure. In reality a driver usually chooses his/her route before starting the trip. The driver makes the decision based on updated route information from media such the Internet or previous experience. In the simulation, the pre-trip route is assumed to be the shortest path (by travel time) resulting from the latest available roadway traffic conditions, termed as *current network condition.* This state is simulated only when a vehicle is generated.
- **Lane-choice state:** Defines a specific lane whenever the vehicle enters a street segment from a turning entry at an intersection. Lane-choice decision is simulated depending on the driver's pre-trip route or en-route plan (Wei et al., 2000). This state is simulated whenever a vehicle is going to turn in a street segment from an intersection.
- **Car-following state:** Defines vehicle location, speed, spatial and temporal relation with the ahead vehicle (if it exists), as well as its reaction to any change of the ahead vehicle's speed at each simulation time step.
- **Lane-changing state:** Recognizes the vehicle's demand and decision on changing lanes, lane-changing type (mandatory, preemptive, or discretionary), lane-changing conditions to determine whether acceptable gaps are available for changing lanes, and lane-changing maneuvers. Location, acceleration, speed, and duration are estimated at each simulated time step during a lane change. This state is simulated as long as the vehicle is moving within a street segment.
- **New-entering state:** Determines status of the vehicle as approaching the next intersection, with update of all above states.
- **En route choice state:** Updates the vehicle's remaining route if and only if the current network condition is changed, updated traveler information is available, and the destination has not been reached. This state

Figure 7. Illustration of primary simulation states

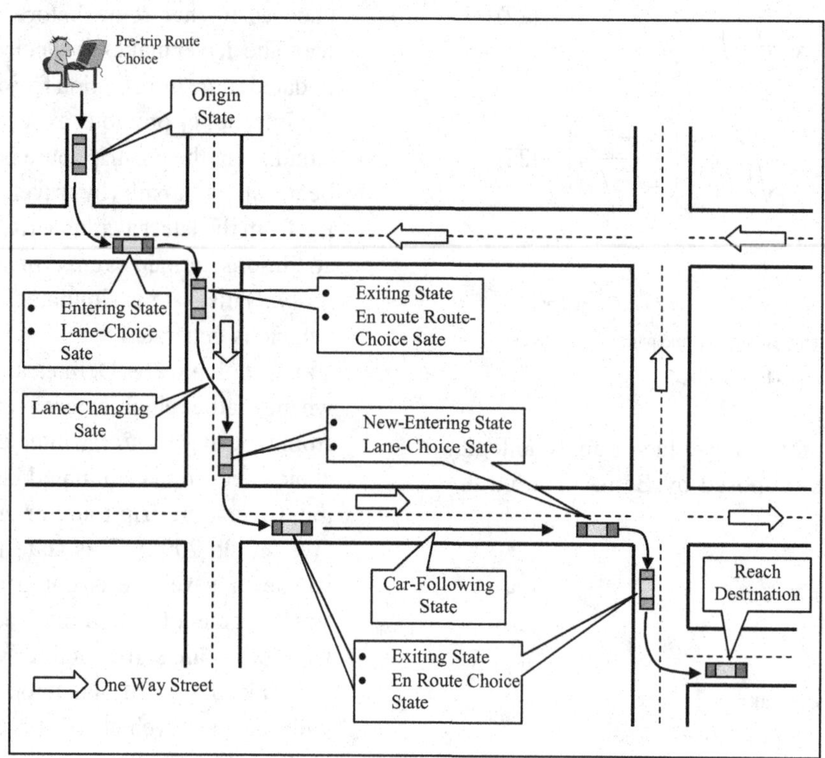

is simulated when the vehicle is entering a downstream street segment.

- **Exiting state:** Checks the vehicle's current lane and its intention as it approaches the end of the current street segment (next intersection) to go straight, turn, or reach its destination. If the approaching intersection is the destination, the vehicle's trip is ended and is no longer traced. Its recorded locations, clock time, speeds, accelerations, and maneuvers are stored in the database when any action occurs that leads to the change of the vehicle's state. This state is simulated when the vehicle is approaching the downstream intersection.

Each state can be viewed as a travel behavior that can be depicted by a corresponding sub-model. Sub-models for pre-trip and en route choice behaviors are discussed in the following sections.

IBRD-Based Route Choice Model

The *indifference band of route delay* simulates a driver's tolerable difference in time between the current route and the dynamic best route resulting from the instant network traffic conditions given by the traveler information system (when the former is greater than the latter). According to Mahmassani and Chang (1985) and Mahmassani and Weimann (2004) studies, the width of the *indifference band of route delay* is suggested to be 10 minutes; Knippenberg and Knippenberg's (1986) study indicates the suggested value of 18 minutes. However, the trip length should be associated with the values of IBRD. On a 60 minute trip, for example, 10 minutes is not such a big difference.

For a 20 minute trip, on the other hand, 10 minute improvement is meaningful to the driver. Fuzzy sets are used to determine the likelihood of a route change if the estimated delay falls into the width of indifference band of route delay.

Figure 8 illustrates the hierarchy of the IBRD-based route choice model with two categories of drivers. In the pre-trip route choice model, the *indifference band of route delay* is the difference in travel time between the driver's primary route γ_p and the dynamic best route γ_b. In en route choice model, it is the difference in travel time between the driver's current route γ_c and the dynamic best route γ_b.

Some basic concepts used in the IBRD-based route choice model (as shown in Figure 8) are introduced as follows

- **Classifications of drivers:** All drivers are generally classified into two categories—aggressive drivers and conservative drivers, denoted by Y_1=1 and Y_1=0, respectively. Meanwhile, all drivers are also either information receivers or information neglecters (i.e., drivers who do not receive information), denoted by Y_2 =1 and Y_2=0, respectively. To clearly describe a driver's classification as a combination of these two parameters, a driver can be denoted by the following symbols.
  - S_1:Y_1 = 1, Y_2 = 1 (an aggressive driver who receives information)
  - S_2: Y_1 = 1, Y_2 = 0 (an aggressive driver who doesn't receive information)
  - S_3: Y_1 = 0, Y_2 = 1 (a conservative driver who receives information)
  - S_4: Y_1 = 0, Y_2 = 0 (conservative driver who does not receive information)

Suppose ∂_1 percent of the O-D trips T_{IJ} between zones I and J are assumed to be aggressive drivers, while (1-∂_1) percent are conservative drivers.

Figure 8. Hierarchy of IBRD-based route choice models

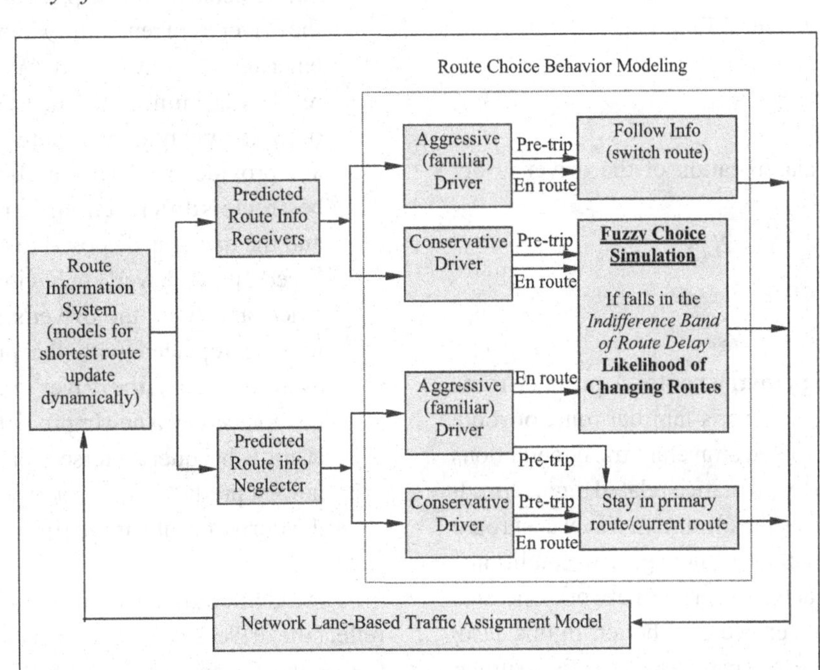

A driver generated during the simulation process can be randomly determined as an aggressive or conservative driver. Assume that a random number ω_1 between [-∝, +∝] is assigned to the driver to represent the driver's aggressiveness. The ω_1 can be converted to a value between 0-100 using the *logsig* neural function:

$$DA1_{nt\_il} = \frac{100}{1+e^{-\omega}} \quad (25)$$

Then, classification of the drivers is described by Y_1 as:

$$Y_{1(nt\_il)} = \begin{cases} 1 & if \;\; 0 \le DA1_{nt\_il} \le \partial_1 \\ 0 & if \;\; \partial_1 < DA1_{nt\_il} \le 1 \end{cases} \quad (26)$$

Similarly, suppose ∂_2 percent of the O-D trips T_{IJ} between zone I and J are assumed to be information receivers, while (1-∂_2) percent are information neglecters. A driver generated during the simulation process can be randomly determined as an information receiver or neglector. Assume that a random number ω_2 between [-∝, +∝] is assigned to the driver to represent the driver's attitude toward information (active or not). The ω_2 can be converted to a value between 0-100 using the *logsig* neural function:

$$DA2_{nt\_il} = \frac{100}{1+e^{-\omega_2}} \quad (27)$$

Then, the classification of the driver is described by Y_2 as:

$$Y_{2(nt\_il)} = \begin{cases} 1 & if \;\; 0 \le DA2_{nt\_il} \le \partial_1 \\ 0 & if \;\; \partial_2 < DA2_{nt\_il} \le 1 \end{cases} \quad (28)$$

- **Driver's primary route:** A primary route simulates a driver's familiar route or route suggested based on average traffic conditions with shortest-distance related algorithm. It is defined as the minimum travel cost route estimated under uncongested conditions, that is, each link in the network operates at level of service C or better. In this case, the volume to capacity ratio, *v/c*, is assumed to be 0.5 or less, and the average speed is assumed to be the posted speed.
- **Dynamic/predicted best route:** A dynamic best route simulates the dynamically updated route for a specific vehicle during a given simulation step. In other words, it is the minimum travel cost route from the current vehicle location to the destination, based on the simulated traffic condition at time *t*. If the vehicle is en route at simulation time step *t*, the cost of the predicted best route includes two parts: experienced route--travel cost of the driver experienced from origin to the current position, and dynamic best route—estimated travel cost of rest of route from the current position to the destination based network condition at *t*. In reality, the nearest place where the driver is able to change the current route is the immediate downstream intersection.
- **Driver's current route:** A driver's current route is the route determined based on the last updated route. A driver starts each trip with a primary route that is determined before departure. The primary route is also the driver's current route when the vehicle is entering the street network. When the vehicle reaches the immediate downstream intersection, its dynamic best route is determined and provided to the driver. If the predicted best route is different from the primary route, and the driver is disposed to change routes based on the driver's behavioral characteristics, and then, the driver's current route will be replaced with the predicted best route. Similarly, the driver's new route may be replaced by a newer predicted best route at any subsequent intersection, provided the newest predicted best route is preferable to the current route at the time.

The likelihood of changing routes is defined to reflect the driver's willingness to alter their route (i.e., to the predicted best route). Assume that the value ranges from 0 to 10, representing the degree of the driver's willingness to change routes. That is, 10 representing the most willingness and 0 representing the least willingness. The control variable is defined as ΔC = *(Cost of Current Route – Cost of the Predicted Best Route)*(30/Primary Route Length in minute).* Figure 9(a) displays a diagram of membership functions (fuzzy sets) of the control variable for the width of IBRD at 0 min, 5 min, and 10 min per 30-minute primary trip, respectively, and the corresponding output curves (probability vs. tendency). When a specific ΔC is obtained (e.g., 7 minutes) and input into the fuzzy system, the output indicates that the driver's tendency of route switch is valued as 6.1, as shown in Figure 9(b). In other words, the driver's degree of willingness to switch to the instant best route is measured as 6.1 out of 10. If the criterion for deciding to change routes is 6.0, then the driver decides to change routes.

The heuristic rules of the pre-trip and en route route-choice models are described as follows:

- **Pre-trip route-choice model:** Before a vehicle begins a trip, the following rules are applied:
  - If ($Y_1 = 1$, $Y_2 = 1$), then the driver chooses the dynamic best route.
  - If ($Y_1 = 1$, $Y_2 = 0$), then the driver chooses the primary route.
  - If ($Y_1 = 0$, $Y_2 = 1$), then the driver's choice of the dynamic best route is dependent on the tendency of the driver to change routes, as illustrated in Figure 9. It is assumed that an aggressive driver is very familiar with the network and can judge the best route instantly by experience.
  - If ($Y_1 = 0$, $Y_2 = 0$), then the driver chooses the primary route. The conservative drivers without notification of updated route information are assumed to be following their habitual routes all the time and are not willing to try other routes.
- **En-route-choice model using fuzzy sets:** Whenever a simulated vehicle passes through an intersection and is entering a downstream segment, the following rules are applied:
  - If ($Y_1 = 1$, $Y_2 = 1$), then the driver switches to the dynamic best route;
  - If ($Y_1 = 1$, $Y_2 = 0$) or ($Y_1 = 0$, $Y_2 = 1$), then the driver's choice of the dynamic best route is dependent on the tendency of the driver to change routes, as illustrated in Figure 9. It is assumed that an aggressive driver is very familiar with the network and can judge the best route instantly by experience. If this is the case, the condition ($Y_1 = 0$, $Y_2 = 1$) applies to the rule.
  - If ($Y_1 = 0$, $Y_2 = 0$), then the driver is in the primary route all the time. The conservative drivers without notification of updated route information are assumed to be following their habitual routes all the time and are not willing to try other routes.

PROCEDURE FOR BUILDING MODELS

There are generally seven steps considered the procedure for building traffic simulation models through application of advanced microscopic simulation software, as summarized by Lieberman and Rathi (2000). Those seven steps are briefly described as follows.

Step 1—Problem statement to:

1. Identify the problems that the model is designated to solve.
2. State the objectives or purposes of the model that is being developed.

Figure 9. Demonstration of the IBRD-based route choice model using the fuzzy sets

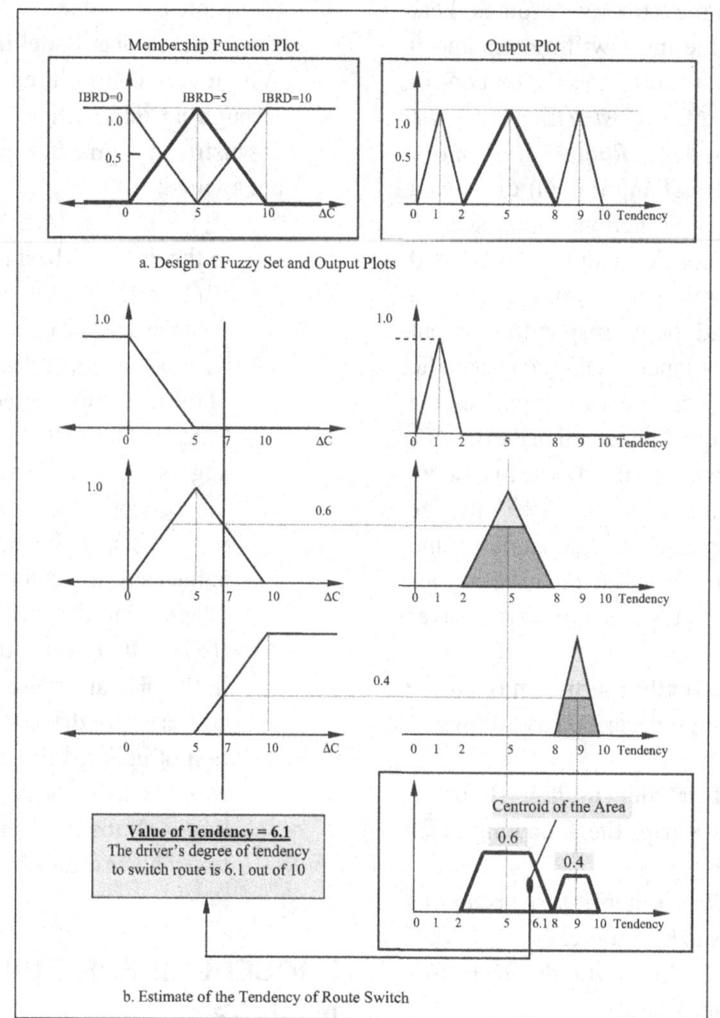

3. Define the information needed for the problem solving solutions.

Step 2—System definition to:

1. Identify major components of the system to be studied.
2. Identify the information as inputs and outputs.
3. Bound the scope of the system to be modeled.
4. Develop the architecture of the system

Step 3—Development of the model to:

1. Classify the sub-models and define their inputs and outputs.
2. Define the flow of data among the above sub-models within the system.
3. Define the functions and processes of the sub-models and other components.
4. Determine the parameters for calibration.
5. Determine the mathematical models that will be used for developing algorithms embedded with each of sub-systems.

6. Create a logical hierarchy for integrating these sub-model and components to support the data flows.
7. Develop interface requirements.
8. Select the software development paradigm, programming language(s), user interface, presentation formats of model results.
9. Design the software: simulation, structured or object-oriented programming language; database, relational/object oriented.
10. Document the logic and all computational procedures.
11. Develop the software code and debug.

Step 4—Calibration of the model to:

1. Set up the procedure of the model calibration.
2. Collect/acquire data to calibrate the model.
3. Define default values of parameters based on calibration results.
4. Introduce this data into the model.

Step 5—Model verification to:

1. Establish that the software executes in accord with the design specification.
2. Perform verification at the model component level.

Step 6—Model validation to:

1. Set up the procedure of the model validation, including collecting, reducing, organizing data for purposes of validation.
2. Establish that the model describes the real system at an acceptable level of accuracy over its entire domain of operation; apply rigorous statistical domain of operation; apply rigorous statistical.

Step 7—Documentation to prepare:

1. Model documentation including algorithms and software system architecture.
2. Executive summary.
3. System users manual.

TECHNIQUES FOR VEHICLE TRAJECTORY DATA COLLECTION

A vehicle trajectory describes the vehicle's path over a period of time. Modeling vehicle travel behaviors with interactions and calibration and validation of microscopic simulation models, relies heavily upon multiple vehicle trajectory data. Other parameters that contribute to microscopic simulation modeling, such as velocity, acceleration, and headway, can be derived from vehicle trajectory data. In recent years, video data collection and subsequent transcription of video data to vehicle trajectories are being attempted by many transportation researchers. As part of the Next Generation SIMulation (NGSIM) program, the Federal Highway Administration's conducted an initial prototype, and three vehicle trajectory data collection efforts (Kovvali, Alexiadis, & Zhang, 2006).

For example, the cameras were used in a fixed camera platform developed by University of California, Berkeley for the Berkley Highway Laboratory for the I-80 data collection effort (Kovvali et al., 2006). This platform provided a rigid system within which the cameras were mounted, as shown by Figure 10. Original raw AVI files are extracted from the video cameras and output as rectified AVI files through the data processor within the NGSIM. Intel® Xeon™ CPU 3.00GHz or faster processor with 2.0 GB of Ram were used for recording the data. These computers provided the NGSIM team with equipment that can be used both for collecting, and then for transcribing the data. One of the concerns for these types of machines are that they are not made for rugged use, so are capable of failing if proper care is not taken. Other data collection efforts have used digital video recorders (DVR) or tape drives, but these mechanisms do not provide adequate storage for 8 hours of continuous video data at 30 frames per second (Kovvali et al., 2006).

Wei, Meyer, Lee, and Feng (2005) developed a methodology for extracting vehicular trajectory

Figure 10. NGSIM camera for I-80 data collection in Emeryville, CA and video snapshot (Kovvali et al, 2006)

Figure 11. Structure of data collection using video-capture technique

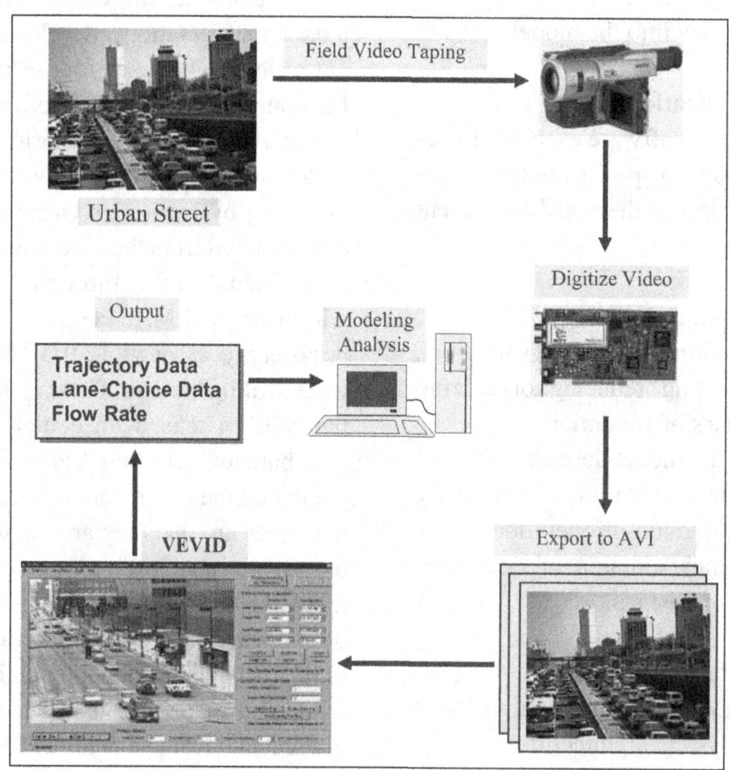

data using a video-capture technique. To help extract traffic related data from the digitized video, Wei developed a computer package, vehicle video-capture data collector (VEVID). VEVID extracts trajectory data from AVI files that have been digitized from videotape using video-capture equipment. Much of the labor traditionally required to extract vehicle trajectory data and to calculate concerned parameters can be eliminated using VEVID. The methodology consists of three basic steps, as shown in Figure 11. First, an urban street is videotaped from an elevated position, and distances between reference points are measured and input into the VEVID parameters file. Sec-

Figure 12. Example of basic form of trajectory output from VEVID

File Name: C:\AVI_Data\Demo1_326KC.tra;
Location:Grand & Pershing, Kansas City, Missouri;
Time:2:55pm,3/26/98

Trajectory of Head Vehicle

#	Time(s)	Position(ft)	Mid-position(ft)	Velocity(ft/s)	Velocity(m/h)	Acceleration(ft/s^2)
0	0	172.73	86.36	---	---	---
1	0.5	190.27	181.50	35.08	23.92	---
2	1	208.45	199.36	36.35	24.78	2.52
3	1.5	223.42	215.93	29.93	20.41	-12.82
4	2	233.93	228.67	21.03	14.34	-17.80
5	2.5	242.72	238.32	17.56	11.97	-6.94
6	3	249.80	246.26	14.16	9.66	-6.78
7	3.5	257.09	253.45	14.58	9.94	0.82
8	4	264.92	261.01	15.66	10.67	2.15
9	4.5	273.07	269.00	16.29	11.11	1.27

Trajectory of Target Vehicle

#	Time(s)	Position(ft)	Mid-position(ft)	Velocity(ft/s)	Velocity(m/h)	Acceleration(ft/s^2)
0	0	112.67	56.33	---	---	---
1	0.5	131.15	121.91	36.94	25.19	---
2	1	147.90	139.52	33.51	22.85	-6.85
3	1.5	162.99	155.45	30.17	20.57	-6.68
4	2	177.41	170.20	28.83	19.66	-2.67
5	2.5	194.60	186.01	34.38	23.44	11.09
6	3	214.02	204.31	38.83	26.48	8.90
7	3.5	231.66	222.84	35.26	24.04	-7.14
8	4	249.80	240.73	36.28	24.73	2.02
9	4.5	269.26	259.53	38.92	26.53	5.27

Trajectory of Lead Vehicle

#	Time(s)	Position(ft)	Mid-position(ft)	Velocity(ft/s)	Velocity(m/h)	Acceleration(ft/s^2)
0	0	223.42	111.71	---	---	---
1	0.5	246.78	235.10	46.72	31.85	---
2	1	267.60	257.19	41.64	28.39	-10.15
3	1.5	287.22	277.41	39.24	26.76	-4.79
4	2	308.62	297.92	42.80	29.18	7.10
5	2.5	328.36	318.49	39.47	26.91	-6.65
6	3	346.37	337.37	36.02	24.56	-6.88
7	3.5	363.61	354.99	34.46	23.49	-3.12
8	4	379.81	371.71	32.41	22.09	-4.10
9	4.5	394.62	387.22	29.61	20.19	-5.58

Trajectory of Lag Vehicle

#	Time(s)	Position(ft)	Mid-position(ft)	Velocity(ft/s)	Velocity(m/h)	Acceleration(ft/s^2)
0	0	0.40	0	---	---	---
1	0.5	23.0	11.73	45.30	30.88	---
2	1	45.87	34.46	45.61	31.10	0.62
3	1.5	69.65	57.76	47.56	32.43	3.90
4	2	93.92	81.79	48.54	33.09	1.94
5	2.5	120.30	107.11	52.75	35.96	8.41
6	3	144.19	132.24	47.79	32.58	-9.91
7	3.5	166.24	155.22	44.09	30.06	-7.40
8	4	186.50	176.37	40.51	27.62	-7.14
9	4.5	205.51	196.00	38.02	25.92	-4.98

ond, a segment of video is digitized into a Video for Windows (AVI) file at a user-specified frame rate. Third, the AVI file is registered in VEVID, and then, in each frame, the user simply clicks the mouse over a distinguishable point of targeted vehicles. Trajectories are output into a trajectory data file along with speeds, accelerations and gaps of targeted vehicles.

Figure 12 shows an example of the basic form of vehicle trajectory data from VEVID. Given the frame rate of 2 frames per second (that reflects 0.5 second between two consecutive frames), all selected vehicles' positions are calculated by VEVID. Then VEVID automatically calculates the vehicles' speeds and accelerations for each time slice. Figure 13 illustrates trajectory curves corresponding with the data in Figure 12. From Figures 12 and 13, it can be seen that VEVID is not only capable of collecting trajectories of vehicles in the same lane, but also targeting multiple lanes simultaneously. This function is very valuable in the study of lane changing behaviors. Moreover, VEVID outputs calculation results of all traffic feature parameters that are useful to simulation modeling, such as gaps, headway and relative speeds between each two vehicles of interest, type of lane changing, duration of lane changing, and so forth.

Vehicular trajectory data also have great value in calibration and validation of existing traffic models. In addition to simulation modeling, vehicular trajectory data could be applied to other traffic analyses such as analysis of work zone merging behavior (Tao, 2002). In Minderhoud and Bovy's study (2001) of improved time-to-collision measures for road traffic safety assessment, vehicle trajectories collected over a specific time horizon for a certain roadway segment are critical inputs to calculate the overall safety indicator value. Trajectory data that present the tracks of vehicles traveling within the merging area of the studied work zone could provide quantitative description of merging maneuvers in terms of gap selecting, merging location selecting, speed

Figure 13. Trajectory curves and lane changing illustration

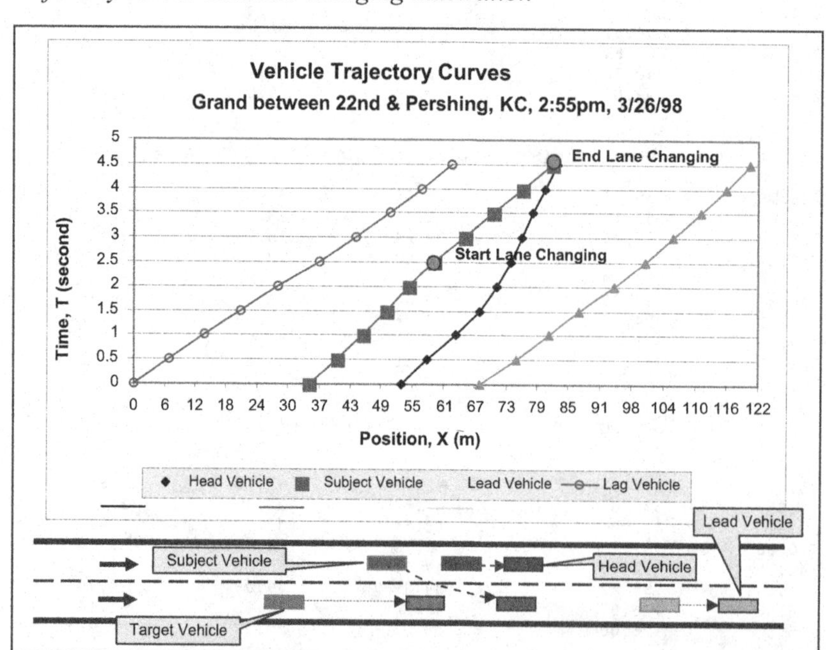

changes, duration of merging, and so forth. As a result, impact of merging behaviors on upstream traffic could be analyzed. Trajectory data could also be used for before-and-after study of work zone traffic control strategies.

Introducing video-capture to traffic data collection, especially multiple vehicle trajectory data for microscopic simulation modeling, is a significant advancement. The methodology proposed provides an effective and economic approach to studying microscopic traffic characteristics. With the help of VEVID, better quality data can be collected more efficiently. This advancement will result in better models of traffic in the urban environment.

The limitation of the video-capture-based approach lies in the extracting trajectory data of the vehicles located over 460 m or 1500 ft. away from the observation site, if a regular (family-use) camcorder is used. The far is the vehicle from the observation location, the longer distance does a pixel present in the image of an AVI frame. Thus, capability to produce high resolution of an AVI frame is one of major factors in selecting camcorder and accuracy testing is needed using sample data. In choosing place to install the camera, the site at which a very oblique camera angle is needed should be avoided at all possible.

CALIBRATION AND VALIDATION OF APPLYING ADVANCED MICROSCOPIC SIMULATION SOFTWARE

Advanced Microscopic Simulation Software

Many simulation models have been developed to evaluate the benefits of transportation operations. Traffic simulation has been in use since the early 1950s, but the recent advancement in computer technology and programming tools has helped to develop more sophisticated software for use in simulation modeling (Narasimha, 2005). As the computing power increases so will the simulation capability to illustrate precise description of roadway and facility conditions on-screen for analysis. To date, typically popular microscopic software for the present includes VISSIM (German for Traffic in Towns - Simulation) models, Paramics (Quadstone) (PARAllel MICroscopic Simulation), and AIMSUN2 (Advanced Interactive Microscopic Simulator for Urban and Non-urban Networks). The major features and functions can be obtained at the Web sites of the software developers (Institute for Transport Studies, 2006). The following sections discussing the experienced procedures for application of above advanced microscopic simulation models.

The general reasons for applying microscopic traffic simulation software to traffic operations and system evaluations include, but are not limited to, the following aspects:

- For its ability to capture the full dynamics of time dependent traffic phenomena.
- As a complementary tool for the detailed evaluation of alternative designs beyond the classical ones.
- For the detailed assessment of traffic management schemes.
- For assessment of advanced traffic management and information systems applications.
- For evaluation of new traffic control methods.
- For accurate emission and fuel consumption modeling.
- For needs of animation (Seeing is believing!).

Calibration and Validation of Simulation Models

Any microscopic simulation model must be calibrated and validated before its application for real problem-solving practice. The calibration involves checking the model results against observed data and adjusting parameters until the model results fall within an acceptable range of error (Chu et al., 2004). The collected data included roadway traffic volume and travel time data. Chu, Liu, Oh, and Recker (2004) summarized an overall calibration procedure based on their experience in study of simulating the I-45 freeway and its surrounding roadway network in California using PARAMICS simulation model. The following four steps of calibration efforts are included in the procedure:

- Calibration of driving behavior models
- Calibration of route choice model
- Origin-Destination estimation
- Model fine-tuning

It also should be noted that the network coding errors are major source of abnormal vehicular movements (Chu et al., 2004). Such errors can be found at any time during the process of the calibration from some. Accordingly, fixing network-coding errors is an important task throughout the whole calibration process. The number of simulation runs is one of contributing factors influencing the calibration accuracy. Before determining the number of simulation runs, the variance of a number of performance measures from simulation results should be estimated. The number of simulation runs could be estimated by the following equation (Chu et al., 2004).

$$N = \left(t_{\alpha/2} \frac{\delta}{\mu\varepsilon} \right)^2 \quad (29)$$

where μ and δ are the mean and standard deviation of the performance measure based on the already conducted simulation runs; ε is the allowable error specified as a fraction of the mean μ; $t_{a/2}$ is the critical value of the t-distribution at the confidence interval of 1-α.

Two objectives of calibration are required to meet: (1) to minimize the deviation between the observed traffic counts (VOL_{obs}) and corresponding simulated traffic counts (VOL_{sim}) at selected measurement locations for the peak hour of the simulation period ($t = 1, T$) ; and (2) to minimize the deviation between the observed travel time (T_{obs}) and corresponding simulated travel time T_{sim} along selected measurement routes (number of sample $n = 1, N$). Those two objective functions are expressed by the following equations:

$$\min \sum_{t=1}^{T} \sum_{n=1}^{N} (VOL_{obs}(n,t) - VOL_{sim}(n,t))^2 \quad (30)$$

$$\min \sum_{t=1}^{T} \sum_{n=1}^{N} (TT_{obs}(n,t) - TT_{sim}(n,t))^2 \quad (31)$$

The major driving behavior models include car-following and lane-changing models, which govern vehicular traffic movement and need to be calibrated for the specific region. The car-following model in a microscopic simulation software such (e.g., AIMSUN2) could be tested and calibrated in various with measured and simulated travel distance within a certain period of time. The error metric used to measure the accuracy of the fitting between measured and simulated values can be expressed by the following equation (Barcelól & Michalopoulos, 2000).

$$Em = \sqrt{\sum_{i=1}^{N} \left[\log\left(\frac{d_{sim}(i)}{d_{obs}(i)} \right) \right]^2} \quad (32)$$

Where, $d_{sim}(i)$ is the distance of the simulated vehicle at i^{th} simulation run, and $d_{obs}(i)$ is the distance measured with the test vehicle, and *log* denotes the logarithm base 10.

Model validation is typically an iterative process linked to each model calibration (Chu et al., 2004). The model validation is generally conducted with a different data set of larger area within the modeling network in order to check if the calibrated model parameters are suitable. Model validation is regarded as a final stage to investigate if each component adequately reproduces observed travel characteristics and the overall performance of the model is reasonable. The measure of goodness of fit could be for validating the calibrated simulation model. Mean absolute percentage error (MAPE) is measure of accuracy in a fitted time series value in statistics, specifically trending. It usually expresses accuracy as a percentage. MAPE is expressed by the following equation (Chu et al., 2004):

$$MAPE = \frac{1}{T}\sum_{t=1}^{T}\frac{M_{abs}(t) - M_{stn}(t)}{M_{abs}(t)} \qquad (33)$$

Where, $M_{abs}(t)$ and $M_{stn}(t)$ are field measured and simulated time-series values during a period of time t.

SUMMARY AND CONCLUSION

This chapter summarizes research results by the author on the core models of microscopic traffic simulations, including lane-choice, lane-changing, and route-choice models, as well as techniques on vehicle trajectory data extraction. Multiple vehicle trajectories provide the basis for the microscopic modeling of traffic on an urban street network. In the past, however, the difficulty of collecting vehicle trajectory data has been an obstacle to deriving verifiable models from empirical data. Introducing video-capture to traffic data collection, especially multiple vehicle trajectory data for microscopic simulation modeling, is a significant advancement. With the help of VEVID, better quality data can be collected more efficiently. In the end, this advancement will result in better models of traffic in the urban environment. Many models introduced in this chapter would not be developed without the previous methodology.

Using video-capture techniques and the VEVID software, the author conducted a lengthy observation of lane-changing behaviors on urban streets and analyses of observed vehicle trajectory data. This study presents new findings from real-world observations. New findings inspired the authors, from the systematic standpoint of view, to explore the hierarchy in recognizing and understanding lane-choice and lane-changing behaviors on urban streets. Based on new findings from observations conducted on four-lane urban streets, the author developed the heuristic structures of a lane-based vehicle assignment procedure along with a lane-choice model and a lane-changing model. The models presented in this research are a significant advancement in lane-specific vehicle-based microscopic simulation modeling, and provides a good basis for conducting further research on six or more lanes streets, as well as improving a microscopic simulation models.

In this chapter, the route choice problem is explored for a lane-vehicle-based microscopic simulation system. Since different categories of drivers have different reactions to the traveler routing information, traditional models assuming that every driver is very familiar with the network and always chooses the shortest path are not applicable to the study of the impact of traveler information on drivers' route choice behaviors. The methodology introduced in this chapter attempts to more realistically simulate route choice behavior. For instance, it is assumed that all drivers must have their primary routes before the trips, based on route information (e.g., from the Internet) or from experience. When they receive updated routing information while en route, aggressive drivers are more likely than conservative drivers to follow the advice. Aggressive drivers who are not exposed to the updated information may still adjust their primary route based on differences between expected and experienced traffic characteristics. But route changes also depend on familiarity with the road network. In general, if a driver on the route decides to change routes, the change cannot occur until the next downstream intersection is reached.

More importantly, drivers do not switch to another route that is predicted to have minimum travel cost if the estimated delay falls into indifference band of route delay. Different categories of drivers have varied criteria of the width of indifference band of route delay. Thus, fuzzy sets may be an appropriate theoretical method to be use for estimation of a specific driver's tendency to change routes. Further investigation and study on threshold values of the width of the indifference band of route delay may be needed for the areas of interest.

This chapter is written through systematically integrating above models into a simulation modeling system while merging some supplementary models and concepts resulted from literature reviews, including vehicle generation model and car-following models. In additionally, to facilitate the applications of the simulation models, procedure for building models and calibration and validation of simulation models are also summarized.

FUTURE RESEARCH DIRECTIONS

Traffic is the result of human behaviors and it is therefore mutual important to find out how traffic decisions are motivated and what results from the complex interactions of various participants (Schreckenberg & Selten, 2004). As a consequence it was not sufficient to model mobility in an entire mechanistic way. The human behavioral parameters need to be better underpinned (Ettema et al., 2003). For example, experiments to test how travelers learn and adjust in a controlled laboratory setting may be one of ways to conduct. Taken into account the fact that traffic decisions are made by individuals on the basis of interactions with other individuals makes the problem highly interdisciplinary and very complex. It will be also important to represent different types of decision makers (Ettema et al., 2003), such as early adaptors, risk takers and risk avoiders, optimizing and satisfying travelers, etc. There are different ways to approach the problem. For example, the widely used approaches include empirical (experimental) and theoretical methods. Regardless of the approaches for building the models, all models must be calibrated and validated prior to their applications.

The speed and capacity of desktop computers is steadily increasing. Tasks that were once the province of mainframe computers can be easily handled by the latest generation of personal computers. Increases in hardware speed generally result in greater capabilities of the models that run on them. Therefore it should soon be possible to see much more advanced micro-simulation models to deal with aspects that today's models consider too computationally expensive. Conventionally, large amount of data required for simulating larger networks is always a question. With increasing functionality of the intelligent transportation systems that automatically collects traffic data through field detection systems, the data collection task is being made easier. Simulation-based analysis of a larger network is expected to become more practical with ease in the future.

As indicated earlier, multi-lane vehicle trajectories are a key in advancing the identification and modeling of traffic characteristics under varied conditions. It is high time to update VEVID to accommodate more requirements for modeling, and most notably, how to relate traffic crime and offenses into the traffic simulation system as a tool to support the analysis of crime prevention strategies is a challenge to traffic simulation modeling. However, this research will apparently need an interdisciplinary research on the similar topics.

REFERENCES

Arentze, T. A., & Timmermans, H. J. P. (2003). Modeling learning and adaptation processes in activity travel choice: A framework and numerical experiments. *Transportation, 30*, 37-62.

Barcelól, J., & Michalopoulos, P. G. (2000). *Implementation of microscopic modeling to traffic simulation for ITS applications*. Presented at the Intelligent Transportation Systems Conference in Torino, Italy.

Ben-Akiva, M., & Bierlaire, M. (1999). Discrete choice methods and their applications to short term travel decision. In R. W. Hall (Ed.), *Handbook of transportation science*.

Ben-Akiva, M. E., Ramming, M. S., & Bkhor, S. (2004). Route choice model. *Human behaviour and traffic networks*. Berlin: Springer-Verlag.

Cascetta, E., & Papola, A. (2001). Implicit availability/perception logit models for route choice in transportatoin network. In *Proceedings of the 8th World Conference on Transport Research*, Antwerp.

Cascetta, E., Nuzzolo, A., Russo, F., & Vitetta, A. (1996). A modified logit route choice results for interurban networks. Transportation and traffic theory. In *Proceedings from the Theirteenth International Symposium on Transportation and Traffic Theory*, Lyon, France.

Chu, L. Y., Liu, H. X., Oh, J.-S., & Recker, W. (2004). A calibration procedure for microscopic traffic simulation. In *Proceedings of the 83th Transportation Research Board Annual Meeting in Washington, D.C.*

Driver's License Examining Bureau (1996, July). *Kansas driving handbook*. Topeka, Kansas.

Ettema, D., Tamminga, G. & Timmermans, H. (2003, August). A micro-simulation model system of departure time and route choice under travel time uncertainty. In *Proceedings of the 10th International Conference on Travel Behaviour Research Lucerne*, (pp. 10-15).

Gipps, P. G. (2001). A model for the structure of lane changing decisions. *Transportation Research, 20B*, 403-414. Institute for transport studies, Leeds University, United Kingdom. Micro-Simulation Tools. Retrieved August 30, 2007, from http://www.its.leeds.ac.uk/projects/smartest/links.html

Kaysi, I., Ben-Akiva, M., & Palma, A. D. (1995). Design aspects of advanced traveler information system. *Urban traffic networks: Dynamic flow modeling and control*. Springer-Verlag.

Knippenberg, C. V., & Knippenberg, A. V. (1986). Discussion on measurement of indifference band. *Transportation Research Record, 1085*, 47-49.

Kovvali, V., Alexiadis, V., & Zhang, L. (2006). Video-based vehicle trajectory data collection. In *Proceedings of the 86th Transportation Research Board Annual Meeting in Washington, D.C.*

Lieberman, E., & Rathi, A. K. (2000). Traffic simulation. *Revised monograph on traffic flow theory*. Update and expansion of the transportation research board (TRB) (Special Report No. 165). Retrieved August 30, 2007, from http://www.tfhrc.gov/its/tft/tft.htm

Mahmassani, H. S., & Weimann, J. (2004). Experiments with route and departure time choices of commuters under real-time information: Heuristics and adjustment processes. *Human behaviour and traffic networks*. Berlin: Springer-Verlag.

Mahmassani, H. M., & Chang, G. L. (1985). Dynamic aspects of departure-time choice behavior in a commuting system: Theoretical framework and experimental analysis. *Transportation Research Record, 1037*, 88-101.

Mahmassani, H. S., & Tong, C. C. (1986). Availability of information and dynamics of departure time choice: Experimental investigation. *Transportation Research Record, 1085*, 33-47.

May, A. D. (1990). *Traffic flow fundamentals*. Englewood Cliffs, New Jersey: Prentice Hall.

Minderhoud, M. M., & Bovy, H. L. (2001). Extended time-to-collision measures for road traffic safety assessment. *Accident Analysis and Prevention, 33*(1), 89-97.

Narasimha, M. A. S. (2005). Application of traffic simulation models in transportation planning. *Design and operations*. White Paper. Korve Engineering, Inc.

Polydoroulou, A., Ben-Akiva, M., and Kaysi, I. (1994). Influence of traffic information on drivers' route choice behavior. *Transportation Research Record, 1453*, 56-65.

Rothery, R. W. (2000). Car following models. *Revised monograph on traffic flow theory*. Update and expansion of the transportation research board (TRB) (Special Report No. 165). Retrieved August 31, 2007, from http://www.tfhrc.gov/its/tft/tft.htm

Schreckenberg, M., & Selten, R. (Eds.). (2004). Route choice model. *Human behaviour and traffic networks*. Berlin: Springer-Verlag .

Small, K. A. (1982). The scheduling of consumer activities: Work trips. *The American Economic Review, 72*, 467-479.

Tao, R. H. (2002). Impact analysis of work zone merging behaviors on upstream traffic. In *Proceedings at the Institute of Transportation Engineers 2002 Annual Meeting.*

Tao, R. H., Wei, H., Wang, Y. H., & Sisiopiku, V. P. (2005). Modeling speed disturbance absorption following SAS chains: Integrated car-following and lane-changing scenarios. *Transportation Research Record, 1934*, 83-93.

Toledo, T. Choudhry, C. F., & Ben-Akiva, M. E. (2005). Lane-changing model with explicit target lane choice. *Transportation Research Record, 1934*, 157-165.

Vaugh, K., Kitamura, R., & Jovanis, P. P. (1995). Experimental analysis and modeling of advice compliance: Results from advanced traveler information system simulation experiments. *Transportation Research Record, 1485*, 18-26.

Vovsha, P. (1997). The cross-nested logit model: Application to mode choice in the Tel-Aviv Metropolitan Area. *Transportation Research Record, 1607*, 6-15.

Wei, H, Lee, J., Li, Q., & Li, C. (2000). Observation-based lane-vehicle-assignment hierarchy: Microscopic simulation on an urban street network. *Transportation Research Record, 1710*, 96-103.

Wei, H. (1999). *Observed lane-choice and lane-changing behaviors on an urban street network using video-capture-based approach and suggested structures of their models.* Unpublsihed doctoral dissertation, University of Kansas.

Wei, H., Meyer, E., & Lee, J. (2001). Models for route-choice reflecting the use of travel information in a vehicle-based microscopic simulation system. In *Proceedings of the 80th Transportation Research Board Annual Meeting in Washington, D.C.*

Wei, H., Meyer, E., Feng, C., & Lee, J. (2002). Characterizing lane-choice behavior to build rules as part of lane-based traffic micro-simulation hierarchy. In *Proceedings of the 81st Transportation Research Board Annual Meeting*, Washington, D.C.

Wei, H., Meyer, E., Lee, J., & Feng, C. E. (2000). Characterizing and modeling observed lane-changing behavior for lane-vehicle-based microscopic simulation on an urban street network. *Transportation Research Record, 1710*, 104-113.

Wei, H., Meyer, E., Lee, J., & Feng, C. E. (2005). Video-capture-based approach to extract multiple vehicular trajectory data for traffic modeling. *ASCE Journal of Transportation Engineering, 131*(7), 496-505.

Zhang, Y. L., Owen, L. E., & Clark, J. (1998). A multi-regime approach for microscopic traffic simulation. In *Proceedings of the 77th Transportation Research Board Annual Meeting in Washington, D.C.*

ADDITIONAL READING

Abdulhai, B., Sheu, J-B., & Recker, W. (1999). Simulation of ITS on the Irvine FOT area using "Paramics 1.5" scalable microscopic traffic simulator: Phase I: Model calibration and validation. *California PATH Research Report*, UCB-ITS-PRR-99-12.

Ahmed, Kazi I., Ben-Akiva, M. E., Koutsopoulos, H. N., & Mishalani, R. G. (1996). Models of freeway lane changing and gap acceptance behavior. In *Proceedings of the 13th International Symposium on the Theory of Traffic Flow and Transportation.*

Barcelo, J., & Casas, J. (2004). Methodological notes on the calibration and validation of microscopic traffic simulation models. In *Proceedings of the 83rd Transportation Research Board Annual Meeting, Washington, D.C.*

Boer, E. R. (1999). Car following from the driver's perspective. *Transportation Research Part F, 2*, 201–206.

Brackstone, M., & McDonald, M. (1999). Car-following: A historical review. *Transportation Research Part F, 2*, 181–196.

Brilon, W., Huber, F., & Schreckenberg, M. (Eds.). (1999). *Traffic and mobility: Simulation - economics - environment.* Springer Verlag.

Gipps, P. G. (1985). A model for the structure of lane-changing decisions. *Transportation Research Part B, 20B*(5), 403-414.

Gipps, P. G. (1981). A behavioural car following model for computer simulation. *Transportation Research-B, 15B*, 105-111.

Helbing D., Hennecke, A., Shvetsov, V., & Treiber, M. (2002). Micro- and macro-simulation of freeway traffic. *Mathematical and Computer Modelling, 35*(5), 517-547.

Helbing, D. (1997). *Traffic dynamics: New physical modeling concepts.* Springer.

Hourdakis, J., Michalopoulos, P. G., & Kottommannil, J. (2003). A practical procedure for calibrating microscopic traffic simulation models. In *Proceedings of the 82nd Transportation Research Board Annual Meeting Preprint.*

Hourdakis, J., Michalopoulos, P. G., & Kottommannil, J. (2003). Practical procedure for calibrating microscopic traffic simulation models. *Transportation Research Record, 1852*, 130-139.

Mahmassani, H. S., & Peeta, S. (1995). System optimal dynamic assignment for electronic route guidance in a congested traffic network. *Urban traffic networks: Dynamic flow modeling and control.* Springer-Verlag.

McNally, M. G., & Oh, J-S. (2002, December). Technical memorandum on calibration/validation of traffic micro-simulation models. *Research report for Orange County Transportation Authority* (OCTA).

Passino, K. M., & Burgess K. L. (1998). *Stability analysis of discrete event systems.* John Wiley adaptive and learning systems for signal processing. Communications and control series.

Rahim, B. (1991). Procedure for validation of microscopic traffic flow simulation models. *Transportation Research Record, 1320*, 190-202.

Ran, B., & Boyce, D. (1996). *Modeling dynamic transportation networks: In intelligent transportation system oriented approach* (2nd revised ed.). Springer.

Resnick, M. (1997). *Turtles, termites, and traffic jams: Explorations in massively parallel microworlds (Complex adaptive systems).* MIT Press.

Takaba, S. (Ed.). (1988). *Simulation in the factory of the future: Simulation in traffic control.* Society for computer simulation (SCS).

Toledo, T., & Koutsopoulos, H. N. (2004). Statistical validation of traffic simulation models. In *Proceedings of the 83rd TRB annual meeting, Washington, D.C.*

Transportation Research Board, National Research Council (2000). *Highway capacity manual.* Washington D.C.

Chapter VII
Simulating Urban Dynamics Using Cellular Antomata

Xia Li
Sun Yat-sen University, China

ABSTRACT

This chapter introduces the concepts of cellular automata (CA) which have been increasingly used for simulating urban dynamics. Simulation and prediction of urban evolution can provide the useful inputs to crime models. However, calibration of urban cellular automata is crucial for simulating realistic cities. Simulation of multiple land use changes using CA is difficult because numerous spatial variables and parameters have to be utilized. The incorporation of neural networks with CA can alleviate the calibration problems. This chapter illustrates how complex land use dynamics can be simulated by the integration of CA and neural networks.

INTRODUCTION

Urban environments have great effects on the distribution of crimes in cities. The simulation and prediction can provide useful information for crime analysis. Urban dynamics is a complex system with open, nonlinear, and uncertain features. The common "top-down" approaches using mathematical equations are considered to be inappropriate in simulating complex urban systems because these approaches cannot capture complex local interactions (Batty, & Xie, 1994). In recent years, there are increasing studies on the development of geographical cellular automata (CA) for simulating complex systems. CA have been applied to the simulation of wildfire propagation (Clarke, Brass, & Riggan, 1994), population dynamics (Couclelis, 1988), and urban evolution and land use changes (Batty, & Xie, 1994; White, & Engelen, 1993).

Cellular automata (CA) were developed by Ulam in the 1940's and soon used by Von Neumann to investigate the logical nature of self-reproducible systems (White, & Engelen, 1993). However, CA has great potentials in simulating urban growth and exploring alternative development forms by using predefined rules. In the last two decades, a set of urban models based on CA techniques were reported with interesting outcomes, such as simulating emerging phenomena and fractal properties of cities (Batty, & Xie, 1994; Batty, & Xie, 1997; Couclelis, 1997; Deadman, Brown, & Gimblett, 1993; Li, & Yeh, 2000; White, & Engelen, 1997; Wu, & Webster, 1998).

Urban CA models differ from the typical CA models to a great extent as described by Wolfram (1984). Some of the strict conditions attached to conventional CA models have to be relaxed to meet the specific requirements of urban simulation. For example, typical CA models have a very limited total number of cells and a small number of temporal iterations (Batty, & Xie, 1994; Wu, & Webster, 1998). Urban CA models involve the use of a large number of cells and iterations. Urban CA models adopt heterogeneous cellular space which is different from that of conventional CA models. There are significant differences between urban CA models and other conventional CA models that have been developed for physics, artificial life, chemistry and biology.

Actually, Hägerstrand's model (1967) could be regarded as an early CA-like model for geography because he used neighborhood effects. Hägerstrand developed diffusion models through "Monte Carlo" simulation techniques. His models were specifically for human migration based on historical population records by using action-at-distance through gravitation effects. It replied on microscopic behavior to describe macroscopic behavior of the system by using simple predefined rules.

Tobler (1979) was perhaps the first to recognize the advantage of CA models in solving geographical problems (White, & Engelen, 1993). In his cellular space model, the state of a cell is determined by the states of a set of "neighbor" cells according to some uniform location-independent rules. The basic principle of such type of models is to use a cell-space representation to realize spatial dynamics.

Couclelis (1985, 1988, 1989) subsequently carried out some pioneering researches on urban simulation using cellular automata. Her studies attempted to explore the links with the theory of complex systems, and examine the possible uses in an urban planning context (White, & Engelen, 1993). She demonstrated that the perplexing dynamics of vole behavior could be simply explained by using CA models (Couclelis, 1988). She showed that CA might be used as an analog or metaphor to study how different varieties of urban dynamics might arise.

Batty and his colleagues (Batty, & Xie, 1994; Batty, & Xie, 1997; Batty, Xie, & Sun, 1999) have also carried out interesting researches on urban CA models. In their early studies (Batty, Longley, & Fotheringham, 1989), a closely related technique, diffusion limited aggregation (DLA) was used to model the growth of built-up areas. DLA models can generate complex forms by using a simple process like CA models. They also develop a general class of CA models which emerged through insights originating in computation and biology (Batty, & Xie, 1994). Their models are very similar to the *Game* of *Life* (Martin, 1970) because each cell can only take on one of two states (dead or alive). However, these models have different features in three ways. First, they are nondeterministic because births and deaths at time t are computed stochastically. Second, a system-wide survival rate is used to control the whole pattern—actual survival rate. Third, a threefold hierarchy of neighborhood is used to decide an actual birth locally. The simulation demonstrates that microprocesses can lead to aggregate development patterns.

CA models can be used for testing hypotheses, simulating urban forms and dynamics, and generating alternative land use plans. However, most of CA models to date have been developed for hypothetical applications (Couclelis, 1997; Batty et al., 1999). They have been focused on testing ideas without providing enough details for realistic representation (White et al., 1997). Most urban CA models are primarily focused on testing urban theories by exploring the mechanisms of urban growth. They are designed to investigate basic questions of urban forms and evolution of urban systems (Couclelis, 1997; White, & Engelen, 1993). These models are useful to explore how local actions give rise to global patterns.

CA models are able to generate cellular cities that have features very similar to those of real cities (White, & Engelen, 1993; White et al., 1997). Recently, much effort has been made to generate greater realism in urban CA simulation. CA models have been experimented to generate detailed and complex urban patterns. There are many aspects of the endeavor by paying attention to fractal structures, higher spatial resolution, inhomogeneous space, urban structure, and sustainability. Fractal structures have been considered as the most important feature of urban geometry. Fractal dimension can be used to evaluate the validity of urban simulation models (Wu, 1998). It has been shown that stochastic disturbance variables can be incorporated into CA models in generating fractal patterns (White, & Engelen, 1993). Batty and Xie (1994) have illustrated how CA can be used to simulate suburban expansion of the town of Amherst in metropolitan Buffalo, New York. White, et al. (1997) also employ CA to simulate the land use pattern of Cincinnati, Ohio. Clarke and Gaydos (1998) apply CA models to simulate and predict urban development in the San Francisco Bay region in California and the Washington/Baltimore corridor in the Eastern United States.

The core of CA is to define transition rules. Transition rules are used to represent a process to be modeled. The configuration of urban CA is affected by researchers' understanding of the nature. There are many ways to configure CA models and different model forms will have impacts on the outcome of CA simulation (Pontius, & Malanson, 2005; Yeh, & Li, 2006). A variety of urban CA models have been proposed to tackle specific problems in urban simulation. Model variations are usually dependent on individual preferences and specifications of applications. It is essential to define transition rules while there is no unique way to do so.

CONFIGURATION OF URBAN CELLULAR AUTOMATA

An urban CA model has four major elements—cells, states, neighborhood, and transition rules. Firstly, urban CA simulation operates on lattice of cells in two-dimensional space. In most situations, the simulation space is divided into uniform regular cells. Secondly, only one state among a set of possible states is assigned to each cell at time *t*, although a "grey" or "fuzzy" state can be used sometimes (Li, & Yeh, 2000). In many urban CA models, there are only two common binary states—urbanized or not. Thirdly, the configuration of neighborhood is to address the influences of neighboring cells in determining the conversion of states. The most common configurations include the use of von Neumann neighborhood or the Moore neighborhood. However, other configurations of neighborhood have been proposed to fit urban environments, such as a circular neighborhood (Li, & Yeh, 2000) and some action-at-distance-windows (Batty, & Xie, 1994). The cells with closer distance to the central cell will have greater influences on the conversion of states at the central cell. Fourthly, transition rules, which are usually expressed by some neighborhood functions, are essential to urban simulation. Iterations are required for the accomplishment of the simulation. Sometimes, stochastic variables are embedded in transition rules to address the influences of unknown factors.

Some studies prefer to use probabilities instead of deterministic rules for urban simulation because of the inherent uncertainties in urban systems. There are many substantial differences between urban CA transition rules and traditional CA transition rules. A variety of urban

CA transition rules have been proposed to satisfy various users' preferences. Unlike traditional CA models, urban CA models have not adopted strict transitional rules

The essential part of CA simulation is to define transition rules. However, the definition of transition rules is not unique, as a large set of transition rules has been proposed from different applications. Rigid transition rules of standard CA only deal with neighborhood effects using either von Neumann neighborhood or Moore neighborhood. A general function can be expressed as follows:

$$S_{ij}^{t+1} = f_N(S_{ij}^t) \quad (1)$$

where S is a set of possible states at location ij, N is the neighborhood of all cells providing input values to the function f, and f is the transition function that defines the change of the state from time t to t+1.

Operational transition rules have to be provided for the implementation of CA. The most famous set of transition rules is related to the *Game of Life*. The rules of the game are extremely simple. If an inactive cell has exactly three live neighbors, it becomes active (born). If an active cell is surrounded by two or three neighbors, it remains alive. An active cell will die under the situations of isolation (surrounded by fewer than two neighbors) or overcrowding (surrounded by more than three neighbors). The simple set of rules can yields patterns of surprising complexity. The complex behavior emerges from these simple rules is rather unexpected, but the patterns can be stabilized after many interactions.

The determination of transition rules for urban CA models is quite relaxed. The transition rules are usually represented by transition probability or transition potentials. A simplified urban CA model can be defined using the following rule-based structure (Batty, 1997):

IF any cell $\{x\pm1, y\pm1\}$ is already developed
THEN $P_d\{x,y\}=\sum_{ij \in \Omega} P_d\{i,j\}/8$
&
IF $P_d\{x,y\}$ > some threshold value
THEN cell$\{x,y\}$ is developed with some other probability $\rho\{x,y\}$

where $P_d\{x,y\}$is urban development probability for cell $\{x,y\}$, cell $\{i,j\}$ are the all cells which from the Moore neighborhood Ω including the cell $\{x,y\}$ itself.

Transition potentials can also be calculated by the combination of a series of factors. White and Engelen (1997) calculate transition potentials according to three factors: (1) the intrinsic suitability of the cell itself; (2) the aggregate effect of the cells in the neighborhood; and (3) a stochastic perturbation. The equation is given as follows:

$$P_z = S_z N_z + \varepsilon_z \text{ for all z,} \quad (2)$$

$$N_z = \sum_{d,i} I_{d,i} w_{z,y,d} \quad (3)$$

where
P_z is the potential for transition to state z;
S_z is the suitability for the cell for activity z; $S_z \in [0,1]$;
N_z is the neighborhood effect;
$W_{z,y,d}$ is the weight applied to cells in state y in distance d;
i is the index of cells in distance zone d;
ε_z is a stochastic disturbance term;

$$I_{d,i} = \begin{cases} 1, & \text{if cell } i \text{ in distance zone } d \text{ is in state } y; \\ 0, & \text{otherwise.} \end{cases}$$

Clarke, et al. (1997) use five factors to control the behavior in urban simulation. The five factors include the factors of *DIFFUSION*, *BREED*, *SPREAD*, *SLOPE_RESISTANCE* and *ROAD_GRAVITY*. Transition rules are given based on these five factors. These factor values, which affect the acceptance level of randomly drawn numbers, were set by the user for every model run and were varied as part of the calibration process.

Wu and Webster (1998) present an integrated CA and multicriteria evaluation (MCE) method to estimate the probability of urban transition in a nondeterministic CA. MCE is used to capture the different blends of government and private developer preferences that govern different development regimes. The development probability is determined by a combined evaluation score r_{ij} and nonlinear transformation is used to discriminate the simulation patterns. The equation is expressed by:

$$p_{ij} = \varphi(r_{ij}) = \exp\left[\alpha(\frac{r_{ij}}{r_{\max}} - 1)\right] \quad (4)$$

where,

α is a dispersion parameter ranging from 0 to 1;

r_{ij} is the combined evaluation score at location ij;

r_{max} is the maximum value of r_{ij}.

The composite evaluation score is calculated from the following linear equation:

$$r_{ij} = (\beta_1 \text{CENTRE} + \beta_2 \text{INDUSTRL} + \beta_3 \text{NEWRAILS} + \beta_4 \text{HIGHWAY} + \beta_5 \text{NEIGHBOR}) \text{RESTRICT} \quad (5)$$

where $\beta_1, \ldots, \beta_5$ are weighting parameters acquired from the AHP analysis of MCE; CENTRE, INDUSTRL, NEWRAILS, HIGHWAY, NEIGHBOR are development factors.

"Grey value" can be defined to represent the "fuzzy" membership of conversion in transition rules (Li, & Yeh, 2000; Yeh, & Li, 2001). It is considered that land use conversion takes place by a gradual course. A "grey value" can be used to indicate the degree of urbanized process for a cell, which is not based on the conventional concept - purely urbanized or not. The "grey value" is calculated by iterations:

$$G^{t+1}_{xy} = G^{t}_{xy} + \Delta G^{t}_{xy} \quad (6)$$

where G is the "grey value" for development which falls within the range of 0~1; and xy is the location of the cell. A cell will be urbanized when the "grey value" reaches 1. ΔG^t is the gain of the "grey value" at each loop; it is calculated by some forms of neighborhood functions and constraints.

Another set of urban CA models is developed based on a different approach employing the concept of life cycle (Batty, & Xie, 1994; Batty et al., 1999). It is considered that activities in urban systems follow life cycles which apply both to the physical stock that gets developed as well as the activities that occupy the stock at different locations. In this type of CA models, urban activities can be defined by new, mature and declining housing, industry and commercial land uses.

Transition rules can become even more complex when CA models are integrated with economic theories and conventional urban models. Urban CA models usually involve not only simple local rules, but also other economic and social factors (Semboloni, 1997). Examples of this mix include the use of social actors, Lowry models and system dynamics in the definition of CA transition rules. Market mechanism governing competition of land use should be emphasized in this type of models. Semboloni (1997) presents a CA model that is closely related to Lowry models. The model is more complex than simple CA models. White and Engelen (1997) also propose a cellular automaton in conjunction with a macro-scale model to represent nonlocal dynamics of population, economy and natural environment. Webster and Wu (1999a, 1999b) infuse many behavioral rules into urban CA models. The transition rules are defined by mixing economic equilibrium and CA paradigms. They are based on behavioral economic models rather than pure heuristics and development potential is measured in monetary value (profit).

There is a question on how to maintain the original simplicity of CA models when they are integrated with other conventional urban models.

They may collapse into other non-CA models if the emphasis of local rules is lost. There are also questions on how to define model structures and parameter values for these complex models. It is almost impossible to calibrate CA models and determine parameter values when these models become too complex and use too many variables. Calibration cannot be carried out by conventional statistical methods to obtain parameter values, such as logistic or multi-logistic regression models. These models are only valid for the simple linear relationships between independent variables and dependent variables.

CALIBRATING URBAN CELLULAR AUTOMATA

It is not easy to define model structures and determine parameter values in urban CA models. There are also very limited studies on calibrating urban CA models because of the complexities (Silva, & Clarke, 2002). A critical issue in CA simulation is to provide proper parameter values or weights so that realistic results can be generated. Real cities are complex dynamic systems that involve the use of many spatial variables in CA simulation. Each spatial variable has a contribution to the simulation. The influence of a spatial variable is determined by its associated parameter or weight in the simulation. A variable associated with a larger parameter value usually indicates that it is more important than other variables. There are usually many parameter values to be defined in a CA model and the results of CA simulation are very sensitive to the parameter values (Wu, 2000; Yeh and Li, 2006).

Most of the existing CA is based on the so-called "trial and error" approach. The visual test is the main method for validating urban CA (Clarke, Gaydos, & Hoppen 1997, White et al., 1997, Ward, Murray, & Phinn, 2000). There are some other attempts to develop more elaborated methods to tackle the problems of uncertainties in defining transition rules and parameter values. Wu and Webster (1998) use multicriteria evaluation (MCE) to heuristically define the parameter values for CA simulation. Calibration can also largely rely on repetitive runs of the same model with different combinations of parameter values (Wu, 2000). Wu (2002) provides a method to estimate the global development probability by using a logistic regression model. The initial global probability is calibrated according to historical land use data. It seems easy to understand the meanings of the coefficients in the logistic regression equation.

Clarke and Gaydos (1998) also provided a more elaborated calibration method by statistically testing the observed against the expected. The method is to find which set of parameter values can lead the model to produce the best fits. The set of parameter values with the best fits are then used for prediction. However, there can be many possible combinations of parameter values. Their experiments have tried more than 3,000 combinations that need a high-end workstation to run several hundreds of hours for the calibration. This method is very time-consuming because it needs to compare all possible combinations of parameter values. Another problem is that the combinations may be extraordinary huge when there are many variables and a sound search procedure is hard to develop for the calibration.

Another method is to use neural networks to deal with the complicated calibration issue in CA urban simulation (Li, & Yeh, 2001). The method has a number of advantages over other methods. The calibration procedure is simple and convenient because the parameter values are automatically obtained using neural networks. The method is more robust by using the well-developed procedure of back-propagation training. Moreover, the model is able to deal with complex interactions among variables. Unlike statistics based approach, variables are not required to be independent of each other in neural networks. The model structure is much simpler and more stable compared with traditional CA models.

A NEURAL-NETWORK-BASED CELLULAR AUTOMATON FOR SIMULATING MULTIPLE LAND USES CHANGES USING GIS

In this study, a new type of CA models based on neural networks is discussed for CA simulation to simplify CA model structure and calibration process. The most attractiveness of neural networks is that the complex nonlinear relationships can be accurately modeled by simple network structures. The parameter values can be automatically obtained by a back-propagation calibration procedure.

The proposed ANN-CA model is devised for simulating multiple land use changes (Figure 1). The output layer of the network represents the transition probabilities of multiple land uses by using multiple output neurons. The parameters that are required for the simulation are automatically determined by a training procedure of neural networks. No explicit transition rules are required in the ANN-CA model. The only task is to train the neural network to obtain parameter values based on empirical data.

The first step is to define the inputs to the network for the simulation. The simulation is cell-based and each cell has a set of n attributes (variables) as the inputs to the neural network. It is assumed that these site attributes decide land use conversion probabilities. These variables can be conveniently obtained by using general GIS buffer and overlay analyses. They can be expressed by:

Figure 1. The flowchart of the neural-network-based CA model for simulating multiple land use changes

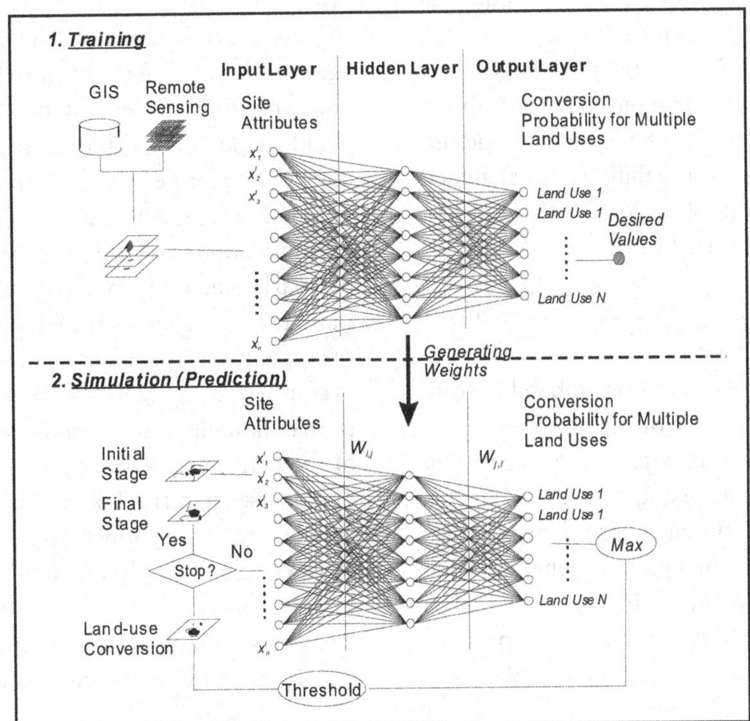

$$X=[x_1, x_2, x_3, \ldots, x_n]^T \quad (7)$$

where x_i is the ith site attribute and T is transposition.

In the hidden layer, the signal received by neuron j from the input layer for cell k at time t is calculated by:

$$net_j(k,t) = \sum_i w_{i,j} x'_i(k,t) \quad (8)$$

where $net_j(k, t)$ is the signal received by neuron j in the hidden layer, $w_{i,j}$ is the parameter or weight between the input layer and the hidden layer, and $x'_i(x,t)$ is the ith scaled site attribute associated with neuron i in the input layer with regard to cell k and time t.

The activation of the hidden layer to the input signal is calculated by:

$$\frac{1}{1+e^{-net\,j(k,t)}} \quad (9)$$

The output layer has a total of N neurons corresponding to N classes of land uses. The lth neuron in the output layer generates a value that represents the conversion probability from the existing type to the lth (target) type of land use. A higher value means that the conversion probability from the existing type to the lth type of land use is greater. Conversion probabilities are calculated by the following formula according to the output function of neural networks:

$$P(k,t,l) = \sum_j w_{j,l} \frac{1}{1+e^{-net\,j(k,t)}} \quad (10)$$

where $P(k, t, l)$ is the conversion probability from the existing to the lth type of land use for cell k at time t, and $w_{j,l}$ is the parameter or weight between the hidden layer and the output layer

A stochastic disturbance term is usually incorporated in CA simulation to generate more plausible results (White, & Engelen, 1993). The disturbance can lead the simulation to produce fractal properties that are found in real urban systems and land use patterns. The error term (RA) can be defined as (White, & Engelen, 1993):

$$RA = 1+(-\ln \gamma)^\alpha \quad (11)$$

where γ is a uniform random variable within the range of 0 to 1, and a is the parameter to control the size of the stochastic perturbation. a can be used as a dispersion factor in the simulation.

The disturbance is incorporated in the neural-network-based CA model for more realistic simulation. The conversion probability is then revised as:

$$P(k,t,l) = \text{RA} \times \sum_j w_{j,l} \frac{1}{1+e^{-net\,j(k,t)}}$$
$$= (1+(\text{-ln}\,\gamma)^\alpha) \times \sum_j w_{j,l} \frac{1}{1+e^{-net\,j(k,t)}} \quad (12)$$

A loop-based neural network is designed to simulate land uses. At each iteration, each neuron in the output layer generates a conversion probability from existing type to another type of land use. Different types of land uses compete against each other for a given cell (e.g., more than two types of land uses can be suitable for a cell simultaneously according to the suitability). The competition can be better explained by a neo-classical bid-rent model (Webster, & Wu, 1999a). In our simulation, land use conversion is decided by comparing the values of conversion probabilities. Land use will convert from the existing type to the type that is associated with the highest value of conversion probability. If the same type of land use has the highest conversion probability, the state of the cell remains unchanged. The simulation of land uses is carried out by running the neural network iteratively until some constraints are satisfied, e.g. the total amount of available land for urban uses.

In most situations, land use changes take place only by a small percentage within a short period.

CA simulation usually involves many iterations to decide whether a cell is converted or not. A predefined threshold value should be used to control the rate of conversion so that land use changes take place step-by-step. If the highest conversion probability is less than the threshold value, the cell remains unchanged. The threshold value may range from 0 to 1. Experiments show that a relatively large value of threshold (e.g., 0.90) can be used to prevent land use from changing too fast in the simulation. The smaller the value, the more cells will be converted at each iteration. A relatively large value of threshold is useful for obtaining the fine patterns of simulation. The threshold can be determined by experiments.

The proposed ANN-CA model was tested by applying it to the simulation of multiple land use changes in a real city, *Dongguan,* in the Pear River Delta in southern China. The study region consists of a city proper and 29 towns with a total area of 2,465 km^2. It was mainly an agricultural area. Tremendous land use changes have occurred in the 1990's due to the fast economic development (Li, & Yeh, 1998). An urban planning CA model was developed to generate urban growth pattern that could minimize agricultural land loss and achieve compact development (Li, & Yeh, 2000). Like most of urban CA models, it only dealt with the conversion between the binary states—urbanized or not. In order to predict what will happen if the current urban development pattern continues, there is a need to develop a CA model that can simulate future urban growth. More ideally, the model should be able to provide detailed information about the conversion between multiple land uses for planning and management purposes. In this study, the simulation involves six types of land uses—cropland, orchards, development sites, built-up areas, forest, and water.

Empirical data should be used to calibrate CA models when the simulation is for real cities. Empirical data usually include the information of location, type, and amount of land use conversion. This type of information can be conveniently obtained from satellite images by employing land use change detection methods. There are many researches on land use change detection using satellite images (Howarth 1986; Jensen, Rutchey, K., Koch, & Narumalani, 1995). In this study, a method based on principal components analysis (Li, & Yeh, 1998) was employed to obtain the information of land use changes for the study area. The 1988 and 1993 TM images were used as empirical data to reveal the fast land use conversion process in the region.

The neural-network-based CA model was implemented in ArcGIS. There are two advantages for programming within the GIS. First, the neural network as data input without any data conversion can directly read GIS data layers. Secondly, the powerful spatial analysis functions of GIS, such as the *Eucdistance* and *Focal* functions of *ARC/INFO GRID,* can be conveniently used in the programming.

The output layer has six neurons, each representing the conversion probability from the existing type to a target type of land use. The model has a total of 12 input neurons to receive these variables (site attributes) for each cell at time *t.* The first three neurons are specified to represent three main types of distance variables. The next six neurons are used to count the amount of each land use type in the neighborhood of 7 × 7 window. When a set of site attributes is passed through the network, each output neuron produces a conversion probability for a target type of land use. Land use conversion at a cell is decided by the competition between different types of land uses. At each iteration, a cell will be converted from one type to another type of land use that is associated with the highest conversion probability. Land use remains unchanged if it is found to be converted to the same type of land use.

The simulation was executed by using the land use in 1988 as the initial state. A mask was used to confine the simulation within the study area. Land use changes outside the study area were masked out. Figure 2b shows the results of simulating multiple land uses in the period of 1988-2005 by using the neural-network-based CA model. It first simulated the land uses in 1993. The goodness of fit was evaluated by comparing the simulation results with the actual land uses that are obtained from remote sensing. Table 1 shows the confusion matrix between the simulated and the actual land uses in 1993 based on overlay analysis. The simulation is quite acceptable because the overall accuracy is 83%.

The next step was to simulate future land use patterns in 2005, assuming the continuation of the current trend and dynamics of urban development (Figure 2c). The same parameter values were used for the network to simulate the future land use changes. Table 2 shows the simulated land use changes by categories. It is found that the future urban growth will lead to a large amount of agricultural land loss if the current land use development process continues. According to the simulation, the built-up areas will increase by 163% while the cropland will drop by 70% in 2005. The prediction of future land use pattern provides useful information for land use planning and management. Potential impacts of land use changes can be further estimated by GIS analysis. Sustainable land development plans can be formulated to mitigate the negative impacts (e.g., control the scale and extent of the land development) before they actually take place.

Table 1. Confusion matrix between the actual and the simulated land usesin 1993 (in percentage)

		Simulated						Total
		Cropland	**Construction Sites**	**Orchard**	**Built-up Areas**	**Forest**	**Water**	
Actual	Cropland	89.3	3.3	7.3	0.1	0.0	0.0	100.0
	Construction Sites	8.4	57.2	9.6	14.3	0.0	10.5	100.0
	Orchard	4.3	8.6	83.1	3.7	0.3	0.0	100.0
	Built-up Areas	0.0	8.6	0.9	79.1	9.6	1.7	100.0
	Forest	0.2	0.0	0.6	1.1	96.4	1.8	100.0
	Water	0.0	0.8	0.0	0.0	4.3	94.9	100.0

Table 2. Simulated land use changes by categories (in hectares)

Land Use	**1988 (Initial)**	**1993**		**2005 (Future)**
		Actual	**Simulated**	
Cropland	100,400.3	77,839.3	84,229.6	57,047.0
Construction Sites	2,031.7	22,753.4	16,118.2	22,886.4
Orchard	63,512.6	62,458.9	59,608.8	70,281.0
Built-up Areas	15,927.3	18,536.1	20,465.1	30,267.4
Forest	40,404.2	41,574.8	41,204.4	41,162.7
Water	17,392.5	16,506.1	18,042.5	18,024.2
TOTAL	239,668.6	239,668.6	239,668.6	239,668.6

Figure 2. Simulation of multiple land use changes using the neural-network-based CA model

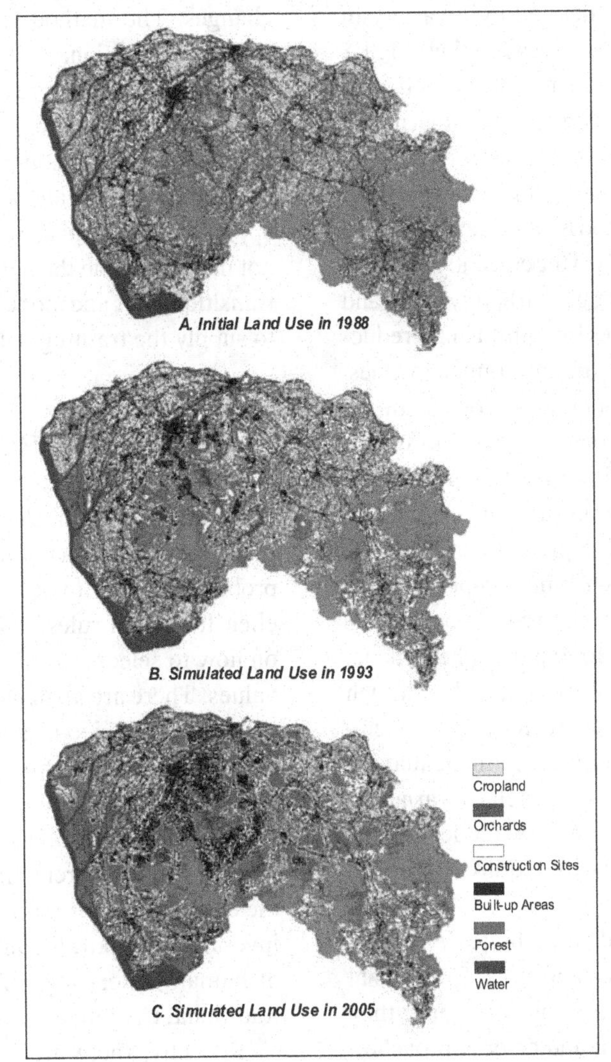

CONCLUSION

CA have become a useful tool for modeling urban spatial dynamics and encouraging results have been documented. These models are often used to simulate urban growth based on the trajectory of historical growth. It is so called 'baseline development' simulation. This type of CA model is usually implemented by the use of GIS. Integrated with GIS, the CA models can benefit much by using social, economic, physical, and environmental data in GIS. The rapid development of GIS helps to foster the application of CA in urban simulation. CA have attracted growing attention in urban simulation because of their capability in spatial modeling that is not fully developed in GIS.

The essential part of geographical cellular automata (CA) is to provide appropriate transition rules so that realistic patterns can be simulated. Transition rules can be defined by a variety of methods, such as multicriteria evaluation (MCE), logistic regression, neural networks, and data mining. This chapter has demonstrated that neural networks can be conveniently integrated with cellular automata for simulating multiple land use changes. The proposed method can overcome some of the shortcomings of the currently used CA models in simulating complex urban systems and multiple land use changes by significantly reducing the tedious work in defining parameter values, transition rules and model structures. Training data from the GIS can be easily used to obtain parameter values by calibrating the model. The model has the advantages in handling incomplete and error input data. The prediction surface is distinctly nonlinear which is much superior to the linear surface of the popular regression models (Lloyd, 1997). In many geographical phenomena, spatial variables are usually correlated with each other. Traditional methods, such as multicriteria evaluation (MCE) techniques, are inadequate in providing correct weights for correlated variables. In the neural-network-based CA model, spatial variables are not necessarily required to be independent of each other.

It is extremely difficult to calibrate CA models when there are multiple land uses. Traditional calibration methods are not robust because they are mainly based on trial and error approaches. These approaches involve the test of many possible combinations of parameter values for seeking the best fit. They are very computation-intensive because there are numerous possible combinations. The calibration algorithms are also application-dependent. Neural networks are quite robust and convenient in calibrating simulation models by using common back-propagation algorithms. In this study, the training process of neural network automatically determines the parameter values. These values are then imported to the model for simulation of multiple land use changes. The method significantly reduces the time of calibration.

The model structure is very simple by using a three-layer network with multiple output neurons to generate conversion probabilities. The model structure is generic and widely applicable to many applications of land use simulation. The users do not need to define the parameter values, detailed transition rules and model structures but just need to supply the training data.

FUTURE RESEARCH DIRECTIONS

Since urban CA models are still under development, they are not without limitations. There are problems on how to define model structures and elicit transition rules. There are no agreements on how to select model variables and parameter values. There are also many ways of incorporating planning objectives and policies in simulation process. Meanwhile, the inherent data error and the modeling uncertainties will also affect the application of CA models. Furthermore, CA models have apparent limitations of reflecting the decisions and behaviors of governments and investors in shaping urban growth. The influences of human factors are difficult to implement in traditional CA models.

Recently, there are increasingly studies on using agent-based systems to simulate complex behaviors of various players in urban systems. The interactions between these micro-agents can give rise to global spatial patterns of cities. The integration of CA and agent-based systems may be a solution to these problems that cannot be explained by using CA models alone. This integration can also provide a useful framework for simulating crime activities by incorporating various physical, social and economic factors.

REFERENCES

Batty, M., & Xie, Y. (1994). From cells to cities. *Environment and Planning B: Planning and Design, 21*, 531-548.

Batty, M., & Xie, Y. (1997). Possible urban automata. *Environment and Planning B: Planning and Design, 24*, 175-192.

Batty, M. (1997). Cellular automata and urban form: A primer. *Journal of the American Planning Association, 63*(2), 266-274.

Batty, M., Longley, P., & Fotheringham, S. (1989). Urban growth and form: Scaling, fractal geometry, and diffusion-limited aggregation. *Environment and Planning A: Environment and Planning, 21*, 1447-1472.

Batty, M., Xie, Y., & Sun, Z. L. (1999). Modeling urban dynamics through GIS-based cellular automata. *Computers, Environment and Urban Systems, 23*, 205-233.

Clarke, K. C., Brass, J. A., & Riggan, P. J. (1994). A cellular automata model of wildfire propagation and extinction. *Photogrammetric Engineering & Remote Sensing, 60*, 1355-1367.

Clarke, K. C., & Gaydos, L. J. (1998). Loose-coupling a cellular automata model and GIS: long-term urban growth prediction for San Francisco and Washington/Baltimore. *International Journal of Geographical Information Science, 12*(7), 699-714.

Clarke, K. C., Gaydos, L., & Hoppen, S. (1997). A self-modifying cellular automaton model of historical urbanization in the San Francisco Bay area. *Environment and Planning B: Planning and Design, 24*, 247-261.

Conclelis, H. (1988). Of mice and men: What rodent populations can teach us about complex spatial dynamics. *Environment and Planning A: Environment and Planning, 20*, 99-109.

Conclelis, H. (1989). Macrostructure and micro-behaviour in a metropolitan area. *Environment and Planning B: Planning and Design, 16*, 141-54.

Couclelis, H. (1985). Cellular worlds: A framework for modelling micro-macro dynamics. *Environment and Planning A: Environment and Planning, 17*, 585-596.

Couclelis, H. (1997). From cellular automata to urban models: New principles for model development and implementation, *Environment and Planning B: Planning and Design, 24*, 165-174.

Deadman, P. D., Brown, R. D., & Gimblett, H. R. (1993). Modelling rural residential settlement patterns with cellular automata. *Journal of Environmental Management, 37*, 147-160.

Hägerstrand, T. (1967). *Innovation diffusion as a spatial process*. Chicago: University of Chicago Press.

Howarth, P. J., (1986). Landsat digital enhancements for change detection in urban environment. *Remote Sensing of Environment, 13*, 149-160.

Jensen, J. R., Rutchey, K., Koch, M. S., & Narumalani, S. (1995). Inland wetland change detection in the Everglades Water Conservation Area 2A using a time series of normalized remotely sensed data. *Photogrammetric Engineering and Remote Sensing, 61*, 199-209.

Li, X., & Yeh, A. G. O. (1998). Principal component analysis of stacked multi-temporal images for monitoring of rapid urban expansion in the Pearl River Delta. *International Journal of Remote Sensing, 19*(8), 1501-1518.

Li, X., & Yeh, A. G. O. (2000). Modelling sustainable urban development by the integration of constrained cellular automata and GIS. *International Journal of Geographical Information Science, 14*(2), 131-152.

Li, X., & Yeh, A. G. O. (2001). Calibration of cellular automata by using neural networks for the simulation of complex urban systems. *Environment and Planning A: Environment and Planning,* 33, 1445-1462.

Martin, G. (1970). The fantastic combinations of John Conway's new solitaire game "Life." *Scientific American, 223*, 120-123.

Pontius, G. R., & Malanson, J. (2005). Comparison of the structure and accuracy of two land change models. *International Journal of Geographical Information Science, 19*(2), 243-265.

Semboloni, F. (1997). An urban and regional model based on cellular automata. *Environment and Planning B: Planning and Design, 24*, 589-612.

Silva, E. A., & Clarke, K. C. (2002). Calibration of the SLEUTH urban growth model for Lisbon and Porto, Portugal. *Computers, Environment and Urban Systems, 26*, 525-552.

Tobler, W. R. (1979). Cellular geography. In S. Gale. & G. Olsson. (Eds.), *Philosophy in geography* (pp. 279-386). D Reidel, Dordrecht.

Ward, D. P., Murray, A. T., & Phinn, S. R. (2000). A stochastically constrained cellular model of urban growth. *Computers, Environment and Urban Systems, 24*, 539-558.

Webster, C. J., & Wu, F. (1999a). Regulation, land use mix and urban performance. Part 1: Theory. *Environment and Planning A: Environment and Planning, 31*, 1433-1442.

Webster, C. J., & Wu, F. (1999b). Regulation, land use mix and urban performance. Part 2: Simulation. *Environment and Planning A: Environment and Planning, 31*, 1529-1545.

White, R., & Engelen, G. (1993). Cellular automata and fractal urban form: A cellular modelling approach to the evolution of urban land-use patterns. *Environment and Planning A: Environment and Planning, 25*, 1175-1199.

White, R., & Engelen, G. (1997). Cellular automata as the basis of integrated dynamic regional modelling. *Environment and Planning B: Planning and Design, 24*, 235-246.

White, R., Engelen, G., & Uijee, I. (1997). The use of constrained cellular automata for high-resolution modeling of urban land-use dynamics. *Environment and Planning B: Planning and Design, 24*, 323-343.

Wolfram, S. (1984). Cellular automata as models of complexity. *Nature, 31*(4), 419-424.

Wu, F., & Webster, C. J. (1998). Simulation of land development through the integration of cellular automata and multi-criteria evaluation. *Environment and Planning B: Planning and Design, 25*,103-126.

Wu, F. (1998). An experiment on the general polycentricity of urban growth in a cellular automatic city. *Environment and Planning B: Planning and Design, 25*, 103-126.

Wu, F. (2000). A parameterized urban cellular model combining spontaneous and self-organizing growth. In P. Atkinson & D. Martin. (Eds.), *GIS and geo-computation* (pp. 73-85). New York: Taylor and Francis.

Wu, F. (2002). Calibration of stochastic cellular automata: the application to rural-urban land conversions. *International Journal of Geographical Information Sciences, 16*(8), 795-818.

Yeh, A. G. O., & Li, X. (2006). Errors and uncertainties in urban cellular automata. *Computers, Environment and Urban Systems, 30*(1), 10-28.

Yeh, A. G. O., & X. Li. (2001). A constrained CA model for the simulation and planning of sustainable urban forms using GIS. *Environment and Planning B: Planning and Design, 28*, 733-753.

ADDITIONAL READING

Benenson, I. (1998). Multi-agent simulations of residential dynamics in the city. *Computers, Environment and Urban Systems*, *22*(1), 25-42.

Brown, D. G., North, M., Robinson, D., Riolo, R., & Rand, W. (2005). Spatial process and data models: Toward integration of agent-based models and GIS [Special Issue]. *Journal of Geographical Systems, 7*(1), 25-47.

Brown, D. G., Page, S., Riolo, R., Zellner, M., & Rand, W. (2005). Path dependence and the validation of agent-based spatial models of land use. *International Journal of Geographical Information Science*, *19*(2), 153-174.

Bura, S., Gue'Rin-Pace, F., Mathian, H., Pumain, D., & Sanders, L. (1996). Multiagent systems and the dynamics of a settlement system. *Geographical Analysis*, *28*(2), 161-178.

Epstein, J. M. (1999). Agent-based computational models and generative social science. *Complexity, 4*(5), 41-60.

Epstein, J. M., & Axtell, R. (1996). *Growing Artificial Societies from the Bottom Up*. Washington, D.C.: Brookings Institution.

Gilbert, N. & Conte, R. (1995). *Artificial Societies: The computer simulation of social life*. UCL Press.

Loibl, W., & Toetzer, T. (2003). Modelling growth and densification processes in suburban regions—Simulation of landscape transition with spatial agents. *Environmental Modelling & Software, 18*, 553-563.

Torrens, P. M., & Benenson, I. (2005). Geographic automata systems. *International Journal of Geographical Information Science*, *19*(4), 385-412.

Chapter VIII
Space-Time Measures of Crime Diffusion

Youngho Kim
University of North Carolina at Charlotte, USA

ABSTRACT

This study proposes methods for space-time diffusion measures and a simulation on crime analyses. A spatial pattern of crimes is a constantly changing and ongoing process. However, prior research on spatial crime analysis has focused primarily on identifying fixed spatial patterns, and has neglected temporal aspects. As a result, the literature has difficulty in explaining the formation and development of such spatial crime patterns. This study investigates both spatial and temporal aspects of crime occurrences, particularly on the space-time diffusion process by using the temporal extensions of local spatial autocorrelation measures. In addition, space-time diffusion simulation is applied based on Hagerstrand's diffusion modeling. Consequently, diffusion modeling and the simulation (1) enables further understanding of the mechanism of how crime patterns are formed, (2) provides an in depth resource for policy makers and police to reduce crimes by considering a temporal dimension of crime, (3) and is readily applicable to other fields such as the epidemiology of disease.

INTRODUCTION

The importance of space has recently been recognized in social science as a key dimension in crime analyses (Brantingham & Brantingham, 1981). Research on the spatial aspect of crime, such as crime hotspot analyses, has been of great interest and has been applied to crime mapping. The major goals of crime hotspot analyses are summarized as follows. First, crime concentrations provide a starting point for understanding the underlying sociological processes, which contribute to the formation of such concentrations (Vigne & Groff, 2001). Second, the identification of more vulnerable areas enables effective allocation of police resources by enforcing more efficient surveillance strategies (Craglia, Haining, & Signoretta, 2001; Reiss & Roth, 1993). Third, the identified hot spots and corresponding sociological explanations are applicable to generating new policies or law enforcement strategies to prevent crime during the planning stages (Sampson, & Groves, 1989; Skogan, 1986).

Spatial crime patterns are formed over time through continuous changes. As Abler, Adams, and Gould (1971) denote, space and time are fundamental dimensions of human existence and enable us to understand people's use of place over time. Therefore, investigating both spatial and temporal aspects of crimes is crucial in understanding spatial crime patterns. However, despite the developments in spatial crime analysis, many crime studies have problems in explaining the formation and development of spatial crime patterns. Instead, the studies merely find spatial patterns of crime without considering temporal aspects. As a result, the studies lack proper explanations, particularly regarding the causes and underlying mechanisms of crime patterns. Uncovering these causes and underlying mechanisms is the most crucial factor in ultimately controlling crime.

While there are various types of space-time patterns in crime occurrences, this study focuses on . is a result of complex adaptive processes that are human reactions to phenomena, representing space-time interaction among human beings (Hagerstrand, 1967). Additionally, the diffusion enables us to understand space as a condition, which determines the level of speed in the diffusion process when analyzed through time (Nijkamp & Reggiani, 1996). Therefore, the crime diffusion process can be analyzed by carefully studying interactions between space and time and enables us to understand the formation and development of spatial crime patterns.

There are several types of depending on how physical or mental objects spread through population over space and time (Morrill, Gaile, & Thrall, 1988). Contagious diffusion, a form of expansion diffusion, indicates a spread from nearby distance to further distance. Hierarchical diffusion, another form of expansion diffusion, denotes spreads by "trickling down" from larger to smaller adopting units. In hierarchical diffusion, distance is not important. Inclusive of contagious and hierarchical diffusion, more agents characterize expansion diffusion after the diffusion process. Relocation diffusion refers to change of agent location. Thus, the agent of diffusion is lost in the source location after the relocation diffusion process. In addition, the number of agents is constant after relocation diffusion. Usually, diffusion occurs in a mixed form of several types. In crime analyses, expansion diffusion, particularly contagious diffusion, has been great interest to the field because spatial proximity is considered as a crucial factor in a crime diffusion process (Messner, Anselin, Baller, Hawkins, Deane, & Tolnay, 1999; Sampson & Morenoff, 2004).

Based on conceptual backgrounds of crime diffusion process (Hollinger, Offer, & Ostrov, 1987; Kellerman, 1966), there has been a recent growth in literature on the crime diffusion process and its identification (Baller, Anselin, Messner, Deane, & Hawkins, 2001; Cohen, & Tita, 1999a, 1999b; Cork, 1999; Craglia, Haining, & Signoretta, 2001; Messner et al., 1999; Sampson, & Morenoff, 2004; Smith, Frazee, & Davison, 2000; Tita & Cohen, 2004). Despite the growing interest, many crime diffusion studies exhibit critical limitations because the studies isolate the underlying mechanism of the diffusion process by using only cross-sectional data without temporal information in the diffusion analyses (Cohen & Tita, 1999a). Therefore, the analyses only consider spatial crime patterns and infer diffusion process from the pattern. However, the diffusion process is presented by changes in spatial patterns over time, which can only be accounted by analyzing both spatial and temporal information simultaneously.

This study overcomes the limitations of spatial crime analysis by measuring changes of spatial crime pattern over time. To achieve this goal, the study provides new methods which measure local spatial autocorrelation over multiple periods. Literature has mentioned the advantages of using local spatial autocorrelation measures in investigating spatial phenomena. The local measures are able to (1) identify the existence of spatial clusters and hotspots; (2) assess the spatial heterogeneity among observations; and (3) recognize distances beyond significant associations (Anselin, 1995; Boots, & Tiefelsdorf, 2000; Getis & Ord, 1996). Considering the capabilities of local measures, the extension from spatial autocorrelation to space-time autocorrelation measures would enable us to analyze (1) the mechanism and process of crime hotspot formation, which are diffused from nearby areas to surrounding areas over time; (2) significant sociodemographic factors regarding of crime occurrences; and (3) patterns of crime in urban areas such as the distance range of a diffusion caused by sociodemographic factors.

For the implementation of the space-time autocorrelation measures, this study simulates an expansion diffusion process, which was originally devised by Hagerstrand (1967) for an innovation diffusion simulation. In the process, hexagon-based areal transformation is applied for Ohio counties. For simplicity in calculation, the diffusion process is simulated by population sizes and connectivity among the counties.

FROM LOCAL SPATIAL STATISTICS TO SPACE-TIME DIFFUSION ANALYSES IN CRIME STUDIES

Application of Local Spatial Statistics to Crime Analyses

Local measures of spatial autocorrelation have been applied widely to crime analyses with the purpose of finding crime hotspots (Craglia, Haining, & Wiles, 2000; Messner et al., 1999; Ratcliffe, & McCullagh, 1999). A feature of the local statistics which identifies local spatial clusters around individual locations (Anselin, & Florax, 1995; Getis, & Ord, 1996) enabled the wide application of the local statistics to crime analyses. In particular, Hanson and Wieczorek (2002) compare local clusters of alcohol mortality in New York using local Moran's I_i and Kulldorff's spatial scan statistics. Baller et al. (2001) present the clustering of homicides in county level using Local Moran's I_i and Moran scatterplot. Mencken and Barnett (1999), and Ceccato, Haining, and Signoretta (2002) applied Getis-Ord G_i statistics to find local clustering.

Even though many spatial crime studies identify crime clusters using local statistics, they overlook a time aspect. Spatial crime patterns are the results of a continuously changing spatial process over time rather than an instantly appeared fixed patterns. Consequently, reliable crime analyses should consider changes of spatial patterns over time. It should be noted that both spatial and temporal aspects are important elements in crime analyses.

Background of Space-Time Modeling and Diffusion Process

Many studies noted the importance of space-time modeling. In particular, Florax and van der Vlist (2003) indicate space-time modeling as a promising area of future research, emphasizing the significance of incorporating spatial, temporal, and space-time correlation. Among various types of space-time human activities, literature in geography has focused on a diffusion process (Berry, 1972; Cliff, Haggett, Ord, & Versey, 1981; Hagerstrand, 1967; Haggett, Cliff, & Frey, 1977), which is defined by Morrill et al. (1988) as "the process by which behavior or characteristics of the landscape change as a result of what happens elsewhere earlier."

Given the notion that violence spreads through a diffusion process (Cohen & Tita, 1999a; Cork, 1999; Messner et al., 1999), spatial crime patterns should reflect the underlying diffusion process

(Baller, Anselin, Messner, Deane, & Hawkins, 2001).

Spatial diffusion emphasizes the features of spatial movements and changes over time. Since the pioneering work of Hagerstrand (1967), which first estimated the stochastic variant of diffusion with probabilities of contacts by distance,[1] diffusion models have presented three major components in the process (Morrill, Gaile, & Thrall, 1988). The three components indicate basic features of diffusion modeling: (1) the logistic relationship is the most commonly observed acceptance pattern in innovation diffusion. As Nijkamp and Reggiani (1996) and Rogers (1993) noted, the logistic function is, in general, "well suitable for representing different speeds of diffusion and irregularities according to different forms of S-shaped time distribution functions"[2]. (2) In most elementary models, the estimated time or intensity of the adoption process is modeled by a function of adoption potential. The adoption potential is usually estimated by spatial interaction models as applied in many studies (Berry, 1972; Cliff & Ord, 1975; Haining, 1983; Nijkamp & Reggiani, 1996; Pederson, 1970; Webber, 1972). (3) There is a clear dependency of the pattern that characterizes the adoption of the phenomena over time.

Space-Time Diffusion Analyses in Crime Study

Crimes are commonly accompanied by the degradation of socioeconomic level in a neighborhood and the corresponding social disorganization (Bursik, 1988; Sampson & Groves, 1989; Shaw & McKay, 1942; Smith, Frazee, & Davison, 2000). Because impoverished areas are usually adjacent to one another, diffusion studies focus on the contagious or expansion diffusion process. For example, crime occurrences would easily diffuse into the areas with low socioeconomic indices,[3] among neighbors who live close to crime hot spot. Loftin (1986) proposes that assaultive violence can be usefully regarded as "analogous to disease," capable of "contagious transmission." As information about violent events is transmitted through social networks and other media of communication, the probability of subsequent violence is likely to increase leading to a definite spatial pattern of violence.

Recently, there are many studies focusing on identifying diffusion in crime analysis (Baller, Anselin, Messner, Deane, & Hawkins, 2001; Cohen & Tita, 1999a, 1999b; Cork, 1999; Messner & Anselin, 2004; Messner et al., 1999; Sampson & Morenoff, 2004; Smith, Frazee, & Davison, 2000; Tita & Cohen, 2004). In growing literature on crime diffusion, studies have examined the diffusion of motor vehicle theft (Rice & Smith, 2002), robbery (Smith, Frazee, & Davison, 2000), drug use (Frischer, Anderson, Hickman, & Heatlie, 2002), and other serious street crimes. In particular, a spatial interdependence of crimes has been widely explored in recent years (Brown, 1982; Craglia, Haining, & Signoretta, 2001; Deane, Beck, & Tolnay, 1998; Land & Deane, 1992; Mencken & Barnett, 1999). The spatial interdependence assumes diffusion as a cause of the interdependence. As Messner et al. (1999) denote, spatial interdependence is "particularly relevant to the provocative claim that violence spreads through a diffusion process". In this context, the diffusion represents the mechanism of the formation of spatial and temporal interdependence in crime occurrences (Tita & Cohen, 2004).

Space-Time Crime Patterns and Characteristics of Crime Analyses

In diffusion processes, crime occurrences have unique features compared to other social phenomena. First, crime occurrences can reflect the degradation process of a neighborhood either directly or indirectly, which results in lack of social control, a function of the regulatory capacity of the community (Sampson, 1986). Second, crime occurrences are easily diffused into geographically adjacent neighborhoods with low socioeconomic indices because a socioeconomic level of a neighborhood plays a crucial role in the crime occurrences. Considering that neighborhood socioeconomic indices tend to be similar in neighboring areas, the corresponding crime diffusion is determined by a similarity in socioeconomic status and proximity in space and time distances. Third, the crime diffusion process has high levels of resistance from various parts of a society, particularly residents of the neighborhoods. Combined with more intensive police patrol and cooperation of neighborhood members, the resistance frequently forms effective barriers to the diffusion process. Given that innovation diffusion is characterized by an adopter's willingness to a new phenomenon, resistance indicates that crime follows a contagious or an expansion diffusion process rather than an innovation diffusion process.

Because of the unique characteristics of the crime diffusion process, most current measures are not appropriate for analyzing crime diffusion process. As a result, many crime studies tend to focus on fixed spatial patterns of crime distribution and infer certain diffusion processes based on a non-random and spatially dependent crime distribution (Baller, Anselin, Messner, Deane, & Hawkins, 2001; Messner et al., 1999). In application, several local spatial autocorrelation measures are widely used to measure spatial pattern of crime incidents (Craglia, Haining, & Signoretta, 2001; Sampson & Morenoff, 2004; Smith, Frazee, & Davison, 2000). Inferring diffusion processes with local spatial measures, Messner et al. (1999) indicated, "if spatial randomness is not present, then there may be a diffusion process at work". However, many studies on crime diffusion have limitations because they do not consider temporal dimensions in the diffusion process. For instance, estimating process only based on local spatial autocorrelation of fixed cross-sectional data would be, at best, probable guesses, lacking thorough investigation of space-time dimension. Consequently, the ignorance of temporal pattern cannot provide reliable diffusion analyses because, as Tita and Cohen (2004) indicate, cross-sectional studies cannot account for the underlying mechanisms that drive certain space-time distribution.

Based on the limitation of current measure in spatial crime diffusion process, this study provides an extended version of local spatial autocorrelation measures: space-time local Moran's I_i and space-time local Getis-Ord G_i in the next section. These newly extended measures provide more thorough and systematic tools for measuring crime diffusion by adding a temporal dimension to conventional spatial autocorrelation measures.

SPACE-TIME DIFFUSION MEASURE BY COMBINING TIME DIMENSION WITH SPATIAL AUTOCORRELATION MEASURES

Space-Time Local Moran's $I_{i,t}$

The space-time autocorrelation measure extends local spatial autocorrelation statistics by including a time dimension. Particularly for the extension of local Moran's I_i statistic, which is refined to as *space-time local Moran's* $I_{i,t}$, a covariance of attributes between one area and neighboring areas is calculated by considering not only spatially proximate values but also temporally proximate values. In Figure 1, conceptual differences between local Moran's I_i and space-time local Moran's $I_{i,t}$ are presented. Whereas local Moran's I_i measure is restricted to spatially proximate values, *space-time local Moran's* $I_{i,t}$ account for temporally proximate values together with nearby spatial values.

The equation form of space-time local Moran's $I_{i,t2}$ is defined as below:

$$I_{i,t2}=\frac{z_{i,t2}}{m_{2,t2}}\sum_j\left(\frac{1}{2}W_{ij,t1}z_{j,t1}+\frac{1}{2}W_{ij,t2}z_{j,t2}\right) \quad j\neq i \tag{1}$$

Figure 1. Conceptual framework of space-time autocorrelation

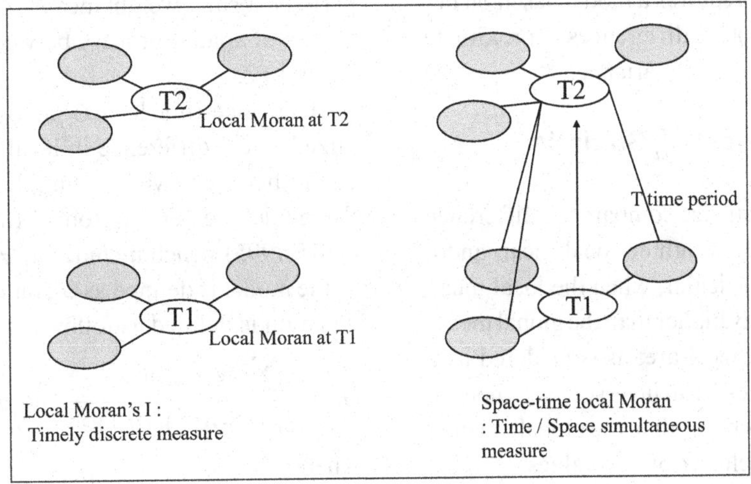

where:

$z_{i,t1} = x_{i,t1} - \bar{x}_{t1}$

$z_{i,t2} = x_{i,t2} - \bar{x}_{t2}$

$\bar{x}_{t1} = \dfrac{\sum_i z_{i,t1}}{n}$

$\bar{x}_{t2} = \dfrac{\sum_i z_{i,t2}}{n}$

$m_{2,t2} = \dfrac{\sum_i z_{i,t2}^2}{n}$ (the second moment of variable at time $t2$)

In the equation (1), $W_{ij,t1}$ and $W_{ij,t2}$ are standardized spatial weight matrix between area i and j for time $t1$ and $t2$. $W_{ij,t1}$ and $W_{ij,t2}$ are the same because spatial connectivity is fixed over time. For the 2 periods applied in equation (1), an identically proportional weight (1/2) is used, assuming that values in each period have the same effect on the measure. Even though only 2 periods are considered in equation (1), more periods can be applied to the equation by using different weights for temporal value. Given that the weight specifies the effects of previous observations in the covariance measure, various weight values can be used based on the features of the dataset or the purpose of analyses. Considering that local Moran's I_i presents covariance among observations, *space-time local Moran's* $I_{i,t}$ measures similarity among spatially and temporally proximate values. Consequently, large values imply high similarity in nearby values among two periods, indicating space-time clusters of a phenomenon. The variance of $I_{i,t2}$ and its generation process are presented in the appendix.

While the covariance type measures are effective in measuring non-random space-time distribution of a phenomenon such as space-time clustering, they may not be appropriate for space-time diffusion measures.[4] Space-time diffusion measures are more concerned with deviations among proximate values, such as how values change in proximate space and time. From this perspective, space-time local Moran's I has minor problems as a space-time diffusion measure. First, the covariance measure cannot differentiate high covariance between low values and high values[5] because both result in high autocorrelation values. Second, including time dimension, high covariance values can be results of either assimilation in space-time proximate values or no change among the values. Based on this limitation, a space-time diffusion measure requires a model based on deviation that can capture differences in proximate space-time rather than covariance.

Space-Time Local $G^*_{i,t}$ Statistic

Local G_i and G^*_i statistics compare the difference between a spatially weighted local mean and a global mean. In particular, when the local mean value is significantly higher than the global mean, the corresponding local area is considered as a cluster of high values. In an inverse case, when the local mean value is lower than the global mean, it is considered as a cluster of low values.

When two spatially weighted local means of different periods are compared, local changes in two periods can be measured because (1) changes in an area value and its spatially proximate values are measured in locally weighted means and (2) the difference in local mean values indicates spatial process among linked values for the period as a result of a diffusion process. Figure 2 presents a simplified spatial process and a change of the values. As a result of the spatial process (expansion diffusion), values of neighboring areas are affected from a source area, and the resulting locally weighted mean values in T2 are increased. Therefore, comparing the difference between two periods' locally weight mean values can provide results of spatial process between two periods: T1 and T2.

The space-time local $G^*_{i,t}$ statistic is conceptualized as the difference in local weighted mean values between two (or multiple) periods. Since this model is extended from $G^*_i(d)$ model (Ord & Getis, 1995) which includes $w_{ii} \neq 0$, the notation of the model is defined as $G^*_{i,t}$ rather than $G_{i,t}$. The equation is defined as follow:

$$G^*_{i,t} = \frac{\sum_j w_{ij}x_{j,t2} - w_{ij}x_{j,t1}}{s\{(nS^*_{1i} - W^{*2}_i)/(n-1)\}^{1/2}}, \quad all\ j \qquad (2)$$

where

$$s = \left(\frac{\sum_j (x_{j,t2} - x_{j,t1})^2}{n} \right)^{1/2}$$

$$W^*_i = \sum_j W_{ij} \quad (all\ j)$$

$$S^*_{1i} = \sum_j w^2_{ij} \quad (all\ j)$$

The applied n by n spatial weight matrix, **W**, is not standardized, and is not necessarily 0 or 1 binary value. The denominator in equation (2) indicates deviations for each locally linked value for two periods, s, and row sum deviations of weight

Figure 2. Conceptual framework of space-time local $G^*_{i,t}$ statistic

T1:

0	0	0
0	2	0
0	0	0

T2:

0	1	0
1	2	1
0	0	0

T1 → T2

Expansion diffusion

Local Mean: 2/9

Local Mean: 5/9

T2 – T1 = 5/9 - 2/9 = 3/9

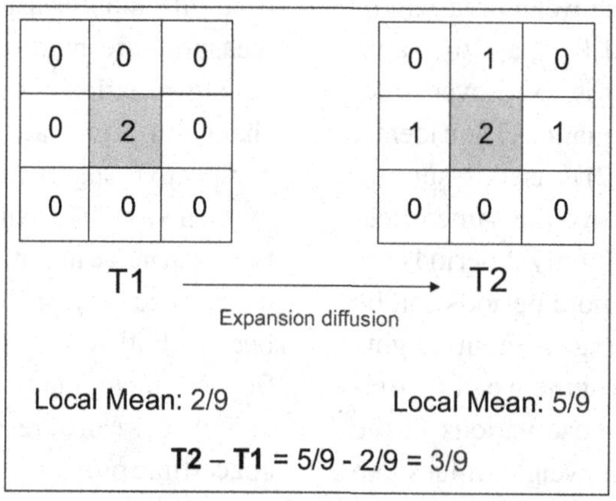

matrix, **W**. Since the weight matrix structure is identical to the original $G_i^*(d)$ equation, the weight deviation applied is based upon Ord and Getis (1995). A large positive value of $G_{i,t2}^*$ indicates a large increase in *i* and neighboring values of *t2* and a large negative value indicates a decrease in *i* and neighboring values of *t2*. Therefore, a large positive $G_{i,t2}^*$ value implies space-time diffusion process in the dataset.

The $G_{i,t}^*$ can be extended to multiple period dataset by including the average value of several past periods, (see equation (3)) α the number of periods in the data.

There are several different features of the two space-time local autocorrelation measures, $G_{i,t}^*$ and $G_{i,t+a}^*$, when compared to the space-time local Moran's $I_{i,t}$ test. While space-time local Moran's $I_{i,t}$ test is based on covariance, the space-time $G_{i,t}^*$ test is based on deviations. Given the deviation-based feature, the space-time $G_{i,t}^*$ measure overcomes the limitation of the Space-time local Moran's $I_{i,t}$ test. Therefore, the space-time $G_{i,t}^*$ test is a more appropriate measure for spatial crime diffusion process.

SIMULATION AND RESULT

Simulation

The diffusion simulation is implemented under strictly controlled settings to exclude unconsidered effects in the process. Many factors may affect an expansion diffusion process, such as geographical distances, accessibilities by transportation networks, and migrations of population. Connectivity and population sizes, however, are considered as the two major components in the simulation. Among several simulation approaches, this study applied Hagerstand's diffusion simulation (1967) to test the performance of space-time local $G_{i,t}^*$ statistics. Focusing only on connectivity and population size, the applied simulation is appropriate for a macro-scale analysis, which the space-time measures are designed for.

For a more specified diffusion simulation in micro-scale analyses, which accounts for various space-time crime agents, cellular automaton (CA) would be an appropriate relevant approach. CA has been applied to space-time simulations in many fields, such as wildfire propagation (Clarke, Brass, & Riggan, 1994), urban evolution (Batty, Xie, & Sun, 1999), and land use changes (White & Engelen, 1993). In particular, a micro-scale space-time crime simulation by Liu, Wang, Eck, and Liang (2005) models crime occurrences based on routine activity theory (Cohen & Felson, 1979). The research specifies three crime factors of the theory (offenders, targets, and crime places) as agents in CA and simulates space-time crime occurrences.

For the simulation in the study, the target areas of diffusion are determined by connectivity to the source area, and the level of diffusion is determined by population size of the target areas. For a random simulation, where every study area has equal chance to be a recipient based on connectivity, a Monte Carlo simulation is applied.

The Monte Carlo diffusion simulation is composed of several steps. First, for the spatial data configuration, Ohio county boundaries are applied. Each county in the data has different connectivity in the number of neighboring counties. The different connectivity between counties

Equation 3.

$$G_{i,t+a}^* = \frac{\sum_j w_{ij} x_{j,\alpha} - \frac{1}{\alpha-1}\sum_{t=1}^{\alpha-1}\sum_j w_{ij} x_{j,t}}{\{(x_{i,\alpha} - \tilde{x}_{i,\alpha}) \text{i} \frac{1}{\alpha-1}\sum_{t=1}^{\alpha-1}(x_{i,t} - \tilde{x}_{i,t}) / \sum_j w_{ij}\}^{1/2} \{(nS_{1i}^* - W_i^{*2})/(n-1)\}^{1/2}}$$

might cause a biased diffusion process in the random simulation because a county with higher connectivity is more likely to be affected in the diffusion process. To control diffusion process based on different connectivity, shapes of counties are transformed into hexagons. The use of a hexagon shape is recommended for specification of planar data (Griffith, 1996). The resulting hexagonal areas are connected to 6 neighboring areas with identical connectivity. Given the goal of random simulation, there's no obligation to use Ohio counties for the simulation. Any set of areal units with population information can be applied to the diffusion simulation. Figure 3 shows the areal configuration of counties in the data and their hexagon transformation.

Second, direction of diffusion is randomly decided that one out of six neighboring counties from a source is randomly selected among the counties. Initially, five randomly chosen counties are set as the sources of diffusion, and one of six neighboring areas from each source is selected as the adoption area. Once an area is chosen for adoption, it becomes an additional source area for the next step. Therefore, as the diffusion process continues, the number of source areas increases exponentially. The number of initial source areas (five randomly chosen counties) for the diffusion is an arbitrary choice. Given that the number of source areas and the total number of area units determine the diffusion pace, the five initial source areas are considered appropriate under 88 area units to have good simulation results five to six time steps later.

Third, the level of diffusion is determined by the size of population for each county. Thus, once an area is selected in the diffusion process, the amount of diffusion is proportional to the area's population. As a result, counties with a relatively large population such as Franklin (Columbus), Cuyahoga (Cleveland), and Hamilton (Cincinnati) counties have a strong effect in the diffusion process when they are selected as adoption areas.

Figure 4 shows the result of diffusion simulation for five periods after the initial selection of five random counties: Butler, Logan, Union, Portage, and Gallia. As conditioned, the diffusion process follows spatially neighboring area units forming expansion diffusion. The expansion condition in the diffusion process results in high values around the initial source areas in latter periods. Between T3 and T5 periods, the western center and southwestern corner regions in the study area have a major increase in crime incidents. Between periods T5 and T6, additional central and south-central areas have experienced increases in crime incidents.

Figure 3. Areal shape transformation of Ohio counties

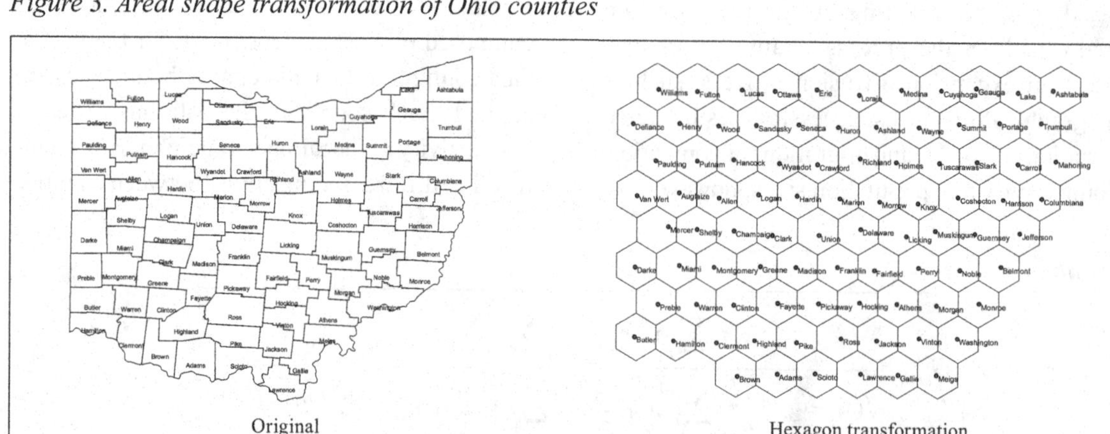

Figure 4. Result of diffusion simulation for Ohio counties

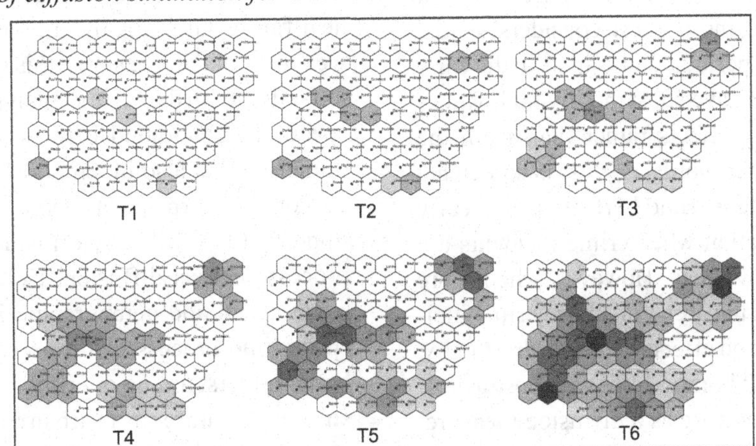

Figure 5. $G^*_{i,t}$ results for spatial expansion diffusion patterns

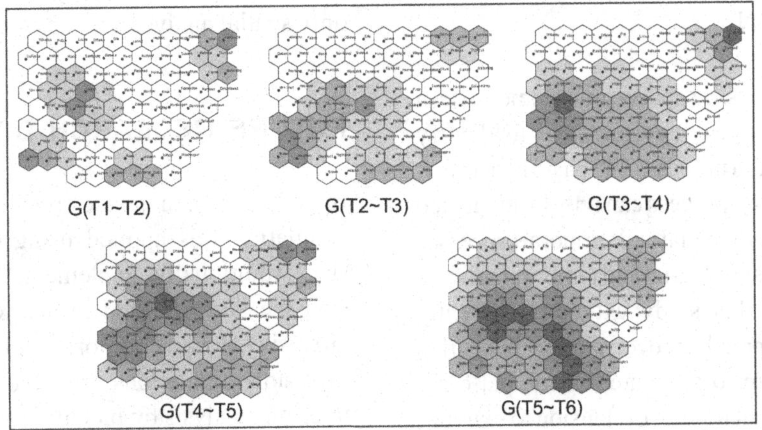

Results

Though the space-time local Moran's $I_{i,t}$ and the space-time $G^*_{i,t}$ are introduced in the previous section, the space-time $G^*_{i,t}$ is applied to test crime simulation because of its appropriateness for the expansion diffusion process. Figure 5 presents the result of $G^*_{i,t}$ test applied to the simulated spatial expansion diffusion process. Each $G^*_{i,t}$ pattern map presents $G^*_{i,t}$ values for space-time patterns between two periods. High $G^*_{i,t}$ values, indicated by the dark areas in Figure 5, imply substantial increase in crime incidents within and surrounding areas of the counties between two periods. Comparing simulation (Figure 4) and $G^*_{i,t}$ value (Figure 5) patterns, the dark counties in Figure 4 merely indicate high crime incidents, while the dark counties in Figure 5 depict level of changes in the crime incidents under consideration of spatial proximity.

Though simulation and the corresponding $G^*_{i,t}$ value provide an appropriate space-time crime pattern analysis result, $G^*_{i,t}$ test exposes a minor limitation. Given the $G^*_{i,t}$ test considers spatial proximity in two periods, some areas in the early periods appear to have substantially high values from neighboring effects rather than from the diffusion[6]. In other words, $G^*_{i,t}$ test is somewhat vulnerable to neighborhood effects in the early periods of simulation when crime incidents are observed in a few areas. However, when more than one-third of the area units have crime incidents, neighborhood effects decrease drastically. Although the neighborhood effects expose a limitation in the $G^*_{i,t}$ statistic as a diffusion measure, general application of crime data, which rarely have zero crime incidents in individual areas, would diminish this problem.

CONCLUSION

This chapter discussed space-time crime pattern analysis and introduced new measures to identify the crime diffusion process. The basic idea is that the crime diffusion process can only be identified by considering both spatial and temporal processes together. To measure spatial and temporal process simultaneously, this study extended currently existing local spatial autocorrelation measures and applied them to simulated crime patterns. By incorporating temporal dimension to existing spatial dimension, the newly devised measures are appropriate to estimate the diffusion process.

From the perspective of space-time crime analysis, the diffusion measures have limitations. Given that the measures only identify crime diffusion, the measures do not take account for related local (neighborhood) characteristics such as urban structural features, socioeconomic backgrounds, and human capital. Based on this limitation, the diffusion measures do not provide specific descriptions of how crimes occur and their structural backgrounds on micro-scale levels. Furthermore, the lack of local characteristics, which commonly functions as catalysts for crime occurrences, disables crime predictions in the near future. Granting the limitations as intrinsic weakness of the measures, this study is expected to facilitate further crime analyses that consider specific neighborhood features, not only in spatial dimension but also in temporal dimension.

For the purpose of crime prevention, it is important to provide information of space-time process such as diffusion. Combined with relevant social and demographic information, the space-time process of crime can contribute to better understanding of crime patterns and their structural features in an urban environment. This study may not significantly contribute to crime control itself. However, when combined with other sociodemographic analyses, this study will provide superior knowledge to administrative policymakers in reducing crimes compared to only spatial analyses.

FUTURE RESEARCH DIRECTIONS

In this study, a space-time crime diffusion simulation was applied using only population size. Additionally, implementation of the diffusion measure resulted in an explorative crime analysis. However, more sophisticated crime diffusion simulations are needed to contribute to crime analysis by including other appropriate demographic attributes. For application, diffusion measures combined with ecological crime analysis using various sociodemographic variables would extend ranges of space-time crime analyses and provide a better understanding of crime occurrences. In particular, information about more localized neighborhood features would contribute to space-time crime analyses on a micro-scale. Also, diffusion simulation can be extended by incorporating appropriate individual agents for neighborhoods.

In spite of the emphasis on temporal aspects in crime analyses, this study lacks the capability to predict future crime occurrences. Given that the diffusion process reflects space-time trends in crime occurrences, it is expected that future research on crime predictions that consider diffusion processes in the past will make more reliable predictions.

REFERENCES

Abler, R., Adams, J. S., & Gould, P. (1971). *Spatial organization: The geographers' view of the world.* Englewood Cliffs, New Jersey: Prentice-Hall.

Anselin, L. (1995). Local indicators of spatial association -LISA. *Geographical Analysis, 27*(2), 93-115.

Anselin, L., & Florax, R. (1995). Small sample properties of tests for spatial dependence in regression models: Some further results. *New directions in spatial econometrics* (pp. 21-74). Berlin: Springer-Verlag.

Baller, R. D., Anselin, L., Messner, S. F., Deane, G., & Hawkins, D. F. (2001). Structural covariates of U.S. county homicide rates: Incorporating spatial effects. *Criminology, 39*(3), 561-590.

Batty, M., Xie, Y., & Sun, Y. (1999). Modeling urban dynamics through GIS-based cellular automata. *Computers, Environment and Urban Systems, 23*, 205-233.

Berry, B. J. L. (1972). Hierarchical diffusion: The basis of developmental filtering and spread in a system of growth centers. In N. Hansen (Ed.), *Growth centers in regional economic development.* New York: Free Press.

Boots, B. N., & Tiefelsdorf, M. (2000). Global and local spatial autocorrelation in bounded regular tessellations. *Journal of Geographical Systems, 2*, 319-348.

Brantingham, P. J., & Brantingham, P. L. (1981). *Environmental criminology.* Beverly Hills, CA: Sage Publications.

Brown, M. A. (1982). Modelling the spatial distribution of suburban crime. *Economic Geography, 58*(3), 247-261.

Bursik, R. (1988). Social disorganization and theories of crime and delinquency: Problems and prospects. *Criminology, 26*, 519-551.

Ceccato, V., Haining, R., & Signoretta, P. (2002). Exploring offence statistics in Stockholm city using spatial analysis tools. *Annals of the Association of American Geographers, 92*(1), 29-51.

Clarke, K. C., Brass, J. A., & Riggan, P. J. (1994). A cellular automata model of wildfire propagation and extinction. *Photogrammetric Engineering & Remote Sensing, 60*, 1355-1367.

Cliff, A. D., Haggett, P., Ord, J. K., & Versey, G. R. (1981). *: An historical geography of epidemics in an island community.* Cambridge: Cambridge University Press.

Cliff, A. D., & Ord, J. K. (1975). Space time modelling with an application to regional forecasting. *Transaction of the Institute of British Geographers, 64*, 119-128.

Cohen, J., & Tita, G. (1999a). Diffusion in homicide: Exploring a general method for detecting processes. *Journal of Quantitative Criminology, 15*(4), 451-493.

Cohen, J., & Tita, G. (1999b). Editors' introduction. *Journal of Quantitative Criminology, 15*(4), 373-378.

Cohen, L. E., & Felson, M. (1979). Social change and crime rate trends: A routine activity approach. *American Sociological Review, 44*, 588-608.

Cork, D. (1999). Examining space-time interaction in city-level homicide data: Crack markets and the diffusion of guns among youth. *Journal of Quantitative Criminology, 15*(4), 379-406.

Craglia, M., Haining, R., & Signoretta, P. (2001). Modelling high-intensity crime areas in english cities. *Urban Studies, 38*(11), 1921-1941.

Craglia, M., Haining, R., & Wiles, P. (2000). A comparative evaluation of approaches to urban crime pattern analysis. *Urban Studies, 37*(4), 711-729.

Deane, G., Beck, E. M., & Tolnay, S. E. (1998). Incorporating space into social histories: How spatial processes operate and how we observe them. *International Review of Social history, 43*, 57-80.

Florax, R., & Vlist, A. V. D. (2003). Spatial econometric data analysis: Moving beyond traditional models. *International Regional Science Review, 26*(3), 223-243.

Frischer, M., Anderson, S., Hickman, M., & Heatlie, H. (2002). Diffusion of drug misuse in Scotland: Findings from the 1993 and 1996 Scottish crime surveys. *Addiction Research & Theory, 10*(1), 83-95.

Getis, A., & Ord, J. K. (1996). Local spatial statistics: and overview. In P. Longley & M. Batty (Eds.), *Spatial analysis: Modelling in a GIS environment* (pp. 261-277). Cambridge: Geoinformation International.

Griffith, D. A. (1996). Some guidelines for specifying the geographic weights matrix contained in spatial statistical models. In S. L. Arlinghaus (Ed.), *Practical handbook of spatial statistics.* Boca Raton: CRC.

Hagerstrand, T. (1967). *Innovation diffusion as a spatial process.* Chicago: University of Chicago Press.

Haggett, P., Cliff, A. D., & Frey, A. (1977). *Locational analysis in human geography.* London: Edard Arnold.

Haining, R. (1983). Spatial and spatial-temporal interaction models and the analysis of patterns of diffusion. *Transactions (Institute of British Geographers), 8*, 158-186.

Hanson, C. E., & Wieczorek, W. F. (2002). Alcohol mortality: A comparison of spatial clustering methods. *Social Science & Medicine, 55*, 791-802.

Hollinger, P. C., Offer, D., & Ostrov, E. (1987). An epidemiologic study of violent death, population changes, and the potential for prediction. *American Journal of Psychiatry, 144*, 215-219.

Kellerman, A. (1966). *Understanding and preventing violence: A public health perspective.* Washington: U.S. Government Printing Offices.

Land, K. C., & Deane, G. (1992). On the large-sample estimation of regression models with spatial effects terms: A two-stage least squares approach. *Sociological Methodology, 22*, 221-248.

Liu, L., Wang, X., Eck, J., & Liang, J. (2005). Simulating crime events and crime patterns. In F. Wang (Ed.), *Geographic information systems and crime analysis* (pp. 197-213). Reading: Idea Publishing.

Loftin, C. (1986). Assaultive violence as a contagious social process. *Bulletin of the New York Academy of Medicine, 62*, 550-555.

Mencken, F. C., & Barnett, C. (1999). Murder, nonnegligent manslaughter, and spatial autocorrelation in mid-south counties. *Journal of Quantitative Criminology, 15*(4), 407-422.

Messner, S. F., & Anselin, L. (2004). Spatial analyses of homicide with areal data. In M. F. Goodchild & D. G. Janelle (Eds.), *Best practices in spatially integrated social science* (pp. 127-144). New York: Oxford University Press.

Messner, S. F., Anselin, L., Baller, R. D., Hawkins, D. F., Deane, G., & Tolnay, S. E. (1999). The spatial patterning of county homicide rates: An application of exploratory spatial data analysis. *Journal of Quantitative Criminology, 15*(4), 423-450.

Morrill, R., Gaile, G. L., & Thrall, G. I. (1988). (Vol. 10). Beverly Hills, CA: Sage.

Nijkamp, P., & Reggiani, A. (1996). Space-time synergetics in innovation diffusion: A nested network simulation approach. *Geographical Analysis, 28*, 18-37.

Ord, J. K., & Getis, A. (1995). Local spatial autocorrelation statistics: Distributional issues and an application. *Geographical Analysis, 27*(4), 286-306.

Pederson, P. (1970). Innovation diffusion within and between national urban systems. *Geographical Analysis, 2*, 203-254.

Ratcliffe, J. H., & McCullagh, M. J. (1999). Hotbeds of crime and the search for spatial accuracy. *Journal of Geographical Systems,* 1, 385-398.

Reiss, A. J., & Roth, J. (1993). *Understanding and preventing violence* (Vol. 1). Washington, D.C.: National Academy Press.

Rice, K., & Smith, W. (2002). Socioecological models of automotive theft: Integrating routine activity and social disorganization approaches. *The Journal of Research in Crime and Delinquency, 39*(3), 304-336.

Rogers, E. M. (1993). The diffusion of innovation model. In I. Masser & H. J. Onsrud (Eds.), *Diffusion and use of geographic information technologies* (pp. 9-24). Dordrecht: Kluwer.

Sampson, R. J. (1986). Crime in cities: The effects of formal and informal social control. In A. J. Reiss & M. Tonry (Eds.), *Communities and crime.* Chicago: University of Chicago Press.

Sampson, R. J., & Groves, W. B. (1989). Community structure and crime: Testing social-disorganization theory. *American Journal of Sociology, 94*(4).

Sampson, R. J., & Morenoff, J. D. (2004). Spatial (dis)advantage and homicide in chicago neighborhoods. In M. F. Goodchild & D. G. Janelle (Eds.), *Spatially integrated social science.* New York: Oxford University Press Inc.

Shaw, C. R., & McKay, H. D. (1942). *Juvenile delinquency and urban areas, a study of rates of delinquents in relation to differential characteristics of local communities in American cities.* Chicago: The University of Chicago Press.

Skogan, W. (1986). Fear of crime and neighborhood change. In J. Albert, J. Reiss, & M. Tonry (Eds.), *Communities and crime* (Vol. 8, pp. 216). Chicago: University of Chicago Press.

Smith, W. R., Frazee, S. G., & Davison, E. L. (2000). Furthering the integration of routine activity and social disorganization theories: Small units of analysis and the study of street robbery as a diffusion process. *Criminology, 38*(2), 489-523.

Tita, G., & Cohen, J. (2004). Measuring of shots fired activity across city neighborhoods. In M. F. Goodchild, & D. G. Janelle (Eds.), *Spatially integrated social science* (pp. 171-204). New York: Oxford.

Vigne, N. G. L., & Groff, E. R. (2001). The evolution of crime mapping in the United States: from the descriptive to the analytic. In A. Hirschfield, & K. Bowers (Eds.), *Mapping and analysing crime data.* New York: Taylor & Francis.

Webber, M. (1972). *The impact of uncertainty on location.* Cambridge: MIT Press.

White, R., & Engelen, G. (1993). Cellular automata and fractal urban form: a cellular modelling approach to the evolution of urban land-use patterns. *Environment and Planning A, 25*, 1175-1199.

ADDITIONAL READING

Anselin, L., Cohen, J., Cook, D., Corr, W. L., & Tita, G. (Eds.). (2000). *Spatial analysis of crime* (Vol. 4).

Casetti, E., & Semple, R. K. (1969). Concerning the testing of hypotheses. *Geographical Analysis, 1*, 254-259.

Cohen, J., Gorr, W. L., & Olligschlaeger, A. M. (2007). Leading indicators and spatial interactions: A crime-forecasting model for proactive police deployment. *Geographical analysis, 39*, 105-127.

Corcoran, J., Wilson, I., & Ware, A. (2003). Predicting the geo-temporal variations of crime and disorder. *International Journal of Forecasting, 19*, 623-634.

Diggle, P. J., Chetwynd, A. G., Haggkvist, R., & Morris, S. E. (1995). Second-order analysis of space-time clustering. *Statistical Methods in Medical Research, 4*, 124-136.

Griffith, D. A. (1987). *Spatial autocorrelation: A primer.* Washington: Association of American Geographers.

Jacquez, G. M. (1996). A k-nearest neighbor test for space-time interaction. *Statistics in Medicine, 15*, 1935-1949.

Knox, G. (1964). The detection of space-time interactions. *Applied Statistics, 13*, 25-29.

Kulldorff, M. (1999). The Knox method and other tests for space-time interaction. *Biometrics, 55*, 544-552.

Liu, H., & Brown, D. E. (2003). Criminal incident prediction using a point-pattern-based density model. *International Journal of Forecasting, 19*, 603-622.

Mantel, N. (1967). The detection of disease clustering and a generalized regression approach. *Cancer Research, 27*, 209-220.

Morenoff, J. D., & Sampson, R. J. (1997). Violent crime and the spatial dynamics of neighborhood trasition: Chicago, 1970-1990. *Social Forces, 76*(1), 31-64.

Murray, A. T., McGuffog, I., Western, J. S., & Mullins, P. (2001). Exploratory spatial data analysis techniques for examining urban crime. *British Journal of Criminology, 41*, 309-329.

Odland, J. (1988). *Spatial autocorrelation.* Newbury Park, California: Sage.

Paulsen, D. J., & Robinson, M. B. (2004). *Spatial aspects of crime: Theory and practice.* New York: Allyn & Bacon.

Rice, K., & Smith, W. (2002). Socioecological models of automotive theft: Integrating routine activity and social disorganization approaches. *The Journal of Research in Crime and Delinquency, 39*(3), 304-336.

Smith, W. R., Frazee, S. G., & Davison, E. L. (2000). Furthering the integration of routine activity and social disorganization theories: Small units of analysis and the study of street robbery as a diffusion process. *Criminology, 38*(2), 489-523.

Strang, D., & Tuma, N. B. (1993). Spatial and temporal heterogeneity in diffusion. *The American Journal of Sociology, 99*(3), 614-639.

Waller, L. A., Carlin, B. P., Xia, H., & Gelfand, A. E. (1997). Hierarchical spatio-temporal mapping of disease rates. *Journal of American Statistical Association, 92*(438), 607-617.

ENDNOTES

1 Hagerstrand generated MIF (Mean Information Field) which provided probabilities of each areal unit for each period with the change in the number of susceptibles. Probabilities of contact is increased as the numbers of adopters at a location rises (for further modification and development of MIF, see Morrill et al., 1988)

2 S-shaped time distribution function is characterized first by a sudden shift to a period

of rapidly accelerating growth, which is followed by a period of stability (see Cliff et al. 1981)

3 The indices are high residential mobility, high family disruption rate, low economic status, and high population density. Those are relevant factors to delinquency rate in social disorganization framework (Kornhauser, 1978; Brusik and Grasmick, 1993; Sampson and Groves, 1989).

4 However, crime literature applied the covariance type measure for analyzing diffusion process (Smith et al., 2000; Craglia et al., 2001; Morenoff 2004)

5 This is the main reason of deriving Moran scatterplot by Anselin (1996)

6 The neighborhood effects implies high $G^*_{i,t}$ values caused by increase in neighboring values even though the areas of high $G^*_{i,t}$ values have no direct influence from diffusion process.

APPENDIX

Variance of $I_{i,t2}$ and Its Generation

The variance of $I_{i,t2}$ is calculated as below. Given that spatial connectivity is constant in different periods, it is reasonable to have $W_{ij,t1} = W_{ij,t2}$. Thus, when the spatial weights are assumed to be $W_{ij,t1} = W_{ij,t2} = W_{ij}$, the original equation can be transformed as:

$$I_{i,t2} = \frac{z_{i,t2}}{m_{2,t2}} \sum_j \frac{1}{2} W_{ij}(z_{j,t1} + z_{j,t2}) \quad j \neq i \tag{4}$$

Seeing that variance is calculated as:

$$Var(I_{i,t2}) = E(I_{i,t2}^2) - E(I_{i,t2})^2 \tag{5}$$

each component is calculated as follow:

$$E(I_{i,t2}^2) = E[\frac{z_{i,t2}^2}{s^4}(\sum_{j \neq i} \frac{1}{2} W_{ij} z_{j,t1} + \frac{1}{2} W_{ij} z_{j,t2})^2]$$

$$= \frac{1}{4m_{2,t2}^2} \sum_{j \neq i} \sum_{h \neq i} W_{ij} W_{ih} E[z_{i,t2}^2 (z_{j,t1} + z_{j,t2})(z_{h,t1} + z_{h,t2})]$$

$$= \frac{1}{4m_{2,t2}^2} \sum_{j \neq i} \sum_{h \neq i} W_{ij} W_{ih} E[z_{i,t2}^2 (z_{j,t1} z_{h,t1} + z_{j,t1} z_{h,t2} + z_{j,t2} z_{h,t1} + z_{j,t2} z_{h,t2})]$$

$$= \frac{1}{4m_{2,t2}^2} \sum_{j \neq i} \sum_{h \neq i} W_{ij} W_{ih} \frac{(-nm_{2,t2} m_{2,t1} + 2m_{2,t2} m_{2,t1})(m_{2,t1} + m_{4,t2})(m_{2,t1} + m_{4,t2})(-nm_{2,t2}^2 + 2m_{4,t2})}{(n-1)^2} \tag{6}$$

Where based on equation (2.39) of Cliff and Ord (1981 p.46):

$$E[z_{i,t2}^2 (z_{j,t1} z_{h,t1})]$$

$$= \frac{1}{(n-1)^2} E_R[z_{i,t2}^2 (\sum_j \sum_h z_{j,t1} z_{h,t1} - \sum_j z_{j,t1}^2 - z_i \sum_j z_{j,t1} - z_i \sum_h z_{h,t1} + z_{i,t1}^2 + z_{i,t1}^2)]$$

$$= \frac{1}{(n-1)^2} E_R[z_{i,t2}^2 (-\sum_j z_{j,t1}^2 + 2z_{i,t1}^2)]$$

$$= \frac{-nm_{2,t2} m_{2,t1} + 2m_{2,t2} m_{2,t1}}{(n-1)^2} \tag{7}$$

$$E[z_{i,t2}^2 (z_{j,t1} z_{h,t2})]$$

$$= \frac{1}{(n-1)^2} E_R[z_{i,t2}^2 (\sum_j \sum_h z_{j,t1} z_{h,t2} - z_i \sum_j z_{j,t1} - z_i \sum_h z_{h,t2} + z_{i,t1}^2 + z_{i,t2}^2)]$$

$$= \frac{m_{2,t1} + m_{4,t2}}{(n-1)^2} \tag{8}$$

equation, $\sum_j z_j = 0$ by definition. The other component $E[z^2_{i,t2}(z_{j,t2}z_{h,t1})]$ and $E[z^2_{i,t2}(z_{j,t2}z_{h,t2})]$ are evaluated in the same way:

$$E[z^2_{i,t2}(z_{j,t2}z_{h,t1})] = \frac{m_{2,t1}+m_{4,t2}}{(n-1)^2} \tag{9}$$

$$E[z^2_{i,t2}(z_{j,t2}z_{h,t2})] = \frac{-nm^2_{2,t2}+2m_{4,t2}}{(n-1)^2} \tag{10}$$

Given:

$$\frac{1}{n}\sum_i z^2_{i,t1} = m_{2,t1}$$

$$\frac{1}{n}\sum_i z^4_{i,t2} = m_{4,t2}$$

$E(I_{i,t2})^2$ component is calculated as follow:

$$E(I_{i,t2}) = \frac{\frac{1}{2}\sum_j W_{ij} E[z_{i,t2}(z_{j,t1}+z_{j,t2})]}{m_{2,t2}}$$

$$= \frac{\sum_j W_{ij} E[z_{i,t2}(-z_{i,t1}-z_{i,t2})]}{2m_{2,t2}}$$

$$= \frac{\sum_j W_{ij}(-k-m_{2,t2})}{2nm_{2,t2}}$$

$$= \frac{(-k-m_{2,t2})}{2nm_{2,t2}} \tag{11}$$

$$E(I_{i,t2})^2 = \left(\frac{(-k-m_{2,t2})}{2nm_{2,t2}}\right)^2 \tag{12}$$

where: $k = \frac{1}{n}\sum_i z_{i,t1}z_{i,t2}$

$\sum_j W_{ij} = 1$ since **W** is row standardized weight matrix.
Over all, the resulting variance would be:

$$Var(I_{i,t2}) = E(I^2_{i,t2}) - E(I_{i,t2})^2$$

$$= \frac{1}{4m^2_{2,t2}} \sum_{j\neq i}\sum_{h\neq i} W_{ij}W_{ih} \frac{(-nm_{2,t2}m_{2,t1}+2m_{2,t2}m_{2,t1})(m_{2,t1}+m_{4,t2})(m_{2,t1}+m_{4,t2})(-nm^2_{2,t2}+2m_{4,t2})}{(n-1)^2}$$

$$-\left(\frac{(-k-m_{2,t2})}{2nm_{2,t2}}\right)^2 \tag{13}$$

Equation (2.39) of Cliff and Ord (1981 p.46)

Since

$$E[z_i z_j]=$$

$$\sum_{j1\neq i}\sum_{j2\neq i}(z_{j1,t1}z_{j2,t1}+z_{j1,t1}z_{j2,t2}+z_{j1,t2}z_{j2,t1}+z_{j1,t2}z_{j2,t2})$$

$$=\sum_{j1\neq i}\sum_{j2\neq i}z_{j1,t1}z_{j2,t1}+\sum_{j1\neq i}\sum_{j2\neq i}z_{j1,t1}z_{j2,t2}$$
$$+\sum_{j1\neq i}\sum_{j2\neq i}z_{j1,t2}z_{j2,t1}+\sum_{j1\neq i}\sum_{j2\neq i}z_{j1,t2}z_{j2,t2}$$

$$\sum_{j1\neq i}\sum_{j2\neq i}z_{j1,t1}z_{j2,t1}$$
$$=z_{j1,t1}z_{j2,t1}+z_{j1,t1}z_{j2,t1}+\ldots+z_{j1,t1}z_{j2,t1}$$
$$+z_{j1,t1}z_{j2,t1}+z_{j1,t1}z_{j2,t1}+\ldots+z_{j1,t1}z_{j2,t1}$$
$$\ldots \qquad \ldots \qquad \ldots$$
$$+z_{j1,t1}z_{j2,t1}+z_{j1,t1}z_{j2,t1}+\ldots+z_{j1,t1}z_{j2,t1}$$

$$=z_{1,t1}(z_{1,t1}+z_{2,t1}+\ldots+z_{i,t1}+\ldots+z_{n,t1})-z_{1,t1}z_{i,t1}$$
$$+z_{2,t1}(z_{1,t1}+z_{2,t1}+\ldots+z_{i,t1}+\ldots+z_{n,t1})-z_{2,t1}z_{i,t1}$$
$$+\ldots \qquad \ldots \qquad \ldots$$
$$+z_{i,t1}(z_{1,t1}+z_{2,t1}+\ldots+z_{i,t1}+\ldots+z_{n,t1})-z_{i,t1}z_{i,t1}$$
$$+\ldots \qquad \ldots \qquad \ldots$$
$$+z_{n,t1}(z_{1,t1}+z_{2,t1}+\ldots+z_{i,t1}+\ldots+z_{n,t1})-z_{n,t1}z_{i,t1}$$

Given $\sum_j z_j=0$, the aforementioned equation is summarized as,

$$\sum_{j1\neq i}\sum_{j2\neq i}z_{j1,t1}z_{j2,t1}=-z_{i,t1}(z_{1,t1}+z_{2,t1}+\ldots+z_{n,t1})+z_{i,t1}z_{i,t1}$$
$$=z_{i,t1}z_{i,t1}$$
$$=z^2_{i,t1}$$

Same procedure is applied to the other component resulting in,

$$\sum_{j1'i}\sum_{j2'i}z_{j1,t1}z_{j2,t2}=z_{i,t1}z_{i,t2}$$
$$\sum_{j1\neq i}\sum_{j2\neq i}z_{j1,t2}z_{j2,t1}=z_{i,t2}z_{i,t1}$$
$$\sum_{j1\neq i}\sum_{j2\neq i}z_{j1,t2}z_{j2,t2}=z_{i,t2}z_{i,t2}$$

Section III
Crime Event and Pattern Simulations

Chapter IX
Synthesis Over Analysis: Towards an Ontology for Volume Crime Simulation

Daniel J. Birks
UCL Jill Dando Institute of Crime Science, UK

Susan Donkin
UCL Jill Dando Institute of Crime Science, UK

Melanie Wellsmith
University of Huddersfield, UK

ABSTRACT

This chapter examines the use of computer simulation, specifically agent-based modeling, as a tool for criminologists and its potentially unique ability to examine, test, refine, and validate criminological theory. It suggests an approach to be taken by those working in this field, through the use of detailed examples of the processes necessary to define, produce, and populate both a simple model of general offending and a more detailed model for domestic burglary. It further suggests methods for evaluating such models, particularly calling for collaborative research and model replication. The authors hope that this chapter will act as a step towards an accepted ontology for volume crime simulation.

INTRODUCTION

In this chapter we will consider the use of simulation—specifically agent-based modeling—as a tool for criminologists. We suggest, from our experience and the research of others, an approach that could be followed by those working in this field, and lay out the beginnings of a framework within which to proceed: an ontology for crime simulation.

The aims of this chapter are: to describe our attempt to create a sufficiently complex and representative simulation that will allow the modeling and evaluation of individual level offender decision-making, thus demonstrating how practical inferences could be drawn from its conclusions; to situate our research within the state of current knowledge; and to propose a structure for further advancement of research in this area.

To this end, we will take the following steps. Firstly, we will consider the three main theories that have informed our research: routine activity theory, rational choice perspective, and crime pattern theory. An overview of these opportunity theories will be provided before we discuss the problems faced when attempting to verify them empirically. We will highlight the gap between the theoretically explained, individual (micro) level decision-making processes and the observed, and thus tested, aggregate (macro) level crime patterns that result from these. We will suggest that one potential method of narrowing this gap is the use of computer simulations of crime, and will show a growing interest in such an approach amongst leading criminologists. We will explain how simulations can be used to test, refine and validate opportunity theories, and the concepts they include, as well as providing an environment for *in silico* experiments. In order to discuss simulation in more detail, we will provide the reader with a brief overview of agent-based modeling and set the scene yet further with a discussion of how this has been, and in the future could be, applied to criminological endeavors. We will specifically focus on how the opportunity theories lend themselves to the decomposition, and subsequent formulism, required by agent-based modeling.

Next, we will turn to the more practical considerations of applying this technique to the theories discussed. In the first instance, we will present a simple model of victimization and detection which is used as an example of theory formalism and model construction. An interactive program will also be provided for the reader. Having laid these foundations, we will introduce the research from which this chapter is born. This will involve a detailed presentation of a bespoke (i.e., custom-made) working agent-based model. We will discuss how to construct and populate the simulation environment and provide an overview of the control paradigm employed and its importance to our approach. We will again show how the theory informing this research is decomposed and formalized into a series of behaviors which determine how the agents in the model perceive, reason and act. In order to do all this, we will highlight a number of assumptions that have to be made. We will explain that, whilst some of these may be unproven, one of the purposes of using simulation techniques is to test the effects such assumptions have on the model output, in order to verify or disprove them.

Having provided sufficient detail about the model we have produced, we will discuss how simulations such as this may be evaluated. We will briefly consider the merits of a replicative approach and make a call for debate in this area. We will then attempt to evaluate, by comparison, our working model, which has been populated with data sets pertinent to domestic burglary. We will describe how the initial output—the pattern produced by an aggregation of individual-level decisions and resulting actions—indicates the presence of spatio-temporal clustering, as observed in analyses of real-world crime data.

Moving away from this specific application, we will finally present a suggested approach to further research in this field, listing a number of considerations which we feel should be followed to best take this method forward. These will be based on what we have learnt from carrying out this research. Specifically, throughout the chapter, we will call for the use of a modular and scalable architecture which allows for the incremental construction of models and efficient sharing and implementation of ideas and relevant research findings. We will detail the steps we intend to take to advance our model, including the use of further datasets and crime schema, and the refinement and addition of agents and their behaviors. We will mention experiments that we would like to carry out using agent-based models and specify a number of potential applications for crime simulations in the future.

To summarize, this chapter will:

- Present a simulation methodology from a criminologist's perspective as a potential tool to bridge the gap between micro level theory and the macro level testing thereof.
- Decompose the opportunity theories discussed into a representation within agent-based modeling.
- Suggest, by example, a modular framework within which to replicate and study the micro level interactions and emerging macro level patterns they give rise to.
- Describe the instances, concepts, attributes and relations required by such a model of crime activities.
- Provide an initial version of the model, using domestic burglary as an example.
- Suggest how the model may be verified and evaluated, illustrate its possible uses and set out the next steps in its development.

UNDERLYING CRIMINOLOGICAL THEORIES

Current understanding of crime and place has been heavily influenced by three theoretical perspectives, often referred to as "opportunity theories": routine activity theory, rational choice perspective and crime pattern theory. Each perspective emphasizes a different element: society, the individual, and the local environment (Rossmo, 2000). However, they are in fact more interlinked than this as each element has an impact upon the other. For example, the routine activities of individuals combine to form a backcloth of neighborhood and societal routine activities, which influence the nature of the local environment in which the rational actor makes his[1] offending "choice". Much event and place-focused research, therefore, tends to take an inclusive approach to these theories, thus providing a more complete understanding of the offence process; it is in this way we intend to proceed.

Routine activity theory stipulates that a direct-contact predatory offence requires three essential elements: a motivated offender, a suitable target, and the absence of a capable guardian (Cohen & Felson, 1979). A motivated, or likely, offender is anyone inclined to commit a crime. A suitable target could be a person or an object considered both vulnerable and rewarding by the likely offender. A guardian is capable if they can protect the crime target. This is unlikely to be a police officer or security guard catching an offender "red-handed", but is more likely to be a security device or ordinary citizen going about his or her daily routine, such as a neighbor or bystander (Felson, 2002). It can be seen, then, that unlike traditional criminological theories, routine activity theory focuses on the criminal event, not the offender. Its proponents argue that, whilst criminal propensity is difficult to predict and tackle, the criminal event can be more easily, and justifiably, identified and manipulated to remove the crime opportunity and, thus, the crime occurrence (Clarke, 1983). In this way, temptation and opportunity are shifted to a central position in terms of both explanation and prevention. At the same time, this, and the other opportunity theories, raise the need for crime-specific explanations, the suitability of a target and the motivation and capability of an offender varying by crime type.

It is the routine activities of all people, including potential victims and offenders, which bring the essential components of the theory together. This works on a group or societal level as well as an individual one. Crime patterns, such as hot spots and crime generators, can be explained as the aggregation of a number of individual routine activities; hot areas have many offender-target-lack of guardian convergences, whilst cool areas do not. In the same way, national crime trends are seen as a result of wide-spread, aggregate activities, such as increasing domestic burglaries resulting from the reduced guardianship of homes as more women entered the workforce (Cohen & Felson, 1979).

In the event of a convergence of the three aforementioned elements, the potential offender needs to make the decision to exploit the opportunity presented to him. The rational choice perspective portrays offenders as rational decision-makers who apply a certain level of preparation and foresight to their crimes: a bounded rationality. The assumption is that offenders are able to adapt their behavior to unforeseen or altering external influences (stimuli), so as to maximize their reward (utility). It is based on three important premises: Firstly, offenders are out to profit in some way from their criminal endeavors, be it for money, status, or excitement (Cornish & Clarke, 1986). Secondly, a crime-specific focus is required if one is to adequately explain criminal choices (Cornish & Clarke, 1986). Finally, though dealing with both crime and criminality, it calls for the development of distinct decision-making models for the involvement process and the criminal event (Cornish & Clarke, 1986). Both Cornish and Clarke (1986) and Gottfredson and Hirschi (1990) point out that decisions about involvement in crime are determined by multiple choices made over considerable time periods. Event decisions, on the other hand, are often based on restricted information, which usually relates to the immediate situation an offender finds himself in. Indeed, these pre-crime situations determine the variable perceptions of risk and reward (Cusson, 2002) and thus vary by crime type. Factors contributing to a crime-attractive situation are: victims (negligence, provocation, vulnerability); targets (interesting objects, CRAVED (Clarke, 1999)); facilitators (weapons, alcohol, drugs, vehicles or other instruments); and the physical environment (obscurity) (Cusson, 2002). Therefore, whilst focusing on the offender and his decision-making process, rational choice perspective also draws on event and environmental information, for it is this that informs much of the offender's perceptions. Indeed, attempting to analyze event-based decision-making *without* considering the environment would be nigh on impossible.

Crime pattern theory focuses on how offenders find suitable targets and crime places within the environment. Including the environment in opportunity explanations of crime provides the backcloth for offender movement and helps to explain target selection (Hearnden & Magill, 2004). Potential offenders come across opportunities within their personal awareness spaces. Such awareness, or activity, spaces are formed around personal activity nodes (such as the home, workplace, and entertainment areas) and the paths between them (Brantingham & Brantingham, 1984, 1993). As an individual spends more time in an area, his awareness of that neighborhood and the opportunities for crime within it increase, resulting in some areas being better known than others. It is postulated that offences are likely to occur where criminal opportunities intersect with these cognitively-known areas (Brantingham & Brantingham, 1993; Clarke & Eck, 2003). Thus, two central concerns of environmental criminology are to explain the spatial distribution of offences and the spatial distribution of offenders (Bottoms & Wiles, 2002).

These three theories, briefly introduced in the previous section, are compatible and mutually supportive (Clarke & Felson, 1993) and it is at times difficult to decide where the distinction, or assignation of certain elements, should be made. Rational choice focuses on the decision-making process, and routine activity theory provides the environmental framework from which hangs the backcloth of choices (Cornish & Clarke, 1986). Crime pattern theory tends to concentrate on where convergences take place, hence where opportunities are spatially and temporally presented. They are now well-established theories, particularly amongst place and event-focused researchers, and there is a growing body of research with results that are compatible with environmental and opportunity explanations.

The three unified opportunity theories all provide a *bottom-up* description of how crime is distributed spatially and temporally, attempting to explain the internal and external mechanisms which dictate where and when the rational actor makes his choice to offend. Situational crime prevention (SCP) aims to reduce the opportunities for crime by manipulating the underlying elements influencing this choice. This can be achieved by increasing an offender's perceived efforts and risks, as well as reducing his perceived rewards, provocations, and excuses for offending (Clarke & Eck, 2003; Wortley, 2001; Clarke, 1995). However, studies of prolific offenders and criminal careers remain at the individual level and are rarely linked to area-level patterns (see Townsley & Pease (2002) for a notable exception). Similarly, area-based studies, which dominate much enforcement-led volume crime analysis, concentrate on retrospective descriptions of small-scale crime patterns. These often utilize aggregate geo-demographic data sets and, consequently, may be vulnerable to the ecological fallacy (Robinson, 1950; Durkheim, 1897). Such analysis often fails to focus upon individual level decisions which wholly contribute to the aggregate patterns observed (Brantingham & Brantingham, 2004; Liu, Wang, Eck, & Liang, 2005) and are the very mechanisms SCP attempts to manipulate. As a result of this, evaluations of SCP-based interventions are usually inherently defined at the area level, data about which are unsuitable for testing the micro-level mechanisms proposed by theory (Eck, 1995), thus a leap of faith is required in ascribing the observed impact to these individual behaviors. Numerous studies have demonstrated the effectiveness of SCP (Clarke, 1997). However, the evaluation gap between the individual and area levels remains. Therefore, the responsibility of the research community must be to provide a greater understanding of the aforementioned interactions, thereby increasing the effectiveness of SCP and allowing practitioners to further optimize the method and targeting of the resources available to them in the fight against crime. Existing analysis techniques such as GIS, regression, multilevel modeling and time series analysis provide considerable tools for those interested in the spatial and temporal distribution of crime. In this chapter we present another tool which, when used alongside other methods, may provide an additional and potentially unique perspective on the explanation of opportunity formation and observed crime patterns.

Recently, computer simulation has presented itself as an alternative to existing techniques, in part due to increases in both computing power and the scope of data collection. The decompositional and subsequently generative nature of simulation lends itself well to the examination of the dynamics connecting individual to area. Simulation's validity or effectiveness is yet to be fully ascertained, and as later discussed, is in many ways more difficult to evaluate than conventional techniques, requiring, to some extent, a methodological shift. These factors withstanding, recent research has described and justified the appropriateness of simulation techniques within environmental criminology, and has provided a conceptual framework of interaction for such models of crime activity (Brantingham & Brantingham, 2004). Additionally, several have demonstrated that simulation models can produce plausible outputs when compared to real world crime observations (Groff, 2006; Liu et al., 2005; Liang, Liu, and Eck, 2001).

This chapter is born out of the authors' interest in examining the dynamics of the victim-offender-location interaction, in the hope of gaining a better understanding of the micro and macro level interactions which give rise to the crime patterns observed at the macro level. The aim of the work described is to investigate the practicality, requirements and applications of simulation techniques in designing a model of crime activities in accordance with rules from environmental criminology, SCP and ecology (Brantingham & Brantingham, 2004). Furthermore, we suggest, by example, a potential specification for individual, area and interaction representations. How this has been achieved will be discussed in the following sections, but first we describe, in more detail, the type of simulation model used and, more precisely, how such models can be incorporated into criminological research.

AGENT-BASED MODELING

Agent-based modeling (ABM) is a well-established method of computer simulation with many real and promising applications across a range of disciplines. Although technically straightforward, its concept is profound (Bonabeau, 2002). Many books and papers have described the subject in great detail (see, for example Jennings & Wooldridge, 1998; Weiss, 1999; Wooldridge & Jennings, 1995). For the sake of this chapter, however, a simple overview is presented, and its potential application within criminology discussed.

Agent-based models are commonly made up of two key elements: autonomous decision-making entities called agents, and some form of network or environment they inhabit. Agents execute a variety of behaviors in accordance with multiple sets of rules that govern how they perceive, reason and act in a given situation. These behaviors define how agents interact with one another, how they observe and analyze particular data from their surroundings and, eventually, how they might alter that environment by performing certain actions. They are used to examine the emergence of macro level patterns by simulating micro level interactions over numerous iterations (cycles) of the model. For this reason they are implemented in a wide variety of disciplines which deal with the examination of complex dynamic interactions. Examples include models of crowd dynamics, urban sprawl, traffic, and consumer behavior. Still, the idea of using ABM applications within criminology is only just beginning to gain momentum (Brantingham, Glässer, Kinney, Singh, & Vajihollahi, 2005a). In terms of the practicalities of following such an approach, there are numerous commercial and open source agent development environments available. These include, but are not limited to, SWARM, NetLogo, Repast, Mason and Agent Analyst. In addition to these "off the shelf" packages, research groups within various fields have developed their own bespoke ABM test-beds.

Agent-Based Modeling in Criminology

The opportunity theories, discussed, appear to provide a logical approach to the explanation of opportunity formation and event-focused decision-making. They are also built upon a number of clearly elucidated elements into which the theory can be decomposed. Such a feature means that they should lend themselves well to ABM, as these elements inform the necessary formalisms, or rules, from which the agents' perceptions and behavior, as well as the environmental backcloth, are built. Elements central to these theories include such things as nodes, activity spaces, guardianship, risk and reward—all of which can be represented within an effective computer simulation. ABM techniques require an environment in which to operate; crime pattern theory and, more broadly, environmental criminology, provide the markers from which this "world" can be built. More specifically, routine activity theory informs how agents will move through the environment and the rules governing this, whilst rational choice perspective is used to formalize their decision-making. To explicitly elucidate the purpose of using such a system: models of offending based upon current theories of opportunity and environment can be created and their subsequent output crime examined for plausibility against existing real world patterns. By implementing a rigorous theory-formalism-test-refine cycle, whereby such theories are formalized within simulation constructs and their emergent patterns of crime examined, simulation models may provide a solution to the existing problems of empirical verification and present a unique opportunity for testing and refinement within a virtual laboratory (Groff, 2006; Liu et al., 2005). This process also affords researchers the ability to perform *in silico* experiments, which would otherwise be impossible for ethical, practical or economic reasons (Groff, 2006; Brantingham, & Brantingham, 2004). In an ideal (and much more advanced) implementation, this would allow for the creation of "what if" type simulations where researchers—or even practitioners—could examine the likely effects of implementing certain tactics within a given area. Additionally, the process of decomposing theories into simulation formalisms, such as the rules which govern agent behavior (Brantingham & Brantingham, 2004), is in itself a useful one in that it provides greater insight, and demands that researchers specify such theories and concepts in explicit terms. This can highlight potential inconsistencies or shortcomings and, by doing so, contributes to the subsequent strengthening of theory.

The publication of this book, as well as recent debates amongst academics and, to some extent, practitioners, are evidence of the degree to which researchers are keen to explore and develop the validity of a simulation approach, as well as showcasing the enthusiasm and expertise of those wishing to get involved. However, current criminological research using such techniques remains in its experimental stages. The main work to date in this area has focused on routine activity theories of crime, although some use has been made of concepts of bounded rationality or utility for agent decision-making (Groff, 2006; van Baal, 2004). A range of simulation environments have also been employed, but those which combine modeling and GIS appear to be finding favor (Groff, 2006; Liang et al., 2001; Liu et al., 2005). More specifically, Liang et al. (2001) use a combination of cellular automata (CA) loose-coupled with GIS. Movement of the agents is determined by a Monte Carlo simulation and they employ an object-oriented design (OOD) paradigm, to consider commercial robbery. However, the purpose of this research was predominantly to "...promote the usage of CA modeling by applying it to invisible phenomenon", in this case crime and its routine activities (Liang et al., 2001, p. 18). This research is taken forward by Liu et al. (2005), this time focusing on street robbery, but utilizing a similar approach. In both cases, the 'results' of the 'experiments' are in keeping with basic crime facts and patterns, although the 2001 research does not calibrate the model, whilst the 2005 research does (Liang et al., 2001; Liu et al., 2005).

Brantingham and Brantingham (2004) make a call for the use of simulation in criminology and describe a method which could be used to address this. They also suggest the use of OOD and focus on routine activity theory, with decision-making and rational choice perspective only referred to in terms of offender "readiness". With others from Simon Fraser University, this call has been developed into a working model and several papers have resulted (Brantingham, Brantingham, & Glässer, 2005; Brantingham et al., 2005a; Brantingham, Glässer, Kinney, Singh, & Vajihollahi, 2005b). Brantingham et al. (2005a) provide a comprehensive review of the work to date. The focus of this research is on crime in urban areas and the spatial and temporal aspects of this, employing multiple agents and multiple targets. In this case, the goal is to validate crime patterns and theories. They use an asynchronous agent-based model known as distributed abstract state machine (DASM), making use of a multi-agent-based system (MABS) modeling paradigm. The environment is populated by autonomous agents that can move between specified nodes (e.g., home, work) by way of a navigation algorithm which makes use of both global and local information. The authors state that the output is less important than the underlying "trace" which has resulted in it (Brantingham, et al., 2005a, p. 14), but believe that validity can be tested by comparing outputs with that expected by theory. No results are presented and they state their intentions to investigate more fully.

In what would appear to be the most comprehensive approach to date, Groff (2006) presents a number of experiments carried out, again using an ABM/GIS package, in this case Agent Analyst (a beta model merging Repast with ArcGIS). The simulation environment is based on Seattle GIS data and the crime focus is, again, on street robbery. This research also centers on routine activity theory, but does make some use of rational choice perspective in terms of agent-decision making. The aim of this work is not prediction, but theory testing by comparison of experimental outputs to those predicted by routine activity theory. No dynamic routing was employed, as this was not supported by the software, and the results of the spatio-temporal constraint experiments appear to have been affected by the repeated clustering of agent movements between designated nodes; that is to say activity spaces were fixed, not dynamic. However, the findings generally support concepts of routine activity theory, such as temporal constraints reducing crime, and the model appears to be robust.

Our model takes a somewhat different approach, using a behavior-based control paradigm in bespoke software built by one of the authors. Rational choice perspective takes a much more central role, although routine activity theory remains important. The working version focuses on domestic burglary which changes the targets to static features (as opposed to other agents) for which many attributes can be specified, and far more environmental backcloth data is introduced. It is to describing this model we will now turn.

In summary, routine activity theory, the rational choice perspective and crime pattern theory all, to some extent, provide *bottom-up* explanations of why crime occurs where and when it does. Conversely, existing analysis and evaluation techniques predominantly approach crime from the *top-down*, examining distributions of crime activities at an aggregate level, whilst having to speculate about the underlying mechanisms which contribute to the spatial and temporal distributions observed. Hence, a separation lies between the theory and how it is tested. The generative nature of simulation, and agent-based modeling in particular, offer the potential to explain the emergence of higher order patterns observed at the area level, from individual level behaviors, therefore bringing the two approaches closer to one another. The initial theories informing such an approach have been presented and we will discuss the formalisms and constructs of such a model. Firstly, however, we present a straightforward example illustrating how some of the concepts discussed could be applied to a simple simulation of victimization and detection.

COPS N' ROBBERS: A SIMPLE AGENT-BASED MODEL

In order to demonstrate the rationale, design, and implementation associated with ABM, we will initially describe a straightforward model of criminal and enforcement activity within a simple "toy-world". Our illustrative model includes concepts which, whilst naïve, still hold in more complex systems, such as that described in the next section. The purpose of providing this example is to take the reader through some of the steps necessary to create a simulation and to show how a simple theory is formalized into agent behavior. The model itself encapsulates simplistic theories of both victimization and detection and allows exploration of the effect that several variable factors might have upon global outputs such as crime and detection rates.

For simplicity's sake, let us imagine a simulation world which is inhabited by three distinct groups of individuals: potential victims, offenders, and law enforcement. We theorize (for the purposes of this illustration):

That *all individuals move around the environment in a totally random fashion*; that *a crime occurs when an offender comes into the same location at the same time as a potential target and in the absence of a capable guardian*; and that *a detection occurs when an offender, target, and guardian all come together at the same point in space and time.*

In the same way that Rossmo (2000) formulized routine activity theory and the opportunity structure for crime as: Crime = (offender + target – guardian)(place + time), in order to build the simulation, we have converted our theory into several algorithmic formalisms. The three algorithms presented in pseudo-code[2] below detail the key behaviors expressed in the theory and thus required of the agents in the simulation[3]: Navigation (dictating how an agent moves within the simulation environment), Victimization (by the offenders) and Detection (by the law enforcement). As we have made no assumptions regarding the environment, we implement a simple toroidal world which allows movement in all directions.

All individuals move around the environment in a totally random fashion:

Navigation

```
select_@_random
(N, S, E, W, NE, NW, SE, SW)
 Move selected direction
```

A crime occurs when an offender comes into the same location at the same time as a potential target and in the absence of a capable guardian:

Victimization

```
if
   (is_present(x,y,t,Offender) &
   is_present(x,y,t,Target) &
   not(is_present(x,y,t,Guardian)))
   Crime occurs
end if
```

A detection occurs when an offender, target and guardian all come together at the same point in space and time:

Detection

```
if
   (is_present(x,y,t,Offender) &
   is_present(x,y,t,Target) &
   is_present(x,y,t,Guardian))
   Detection occurs
end if
```

A model implementing the formalisms has been developed using NetLogo, a cross-platform multi-agent programmable modeling environment, which is freely available from http://ccl.northwestern.edu/netlogo/. An interactive version and instructions concerning the model's usage can be found at http://www.jdi.ucl.ac.uk/people/research/birks/models.php. Briefly, the model allows the user to manipulate the size of each of the potential victim, offender, and enforcement pools and dictate the length, if any, of incarceration associated with detection. Subsequently, users can view the impact of any such alterations on the crime and detection rates and virtual prison population.

The simulation is run for a number of cycles during each of which every agent moves in a random direction in accordance with their movement behavior. In the event of a convergence of victim and offender, or victim, offender and enforcement, a victimization, or detection, is recorded. As the simulation is running, the macro level crime pattern resulting from the summation of these multiple micro (individual) level interactions can be observed. If our theory is to hold, this pattern should be comparable with real world observations (to the extent that such a simplified version can be). Even this unsophisticated model resulted in outputs that were in keeping with observed patterns of crime and predicted by opportunity theories. When an area was flooded with more potential targets the crime rate (number of offences per cycle) increased, as there were more opportunities for existing offenders. The same was true when the number of offenders was increased, thus allowing a greater proportion of targets (opportunities) to be encountered. On the other hand, when the level of law enforcement was raised, the crime rate fell. This was a smaller effect than the previous two scenarios, as detection requires the convergence of all three elements (offender, victim/target, guardian), whilst an offence only requires this of two (offender, victim/target).

By altering the proportions of offenders, targets and guardians we might attempt to ascertain a point of crime prevention "saturation", where recruiting more enforcement personnel has no discernible effect upon crime or detection rates. Additionally, the consequences of differing degrees of incarceration (removal of offender agents from the pool for a fixed period of time upon detection) on crime rates and prison populations could be investigated.

The usefulness of this model has to, of course, be tempered by the assumptions informing it, which may inhibit it from producing realistic models of the individual level decision-making processes we wish to examine. These include:

- The environment itself offers no constraints, inhibitors, or form.
- All entities move around the environment at random.
- Opportunity for crime is distributed randomly throughout the environment, as dictated by the movement of individuals (targets).
- Offender and victim populations are mutually exclusive.
- Offenders do not assess the likelihood of detection, nor are they deterred by enforcement presence and will, therefore, commit an offence regardless of the presence of a guardian.
- Offenders are always motivated, committing an offence whenever an opportunity presents itself.
- Detection can only occur at the exact moment of offence commission (i.e., red-handed) and not retrospectively.

Whilst the empirical evidence may not always exist to prove that these assumptions are incorrect, they may potentially limit the usefulness of our model.

It should be noted, however, that a more complex model attempting to address some of these simplistic assumptions may not necessarily be more useful in examining the mechanisms of the crime event. Instead, such increased complexity could produce results which are more difficult to interpret, or even obscure the impact of experimental changes. However, it is the opinion of the authors that these potential pitfalls should not undermine efforts to advance simulation work. It is hoped that the incremental approach advocated throughout this chapter will minimize the likelihood of these problems through a combination of manageable increases in complexity and repeated output validation.

We have shown, then, how a simple theory can be formalized into a set of behaviors, or rules, to produce an equally simple agent-based model of crime occurrence. We have observed that even this naïve attempt produces an output that is in keeping with real world observations. Further, we have introduced possible *in silico* experiments that could be carried out within this simulation. However, we have also seen that a more sophisticated model will be necessary to encompass the three main opportunity theories informing this research. This will be a complex task, but the authors hope that this chapter will act as both inspiration and blueprint for what must follow to progress such endeavors. With this in mind, the following section presents the first steps to be taken in developing a more complete and practically relevant working system, some of which has been applied to a domestic burglary scenario, about which more detail is provided.

AN AGENT-BASED MODEL OF VOLUME CRIME ACTIVITY

As we have ascertained, in order to examine in more detail the dynamics of the victim-offender-location interaction, we must design a more complex model than that previously described. We now consider more technical aspects of designing and implementing such a working agent-based approach for crime activity simulation. In this section we state our theoretical premise, summarize the modeling approach taken, introduce and describe the features of such a system and discuss their application. For the purposes of implementing and testing our initial version of the model, we have focused on the offence of domestic burglary, having developed a structure, as described below, which allows for the incremental addition of further crimes in the future. Domestic burglary was chosen for the following reasons:

- It involves static targets, which are computationally less demanding.
- High quality target data sets are available at point level.
- It matches well with existing geo-demographic data, such as deprivation indices and classifications of neighborhood areas.
- Research has established observable, and therefore potentially replicable, phenomena such as repeat victimization (Farrell & Pease, 2001; Polvi, Looman, Humphries, & Pease, 1990) and near repeats (Johnson & Bowers, 2004; Townsley, Homel, & Chaseling, 2003).
- Established metrics exist which allow quantitative comparison of simulation and real-world outputs.

Creating a Bespoke Model

As stated, a number of "off the shelf" ABM development environments are available. In the case of the work described, the authors opted not to use one of these; rather, the model presented and its underlying framework has been developed from the ground up with the purpose of examining crime activity in mind. This approach has offered several advantages. Firstly, it allowed a greater level of understanding and control over all low-level implementation decisions—which can have a direct effect on the simulation output, and subsequently the inferences made about it. Additionally, at the time of inception, some of the desired functionality seemed to be lacking in the popular toolkits—for example, several applications did not allow easy integration of both network and grid datasets within a single model. This is desirable, as we wish to represent the nodes and paths of an area's transport network alongside geo-demographic data at a grid-based aggregate level. Further, crime and criminals change over time, as do the environmental and social backcloths, the opportunity structure and the desirability and availability of goods. A working model needs to be adaptable to, and reflect changes in, the real world if it is to fulfill its purpose. Therefore, of utmost importance to the work presented, was the need to build a modular test-bed environment, which would allow for the incremental development of complexity. This is reflected in both the architectural (object-orientation) and representational (behavior-based artificial intelligence) methodologies employed. By designing both suitably modular agent and world models, more complex, valid and accurate representations can be developed as research is carried out and knowledge is increased. This level of flexibility should facilitate refinement and expansion whilst minimizing any hindrance by, and reliance upon, third party solutions.

The Model and Its Underlying Theory

As described in the simple example prefacing this section, key to our approach is the formulation of a theory of offending which we wish to examine. Drawing on the key theories described throughout this chapter, we have assembled, for the purposes of this research, the following statement of offence occurrence:

When an individual of a certain criminal disposition, going about his/her routine activities, comes into the location of a suitable target, which provides an opportunity for gain and which he/she is aware of and capable of exploiting, and when he/she perceives the reward to be sufficient to expend the effort required and endure the risks involved, he/she will commit the offence at the current point in space and time.

It is from this theoretical assembly that we formalize the set of behaviors possessed by each agent which allow us to examine, through synthesis, the target-offender-location interactions they give rise to.

To progress with this, we will need:

- An adequate model of offending behavior (as described in ourtheory).
- A sufficiently detailed model of the environment, which encapsulates all necessary features.

Again, we will begin by attempting to formulize our theory of offence occurrence into pseudo-code:

Crime occurs if
Perception of Opportunity >
current_threshold(propensity,readiness)

Where Perception of opportunity =
Awareness_of_opportunity(target) ×
capability_to_exploit(Opportunity(Target))
AND
Perceived_Reward(Opportunity) >
Perceived_Risk(Opportunity) ×
Perceived_Effort(Opportunity)

Assumptions

As is the case with any modeling of this kind, and as seen in our simple example above, the interactions between elements will necessarily rely on several assumptions that we aim to confirm or falsify through the use of simulation techniques. This chapter provides an example of *one potential investigation* into the application of agent-based modeling within a criminological context. Although the output of all agent-based models can only ever be considered speculative, this is no different from several widely accepted statistical tests, which are similarly tentative. Further, the incremental approach taken will allow the alteration of these assumptions as they are confirmed or disproved, thus permitting us to progress.

In the same way that outputs should be considered speculative, in part so should the remainder of this section. What is provided here is a description of the key concepts required for a simulation of crime activities. Whilst the existing model, which concentrates only on domestic burglary, implements a subset of what is described, such detail and considerations are provided to support the building of a sufficiently open architecture to allow the incremental design and subsequent integration of all the elements discussed below, and more.

Model Elements

In accordance with the three opportunity theories, our model of victim-offender-location interactions includes representations of offenders, potential targets (victims), guardians and a model of the environment which they inhabit. We first consider the representation of this environmental backcloth.

The Environment

In order to create realistic models of offending behavior, agents require a realistic simulation world in which to perceive, reason and act. In other words, the simulation world will need to be reflective of the real world. This is an enormous task, therefore, within our model, we have concentrated on the most important environmental features which affect the perceptions and actions required of the agents. For example, whilst risk perception is offender-centric, its assessment will be driven by environmental features such as visibility of the target or occupancy of premises. The environment within the model described is represented by numerous data sets produced from geo-descriptive and geo-demographic sources. These data sets can predominantly be divided into three classes: node and path networks, point level data, and aggregated environmental data. Node and path networks describe the morphology of the transport network within an area. Point level data include address data representing all buildings within an area. Aggregated environmental data describe certain geo-descriptive and geo-demographic variables, such as building occupancy and pedestrian footfall rates. The following section details these key structures.

The Transport Network

In accordance with crime pattern theory, the morphology of the transport network within an area dictates how individuals, criminal or not, move around, hence determining in part the "where" of crime. Following convention, the transport network within an environment is represented as a network of nodes and paths.

Point Level Data

This can include locations of commercial, residential and industrial premises, car parks, police stations, etc. Many of the targets within the simulation will be represented by point level data. As Cusson (2002) has stated, a key aspect in the formation of opportunities for crime is the number of interesting targets. Such potential targets, however, appear to be everywhere: an open window, an unattended car. Accordingly, any simulation backcloth created should ideally reflect this target-rich environment in which we live.

In the current model, targets fall into two distinct classes—static and dynamic—based on their movement capabilities (or otherwise). Buildings, therefore, are static targets, whilst such things as cars, and events (such as football games) are dynamic, existing, as they do, at different points in space and time.

Targets have several attributes:

- **A type:** Such as "car" or "shop", which allows agents to differentiate between them;
- **A location:** In the form of x,y (which changes over time for dynamic targets);
- **A security rating:** Relevant to the difficulty associated with exploiting the potential opportunity, such as gaining entry to a residential property. Such rating estimations are purely relative in that a house with window locks or an alarm would produce a higher score than one without.[4]
- **Utility value (reward):** One, or several. These may not always be readily apparent, and may be specific to an individual agent or the situation it finds itself in. Utility values are not always, or purely, economic; utilitarian and gratifying rewards should

also be considered. Whilst such simplified descriptions of potential reward are quite limiting, they are practical, open to further refinement and at least a step beyond the usual myopic focus on monetary value.

It should also be noted that interesting targets will vary by crime type and not all potential targets will be seen as such by all potential offenders. The complex interplay of experiences, behaviors and perceptions is, though, what we hope to model and test. It is necessary, therefore, to populate our environment accordingly, with a range of possible targets, and to watch what our agents make of them, based on the crime schema and decision-making processes we have programmed them with. However, in our initial model, such data sets will identify potential targets for domestic burglary and hence are the most important form of point data.

Aggregated Environmental Data

Aggregated data generally include information for which we lack point level data or which have been inferred from other sources, and for which assignation to point level would be inappropriate. Such data sets work at the grid level, placing a virtual lattice over the environment. By doing this, all objects within a grid cell are assigned like values of the concept being represented. For instance, all buildings within the model are allocated one of a set number of occupancy profiles, describing their likely occupancy at certain intervals throughout a simulation day. These values are currently inferred by making some rudimentary assumptions about available data sets, such as neighborhood classifications. For example, a residential area, it can be assumed, will predominantly be occupied overnight, whereas commercial buildings, such as office blocks or shops, are more likely to be occupied during business hours.

Additionally, for simplicity's sake, the current model does not implement all individuals within the environment as agents, only active offenders. Instead, each simulation grid has a pedestrian footfall profile, which, similar to the occupancy profiles of buildings, provides an estimate of the ambient pedestrian footfall level at given intervals throughout the day. Again, the majority of these data have been inferred; for example, central commercial areas, such as shopping precincts, are likely to be busier in the day, and even more so at the weekend. In the same way, we might infer that residential estates, depending upon their occupancy profile, are more likely to have a lower pedestrian footfall during the day. The level of connectivity associated with the grid in question may also have an effect. Connectivity is dictated by the transport network's nodes or paths, which fall within the grid cell. There is substantial research into the movement of individuals within environments; however, the scope of this project means that we have only provided a very simplified implementation, leaving room for the inclusion of more advanced datasets. Other examples of aggregated data sets would include street lighting or CCTV coverage, weather patterns and the location of crime prevention schemes.

Figure 1. An example environment

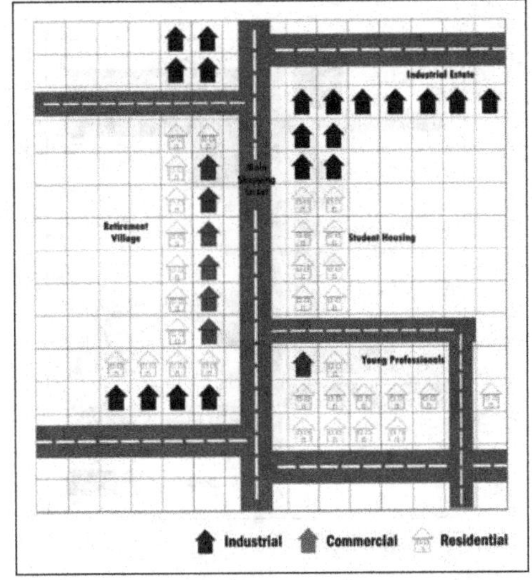

Figure 2. Nodes & Paths

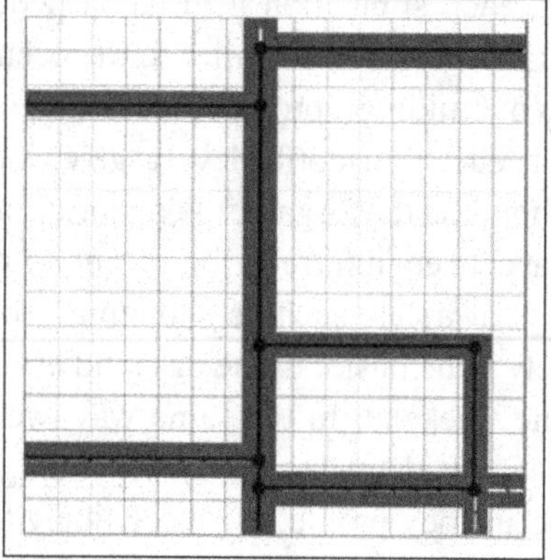

Figure 3. Residential Address Points

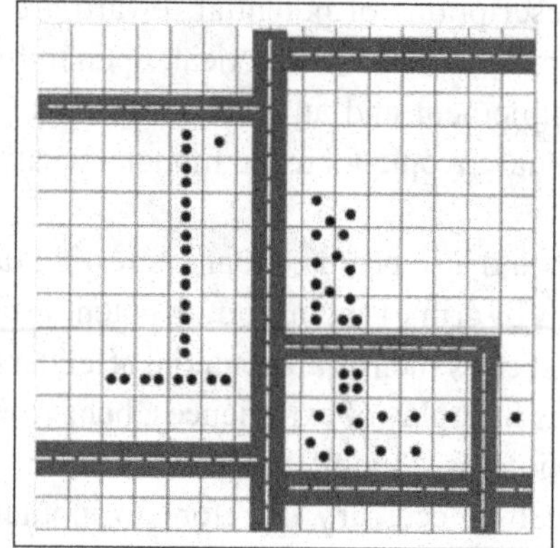

Figure 4. Pedestrian Footfall - Time (t) = 1

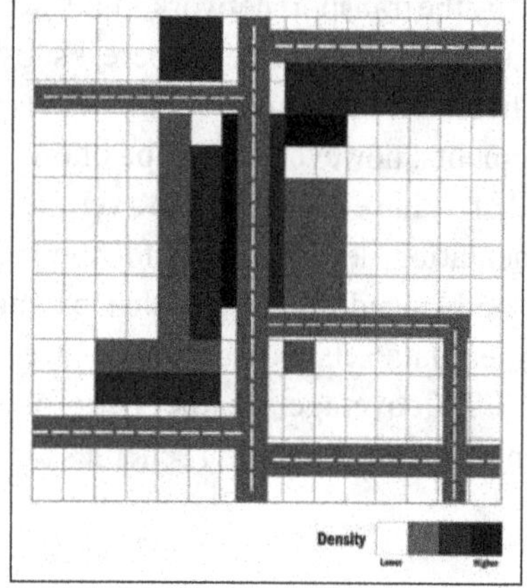

Figure 5. Pedestrian Footfall – Time (t) = 2

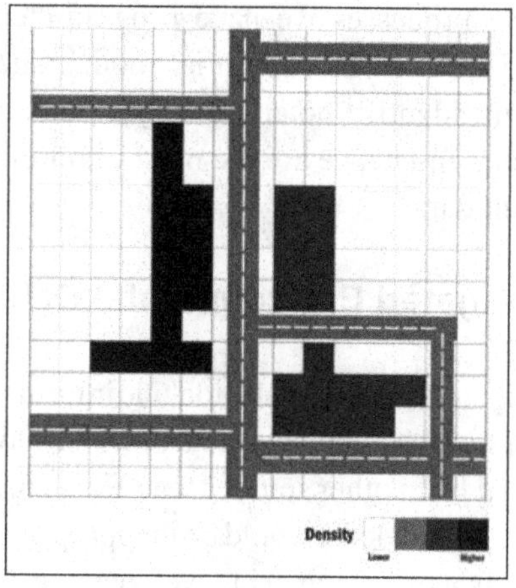

Figure 6. Building Occupancy - Time (t) = 1

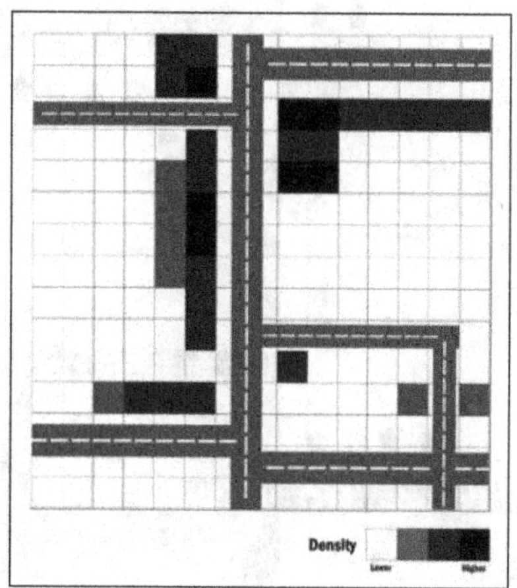

Figure 7. Building Occupancy - Time (t) = 2

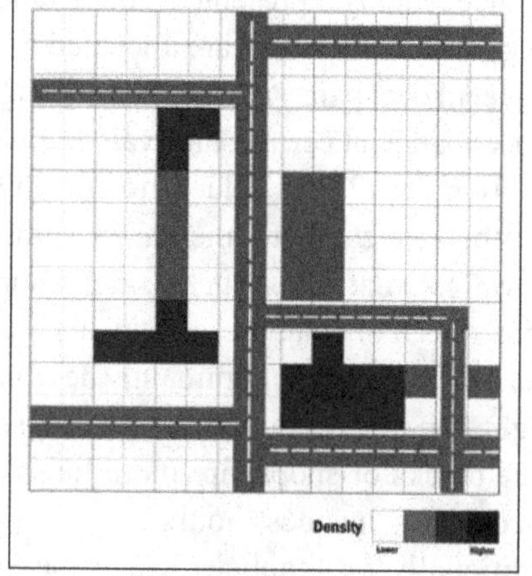

We have now described the key types of data sets which are combined to produce our model of the environment. Some of these environmental features are illustrated in Figures 1 through 7.

The Agents

Now we have described a model of the environment in which we wish to place our offenders, we describe the agents which are used to represent them. The following section describes the control paradigm which governs their decision-making processes, the key attributes they possess and the behaviors they employ.

Behavior-Based Artificial Intelligence

There are a number of control paradigms which could have been used to formalize agent behavior within the simulation. We have chosen to apply an object-oriented implementation (Meyer, 1997) based around behavior-based artificial intelligence (BBAI). BBAI describes intelligence as a series of semi-autonomous modular behaviors, each of which, in our case, is responsible for one perception, reasoning or action element. Such behavioral modules are inhibited or excited by certain perceived stimuli within the environment. Agent activities are dictated by a combination of their currently active internal behaviors. The importance, or weight, of an individual behavior is driven by localized factors from both the current internal agent state and the environment. A more detailed overview of BBAI is provided by Pfeiffer and Scheier (1999), whilst Brooks (1996) and Mataric (1995; 1992) discuss how this approach can be specifically applied to decision-making elements within autonomous agents.

This methodology offers some distinct advantages in both development and implementation. Firstly, the approach is one of inherent modularity. Agent actions are encapsulated as standalone modules (behaviors), which receive a given set of inputs from the environment model and/or their internal state, and subsequently produce a specific output; perhaps a direction of travel or the selection of the next action. In this way, the inputs and outputs of each module are formally specified, but the actual process of transforming input to output can be represented in any way the researcher sees fit. This approach of encapsulation allows behaviors to be altered, refined and/or replaced without the need for the entire model to be redesigned. In the same way, as more conclusions are drawn, further layers of behavior can be added to the model incrementally. Moreover, the approach also allows behaviors to be extensively tested, initially in isolation, and subsequently in interaction with others.

Using this approach, future models can explore the relationship between, and importance of, certain behaviors over one another, as agent priorities can be dynamically altered through a process of reinforcement. In this way, agents may learn to favor one behavior over another or avoid a certain conduct in specific circumstances that were not originally envisaged.

Agent Parameters

Agent parameters specify the characteristics of offenders within the simulation. These key values allow each agent to be unique, with their own routine, awareness space and criminal propensity, allowing researchers to create populations of heterogeneous agents. It is also important to note that the majority of behavioral calculations incorporating these values include stochastic elements, which ensure that the model is nondeterministic.

Propensity

This value represents an offender's penchant for committing crime, dictating the rate at which he will offend (Brantingham & Brantingham, 2004). Gottfredson and Hirschi (1990) argued that an offender's propensity to commit crime is characterized by low self-control, a latent construct that remains relatively stable over the life-course. Individuals with low self-control have a tendency to take advantage of criminal opportunities, fulfilling their need for immediate gratification. Therefore, the propensity value assigned to each agent remains static.

Readiness

This represents the current readiness of an individual to commit an offence. The value is directly related to the propensity of an offender and the time since the last offence committed. As this time increases, so does readiness. Thresholds may then be seen to alter, in that offenders may be willing to take a greater risk or lower reward. As Brantingham and Brantingham (2004) pointed out, in contrast to propensity, readiness is not fixed.

Awareness Space

Individuals have their own awareness space that represents the extent of their knowledge of the local environment. As an offender agent spends more time at a location, it becomes more familiar with it and the opportunities therein. In the same way, if an offender agent commits an offence at a location, its awareness of that location is further increased. Within the simulation this awareness space is simply represented as a two-dimensional array which equates to a grid over the environment. Each grid cell has a numeric value relating to the individual's awareness of it. This value is then used if an agent attempts to ascertain the opportunities at a location. The greater the awareness of an area, the clearer the picture of the opportunities available within it. Following from work on the significance of temporally defined opportunities (Rengert & Wasilchick, 2000) and aoristic analysis (Ratcliffe, 2002), further representations could incorporate temporality into the concept of awareness, whereby offenders are aware of opportunities which may exist only within a fixed time window.

Routine Activity Node Object

This represents a location, and any other relevant information, relating to a routine activity node. For example, routine activity nodes might be the home location, place of work, local drinking establishment, homes of acquaintances, and so forth. The routine activity node object stores the following data:

Location: (x,y)
Type: home, work, social, other
Hours of operation: day, night, and so forth.

Routine Activity Node Array

An individual's routine is represented as an array of routine activity node objects with some associated constraints concerning the times they should be visited. For instance, one may need to be at work between 9am and 5pm. Other constraints, such as hours of operation, may further dictate or influence routines. Some time constraints will be more rigid than others and, as such, play more or less important a role in dictating when an individual will be at a certain location. In turn, this will affect the opportunities they encounter (Ratcliffe, 2006).

Behaviors

In accordance with our BBAI approach, an agent behavior encapsulates a single, but potentially complex perception, process, or action the agent is capable of performing. Agents within the simulation implement several behaviors, some of which represent conscious human decision-making processes, such as making choices about which route to take to a destination. Others represent subliminal processes, such as the updating of memory or redrawing of the cognitive map. These are formalized as individual behaviors for the purposes of implementation; simulating such low-level neurological or autonomic processes being, at least currently, far beyond the scope of this work. With respect to our interests the most important of these behaviors, that is Navigate and Make Rational Choice, as well as associated offending schema, are outlined next. For a more comprehensive view on agent behaviors, Appendix 1 contains a complete description.

Navigate

As discussed, individuals within any environment have certain routine activities, which involve traveling between several key locations, or routine activity nodes. How an agent gets from one point to another is dictated by the transport network of the area, this includes pedestrian thoroughfares, roads (which accommodate pedestrians, cars, buses, among others), and, in future models, mass transit systems.

The cognitive process of route planning is a complex one. The navigational behavior of any agent within a simulation of crime activities is very important, in that any simulation is heavily reliant upon realistic agent movement, as this dictates at least one of the key dimensions within the victim-offender-location interaction. The model described makes use of a dynamic routing algorithm which is implemented via a multilevel variation of the Dijkstra algorithm (1959). It allows an agent to process its current location, internal state and local environmental factors, in order to calculate a suitable route between its current location and its destination. This is accomplished by a combination of ascertaining the shortest, most convenient (where fewer path changes equate to a higher "convenience utility") and best-known route between the current location and intended destination. This approach has its weaknesses, as it assumes that all individuals possess a perfect model of the transport network upon which to calculate routes. It is suggested that a more realistic representation may be accomplished by combining both the existing deliberative approach within areas an individual is aware of, and a rather more reactive algorithm in novel locations which assesses the utility of local route choices spatially. In this way, an agent can build up an awareness of the transport network over time in the same way that one might become aware of crime opportunities within an area. This approach is currently being investigated by the authors. Additionally, subsequent models should implement existing, more complex node path representations which allow for the evaluation of capacity, speed limit and usage levels when routes are selected.

Make Rational Choice

In conjunction with the offending schema (below), this behavior attempts to encapsulate the rational choice of potential offenders: recognition of the presence of a target, and its suitability (within the selected offending schema) alongside assessment of the potential risk, reward and effort of committing an offence. The Make Rational Choice behavior relies on information from both the environment and the agent by evaluating a location with respect to the currently designated crime schema, and an agent's state of readiness and familiarity with the location. An agent at any location will ascertain the presence of an offending opportunity prior to contemplating the risks, rewards and efforts associated with the commission of such an offence. When applying this behavior with the relevant crime schema, if the Make Rational Choice behavior finds favorable conditions for perpetrating an offence (when the offender is suitably motivated and the reward outweighs the risk and necessary effort), a crime is committed. Furthermore, the agent's awareness of the location in question is enhanced, having committed the incident and its associated factors to memory.

The threshold around which this Make Rational Choice behavior is assessed is highly dependent upon the agent's current readiness, therefore an offender who has not come across any opportunities for some time may choose to modify his offending criteria. As reward increases in importance and value, targets which on previous occasions were considered too risky, or required too much exertion, become more feasible. Less attractive opportunities with higher risks are, after all, preferable to a continuation of the dry spell. Either way, an offender's perception of opportunity and its associated factors is offence specific.

Offending Schema

Cornish (1994) introduced the concept of crime scripts as a means to broaden and systematize our understanding of the criminal event. Crime scripts allow modeling of the entire criminal event, focusing on an offender's routine decision-making process as he is confronted with issues such as risk, effort and reward. An offender's perceptions thereof rely heavily upon the crime type for which the individual is evaluating a situation. These scripts, or offending schema, set out a pattern, or structure, for committing a certain crime; they provide the necessary conditions, advantageous and detrimental, for victimization of some kind to occur. For example, a schema for car theft requires the presence of a vehicle, which is of some utility value to the offender, be it economic, utilitarian, or gratifying. Advantageous conditions in this case may be a lack of guardianship, thus minimizing the chance of detection, and a model of vehicle the offender has some experience of stealing. Certain schema "rules" pervade all crime types, such as the negatory presence of a capable guardian, the advantages offered by previous experience of the crime in question, and the minimum effort scenario.

Whilst other factors may seem to apply to all crimes, it is in the specifics of *how* they apply that the schema assist us. It is important to remember that the constitution of the scenario varies by crime type, for example, an open window for burglary, a person carrying cash or a cell phone openly for street robbery, and so on. In some instances, the same phenomena may create conflicting influences for different crime types. For example, burglars are more likely to offend in an area with minimal guardianship or pedestrian footfall, whereas street robbers require a greater level of usage (Felson, 2002), increasing both the number of suitable targets to select from, as well as providing an increased level of anonymity.

Each crime schema should comprise of the following:

- Any crime-specific prerequisites
- A definition of crime-specific risk factors
- A definition of crime-specific reward factors
- A definition of crime-specific effort

In the current version of the model, only one crime schema has been implemented: domestic burglary. This offence has been used as a starting point for reasons described previously. The crime schema for domestic burglary is as follows:

- **Crime-specific prerequisites:** A domestic property.
- **Crime-specific risk factors:** Occupancy of property; pedestrian footfall in the vicinity.
- **Crime-specific reward factors:** Affluence of area; likelihood of property containing 'CRAVED' goods (Hamill, 2000; Hearnden, & Magill, 2004; Felson, 2002).
- **Crime-specific effort:** Security of property in question (e.g., door locks); layout of property (e.g., back alleys).

This schema dictates the formulation of perception of risk, reward and effort for domestic burglary. Therefore, our initial formulism of offence occurrence can be updated to:

Crime occurs if
Perception of Opportunity >
threshold(propensity,readiness)
AND
Schema(domestic_burglary,
(Perceived_Reward(Opportunity))) >
(Schema(domestic_burglary,
(Perceived_Risk(Opportunity)))×
Schema(domestic_burglary,
(Perceived_Effort(Opportunity))))

In accordance with this schema, we can further decompose the perception of opportunity, reward, risk and effort into the following algorithms for use within the simulation[5].

Perceived_Opportunity(x,y)
domestic housing density(x,y) ×
awareness_of_opp =
(me.awareness(x,y) ×
(k+speciality_bonus)
end

Perceived_Reward(Opportunity)
target_density(x,y,t) * *affluence_val(x,y)*
end

Perceived_Risk(Opportunity)
guardianship(x,y,t) ×
security_rating(x,y) ×
(k-speciality_bonus)
end

Perceived_Guardianship
occupancy(x,y,t) +
ped_footfall(x,y,t) +
crime_prev_presence(x,y,t)
end

Perceived_Effort(Opportunity)
security_rating(x,y) ×
(k-speciality_bonus)
end

Simulation Time

As much of simulation's power is in its ability to synthesize a *series* of decisions made by a group of agents, it inherently captures the temporal dimension of the phenomena we wish to observe. As such, a complex representation of time is not required; within the simulation, time is represented by a cyclic variable named *simulation_time* which iterates as time passes. Each cycle has two key phases: the environment phase and the agent phase. During the environment phase the environment model updates. In other words, any of the backcloth data sets with a temporal profile update their values to reflect the new time. Following this, the agent phase proceeds. This can be considered akin to a turn in a game. Each agent within the environment gets a turn, during which it performs its perception-action cycle and perceives, reasons, and acts as described in the next section. After all agents have had their turn, *simulation_time* iterates and the cycle begins again with the next environment phase.

The Agent Perception-Action Cycle

The agent perception-action cycle encompasses the collective actions of an individual agent during one unit of simulation time. Following the behavior-based paradigm previously discussed, the processes within this cycle allow an agent to perceive its local environment and current internal state, and make a decision about the best action to take in the current circumstances. In accordance with our three key theories, an offender agent within our model implements the following key behaviors during each cycle: Follow Routine (broken down into Check Routine and Navigate behaviors), Make Rational Choice (separated into further behaviors: Perceive Opportunity, Risk, Reward and their associated crime schema) and Update Awareness.

In summary, we have envisaged and, using ABM techniques, developed a working model of crime activities which incorporates the mechanisms of routine activity theory, the rational choice perspective and crime pattern theory. We have created an adequately complex model of the environment to facilitate the examination of these theories and populated this with data relevant to domestic burglary. We now move on to discuss how such models might be evaluated and describe the initial observations of our model.

EVALUATION

How to evaluate the output of simulation models, such as the one described is, at present, difficult to ascertain and, thus, open to debate. The aim of our simulation of crime activities is to model, examine and understand the interactions of crime, which give rise to the patterns observed by traditional analysis. In doing so, we aim to gain insight into the interactions between both the criminal and his environment at a micro level, as well as the macro aggregation of numerous individual behaviors, in the hope that we might better be able to divert potential offenders or crime trends respectively.

As previously described, we must therefore attempt to encapsulate what we believe to be the offender decision-making process and then examine its direct impact on a macro level output. However, if this output is akin to that observed in the real world, is it correct to infer that the micro level interactions, which occurred within the simulation, have been dictated by a truly valid operationalization of real world offender decision-making processes? Similarly, if the output does not exhibit the features of observed crime patterns, is this proof of the null hypothesis? Is the behavior we have attempted to formalize irrelevant in terms of crime occurrence or have we simply failed to correctly encapsulate offenders' reasoning or the true interpretation of environmental features? Indeed, should we expect simulated crime outputs to mirror those evidenced in the real world by *recorded* crime data? It is a well-established fact that police crime data and, to a lesser degree victim survey data, are unrepresentative of the true level of crime (Biderman & Reiss, 1967; Maguire, 2002). Were model outputs to accurately reflect such observed levels, we could not, therefore, claim a successful simulation; more likely we would have evidence of significant over-training (see below). However, it is now believed that, although the levels of recorded and actual crime are disparate, the *patterns* of crime (in terms of type, location, etc.) found in the recorded datasets are representative of actual crime patterns for many offences (Farrington, & Langan, 1998). For this reason, comparing the presence of established phenomena such as repeat victimization –where it is the pattern of offending rather than the extent or actual location—remains a potentially suitable technique for model evaluation. This is particularly the case for offences which have relatively high reporting levels, such as homicide, car theft and domestic burglary (Walker, Kershaw, & Nicholas, 2006; Maguire, 2002).

Another potential method of evaluation may be through the application of some form of sensitivity analysis. Through the systematic parameterization of simulation models, experiments which explore the output effects of variance within specific parameters can be performed. This is accomplished by manipulating one simulation variable at a time whilst all others are held static. Any changes in output behavior resulting from this variance can then be examined within the context of the theoretical framework around which the model is based.

A further possible method of evaluating such models, which seems particularly attractive, is that of model replication and verification. This would be similar to the process of replication that occurs when any major scientific discovery is made (and as used in clinical trials), whereby other researchers attempt to replicate the experiment in order to verify or falsify the theory in question. It is suggested that such replications could explore models of offending wholly within different implementation architectures, use new models of offending behavior in existing environmental models, or use existing agents and behavioral models within novel environmental contexts. With regard to the latter, such within-model replication should also be carried out to ensure there has been no over-training of the model. In other words, the simulation should be applied across different times and places to rule out the possibility of bias to the original dataset that could otherwise reduce generalizability and, thus, the utility of any findings. The aim of such replication is to explore the effect of context and, where possible, demonstratively identify any universally applicable representations, thus furthering their theoretical verification. For a more in depth discussion of validation through replication see Townsley and Johnson in this volume.

Whilst the most appropriate techniques for evaluation are further debated, we have chosen to proceed by providing a macro level comparison of simulation and real world domestic burglary offences to test the potential utility of our model. We have previously described several reasons for focusing on this offence, but for the purpose of this evaluation the most compelling are the phenomena of repeat and, for our evaluation, near repeat victimizations (which have been shown to hold true in several studies, across a range of environments, see Farrell & Pease, 2001; Johnson, Bernasco, Bowers, Elffers, Ratcliffe, Rengert, & Townsley, in press, respectively) and the metrics available for their measurement. The following section describes the evaluation process and initial findings from the work described.

Setting Up the Experiment

The features of the current domestic burglary model are explicitly stated below. We suggest it would be most beneficial if this format was adopted by the research community when presenting formalisms of this type.

Aim

Begin examination of opportunity theories by implementing simplistic model of domestic burglary.

Simulation Elements

Environment

Transport network: Road network data

Targets: Residential address points—random allocation of security and affluence rating at aggregate level.

Aggregated environmental data: Household occupancy profiles, pedestrian footfall profiles (both derived from neighborhood classification data)

Agents

Parameters: Propensity, readiness, awareness space, routine activity node array

Key behaviors: Navigate, make rational choice, update awareness

Schema: Domestic burglary (monetary reward only)

Once the selected environment has been digitized into the series of simulation formalisms previously described, the agents themselves are created. In a regular test run, a population of anywhere between one and several hundred offender agents can be created[6]. Each of these is then allocated several parameter values at random, within reasonable bounds. These include the offending propensity

Figure 8. The simulation application

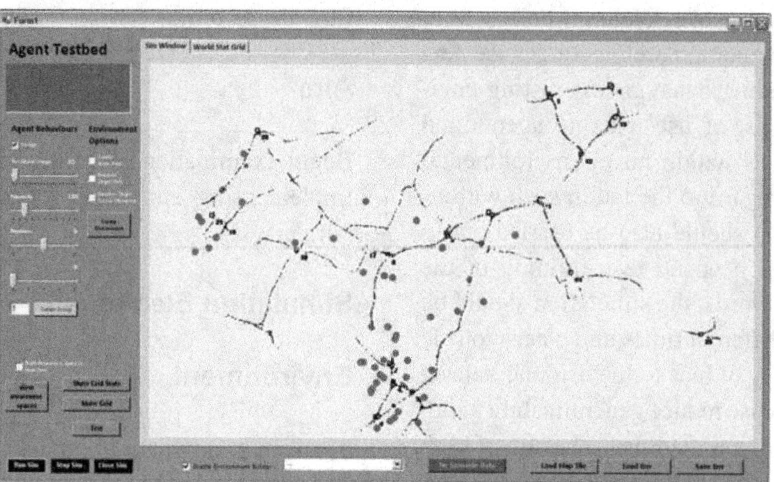

of a given agent, its 'readiness' at simulation start up, a series of routine activity nodes (agents are randomly allocated nodes from a selection of suitable possibilities, for example, the home node should be in a residential area), a routine and, finally, the associated awareness space. Once all these elements are in place, the simulation is started and left to run for a predetermined number of cycles. As it does so, the user is presented with a graphical view[7] similar to that of a GIS, of the agents traversing the environment and, at certain times, performing burglaries. Figure 8 provides an example of the graphical user interface during a simulation test run. At the end of such a run an output file is produced that describes the location, date, time, and offender for all offences committed. Additionally, the user is presented with both a graphical representation of each

Figure 9. Kernel density estimation of simulation output

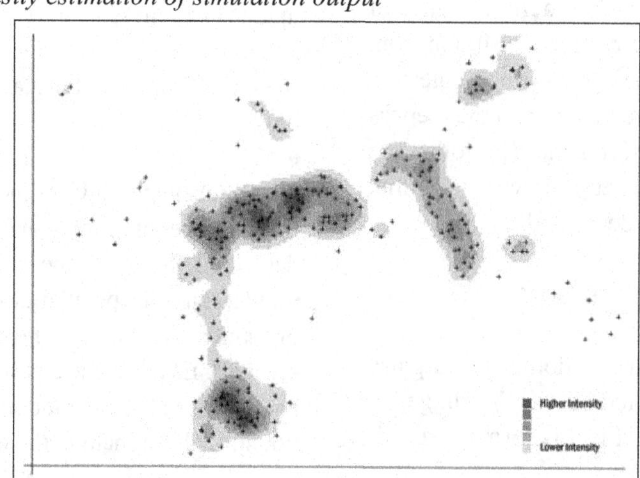

individual agent's accumulated awareness space and of these spaces combined.

Examining the Output

This output can then be examined using existing top-down analysis techniques to ascertain any similarities with real observed crime patterns, allowing the subsequent drawing of inferences about the underlying mechanisms implemented within the simulation. For instance, we may use kernel density estimation to identify the presence of crime hotspots, an example of which is shown in Figure 9.

Near Repeat Victimization

Recent research following from the study of repeat victimization has demonstrated the presence of *near* repeat victimization. This is when offences occur in close spatial and temporal proximity to a previously victimized target. For instance, when a burglary occurs at one home, another is likely to occur swiftly nearby.

Johnson and Bowers (2004) have demonstrated that the risk of domestic burglary appears not only to move, but to cluster in space and time in much the same way as a communicable disease. For this reason the authors utilized an epidemiological metric (Knox & Bartlett, 1964), which allows for the identification and quantification of spatio-temporal clustering occurring within a given dataset. A distinct advantage of this measurement for the current evaluation is that it provides descriptions of spatio-temporal patterns irrespective of their actual locations. This is important as although our environment model is derived from real world datasets, the offenders and therefore their awareness spaces and routine activities are wholly hypothetical. Thus we should not expect the location of simulated offences to mirror real world distributions; rather we are interested in the characteristics of the crime patterns that are formed.

We applied this metric to the output from our models in order to compare the spatio-temporal profiles with those obtained from real world data. This quantitative output was qualitatively assessed and initial results indicate a strong resemblance between the simulation and real world profiles, both showing evidence of near repeat victimization for domestic burglary. Further work is currently being carried out to empirically verify the observed similarities.

Given that there is much debate to be had concerning methods of evaluation it is not appropriate to make conclusions about our theoretical assumptions or simulation representations from this initial comparison. Further testing is required as stated above in addition to sensitivity analysis and cross-validation of the existing model. We further wish to maintain and promote discussion with our peers in the hope of ascertaining the validity and usefulness of the model described through replication and, more widely, through the discussion of simulation techniques within our discipline.

FURTHER WORK AND POTENTIAL APPLICATIONS

The authors recognize that there are likely to be two directions within simulation research: more abstract macroscopic models (such as Cops n' Robbers) and microscopic models that are more representative of the real world environment. As the majority of the research presented here has concentrated on the latter, we now present ideas for further work taking this direction and discuss some potential applications.

A key application of ABM, as stated previously, is to examine, test and refine current theory and the concepts within it. The initial stages of this will need to focus on offender decision-making and routine activities in order to establish the validity of these notions and the ways they have been formalized. Once a consensus has been reached on the success of this stage, efforts can be concentrated on producing a more detailed environmental backcloth, and manipulating features within it. During this phase a number of concepts could be tested. Including sufficiently accurate and detailed land usage data, for example, would allow us to see if crime attractors and crime generators (Brantingham & Brantingham, 1995) appeared naturally and then to compare these facilities to those with particularly low levels of crime. Given a range of crime schema, it would also be possible to consider the relative hetero/homogeneity of offenders and the concepts of self-selection (Chenery, Henshaw, & Pease, 1999; Roach, 2006; Wellsmith, & Guille, 2005) and offender adaptation (Donkin, & Wellsmith, 2006). Due to the time component, and the ability to simulate a number of years of activity in a relatively short period of time, it may be possible to look at the likely impact of an ageing population, the persistency, or otherwise, of hot spots (Johnson & Bowers, 2004; Spelman, 1995) and the criminal careers of places (Sherman, 1995).

Further analysis could be carried out into offenders' journeys to crime, helping to increase our understanding of concepts such as the buffer zones and distance decay observed at the aggregate level (Chainey & Ratcliffe, 2005; Rossmo, 2000; Rengert, Piquero, & Jones, 1999). Through an examination of individual level behaviors we could examine why some offenders travel further to crime than others (Smith, Bond, & Townsley, in press), as well as studying the variability in the directions and routes taken.

On a highly practical level, future models could be used to simulate crime prevention interventions as well as informing resource deployment (the nature and scope of which will be the subject of a future paper by the authors). Simulating interventions as "what if" scenarios would help practitioners select the most appropriate method(s) and target areas for the desired outcome, within practical and budgetary constraints. This could be applied to a range of schemes, from small-scale target hardening or property marking to the redesign of entire estates. It may also be possible to predict patterns of displacement (Barr & Pease, 1990) or diffusion of benefits (Clarke & Weisburd, 1994) and respond to these accordingly. Even the possible effects of changes in general incarceration or, given sufficient intelligence, the removal of specific, prolific offenders could be assessed. In a similar way, the effects of deploying enforcement resources, such as police officers, automatic number plate recognition (ANPR) cameras and mobile CCTV, could be tested and optimal times and locations identified. One specific way in which an agent-based model could inform such activity is by highlighting the routes through an area which are used by the highest number of offenders (generally, or within certain crime schema).

Additionally, new or alternate environments could be constructed and their predicted crime weaknesses identified and designed-out, whilst smaller variations, such as planning or change of use applications, could also be considered in light of the predicted impact upon crime. Changes to the transport system or road network and the blocking of rights of way (Clarke, 2004; Atlas & LeBlanc, 1994) would also be open to such testing.

Another technique which could be developed as a result of ABM is "routine activity profiling". This would be similar to geographic profiling (Rossmo, 2000) and would work by examining an individual's activity history within an area to infer their awareness space, routine activity nodes and, potentially, the locations of their future crimes.

Other analyses or experiments which could be carried out include: the effects of changing working environments (e.g., more people working flexible hours or from home); methods of increasing natural surveillance; the effect on crime rates and distribution of technological advancements in consumer goods; the impact of major events which alter people's routine activities (such as the soccer World Cup); boost and flag (Tseloni & Pease, 2003; Pease, 1998) and side-of-the-street (Bowers & Johnson, 2005) explanations for (near) repeat victimizations; micro analyses of crime distribution within specific facilities (such as hospitals or schools) through the construction of within-premise environments; and even the effects of the weather.

CONCLUSION

Throughout this chapter we have discussed the importance of several factors in aiding the development of simulation as a tool for criminologists. Having done so, we feel that the key issues for those wishing to advance this area of research are:

- Decompose theories of crime and adequately represent them as simulation formalisms.
- Build sufficiently modular and scalable architectures to facilitate incremental development.
- Continue to absorb existing and novel research findings, as well as considering any changes in society, using these to advance models, where relevant.
- Work towards developing a viable evaluation strategy, considering the validity of replication, and interpret any results logically and carefully.
- Most importantly, remember that we need to make some assumptions, but we do so in order to test the validity of them.

Simulation design, implementation, and interpretation are not simple tasks. Therefore, to further endeavors in this area, we suggest the sharing of thoughts, experiences, and representations, thus allowing a cross-pollination of ideas within the research community. From such discussions it may be possible to agree upon ontology for crime simulation, which would facilitate the examination, replication, verification and thus advancement of such an approach and, it is hoped, facilitate its entry into mainstream criminological analysis.

In conclusion, we have demonstrated that the use of agent-based modeling offers those involved in criminological research a new, and possibly unique, method to examine the interactions of crime. This *bottom-up* approach allows for the simulation and subsequent examination of the micro level interactions of crime which wholly contribute to the patterns as we normally observe them: at the aggregate level. In so doing it provides an opportunity to test and refine existing theory through a series of *in silico* experiments which would otherwise be impractical or impossible to implement.

More specifically, we have used a simple model of victimization and detection to describe the processes of theory decomposition and behavioral formalism. We have then described the nature of a much more inclusive model and populated it with data pertinent to domestic burglary. The initial output from this model has included evidence of the real-world phenomena of near repeat victimization. We have summarized our approach to further research in this field and introduced a number of suggestions for others in the research community to consider. These include a call for the cross-pollination of ideas, the use of a shared, modular and scalable architecture and the standardization of representations in order to most effectively take this approach forward, with the ultimate aim of increasing understanding.

FUTURE RESEARCH DIRECTIONS

Our model has been envisaged, and implemented, as an incremental one, allowing an iterative design process as more theoretical concepts are implemented and further data sources added. The scope of such work is vast. Therefore, it is important for developers to possess a roadmap of future extensions to follow. The next section discusses some of the issues we intend to explore. As additional elements are identified and quantified, they can be incorporated into a more advanced model, creating a more realistic and comprehensive representation. Future components should include:

- **Other agents:** Currently, the simulation only implements agents as offenders. An obvious next step is to incorporate non-criminal agents who act as potential targets and guardians, including law enforcement (Groff, 2006).
- **More crime schema:** As the existing model only implements the domestic burglary schema, one of the first steps should be to incorporate further schema for other crime types. These might not be limited to high volume opportunistic crime.
- **Develop additional and more complex agent behaviors:** These could include such things as offenders foraging outside their established awareness spaces, cooperating offenders and the formation of criminal networks. Further, other criminological theories and concepts should be incorporated.
- **Learning agents:** Templates or schema for offending change over time as offenders develop preferences about what makes a good opportunity. Similar mechanisms could be implemented via some form of feedback loop which allows an offender to evaluate the reward gained in any specific circumstances; allowing experience to dictate the perception of a good opportunity. Such mechanisms could be implemented via machine learning algorithms or a neural network.
- **Richer environment data:** The environment ultimately constrains and dictates the choices available to offenders. Hence, additional pertinent data sets should be incorporated into the model as they become available. Convergence on the components within, and representation of, a universal backcloth would significantly aid collaboration and the processes of replication previously discussed.
- **Realistic agent populations:** Create heterogeneous populations of agents which reflect the real area demographics of the environment simulated (Groff, 2006). For example, the population makeup of an area could inform the likely proportion of offenders, via the age crime curve (Farrington, 1986), as well as those available to provide natural surveillance and guardianship.

ACKNOWLEDGMENT

The authors would like to thank their colleagues at the UCL Jill Dando Institute of Crime Science, in particular Ken Pease and Gloria Laycock for their helpful comments. Furthermore, we are grateful to the three anonymous reviewers for their insightful comments and constructive suggestions.

REFERENCES

Atlas, R., & LeBlanc, W. (1994). The impact on crime of street closures and barricades: A Florida case study. *Security Journal, 5*, 140-145.

Barr, R., & Pease, K. (1990). Crime placement, displacement and deflection. In M. Tonry & N. Morris (Eds.), *Crime and justice: A review of research* (Vol. 12). Chicago: University of Chicago Press.

Biderman, A. D., & Reiss, A. J., Jr. (1967). On exploring the "Dark Figure" of crime. *Annals of the American Academy of Political and Social Science, 374*, 1-15.

Bonabeau, E. (2002). Agent-based modeling: Methods and techniques for simulating human systems. In *Proceedings of the National Academy of Sciences of the United States of America (PNAS),* 99(3), 7280-7287.

Bottoms, A. E., & Wiles, P. (2002). Environmental criminology. In M. Maguire, R. Morgan, & R.

Reiner (Eds.), *The Oxford handbook of criminology* (3rd ed.) (pp. 620-656). Oxford: Oxford University Press.

Bowers, K. J., & Johnson, S. D. (2005). Domestic burglary repeats and space-time clusters: The dimensions of risk. *European Journal of Criminology, 2*(1), 67-92.

Brantingham, P. J., & Brantingham, P. L. (1984). *Patterns in crime.* New York: Macmillan.

Brantingham, P. L., & Brantingham, P. J. (1993). Environment, routine, and situation: Toward a pattern theory of crime. In R.V. Clarke & M. Felson (Eds.), *Routine activity and rational choice, Advances in Criminological Theory* (Vol. 5). New Brunswick, NJ: Transaction Publishers.

Brantingham, P. L., & Brantingham, P. J. (1995). Criminality of place: Crime generators and crime attractors. *European Journal on Criminal Policy and Research, 3*(3), 5-26.

Brantingham, P. L., & Brantingham, P. J. (2004). Computer simulation as a tool for environmental criminologists. *Security Journal, 17*(1), 21-30.

Brantingham, P. L., Brantingham, P. J., & Glässer, U. (2005). Computer simulation as a research tool in criminlology and criminal justice. *Criminal Justice Matters, 58.*

Brantingham, P. L., Glässer, U., Kinney, B., Singh, K., & Vajihollahi, A. (2005a). A computational model for simulating spatial aspects of crime in urban environments. In *Proceedings of the IEEE International Conference on Systems, Man and Cybernetics*, Hawaii. Retrieved September 1, 2007 from http://fas.sfu.ca/pub/cs/techreports/2005/CMPT2005-10.pdf

Brantingham, P. L., Glässer, U., Kinney, B., Singh, K., & Vajihollahi, A. (2005b). Modelling urban crime patterns: Viewing multi-agent systems as abstract state machines. In D. Beauquier, E. Börger, & A. Slissenko, (Eds.), In *Proceedings of the 12th International Workshop on Abstract State Machines* (pp. 101-117). Paris: Universite de Paris.

Brooks, R. A. (1996, May). From earwigs to humans. In *Proceedings IIAS The Third Brain and Mind International Symposium Concept Formation, Thinking and Their Development*, Kyoto, Japan (pp.59-66).

Chainey, S. P., & Ratcliffe, J. H. (2005). *GIS and crime mapping.* London: Wiley.

Chenery, S., Henshaw, C., & Pease, K. (1999). *Illegal parking in disabled bays: A means of offender targeting.* Briefing Note 1/99. London: Home Office Policing and Reducing Crime Unit.

Clarke, R. V. (2004). Closing streets and alleys to reduce crime: Should you go down this road. *Problem-oriented guides for police, Response guides series No. 2.* US Department of Justice, Washington, DC: Office of Community Oriented Policing Services.

Clarke, R. V., & Eck, J. (2003). *Become a problem-solving crime analyst.* London: Jill Dando Institute of Crime Science, University College London. Retrieved September 1. 2007, from http://www.jdi.ucl.ac.uk/publications/other_publications/55steps, last accessed October 14, 2006.

Clarke, R. V. (1999). Hot products: Understanding, anticipating and reducing demand for stolen goods. *Police research series, Paper 112.* London: Home Office.

Clarke, R. V. (Ed.). (1997). *Situational crime prevention: Successful case studies* (2nd ed.). Guilderland, NY: Harrow & Heston.

Clarke, R. V. (1995). Situational crime prevention. In M. Tonry & D.P. Farrington (Eds.), *Crime and justice* (Vol. 19). *Building a safer society – Strategic approaches to crime prevention.* Chicago: The University of Chicago Press.

Clarke, R. V. (1983). Situational crime prevention: Its theoretical basis and practical scope. In M.

Tony & N. Morris (Eds.), *Crime and justice: An annual review of research* (Vol. 4) (pp. 225-256). Chicago: University of Chicago Press.

Clarke, R. V., & Felson, M. (1993). Criminology, routine activity, and rational choice. In R.V. Clarke and M. Felson (Eds.), *Routine activity and rational choice, Advances in criminological theories* (Vol. 5). New Brunswick: Transaction.

Clarke, R. V., & Weisburd, D. (1994). Diffusion of crime control benefits: Observations on the reverse of displacement. In R.V. Clarke (Ed.), *Crime prevention studies* (Vol. 2). Monsey, NY: Criminal Justice Press.

Cornish, D. B. (1994). The procedural analysis of offending and its relevance for situational prevention. In R.V. Clarke (Ed.), *Crime prevention studies* (Vol.3). Monsey, N.Y.: Criminal Justice Press.

Cornish, D., & Clarke, R. V. (1986). *The reasoning criminal: Rational choice perspectives on offending.* New York: Springer Verlag.

Cohen, L. E., & Felson, M. (1979). Social change and crime rate trends: A routine activity approach. *American Sociological Review, 44*, 588-608.

Cusson, M. (2002). *Prévenir la délinquance.* Paris: Presses Universitaires de France.

Donkin, S., & Wellsmith, M. (2006). Cars stolen in burglaries: The Sandwell experience. *Security Journal, 19*(1), 22-32.

Dijkstra, E. (1959). A note on two problems in connexion with graphs. *Numerische Mathematik, 1*, 269-271.

Durkheim, E. (1897). *Le suicide.* Paris: F. Alcan.

Eck, J. E. (1995). Examining routine activity theory: A review of two books. *Justice Quarterly, 12*(4), 783-97.

Farrell, G., & Pease, K. (Eds.). (2001). Repeat victimization. *Crime prevention studies* (Vol. 12). Monsey, NY: Criminal Justice Press.

Farrington, D. P., & Langan, P. (1998). *Crime and justice in the United States and in England and Wales 1981-96.* Washington, D.C.: Bureau of Justice.

Farrington, D. P. (1986). Age and crime. In M. Tonry & N. Norris (Eds.), *Crime and justice—An annual review of research.* Chicago: The University of Chicago Press.

Felson, M. (2002). *Crime and everyday life* (3rd ed.). Thousand Oaks: Sage Publications.

Gottfredson, M., & Hirschi, T. (1990). *A general theory of crime.* Stanford, CA: Stanford University Press.

Groff, E. R. (2006). *Exploring the geography of routine activity theory: A spatio-temporal test using street robbery.* Un published doctoral dissertation, University of Maryland. Retrieved September 1, 2007, from https://drum.umd.edu/dspace/bitstream/1903/3775/2/egroff_diss_final.pdf

Hakim, S., & Buck, A. (1991). *Residential burglary: The Hakim-Buck study on suburban alarm effectiveness.* Philadelphia, PA: Temple University, Department of Economics.

Hamill, L. (2000). The introduction of new technology into the household. *Personal Technologies, 4*, 1-16.

Hearnden, I., & Magill, C. (2004). Decision-making by house burglars: Offenders perspectives. *Home office findings* 249. London: Home Office.

Jennings, N. R., & Wooldridge, M. (Eds.). (1998). *Agent technology: Foundations, applications, and markets.* New York: Springer-Verlag.

Johnson, S. D., Bernasco, W., Bowers, K. J., Elffers, H., Ratcliffe, J., Rengert, G., & Townsley, M. T. (in press). *Near repeats: A crossnational assessment of residential burglary.*

Johnson, S. D., & Bowers, K. J. (2004). The stability of space-time clusters of burglary. *The British Journal of Criminology, 44*(1), 55-65.

Knox, E. G., & Bartlett, M. S. (1964). The detection of space-time interactions. *Applied Statistics, 13*(1), 25-30.

Liang, J., Liu, L., & Eck, J. (2001). *Simulating crimes and crime patterns using cellular automata and GIS.* UCGIS Student Award Papers 2001. Retrieved September 1, 2007, from http://www.ucgis.org/f2oppor.html

Liu, L., Wang, X., Eck, J., & Liang, J. (2005). Simulating crime events and crime patterns in a RA/CA model. In F. Wang (Ed.), *Geographic information systems and crime analysis.* Reading, PA: Idea Publishing.

Maguire, M. (2002). Crime statistics: The "data explosion" and its implications. In M. Maguire, R. Morgan, & R. Reiner (Eds.), *The Oxford handbook of criminology* (3rd ed.) (pp. 322-375). Oxford: Oxford University Press.

Mataric, M. J. (1995). Issues and approaches in the design of collective autonomous agents. *Robotics and Autonomous Systems, 16*(2-4), 321-331.

Mataric, M. J. (1992). Integration of representation into goal-driven behavior-based robots. *IEEE Transactions on Robotics and Automation, 8*(3), 304-312.

Meyer, B. (1997). *Object-orientated software construction* (2nd ed.). New York: Prentice Hall.

Pease, K. (1998). Repeat victimisation: Taking stock. *Crime detection and prevention series, Paper 90.* London: Home Office.

Pfeiffer, R., & Scheier, C. (1999). *Understanding intelligence.* Cambridge: MIT Press.

Polvi, N., Looman, T., Humphries, C., & Pease, K. (1990). Repeat break-and-enter victimization: Time course and crime prevention opportunity. *Journal of Police Science and Administration, 17*(1), 8-11.

Poyner, B., & Webb, B. (1993). What works in crime prevention: An overview of evaluations. In R. Clarke (Ed.), *Crime prevention studies* (Vol. 1). Monsey, NY: Criminal Justice Press.

Ratcliffe, J. H. (2002). Aoristic signatures and the spatio-temporal analysis of high volume crime patterns. *Journal of Quantitive Criminology, 18*(1), 23-43.

Ratcliffe, J. H. (2006). A temporal constrain theory to explain opportunity-based spatial offending. *Journal of Research in Crime and Delinquency, 43*(3), 261-291.

Rengert, G. F., & Wasilchick, J. (2000). *Suburban burglary: A tale of two suburbs.* Springfield, IL: Charles Thomas Publishers.

Rengert, G. F., Piquero, A. R., & Jones, P. R. (1999). Distance decay reexamined. *Criminology, 37*, 427-445.

Roach, J. (2006, August). Those who do big bad things also usually do little bad things: Identifying active serious offenders using offender self-selection. In *Proceedings of the 6th Annual Conference of the European Society of Criminology*, Tübingen, Germany.

Robinson, W. S. (1950). Ecological correlations and the behavior of individuals. *American Sociological Review, 15*, 351-357.

Rossmo, D. K. (2000). *Geographic profiling.* Boca Raton, FL: CRC Press.

Sherman, L. W. (1995). Hot spots of crime and criminal careers of places. In J. E. Eck & D.

Weisburd (Eds.), *Crime and place, Crime Prevention Studies* (Vol. 4) (pp. 35-52). Monsey, NY: Criminal Justice Press.

Smith, W., Bond, J. W., & Townsley, M. (in press). Determining how journeys-to-crime vary: Measuring inter- and intra-offender crime trip distributions. In D. Weisburd, W. Bernasco & G. Bruinsma (Eds.), *Putting crime in its place: Units of analysis in spatial crime research*. New York: Springer.

Spelman, W. (1995). Criminal careers of public places. In J. E. Eck & D. Weisburd (Eds.), *Crime and place, Crime Prevention Studies* (Vol. 4) (pp.115-144). Monsey, NY: Criminal Justice Press.

Townsley, M., Homel, R. & Chaseling, J. (2003). Infectious burglaries: A test of the near repeat hypothesis. *British Journal of Criminology, 43*, 615-633.

Townsley, M. T., & Pease, K. (2002). How efficiently can we target prolific offenders? *International Journal of Police Science & Management, 4*(4), 323-331.

Tseloni, A., & Pease, K. (2003). Repeat personal victimization: "Boosts" or "Flags". *British Journal of Criminology, 43*(1), 196-212.

van Baal, P. (2004). *Computer simulations of criminal deterrence: From public policy to local interaction to individual behavior.* Den Haag, Netherlands: BJU Boom Juridische uitgevers.

Walker, A., Kershaw, C., & Nicholas, S. (2006). Crime in England and Wales 2005/06. *Home Office Statistical Bulletin 12/06*. London: Home Office.

Waller, I. (1982). What reduces residential burglary—Action and research in Seattle and Toronto. In H. J. Schneider (Ed.). *Victim in international perspective*. Berlin: Walter de Gruyter.

Weiss, G. (Ed.) (1999). *Multiagent systems—A modern approach to distributed artificial intelligence*. Cambridge: MIT Press.

Wellsmith, M., & Guille, H. (2005). Fixed penalty notices as a means of offender selection. *International Journal of Police Science and Management, 7*(1).

Wooldridge, M., & Jennings, N. R. (1995). Intelligent agents: Theory and practice. *The Knowledge Engineering Review, 10*(2), 115-152.

Wortley, R. (2001). A classification of techniques for controlling situational precipitators of crime. *Security Journal, 14*, 63-82.

ENDNOTES

1. The decision to use the male pronoun when referring to offenders was a stylistic one.
2. Pseudo-code is a generic way of describing algorithms using some of the conventions of programming languages. For example, pseudo-code functions that perform an operation on some input data *x,y* and subsequently produce an output *z* can be described as *function f(input x, input y) = output z*. For example a simple addition function might be represented as *addition(1,1) = 2*.
3. The algorithms assume the use of two functions: *is_present* (x,y,t), which verifies whether an entity is present at a given location in space (x,y) and time (t); and *select_@_random* which uses a stochastic process to select an element at random from a list of possible options, in this case, a random direction from the eight cardinal and ordinal directions.
4. Obviously this makes significant assumptions about whether such things work in dissuading offenders (Poyner & Webb, 1993; Hakim & Buck, 1991; Waller, 1982). We

could synthesize and test the assumptions made about security devices by removing their deterrent effect and examining the subsequent output.

5 Where k is a constant, and *speciality_bonus* represents the offender's expertise in committing the specified offence. This is currently derived from the number of offences of this type previously committed. However, this concept requires further exploration and is currently included only for completeness.

6 Such decisions currently only affect the run-time of a given simulation, although, once more complex interactions between these agents are implemented, there may well be further behavioral ramifications depending on the size of the offender pool.

7 This graphical view is currently used to aid in the development and testing of the navigation behavior, as it allows the researchers to view the impact of a change in behavioral design instantly.

APPENDIX 1

Agent Behaviors

Behavior	What it does	Inputs	Outputs
Run Perception Action Cycle	High level behavior which allows an agent to select and call all relevant behaviors at each simulation cycle.	• Agent Parameters• • Environmental backcloth data	• Calls to Choose Next Destination, Navigate, Make Rational Choice
Choose Next Destination	Allows agents to select destinations from the routine activity node array and some novel activities.	• Routine activity node array • Current time	• Selects next activity node to visit
Navigate	Dynamically navigates between the current location and current destination activity node.	• Current location • Current destination • Awareness space • Road network constraints	• Updates awareness space • Make agent move
Update Awareness Space	Updates the awareness space of an offender so that the more time spent in an area, the more the awareness of that area and its surrounding areas increases.	• Current location • Existing awareness space	• Updated awareness space
Make Rational Choice (about offending)	Allows an agent to use some form of bounded rationality to make a decision whether or not to commit an offence at the current location and time	• Propensity • Readiness • Awareness of current location • Perceived opportunity at current time/place • Perceived reward at current time/place • Perceived risk at current time/place	• Calls commit crime behavior if necessary
Perceive Opportunity	Allows an agent to perceive the opportunity for crime at a given location and time	• Selected crime schema • Environmental backcloth data • Specialty bonus	• Some opportunity value at (x,y,t)
Perceive Risk	Allows agent to perceive the risk of detection involved in committing an offence at current location and time	• Selected crime schema • Environmental backcloth data • Specialty bonus	• Some risk value at (x,y,t)
Perceive Effort	Allows agent to perceive the effort involved in committing an offence at current location and time	• Selected crime schema • Environmental backcloth data • Specialty bonus	• Some effort value at (x,y,t)
Perceive Reward	Allows agent to perceive the reward available by committing an offence at current location and time	• Selected crime schema • Environmental backcloth data	• Some reward value at (x,y,t)
Commit Crime	Propagates a crime at the current point in space and time	• Selected crime schema • Current location and time	• Crime object • Update readiness • Update specialty bonus • Update awareness space

Chapter X
Offender Mobility and Crime Pattern Formation from First Principles

P. Jeffrey Brantingham
University of California, Los Angeles, USA

George Tita
University of California, Irvine, USA

ABSTRACT

Criminal opportunity in most cases is constrained by the fact that motivated offenders and potential targets or victims are not found at the same place at the same time. This ecological fact necessitates that offenders, potential victims, or both move into spatial positions that make crimes physically possible. This chapter develops a series of simple mathematical and agent-based models looking at the relationship between basic movement decisions and emergent crime patterns in two-dimensional environments. It is shown that there may be substantial regularities to crime patterns, including the tendency for crime to form discrete hotspots that arise solely from different movement strategies deployed by offenders.

INTRODUCTION

Foraging theory is the domain of ecology that seeks to model how organisms deploy alternative behavioral strategies to bring themselves into contact with the resources that they need for survival. For stationary organisms such as plants or sessile animals, foraging might mean attempting to establish and control a spatial position within the environment that ensures at least a minimum flow of nutrients past that location. For mobile animals such as large mammalian herbivores or carnivores seeking stationary or mobile prey, foraging may mean developing movement routines that ensure a certain rate of encounter and return from prey items. In exactly the same way, criminal opportunity in most cases is constrained by the fact that motivated offenders and potential targets or victims are not found at the same place at the same time. This ecological fact necessitates that the foraging movements of offenders, potential victims, or both intersect in ways that make crimes physically possible (Cohen & Felson, 1979; Felson, 2006).

Although formal modeling of the foraging behaviors of nonhuman organisms is routine in ecology (see e.g., Altman, 1998; Stephens & Krebs, 1986; Turchin, 1998), much less attention has been directed at modeling the movement patterns of criminal offenders (but see Brantingham & Brantingham, 1981; Groff, in press; Rengert, Piquero, & Jones, 1999; Rossmo, 2000). What we do know is that offenders appear to concentrate their movement in the immediate vicinity of nodal activity points such as a residence, but they occasionally will travel much farther distances along heavily used pathways (Bernasco & Nieuwbeerta, 2005; Flemming, Brantingham, & Brantingham, 1994). While these observations are crucial to crime pattern studies in a general qualitative sense, a quantitative understanding of how individual level movement choices translate into emergent crime patterns is still lacking. If studies from the physical and biological sciences provide any guide (Camazine, 2001; Koch & Meinhardt, 1994; Topaz & Bertozzi, 2004), then there is a strong possibility that very complex spatio-temporal crime patterns may be the product of relatively simple behavioral processes operating at the individual level. Finding this to be true would be consistent with the perspectives of routine activity theory (Felson, 2002), situational crime prevention (Clarke, 1995) and environmental criminology (Brantingham & Brantingham, 1981).

This chapter develops a series of mathematical and agent-based models looking at the relationship between offender movement decisions and emergent crime patterns in two-dimensional environments. These models rely on the simplest behavioral components and represent a "bottom up" modeling strategy. Section 1 of the chapter examines the minimal behavioral elements necessary to model movement in two dimensions. In principle, all we need specify are the rules describing how offenders choose movement distances and movement directions. In some cases it may also necessary to specify the time intervals at which an offender must return to the origin of movement, generally understood to be an activity node such as a residential location (Brantingham & Brantingham, 1993). Section 2 uses these basic components to build a very general and flexible model of offender movement. The model may be used to describe a continuum of offender foraging strategies ranging from simple random walks (Brownian Motion) through to so-called Lévy flights (anomalous diffusion) (Brantingham, 2006). Section 3 examines the hypothetical crime patterns generated by these movement regimes. We address the possible quantitative regularities in crime patterns that may be linked to movement regimes. Finally, we consider the analytical utility of simulating the emergence of crime patterns from first principles.

A MINIMALIST MODEL OF OFFENDER MOVEMENT

Offenders move about their urban environments in response to a complex array of individual and environmental attributes. For instance, the foraging choices of a residential burglar might hinge upon access to private or public transportation, the accessibility of residences, and levels of informal social control or surveillance (Bernasco & Luykx, 2003; Bernasco & Nieuwbeerta, 2005). As demonstrated in ecological studies, however, the simplest possible model of forager movement need only consider two things: (1) the choice of a direction in which to move; and (2) a choice of a movement distance (Brantingham, 2003; Brantingham, 2006; Turchin, 1998). Figure 1 shows how these two essential behavioral variables fit

Figure 1. Minimal components necessary for a model of offender movement. The variable β_i is the bearing for move i in a sequence of i = 1, 2...n moves. The variable δ_i is a distance for move i.

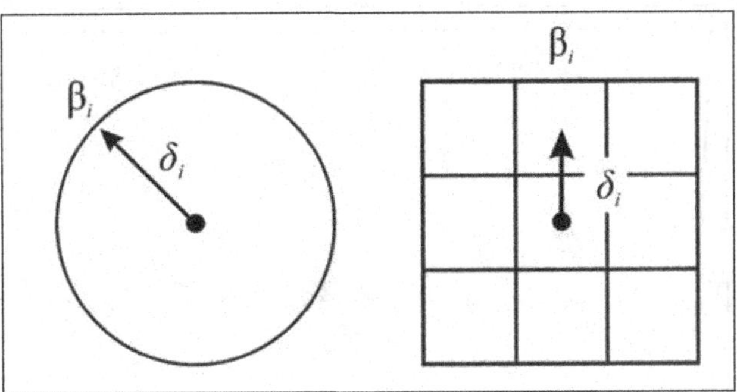

together. Given an initial starting location, a residence for example, we can determine the next spatial location visited by a modeled offender if we know the direction in which that offender is moving and the distance over which he will move. Here we will use the variable β_i to describe the bearing of movement and δ_i the distance for move number i = 1, 2…n in a sequence of n moves. In continuous space β_i is a continuous random variable falling in the interval 1-360° (Figure 1a). On a lattice, β_i is constrained to be in one of the four cardinal directions (Figure 1b). In both continuous and discrete space δ_i may be a fixed, small size, leading to simple random walk models (Turchin, 1998). Alternatively, it may be a random variable drawn on some probability distribution between some minimum δ_0 and maximum δ_{max} possible movement distance. On a lattice, δ_i must be an integer.

For simplicity, we will only describe models where the bearing of movement β_i is a uniform random variable, meaning that all movement directions are equally likely (see Brantingham, 2006; Marthaler, Bertozzi, & Schwartz, 2004; Turchin, 1996). Following a large literature in biology and physics, we model offender movement distances according to the Lévy probability distribution. This so-called Lévy mobility model has been used to study the movement patterns of organisms as different as dinoflagellates (Bartumeus, Peters, Pueyo, Marrase, & Catalan, 2003), bees (Viswanathan, Buldyrev, Havlin, da Luz, Raposo, & Stanley, 1999), albatross (Viswanathan, Afanasyev, Buldyrev, Murphy, Prince, & Stanley, 1996), howler monkeys (Ramos-Fernandez, Mateos, Miramontes, Cocho, Larralde, & Ayala-Orozco, 2004), deer (Viswanathan et al., 1999) and Paleolithic human foragers (Brantingham, 2006). On empirical grounds, therefore, the Lévy mobility model may be expected to provide a good description of offender movement as well.

$$p(\delta_i) = \delta_i^{-\mu} \quad (1)$$

Equation (1) states that the probability that an offender in one instance i moves over a distance δ_i is simply that distance raised to a negative power μ. Offender move distances thus obey a negative power law with properties defined only by the exponent μ (Viswanathan et al., 1999). The distribution corresponding to equation (1) is concave-up, meaning that short distance moves tend to be very common, but long distance moves also occur with a nonzero probability (Figure 3). For example, with $\mu = 2$, an offender faced with a choice to move a distance of 1 km (if measured in these units) will do so with a probability of $p(\delta) = 1$. Movement over a distance of 100 km will occur with a probability of $p(\delta) = .0001$, a rare event but not unlikely over many moves.

Figure 2. Lévy probability distribution describing the probability that an offender moves a distance δ in a single instance.

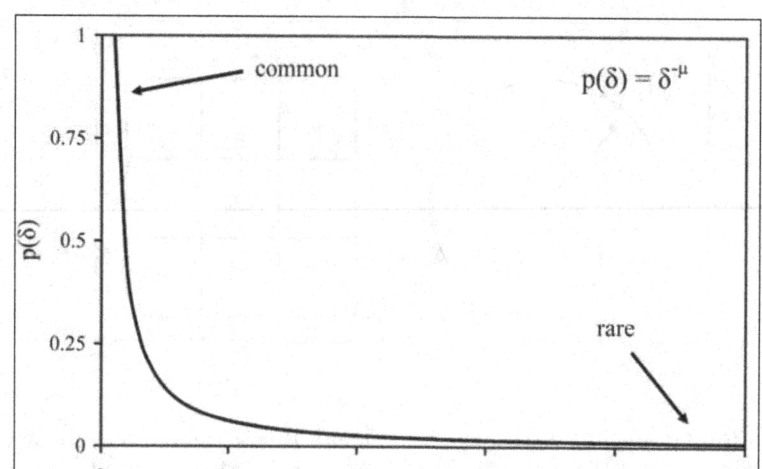

Figure 3. The path followed by of a offender in a continuous 2D environment over 2000 discrete moves. Movement directions are uniformly distributed and movement distances are from equation (1) with $\mu = 3.5$.

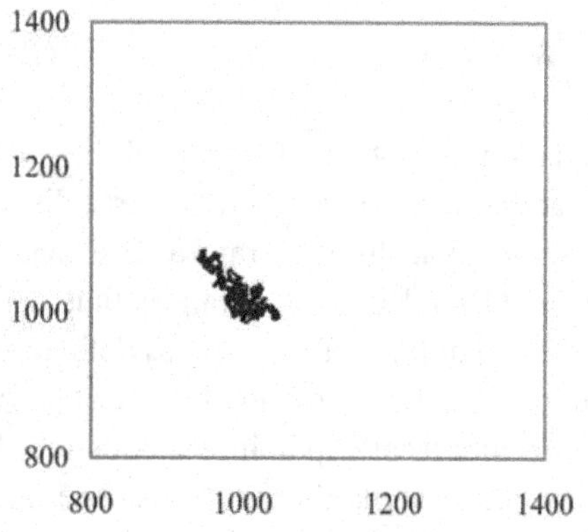

Physical (Nakao, 2000; Shlesinger, Zaslavsky, & Klafter, 1993) and biological (Viswanathan, Bartumeus, Buldyrev, Catalan, Fulco, Havlin, 2002; Viswanathan et al., 1999) studies have shown that qualitatively different forms of behavior appear when $1 < \mu \leq 3$. As μ approaches 3, the probability distribution shown in Figure 2 becomes increasingly concave, meaning that most of the moves that the offender makes will be of short distance. When $\mu \geq 3$, then the average move length is equal to the minimum move length and the pattern of movement is equivalent to a simple random walk (Brownian Motion) (Figure 3) (Viswanathan et al., 1999). At an analytical level therefore values of $\mu = 3.5$ or $\mu = 7.5$ lead to the same behavior. As μ approaches unity, the Lévy distribution develops a "fat tail" and longer distance moves become common (Figure 4). If $\mu = 1$ then there is a finite probability that an offender moves along a path of infinite length, producing a so-called ballistic movement trajectory. When $\mu = 2$, the associated movement pattern displays clusters of short distance moves interspersed with occasional long distance moves (Figure 5). It is reasonable to consider the range of movement routines represented by different values of the Lévy exponent μ as corresponding to the range of movement options available to an offender (see Bernasco & Nieuwbeerta, 2005; see Groff & McEwen, 2006; Wiles & Costello, 2000). Offenders who travel solely on foot such as a teenager, might best be represented by a movement model with $\mu \geq 3$, since this would generate movement patterns dominated by short distance moves. By contrast, offenders who have access to a car such as an experienced commercial burglar might best be represented by a movement model with $\mu \rightarrow 1$ since this would generate movement patterns that show more regular long distance moves.

The movement patterns simulated in Figures 3-5 illustrate cases of unconstrained offender movement. This is typical behavior for foraging animals who do not return to a central place or home base except stochastically (Brantingham, 2006; Ramos-Fernandez et al., 2004; Viswanathan et al., 1996). In the present context, this is the drifter who moves about a city or between cities with no fixed address for any significant period of time. In a technical sense, an offender who commits only one crime from an anchoring address before moving to a new anchor point is itinerant from the perspective of crime pattern formation. The two parameters of the movement model are sufficient to specify the locations of the turning points, strung together end-on-end, along a movement path (Figure 6a).[1] At the other extreme, an offender might return to an activity node such as a residence, place of work or a bar after each individual move (Brantingham & Brantingham, 1993). This is the ideal behavior of a central place forager (see also Canter & Larkin, 1993; Stephens & Krebs, 1986). The two parameters of the current model are sufficient to describe the end points of each individual movement path (Figure 6b). Of course, between these extremes are movement regimes where an offender can string together a number of individual moves end-to-end before returning the origin. For example, Figure 7 illustrates a case where a mobile offender follows ten unique paths each of which strings together 20 individual moves end-to-end before returning to the origin.

FROM MOVEMENT TO CRIME PATTERNS

Very different spatial activity patterns are generated by the above models simply by: (1) varying

Figure 4. The path followed by of a offender in a continuous 2D environment over 2000 discrete moves. Movement directions are uniformly distributed and movement distances are from equation (1) with $\mu = 1.2$. Scale is the same as in Figure 3.

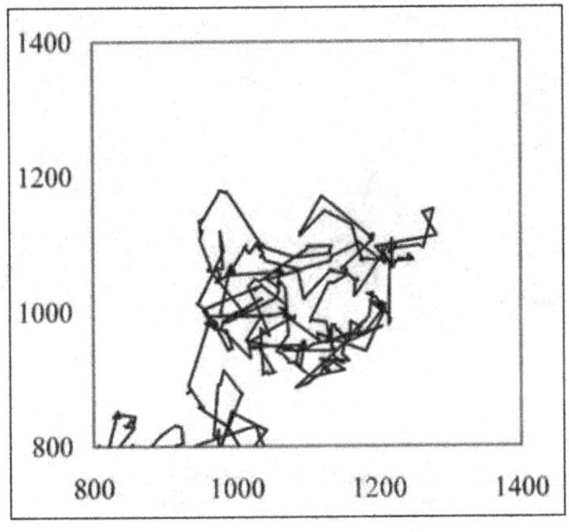

Figure 5. The path followed by of a offender in a continuous 2D environment over 2000 discrete moves. Movement directions are uniformly distributed and movement distances are from equation (1) with $\mu = 2.0$. Scale is the same as in Figure 3.

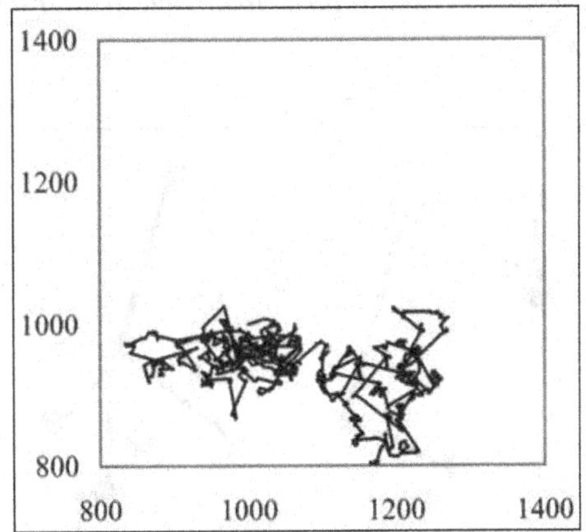

the parameter μ, which controls the relative frequency of movements of different lengths; and (2) imposing different constraints on when a modeled offender must return to the origin of movement. Depending upon the degree of complexity sought, it is relatively straightforward to examine the impact of how these different movement models might lead to different crime patterns. Here we assume that crime opportunities are ubiquitous in the environment and, as a consequence, that crimes occur at the distal end point of each move. An alternative would be to assume that crimes occur at any point along movement paths including both the endpoints and all of the intermediation locations between (see Brantingham, 2006). In the case of an offender that is unconstrained to return to the origin there are dramatic differences in both the overall spread and the local clustering of simulated crime incidence locations (Figure 8). When offender movement patterns are modeled using equation (1) with the exponent $\mu = 3.5$ (Brownian Motion) then crime locations tend to be relatively close to the origin of movement and tend to form dense continuous clusters (Figure 8a). Increasing $\mu = 2$ means that longer distance moves become more common. As a result, crime incidence locations are spread over a much larger area and crime clusters tend to be smaller and isolated (fragmented) (Figure 8b). With $\mu = 1.2$ the spread of crime incidence locations away from the origin of movement is even greater and there is a tendency for crime clusters to be even smaller and more isolated (Figure 8c).

A similar pattern is repeated in the case of an offender that is constrained to return to an origin of movement at some set interval of time. Figure 9 shows the density of crime locations for an offender that returns to the origin after each sequence of 100 moves. In each case, crime locations are mapped in arbitrary space and kernel densities are calculated for the same arbitrary grid size and search radius to ensure comparability of patterns across different simulations. Several general patterns are immediate apparent. When $\mu = 3.5$ and the offender moves out each time from the origin following approximately a simple

Figure 6. The two extreme types of movement topologies an offender might deploy. (a) Itinerant search where the offender is not constrained to return to an origin. (b) Central place movement where the offender returns to an origin after each move.

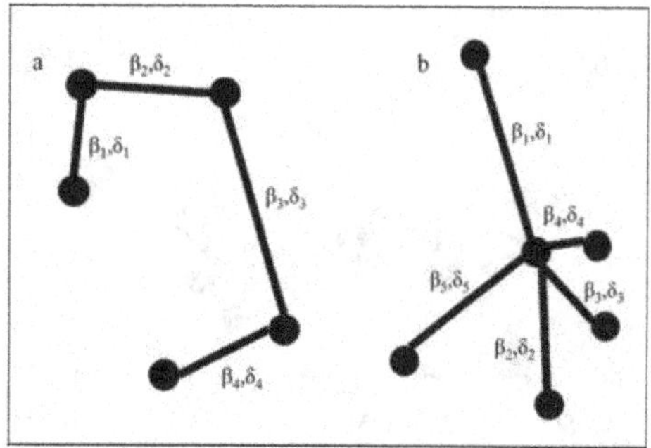

Figure 7. Ten separate paths followed by of a offender in a continuous 2D environment. The offender returns to the origin after each set of 20 discrete moves. Movement directions are uniformly distributed and movement distances are from equation (1) with $\mu = 2.0$. The origin is at 1000, 1000, shown as a gray box.

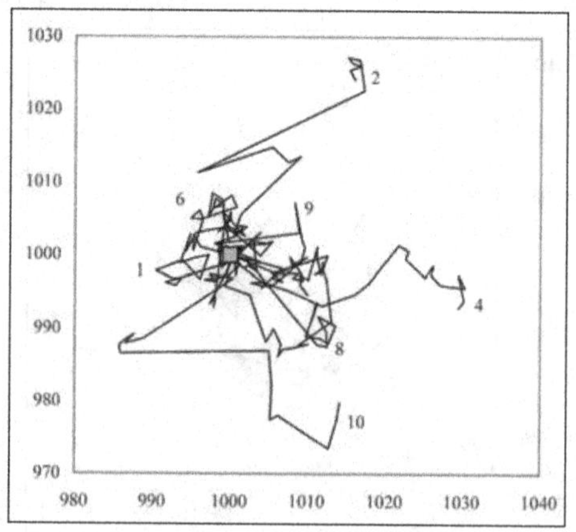

random walk (Brownian Motion) the density of crime locations is very high and compact around the origin and displays a sharp edge that takes the form of a "disc" (Figure 9a). In other words, all areas within this disc are repeatedly victimized a large number (and approximately equal) of times, while areas outside of this disc are victimized rarely. With $\mu = 2$ there is still an area of high

Figure 8. Simulated crime locations for a spatially unconstrained offender in a continuous 2D environment. In all simulations crimes are assumed to occur at the distal end point of each move. Offender movement directions are uniformly distributed. (a) Movement distances are from equation (1) with μ = 3.5. (b) Movement distances are from equation (1) with μ = 2.0. (c) Movement distances are from equation (1) with μ = 1.2. Each simulation consisted of 10,000 individual moves. The origin is at 1000, 1000, shown as a white box. Scale bar in (a) is 50 arbitrary units. Scale bar in (b) and (c) is 200 arbitrary units.

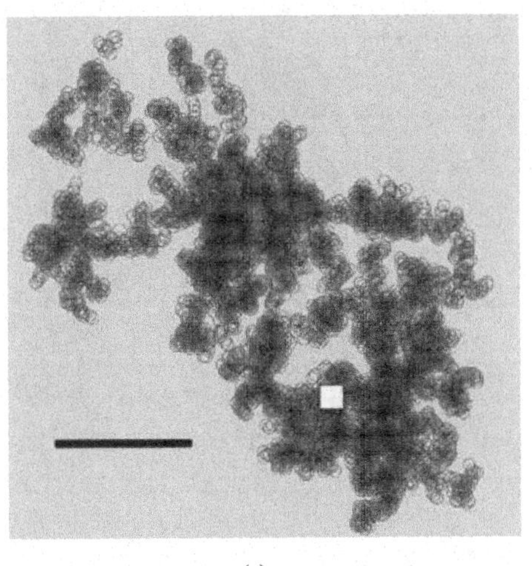

(a)

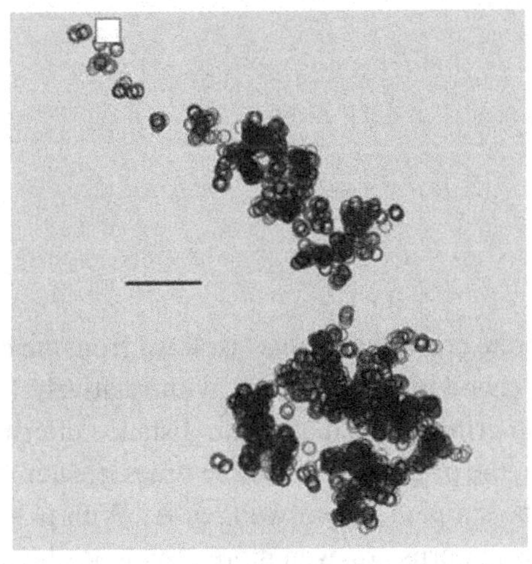

(b)

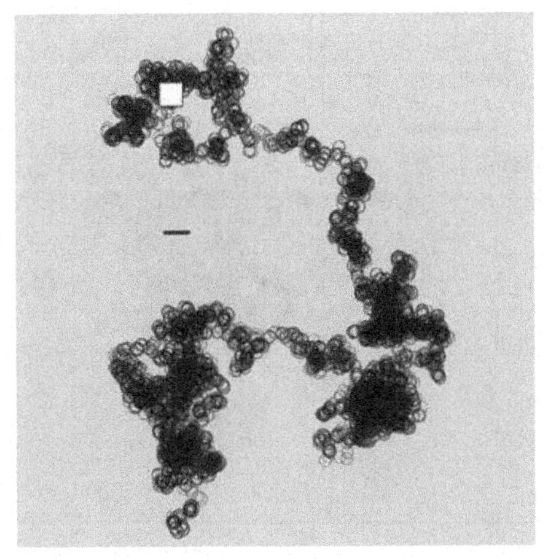

(c)

Figure 9. Density of crime locations for a spatially constrained offender in a continuous 2D environment. In all simulations, the offender was forced to return to the origin after every 100 moves and crimes are assumed to occur at the distal end point of each move.. Movement directions are uniformly distributed. (a) Movement distances are from equation (1) with $\mu = 3.5$. (b) Movement distances are from equation (1) with $\mu = 2.0$. (c) Movement distances are from equation (1) with $\mu = 1.2$. Simulation consisted of 10,000 individual moves. The origin is at 1000, 1000, shown as a white box. Scale bar in each panel is 50 arbitrary units.

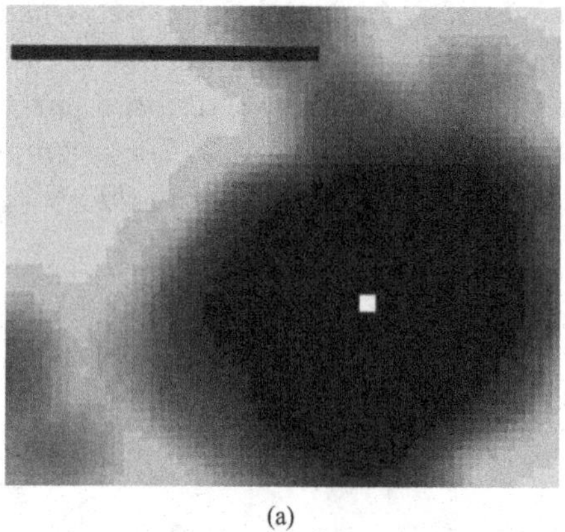

(a)

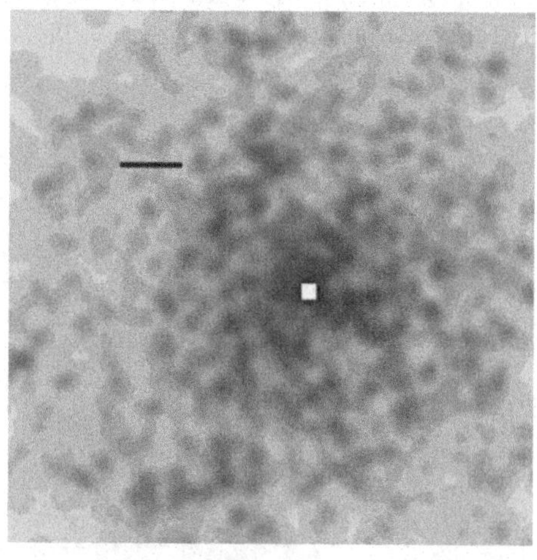

(c)

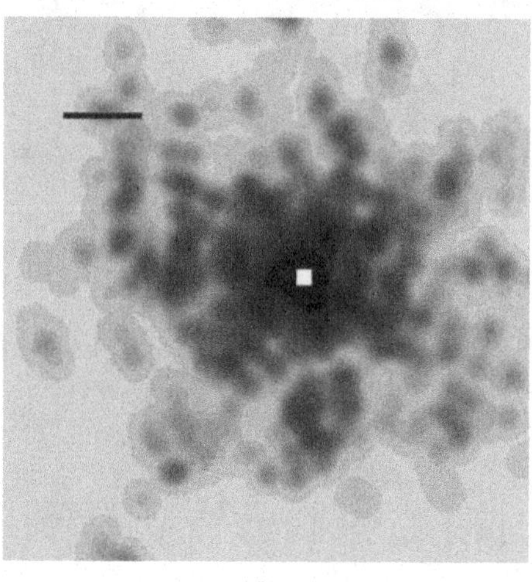

(b)

density crime close to the origin that is both "disc-like" in shape and approximately the same size as with the simple random walk case (i.e., μ = 3.5) (Figure 9b). However, beyond this central region the exterior contours of crime densities become increasingly "rough" with growing distance from the origin until ultimately there are well-formed, discrete crime "hot spots" isolated from the central crime area by regions with relatively little or no crime. The maximum distance of crimes from the origin is about three times greater than in the simple random walk case. With μ = 1.2 these patterns are even more pronounced with a "disc-like" central region of high density crime, a region with a rough exterior contour, a region of isolated crime "crime hotspots" and then finally a dispersed region of isolated crime locations (Figure 9c). The maximum distance of crimes from the origin of movement is approximately 12 times farther than in the simple random walk case. The spatial pattern seen here in the distribution of crime locations has been recognized as a general property random walks under some conditions (Arapaki, Argyrakis, & Bunde, 2004; Larralde, Trunfio, Havlin, Stanley, & Weiss, 1992; Yuste & Acedo, 2000). Despite the apparent regular geometry to the distribution of crimes, note that the abundance of crimes in space is very different between Figure 9a, b, and c. When activity is spread out over a much larger area (e.g., μ = 1.2, Figure 9c) the density of crimes at the origin of movement is much lower compared with the case where movement is concentrated around the origin (e.g., μ = 3.0, Figure 9a).

Figure 9 represents hypothetical crime patterns in an environment assuming that crime opportunities are uniformly distributed in space and that the offender is willing to commit crimes whenever an opportunity is encountered. However, we must also recognize that the interaction between different types of random walks and environmental structure is potentially an important source of spatial pattern generation (e.g., Sole, Bartumeus, & Gamarra, 2005). However, because of the complexities involved in characterizing different types of environmental structure, these issues are beyond the scope of the current paper. It is easier to get a feeling for the impact of local informal social control and surveillance on the spatial patterning of crime. Here we assume that local forms of informal social control will cause

Figure 10. Simulated crime locations for a spatially constrained offender in a continuous 2D environment. (a) Crimes are assumed to occur probabilistically as an increasing function of the distance from the origin of movement. (b) Density of crime locations. The offender was forced to return to the origin after every 100 moves. Movement directions are uniformly distributed and movement distances are from equation (1) with $\mu = 2.0$. Simulation consisted of 10,000 individual moves resulting in 3017 crime locations. Scale bar in (b) is 50 arbitrary units.

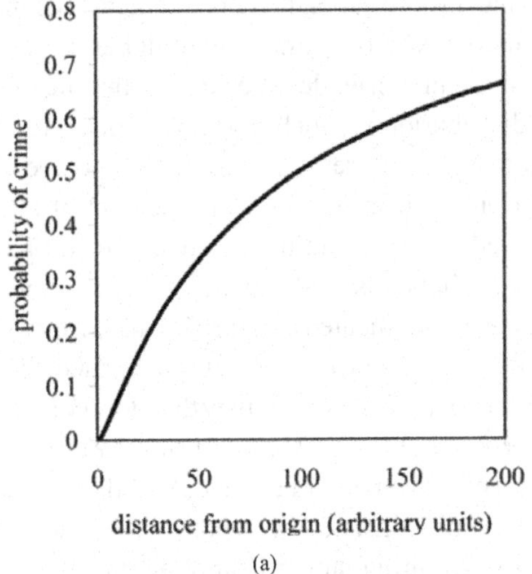

(a)

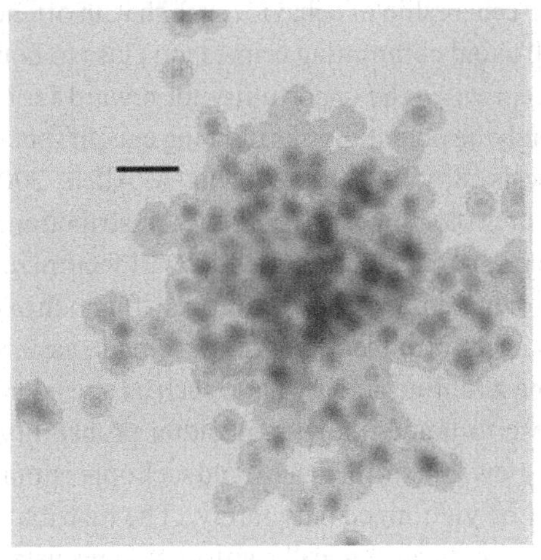

(b)

Figure 11. Simulated crime locations for a spatially constrained offender in a continuous 2D environment. The offender was forced to return to one of two origins after every 100 moves. Return to the lower-left origin occurred 60 per cent of the time. Return to the upper-right origin occurred 40 per cent of the time. Movement directions are uniformly distributed and movement distances are from equation (1) with μ = 2.0. Crimes are assumed to occur at the distal end point of each move. Simulation consisted of 10,000 individual moves. The origins are located at 1000, 1000 and 1106, 1106. Scale bar is 50 arbitrary units.

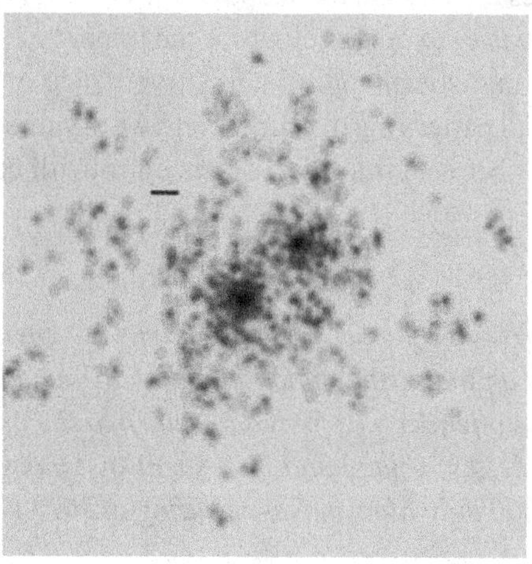

Figure 12. Relationship between the mean crime distance from the origin of movement and the number of crimes along a movement path before returning to the origin. Relationship is shown for three different values of the Lévy exponent μ. Note the log-linear scaling.

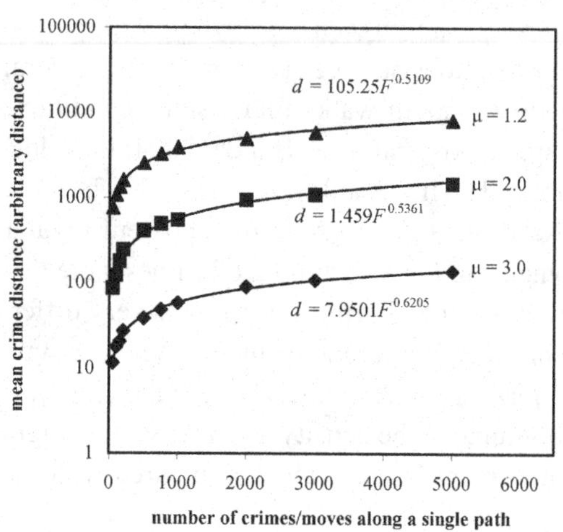

self-censorship of behavior such that an offender will avoid committing crimes too close to home, except when the opportunity for reward far outweigh the potential risks of being caught (but see Kocsis, Rayw.Cooksey, Irwin, & Allen, 2002). Figure 10a shows an hypothetical distribution for the probability that an offender will victimize an encountered crime opportunity as a function of the distance from the origin of movement, assumed to be a routine activity node such as a residence. Close to home, the victimization probability is very low (but still non-zero) and such opportunities will be victimized only rarely. The distribution increases logarithmically with increasing distance from the offender's residence such that far away from the residence crime opportunities are taken with near certainty when they are encountered. Figure 10b shows the results of combining the properties of offender movement modeled as Lévy flights with this self-censoring close to the offender's residence (origin of movement). As in the uncensored cases, there is a general tendency for the density of crimes to be higher closer to the simulated offender's residence, but the overall distribution is much patchier or discrete. In contrast to the previous simulations where the distribution of crimes around the central place covered a large, continuous area, here we have discrete hotspots that are individually smaller and clearly delineated by sharp breaks in levels of crime. Discrete crime hotspots are formed closer to offender's residence and they therefore comprise a greater proportion of the total crime pattern. The origin of movement might be buffered by an area of no crime, consistent with both observation and theory (Brantingham & Brantingham, 1984).

Interestingly, the root causes for discrete hotspot formation are different depending upon distance from the offender's residence. Close to the origin of movement, the offender's decision to self-censor due to local social control and surveillance is the primary reason for the formation of small, discrete hotspots. Far away from the origin of movement, hotspots are generated by constraints on movement; many fewer forays are made out far from the origin and therefore clustering of crime events is entirely the product of these rare stochastic events (see Larralde et al., 1992; Yuste & Acedo, 2000).

DISCUSSION

The simulations presented herein are meant to stimulate thinking about how fundamental features of the ways in which offenders move about their environments in search of suitable targets might be responsible for the generation of crime patterns. Borrowing from foraging theory, we proposed a model of offender movement which uses very limited number of assumptions about how individuals choose: (1) movement directions; (2) movement distances; and (3) when to return to an origin such as a residence location. Furthermore, we have concentrated primarily on the properties of movement distances modeled using the Lévy distribution (equation (1)). Despite the simplicity of the model it is clear that very simple behavioral routines are sufficient to generate a tremendous degree of complexity in hypothetical crime patterns. This observation is in keeping with general perspectives developed in the study of a wide range of complex systems (Camazine, 2001; Hubbell, 2001; Sole & Bascompte, 2006; Turchin, 2003). In particular, we have shown that offender movement strategies that are dominated by single short distance moves (i.e., Brownian Motion) and are directionally unbiased should lead to crime patterns that are concentrated close to the origin of movement, dense and well-bounded; that is there is a relatively sharp edge between areas of high and low crime concentrations (see Figure 9a). If movement routines occasionally include longer distance moves, then an irregular boundary comes to characterize crimes committed farther away from the origin of movement and isolated crime hotspots may also form at even grater distances (see Figures 9b and c). How such general patterns are impacted by differences in the distribution of criminal opportunities in an environment, biases in movement directions or other constraints remains to be investigated. We did briefly explore how self-censoring of criminal activities as a function of proximity to one's residence impacts crime pattern formation with the observation that it tends to enhance the complexity of crime patterns close to home. We anticipate that other constraints will have similarly dramatic impacts. For example, street network structure clearly has a significant impact on empirical crime patterns. Large streets tend to generate more crime simply by virtue of the greater volume of traffic that flows along them (Beavon, Brantingham, & Brantingham, 1994; Cohen, 1980). Similarly, aspects of the environment that serve as crime attractors such as bars or high schools are likely to bias movement in ways that impact crime patterns (Brantingham & Brantingham, 1995; Roncek & Maier, 1991). It seems to us, however, that these are features that should be added once we understand fully the dynamics of the to the baseline models presented here.

The simplicity of the current model brings us to a very important point about the role of simulation (and/or mathematical) modeling in the study of crime. Computer simulation models and especially so-called agent-based models have the advantage that they can be constructed at the scale of observation open to researchers. For example, it is physically possible to go out and observe the behavior of offenders in real environments and then build one's models based directly on these observations. Observation tends to be very rich in detail, however, and there is a real danger that models designed around observation will become bloated with too many variables. We have opted for the alternative in using the smallest number of variables sufficient to model offender movement. Critics of this work would likely claim that the models are either too simplistic and/or too dependent on stochastic mechanisms to actually be of utility in describing something so complex as crime patterns. For example, it might be argued that the present abstract spatial model, where movement anchored to a single activity node, is very unlike how real offenders move about their urban environments (Brantingham & Brantingham, 1993). However, not only is the simple model developed here is flexible enough to describe crime pattern formation around any location that serves as an origin for movement, including school, work, a friend's home, or a bar, but it also is easily extended to deal with an offender that operate from two or more activity nodes. Figure 11 illustrates a case where a single offender with $\mu = 2$ operates from two different activity nodes, returning after every 100 moves. The offender spends 60% of the time moving out from the lower of the two activity nodes and 40% of his time moving out from the other. It is clear not only that the sizes of the crime zones around each of the origins is approximately proportional to the amount of time spent there, but also that the smaller of the two appears more "disc like" in exterior contour and the larger "rougher" in much mimicking variation of the Lévy exponent μ (see Figure 9). There is also a band of hotspots connecting the areas of highest crime density, reminiscent of a path between activity nodes (Brantingham & Brantingham, 1993).[2] In both cases, it is clear that the distribution of crime locations may display regular spatial properties regardless of the specific location of the origin of movement, or how many activity nodes are involved.

Finally, we contend that the use of simple reductionist models provides a degree of analytical and quantitative tractability that are not available in more "holistic" approaches. While we have concentrated on the basics components of a model of offender movement based on the Lévy distribution and the qualitative crime patterns that this model generates, we also note that there are a number of quantitative measures that could be applied to the analysis of such offender movement systems (see Brantingham, 2006; Viswanathan et al., 1999). For example, there is a very regular relationship between the mean distance at which crimes are committed and both the number of crimes committed over a connected series of moves and the Lévy exponent μ (Figure 12). Simulations using different values of μ generate many unique foraging paths, which in turn generate different numbers of crimes. In general, the mean distance increases as the total number of crimes increases along any one foraging path, but the mean also rises much more rapidly for lower values of μ. In practice, this implies that an offender with more limited movement options (modeled as $\mu \rightarrow 3$) such as a teenager without access to a car will see the mean distance between the teenager's residence and each of the teenager's crimes grow slowly. By contrast, an offender with more diverse movement options (modeled as $\mu \rightarrow 1$) will see the mean grow very quickly (see Brantingham, Brantingham, & Wong, 1991). While further simulation testing and model calibration are clearly warranted, aspects of the relationships between offender movement and crime patterns might be highly predictable.

FUTURE RESEARCH DIRECTIONS

Simulation provides a useful tool for translating empirical observations about offenders and targets or victims made at a microscale into predictions about emergent crime patterns at higher spatio-temporal scales. When conducted alongside more rigorous mathematical analyses, simulations may provide a basis for predicting how and why such patterns emerge. While such methods are may lead to interesting insights about the nature of crime pattern formation, they deal mostly with what is possible rather than what actually is. We believe that it is necessary to also seek calibration and testing of models following a hypothetico-deductive framework. While it is by no means satisfying to have one's model rejected based on empirical comparisons, this is exactly how a science of crime pattern formation should preceed. The simple models developed here are thus poised to be rejected, if compared directly with empirical crime patterns, because they make a number of very unrealistic assumptions. Our future research on this problem will attempt to do just this. Subsequently, our goal will be to add measured amounts of complexity to the model, examine how this impacts our understanding of crime pattern formation—using both simulation and analytical tools if possible—and then conduct empirical comparisons in an attempt to reject new model predictions. We expect that the most fruitful areas of model development will be in attempting to understand how environmental structure in the form of street networks and distributions of crime opportunities impact crime patterns.

REFERENCES

Altman, S. A. (1998). *Foraging for survival: Yearling baboons in africa.* Chicago: University of Chicago Press.

Arapaki, E., Argyrakis, P., & Bunde, A. (2004). Diffusion-driven spreading phenomena: The structure of the hull of the visited territory. *Physical Review E, 69*(3).

Bartumeus, F., Peters, F., Pueyo, S., Marrase, C., & Catalan, J. (2003). Helical levy walks: Adjusting searching statistics to resource availability in microzooplankton. *Proceedings Of The National Academy Of Sciences Of The United States Of America, 100*(22), 12771-12775.

Beavon, D. J. K., Brantingham, P. J., & Brantingham, P. L. (1994). The influence of street networks on the pattterning of property offenses. In R. V. Clarke (Ed.), *Crime prevention studies* (Vol. 2, pp. 115-148). Monsey, NY: Criminal Justice Press.

Bernasco, W., & Luykx, F. (2003). Effects of attractiveness, opportunity and accessibility to burglars on residential burglary rates of urban neighborhoods. *Criminology, 41*(3), 981-1001.

Bernasco, W., & Nieuwbeerta, P. (2005). How do residential burglars select target areas? A new approach to the analysis of criminal location choice. *British Journal Of Criminology, 45*(3), 296-315.

Brantingham, P. J. (2003). A neutral model of stone raw material procurement. *American Antiquity, 68*(3), 487-509.

Brantingham, P. J. (2006). Measuring forager mobility. *Current Anthropology, 47*, 435-459.

Brantingham, P. J., & Brantingham, P. L. (1981). *Environmental criminology.* Beverly Hills, CA: Sage.

Brantingham, P. J., & Brantingham, P. L. (1984). *Patterns in crime.* New York: Macmillan.

Brantingham, P. L., & Brantingham, P. J. (1993). Nodes, paths and edges—Considerations on the complexity of crime and the physical-environment. *Journal Of Environmental Psychology, 13*(1), 3-28.

Brantingham, P. L., & Brantingham, P. J. (1995). Criminality of place: Crime generators and crime attractors. *European Journal of Criminal Justice Policy and Research, 3*, 5-26.

Brantingham, P. J., Brantingham, P. L., & Wong, P. S. (1991). How public transit feeds private crime: Notes on the Vancouver sky train experience. *Security Journal, 2*, 91-95.

Camazine, S., Deneubourg, J.-L., Franks, N. R., Sneyd, J., Theraulaz, G., & Bonabeau, E. (2001). *Self-organization in biological systems.* Princeton: Princeton University Press.

Canter, D., & Larkin, P. (1993). The environmental range of serial rapists. *Journal Of Environmental Psychology, 13*(1), 63-69.

Clarke, R. (1995). Situational crime prevention. In M. Tonry & D. Farrington (Eds.), *Building a safer society: Strategic approaches to crime prevention* (Vol. 19, pp. 91-150). Chicago: University of Chicago Press.

Cohen, B. (1980). *Deviant street networks*. Lexigton, MA: Lexington Books.

Cohen, L. E., & Felson, M. (1979). Social-change and crime rate trends—Routine activity approach. *American Sociological Review, 44*(4), 588-608.

Felson, M. (2002). *Crime and everyday life*. Thousand Oaks: Sage.

Felson, M. (2006). *Crime and nature*. Thousand Oaks: Sage.

Flemming, Z., Brantingham, P. L., & Brantingham, P. J. (1994). Exploring auto theft in British Columbia. In R. V. Clarke (Ed.), *Crime prevention studies* (Vol. 3, pp. 47-90). Monsey, NY: Criminal Justice Press.

Groff, E. (in press). Simulation for theory testing and experimentation: An example using routine activity theory and street robbery. *Journal Of Quantitative Criminology*.

Groff, E., & McEwen, T. (2006). *Exploring the spatial configuration of places related to homicide events*. Washington, D.C.

Hubbell, S. P. (2001). *The unified neutral theory of biodiversity and biogeography*. Princeton: Princeton University Press.

Koch, A. J., & Meinhardt, H. (1994). Biological pattern-formation—From basic mechanisms to complex structures. *Reviews Of Modern Physics, 66*(4), 1481-1507.

Kocsis, R. N., Rayw.Cooksey, Irwin, H. J., & Allen, G. (2002). A further assessment of "circle theory" for geographic psychological profiling. *Australian and New Zealand Journal of Criminology, 35*, 43.

Larralde, H., Trunfio, P., Havlin, S., Stanley, H. E., & Weiss, G. H. (1992). Territory covered by n diffusing particles. *Nature, 355*(6359), 423-426.

Marthaler, D., Bertozzi, A. L., & Schwartz, I. B. (2004). *Searches based on a priori information: The biased levy walk*. Los Angeles: UCLA Center for Applied Mathematics Report 04-50.

Nakao, H. (2000). Multi-scaling properties of truncated levy flights. *Physics Letters A, 266*(4-6), 282-289.

Ramos-Fernandez, G., Mateos, J. L., Miramontes, O., Cocho, G., Larralde, H., & Ayala-Orozco, B. (2004). Levy walk patterns in the foraging movements of spider monkeys (ateles geoffroyi). *Behavioral Ecology And Sociobiology, 55*(3), 223-230.

Rengert, G. F., Piquero, A. R., & Jones, P. R. (1999). Distance decay reexamined. *Criminology, 37*(2), 427-445.

Roncek, D., & Maier, P. A. (1991). Bars, blocks and crime revisited: Linking theory of routine activities to the empiricism of hot spots. *Criminology, 29*, 725-753.

Rossmo, D. K. (2000). *Geographic profiling*. Boca Raton: CRC Press.

Shlesinger, M. F., Zaslavsky, G. M., & Klafter, J. (1993). Strange kinetics. *Nature, 363*(6424), 31-37.

Sole, R. V., Bartumeus, F., & Gamarra, J. G. P. (2005). Gap percolation in rainforests. *Oikos, 110*(1), 177-185.

Sole, R. V., & Bascompte, J. (2006). *Self-organization in complex ecosystems*. Princeton: Princeton University Press.

Stephens, D. W., & Krebs, J. R. (1986). *Foraging theory.* Princeton: Princeton University Press.

Topaz, C. M., & Bertozzi, A. L. (2004). Swarming patterns in a two-dimensional kinematic model for biological groups. *Siam Journal On Applied Mathematics, 65*(1), 152-174.

Turchin, P. (1996). Fractal analyses of animal movement: A critique. *Ecology, 77*(7), 2086-2090.

Turchin, P. (1998). *Quantitative analysis of movement: Measuring and modeling population redistribution in animals and plants.* Sunderland: Sinauer Associates.

Turchin, P. (2003). *Complex population dynamics: A theoretical/empirical synthesis.* Princeton: Princeton University Press.

Viswanathan, G. M., Afanasyev, V., Buldyrev, S. V., Murphy, E. J., Prince, P. A., & Stanley, H. E. (1996). Levy flight search patterns of wandering albatrosses. *Nature, 381*(6581), 413-415.

Viswanathan, G. M., Bartumeus, F., Buldyrev, S. V., Catalan, J., Fulco, U. L., Havlin, S., et al. (2002). Levy flight random searches in biological phenomena. *Physica A-Statistical Mechanics And Its Applications, 314*(1-4), 208-213.

Viswanathan, G. M., Buldyrev, S. V., Havlin, S., da Luz, M. G. E., Raposo, E. P., & Stanley, H. E. (1999). Optimizing the success of random searches. *Nature, 401*(6756), 911-914.

Wiles, P., & Costello, A. (2000). *The 'road to nowhere': The evidence for travelling criminals.* London: Home Office.

Yuste, S. B., & Acedo, L. (2000). Number of distinct sites visited by n random walkers on a euclidean lattice. *Physical Review E, 61*(3), 2340-2347.

ADDITIONAL READING

While there are many readings dealing with different aspects of simulation and mathematical modeling, few of these are introductory in nature. As a result, it is often difficult to acquire the conceptual, methodological, and technical skills necessary to build successful models. The additional readings suggested below have been useful to us in explaining the role of modeling in science and in presenting some of the most essential modeling tools.

Camazine, S., Deneubourg, J.-L., Franks, N. R., Sneyd, J., Theraulaz, G., & Bonabeau, E. (2001). *Self-organization in biological systems.* Princeton: Princeton University Press.

Denny, M., & Gaines, S. (2002). *Chance in biology: Using probability to explore nature.* Princeton: Princeton University Press.

Gotelli, N. J. (1998). *A primer of ecology.* Sunderland: Sinauer Associates.

Hubbell, S. P. (2001). *The unified neutral theory of biodiversity and biogeography.* Princeton: Princeton University Press.

Nelson, B. L. (1995). *Stochastic modeling: Analysis and simulation.* New York: McGraw Hill.

Turchin, P. (1998). *Quantitative analysis of movement: Measuring and modeling population redistribution in animals and plants.* Sunderland: Sinauer Associates.

Turchin, P. (2003). *Complex population dynamics: A theoretical/empirical synthesis.* Princeton: Princeton University Press.

ENDNOTES

1. The new location x_j, y_j is given as $x_i + \delta_j \sin \beta_j$ and $y_i + \delta_j \cos \beta_j$ where x_i, y_i is the current location.

[2] The path between corridors is much more apparent if the density surface is calculated using a coarser grained kernel

Chapter XI
Crime Simulation Using GIS and Artificial Intelligent Agents

Xuguang Wang
Environmental Systems Research Institute (ESRI), USA

Lin Liu
University of Cincinnati, USA

John Eck
University of Cincinnati, USA

ABSTRACT

This chapter presents an innovative agent-based model for crime simulation. The model is built on the integration of geographic information systems (GIS) and artificial intelligence (AI) technologies. An AI algorithm (reinforcement learning) is applied in designing mobile agents that can find their ways on a street network. The multi-agent system is implemented as a Windows desktop program and then loosely coupled with ESRI ArcGIS. The model allows users to create artificial societies which consist of offender agents, target agents, and crime places for crime pattern simulation purposes. This is a theory-driven system, in which the processes that generate crime events are explicitly modeled. The simulated crime patterns are shown to have similar properties as seen in reported crime patterns.

INTRODUCTION

Environmental criminologists argue that crime patterns are the result of the complex interactions among offenders, victims and their environment. This complexity includes learning and adaptation by all actors involved in a crime event (Brantingham & Brantingham, 2004; Eck, 2003). The research introduced in this chapter represents an effort to provide a tool to study such complexity and to help develop crime theories and inform crime prevention policy.

The agent-based model presented in this chapter, named spatial adaptive crime event simulation (SPACES), is a crime simulation system for street robbery based on routine activities in an urban area. In a typical simulation designed in SPACES, offender agents and target agents are scheduled to perform routine activities in a spatial environment. The interaction among agents during their routine activities generates crime events and crime patterns for analysis. Offender agents, target agents and crime places are all adaptable, which means that they can modify their actions as a consequence of past offending and victimization experience. Agent routine activity schedules and adaptabilities can be changed to simulate different crime patterns. The simulation process is visual in SPACES as animations. The simulation results could also be exported to commercial GIS software packages for further analysis.

BACKGROUND

Environmental criminology consists of a set of related theories: routine activity theory, crime pattern theory, and rational choice theory. These theories explain crime patterns by focusing on micro crime events.

Routine activity theory (Cohen & Felson, 1979) argues that the occurrence of a direct contact predatory crime event is the result of the convergence of three elements in space and time: a likely offender, a suitable target, and the absence of guardians for the target (Clark & Felson, 1993). Routine activity theory has been expanded to account for third party agents, in addition to guardians, and to explicitly account for crime locations (Felson, 1995). Formalizing expanded routine activity theory, Eck (1995) presented the likelihood of a crime event at a local situation in a mathematical formula. This equation is the foundation of the crime event likelihood evaluation for offender agents in SPACES.

Based on routine activity theory, crime pattern theory (Brantingham & Brantingham, 1993) argues that the distribution of crime events can be explained by the distribution of offenders, targets, and controllers during their daily routines in space and time. Furthermore, it argues that offenders spend most of their time in legal routine activities. They learn an awareness space during legal routine activities. Crime events are most likely to take place in their awareness space. The awareness space defined by routine activities serves as another foundation of SPACES.

In the geographic literature, routine activity is defined as "a recurring set of episodes in a given unit of time" (Golledge & Stimson, 1997, p290). For example, for the daily routine of going from home to work place, from work place to a shopping store, and then returning home, there are three episodes (as shown in Figure 1). The basic element of any complex routine activity is a single episode (as shown in Figure 2). Following this definition, SPACES defines the routine activity of each agent as a set of episodes. At each moment, an agent can only be involved in one episode.

Rational choice theory (Cornish & Clarke, 1986) views a crime event as the result of a series of decisions by offenders. When choosing targets, offenders attempt to increase gains and reduce losses. Human targets, guardians and others also make rational choices. Consistent with this theory,

Figure 1. A three-episode routine activity (arrows indicate movement direction)

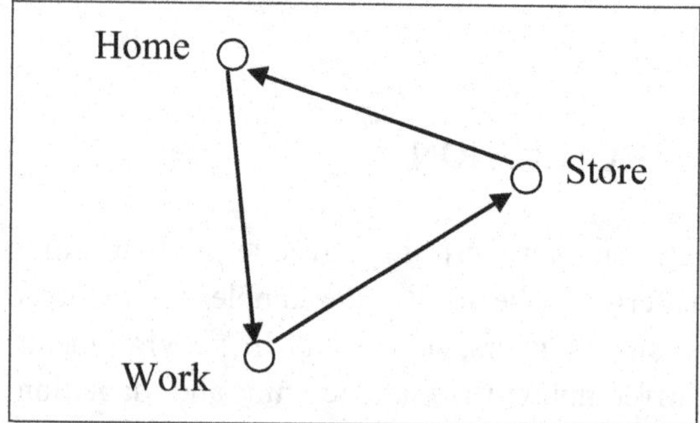

Figure 2. The basic element of a routine activity

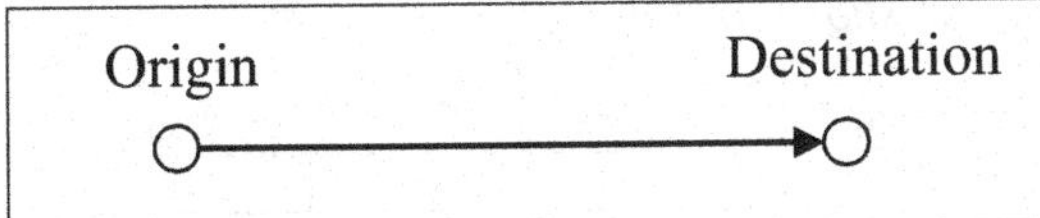

SPACES assumes that offender and target agents have some basic rationality to pursue benefits while avoiding losses. When agents move on the street, they follow the directions that lead to higher rewards and lower costs than the alternative routes available.

CONCEPTUAL MODEL DESCRITION

The SPACES model consists of three basic elements—the environment for the agents to act in, the agents that represent people involved in a crime event, and the rules that control agents' movement and interaction.

The Environment

In SPACES, the spatial environment for street robbery simulation is an urban street network. The street network provides routine activity paths for agents. On the street network, there are routine activity nodes as the origins and destinations of agents' routine activities.

To represent crime places, the street network needs to be in a grid format. According to Eck and Weisburd (1995), a crime place should be no larger than the size of a street address and street corner. Therefore, it is suggested that the cell size of the street network is no larger than the average size of street addresses and street corners. The time represented by each iteration of the simulation is dependent on the cell size of the street network. It equals the time needed by a pedestrian to pass the distance spanned by one cell. For the sample scenarios presented later in this chapter, the cell size is 20×20 feet, and each iteration represents 5 seconds.

The environment has a state variable—tension. As defined by Liu, Wang, Eck, and Liang (2005), tension means the awareness of crime risk at a particular place by the place manager. When a crime event occurs, it adds tension to the crime place. Tension tends to diffuse to nearby crime places and decays with elapsed time.

Types of Agents

SPACES defines three types of agents in a street robbery event—offenders, targets, and place managers. Bystanders on the street can be guardians for potential victims, so the roles of target and guardian are not mutually exclusive (Clarke & Felson, 1993). We assume that nearby targets have the potential to protect each other. So, SPACES does not explicitly define guardian as a new agent type.

Offender agents have one property: Motivation. As offenders learn from past experience their motivation changes. Offender agents also learn offending templates, which are memories of rewards that an offender agent gained at each location in the past.

Target agents have two properties: Desirability and guardian capability. Target agents learn from past experience, and change their desirability and guardianship capabilities after a victimization experience. Target agents also learn victimization templates, which are memories of cost to a target agent caused by the victimization at each location in the past.

Offender agents and target agents are mobile agents. Each mobile agent learns a set of cognitive maps to represent awareness space while exploring on the street network. A mobile agent also relies on cognitive maps to find ways to routine activity destinations.

Place agents represent crime places. Every place agent is a cell on the street network. Each place agent is associated with a place manager. A place manager is also a controller whose presence tends to deter street robberies. These place agents have one property: management effectiveness. Place agent evaluates tension and change management effectiveness according to the local tension level. The changing of tension in space and time is modeled by a cellular automata model, which is discussed in details in Liu, et al. (2005).

Agent Routine Activity Rules

In a SPACES simulation, legal routine activities provide the context of criminal activities. All offender agents and target agents are scheduled to perform legal routine activities during a simulation. During legal routine activities, offender agents may initiate street robbery if the situation allows.

Routine Activity Scheduling

In SPACES, the routine activity of a mobile agent typically involves two or more episodes. Routine activity matrices are used to define the sequence of these episodes, which are saved in text files. In a routine activity matrix, the sequence of episodes is controlled by a transitional probability, which is a stochastic value representing the probability that one episode is followed by another. Each cell value of the matrix represents the transitional probability between the row activity and the column activity. When an agent moves on the street network, it looks up the routine activity matrix to decide which episode to take when one is finished. Figure 3 is a sample routine activity matrix. It shows that an agent has three activity episodes in a simulation. In row #1, the values 0.0, 1.0, and 0.0 mean that the transitional probability between home and home is 0, the transitional probability between home and work is 1, and the transitional probability between home and shopping is 0. This row defines that the agent should go to work after reaching home location. The combination

Figure 3. A matrix that generates the three episode routine shown in Figure 1.

$a_1 \setminus a_2$	Home	Work	Shopping
Home	0.0	1.0	0.0
Work	0.0	0.0	1.0
Shopping	1.0	0.0	0.0

of row #1, row #2 and row #3 defines the activity sequence of going from home to work, from work to shopping, and then returning home.

Assumption of Rationality

During each routine activity episode, an agent moves cell by cell on the street network. At each step an agent must decide which direction to take. As the simplest case, in SPACES we assume that the agent moves in a Neumann neighborhood, which means that the agent moves either vertically or horizontally, but not diagonally (Figure 4). All agents are rational decision-makers; they tend to minimize total cost and maximize total reward received during their routine activities, under constraints of limited information. For offender agents, the cost is distance friction. They are rewarded by crime and gains received at destinations. For target agents, the costs are distance friction and losses from victimization. Their reward is the gain received at destinations. If cost is considered as a negative reward, then the goal of both offender and target agents is to maximize total reward received during their routine activities.

Agent Cognitive Map Learning Rule

In a SPACES simulation, each mobile agent learns an awareness space and establishes routines. Cognitive maps are used to represent an agent's knowledge about its awareness space. A cognitive map is implemented as a spatial variable, which is the same as a street network grid. Each cell of the cognitive map stores the accumulated reward value from the current location to the destination of the current activity episode. The accumulated reward values are used by mobile agents in finding their ways on the street network. At the beginning of a simulation, the accumulated reward values are not available, but are initialized to a constant value across all cells. These values are learned and improved when agents move on the street network. This means that when agents are first released into the street network, the route they choose to the destination is random. But after they gain enough experience by exploring the street network, the cognitive maps are learned well and a routine activity path (typically shortest) is established. The reinforcement-learning algorithm enables agents to accomplish this learning. Rule #1 explains how a mobile agent learns its cognitive map when it moves on the street network.

Rule #1: For each cell (in row i and column j) that an agent visits, it updates the estimated accumulated reward value of that cell with the following equation:

$$V_{(i,j)} = V_{(i,j)} + \alpha(V_{(i',j')} + r_{(i',j')} - V_{(i,j)}) \qquad (1)$$

where $V_{(i,j)}$ is the estimated accumulated reward value stored in the cell (i, j); $V_{(i',j')}$ is the largest accumulated reward value among the four neighboring cells of cell (i, j); $r_{(i',j')}$ is the immediate reward (e.g., distance friction) associated with cell (i', j'); and α is the learning rate ($0 < \alpha < 1$).

Equation (1) is a special case of a reinforcement learning algorithm—Q-learning. A more detailed discussion of reinforcement learning and Q-learning can be found in Sutton and Barto (1998).

The immediate reward r in equation (1) is a spatial variable, which consists of three components: the distance friction, the expected reward of crime, and the reward of legal routine activities. This is shown in equation (2):

$$r_{(i,j)} = d + c_{(i,j)} + l_{(i,j)} \qquad (2)$$

where d is the distance friction. Since all the cells on the street network have the same size, d is constant everywhere. $c_{(i,j)}$ is the expected reward of crime in cell (i, j), which is a value learned from past experience by offender agents or target agents. (c is greater than 0 for offender agents because offender agents gain from a street robbery. c is less than 0 for target agents because target agents lose benefits in a street robbery). $l_{(i,j)}$ is the expected reward of legal routine activities in cell (i, j). $l_{(i,j)}$ is set to 0 for all cells except the destination of a routine activity episode. At the destination cells, positive rewards are assigned to reward agents for finishing the legal routine activities.

Offending Template and Victimization Template Learning Rule

Another characteristic of offender agents and target agents is adaptability. According to Eck (2003), offenders are likely to be reinforced by the positive reward following a crime event at a particular location. Similarly, targets may avoid locations where they have been victimized. In SPACES, offending and victimization templates are designed for offender and target agent adaptation. Templates are defined as memories of the rewards that offenders and targets received in the past. Every agent can have its own template, or multiple agents can share one template if there are communication channels among them. Both templates are implemented as spatial variables using the street network grid. Each cell of the templates stores the expected reward of crime in that cell (the $c_{(i,j)}$ value in equation (2)). At the beginning of the simulation, all cells on both templates are set to 0, meaning that agents have no initial experience of offending or victimization. Rule #2 defines how agents learn offending/victimization templates.

Rule #2: If a crime event occurs in cell (i, j), then the expected reward of crime in cell (i, j) is increased by Δc, as shown in equation (3):

$$c_{(i,j)} = c_{(i,j)} + \Delta c \quad (3)$$

For offending template, Δc is positive. For victimization template, Δc is negative. The offending and victimization templates decay over time. At each iteration, the value in each cell decay for a small proportion p ($0 < p < 1$), as shown in equation (4). This means that agents tend to forget past experiences as the elapsed time since the experiences increase.

$$c_{(i,j)} = c_{(i,j)}(1 - p) \quad (4)$$

Agent Wayfinding Rule

As illustrated in the background section, complex routine activity can be decomposed into individual episodes. Each episode is associated with one destination. In SPACES, when a routine activity scenario is designed, the user specifies the number of episodes and the associated destinations. An agent's routine activity typically has multiple episodes, but an agent can only be involved in one episode at one moment. For the convenience of illustration, the following discussion of agent way finding rule focuses on one episode.

For each episode of the routine activity, each mobile agent is assigned a cognitive map to direct its way finding. Suppose an agent is in cell (i, j) at the current time step. There are at most four possible locations for the agent to step into at the next time step: cell $(i + 1, j)$, cell $(i-1, j)$, cell $(i, j + 1)$, and cell $(i, j - 1)$, as shown in Figure 4. Agents only move in the cells that represent the street. If any of these cells are out of the street, they will not be available for agents to step into. When an agent decides which cell to step into, it checks the accumulated reward values of these neighboring cells from the cognitive map associated with the current episode. Let $V_{(x, y)}$ denote the accumulated reward value stored in cell (x, y) on the cognitive map, Rule #3 is applied when an agent chooses the next cell to step into.

Figure 4. Neumann neighborhood for agent movement

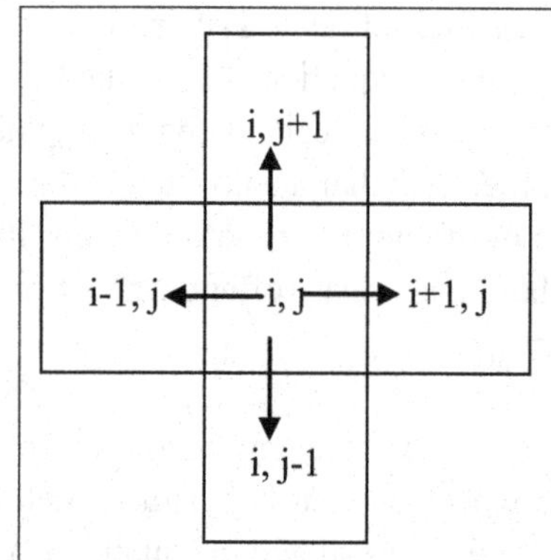

Rule #3: The probability that an agent steps into cell (x, y) is P ($0 < P < 1$) if $V_{(x, y)}$ is the maximum value among the agent's four neighboring cells on the cognitive map. Each of the other three cells has the probability of $(1 - P)/3$. If $V_{(x, y)}$ is equal among all four neighbors, then each cell has the same probability, which is 0.25.

For every decision, the choice of the next step is thus determined by the associated probability for the neighboring cells and the output of a random number generator. According to Sutton and Barto (1998), in a typical reinforcement-learning problem, the value of P needs to be close to 1. This means that agents prefer a direction that leads to maximized accumulated reward. However, P should be less than 1, so that agents have the chance to explore other directions as well to discover possible unknown opportunities.

When an agent steps into the destination cell, the current episode is finished. The agent will then need to decide the next routine activity episode based on the routine activity schedule. After the new routine activity episode is decided, the agent uses the cognitive map associated with the new episode to direct its navigation. Therefore, a mobile agent uses a series of cognitive maps to guide its wayfinding in performing its routine activity.

Figure 5. A mobile agent uses three cognitive maps for a three-episode routine activity

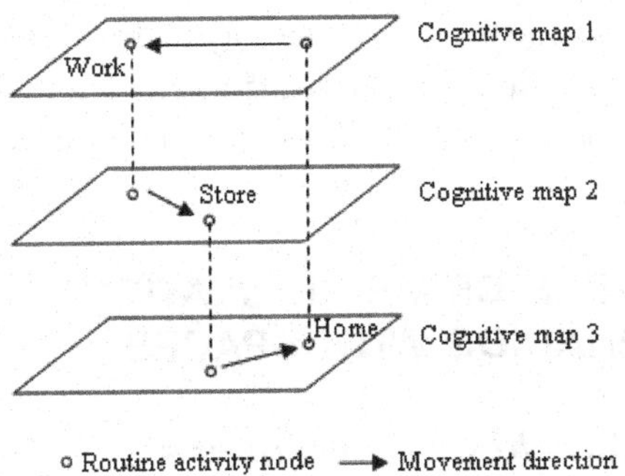

Figure 5 illustrates that a mobile agent follows three cognitive maps to perform a three-episode routine activity. For each routine activity episode, there is an associated cognitive map.

Crime Event Rules

According to routine activity theory, crime events are mostly likely to occur when offender agents and target agents converge in space and time in the absence of a capable guardian. The crime event likelihood evaluation model used by SPACES is based on Eck's formula (1995). Eck's formula represents the crime likelihood in a real world situation. Because the social system in SPACES is only a simplified model, the formula needs to be simplified before it can be used in the simulation. After the simplification, the crime event likelihood model becomes equation (5).

$$L = \frac{\delta\mu}{(1+\varepsilon)(1+\gamma)} \quad (5)$$

where L represents the crime event likelihood, μ is the offender motivation, δ is the target desirability, γ is the target guardian capability, and ε is the place management effectiveness. L, μ, δ, γ, and ε are all values between 0 and 1. Based on equation (5), Rule #4 is specified for judging the occurrence of a crime event:

Rule #4: For every cell that an offender agent steps into, it evaluates the local situation using equation (5). The probability that a crime event occurs is L.

If a crime event occurs, there is still the problem of whether it is successful or not. Rule #5 is specified to give a chance for the crime event to fail.

Rule #5: If a crime event occurs but the crime event likelihood L is less than the failure barrier b_0 $(0 < b_0 < 1)$, then the crime fails.

IMPLEMENTATION

SPACES is implemented as a Windows desktop program using an object oriented programming (OOP) approach. An OOP language provides a natural mechanism for implementing agents as objects. Offender agent and target agent are implemented as two different classes. They are both derived from a base agent class. The base agent class implements the movement and reinforcement learning rules that are common for both offender agent and target agent. Since offender agent initiates robberies, the crime event rules are implemented with the offender agent class.

The interface of SPACES is shown in Figure 6. Command buttons 1, 2, and 3 are for creating, opening, and saving a simulation. After command button 1 is clicked, a dialog box prompts the user to provide the parameters for a new simulation. The parameters of a new simulation include the number of offender agents, the number of target agents, a grid file of the street network, grid files of the routine activity nodes, the duration of the simulation (number of iterations), and the working folders. Command buttons 4, 5, 6, and 7 control the simulation process. A simulation begins when button 4 is clicked. Button 5 pauses the simulation when it is clicked. Button 6 is to run the simulation in a fast forward mode (the screen display is bypassed in this mode). Button 7 is to switch the display between showing crime event distribution and showing agent activities. Command buttons 8, 9, and 10 are for observing from a simulation. Clicking button 8 will bring up dialog 11, which is for viewing/changing simulation parameters during a simulation. Clicking button 9 will bring up a dialog to set breakpoints during a simulation. A breakpoint sets the number of iterations after which the simulation will pause. Button 10 allows the spatial crime pattern and agent properties to be exported for analysis when the simulation is paused.

SPACES contains a multiple document interface, which means that multiple simulations can be opened and run at the same time. The simulation processes are viewable in different child windows (item 14). The settings of agents and the environment are controlled by a dialog (item 11), which allows users to interact with these settings before the simulation is run or when the simulation is running.

The simulation program is loosely coupled with ESRI ArcGIS 9.0. SPACES can read the floating point grid file (.flt) exported from ArcGIS. It can save the final crime pattern in the same format which can then be read by ArcGIS for further analysis. When creating a new simulation, a street network and the routine activity nodes need to be created as shapefile in ArcGIS and then converted into grid format to be used as input to SPACES.

SAMPLE CRIME SIMULATION SCENARIOS WITH SPACES

Routine Activity Scenarios

Building a routine activity scenario is the first step toward designing a crime simulation experiment in SPACES. To design a routine activity scenario, the following parameters should be specified: a street network as the activity area, routine activity nodes as the destinations, number of offender agents and target agents as the actors, and routine activity schedules that agents should follow. Because offender agents and target agents have different lives and the offender group is not likely to communicate with the rest of the population (especially about their criminal activities), they

Figure 6. User interface design of SPACES

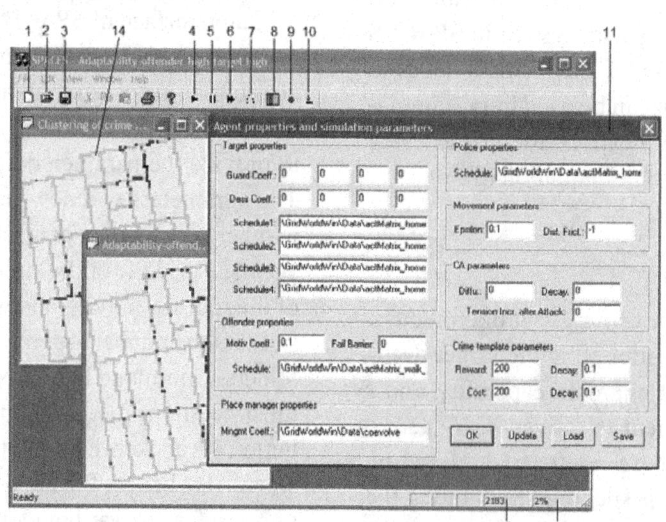

are treated as two different groups. Each group develops its own awareness space.

This section demonstrates two routine activity scenarios designed in SPACES. The purpose is to show that SPACES agents have the capability of performing routine activities in an artificial environment just like human beings do in a real society. In the first scenario, a group of target agents are scheduled to move from home to work place, from work place to a shopping store, and then return home. Figure 7 shows the evolution of agents' activity pattern. Since there are no offender agents, no crime will occur in this area. All the target agents learn the routine activity path based on distance friction. At the beginning of the simulation, agents have no knowledge of the area, so their activity pattern is in chaos (Figure 7(a)). As the simulation continues, agents become more knowledgeable about the area, and their routine activities converge, forming paths (Figure 7(c)). After the simulation runs for 2700 iterations, a path is fully developed (Figure 7(d)). After this point, the street network has become the awareness space for all the agents, and the path shown

Figure 7. Sample routine activity scenario 1. (a) Routine activity nodes. (b) Distribution of agents at iteration #100. (c) Distribution of agents at iteration #1600. (d) Distribution of agents at iteration #2700.

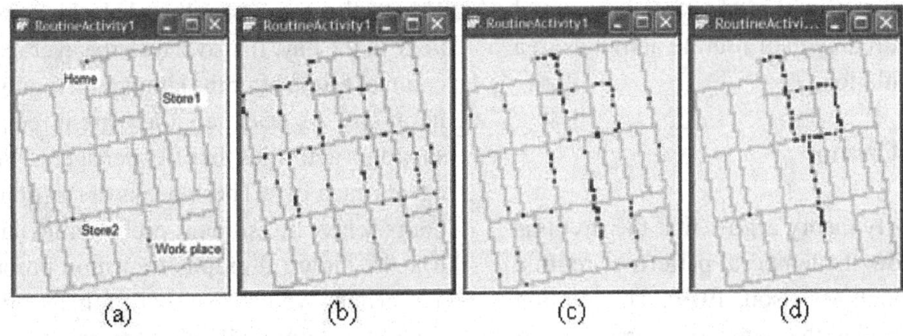

Figure 8. Sample routine activity scenario 2 (crosses represent offender agents and squares represent target agents). (a) Routine activity nodes. (b) Distribution of agents at iteration #100. (c) Distribution of agents at iteration #800.

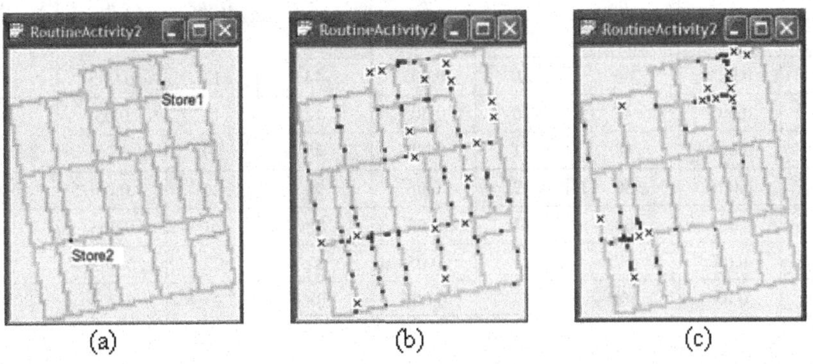

in Figure 7(d) becomes their routine activity path. This result confirms that the rules described in previous sections successfully established routine activity path for agents.

The second scenario is shown in Figure 8. A group of target agents and a group of offender agents are put on the street network. Different from the first scenario, the agents in this scenario are not assigned a home location. They just move randomly on the street network most of the time, and with a small transitional probability (0.01), they go to either one of the two stores. The motivations of offender agents are set to 0, so no crime is to be committed in the area. At the beginning of the simulation, agents are randomly distributed (Figure 8(b)). After the simulation runs for 800 iterations, agents cluster around the two stores (Figure 8(c)). This scenario shows that the distribution of agents in a spatial area is structured by their routine activities in a SPACES simulation.

Timing of Crime

Routine activity theory argues that the rhythms of crime follow the temporal pattern of routine activities (Cohen & Felson, 1979). This section examines whether the same temporal pattern can be replicated in SPACES. Based on the same street network as Figure 7(a), a number of stores are established as destinations (nodes). A group of target agents and a group of offender agents are created. They randomly move on the street network most of the time. With certain transitional probabilities (as shown in Table 1), offender agents and target agents go shopping at the stores. Offender motivation is set to a positive value, so that crime events are likely to occur during the simulation. To force crime to occur at the store locations only, all nonstore locations are masked out in the crime event likelihood evaluation.

To test if more shopping activities leads to more crime, the transitional probabilities from random movement to shopping are set to different values according to the hour of the day. This establishes a routine activity schedule—more shopping at some times of the day than at other times. Table 1 lists the transitional probabilities for every hour in the day. It also shows the average hourly count of crime after the simulation ran for 57,600 iterations. As designed, there are three peaks of shopping activities for offender agents and target agents each day. These peaks correspond to the hours when transitional probabilities are equal to 0.05. Figure 9 graphs transition probabilities and crime. We can see that in this scenario the rhythm of crime follows the temporal pattern of shopping activities.

Table 1. Hourly count of crime (n) and transitional probabilities (p)

Hour	*p*	*n*	Hour	*p*	*n*	*Hour*	*p*	*n*
0	0.005	39	8	0.05	94	16	0.005	65
1	0.005	46	9	0.005	44	17	0.005	43
2	0.005	43	10	0.005	32	18	0.05	99
3	0.005	48	11	0.005	48	19	0.05	95
4	0.005	50	12	0.05	93	20	0.05	81
5	0.005	53	13	0.05	88	21	0.005	63
6	0.05	77	14	0.05	87	22	0.005	45
7	0.05	104	15	0.005	38	23	0.005	45

Figure 9. Hourly count of crime (n) and transitional probabilities (p)

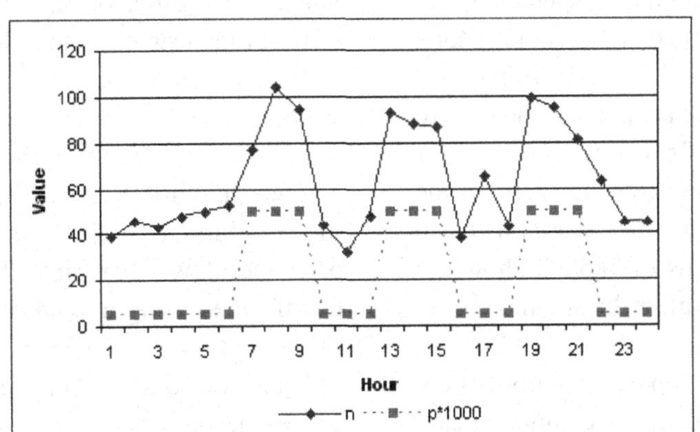

Repeat Location

Research consistently demonstrates that the distribution of crime events across places is highly skewed: of all crime places, a relatively small proportion account for a large proportion of crime (Eck, Clarke, & Guerette, 2007). Spelman (1995) has shown that this skewed distribution of crime events among crime places fits a power law distribution.

Eck (2003) suggests that the skewed distribution of crime events among crime places is caused by the malfunction of controllers (e.g., place managers) at those places. After an offender commits an offense at a place, if the place manager fails to respond to the crime, then the offender gets a positive feedback and may commit more crime at the same place. Such reinforcement learning is one mechanism through which some places may become hotspots. In addition, targets can learn from their victimization experience and change their routine activity destinations. Since targets can protect other nearby targets, the change of target routine activity pattern also changes the local situation of the crime place. Therefore, offender and target adaptation could both contribute to the skewed spatial distribution of crime. This second simulation experiment discussed here is designed to test this hypothesis using SPACES.

This simulation experiment uses the same street network as shown in Figure 7(a). A number of stores are sparsely distributed on the street network as routine activity nodes. To focus the experiment at the store locations, nonstore cells are controlled by setting a high management effectiveness value. Crime events are only possible at the store locations. A group of target agents and a group of offender agents are released to randomly walk on the street network. Occasionally, offender agents and target agents go shopping at the stores.

In order to test whether offender and target adaptation affects the spatial distribution of crime or not, two contrasting simulation models are designed and implemented. In scenario 1, offender agents and target agents are set to be nonadaptable. This is achieved by setting Δc of equation (3) to be 0.0 for both offender agents and target agents, which means that they do not learn the offending/victimization template. The first three columns of Table 2 show the number of crime events at each store location after the simulation ran for 100,000 iterations. In Table 2, the stores are sorted by the number of crime events. X represents rank, n is the number of crime events at the store, and Y is the accumulated percentage of crime events above the current rank among total crime events. In scenario 2, offender agents and target agents are set to be adaptable. The reward of a street robbery (Δc of equation (3)) is greater than 0 for the offender, and less than zero for the target. Other conditions are the same as scenario 1. The last three columns of Table 2 show the number of crime events after the simulation ran for 100,000 iterations.

The final step is to compare the output of the two models. For each model, the column labeled Y in Table 2 indicates that the spatial distribution of crime is skewed. For scenario 1, the top 7 (32%) locations account for 49% of total crime events. For scenario 2, the top 32% locations account for 54% of total crime events. This suggests that the distribution from scenario 2 is more skewed than the distribution from scenario 1. To further support this argument, we fit the Y columns against a power function $Y=aX^b$, where X is the rank of the store and Y is the accumulated percentage of crime above that rank. The data were first transformed using a logarithmic function, then linear regression analysis was used to estimate the values of a and b for the transformed data. The R-square values for both regression analyses are close to 0.99, showing that the data closely fit power functions. The estimated value of b

Table 2. Distribution of crime events by rank

Scenario 1—non-adaptable			Scenario 2—adaptable		
X (Rank)	n	Y	X (Rank)	n	Y
1	109	0.094	1	27	0.118
2	90	0.172	2	25	0.228
3	90	0.250	3	22	0.325
4	77	0.316	4	13	0.382
5	70	0.377	5	13	0.439
6	69	0.436	6	12	0.491
7	60	0.488	7	11	0.539
8	59	0.539	8	11	0.588
9	57	0.588	9	11	0.636
10	48	0.630	10	10	0.680
11	45	0.668	11	10	0.724
12	44	0.706	12	10	0.768
13	43	0.744	13	9	0.807
14	40	0.778	14	9	0.846
15	39	0.812	15	5	0.868
16	38	0.845	16	5	0.890
17	37	0.877	17	5	0.912
18	37	0.908	18	5	0.934
19	36	0.940	19	4	0.952
20	34	0.969	20	4	0.969
21	31	0.996	21	4	0.987
22	5	1.000	22	3	1.000

is 0.75 for scenario 1, and 0.66 for scenario 2. This confirmed that the distribution of scenario 2 is more skewed than scenario 1 because the estimated *b* value is smaller for scenario 2. This experiment shows that the spatial distribution of crime events produced by SPACES is similar to the power function distribution reported by Spelman. The skewed distribution is generated regardless of adaptation. However, adaptation creates more skewed distribution of crime in space.

CONCLUSION

SPACES is designed to simulate crime events and crime patterns. It allows users to create two different types of agents to roam on a raster landscape following certain routine activity schedules. The agents have similar properties as human being in terms of performing daily routines because of the artificial intelligence embedded in these agents. These similarities include way finding and adaptation to changes in the environment. SPACES is loosely coupled with ArcGIS, so that it can make use of GIS data and the analysis functionality from ArcGIS. This will also allow real urban landscape data and routine activity nodes to be used as input to the model. To our knowledge, no other available multi-agent system software packages (such as SWARM and RePast) provide similar artificial intelligent agents and routine activity simulation capability for the purpose of crime simulation.

A few sample routine activities and crime patterns have been presented as a way to validate SPACES. The results show that SPACES can produce crime patterns with similar properties as seen in reported crime patterns in the real world. So far, SPACES is limited in simulating hypothetical routine activity scenarios. This is because at the current stage of the research, the focus is to validate SPACES as a virtual laboratory for theoretical crime pattern simulation before applying it to real cases. More simulation scenarios are needed to test the performance of the agents and the entire model.

There are three potential uses for SPACES. First, it can be used to explore theory. The scenarios described above fit this purpose. Theoretical experiments can be designed to determine how elements of a theory work together, and whether the theory is capable of producing crime patterns as observed in reality; if it is not, then it can be set aside. If it is, then SPACES may be able to generate hypotheses that can be tested using empirical observations.

Second, SPACES can be used as a teaching tool. The authors are planning a graduate seminar for geography and criminal justice students. The goals are to teach students about the creation of crime simulations and how crime patterns arise. Students will design experiments based on environmental criminology theories and test them in SPACES.

Third, it may be possible to use SPACES to "bench test" crime prevention and policing policies. SPACES already uses real world street maps. By adding other theoretically important spatial features, from a real environment, that agents use to make decisions it might be possible to show how patterns change as policies change. Here is a hypothetical example. How would changing a street pattern alter crime patterns? Using an actual street grid, with information about the direction of traffic flow (one way or two way) SPACES could be calibrated to reproduce the current crime pattern. Then after making a change in the street pattern (e.g., changing street directions or blocking off some streets) the new pattern can be observed, and compared to the old pattern. With a sufficiently detailed environment, and agent cognition, SPACES might be useful for urban planning; answering questions such as, how will building a shopping center at a location influence crime? In another example, one could calibrate SPACES to a random police patrol plan, and then compare the resulting crime patterns to those resulting from a hotspots patrol plan.

In summary, SPACES is a promising agent-based modeling approach for crime simulation. It can provide complementary insights to empirical studies. When an experiment is difficult or costly to be implemented in the real world, an agent-based model like SPACES has the potential to be used as an alternative test bed.

FUTURE RESEARCH DIRECTIONS

One of the future research directions is to apply SPACES to simulate real crime patterns and to simulate the impact of crime prevention policy on crime patterns. To model crime patterns in an urban area, SPACES needs to be improved in a number of ways. First, more situational factors can be incorporated into offender decision-making formula. Including such situational factors may require more spatial data layers as input to the model. For example, the presence of street lighting is one of such situational factors. Second, real routine activity schedules need to be used, which defines daily activities for agents (and activity nodes) for a certain amount of time (one month for example, depending on how long the simulation intends to represent). A suitable number of agents should be specified accordingly. Third, in the current version of SPACES, agents make independent decisions. Future versions could include collective decisions to mimic group offending, or group self-protection against offending. Fourth, police agents could be added to help determine how their behaviors could influence crime patterns. Finally, the usability of SPACES can be improved to facilitate the creation of simulation models. For example, when creating a new simulation model, the parameters for offender agents, target agents and crime places are currently located in a single dialog for the current implementation. This could be changed so that the process of taking user parameters is broken down into a series of steps, each step taking the parameters for one type of agent.

ACKNOWLEDGMENT

This chapter is based on a research supported by the National Science Foundation under Grant No. IIS-0081434. Any opinions, findings, and conclusions or recommendations expressed in this chapter are those of the author(s) and do not necessarily reflect the views of the National Science Foundation.

REFERENCES

Brantingham, P. L., & Brantingham, P. J. (2004). Computer simulation as a tool for environmental criminologists. *Security Journal, 17*(1), 21-30.

Brantingham, P. L., & Brantingham, P. J. (1993). Environment, routine, and situation: Toward a pattern theory of crime. In R. V. Clarke & M. Felson (Eds.), *Routine activity and rational choice: Vol. 5. Advances in criminological theory.* New Brunswick, NJ: Transaction Publications.

Clarke, R. V., & Felson, M. (1993). Introduction: Criminology, routine activity and rational choice. In R. V. Clarke & M. Felson (Eds.), *Routine activity and rational choice: Vol. 5. Advances in criminological theory.* New Brunswick, NJ: Transaction Publishers.

Cohen, L. E., & Felson, M. (1979). Social change and crime rate trends: A routine activity approach. *American Sociology Review, 44*, 588-608.

Cornish, D., & Clarke, R. V. (1986). Introduction. In D. Cornish & R. V. Clarke (Eds.), *The reasoning criminal* (pp. 1-16). New York: Springer-Verlag.

Eck, J. E. (1995). Examining routine activity theory: A review of two books. *Justice Quarterly, 12*, 783-797.

Eck, J. E. (2001). Policing and crime event concentration. In R. F. Meier, L. W. Kennedy, & V. F. Sacco (Eds.), *The process and structure of* crime: Criminal event and crime analysis: Vol. 9. Advances in criminological theory, (pp. 249-276). New Brunswick, NJ: Transaction Publishers.

Eck, J. E. (2003). Police problems: The complexity of problem theory, research and evaluation. In J. Knutsson (Ed.), *Problem-oriented policing: From innovation to mainstream: Vol. 15. Crime prevention studies,* (pp. 67-102). Monsey, NY: Criminal Justice Press.

Eck, J. E., Clarke, R. V, & Guerette, R. (2007). Risky facilities: Crime concentration in homogeneous sets of establishments and facilities. In G. Farrell, K. J. Bowers, S. D. Johnson, & M. Townsley (Eds.), *Imagination for crime prevention: Vol. 19. Crime prevention studies* (pp. 225-264). Monsey, NY: Criminal Justice Press.

Eck, J. E., & Weisburd, D. (1995). Crime places in crime theory. In J. E Eck & D. Weisburd (Eds.), *Crime and place: Vol. 4. Crime prevention studies* (pp. 1-33). Monsey, NY: Criminal Justice Press.

Felson, M. (1995). Those who discourage crime. In J. E. Eck & D. Weisburd (Eds.), *Crime and place: Vol. 4. Crime prevention Studies* (pp. 53-66). Monsey, NY: Criminal Justice Press.

Golledge, R. G., & Stimson, R. J. (1997). *Spatial behavior: A geographic perspective.* New York: The Guilford Press.

Liu, L., Wang, X., Eck, J. E., & Liang, J. (2005). Simulating crime events and crime patterns in a RA/CA model. In F. Wang (Ed.), *Geographic information systems and crime analysis.* Hershey, PA: Idea Group Inc.

Spelman, W. (1995). Criminal careers of public places. In J. E Eck, & D. Weisburd (Eds.), *Crime and Place. Crime Prevention Studies, Vol. 4* (pp. 1-33). Monsey, NY: Criminal Justice Press.

Sutton, R. S., & Barto, A. G. (1998). *Reinforcement learning: An introduction.* Cambridge: MIT Press.

Wang, X. (2005). *Spatial adaptive crime event simulation using the RA/CA/ABM computational laboratory.* Unpublished doctoral dissertation, University of Cincinnati, Cincinnati.

ADDITIONAL READINGS

Barnes, G. C. (1995). Defining and optimizing displacement. In J. E. Eck & D. Weisburd (Eds.), *Crime and place: Vol. 4. Crime prevention studies.* Monsey, NY: Criminal Justice Press.

Block, R., & Block, C. R. (2000). The Bronx and Chicago: Street robbery in the environs of rapid transit stations. In V. Goldsmith, P. G. McGuire, J. H. Mollenkopf, & T.A. Ross (Eds.), *Analyzing crime patterns: Frontiers of practice* (pp. 137-152). Thousand Oaks: Sage Publications, Inc.

Brantingham, P. J., & Brantingham, P. L. (1991). Notes on the geometry of crime. In P. J. Brantingham & P. L. Brantingham (Eds.), *Environmental criminology.* Prospect Heights, IL: Waveland Press, Inc.

Brantingham, P. J., & Brantingham, P. L. (1991). Notes on environmental criminology. In P. J. Brantingham & P. L. Brantingham (Eds.), *Environmental criminology.* Prospect Heights, IL: Waveland Press, Inc.

Brantingham, P. J., & P. L. Brantingham (1991). Introduction: The dimensions of crime. In P. J. Brantingham & P. L. Brantingham (Eds.), *Environmental criminology.* Prospect Heights, IL: Waveland Press, Inc.

Brantingham, P. J., & Brantingham, P. L. (2001). The implications of the criminal event model for crime prevention. In R. F. Meier, L. W. Kennedy, & V. F. Sacco (Eds.), *The process and structure of crime: Criminal event and crime analysis: Vol. 9. Advances in criminological theory.* New Brunswick, NJ: Transaction Publishers.

Brantingham, P. J., & Brantingham, P. L. (1984). *Patterns in crime.* New York: Collier Macmillan.

Dibble, C. (2001). *Theory in a complex world: Geograph computational laboratories.* Unpublished doctoral dissertation, University of California at Santa Barbara, Santa Barbara.

Eck, J. E., Gersh, J. S., & Taylor, C. (2000). Finding crime hotspots through repeat address mapping. In V. Goldsmith, . P. G. McGuire, J. H. Mollenkopf, & T. A. Ross (Eds.), *Analyzing crime patterns: Frontiers of practice* (pp. 49-62). Thousand Oaks: Sage Publications, Inc.

Epstein, J. M., & Axtell, R. (1996). *Growing artificial societies: Social science from the bottom up.* Cambridge: MIT Press.

Epstein, J. M (1999). Agent-based simulation models and generative social science. *Complexity, 4*(5).

Felson, M. (1987). Routine activities and crime prevention in the developing metropolis. *Criminology, 25*(4).

Felson, M. (1998). *Crime and everyday life.* Thousand Oaks, CA: Pine Forge Press.

Gabor, T. (1994). Crime displacement and situational prevention: Toward the development of some principles. In R. P. McNamara (Ed.), *Crime displacement: The other side of prevention.* New York: Cummings & Hathway Publishers.

Hollway, W., & Jefferson, T. (2000). The role of anxiety in fear of crime. In T. Hope & R. Sparks (Eds.), *Crime risk and insecurity* (pp. 31-49). New York: Routledge.

Jiang, B., & Gimblett, H. R. (2002). An agent-based approach to environmental and urban systems within geographic information systems. In H. R. Gimblett (Ed.), *Integrating geographic information systems and agent-based modeling techniques for simulating social and ecological processes.* New York: Oxford University Press.

Jeffery, C. R., & Zahm, D. L. (1993). Crime prevention through environmental design, opportunity theory, and rational choice models. In R. V. Clarke & M. Felson (Eds.), *Routine activity and rational choice: Vol. 5. Advances in criminological theory.* New Brunswick, NJ: Transaction Publications.

Kennedy, L. W., & Brunschot, E. G. V. (2001). Routines and the criminal event. In R. F. Meier, L. W. Kennedy, & V. F. Sacco (Eds.), *The process and structure of crime: Criminal event and crime analysis: Vol. 9. Advances in criminological theory.* New Brunswick, NJ: Transaction Publishers.

Meier, R. F., Kennedy, L. W., & Sacco, V. F. (2001). Crime and the criminal event perspective. In R. F. Meier, L. W. Kennedy, & V. F. Sacco (Eds.), *The process and structure of crime: Criminal event and crime analysis: Vol. 9. Advances in criminological theory.* New Brunswick, NJ: Transaction Publishers.

Openshaw, S., & Openshaw, C. (1997). *Artificial intelligence in geography.* Chichester, NY: Wiley.

Sherman, L., Gartin, P., & Buerger, M. (1989). Hotspots of predatory crime: Routine activities and the criminology of place. *Criminology, 27,* 27-55.

Swartz, C. (2000). The spatial analysis of crime: What social scientists have learned. In V. Goldsmith, P. G. McGuire, J. H. Mollenkopf, & T. A. Ross (Eds.), *Analyzing crime patterns: Frontiers of practice* (pp. 137-152). Thousand Oaks: Sage Publications, Inc.

Weiss, G. (1999). *Multiagent systems: A modern approach to distributed artificial intelligence.* Cambridge: MIT Press.

Westervelt, J. D. (2002). Geographic information system and agent-based modeling. In H. R. Gimblett (Ed.), *Integrating geographic information systems and agent-based modeling techniques for simulating social and ecological processes.* New York: Oxford University Press.

Wright, R. T., & Decker, S. H. (1997). *Armed robbers in action: Stickups and street culture.* Boston: Northeastern University Press.

Wu, F. (1999). GIS-based simulation as an exploratory analysis for space-time processes. *Journal of Geographical Systems, 1*, 199-218.

Chapter XII
Characterizing the Spatio-Temporal Aspects of Routine Activities and the Geographic Distribution of Street Robbery

Elizabeth Groff
Temple University and Institute for Law and Justice, USA

ABSTRACT

It is widely recognized that the spatio-temporal components of human behavior strongly influence where and when people converge in space and time. Routine activity theory (Cohen & Felson 1979) ties the frequency of convergence to crime rates. This chapter builds on an earlier agent-based model (Groff, in press-a) by drawing on geographic theory to develop two additional versions of the model in which the agents have more fully developed activity schedules. A series of experiments are conducted which compare the spatial pattern of street robbery events from the original version of the model to the two new versions and to the empirical distribution of street robberies in Seattle, WA. The findings indicate temporally and spatially defined activity spaces have a significant impact on the spatial pattern of crime events produced by the model. The version with spatio-temporal activity spaces produces patterns most like the empirical distribution of street robberies.

INTRODUCTION

Researchers within geography and closely related disciplines have long recognized the importance of considering space and time when examining human behavior (Chorley & Haggett, 1967; Engel-Frisch, 1943; Hägerstrand, 1970;1973; Harvey, 1969; Hawley, 1950; Horton & Reynolds,

1971; Sampson, 1993). In particular, sparked by theoretical developments during the 1970's and 1980's, many criminologists have begun to study how places influence when and where victims and offenders converge (Eck & Weisburd, 1995; Weisburd, 2002). Proponents of this view focus on the study of crime events rather than criminal motivation and rely on a set of "opportunity theories" of crime to explain why crimes occur in one place and not another.[1]

As the importance of place and time in criminological theory has gained recognition, so has the utility of applying a more process-oriented perspective to the study of crime (Sampson, 1993; Weisburd, Lum, & Yang, 2004). This approach recognizes that "social behavior occurs in particular times and places with particular social actors" (Sampson, 1993, p. 429). While the theoretical framework exists for such research, the collection of individual-level data to characterize human interactions in general and crime events in particular remains an on-going barrier to the empirical application of this perspective and one that is unlikely to change due to privacy concerns (O'Sullivan, 2004b).

In response to these challenges, some researchers have begun to consider simulation modeling as an alternative approach (Brantingham & Brantingham, 2004; Eck, 2005; Eck & Liu, 2004; Gilbert & Terna, 1999; Gilbert & Troitzsch, 1999; Gimblett, 2002; Liu, Wang, Eck, & Liang, 2005; Macy & Willer, 2002; Moss & Edmonds, 2005). A subset of these researchers are interested in crime and recognize the value of simulation modeling for: (1) understanding crime in its situational context; and (2) capturing the dynamic interactions taking place at the micro level and examining their relationship to macro level patterns (Brantingham & Brantingham, 2003; 2004; Brantingham & Groff, 2004; Eck & Liu, 2004; Gunderson & Brown, 2003; Wang, Liu, & Eck, 2004). In particular, the Brantinghams (2004) have clearly illustrated the important role of agent-based models in formalizing the context in which a crime event occurs.

One recent study combines theoretical exploration with controlled experiments to study the crime of street robbery (Groff, in press-a). This was accomplished by implementing the assumptions of a theory, in this case routine activity theory (Cohen & Felson, 1979), in a simulation model and then testing them via controlled experiments to discover whether the theoretically-predicted outcomes match the model outcomes (Groff, Forthcoming-a). The model building process emphasized simplicity, focusing on the elements that were directly addressed by the theory (Macy & Willer, 2002) and relied on 'situating' simulation by combining agent-based modeling (ABM) with geographic information systems (GIS) to enable travel on a street network.

The study found support for routine activity theory's core proposition that shifts in routine activities away from home increase the incidence of street robbery. In addition, a spatial analysis demonstrated that the observed clustering in street robbery events is beyond the degree that would be expected based on the configuration of the streets alone. The approach taken in the study represented a middle ground for theory exploration between the verbal formulation of the theory and the testing of theory with empirical data (Eck, 2005); some characterize it as a way of "experimenting on theories" (Dowling, 1999).

This chapter extends Groff (in press-a) by incorporating routine activity spaces into agent behavior. This is accomplished by creating two new versions of the original agent-based model of street robbery; one adding defined temporal schedules and the other spatio-temporal schedules. Systematically adding complexity to the original model makes it possible to isolate the effects of time and space on the amount and spatial distribution of street robbery. The research then examines whether the changes in the structure of agent activity spaces significantly alter the spatial distribution of street robberies.

CONCEPTUALIZING HUMAN ACTIVITY SPACES

Representing the spatio-temporal aspects of human behavior (i.e., routine activities) that facilitate convergence is a critical element in modeling street robbery events since it is the interactions between humans and their environment that serve as the source of explanation of observed spatial patterns (Aitken, Cutter, Foote, & Sell, 1989; Golledge & Timmermans, 1990; Walmsley & Lewis, 1993). A variety of scholars have recognized that capturing only a single dimension leaves more questions than are answered (Hägerstrand, 1970;1975; Pred, 1967; Thrift & Bennett, 1978; Thrift & Pred, 1981) and that examining space-time together yields a different and more complete representation of a situation than studying temporal variation or patterns in space individually (Pred, 1996).

Fortunately, a substantial literature exists that is dedicated to the examination of issues surrounding time-space geographies (please see Groff, 2006 for a more complete review). The approach taken here relies heavily on the time-geographic perspective developed by the Lund School in Sweden which focuses on developing a set of probable behaviors, not on trying to predict activity spaces based on empirical data; and emphasizes increased understanding as a goal (Hägerstrand, 1975). Time-geography, as developed by Hägerstrand (1970; 1975), offers the initial conceptual framework taking into account the spatio-temporal aspects of human behavior as situated within larger social processes (Thrift & Pred, 1981). Several other perspectives have also examined human activity and taken together they provide a foundation for agent movement and routine activities in the model.

In general, these perspectives agree that each person has what is termed here an *activity space*; a geographic area within which they conduct their daily activities (Horton & Reynolds, 1971). This area is equivalent to Hägerstrand's (1970; 1975) *domain* and Miller's (Miller, 1991) *potential path area* which encompass both the locations that are visited and the paths taken among those locations. Locations that are visited are called *nodes* (Brantingham & Brantingham, 1981; Brantingham & Brantingham, 1993; Lynch, 1960; Miller, 1991) or *anchorpoints* (Golledge & Stimson, 1997; Rengert, 1988) and represent the places where the majority of human interaction occurs. The routes taken among the locations are termed *paths* (Lynch, 1960; Miller, 1991) and often represent the shortest route between two places (Felson, 1987). Most importantly for the current research, Miller (1991) identifies the following elements necessary for defining an activity space: (1) locations that function as the origin/end of trips; (2) locations of activities; and (3) the arcs and nodes describing the travel environment. None of these elements are static, for example, activity spaces can change as people change jobs or as their circumstances change (Hägerstrand, 1970).

An individual's activity patterns are influenced by constraints (temporal, economic and spatial) on their ability to take advantage of opportunities for housing, employment, recreation, and so forth. Focusing on individual opportunities and constraints as they play out within a particular context is essential to understanding why events, in this case street robberies, occur sometimes and not others (Pred, 1996). Constraints shape both the destinations and the route taken by individuals as they go about their daily activities (Hägerstrand, 1970). In addition, constraints structure the timing and thus the "spacing" of discretionary activity, an important element in criminal behavior (Ratcliffe, 2006). An individual's actual travel distance depends on several factors including mode of transportation, street network, and speed limits; all of which factor into the amount of distance that can be covered in the time allotted. For example, a person who can afford a car has greater mobility than someone who walks. Key to this research is how constraints interact with fixed locations to limit travel (e.g., individuals can travel no farther away from home or work than the amount of time needed to return). Thus, models of routine activities must include both individual behavior and urban form if we are to better understand how the two are related and how they together produce human travel behavior (Hägerstrand, 1975).

Regardless of the terminology, these perspectives share the following characteristics. Individuals' travel patterns are influenced by temporal, economic and spatial constraints that limit their choices related to housing, employment, recreation etc. Home tends to be the dominant *node* and travel is concentrated along certain routinely frequented paths. Frequently traveled *paths* are hypothesized to be important factors in determining aggregate crime patterns because they bring offenders and victims together in space and time. *Activity spaces* represent the areas with which an individual has routine interaction. The formulation of activity spaces in this model combines elements from the perspectives just discussed and relies heavily on the notion of an integrated time-space approach to modeling human behavior in the urban environment.

SIMULATION FOR VIRTUAL EXPERIMENTATION

While many researchers use simulation modeling for prediction and forecasting (Maguire, Batty, & Goodchild, 2005; Miller, Hunt, Abraham, & Salvini, 2004; Miller, Roorda, & Carrasoc, 2005), others emphasize the potential of simulation for elaborating theory (Albrecht, 2005; Eck, 2005; Macy & Willer, 2002) and for conducting systematic experiments in virtual laboratories (Dibble, 2001; Epstein & Axtell, 1996; Gilbert & Terna, 1999; Macy & Willer, 2002). One recent study combines approaches and makes the case for testing theory via experimentation with virtual societies (Groff, 2007a).

These researchers argue that simulation can be a valuable tool for strengthening theories because it requires a more rigorous level of formalization and enables the use of experiments within a virtual laboratory. The vast majority of social science theories are verbal, that is they are communicated with words rather than with equations. This means they are rich in detail but lack the formalization and specificity of mathematical models (Ostrom, 1988). Simulation models require that verbal theories undergo a process of formalization in order to identify their core elements and the relationships between those elements prior to implementation. During this process, gaps and inconsistencies can be identified and addressed. In this way, the process of translating verbal theories into programming code acts to strengthen the internal consistency of the theory.

Finally, the ability to conduct and replicate experiments adds a level of scientific rigor to the process. Simulation enables the modeler to systematically manipulate one aspect of the model while holding all others constant. Random number generators play an important dual role in agent-based models by enabling scientific experimentation and providing the stochastic elements in the model. When a random number seed is defined at the start of a simulation the random number generator produces the same sequence of random numbers each time the model is run making experiments repeatable. This characteristic forms the basis for using simulation as a laboratory for experimentation because it enables any differences in the outcome variable to be attributed to the manipulated variable and not to other sources (Axelrod, in press; Groff, in press-a; Lenntorp, 1978).

RESEARCH APPROACH

This section describes the methodology used to implement two additional versions of a basic model of street robbery. It begins with a brief description of the original simulation model (Groff, 2007a) and then describes the two new versions of the model. The section ends with the technical details such as data, software, and experiments.

Original Street Robbery Model

The original model of street robbery is primarily based on routine activity theory (Cohen & Felson, 1979) but relies on rational choice theory for the specifics of offender decision-making (Clarke & Cornish, 1985; 2001). The central premise of Cohen and Felson's (1979) routine activity theory is that increases in crime are the result of a shift of routine activities away from home. As originally conceptualized, the theory identifies the convergence of *motivated offender, suitable target,* and the *lack of* a *capable guardian* at a particular place and time as the core elements necessary for a crime to occur. A fourth element, *routine activities,* influences when and where victims and offenders converge. Routine activities are the key dynamic element in determining aggregate crime rates because this element affects the convergence of the three other elements necessary for a crime, motivated offender, suitable target, and guardianship. In summary, crimes occur when the normal, everyday activities of offenders and victims converge in space and time with no guardian present. Changes in routine activities directly impact the frequency of convergence among these elements, which in turn, increases or decreases overall crime rates.

In the implementation of the original agent-based model there are two types of people, civilians (n = 1,000) and police (n = 200). The civilians represent the general population of Seattle. Each civilian in the model has a unique set of characteristics that include criminal propensity, time to stay at home (varies with experimental condition), and wealth. Random number distributions are used to assign characteristics to individual agents. Criminal propensity differentiates agents who are interested in committing robbery from all other agents in the model. Civilians with criminal propensity can potentially take on any one of three roles: offender, victim, or guardian. Civilians without criminal propensity can be either victims or guardians. In all other ways, civilians with criminal propensity are exactly the same as those without. While only agents with criminal propensity can make the decision to offend, it is the particular constellation of individual and contextual dynamics that determines whether a crime is committed. In this way, patterns of offending and victimization are allowed to emerge from decisions made by individuals in particular contexts. In addition to criminal propensity civilian agents are assigned a time to spend at home that is static over a model run, and a wealth that can change. Civilian agents get paid every other week and can gain or lose money by robbing or becoming a victim. Related to geography and movement, the agents are randomly distributed across the nodes. All agents move randomly along a real street network and each day begins at the node where the previous one ended. Agents are at risk of being robbed or robbing whenever they are not at home.

Police agents represent formal guardians and their presence automatically prevents a crime from occurring. They have no individual characteristics and exist only to patrol. At the start of the simulation police agents are randomly distributed across the nodes and they follow a "random walk" movement pattern in which they move one node at a time and only to an adjacent node.

Upon convergence, guardianship and suitability of target are considered by the active offender when making the decision whether or not to commit a robbery. The decision to offend is made as follows. At each model tick (i.e., each minute of the model year) all nodes with at least one agent present are evaluated. Active nodes meeting the following three criteria are evaluated further: (1) no police present; (2) at least two civilians present; and (3) at least one of the civilians must have criminal propensity. If there is only one offender at the node, that agent automatically becomes the active offender. Otherwise, the active offender is randomly selected from the list of agents with criminal propensity who are at the node. Offender agents who are not selected to be active are at risk of becoming victims. The active agent considers both the number of other agents at the node (i.e., guardianship) and the amount of wealth each agent has (i.e., suitability of targets).[2] When an agent commits a robbery, one unit of wealth is taken from the victim and transferred to the offender. Once the active offender at each of the active nodes evaluates their situation, all agents move and the decision structure repeats.

Enhancements to the Original Model

The original agent-based model (Groff, in press-a) implemented only a simple notion of activity space in which agents were either at home or away from home and they traveled randomly along a street network. I argue a more complex representation of activity spaces is required to represent the space-time aspects of human behavior and to dissect their effect on outcomes. Including agent activity spaces both represents the *routine activities* element of routine activity theory and provides a systematic way of testing the impact of time and time-space schedules on the incidence and distribution of street robbery. The following hypotheses related to the spatial distribution of street robbery can be examined:

H_1: As the average time spent by civilians on activities away from home increases, the spatial pattern of robberies will change.

H_2: The temporal and spatio-temporal schedules of civilians while away from home change the spatial pattern of robbery events.

The first hypothesis is replicated from the original study and compares the outcome distributions of street robberies from the experimental conditions (i.e., changing societal time spent away from home) to one another. The second hypothesis explores the impact of changing the temporal and spatio-temporal structure of routine activities on the spatial distribution of robbery events. Since this is the first test of the effect of spatio-temporal schedules on the spatial pattern of street robberies, the hypotheses do not describe the potential outcome pattern but simply note it will be different.

In the model, the routine activity spaces of individuals are implemented as a set of nodes (places) and paths (list of places traversed when traveling from one node to another) (Hägerstrand, 1970; 1975; Miller, 1991). Specifically, each civilian agent is assigned four nodes representing a home, a main (e.g., work, school etc.) and two activities (e.g., recreation, social, and retail places). The nodes are assigned based on the distributions of population, jobs and activities in Seattle (e.g., if 10% of the population lives in a particular blockgroup then 10% of the agents are assigned to that blockgroup). In this way, the size and form of activity spaces is influenced by the distribution of residential housing, jobs, schools, retail, and services (Kwan, 1998; Weber & Kwan, 2003). The outcome is that each civilian has a unique activity space reflecting their origin/end place, the places they visit, and the routes among those places.[3]

The agent activities are attached to a series of street intersections rather than street addresses or street blocks.[4] Street intersections are used to represent "interchange points for journeys from stations to the road network and *vice versa*" (Lenntorp, 1978, p. 168). It is at street intersections that agents change travel status (e.g., from work to travel) and that the potential for street robbery exists. Intersections also provide a convenient heuristic to represent the dual nature of many places; a bank may be a workplace to an employee and a discretionary activity to customers (Lenntorp, 1978).

In addition, activity spaces evolve (Hägerstrand, 1970). Accordingly, each civilian agent has two potential activity spaces; one activity space is used while employed and the other while unemployed. Since becoming unemployed does not automatically change residence and other activities, the two activity spaces are identical except that the work location is dropped from the unemployed path and a new activity location is added. The home location and the locations of the original two activities do not change.

Using activity spaces that vary by whether an agent was employed or unemployed requires that agents have an employment status. Employment status also provides a way for employed agents to accumulate more wealth than those not employed. Those agents who are employed receive regular but static infusion of wealth every two weeks over the model year but civilians who are unemployed do not get paid. Every month, 3% of unemployed agents become employed and are replaced by a new random selection of employed agents who become unemployed. It is important to note that the employment status is assigned independently of the criminal propensity indicator; civilians with criminal propensity can be employed in the model, as they are in life.

Following time-geographic principles each agent is indivisible, they can be in only one place at a time, movement across space takes time, and all activities have duration. These principles are reflected in the existence of a temporal schedule for each that incorporates the temporal constraints on their travel (Miller, 2005). Each agent's temporal schedule is primarily based on the daily amount of time the agent is assigned to stay at home and the size of their activity space. The amount of time to stay at home is assigned first and is static so that the average time spent away from home for the societal experimental condition will be accurate. Next, the amount of time needed to travel among the activity nodes is calculated since, as noted earlier, it limits the time available to spend at activities. The remaining time in the day is randomly allocated to the Main, Activity 1 and Activity 2.

The final element important to human activity is the street network. The paths taken to travel among activity place are structured by the street network (Hägerstrand, 1970, 1975; Miller, 1991). Movement in the model is either random or directed. Random movement follows a random walk process in which a node is randomly chosen from the set of adjacent nodes (Chaitin, 1990). Random movement is used by the police agents in all three versions and by the civilians in two versions of the model.

Agents with predefined spatio-temporal activity spaces (i.e., those in the Activity Space version) are the only ones who use directed movement. Their activity locations and the path among those places are generated in ArcGIS before the start of the model. Each agent starts at home and then moves along the shortest path from activity place to activity place according to a temporal schedule and following a ring pattern so they end at home (Hägerstrand, 1970; Lenntorp, 1978; Miller, 1991). While research has shown that the shortest topological path is frequently not taken, it offers a standardized and convenient heuristic for this initial model (Kent, Leitner, & Curtis, 2006). In this way, movement along the street network and activity spaces provide the basis for modeling how the routine nature of spatio-temporal behavior influences the convergence of individuals at a place-time.

One limitation of the activity spaces in the model is that they are static while human behavior often changes daily. Ideally, each the agent's activity space would be dynamic during the model run enabling them to choose locations for activities within their potential path area given existing temporal constraints. However, current software limitations preclude dynamic activity spaces. While the software limitation is disappointing, the implementation of routine activity spaces with temporal and spatio-temporal constraints represents an advance and is tested here.

The two new versions of a street robbery model are compared to the original version (Table 2).

The Simple version is from the original study and is included to offer a counterpoint to the two new versions (Groff, in press-a). The Temporal and Activity Space versions differ in that one has only temporal constraints and the other has both spatial and temporal constraints on agent behavior. The Temporal version has civilian agents who are randomly distributed across the nodes and follow a temporal schedule for random travel when not at home (i.e., they have defined times to spend at a main activity and two other activities). Civilians in the temporal and Activity Space models share the same temporal schedule for activities and travel and consequently those agents spend the same amount of time at risk for street robbery. While at home or at work the agent is not at risk of participating in a street robbery. Thus, the amount of time at home or at work reduces risk of street robbery, while time spent traveling or engaging in other activities increases it. This representation of risk is in keeping with the crime being studied. By definition, street robbery happens only on the street or in public places, not in a home or inside a workplace.[5] The Activity Space version civilians have assigned places they live, work, and visit as well as routes to take among those places. The decision to offend is the same across all three versions.

Table 1. Parameters in the model

Variable	Rationale
Society Level	
Number of Agents = 1,000	Represents a balance between ensuring there are enough agents so that interactions can occur and the computational overhead from using more agents
Number of Cops = 200	Chosen to ensure that cops would be present at some of the convergences that occur across the 16,035 places in Seattle.[13]
Unemployment Rate = 6%	The unemployment rate of 6% is based on the 2002 unemployment rate for Seattle (Bureau of Labor Statistics, 2003).[14]
Rate of Criminal Propensity = 20%	Given that 20% of the population has committed a crime, 20% of civilians are assigned criminal propensity using a uniform distribution (Visher, & Roth, 1986).
Time To ReOffend = 60	Parameter value chosen as a starting point since the author could find no empirical data on which to base time to reoffend.
Random Number Seed = 100 (seed also tested at 200, 300, 400 and 500)	An explicit random number seed based on the Mersenne Twister (MT) algorithm is used as the basis for all random number distributions used in the model. MT is currently considered to be the most robust in the industry (Ropella, Railsback, & Jackson, 2002).
Agent Level	
Societal Time Spent Away From Home = 30% (40%, 50%, 60%, 70%)	Assigned based on a normal distribution with a mean of 432 minutes (for the 30% condition) and a standard deviation of 10% of the mean (sd = 43).[15]
Initial Wealth = 50	Initial wealth is assigned with a mean of 50 and a standard deviation of 20 units.
Amount of wealth received each payday = 5	No empirical evidence available. Parameter chosen is a starting point.
Amount of wealth exchanged during robbery=1	No empirical evidence available.[16] Parameter chosen is a starting point.
Situation Level	
Guardianship Perception = U(-2,2)	The guardianship perception value can add or subtract zero, one or two guardians from the actual number present. This represents the stochastic element in the offender's perception of the willingness of a guardian to intervene.
Suitable Target Perception = U(-1,1)	The value in suitable target can increase or decrease the suitability or leave it unchanged. This enables the offender to sometimes decide a target is not suitable even when they have more wealth.

Table 2. Implementation versions of the conceptual street robbery model

	Simple	Temporal	Activity Space
Civilian Movement	Random*	Random*	Defined Activity Space
Police Movement	Random*	Random*	Random*
Civilian Characteristics			
Criminal Propensity	Yes	Yes	Yes
Wealth	Yes	Yes	Yes
Activity Space	No	Temporal	Spatio-temporal
Employment Status	No	Yes	Yes

** Agents are randomly distributed to start and travel randomly during the simulation.*

Implementation Software

Agent Analyst is again used to build the two additional versions of the original model (Groff, in press-a).[6] Agent analyst combines two of the most popular packages for ABM and GIS; for ABM it relies on the recursive porous agent simulation toolkit for python (RepastPy) (North, Collier, & Vos, 2006) and for GIS it uses ArcGIS (ESRI, 2005). Once the agent analyst toolbox is added into an ArcGIS session individual models can access shapefiles allowing: (1) individual agents to become spatially aware and (2) the visualization of agent movement and decision outcomes (e.g., locations of crimes).

A combined ABM/GIS simulation model integrates the advantages of autonomous agents found in agent-based modeling with the spatial explicitness of a geographic information system (Albrecht, 2005; An, Linderman, Qi, Shortridge, & Liu, 2005; Brown, Riolo, Robinson, North, & Rand, 2005). Both are necessary to move from artificial environments to "real" ones. The agents interact on city streets and their activities during the simulation are impacted by the distribution of opportunities for housing, employment, shopping and recreation across the urban backcloth. This allows the spatial behavior of agents based on real landscapes to be more representative of actual human behavior.

Data

The model uses input data describing the land use and street network of Seattle, Washington. Four datasets describing conditions in Seattle are used to inform the activity spaces of agents in the model: (1) total population; (2) total employment; (3) total potential activities; and (4) streets. Blockgroup level population figures describe the distribution of residences across Seattle (U.S. Census Bureau, 2000). Employment data provide the number of employees per zip code area (U.S. Census Bureau, 2002). Potential activity locations are quantified through the use of retail, recreation and service establishments (e.g., grocery stores, convenience stores, dry cleaners, gyms etc.) (ESRI, 2003). Finally, the King County Street Network Database (SND) file is used to structure the agent's movements. There are 16,035 street intersections/nodes in Seattle and these locations represent places at which a street robbery may occur. In addition to the input data describing Seattle, the 12 parameters described earlier are set prior to the model run (Table 1).

Experiments

In keeping with the original study, the same series of five experiments are conducted on each of the two new versions of the street robbery model.

That is, both the Activity Space and the Temporal versions of the model are run 5 times assuming 5 different societies which vary from 30% of time spent away from home to 70%. The outcomes from the experiments are then compared to test the impact of the following on spatial patterns of street robbery: (1) changes in the amount of time spent away from home; and (2) the addition of temporal and spatial constraints to routine activities. As in life, the societal average represents the average time spent away from home for the agent population as a whole; individual agents have different times spent away from home.

CHALLENGES TO LEARNING FROM MODELS: CALIBRATION AND VALIDATION

Before turning to the results of the theoretical experiments outlined here, it is prudent to examine some of the challenges in learning from simulation models especially those for which prediction is the goal. The main challenge is termed the "equifinality problem" and is not unique to simulation but involves all numerical models (Oreskes, Shrader-Frechette, & Belitz, 1994; O'Sullivan, 2004a). The equifinality problem concerns the fact that more than one model can produce the same result. Thus, even the best-calibrated and most rigorously tested models can account for the same observed outcome using different mechanism. In response, O'Sullivan (2004a) suggests the following approach.

> It is clear that assessment of the accuracy of a model as a representation must rest on arguments about how competing theories are represented in its workings, with calibration and fitting procedures acting as a check on reasoning. So, while we must surely question the adequacy of a model that is incapable of generating results resembling observational data, we can only make broad comparisons between competing models that each provides a 'reasonable' fit to observations. Furthermore, critical argument and engagement with underlying theories about processes represented in models is essential: no purely technical procedure can do better than this. (O'Sullivan, 2004a, p. 291)

Another challenge to validating simulations of crime is lack of a reliable dependent variable. Official crime data are most frequently used but they reflect an unknown fraction of the actual crime events that occur. A simulation model is set up to generate actual numbers of crime; as if all crimes were reported by victims and all were judged valid by police. Thus simulation models are built to reflect all crime while official crime data captures an unknown portion of total crimes committed. However, it is possible to evaluate the plausibility of the patterns and numbers of crime produced by models. Under this standard, model results are judged on how well they reproduce the general characteristics of crime patterns and volume (Batty, & Torrens, 2005). Specifically, to be credible the crime patterns produced would have to have the following characteristics: (1) spatially concentrated rather than dispersed (i.e., a few locations should have many crimes and many locations should have just a few); and (2) include both repeat offenders and repeat victims (Liu, Wang, Eck, & Liang, 2005).

The potential for learning is a product of the entire model building process from formalization of theories, to sensitivity testing and calibration, to comparison with observed data: under this framework models are heuristic devices, representations that can aid in understanding and illuminate mechanisms at work for further study (Batty, & Torrens, 2005; Dowling, 1999; Oreskes et al., 1994; O'Sullivan, 2004a). Although the current research emphasizes the representation of theory in models, and how we can learn from that process, it also takes issues of calibration and validation seriously and these are discussed next.[7] Choices of the parameter values and distributions used in the model are included under the rubric of calibration. Explorations of the parameter space assist with the understanding of mechanisms at work in the model. While the concept of validation is centered on the level of confidence we can have in a model, namely do both the mechanisms and the results of the model reflect reality (or at the very least the reality of imperfect data). Validation involves comparing model results to actual data.

Related to calibration, the choice of parameter values is a critical aspect of modeling that deserves special attention because of the potential impacts on the model outcomes. Modelers try to use theoretically-based empirical values whenever possible and plausible ones when empirical ones are not available. Some modelers use sensitivity testing to quantify the robustness of the model results (Manson, 2001; O'Sullivan, 2004a). This is accomplished by systematically varying the initial parameters and the random number seed and testing the impact on the model results. Others use calibration to "fit a real data set" (Liu et al., 2005, p. 208; Oreskes et al., 1994). In this process, the parameters are systematically changed to attempt to match the empirical data pattern and intensity.

This study evaluates the robustness of the findings through the systematic variation of five of the key parameter values and by varying the random number seed used across the new versions of the model. The five parameter values are systematically increased (i.e., number of police, time to wait before able to re-offend, initial wealth distribution, perception of target suitability random term, and the perception of guardianship random term), the model runs are repeated for all five experimental conditions, and a one-way ANOVA is applied to analyze the results. Finally, the entire sensitivity testing process of varying the five parameter values is repeated four more times using different random number seeds to test the effect of changing the random number seed on the outcomes of the model.

Sensitivity testing demonstrates the original and the new model versions are robust to changes in parameters and random number seeds. The absolute number of robberies increased or decreased

Figure 1. Conceptual model of street robbery for all versions

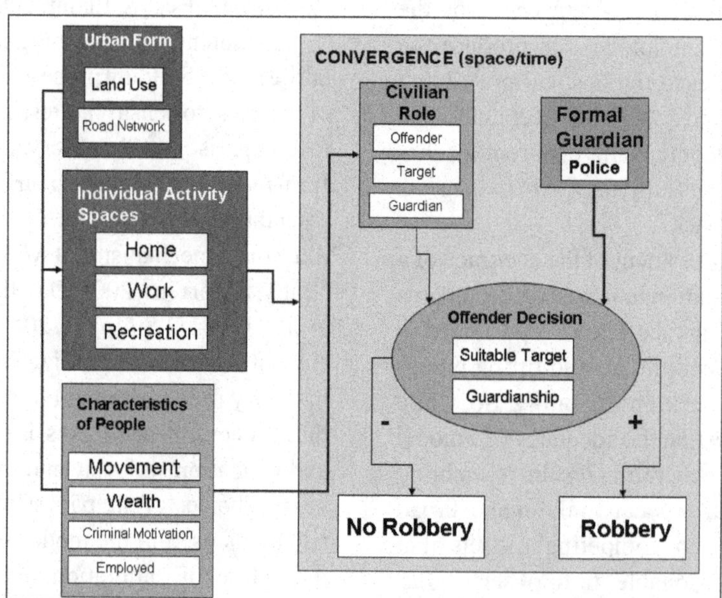

Table 3. Place-level model outcomes

	Empirical Data	Experimental Condition				
	Seattle 2002	30%	40%	50%	60%	70%
Total Robberies	1,156	54,637 (S) 12,807 (T) 32,326 (AS)	76,032 (S) 13,671 (T) 34,628 (AS)	95,219 (S) 15,183 (T) 38,331 (AS)	118,085 (S) 16,196 (T) 41,266 (AS)	139,007 (S) 17,181 (T) 46,085 (AS)
Average robberies per node	0.07	3.41 (S) .80 (T) 2.02 (AS)	4.74 (S) .85 (T) 2.16 (AS)	5.94 (S) .95 (T) 2.39 (AS)	7.36 (S) 1.01 (T) 2.57 (AS)	8.67 (S) 1.07 (T) 2.87 (AS)
Total places with a robberya	789	13,376 (S) 6,689 (T) 1,535 (AS)	13,925 (S) 6,641 (T) 1,499 (AS)	14,309 (S) 6,549 (T) 1,472 (AS)	14,531 (S) 6,441 (T) 1,475(AS)	14,683 (S) 6,568 (T) 1,498 (AS)
Percent of places with a robbery	5.9%	83.4% (S) 41.7% (T) 9.6% (AS)	86.8% (S) 41.4% (T) 9.4% (AS)	89.2% (S) 40.8% (T) 9.2% (AS)	90.6% (S) 40.2% (T) 9.2% (AS)	91.6% (S) 41.0% (T) 9.3% (AS)
Total places with more then one robbery	189	11,157 (S) 3,130 (T) 1,179 (AS)	12,175 (S) 3,183 (T) 1,171 (AS)	12,995 (S) 3,225 (T) 1,128 (AS)	13,303 (S) 3,254 (T) 1,134 (AS)	13,572 (S) 3,197 (T) 1,142 (AS)
Percent of places with more then one robbery	1.2%	69.6% (S) 19.5% (T) 7.4% (AS)	75.9% (S) 19.9% (T) 7.3% (AS)	81.0% (S) 20.1% (T) 7.0% (AS)	83.0% (S) 20.3% (T) 7.1% (AS)	84.6% (S) 19.9% (T) 7.1% (AS)

(S) Simple (T) Temporal (AS) Activity Space

depending on the parameter being varied. However, findings related to routine activity theory's core proposition remain consistent across the vast majority of the tests lending additional support for robustness of the model even as parameters are varied. The two exceptions are found in one of the random number seed tests and the time spent away from home. One of the random number seed variations produces a significant result for the Activity Space version. Otherwise, the results of the model are shown to be robust to changes in the random number seed. Increasing the time an agent with criminal propensity has to wait to commit another street robbery makes the ANOVA for the Temporal version non significant and points to the importance of timing in the decision to offend.

FINDINGS

The impact of schedule constraints on the spatial distribution of street robbery is evaluated by comparing the findings from the Simple version to those from the Temporal and Activity Space versions across the five experimental conditions using kernel density and Ripley's *K*. Kernel density surfaces offer a means of evaluating the existence of global trends in the distribution of street robberies and for comparing the relative density of robberies across experimental conditions (Bailey & Gatrell, 1995; Levine, 2005; Mitchell, 1999; Williamson, Mclafferty, McGuire Philip, Ross, Mollenkopf, Goldsmith, 2001). Ripley's *K* provides more formal test of the relative spatial distributions. All of these measures are distance-based and characterize the spatial patterning of the street robbery locations as conditioned by the pattern of street nodes. In addition, the spatial patterns of the model are compared to the pattern of one year of street robberies in Seattle, WA to determine which of the representations comes closest to the actual distribution of street robberies.

The following interpretational caveat should be kept in mind when considering the Ripley's *K* results. The outcome data from the model are somewhat unique in that convergences and robbery events can only occur at the street nodes thus a comparison to complete spatial randomness is inappropriate. Instead, the *K* function is calculated for the street nodes and then compared to CSR. The original study found both the street nodes and the robberies were significantly more clustered than would be expected under CSR (Groff, in press-a).

There is support of the first hypothesis; *as the average time spent by civilians on activities away from home increases, the spatial pattern of robberies will change* (Table 3). While the average robberies per node increase with time spent away from home for all versions of the model, there are differences in the distribution of those events across nodes. In the Simple version, both the total places that experience a single robbery and multiple robberies increase steadily as more time is spent away from home. In contrast, those figures are essentially flat for both the Temporal and Activity Spaces versions. To examine the spatial distribution of robberies across places, spatial statistics such as kernel density maps and the Ripley's *K* statistic are necessary.

One way of characterizing the spatial pattern of robberies is via a kernel density.[8] Two maps describe the spatial pattern of robberies that emerges for each version of the model at the 30% and 70% conditions (Maps 1 and 2).[9] Once again there are differences between the versions. In both the Simple and Temporal versions as civilians spend more time away from home, the robbery concentrations visible at the 30% condition become more intense while new areas emerge and become hotspots; this outcome is most likely due to the random movement pattern and the increased likelihood of convergence as agent's spend more time away from home. Under random movement, the more time an agent has to travel the farther they can go in one day which contributes to

Map 1. Kernel density for 30% time spent away from home

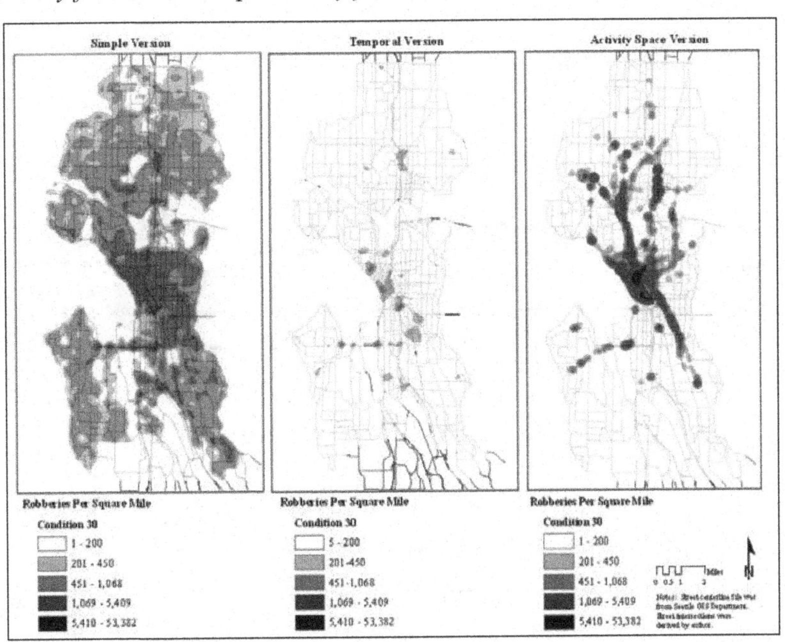

Map 2. Kernel density for 70% time spent away from home

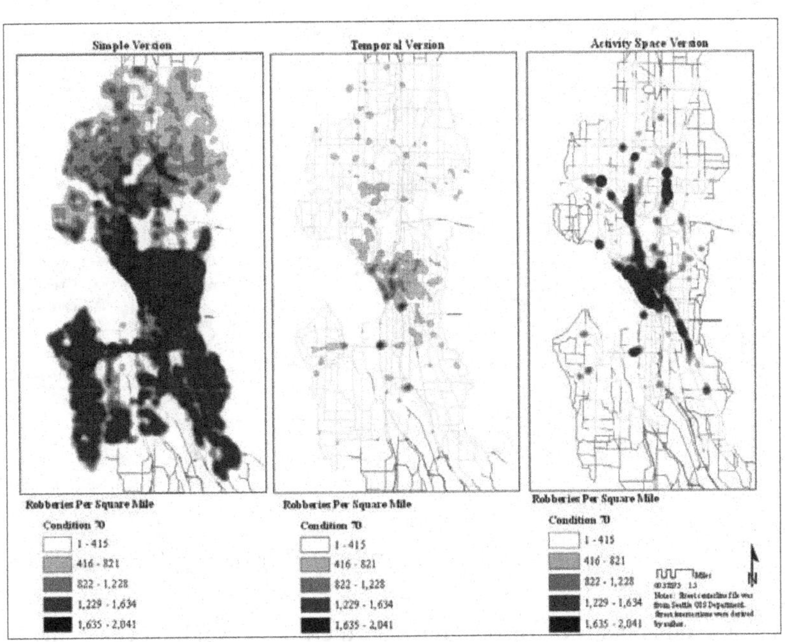

Figure 2. Ripley's K analysis: Effect of time spent away from home for model produced and real robbery events

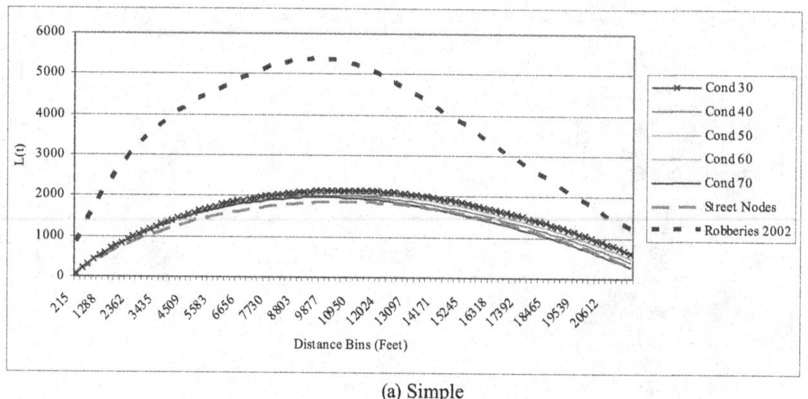

(a) Simple

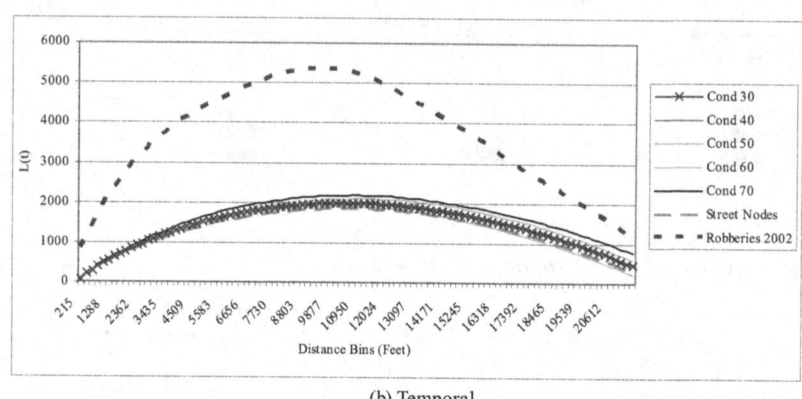

(b) Temporal

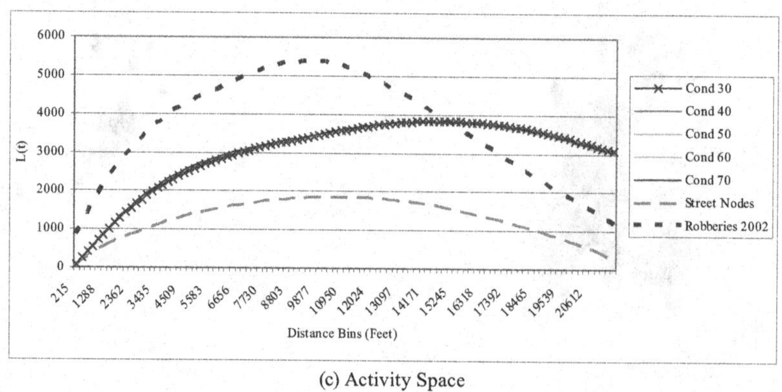

(c) Activity Space

the formation of new hotspots (i.e., dispersion of robbery). Under the Activity Space version, there are spatially constrained hotspots at 30% that follow major transportation routes. At 70% there are fewer but even hotter hotspots of crime. This visual inspection of the map series indicates support for the first hypothesis and illustrates the importance of considering the spatio-temporal structure of routine activities.

Ripley's *K* offers a more formal test of the form of the distribution across experimental conditions.[10] Figure 2 compares the concentration of street robberies under all five of the experimental conditions to the concentration of the street network's nodes, and to a reference distribution of one year of street robberies in Seattle. In the Simple version of the model, robberies are much less concentrated than real street robberies but slightly more concentrated than would be expected based on the street network alone. Related to time spent away from home. There is slight variation by amount of time. Model robberies are most concentrated when society spends 30% of time away from home and the concentration decreases as time spent away from home increases. This is a plausible outcome since as agents spend more time away from home they can also get farther away from home so the pattern becomes more and more dispersed.

Temporal version model robberies are once again much less concentrated than the actual distribution in 2002 at all distances. In a reverse from the Simple version, the 70% condition is the most clustered for the Temporal version. Temporal version robberies track the clustering in street nodes until about a quarter of mile when they become and then remain more clustered at all distances. The one exception is for 50% condition which exhibits the same level of clustering as the street nodes at distances less than about one mile and greater than two miles.

The Activity Space *K* function lines are significantly more clustered than the street nodes at all distances and under all five experimental conditions (Figure 2c). The pattern of model-produced robberies is most similar to the sample pattern of actual street robberies. Unlike the Temporal and Simple versions, there is very little variation among the individual experimental condition lines for the Activity Space version.

An additional analysis of the distribution of visits (i.e., number of times a civilian agent is at a node) enables the separation of clustering due to everyday travel patterns from that of street robbery. The outcome shows that the patterns for visits and robberies are very similar across all model versions with robberies exhibiting slightly more clustering than would be expected based on the network. This provides evidence of the existence of additional factors, beyond routine travel, that are contributing to the greater concentration of street robbery events.[11]

Results also support the second hypothesis that *the temporal and spatio-temporal schedules of civilians while away from home change the spatial pattern of robbery events.* Outcome measures reveal both increases in concentration and spread of street robberies as time spent away from home increases (Table 3). Mean robberies per node are lowest in the Temporal model followed by the Activity Space model. The more time that is spent away from home, the bigger the disparity among the versions. A different pattern emerges when looking at the percent of street nodes with only one robbery and the percent with more then one robbery. The Simple version has the highest proportions of both, followed by the Temporal version. Less than 10% of all nodes in Activity Space version ever have a robbery.

Kernel density maps (Maps 1 and 2) reveal the existence of interversion differences in the spatial patterns of street robbery at the 30 and 70% conditions. In general, the Simple condition has a more dispersed pattern then the Temporal version and the clusters represent higher density areas regardless of the experimental condition. The location of the densest clusters are in the same general area (e.g. in and near the downtown) for both versions but the distribution for the rest of the city is very different. The Simple model results indicate higher robbery density over most of the central and southern Seattle while the Temporal version has lower robbery density and mostly in the central city with some hot spots in both the north and south. As the only spatially-defined version, the Activity Space version has a pattern distinctly different from the other versions; one

Figure 3. Ripley's K analysis: Distribution of street robberies by model version

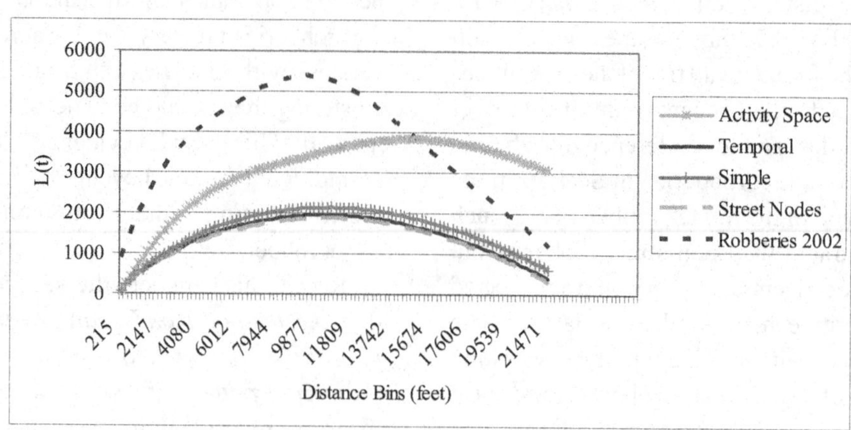

(a) Condition 30: Society Spends 30% of Time Away From Home

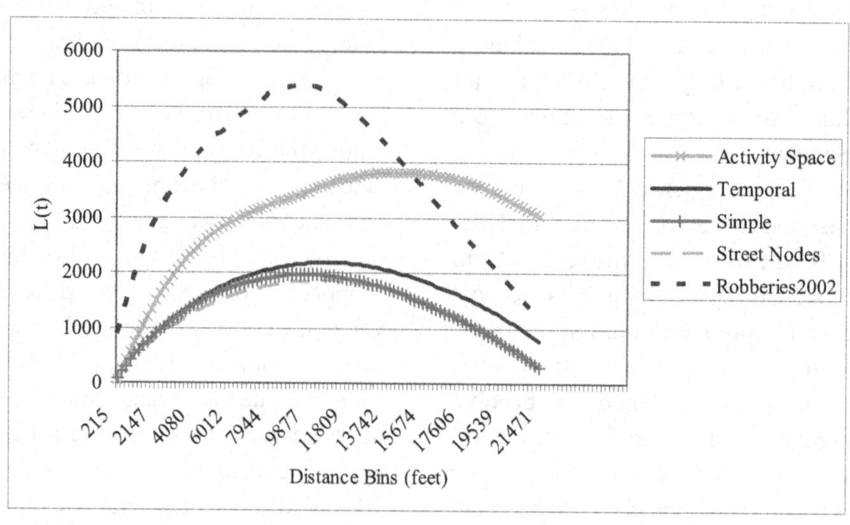

(b) Condition 70: Society Spends 70% of Time Away From Home

that reflects the distribution of opportunities and the unchanging activity spaces of the agents in the model.

Another way to examine the differences in the spatial pattern of street robberies produced by the addition of time and then time-space to the civilian's activities is to use the Ripley's *K* calculated earlier but compare the distributions produced by the model versions at the 30 and the 70% experimental conditions (Figure 3).[12] The street robbery pattern produced by the Activity Space version is significantly more clustered than the other versions, and than would be expected based on the street node network regardless of experimental condition. This result is reasonable because the Activity Space version specifically restricts civilians to pre-defined activity spaces for the duration of the model run.

On the other hand, the pattern of clustering in the Simple and Temporal versions relative to one another changes depending on time spent away from home. Although both are more clustered then the street nodes at distances under two miles, the strength of that clustering varies with experimental condition. The Simple version exhibits higher levels of clustering at distances under two miles for 30% condition. At 70% the results are identical at shorter distances but after about a mile they two versions switch roles and the Temporal version exhibits greater clustering because of the smaller activity spaces. Overall, temporal constraints reduce clustering in the distribution at distances between one-half and two miles but only in societies in which civilians spend up to half of their time away from home. In sum, adding spatial constraints produces a much larger clustering effect than adding temporal ones.

A comparison of the simulated results to the empirical distribution of street robberies in 2002 (N = 1,256) reveals that all three models over-predict the absolute number of street robberies (Table 3). Using the 30% condition for comparison, the Temporal model comes the closest with roughly ten times as many robberies over a year period. Relatedly, the Temporal model is also closest to the empirical distribution on average number of robberies per node (.80 vs. .07 respectively). But on all other measures the Activity Space model comes closer because it is the model that predicts the most concentration in street robberies; 100% of the robberies occurred at only 5.9% of places empirically and 9.6% of places in the Activity Space version. The visual comparison of Kernel density maps confirms the concentration of robberies in the Activity Space versions (Map 1 and 2) to be more similar to the actual pattern (Map 3). Finally, the Ripley's K graphs (Figure 3) provide further evidence in favor of the Activity Space version showing that the empirical distribution is most concentrated followed by the Activity Space model results.

Map 3. Comparison of Kernel density for empirical street robberies vs. activity space version

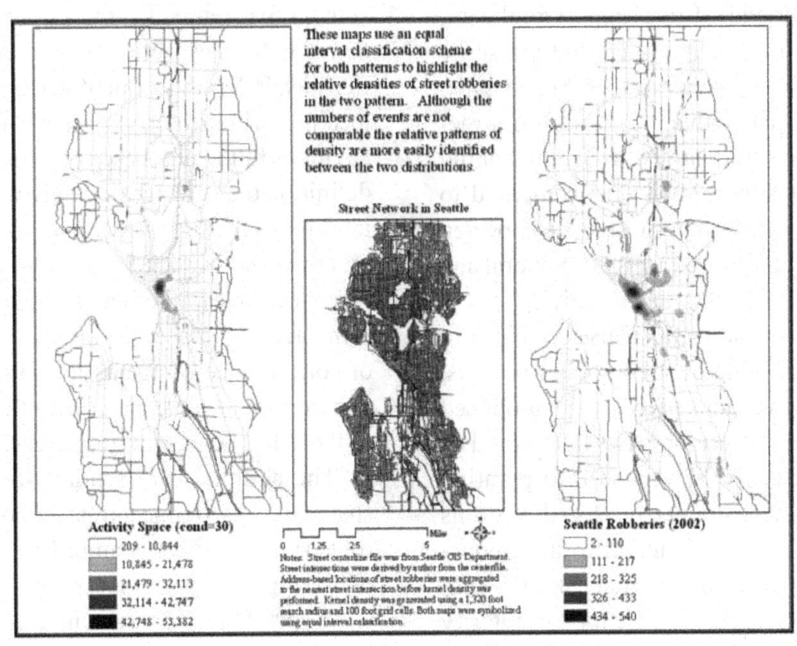

DISCUSSION

This chapter extends earlier work that presented the case and provided the method for testing routine activity theory using simulation and found support for the theory's main premise that the shift of routine activities away from home increases rates of street robbery (Groff, in 2007a). However, the earlier study left unexamined the temporal and spatio-temporal aspects of routine activities in the model. This chapter creates two additional versions of the basic model of street robbery that implement activity spaces for agents (Groff, in 2007b). One version adds time schedules to the civilians so that their time at risk of committing or being a victim of street robbery is varied. The other version defines both the spatial and temporal schedules of the civilians by having them travel among a set of locations spending the same amounts of time traveling and at activities as in the Temporal version. In this way, the current work is able to explore the impact of progressively more complex temporally and spatio-temporally explicit activity spaces on the spatial distribution of street robbery events.

The results provide strong support for the important role of time and particularly time-space in the definition of activity spaces. Specifically, routine activity spaces that include time or time-space produce significantly different spatial distributions of street robbery as compared to the original model. In other words, as expected based on theory, the introduction of temporal and spatio-temporal elements to the activity spaces of the civilians in the model causes changes in the spatial distribution of street robbery events. Although all the versions of the model produced significantly more street robberies than would be expected empirically, the version incorporating spatio-temporal constraints produced patterns with characteristics most similar to the empirical distribution (i.e., highly concentrated with relatively few places responsible for the majority of robberies).

Explanations for the findings just described have their roots in the simple rules governing agent behavior and interaction. The separate influences of temporal and spatio-temporal schedules and the movement rules of the agents underlie the finding that time and space each have an effect on the spatial distribution of street robbery events. Temporal schedules reduce both: (1) the time agents are "at risk" of becoming victims or offenders; and (2) the size of the agent's activity spaces. Agents with a temporal schedule spend time at their activity nodes which means: they travel for less time, and thus less distance; and are not vulnerable to street robbery for as much time each day.

Empirically-informed spatio-temporal activity spaces in the Activity Space version of the model counteract the reduced risk from the temporal schedule by increasing convergence. The inherent clustering of agent's homes, jobs, and activity nodes increases convergence as compared to a random distribution. This concentration of origins and destinations means civilians are funneled along many of the same roads to reach many of the same areas. In addition, the use of a defined activity space embodies the routine nature of daily travel and its restriction to a potential path area in which individuals can travel to all the required locations within their time schedule (Miller, 1991). Civilians following these predefined paths are by definition then converging only with other civilians' paths that physically intersect their own. In this way, spatially-defined activity spaces act to: (1) concentrate the activities of agents sharing the same activity space; (2) increase the frequency of convergence of agents in the model; and (3) increase the deterrence effect of police who are in those high concentration areas.

The addition of a spatially-defined activity space also acts to concentrate the hotspots of street robbery. This effect is amplified since there are only two potential activity spaces for each agent in the model. This creates an unrealistically focused travel pattern for society. While the essentially routine nature of activity is well-known, accessibility research indicates there is typically more variety in daily paths (Kwan, 1998; Weber, & Kwan, 2002). As a consequence of this restricted interaction in the model, the places where convergence is possible are more concentrated and involve the same agents each time.

In sum, this research demonstrates how geographical perspectives can inform the spatio-temporal representation of human behavior in a criminological theory and in doing so advance the body of knowledge in both disciplines. The research breaks new ground by extending an existing model so that it is capable of accommodating both the empirically-based activity spaces and the individual-level interactions necessary to represent crime events. The findings from the model provide evidence for the important role of the individual-level, spatio-temporal aspects of human spatial behavior in contributing to the distribution of street robbery events.

While this initial research points to the integration of both space and time as key to producing simulated street robbery distributions, further model enhancements are needed to more completely reflect theory about human behavior in space-time. Sensitivity testing suggests that adjustments to the time until an offender re-offends would be one fruitful path. The following discussion highlights the directions for future work with the greatest promise for better representing activity spaces in the model.

FUTURE RESEARCH DIRECTIONS

This discussion begins with enhancements to the temporal and then spatial aspects of routine activity spaces. Of the many enhancements that could be added to model, incorporating a more realistic representation of time is perhaps the most intriguing. Adding time of day would allow for a more fully developed representation of temporal constraints to be included in the model (Miller, 2005). Temporal constraints are particularly important to offender behavior because they shape the spatio-temporal patterns of opportunity to commit crime (Ratcliffe, 2006). The requirement that an individual be at certain places at certain times and the existence of discretionary time (i.e., time not allocated to a task or to travel) constrain the shape and size of activity spaces. Incorporating time of day would have the added benefit of enabling the model to reflect more general temporal patterns such as the fact that more people are away from home during the day and early evening than during the night time (i.e. when most people are sleeping).

Additional temporal constraints related to mode of transportation and characteristics of the street network could enhance the notion of "at risk" status. Individuals who are walking or using public transportation are at greater risk of street robbery than those in automobiles. Mode of transportation also impacts the distance that can be traveled in a particular time period which could be included in the model. The inclusion of speed limits and one-way streets would provide more realistic travel times and routes.

Beyond temporal constraints, the representation of activity spaces in general deserves more attention. Ideally, activity spaces would be dynamically generated during each day of the model. This would allow the activity spaces to emerge during the course of a simulation and become the object of a study. Unfortunately, this strategy would require that the necessary software classes be developed so the appropriate data structures could be accessed during model runs. In the interim, a relatively straightforward improvement would be to generate multiple activity spaces per agent. By increasing the number of activity spaces available to agents, the model will better reflect the variety found in activity spaces.

Finally, replication is necessary to improve the external validity of the model. The testing of different cities with varying street networks and land use patterns would provide additional insight into the role of the built environment in shaping the pattern of crime events.

REFERENCES

Aitken, S. C., Cutter, S. L., Foote, K. E., & Sell, J. L. (1989). Environmental perception and behavioral geography. In Wilmott & Gaile (Eds.), *Geography in america* (pp. 218-238).

Albrecht, J. (2005). A new age for geosimulation. *Transactions in GIS, 9*(4), 451-454.

An, L., Linderman, M., Qi, J., Shortridge, A., & Liu, J. (2005). Exploring complexity in a human-environment system: An agent-based spatial model for multidisciplinary and multiscale integration. *Annals of the Association of American Geographers, 95*(1), 54-79.

Axelrod, R. (in press). Advancing the art of simulation in the social sciences. In J.-P. Rennard (Ed.), *Handbook of research on nature inspired computing for economy and management*. Hershey, PA: Idea Group.

Bailey, T. C., & Gatrell, A. C. (1995). *Interactive spatial data analysis*. Essex: Longman Group Limited.

Batty, M., & Torrens, P. M. (2005). Modelling and prediction in a complex world. *Futures, 37*, 745-766.

Brantingham, P. J., & Brantingham, P. L. (1981). Notes on the geometry of crime. In P. Brantingham & P. Brantingham (Eds.), *Environmental criminology* (pp. 27-54). Prospect Heights, IL: Waveland Press, Inc.

Brantingham, P. L., & Brantingham, P. J. (1993). Nodes, paths and edges: Considerations on the complexity of crime and the physical environment. *Journal of Environmental Psychology, 13*, 3-28.

Brantingham, P. L., & Brantingham, P. J. (2003). *Computer simulation as a tool for environmental criminologists*. Paper presented at the presented at 11th International Symposium on Environmental Criminology and Crime Analysis, University of Cincinnati.

Brantingham, P. L., & Brantingham, P. J. (2004). Computer simulation as a tool for environmental criminologists. *Security Journal, 17*(1), 21-30.

Brantingham, P. L., & Groff, E. R. (2004). *The future of agent-based simulation in environmental criminology*. Paper presented at the American Society of Criminology, Nashville, TN.

Brown, D. G., Riolo, R., Robinson, D. T., North, M., & Rand, W. (2005). Spatial process and data models: Toward integration of agent-based models and GIS. *Journal of Geographic Systems, 7*, 25-47.

Bureau of Labor Statistics. (2003). *Metropolitan area employment and unemployment: January 2003*. Bureau of Labor Statistics, United States Department of Labor. Retrieved September 2, 2007, from the World Wide Web: www.bls.gov/news.release/archives/metro_03262003.pdf

Chaitin, G. (1990). *Information, randomness and incompleteness* (2nd ed.). Singapore: World Scientific.

Chorley, R. J., & Haggett, P. (Eds.). (1967). *Models in geography*. London: Methuen & Co.

Clarke, R. V., & Cornish, D. B. (1985). Modeling offender's decisions: A framework for Research and policy. In M. Tonry & N. Morris (Eds.), *Crime and justice: An Annual Review of Research* (Vol. 6). Chicago: University of Chicago Press.

Clarke, R. V., & Cornish, D. B. (2001). Rational choice. In R. Paternoster & R. Bachman (Eds.), *Explaining criminals and crime* (pp. 23-42). Los Angeles: Roxbury Publishing Co.

Cohen, L. E., & Felson, M. (1979). Social change and crime rate trends: A routine activity approach. *American Sociological Review, 44*, 588-608.

Dibble, C. (2001). *Theory in a complex world: GeoGraph computational laboratories.* Unpublished doctoral dissertation, University of California Santa Barbara, Santa Barbara.

Dowling, D. (1999). Experimenting on theories. *Science in Context, 12*(2), 261-273.

Eck, J. E. (2005). *Using crime pattern simulations to elaborate theory.* Paper presented at the American Society of Criminology, Toronto.

Eck, J. E., & Liu, L. (2004). *Routine activity theory in a RA/CA crime simulation.* Paper presented at the American Society of Criminology, Nashville, TN.

Eck, J. E., & Weisburd, D. L. (1995). *Crime and place.* Monsey, NY: Willow Tree Press.

Engel-Frisch, G. (1943). Some neglected temporal aspects of human ecology. *Social Forces, 22*(1/4), 43-47.

Epstein, J. M., & Axtell, R. (1996). *Growing artificial societies.* Washington. D.C.: Brookings Institution Press.

ESRI (2003). *Business location data.* Redlands, CA: Environmental Systems Research Institute.

ESRI (2005). *ArcGIS 9.1.* Redlands, CA: Environmental Systems Research Institute.

Felson, M. (1987). Routine activities and crime prevention in the developing metropolis. *Criminology, 25*(4), 911-931.

Gilbert, N., & Terna, P. (1999). *How to build and use agent-based models in social science.* Discussion Paper. Retrieved September 2, 2007, from http://web.econ.unito.it/terna/deposito/gil_ter.pdf

Gilbert, N., & Troitzsch, K. G. (1999). *Simulation for the social scientist.* Buckingham: Open University Press.

Gimblett, H. R. (Ed.). (2002). *Integrating geographic information systems and agent-based modeling techniques for simulating social and ecological processes.* Oxford: Oxford University Press.

Golledge, R. G., & Stimson, R. J. (1997). *Spatial behavior: A geographical perspective.* New York: Guilford Press.

Golledge, R. G., & Timmermans, H. (1990). Applications of behavioural research on spatial problems I: cognition. *Progress in Human Geography, 14*, 57-99.

Groff, E. R. (2006). *Exploring the geography of routine activity theory: A spatio-temporal test using street robbery.* Unpublished Dissertation, University of Maryland, College Park, MD.

Groff, E. R. (2007). Simulation for theory testing and experimentation: An example using routine activity theory and street robbery. *Journal of Quantitative Criminology, 23*(2), 75-103.

Groff, E. R. (2007). 'Situating' simulation to model human spatio-temporal interactions: An example using crime events. *Transactions in GIS, 11*(4), 507-530.

Gunderson, L., & Brown, D. (2003). *Using a multi-agent model to predict both physical and cyber crime.* Retrieved September 2, 2007, from http://vijis.sys.virginia.edu/publication/SMCMultiAgent.pdf

Hägerstrand, T. (1970). What about people in regional science? *Papers of the Regional Science Association, 24*, 7-21.

Hägerstrand, T. (1973). The domain of human geography. In R. J. Chorley (Ed.), *Directions in geography* (pp. 67-87). London: Methuen.

Hägerstrand, T. (1975). Space, time, and human conditions. In A. Karlqvist, L. Lundqvist, & F. Snickars (Eds.), *Dynamic allocation of urban space* (pp. 3-14). Farnborough: Saxon House.

Harvey, D. (1969). *Explanation in geography.* London: Edward Arnold Publishers.

Hawley, A. H. (1950). *Human ecology.* New York: The Ronald Press Company.

Hindelang, M. J., Gottfredson, M. R., & Garofalo, J. (1978). *Victims of personal crime.* Cambridge: Ballinger.

Horton, F. E., & Reynolds, D. R. (1971). Action space differentials in cities. In H. McConnell & D. Yaseen (Eds.), *Perspectives in geography: Models of spatial interaction* (pp. 83-102). Dekab, IL: Northern Illinois University Press.

Kent, J., Leitner, M., & Curtis, A. (2006). Evaluating the usefulness of functional distance measures when calibrating jouney-to-crime distance decay functions. *Computers, Environment and Urban Systems, 30*, 181-200.

Kwan, M.-P. (1998). Space-time and intregral measures of individual accessibility: A comparative analysis using a point-based framework. *Geographical Analysis, 30*, 191-216.

Lenntorp, B. (1978). A time-geographic simulation model of individual activity programmes. In T. Carlstein, D. Parkes, & N. J. Thrift (Eds.), *Human geography and time geography* (pp. 162-199). New York: Halsted Press.

Levine, N. (2005). *CrimeStat: A spatial statistics program for the analysis of crime incident locations (v 3.0).* Washington, D.C.: Ned Levine & Associates, Houston, TX, and the National Institute of Justice.

Liu, L., Wang, X., Eck, J., & Liang, J. (2005). Simulating crime events and crime patterns in RA/CA model. In F. Wang (Ed.), *Geographic information systems and crime analysis* (pp. 197-213). Singapore: Idea Group.

Lynch, K. (1960). *The image of the city.* Cambridge: M.I.T. Press.

Macy, M. W., & Willer, R. (2002). From factors to actors: Computational sociology and agent-based modeling. *Annual Review of Sociology, 28*, 143-166.

Maguire, D. J., Batty, M., & Goodchild, M. F. (Eds.). (2005). *GIS, spatial analysis, and modeling.* Redlands, CA: ESRI Press.

Manson, S. M. (2001). Calibration, verification, and validation (Section 2.4). In D. C. Parker, T. Berger, S. M. Manson, & W. J. M. (mng. ed. (Eds.), *Agent-based models of land-use and land-cover change.*

Miller, E. J., Hunt, J. D., Abraham, J. E., & Salvini, P. A. (2004). Microsimulating urban systems. *Computers, Environment and Urban Systems, 28*(2004), 9-44.

Miller, E. J., Roorda, M. J., & Carrasoc, J. A. (2005). A tour-based model of travel mode choice. *Transportation, 32*, 399-422.

Miller, H. J. (1991). Modelling accessibility using space-time prism concepts within geographical information systems. *International Journal Geographical Information Systems, 5*(3), 287-301.

Miller, H. J. (2005). A measurement theory for time geography. *Geographical Analysis, 37*, 17-45.

Mitchell, A. (1999). *The ESRI guide to GIS analysis: Vol. 1. Geographic patterns & relationships.* Redlands, CA: Environmental Systems Research Institute Press.

Moss, S., & Edmonds, B. (2005). Sociology and simulation: Statistical and qualitative cross-validation. *The American Journal of Sociology, 110*(4), 1095-1131.

North, M. J., Collier, N. T., & Vos, J. R. (2006). Experiences creating three implementations of the repast agent modeling toolkit. *ACM Transactions on Modeling and Computer Simulation, 16*(1), 1-25.

Oreskes, N., Shrader-Frechette, K., & Belitz, K. (1994). Verification, validation, and confirmation of numerical models in the earth sciences. *Science, 263*(5147), 641-646.

Ostrom, T. M. (1988). Computer simulation: The third symbol system. *Journal of Experimental Psychology, 24*, 381-392.

O'Sullivan, D. (2004a). Complexity science and human geography. *Transactions of the Institute of British Geographers, 29*, 282-295.

O'Sullivan, D. (2004b). Too much of the wrong kind of data: Implications for the practice of micro-scale modeling. In M. F. Goodchild & D. G. Janelle (Eds.), *Spatially integrated social science* (pp. 95-107). New York: Oxford University Press.

Pred, A. (1967). *Behavior and location: Foundations for a geographic and dynamic location theory, Part I.* Gleerup: Lund.

Pred, A. (1996). The choreography of existence: Comments on Hagerstrand's time-geography and its usefulness. *Economic Geography, 53*, 207-221.

Ratcliffe, J. H. (2006). A temporal constraint theory to explain opportunity-based spatial offending patterns. *Journal of Research in Crime and Delinquency, 6*(3), 261-291.

Rengert, G. (1988). The locations of facilities and crime. *Journal of Security of Administration, 11*(2), 12-16.

Ropella, G. E., Railsback, S. F., & Jackson, S. K. (2002). Software engineering considerations for individual-based models. *Natural Resource Modeling, 15*(1), 5-22.

Sampson, R. J. (1993). Linking time and place: Dynamic contextualism and the future of criminological inquiry. *Journal of Research in Crime and Delinquency, 30*(4), 426-444.

Thrift, N. J., & Bennett, R. R. (Eds.). (1978). *Towards the dynamic analysis of spatial systems.* London: Pion Limited.

Thrift, N. J., & Pred, A. (1981). Time-geography: A new beginning. *Progress in Human Geography, 5*(2), 277-286.

U.S. Census Bureau (Cartographer) (2000). *Census 2000: Summary tape file 1 (SF1)*

U.S. Census Bureau (2002). *County business patterns.* U.S. Census Bureau. Retrieved, September 2, 2007, from http://censtats.census.gov/cbpnaic/cbpnaic.shtml

Visher, C. A., & Roth, J. A. (1986). Participation in criminal careers. In A. Blumstein, J. Cohen, J. A. Roth, & C. A. Visher (Eds.), *Criminal careers and "Career Criminals"* (Vol. I, pp. 211-291). Washington, D.C.: National Academy Press.

Walmsley, D. J., & Lewis, G. J. (1993). *People and environment: Behavioral approaches in human geography.* Essex: Longman Scientific & Technical.

Wang, X., Liu, L., & Eck, J. (2004). *A spatial dynamic simulation of crime using Agent-based modeling.* Paper presented at the Association of American Geographers, Philadelphia, PA.

Weber, J., & Kwan, M.-P. (2002). Bringing time back in: A study on the influence of travel time variations and facility opening hours on individual accessibility. *The Professional Geographer, 54*, 226-240.

Weber, J., & Kwan, M.-P. (2003). Evaluating the effects of geographic contexts on individual accessibility: A multilevel approach. *Urban Geography, 24*(8), 647-671.

Weisburd, D. L. (2002). From criminals to criminal contexts: Reorienting crime prevention. In E. Waring & D. Weisburd (Eds.), *Crime & social organization* (Vol. 10, pp. 197-216). New Brunswick, NJ: Transactions Publishers.

Weisburd, D. L., Lum, C., & Yang, S.-M. (2004). *The criminal careers of places: A longitudinal study.* Washington, D.C.: US Department of Justice, National Institute of Justice.

Williamson, D., Mclafferty, S., McGuire Philip, G., Ross, T. A., Mollenkopf, J. H., Goldsmith, V., & Quinn, S. (2001). Tools in the spatial analysis of crime. In A. Hirschfield & K. Bowers (Eds.), *Mapping and analysing crime data: Lessons from research and rractice* (pp. 187-203). London: Taylor & Francis.

ADDITIONAL READING

Brantingham, P. J., & Brantingham, P. L. (1991 [1981]). *Environmental criminology.* Prospect Heights, IL: Waveland Press, Inc.

Calthrope, P. (1993). *The next American metropolis: Ecology, community and the American dream.* New York: Princeton Architectural Press.

Duaney, A., & Plater-Zyberk, E. (1993). The neighborhood, the district and the corridor. In P. Katz (Ed.), *The new urbanism: Toward an architecture of community.* New York: McGraw-Hill.

Meier, R. F., Kennedy, L. W., & Sacco, V. F. (2001). Crime and the criminal event perspective. In R. F. Meier, L. W. Kennedy, & V. F. Sacco (Eds.), *The process and structure of crime: Criminal events and crime analysis: Vol. 9. Advances in criminological theory* (pp. 1-28). New Brunswick, NJ: Transaction Publishers.

Nelessen, A. C. (1994). *Visions for a new American dream: Process, principle and an ordinance to plan and design small communities.* Chicago: Planners.

Sargent, R. G. (1999). *Validation and verification of simulation models.* Paper presented at the Winter Simulation Conference, Phoenix, AZ.

ENDNOTES

1 Space constraints prohibit a full discussion of opportunity theories which include: routine activity theory (Cohen & Felson, 1979), environmental criminology (Brantingham & Brantingham, 1991 [1981]); lifestyle theory (Hindelang, Gottfredson, & Garofalo, 1978) and the criminal event perspective (CEP) (Meier, Kennedy, & Sacco, 2001).

2 Suitability is evaluated as $S = (W_T - W_A) + P_S$. Wealth of the target compared to the wealth of the active criminal agent plus an error term (P_S) that varies between -2 and 2. Guardianship levels are perceived using the following: $G = (N_A - 2) + P_G$. The number of agents at the node minus two agents (i.e., active offender and potential target) plus an error term (P_G) that varies from -1 to 1. The error terms are generated using a Mersenne Twister uniform random number generator.

3 This relatively simple representation of human spatial behavior does not incorporate other aspects of trip decision making (e.g., trip purpose, model of travel, order of travel, time of day etc.) which affect travel but it does provide a starting point.

4 This follows the method used by Miller (1991) but for different reasons. His was to simplify the representation in GIS. Here the use of street intersection reflects a software limitation. Agent Analyst cannot read network or geodatabase files from ArcGIS so agents must travel from intersection/node to intersection/node.

5 The designation of 'at risk' is simplified from real life. A person who is shopping in a retail store also cannot be a victim of street robbery but is considered "at risk" in the model. The main purpose of the designation is to vary the time a civilian agent is at risk based on their activities.

6 Agent analyst is under development as a partnership between ESRI and Argonne National Laboratories; the parent companies of ArcGIS and Repast respectively. Agent Analyst is free and can be downloaded at http://www.institute.redlands.edu/agentanalyst/.

7 Verification of models is also an important consideration that is not discussed here because of space constraints. Please see the following works for more information (Maguire et al., 2005; Manson, 2001; Ropella, Railsback, & Jackson, 2002; Sargent, 1999).

8 The purpose of the kernel density surface use here is to represent the overall changes in intensity across the city of Seattle. Therefore, a bandwidth of 1,320 feet (one quarter mile) and a cell size of 100 feet are the basis for all kernel density surfaces. The quarter mile distance is often employed to represent the potential walking area for individuals in urban areas and by extension their potential area of interaction around a given point (Calthrope, 1993; Duaney & Plater-Zyberk, 1993; Nelessen, 1994). The surfaces are generated in ArcGIS version 9.1 and the output is in robberies per square mile (Mitchell, 1999).

9 Kernel density maps of the 30, 40, 50 and 60% conditions are not shown here but are available from the author.

10 The reported Ripley's *K* functions are generated using CrimeStat III (Levine, 2005). Following the original study, no edge correction is applied since approximately three quarters of the perimeter of Seattle is bounded by water.

11 Due to space constraints the kernel density and Ripley's *K* results for the analysis of visits are not included in the chapter but are available upon request from the author.

12 Only the 30 and 70% graphs are included in the chapter. Results from the 40, 50, and 60% conditions are available from the author.

13 The police/citizen ratio of 1 to 5 is recognized as unrealistic when compared to the actual ration of approximately 1 to 471.

14 Since the jobs data are from 2002, the corresponding year's unemployment rate is used.

15 The time spent away from home is systematically varied to test the core proposition of routine activity that as time spent away from home increases crime will increase.

16 A request to the Seattle Police Department for the average amount of cash taken during street robberies remains unanswered.

Chapter XIII
Mastermind:
Computational Modeling and Simulation of Spatiotemporal Aspects of Crime in Urban Environments

P.L. Brantingham
Simon Fraser University, Canada

U. Glässer
Simon Fraser University, Canada

P. Jackson
Simon Fraser University, Canada

B. Kinney
Simon Fraser University, Canada

M. Vajihollahi
Simon Fraser University, Canada

ABSTRACT

Pattern and routine activities theories suggest that through a combination of decisions and innate understandings of environmental cues, likely offenders are able to separate good criminal opportunities from bad risks. The nature of this process is highly structured and allows researchers to anticipate likely concentrations for a variety of regular, daily activities, including criminal offences. This chapter sets out to model and test these theoretical principles. Mastermind represents an interdisciplinary research project in computational criminology jointly managed by ICURS and the Software Technology Lab at Simon Fraser University. Using the abstract state machine (ASM) formalism in combination with a multi-agent based modeling paradigm, we devise a formal framework for semantic modeling and systematic integration of the theories for crime analysis and understanding crime patterns. We focus on crime in urban areas and model spatial and temporal aspects of crime potentially involving multiple offenders and multiple targets. Mastermind is used in a hypothetical analysis of motor vehicle theft.

INTRODUCTION

Crimes are complex, multidimensional events comprised of at least four necessary dimensions—the law, the offender, the target and the place (Brantingham & Brantingham, 1978, 1984, 1991). For several decades, criminologists have contended that there is definite patterning in the temporal and spatial characteristics of physical crime (Bottoms, Claytor, & Wiles, 1992; Kennedy & Forde, 1990; Roncek, 1981; Sherman, Gartin, & Buerger, 1989). In particular, environmental criminology argues that in spite of their complexity, criminal events can be understood against the context of people's movements in the course of everyday routines. Environmental criminology posits that the large majority of offenders will commit most of their offenses near places they spend most of their time, and similarly, victims are victimized near places where they spend most of their time (Brantingham & Brantingham 1993b; Felson, 1987). Pattern and routine activities theories contend that crime locations are not random, but rather, are determined through a combination of normal movement and activity patterns, each of which is at least partly determined by the perceptions of the physical and social environment. Through both rational decisions (c.p., Cornish & Clarke, 1986) and innate understandings of environmental cues, likely offenders are able to separate good criminal opportunities from bad risks. This decision-making process takes place within, and is predicated upon, the nature of the built environment. In most cities, these important features include street and transportation networks, as well as land use features. Each of these topographical entities are formative features in guiding the movement of people in space-time, and as such, represent a valuable source of information about what situational and ecological contexts attract crime, and under what conditions.

The structured nature of this process allows researchers to anticipate likely concentrations for a variety of regular, daily activities, including criminal offences. The importance of street networks in the distribution of social events (criminal or otherwise) cannot be overstated; major transportation pathways and the attractiveness of certain land uses (entertainment districts, shopping malls, licensed premises, or schools, for example) are well known in criminology (Brantingham & Brantingham, 1984). What is new to the field, however, is the recent energy devoted to developing computational methodologies for testing these principles against both archival data and in simulations.

Conventional research in crime analysis strongly supports this theoretical framework for a broad range of crimes (Bottoms & Wale, 2002; Rossmo, 2000; Wright, & Decker, 1997), but such work, although empirical in nature, tends to use methods that rely upon past data. However, empirical deduction and inference are no longer sufficient. Although theories of crime are well established, the lack of a unifying framework for integrating the four dimensions of crime (e.g., a law, offender, a victim/target, and a setting converging in space-time) in a coherent and consistent way inhibits their applicability to real-life scenarios. Novel research directions (Bowers, 2007; Brantingham & Brantingham, 2004; Brantingham, Brantingham, & Glässer, 2005a; Groff, 2006; Gunderson & Brown, 2000; Liu, Wang, Eck & Liang, 2005), however suggest a fundamentally different approach to overcome limitations of statistical methods that are based on measures of association on observed or measured data. High levels of autocorrelation, lack of independence of observations, and analyses that make it difficult to track individuals in a changing environment create limits to statistics as the model building technique. The need to handle continual change and the interdependence of dimension and individual entities or agents calls for methods that facilitate model building based on abstract definition of the theoretical structure and a process that makes it possible to move incrementally towards complexity. The complex dynamics and the intricate structure of these underlying social systems demand the systematic, formalized, and replicable use of mathematical modeling techniques combined with computational methods and tools. Computer models can serve as a practical instrument for studying crime patterns and for reasoning about likely scenarios, facilitating the understanding of and experimenting with crime patterns (Brantingham, Glässer, Kinney, Singh, & Vajihollahi, 2005b).

Given the predictive nature of most crime analyses, especially those working from what is broadly construed as environmental criminology perspective, the blending of criminology, computing science, and mathematics is a natural fit (Brown, 1998; Clarke, 2004; Gunderson, & Brown, 2000). Exciting work is already underway in a number of criminological and computing science fields, such as hotspot analysis (Hua & Brown, 1998; Kianmehr & Alhajj, 2006; Xue & Brown, 2003), offender profiling (Baumgartner, Ferrari, & Salfati, 2005), database, and information systems management (Bettini, Wang, & Jajodia, 1998; Borne, Fayech, Hammadi, & Mauche, 2003; Fang, Hipel, Kilgour, & Peng, 2003; Hendrick, Howell, London, Luehrs, Saliba, Brown, 2004), among others.

Not only is the social and physical environment complex, but so too are the relevant sources of data and the methods required for building truly interoperable and "silo-free" repositories needed to form the basis of *decision support systems* (e.g., Fang et al., 2003; Mikhailov & Singh, 2003). Decision support systems (DSS) are a popular class of computer-based information or knowledge based systems that support decision-making activities. Specifically, Intelligent DSS often use multiple intelligent agents interacting based on decentralized coordination models to assist decision makers in analyzing a situation (Guerlain, Brown, & Mastrangelo, 2000; Gupta, Forgionne, & Mora, 2006); they can provide effective, reliable, and replicable instruments for evidence based policy making.

Mastermind is an interdisciplinary research project in computational criminology jointly managed by ICURS and the Software Technology Lab at Simon Fraser University.[1] The project aims at devising a comprehensive computational framework for abstract semantic modeling, discrete event simulation and machine-assisted evaluation and validation of discrete event models used in crime analysis and prevention. The specific focus here is on spatiotemporal characteristics of crime in urban environments, potentially involving multiple offenders and multiple targets. Crossing boundaries of research disciplines, the Mastermind project is linked to a wide range of research areas and application fields spanning criminology, computing, mathematics, psychology and systems science. Any attempt to systematically integrate such diverse views within one unifying computational framework in a coherent and consistent way naturally poses a considerable challenge. From a systems theory perspective, the system under study is best characterized as a combination of *cognitive system* and *reactive system*. Cognitive aspects relate to persons, namely offenders, victims, police officers and security personnel, whereas reactive aspects refer to properties of the physical environment, such as traffic, road and weather conditions. Another challenging aspect is the question of how to draw the boundaries of any such system, clearly delineating the system from the environment into which it is embedded.

We define the Mastermind system model using common notions and structures of discrete mathematics and computational logic. Given the experimental subject nature and the evolutionary system development context, robustness and scalability are key aspects in the design of a computational framework for the construction, refinement and validation of discrete event models of crime. This requirement calls for an abstract and mathematically well-defined semantic foundation, one that allows for the separation of high-level semantic concepts from low-level coding which predominantly focuses on syntactic aspects. Hence,

Mastermind is devised based on the *abstract state machine* (ASM) formalism and abstraction principles (Börger & Stärk, 2003), a universal computational paradigm for mathematical modeling of discrete dynamic systems.[2] This choice offers considerable flexibility for integrating a multitude of divers system views—for instance, related to environmental criminology, formal methods, algorithms, systems engineering, AI and artificial life—in a unifying semantic model. Following a top-down approach, our Mastermind model will be introduced in several steps starting with a high-level description of the overall system architecture. This model will then be refined at various layers of abstraction, all the way down to an implementation level, where the latter will only be sketched for illustrative purposes.

The target audience of the Mastermind system can be (a) criminologists: using it for validation of crime patterns, verification of hypothetical theories; (b) modern policing agencies: using it for prediction of criminal activities, investigation support to identify and prioritize potential suspects; and (c) city planners: for effective urban planning by taking the geography of crime into account.

As will be shown in this chapter, Mastermind is a system that could be used for modeling spatially dependent crimes such as burglary, robbery, motor vehicle theft and vandalism. It is not designed currently to handle crimes that involve people moving through the cyberspace or crimes that depend on telephone connections.

Related Work

In examining the theoretical foundation of the Mastermind project, two articles should be mentioned. The Virginia Institute for Justice Information Systems (VIJIS) group at the University of Virginia applies statistical methods to the analysis of both physical and cyber crime. In an outline of a design for a multi-agent simulation system (Gunderson & Brown, 2000) the authors examine central aspects of criminological analysis, including spatial mobility, rational choice and routine activities theories and unveil important issues to consider when building such a system and the elements that it requires. Three hypotheses of criminal activity are examined in detail: spatiality, rational choice and routine behavior. Their justification for the value of a multi-agent system is worthy of consideration. We have also found many of the points raised to be important in the development of Mastermind. In Xue and Brown (2003), criminal incidents are viewed and analyzed as spatial choice processes. The authors propose two models for criminal site selection, which they obtain by modifying a traditional discrete choice model. In a comparison based on real crime data both spatial choice models outperform the hot spot model they are compared to in their predictions of future spatial choices for crimes.

The second article to look at is the result of a different project from our own group. In our research, we emphasize the use of abstract state machines as a practical instrument for the systematic development and analysis of complex discrete event models. In Glässer, Rastkar, and Vajihollahi (2006), the use of probabilistic methods and supporting tools to evaluate airport security systems is discussed. Where Mastermind is more of a tool for experimental analysis, the focus of the airport security project is on probabilistic model checking. However, both projects share a common foundation in that distributed abstract state machines are used to assist with model validation, verification, and refinement.

In terms of experimental focus, the mathematical and simulation modeling of crime project being undertaken at the University of California (UC MASC) shares several important characteristics with Mastermind (Brantingham, Bertozzi, Tita, & Chayes, 2006). The value of agent-based modeling in understanding offender behavior is highlighted in their work, and statistical and mathematical methods are employed to determine the movement of agents within the simulation environment. They also mention the use of geographic information systems for the comparison to real-world results and verifying the accuracy of the model. Their work is more focused on large-scale patterns: they base their methods on the mechanics of swarm behavior, while the Mastermind project looks more carefully at the decisions and planning made at the individual level. However, it is important to heed the warning of the UC MASC project: the results of a simulation are only as good as the veracity of the elements used to build it.

Another project with related subject matter is the SimDrug project (Perez, Dray, Ritter, Dietze, Moore, & Mazerolle, 2003), which looks at the trade and use of heroin in Melbourne, Australia during the drug "drought" of 2000. It differs from Mastermind because it is more concerned with inter-agent activity, and also because it takes place in an abstract environment. An interesting contrast is emphasis on the value of complexity. By including many sources of real-world data, the authors hope to give the results generated a better grounding in reality. With Mastermind, the process of abstraction has encouraged us to value simplicity in our models. However, it is also important to recognize the point that SimDrug presents: computing is an ideal tool for the analysis of data-rich simulations.

COMPUTATIONAL CRIMINOLOGY

Social ecologists have long been interested in the geographic patterning of crime and deviance in the built (urban) environment. In the first quarter of the 20th century researchers tracked distributions of criminal and delinquent events across urban space and quickly that concentrations of each in certain neighborhoods. This rather simple descriptive work evolved into ever more complex collection of statistical and methodological techniques. Environmental criminology is part of this rich tradition (Brantingham & Brantingham, 1984). Key concepts include the routine nature of many of our daily activities (Felson, 1987), and the structured way in which we become aware of, and interact with, our environment (Brantingham & Brantingham, 1991, 1993a). The theoretical constructs and empirical methods of environmental criminology are used in the analysis of a broad spectrum of crime events, including key index crimes tracked in the Uniform Crime Reports surveys used in the United States and other countries. Serial violent and property offenses ranging from homicides to burglary are particularly well represented in the environmental criminology research literature (Rossmo, 2000; Wright & Decker, 1997; Wiles & Costello, 2000).

In spite of the notable problems with testing social science theories "in the field"—primarily a lack of experimental controls—a substantial empirical research base has led to a general agreement among environmental criminologists that the clustering of crime events can be reliably predicted in the aggregate and explained at an individual offender level (Brantingham et al., 2005a). Building on this research base, computational criminology pushes these techniques even further, particularly in collaboration with mathematics and computing science. This interdisciplinary work seeks to develop models that take advantage of the structured nature of offender movements and routines as suggested by the crime event research, and formalizes these social "routines" in a computer-modeling environment.

Although the computational criminology approach using ASM described in this chapter is complex in that it models the urban environment, complete with travel paths, major residential, work and entertainment "zones," the key principles can be mapped briefly here. We begin by placing an agent (or criminally intending offender) on a vector representation of an urban environment. The agent is "free" to make decisions about how to move about in this space, but for simplicity, our hypothetical agent/offender can only travel along actual street networks (bidirectional graphs).

In order to simulate crime in a space one must first imbue the agent with a set of well-understood (familiar) nodes which will serve as anchor, or starting points, and further, to populate the environment with typical census (e.g., income, population and other demographic data) and cadastral (or land use) variables from which the agent can make "decisions" about exploiting recognized crime opportunities.

Research suggests that both offenders and non-offenders alike move around cities and towns in similar ways, and further, that everyone is tied to at least three main classes of activity nodes: home, work and recreation. We also know from this literature something of how people structure their trips to and from these nodes, a process known as "way finding" (Brantingham & Brantingham, 1993b). Given the primacy of key nodes, people know a great deal about the immediate surrounds of these micro spaces. Individuals often favor the same pathways between each of these nodes, a principle that allows researchers to predict likely travel paths based on shortest distance or other metrics. As individuals make their node-to-node trips, they will eventually develop a specific and detailed knowledge of that area as *activity space*—that is the services and facilities (shopping, entertainment or other services) of interest in the immediate environment. Just as noncriminal opportunities for fun and commerce are noted, so too are crime opportunities noted by some of these individuals who are also "criminally aware" (Brantingham & Brantingham, 1993b). Each agent also possesses an *awareness space* that characterizes the working knowledge of the wider environment. Under normal conditions individuals are relatively free to adjust their travel routines and to explore new areas, but often these excursions remain tied to the use of awareness and activity spaces as navigational aides. At a conceptual level, methods to replicate such travel and activity decisions, through the use of nodes and pathways, have been available for over a decade. Computational criminology takes this theoretical framework, and through agent-based simulation methods and models, provides a new way to validate both tools and theory.

If the agent starts the day at home, and then travels to either work (or school), for example, the agent will typically take the most direct and most easily navigated route (with, of course, the occasional choosing of alternative paths). Along the way, the agent will take notice of a range of phenomena in the activity space. For example, the agent might see a favorite coffee house, or take notice of a particular shopping opportunity along the way to the work node. Even if the agent does not stop and interact specifically with potential activity sites, the agent will often remember such sites the next time the agent wants to purchase a cup of coffee or to patronize a particular business. The same learning process applies to the travel paths to and from other significant activity spaces. Environmental criminologists view the learning and decision-making process for crimes to be much the same as those for non-criminal activities. Criminals are rarely criminal all of the time. Everyone has a degree of criminal potential; what differs is the level of criminal propensity that each person "brings along with us" on our daily routines. More criminally predisposed agents will respond to observed crime opportunities more frequently than people with low (or very low) crime potentials. What requires modeling is the process by which agents move from node to node, and when, if at all, does the agent act upon an observed criminal opportunity.

The process of choosing a target of opportunity involves target templating (Brantingham & Brantingham, 1993a). Each agent compares potential criminal opportunities to the agent's crime template in order to assess the value of potential rewards against the risks or degree of energy required for successful execution (Cornish & Clarke, 1986; Rengert, 1992).

A typical crime in large cities is that of burglary, otherwise known as "break and enter", or "B & E". In the large majority of cases, for the agent to be aware of a potential target, the site must be located within the agent's activity space—which, in turn, is defined by the set of common activity nodes, as discussed earlier. The burglar would travel from Node 1 (home) to Node 2 (work), as the routine may require. Along the way the burglar recognizes a residential building that is suggestive of a "good" target, as it "fits" within that particular agent's crime template. Research on burglars (Ekblom & Tilley, 2000; Rengert, 1991, 1992) suggests that variables such as property value, lack of occupants or potential witnesses capable of intervening, and obvious entry opportunities, all form "cues" (Eck & Weisburd, 1995) from which the agent assesses quickly to determine if either the criminal event will be attempted, or at least investigated further.

Related modeling and simulation work in criminology (Brantingham & Brantingham, 2004; Hooimeijer & Oskamp, 1999), suggest the value of pursuing computational methods to predict patterns in crime. Although a "new" area for criminology, this area is showing signs of gaining momentum.

COMPUTATIONAL TECHNIQUES

Social simulation uses many mathematical approaches that range from differential or difference equations through stochastic processes, game theory or cellular automata to name a few. One core technique, distributed artificial intelligence (multi-agent systems), explores the actions / behavior of individual entities within a context. Multi-agent simulations are gaining importance in understanding decision making of objects active within a dynamic environment. We use a multi-agent paradigm to simulate the target choice behavior of potential offenders. Our model is linked to the underlying context of the social system through an intermediate layer that defines the multi-agent system. The formal multi-agent framework we use is called abstract state machines. As its name implies, the framework starts with conceptually abstract formalism and works towards the complex by adding incrementally specificity and layering a sequence of smaller decisions into complex rules. The following section provides an overview of abstract state machines.

Abstract State Machines

Abstract state machines (Börger & Stärk, 2003) have been proposed as a universal mathematical framework for semantic modeling of *discrete dynamic systems* and studied extensively by researchers in academia and industry in Europe and in North America. The ASM formalism and abstraction principles are particularly known for their versatility in high-level design, experimental validation, and formal verification of algorithms, architectures, languages, protocols and virtually all kinds of sequential, parallel, and distributed systems.[3]

We briefly sketch here the basic concepts at an intuitive level of understanding using common notions and structures from discrete mathematics and computing science. For further details, we refer the reader to the existing ASM literature on the underlying theory (Gurevich, 2000; Blass & Gurevich, 2003) and its practical applications (Börger & Stärk, 2003). For a tutorial introduction to DASMs, see Farahbod and Glässer (2006).

We concentrate on using an asynchronous ASM model, called *distributed ASM*, or DASM. Using DASM allows for formal modeling of concurrent and reactive system behavior by distributed abstract machine *runs*. That is, the DASM model M is defined over a given vocabulary V_M by its distributed program P_M with a non-empty set I_M of initial states. The vocabulary V_M consists of symbols denoting various semantic objects and their relations in the formal representation of M. Distinctions are made between *domain symbols*, *function symbols* and *predicate symbols*. There are two types of symbols: static and dynamic. As would be expected by the words, symbols having a fixed interpretation regardless of the state of M are called *static.* When there are different interpretations in different states of M, the symbols represent *dynamic interpretation.* The distinction between static and dynamic is an important component of DASM. A given state S of M yields an interpretation of all the symbols in V_M.

Concurrent control threads in a run of P_M are modeled through a dynamic set AGENT of autonomously operating *agents.* That is agents interact with each other by exchanging (reading and writing) shared locations of global machine states. The underlying semantic model regulates such interactions. Expected conflicts are resolved according to the semantics of *partially ordered runs*, as defined in Gurevich (1995).[4]

The distributed program P_M consists of a collection of statically defined agent programs with associated state transition rules. A transition from a given state S of M results in a new, updated state S' of M (associating a different interpretation to one or more of the symbols in V_M). Each agent program defines the behavior of a certain *type* of agent through state transition rules. A DASM model contains multiple classes of agents with associated transition rules. Within P_M, the canonical rule for an agent is an update instruction of the form $f(t_1,t_2,...,t_n):= t_0$, where f is an n-ary dynamic function symbol and each t_i $(0 \leq i \leq n)$ is a term defined over the symbols of V_M. Intuitively, this can be seen as a *dynamic function table* where each row associates a sequence of argument values with a function value. An update instruction specifies a pointwise function update, that is, an operation that replaces an existing function value by a new value to be associated with the identifiable arguments. Complex rules are formed inductively from the simple update instructions using rule constructors.

It is important to see how M is embedded within a representation of a defined operational environment—the *external world.* The recorded actions and events are virtual artifacts of the interface of agents and rules with the operationalized external world. With a DASM model the external world affects operations of M through the use of externally controlled monitoring functions. Such functions, however, change their values dynamically over runs of M, but not by agents of M. A most straightforward example is the representation of time through a nullary monitored function *now* taking values in a metrically ordered domain TIME. Intuitively, the function *now* in any given state of M represents the global time measured by some externally controlled clock.

Multi Agent Systems: Linking Social Systems to Abstract State Machines

Multi-agent systems (MAS) (Ferber, 1999; Sycara, 1998; Wooldridge, 2002a, 2002b) have gained widespread popularity and support as a modeling paradigm for distributed systems, open dynamic environments, and systems that can naturally be regarded as a society of interacting agents (Gilbert & Doran, 1994). Specifically, MAS support and success for simulating social systems is justified by its long history (Attoui, 2000; Doran, Palmer, Gilbert, & Mellars, 1994; Drogoul & Ferber, 1994; Gilbert & Troitzsch, 1999; Wooldridge, 2002a).

It is particularly interesting that MAS modeling is interdisciplinary. This chapter is an example of the need to bring specialists in agent-based computing together with social scientists and experts in computer simulation in general (Davidsson, 2002). Pertinent to our context, MAS brings together theorists and practitioners from the social sciences and computing science together with a theoretical modeling framework for incrementally refining a model by integrating approaches from other disciplines such as AI and criminology.

The underlying social environment that is the basis for modeling involves different types of entities. We use a generic classification of entities divided in three different categories:[5] *passive objects*, *active objects* and *autonomous agents.* The core of this classification is based on the essentials of the belief desire intention (BDI) agent architecture (Bratman, Israel, & Pollack, 1988, Wooldridge, 2002b) and the framework for *agency and autonomy* (Luck & d'Inverno, 1995).

A *passive object*, as its name implies, is an entity that has a fixed set of static *attributes*. With an *active object* the attributes may change, but the change (defined as the *behavior* of the object) is induced by the environment. An *autonomous agent* has attributes and behavior, but it also has *rules, motivation* and a *memory*. There is an important difference between *passive, active* and *autonomous* agents. Behavior for an autonomous agent is generated by rules triggered by the agent itself to change its internal state or the environment. An autonomous agent generates its own behavior using given goals or incentives (motivations), and its knowledge of the environment is stored in a memory.[6]

A criminal offender is an autonomous agent (consistent with core elements of environmental criminology). The offender/agent has attributes (e.g., a personal profile), behavior (e.g., commuting, visiting friends, offending), motivations (e.g., greed, risk taker, revenge), and a memory (e.g., storing of likely targets and past successful crimes). In the model there are also multiple classes of agents that can have different attributes (profile, travel goals and motivations). It is a combination of these entities that makes it possible to model a broad range of criminal activities in an urban environment, such as robberies, auto thefts, burglary or shoplifting.

MASTERMIND: THE MODEL

Given that there is a bewildering list of notions of agents (Franklin & Graesser, 1997), for our purpose, we adopt a generic definition of an agent that subsumes most extant views. We define an agent as an active entity that is situated in an environment of which it has a partial representation, possesses resources and skill sets (Ferber, 1999), exhibits autonomy, social ability, reactivity, and pro-activeness (Wooldridge, 2002b). A multi-agent system is then a collection of passive and active objects, and autonomous agents interacting with each other in a given environment according to the given laws of action (Ferber, 1999).

The Mastermind model is built on a multi-agent system view where the behavior of agents is defined by two different sets of rules, *reactive rules* and *cognitive rules*. Agents operate in a highly dynamic, discrete environment. We propose a mechanism for *reasoning* and *learning*, based on the foundations of case-based reasoning; that is, the agents learn from past experiences and use them in solving new problems rather then solving the problems from scratch every time. Thus, the agents reason and learn using a form of *behavioral reinforcement learning* where, based on experiences made in the past, certain preferences are developed that may influence future choices that an agent will make.

The model captures spatial and temporal aspects of the agents' behavior by considering both the surrounding environment and time factors. Past experiences, defined in terms of space and time (i.e., where and when), form the basis for reasoning and learning and are used in the analysis of criminal behavior.

Agent Architecture

The key component of our model is called *person agent* and represents an autonomously acting entity defined to model the spatial and offence occurrence behavior of offenders. The person agent architecture is a pragmatic BDI-based model—Beliefs, desires, and intentions based model—(Bratman et al., 1988), which has a strong philosophical foundation and a pragmatic functionality. We start with a BDI-theoretic core and use incremental refinements based on the pragmatics of other problem-solving techniques such as case-based reasoning (Kolodner & Leake, 1996) and model-based reasoning (Russel & Norvig,

2003). Our concrete BDI-based architecture can be seen as a system of concurrent subsystems, that provides a firm computational semantics for the initial abstract architecture.

Figure 1 illustrates the structural decomposition of a person agent into its constituent logical components (or modules) following a classical Divide and Conquer[7] approach. The proposed architecture has well-known advantages of a modular design, specifically robustness and scalability, providing ease of change and flexibility for future extensions. The figure reflects a functional perspective of the architecture, within the philosophical foundations of the BDI model. The agent in this model has goals and the capacity to form decisions based on case or situation specific states. Cognition, memory and action rules are the foundations for the model.

The cognition, memory formation and decision rules in the model are based on the research on how individuals move about in an urban environment and how offenders choose targets. BDI-based models fit well with the theoretical framework of environmental criminology where offenders develop routines, a knowledge base for criminal and non-criminal activities, and cue templates that trigger a decision to commit a crime.

The agents in our model are autonomous. To reflect the independence of individuals from their surrounds but maintain how individuals interact with their environment, the environment in its entirety is divided into two broad categories (Brunswick, 1952; Koffka, 1967): the *objective* and the *subjective* environment. In our abstract model the objective environment is called *geographic environment*. It is external to the agent and represents the totality of all things forming the physical reality. We assume here that all the elements of the geographic environment have some finite representation. Intuitively, the geographic environment for a given urban surrounding can be conceived as an abstract image of the urban

Figure 1. Person agent architecture

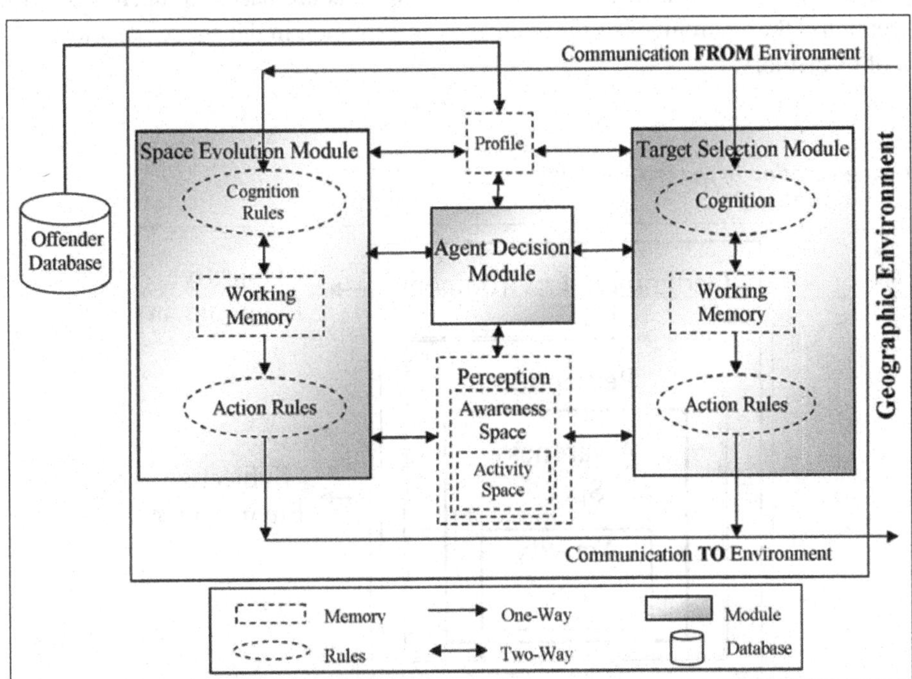

landscape as represented by one or more graphic information system (GIS) in combination with additional real-time information on dynamically changing environment conditions. The dynamic aspects pertain to road conditions, traffic situations and weather conditions.

The subjective environment (*Perception*), maintains a filtered view of the geographic environment and represents the environment as the agent "perceives" it; it thus models the subjective reality and is constantly updated by the agent. The subjective environment is further divided into subcategories (Sonnenfeld, 1972). The part of the perception that an agent is aware of by way of current events and past experiences forms the *awareness space* of the agent. The *activity space* is the part of the awareness space that the agent has visited more frequently over a recent period of time. The agent typically has very detailed information about this part of the environment. This categorization of environment is illustrated in Figure 2.

The agent's memory is a collection of facts/beliefs/knowledge—present and past—which may change dynamically over time. As such, the agent's perception of the environment is the main component of its memory.

There are three core space related modules: the space evolution module (SEM); the target selection module (TSM); and the agent decision module (ADM).

The space evolution module (SEM) creates the *activity space* and the *awareness space* of the person agent. This is done using a navigation algorithm to move the agent from a specified origin to a destination node on a given road network, which considers the particular preferences of the agent. Preferences include a variety of aspects: choosing shorter routes, avoiding traffic or blocked roads, using familiar roads, and so forth.

The target selection module (TSM) monitors potential targets at activity nodes or on the routes taken by the agent between nodes, and selects attractive targets based on specified selection criteria. This module gradually creates the *opportunity space* and the *crime occurrence space* of the agent.

The agent decision module (ADM) is a decision/ choice module that selects 'what to do' next. The decision information is passed to the TSM or the SEM to identify a 'how to do it'. The agent's decisions are based on agent's motivations and information in the agent's memory.

Figure 2. Categorization of the environment

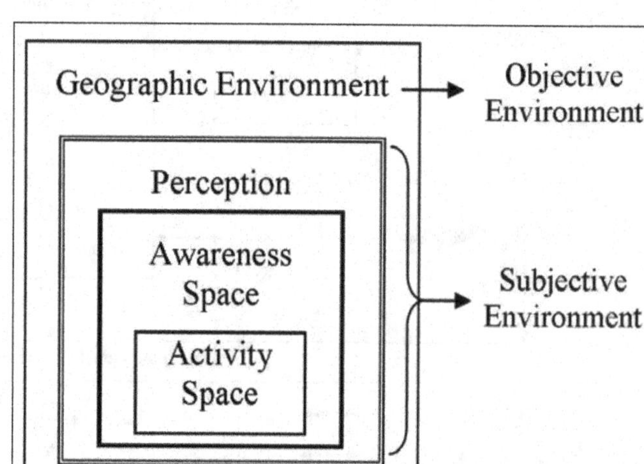

The SEM and the TSM both use *action rules* and *cognition rules*. While cognition rules modify the state of the internal memory, action rules affect the environment. Each of these modules is further modeled by an ASM agent and the corresponding rules form the program of this agent. Each module also has an internal memory component, called *working memory*, which stores volatile information needed for path computation or target selection.

Finally, the *profile* represents the personal attributes of the agent and stores information such as preferences, skills, home locations and demographic factors that are taken into account for determining certain aspects of an agent's individual behavior when moving in space and time.

The Environment

Mastermind abstractly represents the physical environment of a given urban landscape in terms of an attributed directed graph. This model of the physical environment includes everything from road and rail traffic networks to walkways and hiking trails in city parks. In principle, it can also include the layout of other public spaces such as shopping malls, underground stations and airports. Here, we will however restrict our agent to street networks for explanatory reasons, although the same modeling approach applies to virtually any type of urban traffic and transportation system. We gradually define the physical environment model in several steps as follows.

Let $H = (V, E)$ be a directed connected graph representing the complete street network of some urban area as specified by a city map or a geographic information system (GIS). Let V be a set of vertices, $V = \{v_1, \ldots, v_n\}$, representing the intersections or points of interest on the map; and let E be a set of edges, $E \subseteq V \times V$, representing all major and minor roads with unidirectional roads being represented by single edges and bi-directional ones by a pair of oppositely directed edges connecting the same two vertices.[8] Figure 3 sketches the graph structure.

For labeling the edges and vertices of H, let Θ_v and Θ_e denote finite attribute sets for vertices and edges respectively. Vertex attributes, for instance, specify geographic coordinates and points of interest. Edge attributes yield information on distances, road types, road conditions, speed limits, traffic situations, et cetera. Intuitively, Θ_e splits into two disjoint subsets, Θ_e^{static} and $\Theta_e^{dynamic}$, the edge attributes that are *statically* defined—such as distances, road types and speed limits—and those that may, and normally do, change *dynamically*—like traffic conditions and road conditions. Examples of the latter type are road blockings

Figure 3. Representation of streets and intersections

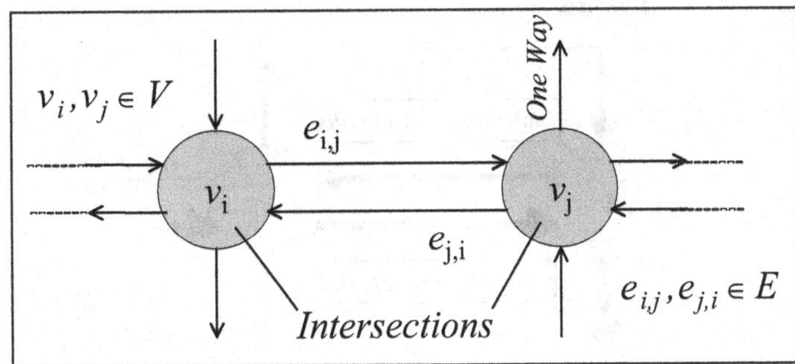

and closures, construction work, and weather related phenomena like snow, ice and flooding as illustrated in Figure 4.

We can now define the *geographic environment* G_{GeoEnv} as an attributed directed graph, $G_{GeoEnv} = (H,\Theta)$, by labeling the vertices and edges of H. Formally, this is expressed by introducing an attribution scheme $\Theta = (\Theta_v, \Theta_e)$, with $\Theta_e = (\Theta_e^{static}, \Theta_e^{dynamic})$, consisting of three finite mappings:[9]

- $\boldsymbol{\Theta_v} : V \rightarrow P(\Theta_v)$ assigns a set of vertex attributes to each vertex in V
- $\boldsymbol{\Theta_e^{static}} : E \rightarrow P(\Theta_e^{static})$ assigns a set of static edge attributes to each edge in E
- $\boldsymbol{\Theta_e^{dynamic}} : E \rightarrow P(\Theta_e^{dynamic})$ assigns a set of a dynamic edge attributes to each edge in E

G_{GeoEnv} represents the objective physical environment and provides the basis for defining the subjective environment of each individual agent, effectively reflecting an agent's perception of the objective environment. Perception is modeled by introducing an additional attribution scheme defined on top of G_{GeoEnv}. The fact that each agent perceives the geographic environment differently in conjunction with the fact that every perception is logically linked to one of the agents implies that the mapping from agents to their subjective environments is always a bijection, that is, is both injective and surjective. Injectivity means that no two agents have an identical perception of G_{GeoEnv}. Surjectivity ensures that each perception belongs to one of the person agents in any given model.

Let λ_v and λ_e denote additional attribute sets for vertices and edges respectively. The formal model of the physical environment, including both the subjective environment and the objective environment, is defined as an attributed directed graph $G_{Env} = (G_{GeoEnv},\lambda)$, with $\lambda = (\lambda_v,\lambda_e)$. In this model, λ abstractly represents the agent-specific labeling of vertices and edges (see also Figure 5) by means of two injective mappings such that:

Figure 4. Representation of road types, road conditions and points of interest

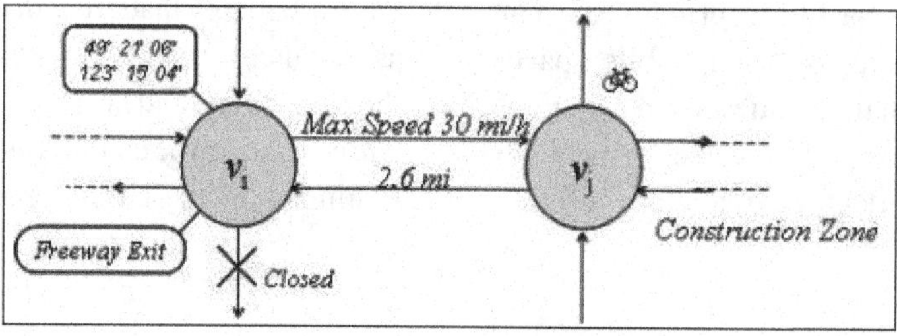

Figure 5. Attributes related to individual agents

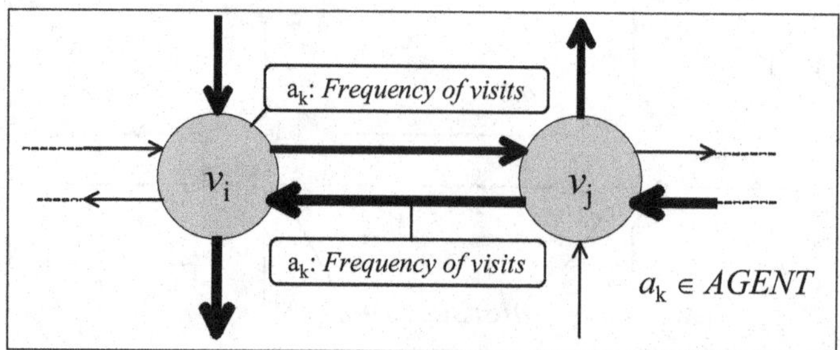

- $\lambda_v : AGENT \times V \rightarrow P(\lambda_v)$, for each agent in *AGENT* and each vertex in *V*, yields a non-empty set of vertex attributes.
- $\lambda_e : AGENT \times E \rightarrow P(\lambda_e)$, for each agent in *AGENT* and each edge in *E*, yields a non-empty set of edge attributes.

G_{Env} can be seen as an attributed directed graph with colored attributes, where each color refers to the unique perception of an individual agent. Attribute values in λ_v, for instance, specify the frequency of visits of an agent to a specific location and the agent's subjective interest in a location. Attribute values in λ_e, for instance, specify the frequency of using a particular road, reinforcement factors, intensity of awareness, et cetera as illustrated in Figure 5.

Finally, the awareness space and the activity space of each agent, in a given system state, are computed by means of operations defined on G_{Env}. These operations effectively access and manipulate the data associated with the physical environment by viewing G_{Env} as an abstract data structure. This way, the activity space, for instance, is obtained as the subset of edges of G_{Env} with an associated intensity value (frequency of visits) above a certain threshold. Likewise, the crime occurrence space is computed for a certain type of crime (assuming a defined encoding of potential targets within a given opportunity space) as the intersection of the opportunity space and the activity space of an agent.

Abstract Model

The behavior of an offender is captured by three operational units: Space evolution module (SEM), target selection module (TSM), and agent decision module (ADM). Hence, an offender is modeled by a collection of interacting ASM agents. A master agent of type PERSON, called "person agent", and three subordinate agents operating under the control of the master. Each subordinate agent represents one of the three operational units. A function *parentAgent* defined on subordinate agents links these agents to their person agent.

$$AGENT \equiv PERSON \cup SEM \cup TSM \cup ADM$$

Asynchronous interaction between the various agents is based on an event triggering mechanism using a discrete signaling framework in which each signal specifies its sender and receiver and may carry any type of data. For further details, the reader is referred to Farahbod (2004).

The following sections introduce the SEM and the navigation algorithm in more detail. For more information on the TSM and its functionality, the reader is referred to Brantingham, Glässer, Singh, and Vajihollahi (2005c).

Space Evolution

The main responsibility of the SEM is to control how the person agent navigates an urban environment G_{Env} based on personal preferences. As a byproduct of navigation, a person agent's activity space evolves as this agent visits more places or repeatedly visits the same location within certain time intervals, thus affecting the attribute values of G_{Env}. SEM agents access and manipulate such attributes through operations on the graph structure, which will be introduced and explained on the fly.

The algorithm used by the SEM for path finding (called navigation algorithm) reflects natural and intuitive choices a person makes while moving in an urban landscape. The path taken might not be a globally optimal and best one, but a more natural and 'good-enough' one. The algorithm takes into account the factors that are known to influence human path planning and is developed in collaboration with the domain experts (Løvås, 1998; Hochmair & Karlsson, 2004). Overall, navigation is modeled as a combination of *exploration* and *learning*, the details of which are described in the next section.

Generally, a person agent has some global information about its environment, which is influenced in turn, by perception and past experiences. This global information is utilized by the SEM to perform *global path planning.* On the other hand, local information discovered on the fly is also considered for performing *local replanning,* whenever necessary. This allows the agent to examine changes in highly dynamic factors such as traffic and road conditions and revise its decision accordingly. Formally, the behavior of the SEM is defined in terms of a *control-state abstract state machine*[10] as shown in Figure 6.

In order to move an agent from an origin to a destination, the SEM steps through *modes* as represented by the *control states.* Initially, the SEM is in the *idle* mode, and when a new destination is passed to it from the ADM, the mode switches to *pathPlanning,* where the process of finding an intuitive path to the destination begins. This path, called *suggestedPath,* is calculated using the global information that the agent has about its environment. This can include referring to agent's memory, if the destination is previously known, or using a map depending on an agent's personal preferences. In other words, this state is where *global path planning* is achieved.

Next, the mode changes to *roadSelection,* where the roads on the suggested path are examined on the fly. While in the *roadSelection* mode, the agent is essentially moving toward the destination. Once the destination is reached, the mode switches to *pathCompleted* and the trip is finalized. On the other hand, if the agent's original decision changes during the trip (*signalFromADM*), the mode switches back to *pathPlanning* to accommodate revised decisions. Otherwise, a single road, called *suggestedEdge,* is selected to be taken by the agent. This choice can either result from the suggested path that the agent had in mind, or it might be a random edge (which models unexpected random behavior of the agent).

Once the road is selected, the mode changes to *localRePlanning,* where the selected road is examined with respect to its local conditions such as traffic, construction work, etc. If the local condition of this road is unacceptable, a new path to the destination needs to be found; thus, the mode

Figure 6. Control-state ASM of the space evolution module (SEM)

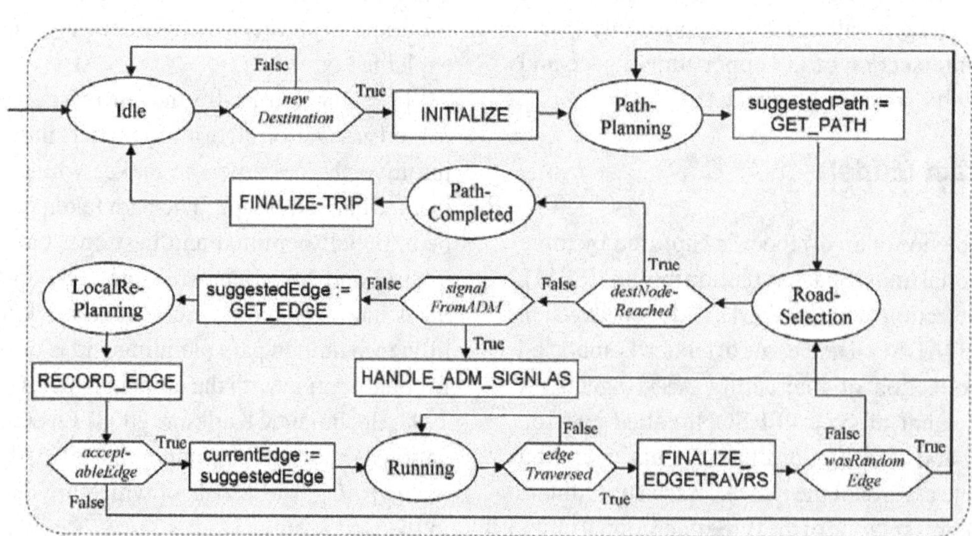

changes back to *pathPlanning.* Otherwise, the suggested road is identified with the *currentEdge,* and the mode changes to *running*, meaning that the road is being traversed. At this point, the mode normally switches back to *roadSelection* to select the next road on the suggested path. However, in cases where the agent takes a random edge, a new path to the destination must be figured out; hence, the mode changes to *pathPlanning.* Once the trip is completed (*pathCompleted*), the ADM is informed that the agent has reached the final destination, and specific information regarding the taken path is recorded in the agent's memory. The SEM then remains idle until the agent decides to move to a new destination.

Navigation Algorithm

The SEM uses a combination of *global planning* and *local re-planning* to lead the agent to its destination. As described previously, local replanning is achieved through on the fly evaluation of local characteristics of candidate roads. On the other hand, global planning of the path builds on what the agent has *learned* so far, and its ability to *explore* the environment. Hence, a mechanism of *hybrid reasoning*—based on case-based reasoning (CBR) and model-based reasoning (MBR)—is used to perform global path planning. Here, we briefly describe the reasoning mechanism; however, for a comprehensive description, the reader is referred to Singh (2005).

The role of CBR resembles human problem solving by remembering and recollecting past experiences. In contrast, the role of MBR resembles problem solving right from scratch, exploiting more complex algorithmic procedures. In our model, the MBR component is called *path explorer.* Typically, when searching for a path to a new destination, the CBR is called first to provide a solution. If a satisfactory solution is not available (e.g., an exact path to a destination does not exist in the memory), the CBR is used in conjunction with the path explorer (e.g., using a partial path from the CBR and then utilizing the explorer to complete the path). The path explorer can also be used stand alone to find a path without referring to the memory, or when exploring new territory.

The path explorer finds a path with a highest *preference* reflecting natural and intuitive decisions a person makes while moving in an urban landscape. The algorithm assumes a model of the underlying urban environment in terms of a directed attributed graph. The preference of a path is defined as the sum of the preferences of all the edges comprising the path. Intuitively, edge preference is defined in terms of the factors that are known to influence human path planning, including distance, type of the road (e.g., major vs. minor), number of intervening stops, angle toward the destination, traffic, familiarity with the road, and so forth. These factors work as proxies through which a person agent perceives the environment.

Generally, a person agent has some global information about its environment through perception and past experiences. Thus, the values of certain factors, such as distance and road type, are initially derived from the underlying geographic environment. Other factors, such as familiarity with a particular road, are more subjective and may change based on the agent's experience. In this way, subjective human perception is incorporated into calculating paths preferences. Other factors, such as angle and number of stops, are dependent on the orientation and length of the path, and hence are computed alongside by means of the path finding algorithm.

Furthermore, a *factor weight* associated with each factor determines the importance of that factor in the overall edge preference. These weights reflect personal preferences and vary from individual to individual. The overall preference of an edge is then a weighted sum of all the aforementioned factors.[11] (See Box 1).

Technically, the algorithm used by the explorer to find a path with a highest preference is based on Dijkstra's shortest path algorithm (Dijkstra, 1959).

Discrete Event Simulation

The ASM model presented so far serves as a *ground model* of the behavior of a potential offender. A ground model provides a mathematically well-defined abstract description of the key functional requirements of a system under study with a degree of detail and precision that is considered most appropriate; it is meant to serve as a "blueprint" of the high-level system design and should be understandable by both the domain experts and system designers; it also has a precise semantic foundation which allows for inspection by analytical means as well as experimental validation through simulation and testing (Börger & Stärk, 2003). Such a ground model can be systematically refined into an executable model for running discrete event simulations. The simulation model presented here is written in Java (Sun Microsystems, 2006); however, it is directly built on top of the ASM model. The following sections outline the construction of the simulation model and elaborate some technical issues.

Refinement

From the abstract ASM model (Figure 6), we obtain a hierarchy of intermediate models through stepwise refinements. At each refinement step, the model becomes more concrete by adding certain details to capture certain behavior that was

Box 1.

$$edgepreference(agent, edge) = \sum_{f \in FACTOR} factorValue(agent, edge, f) \times factorWeight(agent, f)$$

Figure 7. An example of transforming the ASM model into Java code

```
rule FINALIZE_TRIP ≡
 trigger s: INFORM_ARRIVAL,decisnModule(parentAgent)
  arrivalTime(s) := now
  path(s) := takenPath

  SEND_FEEDBACK_TO_CBR(curProb,pathCBR,takenPath)
```

a) Abstract State Machine Specification of FINALIZE_TRIP

```
private void finalizeTrip(){
 InformArrivalSignal s = (InformArrivalSignal)
              Main.createSignal(
              InformArrivalSignal.class,
              this, this.parentAgent.
              getDecisionModule());
 s.setArrivalTime(SimMain.now());
 s.setTakenPath(takenPath);
 Main.trigger(s);

 sendFeedbackToCBR(curProb,pathCBR,takenPath);
}
```

b) Java Implementation FINALIZE_TRIP

previously left abstract. Such a concrete formal model provides a precise blueprint for building the simulation model and makes the transition to the implementation almost mechanical. Here, we provide an example of such a transition.

Figure 6 shows the high-level definition of the SEM where certain rules are left abstract. These rules are refined in the subsequent refinement steps. For instance, the FINALIZE_TRIP rule is refined using an event triggering mechanism to inform the ADM of agent's arrival at the destination (Figure 7a). The concrete rule is then directly converted to Java code using an implementation of the event triggering mechanism in Java (Figure 7b).

Although, the transformation is not always as trivial as this example, the concrete formal model provides a comprehensive definition of the system, and leaves very few details for the implementation, which allows for systematic construction of discrete event simulations.

Simulation

An implementation of our model in the Java programming language was developed for presentation at the 14th Environmental Criminology and Crime Analysis (ECCA) conference 2006 (Brantingham et al., 2005b). The goal was to demonstrate the application of the project in both criminology research and crime prevention by simulating the creation of awareness space as agents go about their daily activities. This chapter takes the development of the model one step further and explores the potential impact of the awareness space of individual agents on choice of targets.

The first step in the simulation process is the generation of a graph to be used as the simulation of the road network used by the agent for moving around in the environment. To allow for further validation of the model, it is important for implementation to accommodate real-world data.

Figure 8. The Mastermind program at the beginning of a run. The road network mirrors that of downtown Vancouver. The icons represent agents, targets and locations of importance.

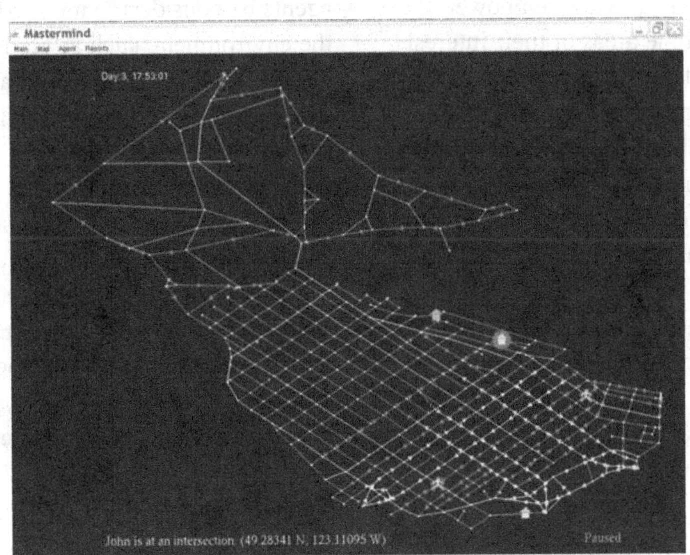

For that purpose, the underlying road network environment is created by transforming standard road network files into a graph data structure. The simulation environment can be built from any subsection of the road network. That is, new simulation environments can be created by using another street network from another city or another part of a city. The flexibility of Mastermind allows the size of the simulation area to be tailored to the user's wishes. Currently, available CPU processing power and memory create an upper limit on the size of the area that can be considered. At present, the downtown core of the city of Vancouver is of an easily manageable size for the application (416 intersections; 710 street sections), but the city as a whole is too large (5303 intersections; 8966 street sections). Figure 8 shows a snapshot of the simulation environment using downtown Vancouver as the underlying street network.

In conjunction with Java, we used the OpenGL graphics engine (OpenGL Architecture Review Board & Shreiner, 2004) to create the visualization capabilities of the application. Both Java and JOGL (Java OpenGL libraries) enabled quick development of a user-friendly and flexible simulation. Small considerations, such as allowing panning and zooming of the map view, empower the end-users to focus on the areas of their interest. Similarly, attributes of the agents and the environment can be altered within the program. A detailed data output of simulation runs is also available, so that the results can be also analyzed by other methods. For example, statistical methods may give the user supplementary insight into what has taken place.

Our current stage in implementing Mastermind uses provincial road network data to create a geographical model of an urban area, with the street block the natural level of analysis. At this stage we consider the crimes interesting at this level of detail. Such crimes include car theft, burglary and robbery of banks or at ATMs. The example presented in this chapter is motor vehicle theft.

The model is set up so that the user of the model could hypothetically place potential targets anywhere in the simulation environment. An agent, however, is only aware of potential targets when the routine path crosses the location of the potential target. This means that agents starting in different locations in the environment and developing different regular routes will encounter a different set of targets. Effectively the number of targets considered is limited by what the agent may notice, not the total number of targets in the environment. A car thief will not be interested in nor "know" about the availability of any target other than cars on the thief's routine path. In this way, the perceptual space of the agent defines the number and location of targets introduced into the system. This allows us effectively to consider a large number of targets of different types (e.g., temporary/mobile) in the simulation.

The target selection behavior of an agent includes evaluating targets as they are generated by the system, and reacting appropriately when a viable target is found. This could either be simply recording the details of that target or as complex as committing a crime. We are currently working on improving the target selection behavior of the agents by considering more complex features of the environment, such as land use, specific sites and SES background information for areas, so that in the next step criminal behavior can be simulated more precisely.

This interaction between two parts of the model, navigation and target selection, is an example of one of the strengths of an ASM approach. The modular structure of the Mastermind program allows for integrating other functionality as research progresses. These can be specific modules for use in a single experiment, or extensions and improvements of existing functionality.

Results

Our first experiment with the Mastermind program consisted of 10 runs, each of which simulated the actions of two criminal agents over a period of one week. The two agents (named Jack and John) had different navigation preferences, but were otherwise identical. They shared the same activity nodes (home, work, and recreational locations) and were assumed to move around the environment on foot. In regards to navigation, Jack preferred quick trips along main roads. John had no such preference, and was willing to "take the scenic route" to get to his destination. The simulation environment was based on the road network for the downtown section of Vancouver, a densely populated peninsula.

The following items were measured:

- **Targets selected:** The number of potential targets evaluated as "good" by the agents over the time period (one week).
- **Visit frequency:** How many times the road section a target was found on was visited during the time period.
- **Minimum distance to activity node:** The shortest distance from a target to one of the agent's activity nodes (work, home, or recreation). The number given is relative to the simulation: in this case, a score of five roughly corresponds to two city blocks.
- **Targets in activity space:** The proportion of targets selected that fell within the agent's activity space. For the purpose of this experiment, activity space was defined as the places an agent visited on average at least twice a day (see Table 1).

Looking at the results, it is possible to notice some interesting properties. First of all, the agent willing to travel longer distances in his daily activity, John, usually found more targets. Despite this, the average visit frequency for both agents is very close, at just below 9, or slightly more than one visit on average per day. However, John had a larger standard deviation for this result, indicating a wider variety of locations targets were chosen from. In both cases, the proportion of targets chosen within the activity space was very low, but the visit frequency suggests that targets were found in the awareness space.

The program includes an inhibition function to discourage agents from choosing targets near their activity nodes. It is interesting to note that the average minimum distance to activity node is close to the cut-off for the inhibition function (5.0) for both agents. In Jack's case, it falls slightly under the cut-off. This would suggest that the targets he chose were perhaps somewhat too close to his activity nodes, but not overly so. In his case, the direct routes he took between activity nodes most likely limited his choices. However, for both agents, the standard deviation is relatively high, indicating that activity node distance was not an overwhelming factor in target selection.

Table 1. Agent activity spaces and target selection

		Jack	John	All Agents
Targets selected	Average	6.0	8.7	7.35
	Standard deviation	2.98	2.63	3.07
Visit frequency	Average	8.63	8.90	8.79
	Standard deviation	3.17	6.40	5.31
Min. distance to activity node	Average	4.24	6.34	5.48
	Standard deviation	3.15	3.91	3.75
Targets in activity space		0%	14.94%	8.84%

The road network database the simulation environment was built from categorizes roads according to the amount of traffic they are designed for. The agent Jack had a noticeable preference (73.3%) for the busiest type of roads. This makes sense considering Jack's preference for quick routes along main roads. On the other hand, John showed no such preference, distributing his choice of targets relatively equally among the three main road types in the area. Again, since John does not consider speed of travel important, it is more likely that he will visit side streets and residential areas. This data is not surprising, but its suggestion of a relationship between navigation choices and target discovery is worthwhile for follow-up research.

The results gathered so far are of the most preliminary nature. They are not enough to make any conclusions, but they raise some interesting questions. However, they are still useful for two reasons. The first is that they can help us to improve our model. If some behavior seems unrealistic, we can use that to see if some of our assumptions are either incorrect or poorly formalized. The second valuable aspect of the results is that they are able to help us develop ideas. A connection suggested by the results can be refined into an interesting problem and used in a more rigorous investigation. The dynamic nature of the simulation model is most valuable in its ability to spur its users on to further research developments.

Model Validation

Computational modeling of real-world phenomena seems meaningless, unless one can actually establish the validity of a model and assess the quality of the results it produces. Since there is no way to prove in a rigorous mathematical sense the validity of a model, the best one can hope for is a conclusive justification—to be provided conceptually, mathematically and experimentally—that a model is faithful to reality. To make sure that the proposed Mastermind model is sound from both a computational as well as a criminological perspective, we combine a number of qualitative and quantitative techniques for reasoning about the model and evaluating its behavior.

Qualitative aspects include the internal consistency of the symbolic representation of the model and its conceptual consistency with regard to the underlying theories of crime. Specifically, we exploit the ASM ground model method for checking consistency and validity by providing a framework that allows for inspection by analytical means and for performing experiments that based on objective criteria "allow for systematic attempts to 'falsify' the model in a Popperian sense (Popper, 1959) against the to-be-encoded piece of reality" (Börger, 2004).

Quantitatively, one can evaluate the model in at least two different ways. One is to compare results of simulation runs to results produced by other prediction models, for instance, using statistical methods (Xue & Brown, 2003). The other one is to use real-world data from crime databases as a basis for comparison. In this case, the goal is to reproduce spatial characteristics matching those derived from real-world data of comparable scenarios. Both approaches provide feedback mechanisms for calibrating the various model parameters.

Beyond prediction of likely scenarios, the model serves as a subject for further study. Due to its descriptive nature, it facilitates the inspection of its conceptual and mathematical foundation by analytical means. This includes aspect such as: (a) identification of behavior characteristics from response patterns generated by simulations; and (b) identification of the system boundary and the factors that influence the behavior of interest. Clearly, the key issue is not to obtain a simulation response as the main result but to inspect the underlying trace that generated the response and suggest changes on that basis.

FUTURE RESEARCH DIRECTIONS

In this chapter we propose a novel approach to computational modeling of crime patterns, one that takes advantage of the structure afforded by the ASM paradigm for mathematical modeling of discrete dynamic systems. Within this formal framework, it is possible to better understand crime patterns, but also to test crime pattern and prevention theory (Brantingham et al., 2005a). We model spatial and temporal aspects of crime in urban environments as a foundation for the systematic development of simulation models. Mastermind is scalable and applicable to a broad range of crime events in the urban environment, but it is also usable in specific, smaller scale facilities. Centralized and high-volume activity spaces that require strict controls of user movements, such as airports, ports, will benefit from discrete event simulations to test new controls or other environmental interventions. Similarly, this type of modeling is of potential value in modeling crime and conflicts in more free-flowing settings such as shopping centers, major sporting and entertainment facilities.

As a systematic and portable methodology, computational modeling of crime patterns has direct value in a range of criminal justice applications. The use of ASM models and simulations is new to social situations, but the development and testing of these models could be of value in policies and operations. Law enforcement possibilities are obvious: crime prevention interventions can be modeled prior to physical implementation, allowing modification to improve desired impacts and, just as importantly, anticipate unintended consequences. While not covered in this chapter, Mastermind could be used for estimating potential displacement and abatement of crime reduction interventions. Forecasting is essential in intelligence led policing, and in proactive crime reduction and prevention. Models such as Mastermind would provide program planners and analysts with another tool to predict likely activity spaces for both typical street crimes and those requiring more focused and long-term investigations, such as those involving serial or persistent (chronic) offenders.

Although unconventional, the application of the ASM modeling paradigm to social systems turns out to be a promising approach; it seamlessly combines with the established view of multi-agent modeling of social systems, providing a precise and well-defined semantic foundation for the latter. Our main theoretical result is the abstract behavior model of person agents (based on the *agent architecture*) interacting with their objective and subjective environments. Our main practical result is an executable version of Mastermind implemented in Java. Together with an advanced GUI for interactive control and visualization of Mastermind runs, the executable model serves as a platform for the construction and experimental validation of discrete-event simulation models. Our future research will concentrate on extending Mastermind by gradually integrating other dimensions of crime so as to express a multitude of aspects within a unifying framework in a coherent and consistent way. Specifically we will consider computational models of dynamic aspects of social networks and networks with complex relations allowing for agents with multiple identities, for instance, as required to reflect organized crime and the behavior of criminal organizations.

From a pure research point of view, the ASM formalism and underlying abstraction principles provide a firm semantic foundation for integrating different theories of crime, and allows researchers to test theoretical expectations directly in ways not possible in real world environments. As such, using the ASM modeling framework in computational criminology provides a research paradigm that supports evidence based policy and planning efforts to advance best practices in crime prevention and crime reduction programming.

REFERENCES

Attoui, A. (2000). *Real-time and multi-agent systems*. Berlin: Springer-Verlag.

Baumgartner, K. C., Ferrari, S., & Salfati, C. G. (2005). Bayesian network modeling of offender behavior for criminal profiling. In *Proceedings of 44th IEEE Conference on decision and control and 2005 European Control Conference* (pp. 2702- 2709).

Bettini, C., Wang, X. S., & Jajodia, S. (1998). Temporal semantic assumptions and their use in databases. *IEEE transactions on knowledge and data engineering, 10*(2), 277-296.

Blass, A., & Gurevich, Y. (2003). Abstract state machines capture parallel algorithms. *ACM transactions on computation logic, 4*(4), 578-651.

Börger, E. (2004). *The ASM ground model method as a foundation of requirements engineering.* In N. Dershowitz (Ed.), *Verification: Theory and practice: LNCS 2772* (pp. 146-161). Springer.

Börger, E., & Stärk, R. (2003). *Abstract state machines: A method for high-level system design and analysis.* Springer-Verlag.

Borne, P., Fayech, B., Hammadi, S., & Maouche, S. (2003). Decision support system for urban transportation networks. *IEEE transaction on systems, man and cybernetics, Part C, 33*(1), 67-77.

Bottoms, A. E., & Wale, P. (2002). Environmental criminology. In M. Maguire, R. Morgan & R. Reiner (Eds.), *The Oxford handbook of criminology* (3rd ed., pp.620-656). Oxford: Oxford University Press.

Bottoms, A. E., Claytor, A., & Wiles, P. (1992). Housing markets and residential community crime careers: A case study from Sheffield. In D. J. Evans, N. R. Fyfe & D. T. Herbert (Eds.), *Crime, policing and place: Essays in environmental criminology* (pp. 118-144). London: Routledge.

Bowers, K. (2007) Crime risk models: Specifying boundaries and environmental backcloths. In *Proceedings of the Crime Hot Spots: Behavioral, Computational and Mathematical Models, IPAM, UCLA.*

Brantingham, P. J., & Brantingham, P. L. (1978). A theoretical model of crime site selection. In M. Krohn, & R. L. Akers (Eds.), *Crime, law and sanctions.* Beverly Hills, CA: Sage Publications.

Brantingham, P. J., & Brantingham, P. L. (1984). *Patterns in crime.* New York: Macmillan Publishing Company.

Brantingham, P. J., & Brantingham, P. L. (1991). Introduction: The dimensions of crime. In P. J. Brantingham, & P. L. Brantingham (Eds.), *Environmental criminology* (pp.7-26). Waveland Press.

Brantingham, P. J., & Brantingham, P. L. (1993a). Environment, routine and situation: Toward a pattern theory of crime. In R. V. Clarke, & M. Felson (Eds.), *Routine activity and rational choice: Advances in criminological theory* (Vol. 5., pp. 259-294). New Brunswick, NJ: Transaction Publication.

Brantingham, P. J., & Brantingham P. L. (1993b). Nodes, paths and edges: Considerations on the complexity of crime and the physical environment. *Journal of Environmental Psychology, 13*, 3-28.

Brantingham, P. J., & Brantingham P. L. (2004). Computer simulation as a tool for environmental criminologists. *Security Journal, 17*, 21-30.

Brantingham, P. J., Brantingham P. L., & Glässer, U. (2005a). Computer simulation as a research tool in criminology and criminal justice. *Criminal Justice Matters, 58*, 18-19.

Brantingham, P. J., Bertozzi, A., Tita, G., & Chayes, L. (2006.). *UC mathematical and simulation modeling of crime project.* Retrieved September 5, 2007, from http://paleo.sscnet.ucla.edu/ucmasc.htm

Brantingham, P. L., Glässer, U., Kinney, B., Singh, K., & Vajihollahi, M. (2005b). A computational model for simulating spatial aspects of crime in urban environments. In *Proceedings of 2005 IEEE International Conference on Systems, Man, and Cybernetics, Hawaii, USA* (pp. 3667- 3674).

Brantingham, P. L., Glässer, U., Singh, K., & Vajihollahi, M. (2005c). *Mastermind: Modeling and simulation of criminal activity in urban environments* (Tech. Rep. SFU-CMPT-TR-2005-14). Burnaby, Canada, Simon Fraser University. Revised version of SFU-CMPT-TR-2005-01.

Bratman, M. E., Israel, D., & Pollack, M. E. (1988). Plans and resource-bounded practical reasoning. *Computational Intelligence, 4*, 349-355.

Brown, D. E. (1998). The regional crime analysis program (ReCAP): A framework for mining data to catch criminals. In *Proceedings of 1998 IEEE International Conference on Systems, Man, and Cybernetics, San Diego, California* (pp. 2848-2853).

Brunswik, E. (1952). The conceptual framework of psychology. *International Encyclopedia of Unified Science, 1*(10).

Clarke, R. V. (2004). Crime proofing of products: The idea and the substance. *IEEE Technology and Society Magazine, 23*(3), 21-27.

Cornish, D., & Clarke, R. V. (1986). Introduction. In D. Cornish & R. V. Clarke (Eds.), *The reasoning criminal: Rational choice perspectives on offending* (pp. 1-16). New York: Springer-Verlag.

Davidsson, P. (2002). Agent based social simulation: A computer science view. *Journal of Artificial Societies and Social Simulation, 5*(1).

Dijkstra, E. W. (1959). A note on two problems in connection with graphs. *Numerische Mathematik, 1*, 269-271.

Doran, J., Palmer, M., Gilbert, N., & Mellars, P. (1994). The EOS project: Modelling upper paleolithic social change. In N. Gilbert & J. Doran (Eds.), *Simulating society: The computer simulation of social phenomena* (pp. 195-221). London: UCL Press.

Drogoul, A., & Ferber, J. (1994). Multi-agent simulation as a tool for studying emergent processes in societies. In N. Gilbert & J. Doran (Eds.), *Simulating society: The computer simulation of social phenomena* (pp. 127-142). London: UCL Press.

Eck, J. E., & Weisburd, D. (1995). Crime places in crime theory. In J. E. Eck & D. Weisburd (Eds.), *Crime and place.* Monsey, NY: Criminal Justice Press.

Ekblom, P., & Tilley, N. (2000). Going equipped: Criminology, situational crime prevention and the resourceful offender. *British journal of criminology*, 40(3), 376-398.

Fang, L., Hipel, K. W., Kilgour, D. M., & Peng, X. (2003). A decision support system for interactive decision making-Part I: Model formulation. *IEEE Transactions on Systems, Man and Cybernetics, Part C, 33*(1), 42-55.

Farahbod, R. (2004). *Extending and refining an abstract operational semantics of the web services architecture for the business process execution language.* Unpublished master's thesis, Simon Fraser University, Burnaby, Canada.

Farahbod, R., & Glässer, U. (2006). Semantic blueprints of discrete dynamic systems: Challenges and needs in computational modeling of complex behavior. In *Proceedings of the 6th Int'l Heinz Nixdorf Symposium*, Paderborn, Germany.

Felson, M. (1987). Routine activities and crime prevention in the developing metropolis. *Criminology, 25*, 911-931.

Ferber, J. (1999). *Multi-agent systems: An introduction to distributed artificial* intelligence. Harlow: Addison Wesley Longman.

Franklin, S., & Graesser, A. (1997). Is it an agent, or just a program? A taxonomy for autonomous agents. In *Proceedings of the workshop on intelligent agents III, agent theories, architectures, and languages ECAI '96* (pp. 21-35). London: Springer-Verlag.

Gilbert, N., & Doran, J. (1994). *Simulating societies*. UCL Press.

Gilbert, N., & Troitzsch, K. G. (1999). *Simulation for the social scientist*. Open University Press.

Glässer, U., Rastkar, S., & Vajihollahi, M. (2006). Computational modeling and experimental validation of aviation security procedures. In S. Mehrotra, D. D. Zeng, & H. Chen (Eds.), *Intelligence and security informatics: Vol. 3975 of LNCS* (pp. 420-431). Berlin: Springer-Verlag.

Groff, E. (2006). *Exploring the geography of routine activity theory: A spatio-temporal test using street robbery*. Unpublished doctoral dissertation, University of Maryland, Maryland.

Guerlain S., Brown D. E., & Mastrangelo, C. (2000). Intelligent decision support systems. *IEEE International Conference on Systems, Man, and Cybernetics, 3*, 1934 – 1938.

Gunderson, L., & Brown, D. (2000). Using a multi-agent model to predict both physical and cyber criminal activity. In *Proceedings of the IEEE International Conference on Systems, Man, and Cybernetics, 4*, 2338-2343.

Gupta, J. N. D., Forgionne, G. A., & Mora, T. M. (Eds). (2006). Intelligent decision-making support systems: Foundations, applications and challenges. *Decision engineering*, Springer.

Gurevich, Y. (1995). Evolving algebras 1993: Lipari guide. In E. Börger (Ed.), *Specification and validation methods* (pp. 9-36). Oxford University Press.

Gurevich, Y. (2000). Sequential abstract state machines capture sequential algorithms. *ACM Transactions on Computational Logic, 1*, 77-111.

Hendrick, J. S., Howell, T. J., London, D. M., Luehrs, E. M., Saliba, M., Brown, D., et al. (2004). Webcat: The design and implementation of the web-based crime analysis toolkit. In *Proceedings of the 2004 IEEE systems and information engineering design symposium* (pp. 95-103).

Hochmair, H. H., & Karlsson, V. (2004). Investigation of preference between the least-angle strategy and the initial segment strategy for route selection in unknown environments. In C. Freksa, M. Knauff, B. Krieg-Brückner, B. Nebel, & T. Barkowsky (Eds.), *Spatial cognition IV: LNCS 3343* (pp. 79-97). Berlin: Springer-Verlag.

Hooimeijer, P., & Oskamp, A. (1999) Advances in the microsimulation of demographic behavior. In Van Wissen L. J. G., & Dykstra P. A. (Eds.), *Population issues: An interdisciplinary focus* (The Plenum series on demographic methods and population analysis) (pp. 229-263). New York: Plenum Press.

Hua, L., & Brown, D. E. (1998). Spatial-temporal event prediction: A new model. In *Proceedings of 1998 IEEE International Conference on Systems, Man, and Cybernetics, San Diego, California*, (pp. 2933-2937).

Kennedy, L. W., & Forde, D. R. (1990). Risky lifestyles and dangerous results: Routine activities and exposure to crime. *Sociology and Social Research, 74*(4), 208-211.

Kianmehr, K., & Alhajj, R. (2006). Crime hotspots prediction using support vector machine. In *Proceedings of 2006 IEEE International Conference on Computer Systems and Applications* (pp. 952- 959).

Koffka, K. (1967). *Principles of gestalt psychology*. Harcourt.

Kolodner, J., & Leake, D. (1996). A tutorial introduction to case-based reasoning. In D. Leake (Ed.), *Case-based reasoning: Experiences, lessons, and future directions* (pp. 31-65). AAAI Press.

Liu, L., Wang, X., Eck, J., & Liang, J. (2005). Simulating crime events and crime patterns in a RA/CA model. In F. Wang (Ed). *Geographic information systems and crime analysis* (pp. 197-213). Reading, PA: Idea Publishing.

Løvås, G. G. (1998). Models of wayfinding in emergency evacuations. *European Journal of Operational Research, 105* (3), 371-389.

Luck, M., & d'Inverno, M. (1995). A formal framework for agency and autonomy. In V. Lesser & L. Gasser (Eds.), In *Proceedings of the First International Conference on Multi-Agent Systems (ICMAS-95), San Francisco, California,* (pp. 254-260). AAAI Press.

Mikhailov, L., & Singh, M. G. (2003). Fuzzy analytic network process and its application to the development of decision support systems. *IEEE Transactions on Systems, Man and Cybernetics, Part C, 33*(1), 33-41.

OpenGL Architecture Review Board & Shreiner, D. (2004), *OpenGL(R) reference manual: The official reference document to OpenGL, Version 1.4* (4th Edition). Addison-Wesley Professional.

Perez, P., Dray, A., Ritter, A., Dietze, P., Moore, T., & Mazerolle, L. (2003). Simdrug: A multi-agent system tackling the complexity of illicit drug markets in Australia. In N. Gilbert, N. Ferrand, D. Batten, & P. Perez (Eds.), *Complex science for a complex world. Exploring human ecosystems with agents* (pp. 193-223). Canberra Australia: ANU E Press.

Popper, K. (1959). *The logic of scientific discovery.* Hutchinson & Co.

Rengert, G. F. (1991). Burglary in Philadelphia: A critique of an opportunity structure model. In P. J. Brantingham & P. L. Brandtingham (Eds.), *Environmental criminology* (pp. 189-201). Prospect Heights, IL: Waveland Press Inc.

Rengert, G. F. (1992). The journey to crime: Conceptual foundations and policy implications. In D. J. Evans, N. R. Fyfe, & D. T. Herbert (Eds.), *Crime, policing and place: Essays in environmental criminology* (pp.109-117). London: Routlede.

Roncek, D. W. (1981). Dangerous places: Crime and residential environment. *Social forces*, 60(1), 74-96.

Rossmo, D. K. (2000). *Geographic profiling.* Boca Raton, FL: CRC Press.

Russel, S. J., & Norvig, P. (2003). *Artificial intelligence: A modern approach* (2nd ed.). Prentice Hall.

Sycara, K. P. (1998, Fall). Multiagent systems. *AI magazine*, 79-92.

Sherman, L. W., Gartin, P. R., & Buerger, M. E. (1989). Hot spots of predatory crime: Routine activities and the criminology of place. *Criminology, 27*(1), 27-55.

Sonnenfeld, J. (1972). Geography, perception and the behavioral environment. In P. W. English & R. C. Mayfield (Eds.), *Man, space and the environment* (pp. 244-251). New York: Oxford University Press.

Singh, K. (2005). *An abstract mathematical framework for semantic modeling and simulation of urban crime patterns.* Unpublished master's thesis, Simon Fraser University, Burnaby, Canada.

Sun Microsystems (2006). *Java platform, standard edition.* Retrieved September 5, 2007, from http://java.sun.com

Wiles, P., & Costello, A. (2000). The "Road to Nowhere": The evidence for traveling criminals. *Home Office research study No. 207.* London: Home Office Research.

Wooldridge, M. (2002a). Intelligent agents: The key concepts. In M. Luck, V. Marik, O. Stepankova, & R. Trappl (Eds.), *Multi-agent systems and applications II* (pp.3-43). Springer.

Wooldridge, M. (2002b). *An introduction to multiagent systems*. John Wiley and Sons Ltd.

Wright R. T., & Decker S. H. (1997). *Armed robbers in action: Stickups and street culture*. Boston: Northeastern University Press.

Xue, Y., & Brown, D. E. (2003). A decision model for spatial site selection by criminals: A foundation for law enforcement decision support. *IEEE Transactions on Systems, Man and Cybernetics, Part C, 33*(1), 78-85.

Additional Readings

Abstract State Machines

Börger, E., & Stärk, R. (2003). *Abstract state machines: A method for high-level system design and analysis*. Springer-Verlag.

This book is a combination of a text and a reference book with proofs, examples and clear descriptions of ASM.

Börger, E. (2004). *The ASM ground model method as a foundation of requirements Engineering*. In N. Dershowitz (Ed.), *Verification: Theory and practice: LNCS 2772* (pp. 146-161). Springer.

Excellent description of ground models, a fundamental intellectual part of ASM that helps design with the understanding of human cognitive meaning and dynamically changing environment.

Farahbod, R. & Glässer, U. (2006). Semantic blueprints of discrete dynamic systems: Challenges and needs in computational modeling of complex behavior. In *Proceedings of the 6th International Heinz Nixdorf Symposium*, Paderborn, Germany.

This article describes the importance of semantics in modeling complex behavior.

Gurevich, Y. (1995). Evolving algebras 1993: Lipari Guide. In E. Börger (Ed.), *Specification and validation methods* (pp. 9-36). Oxford University Press.

Provides the background and origins of ASM and validation approaches.

Zimmermann, W., & Thalheim, B. (2004). Abstract state machines 2004: Advances in theory and practice. In *Proceedings of the 11th International Workshop, ASM 2004*. Springer

This is a book of proceeding that provides an overview of recent advances in ASM through a series of chapters.

Agent Based Approaches

Attoui, A. (2000). *Real-time and multi-agent systems*. Berlin: Springer-Verlag.

Detailed account of real-time systems and multiagent requirements.

Davidsson, P. (2002). Agent based social simulation: A computer science view. *Journal of artificial societies and social simulation, 5*(1).

Example of use of agent based modeling in social situations.

Gimblett, R. (2002). *Integrating geographic information systems and agent-based modeling techniques for simulating social and ecological processes*. Santa Fe Institute Studies in the Sciences of Complexity: Oxford University Press.

Overview of use of the Santa Fe agent based modeling in a range of ecological and environmental areas..

Simulation Modeling in Criminal Activity

Brantingham, P. J., Brantingham, P. L., & Glässer, U. (2005a). Computer simulation as a research tool in criminology and criminal justice. *Criminal Justice Matters, 58*, 18-19.

An overview for the general professional within the justice system.

Brown, D. E. (1998). The regional crime analysis program (ReCAP): A framework for mining data to catch criminals. In *Proceedings of 1998 IEEE international conference on systems, man, and cybernetics,* San Diego, CA, (pp. 2848-2853).

The use of innovative analysis processes in studying criminal behavior.

Hendrick, J. S., Howell, T. J., London, D. M., Luehrs, E. M., Saliba, M., Brown, D., et al. (2004). Webcat: The design and implementation of the Web-based crime analysis toolkit. In *Proceedings of the 2004 IEEE systems and information engineering design symposium* (pp. 95-103).

Practical toolkit and description of crime analysis.

Liu, L., Wang, X., Eck J., & Liang. J. (2005). Simulating crime events and crime patterns in a RA/CA Model. In F. Wang (Ed). *Geographic information systems and crime analysis* (pp. 197-213). Reading, PA: Idea Publishing.

Full description of use of CA in simulating crimes patterns in an urban context.

Criminology

Bottoms A. E., & Wale P. (2002). Environmental criminology. In Mike Maguire, R. Morgan, & R. Reiner (Eds.), *The Oxford handbook of criminology* (3rd ed.) (pp.620-656). Oxford: Oxford University Press.

Overview of field of environmental criminology.

Brantingham, P. J., & Brantingham, P. L. (1993b). Nodes, paths and edges: Considerations on the complexity of crime and the physical environment. *Journal of Environmental Psychology, 13,* 3-28.

Review of important of travel routes in determining awareness spaces and crime patterns.

Brantingham, P. J., & Brantingham, P. L. (1993a). Environment, routine and situation: Toward a pattern theory of crime. In R. V. Clarke & M. Felson (Eds.), *Routine activity and rational choice: Advances in criminological theory* (Vol. 5) (pp. 259-294). New Brunswick, NJ: Transaction Publication

Detailed description of crime pattern theory.

Eck, J. E., & Weisburd, D. (1995). Crime places in crime theory. In J. E. Eck & D. Weisburd (Eds.), *Crime and place.* Monsey, NY: Criminal Justice Press.

Description of the importance of the characteristics of a locale, the making of a place, for crime.

ENDNOTES

1. The Mastermind research project is partly funded by the RCMP "E" Division.
2. Although the original definition of ASMs is intended to capture any kind of discrete dynamic system, their application to social systems is original and unprecedented.
3. See also the ASM Web site at www.eecs.umich.edu/gasm/ for numerous applications and case studies.
4. Abstract state machines were originally called evolving algebras.
5. Despite being generic, this categorization is not intended to be universal; it is only meant to capture the dynamics of our target system.
6. This is analogous to a BDI architecture, whereby, memory represents the beliefs, motivations represent the desires, and the rules represent the deliberative and means-end reasoning phase of the BDI agents.

7 Our Divide and Conquer approach to model criminal behavior of intelligent agents emphasizes a clear separation of concerns, effectively breaking a complex computational problem into a number of individual subproblems that can be addressed separately. Each sub-problem is defined as a module focusing on a specific aspect of the behavior, such as navigation or target selection. The solutions to the subproblems are then combined to provide a solution to the original problem.

8 Depending on the resolution that is required, one can in principle also represent each individual lane of each road by a separate edge using a labeling scheme for distinguishing different lanes of the same road.

9 For any given set *S*, P(*S*) denotes here the power set (i.e., the set of all subsets) of *S*.

10 Control state ASMs represent "a normal form for UML activity diagrams and allow the designer to define machines which below the main control structure of finite state machines provide synchronous parallelism and the possibility to manipulate data structures." (Börger, & Stärk, 2003)

11 The factor values are normalized to real positive numbers between 0 and 1.

Chapter XIV
The Simulation of the Journey to Residential Burglary

Karen L. Hayslett-McCall
The University of Texas at Dallas, USA

Fang Qiu
The University of Texas at Dallas, USA

Kevin M. Curtin
The University of Texas at Dallas, USA

Bryan Chastain
The University of Texas at Dallas, USA

Janis Schubert
The University of Texas at Dallas, USA

Virginia Carver
The University of Texas at Dallas, USA

ABSTRACT

This chapter presents an innovative approach to the study of the journey to residential burglary. We demonstrate a simulation model that is built upon the integration of cellular automaton (CA) and multi-agent system (MAS). The model utilizes both social disorganization (SD) and routine activity (RA) theories to predict locations of residential burglary targets. The model simulates an offender as an intelligent agent of MAS that interacts with the target and place automata of CA. The likelihood of a residential burglary is modeled as a function of offender's motivation, target desirability and place guardianship, which in turn are determined by the offender's individual characteristics often used by RA and the target and place's neighborhood properties frequently utilized in SD. The model was initialized and parameterized using "real" crime data from Dallas, Texas Police Department. Results under two different weighting scenarios were obtained and compared with the actual distribution of offense locations, revealing the flexibility of model in its capability to assessing the influence of the two theories in burglary crime simulation. In closing we propose possible modifications that could be made to the model in the future.

INTRODUCTION

In this chapter, the offender and the residential location that was targeted for burglary are discussed in the terms of modeling them as agents and automata in a cellular automaton (CA) and multi-agent system (MAS) modeling. The offender agent has the following properties: age (i.e., experience), race, and gender that are related to motivation (i.e., poor neighborhood burgling in a wealthier neighborhood). In addition to its location, the target has properties such as income level (i.e., wealth of neighborhood) and race composition that determines its desirability. The residential location also has several properties that define the lack of guardianship (e.g., commuting time of residents and tenure, etc.). Our model is developed based on the essential components of routine activity (RA) and social disorganization (SD) theories, calibrated and validated utilizing the attributes of both the offenders and residential targets from the reports database from the Dallas Police Department (Dallas, TX). Our models are also supported by publicly available neighborhood attribute information (e.g., U.S. Census and tax parcel data), and location and distance information derived through geographic information systems (GIS) techniques in the model of the journey to crimes of residential burglary.

JOURNEY TO CRIME

The study of journey to crime is an evaluation of offense patterns—exploring the distance traveled between an offender's residence and the offense location. "Distance, so far as it enters into human relationships, is thus entirely relative to the available techniques for overcoming the friction of space" (Hawley, 1950: 237). Time and space are obstacles in human movement; criminal behavior is not exempt from these constraints. Research demonstrates that offenders generally commit crimes close to home, although significant differences exist by type of crime. The average crime trip is relatively short, reported as 1.66 miles (White, 1932), 1.43 miles (Philips, 1980), 1.22 miles (Gabor & Gottheil 1984), 1.93 miles (Costello & Wiles, 2001) and 0.4 miles (Turner, 1969). Many of the studies that measure crime trips as distances report a significant percent occurring over less than one mile (Costello & Wiles 2001; Rengert, Piquero, & Jones, 1999; Turner, 1969). When compared, property offenses are consistently committed farther from the home than crimes against persons (DeFrances & Smith, 1994; Pyle, 1976; Rand, 1986; Rhodes & Conly, 1981; White, 1932). The difference is related to the motivations behind crimes and the availability of suitable targets.

Considerations of the journey to burglary must account for a target selection process. Burglars begin in a general area, from which they select a specific target (Wright & Decker, 1994). An area's attractiveness can influence the direction and timing of burglaries (Rengert, 1981). Burglary follows the typical journey-to-crime pattern: many offenses are located within a few miles of the burglar's home (Costello & Wiles, 2001; Ratcliffe, 2001; Snook, 2004) and the number of burglaries committed decreases as the distance from the offender's home increases (Rengert,

Piquero, & Jones, 1999). Offenders are "likely to minimize the time and energy involved in criminal activities by selecting crimes that can be executed at relatively short distances from their homes as opposed to long distances" (Rengert, et al., 1999:429).

MODELING BURGLARY WITH SOCIAL DISORGANIZATION AND ROUTINE ACTIVITY THEORIES

The most popular theories on burglary are probably social disorganization theory and routine activity theory, using both neighborhood and residential characteristics as important tenets. For example, the commission of a crime requires a suitable target. In the case of residential burglary, that target is going to be a place of residence: a house, an apartment, a trailer, and so forth. Ratcliffe (2001) also reports on the timing of burglaries based on activity patterns. Residential and public spaces are burgled at opposite times, with residential offenses occurring mostly during the day while residential owners are at work. In addition to distinct temporal patterns of area traffic and subsequent crime, the presence of targets in a neighborhood influences offender behavior.

Social disorganization theory and routine activity theory are compatible explanations of the neighborhood-crime relationship. Both theories are control theories, in that they both assume that "people would commit crime if left to their own devices" (Vold, Bernard, & Snipes, 1998, p. 201). Social disorganization theorists believe that control mechanisms are present in neighborhoods, and that these controls have varying degrees of effectiveness in deterring or preventing predisposed offenders from committing crime. Routine activity theorists also discuss control, in that motivated offenders are assumed to be disinhibited and will commit crime against suitable targets when a capable guardian is not present. Both social disorganization and routine activity theorists agree that when controls are in place, predisposed offenders will be less likely to act even when an opportunity is present. In the case of social disorganization theory, the social controls include the three levels of social control (private, parochial, and public) (Hunter, 1985), while routine activities discusses control in terms of the presence of the capable guardian (Cohen & Felson, 1972).

In the last 20 years, social disorganization theorists have focused more closely on neighborhood-level financial resources and activity patterns, including criminal activity patterns. The systemic social disorganizationists have explored a series of new variables, beyond the variables of the original linear model, which have identified levels of social disorganization by a neighborhood's social composition patterns. These theorists have developed a body of research that studies the linear disorganization variables including neighborhood level of poverty and the amount of residential mobility. In addition, they have updated the model to include variables such as: the percentage of residents that rent vs. own, a higher number of abandoned buildings, the percentage of female-headed households, length of tenure, and high crime rates (Morenoff & Sampson, 1997; Sampson, 1985, 1987; Sampson & Groves, 1989; Sampson, Morenoff, & Earls, 1999; Sampson, & Raudenbush, 1999; Skogan, 1990; Taylor, 1997; Warner & Pierce, 1993). Where these variables are present, researchers have used this expanded list of important neighborhood factors to define "disorganization" within neighborhoods. Of these variables, we focus on the length of tenure in our study. This measure operates as a guardianship function for our 'targets.'

Of interest to the current study is the work by Sampson et al. (1987; 1997), who found that social integration factors, such as mobility, affected individual likelihood of being the victim of a crime. Indeed, some research has shown that neighborhoods still capable of exercising some level of informal social control could reduce their collective likelihood of criminal victimization Sampson, Raudenbush, and Earls (1997) found that the relationships between concentrated disadvantage and violent victimization as well as between neighborhood residential instability and victimization were mediated significantly by collective efficacy. Collective efficacy was defined as the "social cohesion among neighbors combined with their willingness to intervene on behalf of the common good" (Sampson et al. 1997, p. 918). Thus, neighborhoods that were willing to act for the common good were able to affect the number of victimizations that occurred within their boundaries.

Unlike previous research, Smith et al. (2000) found several interactions between "individual risk factors (as specified by routine activity theory) and type of neighborhood (as specified in social disorganization theory)" (p. 491). Overall, according to docial disorganization theory, along with a higher rate of offenders, residents are less likely to engage in active guardianship (i.e., collective efficacy). Disorganization results in high rates of instability and anonymity. Weak guardianship and motivated offenders, two of the three tenets of RA theory, are present in disorganized neighborhoods. The third tenet, presence of suitable targets, varies by the type of crime.

All of these factors from RA and SD theory can be applied in a simulation to the journey to residential burglary. They are given as characteristics to each of the following: the offender, the target agent, and the place agent.

CELLULAR AUTOMATA AND MULTI-AGENT SYSTEMS APPLIED IN THE SIMULATION OF CRIME

Cellular automata have been integrated into GIS through the fundamental operations of map algebra (Takeyama & Couclelis, 1997). They have been accepted as a structure for the modeling of space-time processes in GIS (Wu, 1999), and they have been identified as one of the prominent advances in GIS modeling (Goodchild, 2003).

Cellular automata (CA) is a discrete model consisting of an infinite number of regular grid cells, each in one of a finite number of states. However, in reality the model generally consists of a finite number of cells. The state of a cell at time t is a function of the states of a finite number of cells (or neighborhood) at time t-1. These neighbors are a selection of cells relative to the specified cell. Two standard neighborhood types are the "Moore" neighborhood and "von Neumann" neighborhood (Benenson & Torrens 2005). The former includes neighbors of single-point adjacency (similar to a queen's moves on a chessboard), while the latter does not (similar to a rook's moves on a chessboard). Every cell has the same rule for updating, based on the values in this neighborhood. In general, the state of an automaton can be defined as a function of the states of the automaton of the focal cell and its neighbors, the set of transition rules needed to adapt the automaton over time (Benenson & Torrens 2005). CA was first conceived by John von Neumann in the late 1940's and early 1950's, and then in the 1980's Stephen Wolfram made it famous for use in other fields (von Neumann, 1949; Wolfram, 1986). Soon after, the spatial aspects of CA were examined (Couclelis, 1985, 1988, 1989; Hogeweg, 1988; Green et al., 1990; Phipps, 1989; Smith, 1991; White & Engelen, 1992). One distinct feature of CA is the stationarity of the automata. The cell positions and most of time the spatial relations of their neighborhoods remain constant over time. Information can be exchanged with neighbors over time, which allows for spatial information propagation.

Multi-agent systems (MAS) have the ability to consider individual-oriented behavior. Their interpretation of automata states and transition rules allow for the design of autonomously behaving agents. These agents can be designed to make human-like decisions (to a certain degree), and are capable of moving through space. This capability is the key distinguishing feature from CA, in which automata are fixed. The variety of spatial relationships between automata can be relaxed in MAS, allowing for arbitrary neighborhood assignments between automata.

Franklin and Graesser (1996) define an agent as: "*An autonomous agent (1) is a system situated within and part of an environment; (2) that senses that environment and acts on it, over time; (3) in pursuit of its own agenda, and (4) so as to effect what it senses in the future.*" Cellular automata do not appear to meet at least two of these rules. The cells in CA do not have their own agenda nor do they sense the future. More importantly, they do not act by themselves. An agent should be able to "act", "pursue its own agenda", and "sense the future."

Beyond this, agents are heterogeneous—other modeling simply looks at the "average" individual. In MAS, agents have the ability to be anywhere on the spectrum, and can be modeled to fit a known distribution, if desired. Agents are proactive about reaching their set of goals (Terna, 1998). For example, geographic agents can be set to follow certain paths. In terms of residential burglary, agents can be set to seek targets of "best opportunity" (i.e., perceived gain of wealth). Similar to automaton in the neighborhoods of CA, agents are also perceptive of their environment and are able to sense their surroundings. We hypothesize that residential burglars are sensitive to their environments. We know from the literature that individuals preferred to offend in neighborhoods composed mainly of their own race (Reppetto, 1974). In addition, MAS agents are sensitive to the other agents and are aware that socially disorganized neighborhoods have higher success rates of offences, and residents are less likely to engage in active guardianship. Unlike CA, however, agent perception is not constrained to a neighborhood, because of their ability to travel. In closing, agents are also able to adapt to their environment. Agents are able to modify their behavior based on experience gained during the model lifespan.

Cellular automaton and related agent based models have been used to explore some crime-related issues, but the investigation of crime through CA is still in its infancy. CA has been used to study the prisoner's dilemma (Alonso, Fernandez, & Fort, 2006), in modeling the outbreak of infectious disease, and in planning for crowd control (Batty, Desyllas, & Duxbury, 2003). CA have been used in transportation applications including the modeling of pedestrian behavior (Blue & Adler, 2001) and the simulation of road traffic states (Wahle, Neubert, Esser, & Schreckenberg, 2001). In a geographic context a substantial amount of research has focused on the use of CA for simulating urban dynamics (Batty, 2005; Batty, Xie, & Sun, 1999), growth (Barredo, Kasanko, McCormick, & Lavalle, 2003; Clarke & Gaydos, 1998), and sprawl (Torrens, 2006), with very limited mention of crime.

Not explicitly following the paradigm of cellular automata though, rule based systems for the support of police operations have been implemented (Brahan, Lam, Chan, & Leung, 1998), and economic simulations of criminal offenses have been modeled (Winoto, 2002). All of these elements (CA, GIS, and criminology) have come together in a recent work that used CA to model the criminological theory of routine activities and street robbery and implemented this model in a GIS context (Liu, Wang, Eck, & Liang, 2005).

COMPONENTS OF RESIDENTIAL BURGLARY CRIME

For residential burglary crimes, we have identified three major players: offender, target, and place. In this study, we integrated both the MAS and CA approaches into our model of these three components. An offender, a mobile individual with autonomous behavior to response perceived environment, is modeled as agent. Target and place, with stationary locations in the case of residential crime, are simulated as automata as in a typical CA model. Each of these components has been assigned a set of properties and behaviors according to our hypotheses, which are based foremost on previous studies in social disorganization and routine activity theories.

THE OFFENDER AGENT

Offender agents have several properties relative to committing residential burglary, such as location, age, race and gender of the offender.

First is the home location of the offenders, which is often recorded in crime report. For the purposes of this chapter, we have to assume that this is the location from which the offender agents begin their journey to crime. These are known offenders that have burgled in the Dallas area. We have data from the Dallas Police Department regarding both the place of residence and the place of offense. This data will be used to both initialize our model and to validate our findings. We are limited in that we have no other information other than where the offender lives and where the offender offended—thus, we must assume that they are starting from their home locations. However, this is a reasonable assumption, as crime researchers have found that the journey to crime is generally inversely related to the distance from an offender's residence (Brantingham & Brantingham, 1991).

In addition to the offender's location is the offender's motivation. With residential burglary, the motivation of an offender is often influenced by his individual characteristics, such age, race, and gender. Often assumed to be positively correlated with distance traveled, age has received limited attention in prior research. The inconsistent ranges used to evaluate age compound the problem. When evaluated in journey to crime research, age is classified arbitrarily, eliminating the ability to detect a pattern among research. The varied age categories prevent cross-comparisons of findings, so that although age is assumed to increase mobility, empirical evidence is lacking. Increased mobility afforded by access to transportation and a wider knowledge of surrounding areas is presumed to increase an offender's range. While youth is commonly stated as a factor limiting distance to offense, few studies have effectively evaluated its impact and results have been conflicting. Some find age positively correlated with mobility (Gottheil & Gabor, 1984; Turner, 1969; Phillips, 1980; Warren et al., 1998), while others report no effects (Canter & Gregory, 1994; Costello & Wiles, 2001; Tita & Griffiths, 2005).

The impact of race is also relevant to motivation. However, in previous research, the impact of race on offender mobility is unclear. Some studies report no effect on offender distance due to race (Messner & Tardiff, 1986; Rand, 1986). One found black offenders stayed closer to familiar locations, branching out less than white offenders (Carter & Hill 1979). Both white and black subjects preferred to offend in neighborhoods composed mainly of their own race (Reppetto, 1974). With one study suggesting that black offenders stayed closer to familiar locations than their white counterparts (Carter & Hill 1979). Based on the general demographic patterns of racial residential patterns in Dallas, Texas, we expect that black offenders would be less motivated to travel long distances. Previous researches have seldom studied Hispanic journey to crime. We speculate that their travel distance is probably the shortest among the three races, because they are geographically dispersed throughout the city more than are African Americans and Whites.

Little work has examined the difference between the male and female journey to crime. In our research sample of 148 residential burglaries, the females were likely to travel further to commit a residential burglary. This may be due to selection of targets that are suitable for their physical abilities. For example, Dallas has large numbers of tall privacy fences (e.g., six and eight feet) that may be more difficult for a female to climb than a male.

THE TARGET AUTOMATON

A target automaton in the residential burglary crime is a house or an apartment unit, instead of a human victim. Previous research suggests that both potential costs and rewards factor into the selection of a target. A target is attractive when an offender perceives a large gain, the crime requires little investment, and there is a minimal perceived chance of apprehension (Rhodes & Conly, 1981). We identified three important properties for target: location, income and race composition of the residential area. The location of offenses is also reported in the data. For a residential burglar, the location is usually the home address of the target. The distance between the offender's location and offenses location basically provides the length of the journey to crime.

Except for the items that were stolen, we may not have much information about the target itself in the crime report. As a residential location has no true "routine activities" of its own, it assumes those of the people that reside within it and around it. That is, we are constrained to assign the target the average socioeconomic status (SES) of the members of the blockgroup within which the residence falls.[1] In this study, we used medium household income of the census blockgroup and assigned to all cells in it to represent the desirability of the potential targets. We use income level as a surrogate for desirability because the distance an offender is willing to travel will not be great, unless the reward is great. Further, no offenders was found to prefer to offend in neighborhoods composed mainly of the opposite race (Reppetto, 1974), thus we expect that motivation would be less to offend in a neighborhood where the racial make-up was markedly different from the offender's race.

THE PLACE AUTOMATON

Place automaton is the target residence's neighboring area in this case. Place has several properties, such as mean commute time, and mean length of residential tenure, which is often related to the guardianship of the target. For a house to be burgled, the house's own resident must be absent or unaware of the entry. Thus, the only place managers that are left to guard the house are the residence's neighbors. We suggest that the strength of place managers (i.e., the effectiveness) is determined by the average tenure and the average commute time of neighborhood residents.

Even as early as 1938, Wirth noted the growing sense of anonymity even in residential neighborhoods. He felt that residential neighborhoods had long been the harbor for interpersonal knowledge of those persons who lived nearby. Simply put, historically neighborhoods were viewed as a location where people living on the same block would know each other. Wirth believed that anonymity was evidenced by the loss of primary contacts, and the effects of formal control replacing traditional informal neighborhood controls. Further works, which later became known as social disorganization theory (Shaw & McKay, 1942), introduced the notions that residential mobility led to the disruption of a community's social organization and community solidarity, which led to crime. Residential tenure (i.e., staying in the same neighborhood for longer periods of time) and commute time are key factors for the place automaton, and are crucial according to social disorganization theory (Bursik & Grasmick, 1993; Hunter, 1985, Sampson, 1987; Sampson & Groves, 1989). Longer periods of residential tenure will strengthen the effectiveness of the guardianship. The longer the average commute that neighborhood residents have outside of their neighborhood, the fewer available guardians and the weaker the guardianship capacity of the place.

THE JOURNEY TO RESIDENTIAL BURGLARY SIMULATION MODEL

Based on the previously discussed theories and criminological research, the journey to residential burglary is related to an interaction between the offender, the targeted residential unit and the complex neighborhood structure within which the target resides. The likelihood of a residential burglary is primarily based on the motivation of the offender, the desirability of the target, and the lack of guardianship of the place. While RA assumes that all persons are potential offenders, some may be more motivated than others. Following SD theory we would possibly suspect that, offenders might be more motivated to travel further if they are older or a female. Offenders of different races may choose to commit the burglary either closer or further from their homes. The desirability of the target is positively correlated with the income value of its contents. This desirability may be curtailed by their desire to offend in neighborhoods where they may be more likely to racially "blend" with residents. Place guardianship is enhanced by longer tenures and is weakened by longer commute times.

We have developed a model that applies both cellular automata (CA) and multi-agent systems (Gottheil & Gabor, 1984) to simulate the distribution of residential burglary in space and time using 2000 Dallas Police data. In 2000, there were 148 burglaries that were "cleared," or solved. Thus, we have the locations of 148 offenders' residences and target locations. These were all addressed utilizing geocoding capability in GIS. The average age of our offenders was 26.64, but the vast majority was under the age of 25. We had 137 males and 11 females in our sample, suggesting that males either commit more residential burglaries, or at least that they get caught more often in Dallas. We only had three races represented in our sample: White (26), Black (82), and Hispanic (40). In addition to the offender data, we gathered information from the 2000 U.S. Census. This information was selected on the basis of supporting either RA or SD theory. We included such variables as: racial composition of neighborhoods (i.e., block groups), commute time, length of tenure, and income.

The model was developed with ArcGIS software development kit (ArcObjects SDK) using Visual Basic. Similar to other CA models, we utilize cellular space, which consists of interconnected rectangular cells. These also become our places, within which the targets reside. The grid of these rectangular cells is overlain on the census blockgroup layer in order to transfer those area properties to the cells. These properties become our state variables. The offenders are modeled as intelligent agents in the simulation through vector points, because they are able to move around based on the choices they make. Unlike most of the simulation models that generate random offenders, we use the actual offenders from the Dallas Police records as our agents. The offenders are sorted based on the time and date of offenses so that we can simulate the residential burglaries across the full calendar year and compare the outputs from the model to that of the actual offenses that occurred in 2000.

The neighborhood template is often modeled in the literature as one of the two standard neighborhood types, the "Moore" neighborhood and "von Neumann" neighborhood (Benenson & Torrens, 2005). The template that we choose for our model can be extended as large as the whole blockgroup, because our offenders now can move at any distance and in any direction due to the flexibility provided by vector based MAS.

The primary variable to be simulated is the distance that a burglar is willing to travel, determined by the likelihood of such crime in a location, which is a function of motivation, target desirability and place guardianship. Currently, the distance the offender is willing to travel to commit the residential burglary is modeled as the Euclidean distance to the offender's home address. In our future studies, we will improve this model by adopting street network distance.

Motivation

Burglary is more often committed within a certain distance from the criminal's home because the offender does not want to be recognized in the offender's own neighborhood (Brantingham & Brantingham, 1993, Costello & Wiles, 2001; Ratcliffe, 2001; Snook, 2004; Rengert et al., 1999). Previous studies have assigned a threshold distance within which no burglary crime will happen. This treatment runs into a risk that would completely exclude offenses inside the offender's own community, which happens, although not so frequently. The motivation is usually increased with the distance within a certain range, after that willingness to travel further becomes diminished with the distance. Therefore, we chose use a Gaussian function to model the offender's motivation as a function of distance from his home address. For each offender, this Gaussian function can be parameterized based on the burglar's personal characteristics, which include race, age and gender of the offender. To obtain these parameters, we performed descriptive statistics on the Dallas Police data to derive the mean and standard deviation for each age, race and gender group (Table 1).

According to the statistics in Table 1, whites travel the longest of the three races. Blacks travel shorter distances than whites, as may be anticipated by social disorganization theory. Social disorganizationists, and others, have found that African Americans have historically found themselves to be the most segregated of the races (Sampson & Wilson, 1995). Research suggests that races will stay within their own comfort zone or in mixed race neighborhoods. Thus, the distance to travel for African Americans will be altered by the neighborhood patterns of racial differences in Dallas, TEXAS. On the other hand, Hispanics have typically integrated into wider parts of the Dallas area, which may be reflected in their travel distance. Hispanics travel the shortest distances to residential burglaries compared to their counterparts in the other two race categories.

Offenders between the ages of 35-40 (N= 18) travel the furthest with the second furthest traveling offenders being between the ages of 25-30 (N= 16). This first group of individuals is more likely to belong to the professional burglar status. The most active age group was the most youthful age group (N=48), however, they traveled the second fewest miles to commit their offenses. Thus, our statistics in Table 1 finds some support that suggests that age is positively correlated with mobility (Canter & Gregory, 1994; Costello & Wiles, 2001; Gabor & Gottheil, 1984; Phillips, 1980; Turner, 1969; Tita & Griffiths, 2005; Warren et al., 1998). We see two separate peaks in our data.

Within the Dallas database, females traveled further than their male counterparts (Table 1). Females traveled an average distance of 5.49 miles. Males traveled the average distance of 2.49 miles. As noted above, this may be due to the physical differences in the genders to cope with barrier (i.e., tall privacy fences in Dallas).

Desirability

In this study, desirability of the target is determined by the income and race composition data of the community it resides, due to the lack of individual level information for the target. Offenders often select targets that have a higher income level than their own and they usually avoid impoverished areas which would not have much to steal. However, this is not always the case, because occasionally offenders may select targets within their own income bracket or even lower (albeit rare). Additionally, in some locations, high income residences may be unavailable to offender because they may be within gated communities, have security guards and/or alarm systems. While the higher the income of the targets, the more desirable in general, a simple linear function is not appropriate for our model.

We used Gaussian function again to model the relationship between desirability and the income level based on the statistics obtained from Dallas census blockgroup data (Table 1). In this way, both very low and very high median household incomes would have a low desirability while medium and medium high household incomes would have a high desirability.

Generally speaking, we know that black neighborhoods are disproportionately segregated and concentrated in various zones in cities. This follows along the lines of SD theory and the notions of the "American Apartheid" (Wilson, 1987; Sampson & Wilson, 1987). In the case of Dallas, Texas, large African American communities are segregated in the South quadrant of the city. Thus, the very distribution of the neighborhoods within the city impact the offender, as we know that offenders prefer to offend within their comfort zone (within race or within a mixed race neighborhood). For example, white offenders prefer white dominant area first, and then mixed or Hispanic zone, with the least preference in a black dominant neighborhood. In order to determine a neighborhood's desirability based on race, the census statistics for the percentage of population that is white, black, and Hispanic are combined and weighted in such a fashion as to reflect an offender's general tendency to stay in a neighborhood of similar racial diversity as his own (Table 1). For whites, the desirability for target is,

$$P_w = 0.6 \times \%white + 0.3 \times \%Hispanic + 0.1 \times \%black$$

Similar formulas are used for both African Americans and Hispanics as seen in Table 1.

Guardianship

Offenders often select communities that lack of guardianship to commit burglary crimes. The lack of guardianship in this study is defined by mean commute time and mean residential tenure (% of less than 5 years' tenure). In general, the longer the commute time of neighborhood residents and the higher the percentage of new comers to the community, the higher degree the lack of guardianship. After several experiments, both variables that are used to measure lack of guardianship are transformed from raw blockgroup census data into normally-distributed values using a power transformation (Table 1). The output are then rescaled to the range from 0 (meaning very low degree of lack of guardianship), to 1 (indicating extremely high degree lack of guardianship).

Likelihood

Our study extends previous work by Eck (1995) and Liu, Wang, Eck, and Liang (2005), We have theoretically focused on the property crime of residential burglary by imitating the relationship between the offender's motivation, the target's desirability, and the place's guardianship. The interaction of these three elements determines the likelihood of a residential burglary, which is defined by a two levels of weighted linear combinations, with the weights customizable and summing up to 1. First, the likelihood of a burglary crime is a weighted linear combination of the offender's motivation, the target's desirability and the place's degree of lack of guardianship.

$$L_{tij} = w_m \cdot M_{tj} + w_d \cdot D_{ti} + w_{lg} \cdot LG_{ti}$$

L is the likelihood for residential burglary committed at time t, at place (and target) i, by offender j. M stands for the offender's motivation, D is the target's desirability and LG denotes the degree of lack of guardianship for the place. w_m, w_d and w_{lg} are the weights for motivation, desirability and lack of guardianship, respectively. At the second level, motivation is a weighted linear combination of those defined by age (M_{tja}), race (M_{tjr}) and gender (M_{tjg}), with w_a, w_r and w_g are the corresponding weights for age, race and gender, respectively,

$$M_{tij} = w_a \cdot M_{tja} + w_r \cdot M_{tjr} + w_g \cdot M_{tjg}$$

Desirability is a weighted linear combination of those defined by income (D_{tic}) and race composition (D_{tie}) of the target community with their corresponding weights being w_c and w_e respectively.

$$D_{ti} = w_c \cdot D_{tic} + w_e \cdot D_{tie}$$

Lack of guardianship is a weighted combination of those defined by commute time (LG_{tiu}) and % of less than 5 years' tenure (LG_{tin}) with their corresponding weights being w_u and w_n respectively.

$$LG_{ti} = w_u \cdot LG_{tiu} + w_n \cdot LG_{tin}$$

Target Selection

Based on the two levels of weighted linear combinations, a likelihood surface is generated, covering the whole study area for each individual offender. A random surface is then produced programmatically for the offender and compared with the offender's likelihood surface. If the likelihood is greater than the random value at that location, the location will be selected as a potential target. In our one year database, there is only one offense committed by a unique offender. Therefore, the model chooses the location with the highest

Table 1. Model parameters derived from the statistics of Dallas, TX Crime Data

Components	Properties	Representation	Weights	2nd Scenario
Offender: Motivation	Race	Average distance (and standard deviation) in miles: • Whites: 3.23 (3.0065) • Blacks: 2.96 (4.4130) • Hispanic: 1.87 (3.6456)	33.3%	40%
	Age	Average distance (and standard deviation) in miles: • 16-20: 2.13 (3.47) • 20-25: 3.51 (5.09) • 25-30: 3.32 (4.70) • 30-35: 1.07 (1.44) • 35-40: 3.83 (4.39) • 40+: 2.19 (2.12)	33.3%	
	Gender	Average distance (and standard deviation) in miles: • Males: 2.49 (3.74) • Females: 5.49 (6.03)	33.3%	
Target: Desirability	Income	Average income (and standard deviation) in dollars: • Income : 46,413 (32049)	33.3%	30%
	Race composition	• For white $P_w = 0.6 \times \%white + 0.3 \times \%Hispanic + 0.1 \times \%black$ • For black $P_b = 0.1 \times \%white + 0.3 \times \%Hispanic + 0.6 \times \%black$ • For a Hispanic $P_h = 0.2 \times \%white + 0.6 \times \%Hispanic + 0.2 \times \%black$	66.7%	
Place: Lack of Guardianship	Length of tenure	$(Y^{0.5} - 1)/0.5$ This result is then rescaled to fall between 0-1	50%	30%
	Commute Time	$(Y^{0.4} - 1)/0.4$ This result is then rescaled to fall between 0-1	50%	

likelihood among the selected ones as the final target for the burglar. Then the model moves to the burglar that was caught next in time sequence from the temporally sorted database.

For the simulation of each subsequent burglar, if there are offenses within a neighborhood in the past 60 days, a multiplier will be derived to decrease the combined degree of the lack of guardianship (or increase of guardianship). However, unlike Liu's work, we do increase the motivation of the offenders because our one year dataset does not contain uncaught (or unsolved) offenders. There are also no updates on the target desirability, due to fact that the major variables determining desirability (income and race composition) do not change often in a short period of time.

RESULTS AND DISCUSSION

The model that we developed to simulate burglary crimes embraced both social disorganization and routine activity theories. The information related to the motivation of the offenses (i.e. age, race and gender) is available at the individual level, which is usually what the routine activity theory attempting to examine. The variables used to derive target desirability and lack of guardianship of place (i.e. income, race composition, commute time, and % of less than 5 years tenure) are only available at the neighborhood level, which is primarily what we are limited to using in order to gather information on the impact of various measures of social disorganization.

To test how much these two theories contribute to the explanation of journey to burglary crime in Dallas, we configured the model with two different weights. For the first scenario, we assume equal importance of all variable and assign equal weights to factors at both levels. This means, at the first level, motivation, desirability and lack of guardianship are equally weighted with a 33.3% influence for each. At the second level, each element of the first level factor is also

Figure 1. The distribution of actual burglary offenses (targets) in Dallas, TX (2000)

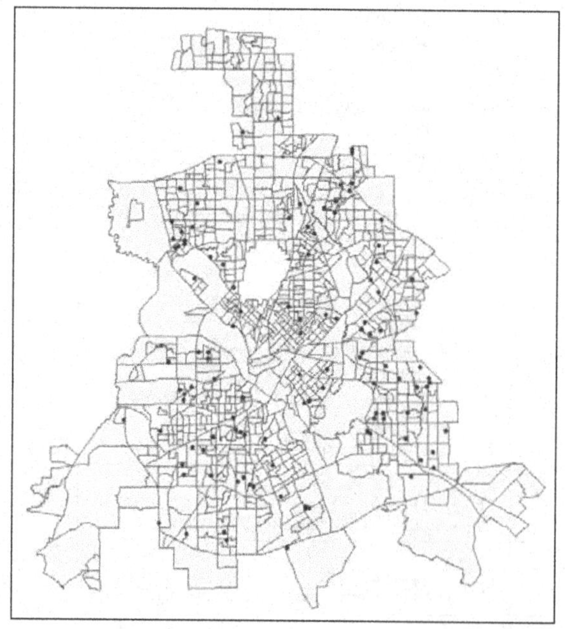

treated the same. For example, for motivation, age, race and gender of the offender are associated with a 33.3% weight each, while for desirability, income and race composition each receive a 50% weight. Figure 1 displays the actual distribution of all the burglary targets and Figure 2 shows the results of the model simulation with equal weights at both levels. This modeled result appears to be noticeably clustered, while the actual distribution of targets is more spread out. This is likely due to the fact that with equal weighted scenario, the factors related to social disorganization theory are more emphasized. Two of the first level factors and four of the second level factors are neighborhood level variables, which causes an over-clustering of predicted targets at certain census block groups.

In the second scenario, we modified the weights so that some of the factors are of unequal importance at different levels (Table 1). At the first level, we assign a weight of 0.4 for offender motivation to increase the influence of routine activity theory, while giving both target desirability and lack of guardianship a lower weight of 30%. At the second level, for target desirability, we downplay the influence of income factor (33.3%) compared to race composition (66.7%). Figure 3 shows the results of this second scenario. As a consequence of the modified weights, it is observed that the amount of clustering seen in the equal-weights model is greatly reduced. The modeled distribution of offenses appear to be more spread out, much closer to that of actual data, which suggests that the routine activity theory may better explain the distribution of burglary crimes than social disorganization theory, although both are regarded necessary and considered in this model. For future study, we will develop an automatic model calibration approach to derive an optimal weight configuration to achieve a prediction that is closest to the actual data.

Figure 2. The distribution of burglary offenses (targets) by an equally weighted simulation model

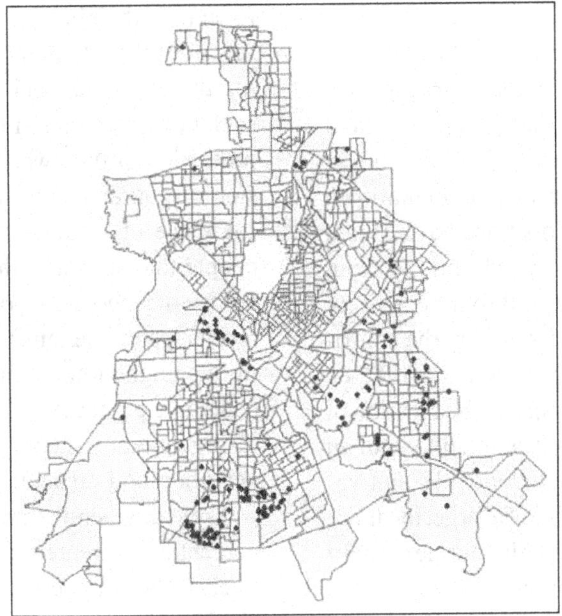

Figure 3. The distribution of burglary offenses (targets) by an unequally weighted simulation model

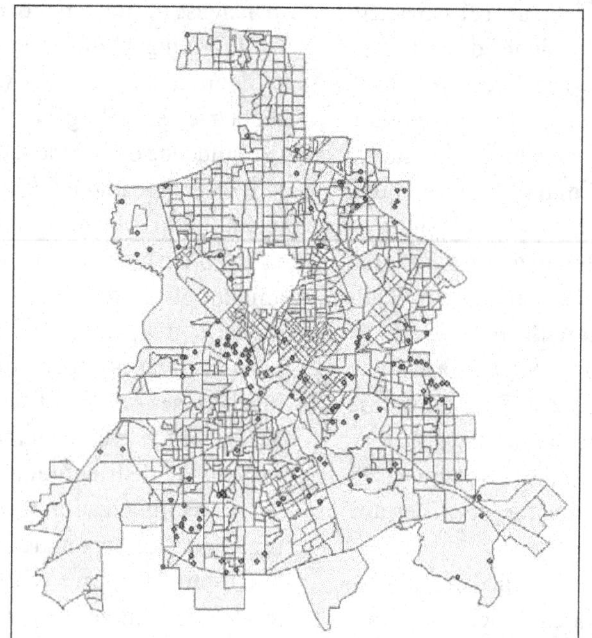

CONCLUSION AND FUTURE RESEARCH

The complex social fabric that encompasses neighborhood phenomena, including residential burglary, is difficult to explain with a linear formula and linear theoretical explanations. Different from previous works, we have used a multifaceted theoretical approach pulling from both social disorganization and routine activity theory. Routine activity theory offers the contributions of understanding the person that offends (i.e., the motivated offenders), and the location of the offense (i.e., the target). The likelihood of an offense is a function of the individual's motivation and individual preference of a target location, both of which are key concepts in routine activity theory. Social disorganization helps to explain the guardianship for residential burglary better for residential burglary. The very definition of burglary denotes the lack of human inhabitants in the dwelling during the course of the crime (or at least their being unaware of another person invading their home). However, when examining the place manager of a residential burglary, social disorganization theory would explain the protection of the dwelling regarding the expansion of guardianship into the larger geographical space of a "neighborhood." This pocket of people that surround the house can offer an effective management strategy by being long-term residents that are familiar with those that belong in the neighborhood and those that do not (i.e., collective efficacy). Further, according to social disorganization theory, the effectiveness of this neighborhood structure, the place manager, is weakened, when the neighborhood has a higher percentage of renters and individuals are more likely to be strangers to one another.

Our chapter provides a unique insight into the application of simulation modeling into property crimes, such as residential burglary, by integrating the traditional CA model with an innovative MAS. As such, our line of research extends previous work by Eck (1995) and Liu, Wang, and Eck (2005) through the discussion of a very different formulation of a state variable—the journey to crime. We have applied a dynamic system similar to that described by Liu, Wang, and Eck (2005), however we have theoretically focused on the property crime of residential burglary. We model our offenders, targets, and places as artificial agents and automata, which imitate what we propose above to be the relationship between these three elements.

Our model provided several advancements. First, we utilized "real" data to configure our model parameters and the initial states of the automata with statistics obtained from the Dallas, TEXAS Police Department. This data driven nature of our model freed us from the restriction of random placement and general validation modeling. Second, in addition to model configuration, our model simulates true offenders as intelligent agents, so that year-round crime activities in Dallas, Texas can be modeled. Again, we were able to avoid general randomization in most simulation studies, which made our model results more comparable to the actual offense data. Third, we were able to assign unequal importance to the various factors that were utilized to simulate burglary likelihood (e.g., offender motivation, guardianship, etc.). This allowed us to test the model to determine which factors were acting more 'strongly' in the activity pattern of the offender agent. As a result, we were able to evaluate the different contributions made by SD and RA theory components.

We are limited, in that we cannot address an offender's "awareness space" (Brantingham & Brantingham, 1991). Our only alternative would be to place our offenders randomly on the grid, and we do not feel that this would provide a quality model. We simply do not have that level of data available at this time. We also imagine that our findings would only be generalized to American, and perhaps Canadian, cities due to the theoretical approaches that we have chosen to present. Future research may want to test these models in other parts of the country and world. Future researchers may also enhance our modeling by adding information on the amount of goods stolen from each actual residential burglary.

REFERENCES

Alonso, J., Fernandez, A., & Fort, H. (2006). Prisoner's dilemma cellular automata revisited: Evolution of cooperation under environmental pressure. *Journal of Statistical Mechanics: Theory and Experiment, P06013*, 1-15.

Barredo, J. I., Kasanko, M., McCormick, N., & Lavalle, C. (2003). Modelling dynamic spatial processes: Simulation of urban future scenarios through cellular automata. *Landscape and Urban Planning, 64*, 145-160.

Batty, M. (2005). Agents, cells, and cities: New representational models for simulating multiscale urban dynamics. *Environment and Planning A, 37*, 1373-1394.

Batty, M., Desyllas, J., & Duxbury, E. (2003). Safety in numbers? Modelling crowds and designing control for the Notting Hill carnival. *Urban Studies, 40*, 1573-1590.

Batty, M., Xie, Y., & Sun, Z. (1999). Modeling urban dynamics through GIS-based cellular automata. *Computers, Environment and Urban Systems, 23*, 205-233.

Benenson, I. & Torrens, P.M. (2005). *Geosimulation: Automata-based modeling of urban phenomena.* London: John Wiley & Sons.

Blue, V. J., & Adler, J. L. (2001). Cellular automata microsimulation for modeling bi-directional pedestrian walkways. *Transportation Research Part B, 35*, 293-312.

Boggs, S. L. (1965). Urban crime patterns. *American Sociological Review, 30*, 899-908.

Brahan, J. W., Lam, K. P., Chan, H., & Leung, W. (1998). AICAMS: artificial intelligence crime analysis and management system. *Knowledge-Based Systems, 11*, 355-361.

Brantingham, P.J. & Brantingham P. L. (1991). *Environmental Criminology.* (2nd Ed.) Prospect Heights, IL: Waveland Press.

Bursik, R. J., & Grasmick, H. G. (1993). *Neighborhoods and crime.* San Francisco: Lexington Books.

Byrne, J. M., & Sampson, R. J. (1986). *The social ecology of crime.* New York: Srpinger-Verlag.

Canter, & Gregory. (1994). Identifying the residential location of rapists. *Journal of Forensic Science, 34*, 169-175.

Canter, & Larkin. (1993). The environmental range of serial rapists. *Journal of Environmental Psychology, 13*, 64-70.

Carter, R. L. (1979). *The criminal's image of the city.* New York: Pergamon Press.

Clarke, K. C., & Gaydos, L. (1998). Loose-coupling a cellular automaton model and GIS: Long-term urban growth prediction for San Francisco and Washington/Baltimore. *International Journal of Geographical Information Science, 12*, 699-714.

Cohen, L. E., & Felson, M. (1979). Social change and crime rate trends: A routine activity approach. *American Sociological Review, 44*, 588-608.

Costello, A. & Wiles, P. (2001). GIS and the journey to crime: An analysis of patterns in South Yorkshire. In A. Hirschfield & K. Bowers (Eds.), *Mapping and analysing crime data: Lessons from research and practice* (pp. 27-60). London: Taylor and Francis.

Couclelis, H. (1985). Cellular worlds: A framework for modeling micro-macro dynamics. *Environment and Planning A, 17*, 585-596.

Couclelis, H. (1988). Of mice and men: What rodent populations can teach us about complex spatial dynamics. *Environment and Planning A, 20*, 99-109.

Couclelis, H. (1989). Macrostructure and microbehavior in a metropolitan area. *Environment and Planning B, 16*, 141-154.

DeFrances, C. J., & Smith, S. K. (1994). *Crime and neighborhoods.*

Eck, J. E. (1994). Examining routine activites theory: A review of two books. *Justice Quarterly, 12,* 783-797.

Franklin, S., & Graesser, A. (1996) Is it an agent, or just a program?: A taxonomy of autonomous agents. Intelligent Agents III: In *Proceedings of the Third International Workshop on Agent Theories, Architectures, and Languages*, (ATAL'96), Lecture Notes in AI, Third International Workshop on Agent Theories, Architectures, and Languages, (ATAL'96), Springer-Verlag.

Goodchild, M. F. (2003) Geographic information science and systems for environmental management. *Annual Review of Environmental Resources, 28*, 493-519.

Gottheil, E., & Gabor, T. (1984). Offender characteristics and spatial mobility. *Canadian Journal of Criminology, 26*, 267-281.

Green, D., Tridgell, A., & Malcom, G. A. (1990) Interactive simulation of bushfires in heterogeneous fuels. *Mathematical Computation and Modelling, 13*, 57-66.

Hawley, A. (1950). *Human ecology.* New York: Ronald Press Co.

Hesseling, R. B. P. (1992). Using data on offender mobility in ecological research. *Journal of Quantitative Criminology, 8*, 95-112.

Hogeweg, P., (1988) Cellular automata as a paradigm for ecological modeling. *Applied Mathematics and Computation, 27*, 81-100.

Hunter, A. J. (1985). Private, parochial, and public social orders: The problem of crime and incivility in urban communities. In G. D. Suttles & M. N. Zald (Eds.), *The challenge of social control: Citizenship and institution building in modern society* (pp. 230-242). Norwood, NJ: Ablex Publishing.

Liu, L., Wang, X., Eck, J., & Liang, J. (2005). Simulating crime events and crime patterns in a RA/CA model. In F. Wang (Ed.), *Geographic information systems and crime analysis* (pp. 197-213). Hershey, PA: Idea Group Publishing.

Messner, S. F., & Tardiff, K. (1986). *The social ecology of urban homicide: An application of the 'Routine activities approach. Criminology, 22*, 241-67.

Morenoff, J. D., & Sampson, R. J. (1997). Violent crime and the spatial dynamics of neighborhood transition: Chicago, 1970-1990. *Social Forces, 76*, 31-64.

Phipps, M. (1989). Dynamical behavior of cellular automata under constraints of neighborhood coherence. *Geographical Analysis, 21*, 197-215.

Phillips, P. D. (1980). Characteristics and typology of the journey to crime. In D. E. Georges-Abeyie & K. D. Harries (Eds.), *Crime: A spatial perspective* (pp. 167-180). New York: Columbia University Press.

Pyle, G. F. (1976). Spatial and temporal aspects of crime in Cleveland, Ohio. *American Behavioral Scientist, 20*, 175-198.

Rand, A. (1986). Mobility triangles. In R. M. Figlio, S. Hakim, & G. F. Rengert (Eds.), *Metropolitan crime patterns.* Monsey, NY: Criminal Justice Press.

Ratcliffe, J. H. (2001). Policing urban burglary. *Trends and issues in crime and criminal justice (No. 213).* Canberra: Australian Institute of Criminology.

Rengert, G. F. (1981). Burglary in Philadelphia: A critique of opportunity structure model. In P. Brantingham & P. Brantingham (Eds.), *Environmental criminology* (pp.167-188). Beverly Hills, CA: Sage Publications.

Rengert, G., Piquero, A. R., & Jones, P. R. (1999). Distance decay reexamined. *Criminology, 37*, 427-445.

Reppetto, T. A. (1974). *Residential crime.* Cambridge: Ballinger.

Rhodes, W. M., & Conley, C. (1981). Crime and mobility: An empirical study. In P. J. Brantingham & P. L. Brantingham (Eds.), *Environmental criminology.* Beverley Hills, CA: Sage Publications.

Sampson, R. J. (1985). Neighborhood and crime: The structural determinants of personal victimization. *Journal of Research in Crime and Delinquency, 22*, 7-40.

Sampson, R. J. (1987). Does an intact family reduce burglary risk for its neighbors? *Sociology and Social Research, 71*, 204-207.

Sampson, R. J., & Groves, W. B. (1989). Community structure and crime: Testing social-disorganization theory. *American Journal of Sociology, 94*, 774-802.

Sampson, R. J., & Wilson, W. J. (1995). Race, crime and urban inequality. In J. Hagan & R.D. Peterson (Eds.), *Crime and inequlity* (pp. 37-54), Stanford University Press.

Shaw, C. R., & McKay, H. D. (1942). Juvenile Delinquency and Urban Areas. Chicago, IL: University of Chicago Press.

Skogan, W. (1990). *Disorder and Decline: Crime and the Spiral of Decay in American Neighborhoods.* New York: The Free Press.

Smith, R., 1991, The application of cellular automata to the erosion of landscapes. *Earth Surface Processes and Landforms, 16*, 273-281.

Smith, S. K., & DeFrances, C. J. (1994). *Crime and Neighborhoods.*

Snook, B. (2004). Individual differences in distance traveled by serial burglars. *Journal of Investigative Psychology and Offender Profiling, 1*, 53-66.

Takeyama, M., & Couclelis, H. (1997). Map dynamics: Integrating cellular automata and GIS through Geo-Algebra. *International Journal of Geographical Information Science, 11*, 73-91.

Taylor, R. B. (1997). Social order and disorder of street blocks and neighborhoods: Ecology, microecology, and the systemic model of social disorganization. *Journal of Research in Crime and Delinquency, 34*(1), 113-155.

Terna, P. (1998) Simulation tools for social scientists: Building agent based models with SWARM. *Journal of Artificial Societies and Social Simulation.*

Tita & Griffiths. (2005). Traveling to violence: The case for a mobility-based spatial typology of homicide. *Journal of Research in Crime and Delinquency, 42*, 275-308.

Torrens, P. (2006). Simulating sprawl. *Annals of the Association of American Geographers, 96*, 248-275.

Turner, S. (1969). Delinquency and distance. In J. T. Sellin & M. E. Wolfgang (Eds.), *Delinquency: selected studies*. New York: Wiley.

Vold, G. B., Bernard, T. J., & Snipes, J. B. (1998). *Theoretical criminology* (4th ed.). New York: Oxford University Press.

von Neumann, J. (1949) Theory and organization of complicated automata. In A. W. Burks (Ed.), *Theory of self-reproducing automata (Part One)* (pp. 29-87). Urbana: University of Illinois Press.

Wahle, J., Neubert, L., Esser, J., & Schreckenberg, M. (2001) A cellular automaton traffic flow model for online simulation of traffic. *Parallel Computing, 27*, 719-735.

Warner, B. D., & Pierce, G. L. (1993). Reexamining social disorganization theory using calls to the police as a measure of crime. *Criminology, 31*(4), 493-517.

Warren, J., Reboussin, R., Hazelwood, R. R., Cummings, A., Gibbs, N., & Trumbetta, S. (1998). Crime scene and distance correlates of serial rape. *Journal of Quantitative Criminology, 14*, 35-59.

White, C. R. (1932). The relation of felonies to environmental factors in Indianapolis. *Social Forces, 10*, 498-509.

White, R., & Engelen, G. (1992). *Cellular dynamics and GIS: Modelling spatial complexity*. Working Paper 9264, Research Institute for Knowledge Systems, Maastricht, The Netherlands.

Wilson, W. J. (1987). *The truly disadvantaged: The inner city, the underclass, and public policy.* Chicago: University of Chicago Press.

Winoto, P. (2002). A simulation of the market for offenses in multiagent systems: Is zero crime rates attainable? In *Proceedings of the Multi-Agent-Based Simulation, Third International Workshop*, Bologna, Italy.

Wolfram, S. (1986). *Theory and applications of cellular automata*. Singapore: World Scientific.

Wright, R., & Decker, S. H. (1994). Choosing the target. *Burglars on the job: Streetlife and residential break-ins*. Boston: Northeastern University Press.

Wu, F. (1999). GIS-based simulation as an exploratory analysis for space-time processes. *Journal of Geographical Systems, 1*, 199-218.

ADDITIONAL READINGS

Brantingham, P. J., & Brantingham, P.L. (1981). Environmental criminology. Beverly Hills, CA: Sage Publications,.

Liang, J. (2001). *Simulating crimes and crime patterns using cellular automata and GIS*. Department of Geography. University of Cincinnati.

Rengert, G. (1989). Spatial justice and criminal victimization. *Justice Quarterly, 6*, 543-564.

Rengert, G. F. (1992). The journey to crime. In N. R. Fyfe, D. J. Evans, & D. T. Herbert (Eds.), *Crime, policing and place: Essays in environmental criminology*. London: Routledge.

Rengert, G. F., & Wasilchick, J. (2000). *Suburban burglary: A tale of two suburbs* (2nd ed.). Springfield, IL: Charles C. Thomas.

Takeyama, M. & Coucelis, H. (1997). Map dynamics: Integrating cellular automata and GIS through Geo-Algebra. *International Journal of Information Science, 11*(1), 73-91.

Wu, F. (1998). GIS-based simulation as an exploratory analysis for space-time processes. *Journal of Geographic Systems, 1*, 199-218.

ENDNOTE

1 By assigning the individual residence the average SES of the blockgroup, we are breeching into a form of ecological fallacy. However, due to data constraints, this is the best measure that we have of the residence's inner contents which the burglar would be interested in stealing.

Chapter XV
Simulating Crime Against Properties Using Swarm Intelligence and Social Networks

Vasco Furtado
University of Fortaleza, Brazil

Adriano Melo
University of Fortaleza, Brazil

André L.V. Coelho
University of Fortaleza, Brazil

Ronaldo Menezes
Florida Institute of Technology, USA

Mairon Belchior
University of Fortaleza, Brazil

ABSTRACT

Experience in the domain of criminology has shown that the spatial distribution of some types of crimes in urban centers follows Zipf's Law in which most of the crime events are concentrated in a few places while other places have few crimes. Moreover, the temporal distribution of these crime events follows an exponential law. In order to reproduce and better understand the nuances of such crime distribution profile, we introduce in this chapter a novel multi-agent-based crime simulation model that is directly inspired by the swarm intelligence paradigm. In this model, criminals are regarded as agents endowed with the capability to pursue self-organizing behavior by considering their individual (local) activities as well as the influence of other criminals pertaining to their social networks. Through controlled experiments with the simulation model, we could indeed observe that self-organization phenomena (i.e., criminal behavior toward crime) emerge as the result of both individual and social learning factors. As expected, our experiments reveal that the spatial distribution of crime occurrences achieved with the simulation model provides a good approximation of the real-crime data distribution. A detailed analysis of the social aspect is also conducted here as this factor is shown to be instrumental for the accurate reproduction of the spatial pattern of crime occurrences.

INTRODUCTION

Recently, an extensive analysis conducted over real-crime data related to a large Brazilian metropolis (Cansado, 2005) has demonstrated that the spatial distribution of crimes as robbery, thefts, and burglaries follows a power law, specifically the Zipf's one (Zipf, 1949). This means that the frequency of crime occurrences per type of an attacked geographic area tends to scale according to the following rule: The number of crime occurrences at the most frequently attacked area would be roughly n times higher than the number of crime occurrences at the nth most frequently attacked area, which, in turn, would be n times higher than that of the n^2th most frequently attacked area, and so on. In the same work (Cansado, 2005) an analysis of the temporal aspect shows that these crimes follow an exponential distribution per period of analysis.

Although knowing the crime distribution profile for a given moment may be necessary for the better conduction of some police decision-making activities, it is not enough to help one gain further insights into crime in its totality. Crime is a dynamic process, and the decision of protecting a frequently attacked target in a moment will eventually lead to the exposure of other potential targets in the periods that follow due to a range of limitations in terms of resources availability (e.g., human resources).

In this sense, we advocate that a better understanding of the trends of crime activities as well as of the types of reactions criminals might potentially undertake is a crucial task to be pursued. In this context, the goal of the research we are conducting is to produce a crime simulation system that reproduces crime phenomena as realistically as possible.

In this chapter, we give one step in the direction of the aforementioned goal by introducing a dynamic model of crime against properties that evidences experimentally how this type of crime evolves spatially and in time. The main challenge behind this effort lies in the definition of a simulation model that could generate crimes according to a spatial Zipfian distribution, and at the same time be in agreement with the results brought forth by sociological and criminological studies on crime. For such a purpose, we have designed a multi-agent-based criminal model that mimics real-life criminal behavior (with respect to sociological studies), taking into account the following facts: (1) criminals improve their performance through time by creating preferences according to their experience in crime; and (2) social communication between criminals must also be properly modeled because criminal behavior depends not only on individual incentives but also on the behavior of their peers and neighbors (Sutherland, 1947), (Akers, Krohn, Lanza-Kaduce, & Radosevich,1979).

This criminal model resorts to concepts related to self-organizing systems inspired by the ant colony optimization algorithm (Bonabeau, 1999). The rationale behind this choice is also twofold. These systems account for both the individual and social aspects that we intend to consider in our crime simulation model, and, at the same time, as we have identified experimentally, their formal model is capable of generating spatial/temporal behaviors of a power-law nature. By this means, criminals are regarded as agents endowed with the capability to pursue self-organized behavior by considering their individual (local) activities as well as the influence of other criminals in the community they live in.

Through controlled experiments with the simulation model, we could have indeed observed that self-organization (i.e., criminal behavior toward crime) emerges as the result of both individual learning and social interaction factors. At the same time, our experiments have revealed that the simulation provide a good match between the spatial distribution of crime and the actual data of crime distribution concerning a large Brazilian urban center named Fortaleza. To better understand why this prediction could be possible, we provide an analysis of the social aspect. By comparing the results produced from simulations in which criminals interact through different social network topologies against those in which there is no social interaction, we show that the social aspect is a major factor for generating crimes that follow Zipf's Law.

The remainder of the chapter is structured as follows: Initially, we describe related work that has offered the theoretical basis upon which we have constructed and calibrated our crime simulation model, and then we focus on the characterization of the current version of the model. We pay special attention to the description of the criminal learning behavior. The results come in the sequence and reveal how the crime distribution generated from the simulation model is closely related to the real data, and how important the social factor is in this process. We conclude by describing the relevance of these findings, and our future work.

BACKGROUND KNOWLEDGE

In this section, we briefly touch upon some important concepts coming from related areas of research that are associated with our crime simulation model.

Multi-Agent Simulation

Multi-agent systems (MAS) primarily study the behavior of autonomous and organized groups of agents with the purpose of providing distributed, emergent solutions to complex problems that could not be achieved by each individual agent alone. Conversely, the deployment of simulations for the purpose of gaining insights along a given decision-making process can be a very effective approach one could resort to, as computer simulations usually allow the focused analysis of important issues by investigating their influences either separately or conjointly.

Multi-agent systems have been successfully adopted in conjunction with simulation models as the inherent characteristics of the former (e.g., agent autonomy, reactivity, and pro-activity) facilitate the constructing and simulating more realistic and dynamic models, thus contrasting directly with conventional computer simulation approaches. The outcome is generally referred to by multi-agent-based simulation (MABS) systems, which, according to (Gilbert & Conte, 1995), are especially appropriate when one has to deal with very interdisciplinary problem domains (like the public-safety one investigated here). We suggest that the multi-agent approach (bottom-up in nature) is appropriate for the study of social and urban problems, since social or urban environments are dynamic, nonlinear, and composed of a great number of variables and entities. As pointed out by (Drogoul & Ferber, 1992), the main objectives behind the construction of MABS systems are the following:

- To test hypothesis related to the emergence of macro-level behavior from interactions occurring at micro levels.
- To build theories that can contribute to a better understanding of sociological, psychological, and ethological phenomena.
- To integrate partial theories coming from different disciplines (e.g., sociology, cogni-

tive psychology, and ethology) in a common theoretical framework.

Swarm Intelligence

The study of agent self-organization and related concepts such as emergence is responsible for a major revival within intelligent systems. The basic idea is that societies of agents demonstrate intelligent behavior at the collective level out of simple rules at the individual level. Moreover, these individual rules often do not explain the behavior that is attained at the collective level. Swarm intelligence is characterized (1) by strictly local communication; (2) by the formation of emergent spatial-temporal structures; and (3) by the agent's taking stochastic decisions based solely on the local information available. One of the branches of swarm intelligence is ant-colony optimization (ACO), proposed by Bonabeau (Bonabeau et al, 1999). ACO is a meta-heuristic model for solving combinatorial problems that can be represented as graphs. ACO gets inspiration from other areas of science; in this case informed by biological sciences. From the start, it became clear that ACO had many strengths when compared to other meta-heuristics. One of the strengths is the ability to adapt to dynamic settings.

In a nutshell, ACO works by allowing agents (ants) to explore a search space, but it requires these ants to leave feedback information about locations with good solutions on the space itself. Agents are then attracted by the feedback left in the environment—the larger the amount of information (pheromone), the more attractive the agents find the position in the environment. In order to avoid early convergence to local optima, the approach assumes that the information left is volatile and impermanent—if no other activity occurs, a piece of information left in the environment "expires" or disappears over a certain period of time.

Although never explored as a model for criminal behavior, ACO's characteristics appeared from the start to be an ideal fit to our purposes. As we will discuss later, the distribution of crime generated by our ACO simulation model follows a power law distribution, more specifically a Zipfian distribution.

We investigate two variations of this learning: with and without a social factor. The former assumes criminal agents who are part of the same community and share their knowledge about crime targets with other criminals. The latter considers learning using only the aforementioned ACO-inspired approach.

Social Networks

In order to be part of a society, it is imperative for an individual to establish social links with other peers. However, the way an individual relates to others may vary significantly in accordance with a range of aspects, such as the level of acquaintance, the regularity of interaction, the physical coexistence, and the sharing of interests. Moreover, different forms of interaction among the same individuals, even considering small groups, may take place simultaneously, and may vary in different paces through time. One usual means to represent and analyze the (evolving) social structure underlying an organization of individuals is by resorting to the concept of social networks (Scott, 2000).

Roughly speaking, a social network alludes to any formal, graph-based structure where target individuals (agents) are represented by nodes and the prominent social relationships that unite them are represented by links (ties) between those nodes. The shape (topology) of a social network is an important issue to be considered in its analysis as it helps to determine the network's usefulness (from the viewpoint of the individuals that participate in the network). For example, the number of direct connections that a node has (that is, its degree) gives an indication of its level of activity (importance or influence) in the network. Nodes with high degree numbers in a network are referred to as its hubs. However, to be effective in its activities, a hub should also establish connections to individuals lying outside its immediate cluster (i.e., its clique in the graph). On the other hand, it is known that smaller, tighter, networks can be less useful to their members than networks with numerous loose connections (weak ties) to individuals outside the main network. Such "open" networks, with many weak ties and social connections, are usually more likely to introduce new ideas and opportunities to their members than closed networks with many redundant ties. Through this perspective, a successful individual is one that establishes connections to a variety of networks rather than having many connections within a single network. Individuals that follow such strategy can thus exercise influence on a much broader scale, acting like brokers who bridge two or more networks that are not directly linked.

INDIVIDUAL AND SOCIAL LEARNING IN CRIME

The social interaction and learning aspects that underlie the criminal activities were investigated in Sutherland's seminal work that proposed the differential association theory (Sutherland, 1947), which advocates the notion that interaction with others who are delinquent increases the likelihood of someone becoming and remaining a delinquent. Thus, peers can play a crucial role in the development of values and beliefs favorable to law violation. In this theory, Sutherland elaborates nine postulates, among which three are particularly relevant for our study:

- Criminal behavior is learnable. This means that behavior toward crime is not an inherited trait and is not something to be acquired only by wish.
- Criminal behavior can be especially learned through the interactions one establishes with other persons, typically through a verbal communication process.
- The principal part of the learning of criminal behavior occurs within intimate personal groups.

Recently, different perspectives on the study of crime in human societies have appeared, capitalizing from the theoretical resources made available in the area of social network analysis. Some works have focused on characterizing the impact of social network topologies (*viz.* scale-free and small-world settings) on the development and growth of special types of criminal activities, like those related to narcotics (Kaza, 2005). By other means, (Calvó-Armengol & Zenou, 2004) have studied, through a game-theory stance, how the levels of criminal activity on a given territory are influenced by the competitive-cooperative relationships established by delinquents dwelling within it. The authors concluded that the various equilibria produced by the game, representing different numbers of active criminals and their levels of involvement in criminal activities, are only driven by the geometry of the social links connecting the delinquents. Other researchers, like (Houtzager & Baerveldt, 1999), have verified the influence of social relations on the motivation of young boys to commit petty crimes. Basically, the general conclusions taken from all these studies, which are especially relevant for our purposes, are that criminal behavior depends not only on individual incentives but also on the behavior of their peers and neighbors. In other words, an individual is more likely to commit crimes if his/her peers usually commit crimes.

Finally, another particularly important indication coming from these works is that social network models are a natural way to explain the concentration of crimes per area. Criminal data analyzed from different regions, and even countries, usually reflect the fact that there are huge spatial (but also temporal) variations in the crime rate between different cities and between different regions in a city. In fact, (Glaeser, Sacerdote, & Scheinkman, 1996) have shown that less than 30% of the spatial variation of crime (both inter- and intra-city) can be explained by differences in local attributes. The 70% left can be explained by social interactions, which means that the agents' decisions about crime are somewhat positively correlated. The authors show that the impact of social relations is greater in thefts, burglaries, assaults, and robberies (i.e., crimes against properties) than in homicides.

SIMULATING CRIME AND POLICE PATROL

One of our claims in this chapter is that ant-optimization systems, augmented with social network concepts, comprise an adequate strategy for modeling criminal behavior. There are some reasons that ratify this choice. In general, criminals prefer to commit crime in locations known to be vulnerable, with high payoff, and so forth. In other words, their choice considers their preference and knowledge about the crime points. The link here to ACO is that ants always choose their next location in the environment (where they are going to move to) via a mechanism of preferential attachment. Hence the insect's choice as the basis for our crime model here.

Another interesting characteristic that ACO offers to our purposes is the implicit notion of social relationship. Clearly, we are not referring to social concepts as in humans, but rather concepts intrinsically linked to the idea of the collective. Social characteristics belong to groups and not individuals. Individuals are actors that influence the characteristics of the group but have no mandate to dictate the group behavior by themselves. In ACO, ants perform their local tasks without dictating colony (group) behavior, which is emergent from these combination of all the local activities.

Our model abstracts ants as criminals that make decisions based on: (1) information they learn about the points (pheromone/attractiveness to these points); (2) some static information about the point that could be the distance to the point; and (3) some social information about the point, that is, how other criminals see the points (their attractiveness to the points). We investigate these approaches separately as variations of learning: with and without a social factor. The former assumes criminal agents are part of the same community and share their knowledge about crime targets with other criminals.

For doing this, we have defined, in our simulation model, guardians, targets and criminals. Each of these agents can be defined as a triple of components $Ag = (O, D, R)$. O stands for the ontological aspects of an agent, meaning the definition of its concepts and properties. The component D is in regards to the rules and criteria used by the agent to decide about its next actions or about how its state will change. R defines how the activities the agent must realize should be implemented. These activities are a consequence of the decisions taken by the component D.

The Police Team

There is a set of police teams available, each one associated with a monitoring route passing through some locations of the urban territory being considered. A police patrol route is a set $R_t = \{P_{t1}, P_{t2}, \ldots, P_{tm}\}$ and each P_t member of R_t is a triple $P_t = (T_g, \Delta_t, P)$, where T_g is the target, Δ_t the interval of time the police team stays in the target, and P is the daily period the routes refer to. P can assume one of the following values: morning (6 a.m. to noon), afternoon (noon to 6 p.m.), evening (6 p.m. to midnight), and night (midnight to 6 a.m.). There is no distinction, in terms of skills, between the police officers allotted to the different police teams. Different teams may be associated with different-length routes, which, in turn, can overlap and/or share common points of surveillance.

Targets

The locations to be patrolled are referred to as targets, which can be differentiated with respect to the type of commercial/entertainment establishment they represent (viz. drugstores, banks, gas stations, lottery houses, squares, and stores). Targets are distributed in a geographic area, which, in turn, is represented by a grid of squared cells. Mobile targets are not modeled, since we are initially concentrating our study on crimes against property. Targets have a state of vulnerability that can be either active or inactive. A vulnerable target means that it is perceivable to a criminal. Otherwise, it would not take part in the set of choices of the criminal. Each target has a probability of being vulnerable, which follows the temporal distribution of real crime data for the associated target type. In doing so, we are modeling a control parameter that allows reproducing the pace of crimes per type as it happens in real life. Crime temporal distribution varies on day-time basis. We have modeled this variation in four periods of six hours each, in the same way as for the police teams' patrol shifts mentioned before. For each period and type of target, a value for a configurable parameter, λ, must be determined at the start of the simulation in order to define the pace of occurrence of crimes. For instance, at evening, a drugstore robbery may follow a distribution based on a given value for λ; whereas at daylight periods, the crime temporal distribution might shift, achieving values four times higher for λ. In any simulation tick, at least one target is made vulnerable in accordance with the temporal distribution associated with its type.

Criminals

There is a set of criminals representing the agents that frequently try to commit the crimes. Each criminal is endowed with a limited sight of the environment, measured in terms of grid cells. For instance, with a vision of 1,000 meters, if each cell has 100-meter sides, the radius of the criminal's sight will be 10-square cells around the criminal agent. Criminals have one or more points of departure that we call "gateways". Such points of departure represent places where criminals probably start out, for example, their residences, metro stations, bus stops, and so forth. It is also assumed that, at the end of each day, each criminal always returns back to the initial gateway, something that does not depend upon the number of crimes the criminal has committed in that day. As the ultimate scope of our work is the preventive policing, we assume that the number of criminals is always constant during a simulation. The preventive police-planning goal is to define strategies to cover the urban space in a way that could prevent crimes to occur; thus events that change the number of criminals, such as arrests, are irrelevant. Interactions between the preventive and repressive aspects are outside of the scope of this work as well.

Target selection is probabilistic (see next section for a formalization of the adopted strategy) based on the target vulnerability and distance, and on the criminal's experience. Having probabilistically selected the next type of target, the time spent to reach the target is calculated based on the speed at which the criminal is able to move and the distance to the target. The shortest period of motion, considering all criminals, is taken as reference, so that the criminals are allowed to move only during this time period. It should be noted that only vulnerable targets are considered in the target selection process. Finally, the decision whether to commit a crime or not is made based on the existence of one or more police teams within the radius of the criminal's sight. If the offender decides to not commit a crime, then the offender will select a new target to approach, leaving the current location. Otherwise, we assume that a crime will be committed and another target will be selected in the sequence.

Learning Ability of the Criminal

Criminal behavior has a learning component that exploits its own experience with each target in conjunction with the information coming from other criminal agents. The success rate of individual agents is computed as the ratio of the number of successful crimes in their lifetime to the overall number of crimes attempted (also in their lifetime). Criminals form communities wherein hints are shared. The agents in a community communicate with each other at the end of a day period. Due to the interconnection of the communities, such hints could be relayed to other criminals in other communities, and the rate at which this happens depends directly on the topology of the network of communities.

In this chapter, we consider two types of topologies to represent the network of criminals: a small-world and a scale-free topology. This assumption is based on both works on social networks that emphasize the adequacy of these kinds of topology for human relations Buchanan and works on criminology that have identified small-world structures in different instances of real criminal networks (Kaza, 2005). Beyond the small-world structure, instead of randomly defining the brokers of the network, we have opted to make use of the concept of hubs (nodes with the highest number of acquaintances) in a community. By doing so, the outcome is a scale-free network, according to the model of Barabási (Barabási, 2002).

Swarm-Based Criminal Agent Behavior

In our model, each criminal has three possible actions: commit a crime, not commit a crime, and move to a certain location. In order to reach a decision whether to commit a crime or not, criminals utilize a probability equation generally exploited in ant-foraging-based swarm systems Bonabeu (Bonabeu, 1999). In the equation, p_{cn} represents the probability of a criminal agent, c, choosing a crime target, n:

$$p_{cn} = \frac{[\tau_{cn}]^{\alpha} \times [\phi_{cn}]^{\beta}}{\sum_{\forall p \in N} [\tau_{cp}]^{\alpha} \times [\phi_{cp}]^{\beta}} \qquad (1)$$

where τ_{cn} represents the learned experience of a criminal c with relation to crime target n, and N is the set of all crime targets the criminal c is considering in his decision of where to commit the crime. The other parameter, φ_{cn}, is the inverse of the distance between the location of criminal c and the crime target n; we assume that the criminal has the knowledge necessary to localize the closest exemplar target on the map. Empirical evidence Brantingham (Brantingham, 1979) suggests that many criminals do not travel great distances to commit a crime. Most crimes against property are committed in neighborhoods near, but not too close to, criminals' residences. Then, we decided to model the probability of a criminal going to a place as the inverse of the distance of that place to the criminal's location at the moment of the simulation. The parameters α and β in equation (1) are employed to balance the importance of τ_{cn} against φ_{cn}. As φ_{cn} is the inverse of the distance, when β increases, the learning factor becomes more relevant.

Equation (1) is applied to all currently vulnerable targets, and the decision is made with regard to which target to attempt the next crime on. Once the target is chosen, the criminal will attempt to commit a crime; this is represented by CT_{cn} and CT_c, which stands for the number of crime attempts on a specific target n in the last day, and the cumulative (all days) for all targets in the environment, respectively. The number of attempts can be subdivided into:

- Successful attempts (crimes effectively occurred), represented by CO_{cn} and CO_c, again representing local (at a given target) and global counters.

- Attempts that were prevented by the police (we do not use the global variant of this counter).

One should note that CT_{cn} is the summation of crimes occurred and crimes attempted, all related to criminal c at target n, and accumulated for the last day only—these counters are reinitialized every day in the simulation.

From equation (1), we have τ as a learned factor for the criminals. For every criminal, c, and target, n, the learned factor is given by τ_{cn}, which is calculated by,

$$\tau_{cn} = \mu \times [\tau_{own}(c)] + (1-\mu) \times [\tau_{own}(c)] \qquad (2)$$

where

$$\tau_{own}(c) = \rho \times \tau_{cn} + (1-\rho) \times \Delta\tau_{cn} \qquad (3)$$

$$\tau_{social}(c) = \frac{\sum_{\forall k \in S(c)} (\tau_k \times \tau_{kn})}{\sum_{\forall k \in S(c)} \tau_k} \qquad (4)$$

The update rule for the learned factor is given in equation (2). Conversely, in equation (3), one can see the individual learning of the agent, which includes a negative feedback factor ρ, which is the level of forgetfulness of a criminal or the extent to which the agent considers the experience taken from the last day $\left(\Delta\tau_{cn} = {CO_{cn}}/{CT_{cn}}\right)$ in relation to the experience it already has at the target n. It is worth noticing here that, in terms of foraging-based swarm systems, the parameter ρ is used to represent a pheromone evaporation rate. In our criminal model, we use this parameter to represent the rate at which agents forget events.

Equation (4) states the social learning of the agent. The importance of this social learning (coming from all members of the social network) is controlled by the parameter μ in equation (2). Note that the social network is directly related to the criminal agent c (indicated by the set $S(c)$). Hence, given that τ_{cn} represents the level of confidence of a criminal with a target, we emphasize that every day (or every fixed interval of time) the agent forgets a little of his/her previous experience and is influenced more by the new one.

Equation (2) also shows that an initial streak of failures or successes will lose its influence over the agent's lifetime. In addition, every day, the agent's own experience is weighted against the experience of all the others pertaining to the agent's social network. It is also important to discuss equation (4). The value of τ_{social} represents the consensual judgment the acquaintances of c have with respect to the target being considered (n). In other words, all contacts of c tell him/her separately what they think about target n. Such hints are then aggregated. For this purpose, as all criminal agents have different success rates, we weigh the experience τ_{kn} of each companion k of c in relation to that target by the overall experience that criminal has regarding all targets $\left(\tau_k = {CO_k}/{CT_k}\right)$. The interpretation is that a successful criminal has higher influence than an unsuccessful one.

EXPERIMENTAL EVALUATION METHODOLOGY AND RESULTS

In order to evaluate the performance of our approach, several simulation experiments were carried out on the basis of two case studies defined over the same artificial urban environment that mimics one well-known neighborhood of Fortaleza, a 2.5-million inhabitant metropolis in Brazil.

In the first case study, which we call *core evaluation scenario*, the multi-agent simulation parameters were set as follows. As shown in Figure. 1, we modeled all existing 41 fixed targets in the neighborhood, such as drugstores, gas stations, lottery houses, banks, squares, and stores, in a 64×64 grid. The location of these targets represents an approximation of their actual distribution across the urban space. G1 and G2 are also depicted, representing the gateways where the criminals start out in the simulation. Gateway G1 represents a slum in the corner of the area whereas the G2 gateways mimic four equally distributed bus stations.

Conversely, in the second case study, referred to in the following as *parameter sensitivity analysis scenario*, we refrained ourselves from having to reproduce precisely the physical characteristics of the actual neighborhood, as our main purpose was to assess the sensibility of our crime simulation model to the calibration of some of its important control parameters (*viz.* parameters related to the criminal model). Our idea was to represent a sort of group of neighborhoods, leading to a higher number of potential targets and, consequently, to an increase in the criminals' activities.

In both scenarios, most of the simulation aspects (described in the next section) were kept the same; one exception is the fact that the covered area for the second scenario was modeled as a 240×240 grid of cells and the number of potential targets was augmented to 240. In both scenarios, each grid cell represents a block of 100 meters.

It is pertinent to mention again that the temporal distribution of crime in our simulations follows an exponential distribution profile, as identified by (Cansado, 2005) from real crime data analysis. Thus, the probability of a target being vulnerable follows an exponential distribution and consequently drives the crime occurrence at that temporal pace. It is worth to remember that the crime exponential distribution depends also on the period of the day at which the crime occurs.

Twenty-four police teams were allotted to patrol the area (six per period). This number is what has been used (on average) by the police headquarters in Fortaleza for the surveillance of the given area. The police patrol routes used in the simulation had a similar configuration to those typically used by the police department for that region. The simulated routes covered four targets per period and the time of stay at each

Figure 1. Simulated environment for the core evaluation scenario

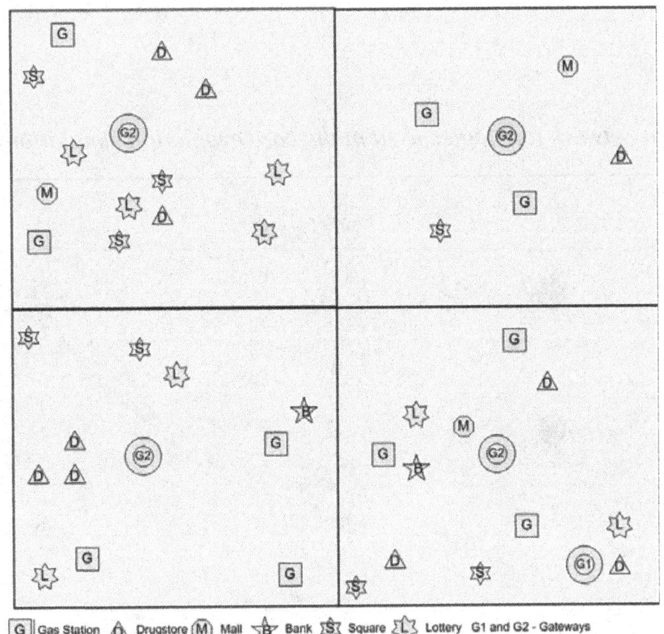

target was divided equally. The number of criminals was set as 16 because: (1) the number and frequency of crimes committed by that number of criminals was already close enough to what has been observed in real data; and (2) as we provide empirical evidence in the end of the next section, increasing the number of criminals did not cause any sort of relevant qualitative alteration in the results achieved. For these reasons we decided to maintain the same number of criminals in the second case study, even though the coverage area was much higher.

Specifically in the *core evaluation scenario*, in order to evaluate the impact of social learning on crime distribution, we ran simulations with different network topologies, namely a small-world, a scale-free, and a fully-connected network. Simulations with no communication between the criminals were also performed. Conversely, in the second scenario, only the scale-free topology was taken into account.

Core Evaluation

Figure 2 shows instances of scale-free (left) and small-world (right) networks randomly produced for the first class of simulation experiments in consideration (we have used the JUNG framework (JUNG, 2006)). The learning parameters of the criminals were set as $\alpha = 0.5$, $\beta = 2$ (since our primary intention is to investigate situations where the choice of the target is based mainly on the agent's past experience rather than in the distance to the target), $\mu = 0.2$ (giving higher importance to the social communication), and $\rho = 0.4$ (meaning that the experience on the last day prevails over the agent's history).

We ran ten simulations for each different gateway setting. The results of each simulation were visually analyzed. Zipf's Law is most easily observed by scatterplotting the data in a log-log chart (rank order X frequency). If the points were close to a single straight line downwards, that means that the distribution follows Zipf's Law.

Figure 3 shows the crime distribution per target produced by a simulation run in which criminals start out in gateway G2 and a scale-free network was used for modeling criminal communication. The targets are ranked in descending order, meaning that the first target has the highest number of crimes. We have also computed the linear regression coefficient R^2 for each distribution to

Figure 2. Two different network topologies used in the core evaluation simulations

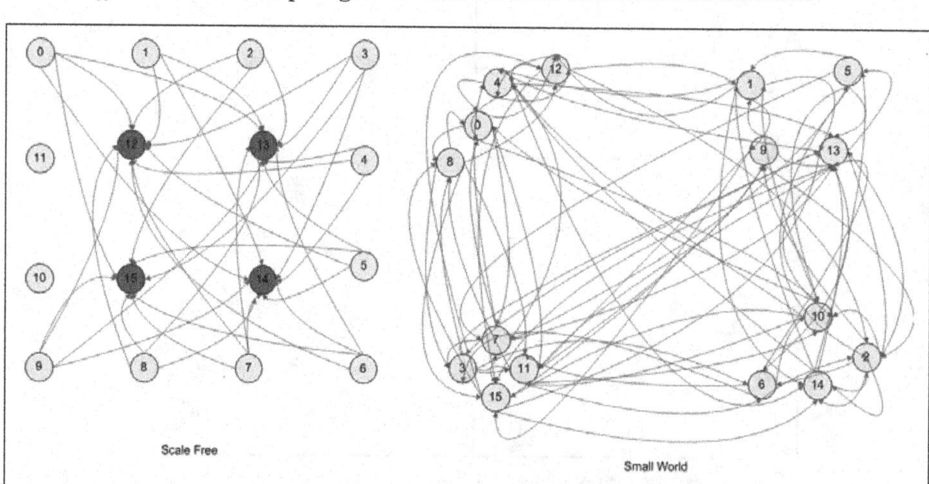

Figure 3. Crimes per target following Zipf's Law distribution

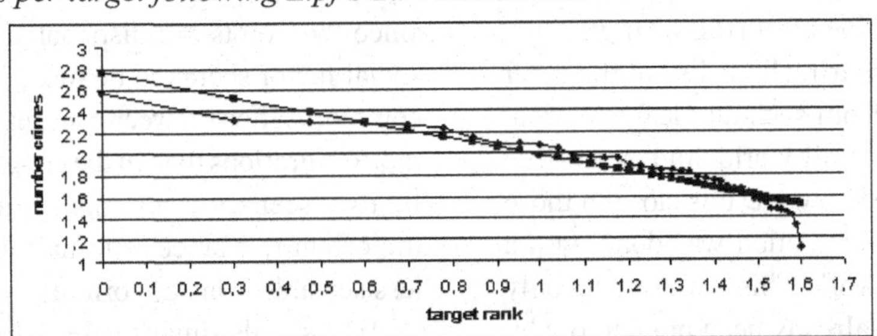

numerically measure the distance between the simulated data and a linear curve. The average values of R^2 for each simulation with G1 and G2 gateway settings are plotted in Figures 4a and 4b, respectively. These results also indicate that the Zipf factor is somewhat correlated with the social factor. The three simulation variants with social communication (namely, with a small-world, scale-free, or fully-connected network) show high regression values (≈ 0.85) indicating that a Zipfian profile is indeed present (we consider those values as Zipfian-like because it is a stochastic phenomenon and uses the average of simulations. Moreover, the slope values were close to 1 like a typical Zipfian distribution). The regression factor is sensibly reduced whenever there is no criminal communication (*no network* in Figure 4). By varying the topology of the social network, we could analyze how sensitive the model is to a particular topology.

The scale-free and small-world networks have similar associated results. Even though a fully-connected network is not feasible in real life, this would represent an ideal situation where

Figure 4. Evolution of R^2 for the scenario with gateways G2 (a) and gateway G1 (b)

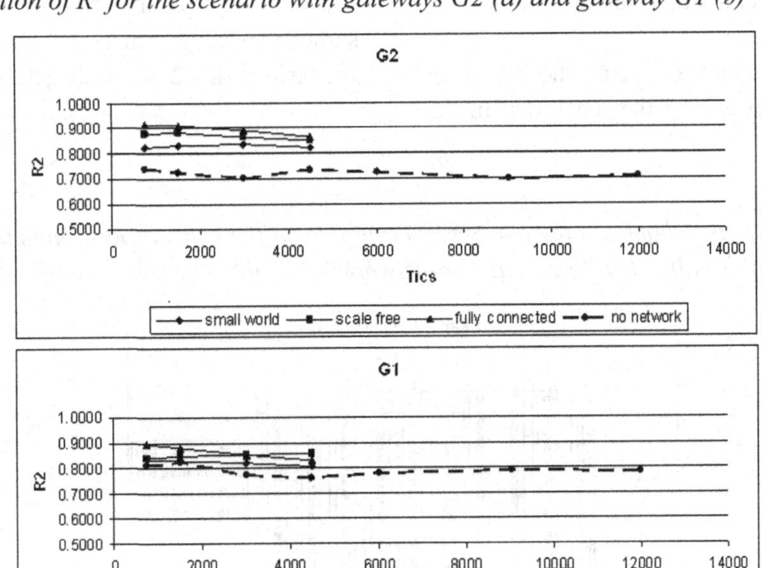

every criminal communicates with every other. Thus the results obtained from this configuration were useful for measuring how distant the other configurations are from such an ideal situation. Simulations with small-world and scale-free configurations have shown results close to those obtained when the simulation was done with a fully-connected network. This achievement only reinforces what has already been pointed out by some sociological studies (Buchanan, 2002), i.e., that small-world and scale-free network settings seem to be very efficient topologies for agent interaction and information dissemination. This is may be because small degrees of separation between nodes allow fast rates of message flow as well as high degrees of interconnectivity between criminals.

Indeed, as one can observe in the scale-free setting of Figure 2, the criminals exchange information with other five peers on average. Nodes 13-16 concentrate, proportionally, the highest numbers of outcome links (i.e., they are hubs). Each of these nodes lies in a different cluster distributed in one of the four corners of the grid. This explains why communication of hints is so efficient, disseminating rapidly among the criminals.

It is also important to discuss the impact of the criminal gateways on the scenarios. In the scenario with gateway G2, which is more realistic since the points are distributed in the area, the social factor seems to be more relevant because communication between criminals would provoke more migrations than in the G1-gateway scenario. In that scenario, communication plays a less important role since criminals are clustered and less sensible hints are offered.

We have also investigated whether a society of criminal agents with no interaction could produce a Zipfian crime pattern in the long run. We would like to know if the social effect was merely to accelerate the Zipf distribution formation or if it is a necessary condition. In order to do so, we ran simulations representing two, four, six, and eight months (a 1,500-tick-simulation represents approximately one month). Figure 4 shows that the R^2 factor for the *no-network* option, in any scenario, does not increase with time.

Finally, as we mentioned before, we have also conducted some experiments assessing the impacts of a possible change in the number of criminals living in the artificial society on the reproduction of the Zipf's Law behavior. In this case, 36 criminals, instead of 16, were allowed to roam, interact, and commit crimes over the same urban environment (i.e., the core evaluation scenario with G2 points as gateways).

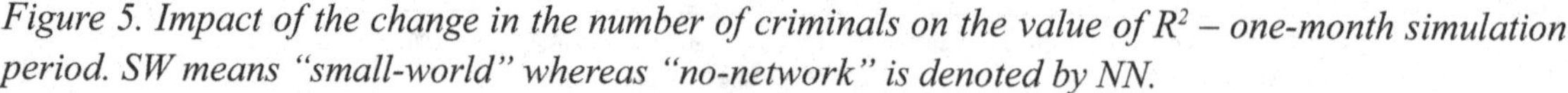

Figure 5. Impact of the change in the number of criminals on the value of R^2 – one-month simulation period. SW means "small-world" whereas "no-network" is denoted by NN.

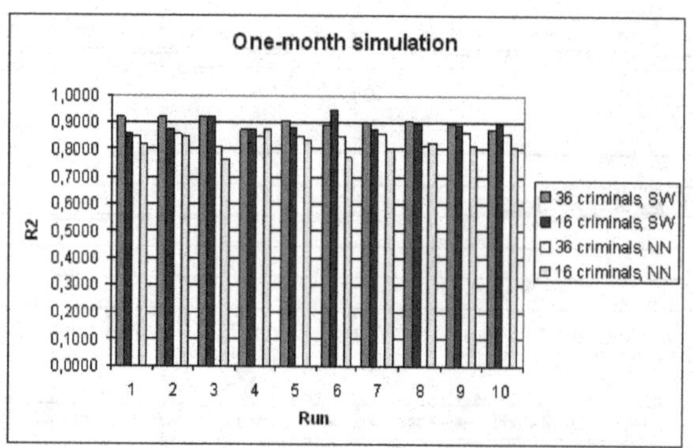

Moreover, one- to four-month simulation runs were conducted so as to reveal whether or not an increase in the number of criminals could accelerate the formation of the Zipf's Law. In this regard, Figures. 5-7 show some results related to these novel experiments.

When considering the small-world setting, on average, an increase in the number of criminals has not shown a significant impact on the achievement of the power-law behavior, irrespective of the number of simulation months considered; however, in some runs, it has incurred better values for the R^2 factor. We thought initially that this nonsignificance of the number of criminals as a parameter to control the formation of Zipf's Law was a side-effect for considering only four gateways in our scenario. Indeed, by this mean, either with four or nine criminals per gateway, there is a rapid spread of hints among the criminals with respect to the most vulnerable targets discovered in the early simulation iterations, leading the criminals to quickly cluster around these targets. However, we have conducted the same sort of experiments with a higher number of gateways (fourteen), and the same qualitative results have been obtained. This suggests that, in

Figure 6. Impact of the change in the number of criminals on the value of R^2 – two-month simulation period. SW means "small-world" whereas "no-network" is denoted by NN.

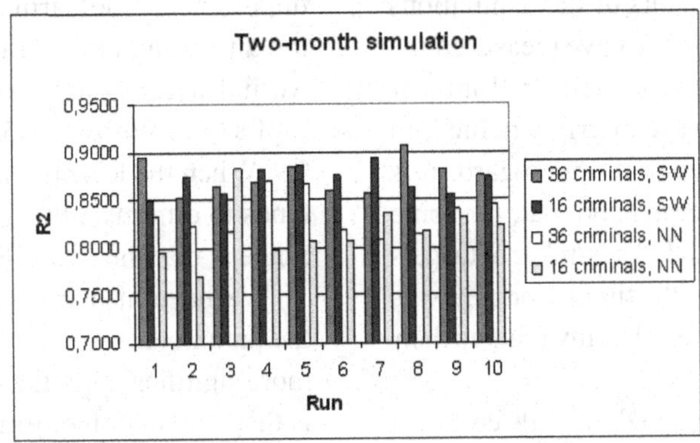

Figure 7. Impact of the change in the number of criminals on the value of R^2 – four-month simulation period. SW means "small-world" whereas "no-network" is denoted by NN.

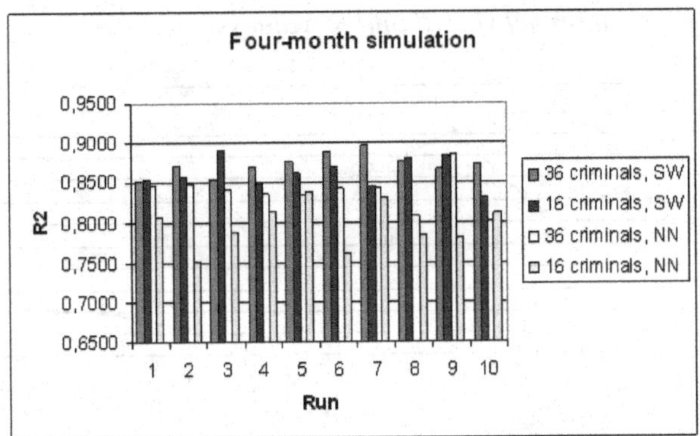

fact, the number of criminals is not a parameter of primary importance when taking into account the social interactions among them. Such result contrasts directly with that observed for the "no-network" setting. In this case, as we already expected, an increase in the number of criminals tends to augment the value of the R^2 factor. This can be better noticed for the two- and four-month simulations.

Parameter Sensitivity Analysis

Since we employ several parameters in our crime simulation model, it is important to analyze the possible variations in the simulation results that are yielded from different parameter settings. To this end, we have changed the values of some of the criminal model's parameters individually and then evaluate the results of the simulations in terms of R^2 variability. We have measured the variability of R^2 with respect to the overall number of crimes and also per type of crime (which, in turn, relates to target type); in this regard, it is important to mention beforehand that, for some types of crimes considered, the number of targets effectively attacked along the simulation runs was insignificant, something that has invalidated their associated R^2 calculus.

It should be remembered that three main parameters drive the criminal's target choice: β, which determines the importance of the target distance to criminal's choice; α, which determines the importance of the learning factor; and μ, which denotes the importance of the hints. We have firstly investigated the impact of varying the importance given to the distance from the criminals to the target. For this purpose, we have varied the β value, maintaining a fixed value for the parameter α—note that the lower the β is, the more relevant the distance factor becomes. We ran simulations varying the β value within the range [0.5;4], with a step of 0.5, and the results confirm that β and R^2 are positively correlated. Figure 8 evidences that a threshold exists at 1.5, after which the higher the β value, the lower the value of R^2 tends to be. In the region [2.5;4] the correlation practically stagnates.

On the other hand, the evaluation pertaining to the value of α indicates that, by increasing the importance of the learning factor (i.e., by reducing the α value and maintaining a fixed value for β), we find that criminal activity more closely follows Zipf's Law. With α = 0.5, the value of R^2 is nearly 0.9. When the learning factor is reduced, R^2 also tends to diminish, though the correlation in this range is nonlinear (see Figure 9).

We have also investigated the influence of the parameter μ on the criminal's behavior. The more significant qualitative result in this context is that a reduction of μ (i.e., simulations become more social-oriented) leads to a slightly better fit of crimes with Zipf's Law. By looking at Figure

Figure 8. Analysis of the correlation between β and R^2 values

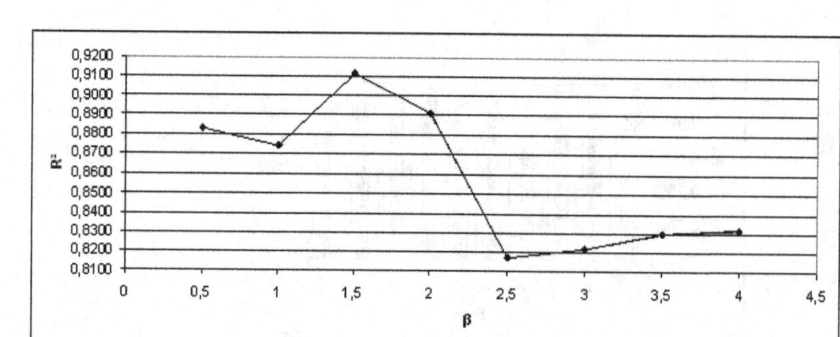

Figure 9. Analysis of the correlation between α and R^2 values

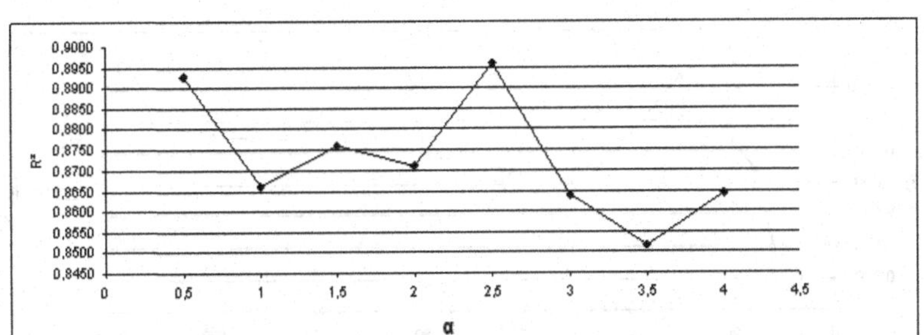

Figure 10. Analysis of the correlation between μ and R^2 values

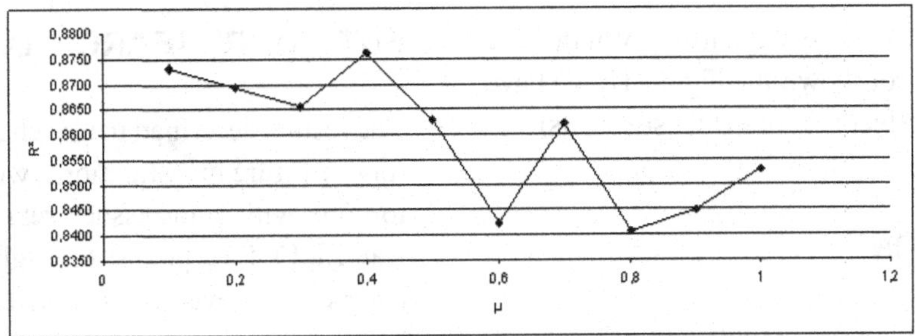

10, one can readily observe that, for μ = 0.1 and μ = 1, the values of R^2 are approximately 0.87 and 0.85, respectively. On the other hand, when assessing the profile assumed by R^2 per type of crime, we observe that, specifically for μ = 0.1, the values assumed by R^2 are approximately 0.92, 0.94, and 0.94, respectively, for the following types of targets: banks, drugstores, and gas station. For μ = 1, the results indicate that $R^2 \approx 0.83$, 0.84, and 0.84, respectively, for the types of crimes mentioned previously. These results conform to sociological findings that have identified a positive correlation between social relations and selective concentration of crimes as already mentioned in the background knowledge section.

The last results we present assumes a different character from the others we have discussed so far in this section, as they do not involve an analysis over a simulation parameter alone (albeit we have also exploited the features of the bigger coverage area). The purpose is just to provide a sense of the time needed for the formation of a Zipfian distribution in our simulated experiments.

In less-than-a-month simulations, as the number of crimes is still small, the R^2 factor is not good enough to characterize alone the truthfulness of Zipf's Law assumption. For this purpose, it is also necessary to observe the slope of the curve. We have verified that, when social communication among the criminals is allowed, a half-month period of simulation seems to be enough for a Zipfian distribution to start emerging ($R^2 \approx 0.87$ and slope ≈ 0.75). Looking at Figure 11, one can observe that, after 40 days of simulation, there is practically no increase in the value of the R^2 factor. This happens because police patrol routes do not change, giving criminals no incentive to look for new target. The crimes become more clustered,

Figure 11. Formation of R^2 values

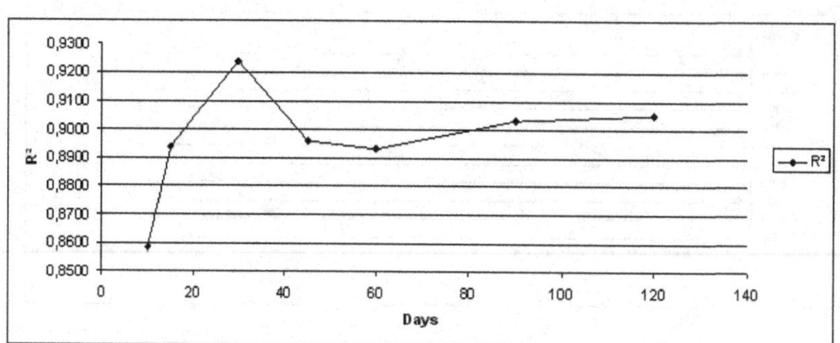

and Zipf's Law tends to stagnate or even decline (though this is not shown the Figure 11, we have observed this effect in more extensive tests).

CONCLUSION

Simulation of criminal activities in urban environments is an asset to decision makers seeking preventive measures. Law enforcement authorities need to understand the behavior of criminals and their response to possible actions or patrol configuration. We have shown that ant-optimization systems augmented with social network concepts constitute an adequate strategy for modeling criminal behavior. Using these technologies we can model the important role of criminal preference—criminals follows their preferences when committing crimes and those preferences depend on past experience and social communication. In other words, a criminal act incorporates the criminal's preference and prior knowledge of the crime points. ACO allows for crime target selection via a mechanism of preferential attachment. Therefore, the simulation model yields a spatial distribution of crime according to Zipf's Law (the expected). We have also shown the effect of learning and social connections on criminals.

FUTURE RESEARCH DIRECTIONS

The results described in this chapter are the basis for our future investigations, which are intended to cope with some issues related to this work. Can Zipf's Law persist through time even after a series of preventive strategies takes place? If not, how long does it take for one to notice the reestablishment of this law? Is it somehow possible to avoid such reestablishment? Furthermore, we are also designing an evolutionary approach that integrates with the simulation tool and is devised to assist police officers in the design of effective police patrol routes. Our approach is inspired by the increasing trend of hybridizing multi-agent systems with evolutionary algorithms. Our idea is to uncover strategies for police patrolling that cope with the dynamics of the crime represented by criminals that learn on the fly. To uncover good police patrol routes in this context, we are integrating a genetic algorithm into the simulation model. Preliminary results (Reis, Melo, Coelho, & Furtado, 2006) have shown that such an approach is very promising. We are working on that issue by tackling the problem by designing optimal patrol routes and, particularly, by investigating two related questions, namely: (1) how far from the optimal patrolling routing strategies are those actually adopted by human police managers, and (2) how complex do such optimal patrolling routes need to be in terms of their total lengths and urban area coverage?

REFERENCES

Akers, R., Krohn, M., Lanza-Kaduce, L., & Radosevich, M. (1979). Social learning and deviant behavior: A specific test of a general theory. *American Sociological Review, 44,*(4), 636-655.

Barabási, A. (2002). *Linked: The new science of networks.* Cambridge: Perseus Pulishing.

Bonabeau, E., Dorigo, M., & Theraulaz, G. (1999). *Swarm intelligence: From natural to artificial systems.* Santa Fe Institute Studies in the Sciences of Complexity Series: Oxford Press.

Brantingham, P., & Brantingham, P. (1979). Environment, routine, and situation: Toward a pattern theory of crime. In R. Clark & M. Felson (Eds.), *Routine activity and rational choice* (Vol. 5) (pp. 259 – 294).Transaction Books

Buchanan, M. (2002). Nexus: Small worlds and the groundbreaking science of networks. New York: W. W. Norton.

Calvó-Armengol, A., & Zenou, Y. (2004). Social networks and crime decisions: The role of social structure in facilitating delinquent behavior. *International Economic Review, 45*(3), 939-58.

Cansado, T. M. L. (2005). *Alocação e despacho de recursos para combate à criminalidade.* Master dissertation, UFMG, Belo Horizonte.

Drogoul, A., & Ferber, J. (1992). Multi-agent simulation as a tool for modeling societies: Application to social differentiation in ant colonies. In *Proceedings of 4th European Workshop on on Modelling Autonomous Agents in a Multi-Agent World, Artificial Social Systems* (MAAMAW), Lecture Notes in Computer Science (Vol. 830, pp. 3-23).

Gilbert, N., & Conte, R. (1995). *Artificial societies: The computer simulation of social life.* London: UCL Press.

Glaeser, E., Sacerdote, B., & Scheinkman, J. (1996, May). Crime and social interactions. *Quarterly Journal of Economics, 111*(2), 507-48.

Houtzager, B., & Baerveldt, C. (1999). Just like normal: A social network study of the relation between petty crime and the intimacy of adolescent friendships. *Social Behavior and Personality, 27*(2), 117–192.

Java Universal Network/Graph Framework. Retrieved September 6, 2007, from http://jung.sourceforge.net/

Kaza, S., Xu, J., Marshall, B., & Chen, H. (2005). Topological analysis of criminal activity networks in multiple jurisdictions.

Reis, D., Melo, A., Coelho, A. L. V., & Furtado, V. (2006). *GAPatrol: An evolutionary multi-agent approach for the automatic definition of hotspots and patrol routes. In* J. S. Sichman, H. Coelho, & S. Oliveira (Eds.). In *Proceedings of IBERAMIA/SBIA 2006,* Lecture Notes in Artificial Intelligence (LNAI) 4140, pp. 118-127.

Scott, J. P (2000). *Social network analysis: A handbook.* Sage Publications.

Sutherland, E. (1974). *Principles of criminology* (4th ed.). Philadelphia: J. B. Lippincott Company.

Zipf, G. K. (1949). Human behaviour and the principle of least-effort. Cambridge: Addison-Wesley.

ADDITIONAL READING

Almeida, A., Ramalho, G. L., Santana, H. P., Tedesco, P., Menezes, T. R., Corruble, V., & Chevaleyre, Y. (2004). Recent advances on multiagent patrolling. In A.L.C. Bazzan & S. Labidi (Eds.), Advances in artificial intelligence – SBIA 2004:

In *Proceedings of the 17th Brazilian Symposium on Artificial Intelligence*, LNAI 3171, (pp. 474-483). Berlin: Springer.

Becker, G. (1968). Crime and punishment: An economic approach. *Journal of Political Economy, 76*, 169-217

Camazine, S., Deneubourg, J-L., Franks, N. R., Sneyd, J., Theraulaz, G., & Bonabeau, E. (2001). *Self-organization in biological systems*. Princeton University Press.

Cohen, L., & Felson, M. (1979). Social change and crime rate trends: A routine approach. *American Sociological Review, 44*, 588-608.

Davidsson, P., Logan, B., & Takadama, K. (2004) (Eds.). Multi-agent and multi-agent-based simulation. In *Proceedings of the Joint Workshop MABS 2004*, New York. July 19 and Jaime Simão Sichman, Luis Antunes (Eds.): Multi-Agent-Based Simulation VI, International Workshop, MABS 2005, Utrecht, The Netherlands.

Dorigo, M., & Stützle, T. (2004). *Ant colony optimization*. The MIT Press.

Furtado, V., & Vasconcelos, E. (2006). A multiagent simulator for teaching police allocation. *AI Magazine, 27*(3).

Gaston, M. E., & desJardins, M. (2005). Social network structures and their impact on multiagent system dynamics. In *Proceedings of the Eighteenth International Florida Artificial Intelligence Research Society Conference*, (pp. 32–37).

Kennedy, J., & Eberhart, R. C. (2001). *Swarm intelligence*. Morgan Kaufmann.

Leighton, B. (1988). The community concept in criminology: Toward a social network approach. *Journal of Research in Crime and Delinquency, 25*(4), 351-374.

Liu, L., Wang, X., Eck, J., & Liang, J. (2005). Simulating crime events and crime patterns in a RA/CA model. In F. Wang (Ed.), *GIS and crime analysis* (pp. 197-213). Hershey, PA: Idea Group.

Machado, A., Ramalho, G. L., Zucker, J.-D., & Drogoul, A. (2003). Multi-agent patrolling: An empirical analysis of alternative architectures. In J. S. Sichman, F. Bousquet, & P. Davidsson (Eds.), In *Proceedings of the Multi-Agent-Based Simulation II, Third International Workshop* (MABS 2002), LNAI 2581 (pp. 155-170). Berlin: Springer.

Mamei, M., Menezes, R., Tolksdorf, R., & Zambonelli, F. (2006). Case studies for self-organization in computer science. *Journal of System Architecture, 52*(8), 443-460.

McIllwain, J. S. (1999). Organized crime: A social network approach. *Crime, Law and Social Change, 32*(4), 301-323(23).

Sherman, L., Gartin, P., & Buerger, M. (1989). Hot spots of predatory crime: Routine activities and the criminology of place. *Criminology, 27*, 27-56.

Sparrow, M. (1991). The application of network analysis to criminal intelligence: An assessment of the prospects. *Social Networks, 13*, 251–274.

Wasserman, S., Faust, K., Iacobucci, D. (1994). *Social network analysis: Methods and applications*. Cambridge University Press.

Weiss, G. (1999). (Ed.). *Multiagent systems: A modern approach to distributed artificial intelligence*. The MIT Press.

Winoto, P. A. (2003). Simulation of the market for offenses in multiagent systems: Is zero crime rates attainable? In J. S. Sichman, F. Bousquet, & P. Davidsson (Eds.). Multi-agent-based dimulation II. In *Proceedings of the Third International Workshop (MABS 2002)*, LNAI 2581 (pp. 181-194). Berlin: Springer.

Zenou, Y. (2003). *The spatial aspects of crime*. Center for Economics Policy research (Discussion Papers No. 4028).

Chapter XVI
FraudSim:
Simulating Fraud in a Public Delivery Program[1]

Yushim Kim
Arizona State University, USA

Ningchuan Xiao
The Ohio State University, USA

ABSTRACT

This chapter shows that white-collar crime can be approached using an agent-based model. Fraud in public delivery programs often involves several entities that are loosely interrelated and interact dynamically. However, the crime literature has not paid sufficient attention to these characteristics, thus providing limited utility for public managers. This chapter frames a public delivery program as a complex system. The patterns of fraud in such a system are simulated using an agent-based model called FraudSim. We demonstrate that FraudSim closely replicates the statistical and spatial patterns of fraud and provides a framework for future work in this area.

INTRODUCTION

Fraud is a crime that violates social norms, uses secretive processes, injures victims, and benefits perpetrators unfairly (Barker & Roebuck, 1973; Vandenburgh, 1999). In the public sector, fraud in welfare and health care programs has been well-documented (GAO, 1998, 2005). To minimize fraud, public agencies have utilized several fraud prevention and detection mechanisms (Bolton & Hand, 2002). For example, fraud prevention focuses on procedures to avert fraud, using methods such as watermarks and personal identification documents before fraud occurs. Fraud detection focuses on identifying those who committed fraud after it has occurred using statistical methods or actual investigations. However, many of these traditional mechanisms maybe static and ineffective in preventing or uncovering complex interactions among corrupt agents (Fawcett & Provost, 1997; Glover & Aono, 1995). Therefore, there is a need to develop an alternative framework to address such complex and adaptive problems in public management. In this research, we developed an agent-based model called FraudSim that can be used to simulate and analyze crime patterns in public service delivery programs. In the remainder of this chapter, we first discuss the context of our research based on a literature review of white-collar crime and related issues. We then discuss our agent-based modeling framework and its implementation. This model is then tested against empirical data for the purpose of evaluation. We conclude this chapter with a discussion on the limitation and future of this research.

BACKGROUND

Traditional sociologists recognize crime to be influenced by multiple dimensions of social life. A traditional theory of criminal behavior finds criminality to be caused by poverty or the psychopathic and sociopathic conditions associated with poverty. Crime is a function of socioeconomic factors, or possibly biological factors. Criminals are similar to those who are irrational or have mental illness due to societal oppression or disease. An appropriate way to eliminate crime is to attack the root cause of crime through job creation and income maintenance (Cooter & Ulen, 2000).

Sutherland (1940) argued that the traditional conception of crime and explanations were misleading and incorrect. He argued that the traditional theory was derived from data provided by criminal justice agencies, which focused on lower class crime. A general theory of crime should include white-collar crime, and white-collar criminality is not different from the criminality of the lower class. Both types of criminality are *learned* rather than simply influenced by the psychopathic and sociopathic conditions.

While Sutherland (1940) provided a compelling view of criminality as learning behavior regardless of social class, white collar crime has primarily been interpreted as crime committed by a person of respectability and high social status in the course of his occupation (Baker, 2004; Braithwaite, 1985). White-collar criminals are mostly recidivists, and their illegal behavior is much more extensive. They often do not lose status among associates, even after violating the laws designed to regulate business (Sutherland, 1982). However, the usefulness of the distinction of crime by social status has been a source of debate in crime theory (Griffin, 2002; Hirschi & Gottfredson, 1987; Lynch, McGurrin, & Fenwick, 2004). Empirical studies on social class and punishment have also yielded mixed results (Benson & Walker, 1988; Wheeler, Weisburd, & Bode, 1982).

The current definition of white-collar offenses by the Department of Justice shows that it constitutes those nonviolent illegal activities, which principally involves traditional notions of deceit, deception, concealment, manipulation, breach of trust, subterfuge, or illegal circumvention (Baker, 2004). Levitt and Dubner (2005) argued that "despite all the attention paid to rogue companies like Enron, academics know very little about the practicalities of white collar crime" (p. 46). Friedrichs (2004) suggested an integrated theoretical approach, describing cases such as the Enron scandal as "an outcome of a complex interaction of many different factors and variables, operating on various levels" (p.116).

Crime Opportunity

A group of criminologists has focused on crime as events and actions. The studies rooted in routine activity theory are interested in spatio-temporal dynamics of crime (Cohen & Felson, 1979; Felson, 1994). Routine activity theory is a micro-level theory and an individual is the unit of analysis (Eck, 1995). A main thrust of this theory is that crime depends upon opportunities presented by the routine activities of everyday life where motivated offenders and suitable targets without guardianship are converged in time and space (Felson, 1994; Eck, 1995). These recurrent and prevalent activities deliver crime opportunities to the offender (Cohen & Felson, 1979; Felson, 1987). Place is also central to this theory, facilitating or inhibiting crime as a crime promoter (e.g., abandoned building) or a crime suppressor (e.g., place manager).

Routine activity theory may predispose some persons to greater risks as targets or to greater motivation as offenders. The theory frames that the selection of a particular target within a socio-temporal context is determined by the expected utility of one target over another (Miethe & Meier, 1990). However, Osgood, Wilson, O'Malley, Bachman, and Johnston (1996) argue "this sharp distinction between offender and victim is not applicable to a large share of illegal or deviant behavior" (p. 636). The motivation for deviant behavior is inherent in the situation rather than in the person. To participate in illegal or deviant behavior, one needs to be there when the opportunity arises and when others are willing.

Building a Framework from a Management Perspective

The literature offers substantial accounts of the nature and causes of criminality and crime. However, it is rare to see the literature that has paid attention to the mechanisms underlying the practice of fraud, particularly in public delivery programs, where several entities are dynamically and loosely interrelated (Weick, 1979). Public delivery programs consist of interdependent, but incongruent entities. They pursue different goals while working together. For example, public agencies attempt to efficiently deliver public services to recipients by frequently contracting with private entities. While these private entities are responsible for delivering the services on behalf of public agency, they also attempt to maximize profit from the delivery. Program recipients are supposed to improve their physical/economic conditions by complying with program policy and consuming the services. Public services are designed and delivered through routine procedures among these players under the assumption that each player will comply with policy for the common good. In reality, however, policy intention is not implemented as designed. For example, fraud occurs when some players who have specialized access behave opportunistically in order to take an advantage of a system.

Given the characteristics of public delivery programs, Sutherland's view on criminality and crime opportunity together provide a useful theoretical framework to explore fraud. It is our contention that the players are vulnerable to the temptation to commit fraud in the policy system and there is no sharp distinction between those who will be involved in fraud and those who will not. Some individuals are more likely to succumb to temptation than others depending upon their propensity toward illegal behavior. Further, we claim that noticeable spatio-temporal macro patterns emerge from the routine activity and opportunistic behavior of individual players at micro-levels.

A few scholars have recently attempted to understand fraud as outcome of complex interactions (Friedrichs, 2004; Provost, 2002; Wilhelm, 2004). They recognize that fraud is an issue that requires a dynamic, evolving, and adaptive approach due to its complexity. However, the adaptive nature of fraud is not well-addressed in traditional frameworks. It requires a dynamic and equally adaptive approach. Spatio-temporal patterns need to be carefully considered in order to effectively address the issue. Recent advances in complexity science see natural, human, or social phenomena as complex adaptive systems. Complex systems consist of a network of interacting adaptive agents who exhibit a dynamic aggregate behavior emerging from individual activities of the agents (Holland & Miller, 1991). Agent-based models have been developed as operational models of this approach (Bankes, 2002; Epstein & Axtell, 1996). This model provides a solid methodological framework to examine our contention.

METHODS

The Special Supplemental Nutrition Program for Women, Infants, and Children (WIC) program aims to safeguard the health of low-income women, infants, and children up to age five who are at nutritional risk. The program provides nutritious supplemental foods, nutritional education, and referrals to health care and other social services. In Ohio, WIC serves approximately 277,000 participants each month with a budget of over $150 million each year. Ohio WIC has contracts with over 200 local clinics and 1,400 vendors. These participants, local clinics, vendors, and the state agency are the major players in Ohio WIC. Because the operation of WIC is mainly at state and local levels, we do not consider federal government in this research.

Figure 1 illustrates the business model of the Ohio WIC program. Each month, participants receive three or four vouchers with food benefits at local clinics. These participants are expected to redeem their benefits at WIC retail vendors within a specified period. These vendors are convenience marts or national grocery chains. When they receive their vouchers, participants are informed available vendors for their use within their county. Each voucher specifies the products and quantities a participant can purchase, as well as the maximum prices that the state will pay for an allowable food. The state pays for the vouchers collected from the vendors. The state also monitors the overall flow of transactions in the WIC system.

The WIC program is subject to managerial and operational breakdowns and their undesirable consequences. Fraud can significantly contribute to such a breakdown. Fraud has been detected among vendors (approximately 9% of all ven-

Figure 1. Business mechanism in Ohio WIC

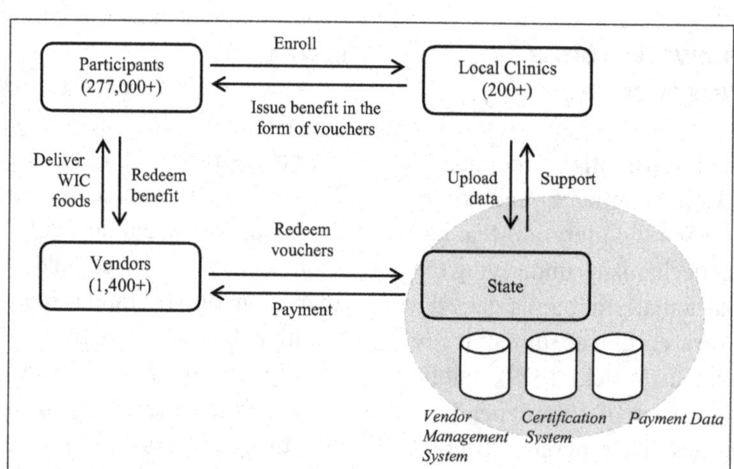

Note: The figure shows how players in Ohio WIC interact. Numbers inside boxes present how many participants, local clinics, and vendors are of Ohio WIC.

dors), participants (0.14%), and employees (4%) (GAO, 1999).[2] This shows that fraud in public programs is not committed by any specific player. Although they were not supposed to be involved in illegal activities, all players are vulnerable to the temptation to commit fraud. In addition, the reality of fraud in public delivery programs is more complex.

In the WIC program, four possible fraud mechanisms can be noted. First, fraud can occur through illegal exchanges of benefit between vendors and participants. For example, vendors overcharge when participants redeem their benefits. Some other illegal activities include forcing a participant into unwanted purchases, substitutions of WIC foods for unauthorized items (substitution), and exchanges of public service benefits for cash (trafficking). Second, fraud can occur through the improper exchange of benefits among participants, though the WIC policies and guidelines require that they do not hand over the benefits to non-WIC participants or other WIC participants. In reality, compliance on this contract is uncertain in some cases. Third, fraud can also occur through a network of corrupt vendors. In addition to all these improper conducts, there is a chance that a third party can be involved.

While other mechanisms are relevant, the focus of this chapter is placed on fraud committed by the interactions between vendors and participants because these are more common in the WIC system than other types of fraud. An agent-based model is developed to capture macro patterns emerged from their interactions. The simulated crime patterns are compared with the observed in an empirical dataset.

Data

For a case study, one month of payment data from an Ohio county were examined to obtain an estimate of the distribution of the risk status of vendors. Vendors are a key target to be monitored in terms of fraud. In the sample county,[3] a total of 188 vendors were included, along with a total of 28,887 participants who redeemed their benefits in April 2004.[4] On average, a vendor has 6 checkout lanes, ranging from 1 to 30 lanes. The state paid, on average, $8,976 to each vendor while the total cost from collected vouchers was an average of $11,589 at each vendor. The vendor redemption ratio was approximately 82% of the state's voucher costs. Average WIC sales per checkout lane were $2,520 per month. Average food costs per participant at the vendor were approximately $40, ranging from $7 to $76. This information is provided in Table 1.

Table 1. Descriptive statistics in a WIC county in Ohio in April 2004 (number of vendors = 188)

	Mean	Std. Dev.	Min	Max	Note [1]
Checkout lanes (#)	6	6	1	30	
State payment to vendors ($)	8,976	10,008	28	56,884	
Voucher costs ($)	11,589	13,988	38	82,263	
Participants per vendor (#)	223	248	4	1,402	
Risk indicators					
Vendor redemption ratio (%)	82.0	10.7	60.0	100.0	6.4%
WIC sales per checkout lane ($)	2,520	2,706	3	16,673	9.6%
Food costs per participant at vendors ($)	40	12	7	76	8.5%

[1] *Percentage of vendors who met each risk indicator*

Here we focus on the pattern of WIC sales volume in order to identify vendors who involve in fraud or have a high potential of committing fraud. WIC sales volume is investigated for (1) vendor redemption ratio (state payment to vendors / voucher costs), (2) WIC sales per checkout lane (state payment to vendors / checkout lanes), and (3) food package costs per participant at the vendor (state payment to vendors / participants per vendor). These indicators are based on a data-driven risk assessment in the state system that serves to identify outliers (i.e., over 90th percentile for each indicator). In the state vendor monitoring system, vendors meeting more than one risk indicator (out of three) are considered to be high risk. The percent of vendors identified as outliers by each indicator is also reported in Table 1. The information from the empirical data is used as a reference for the following simulation model.

FraudSim: Agent-Based Modeling

FraudSim is developed within the programming structure of MASON[5] that serves as the basis for a wide range of multi-agent simulation tasks (Balan, Cioffi-Revilla, Luke, Panait, & Paus, 2003; Luke, Cioffi-Revilla, Panait, & Sullivan, 2004). Players in Figure 1 are modified and used as basic agents. In Figure 2, agent "public agency" provides the functions of local clinics and state administration, such as program maintenance and monitoring. A "vendor" agent is responsible for delivering food and nutritional supplements to "participant" agent, who redeems their vouchers. The public agency agent is not spatially explicit, while the other types of agents are spatially referenced.

In terms of key properties, risk propensity and vendor size are crucial on which this chapter focuses. Risk propensity is a hypothetical property used to model the change of an agent's propensity toward risky behavior. It is assumed that at the initial stage, agents' risk propensity follows a truncated Gaussian distribution with a mean of 0.40 ranging from min 0.00 to max 1.00 for both participant and vendor agents, regardless of other properties. The assumption is that the higher the assigned risk propensity, the higher the probability of committing fraud will be.

Figure 2. The framework of FraudSim for Ohio WIC

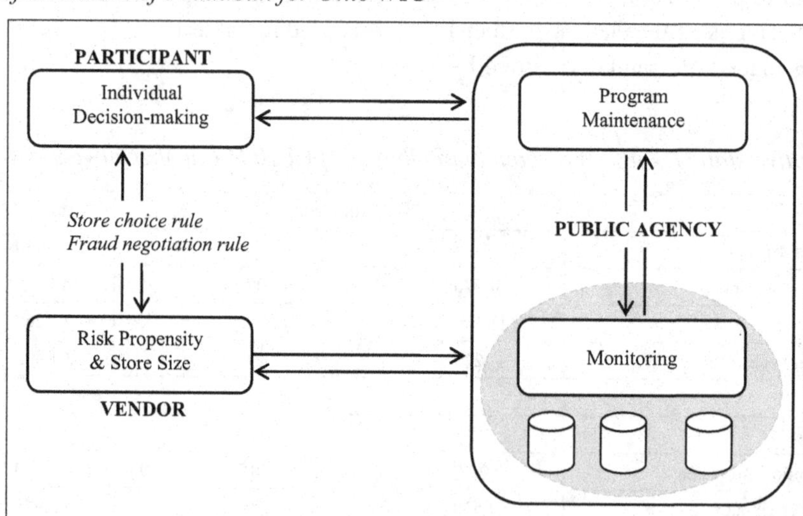

Note: The figure defines agents, interdependency, and interactions for an agent-based model of the Ohio WIC system. Capital letters represent agents and italics show interaction rules.

In the simulation, vendors' involvement in fraud is influenced by store size and dynamically changing risk propensities. Store size is a proxy of business type in the WIC program. Larger vendors are most likely to be national chains, while small vendors with one or two lanes are generally family owned. Fraud occurs more frequently among small vendors than among large vendors (USDA, 2001); hence, the smaller the vendor, the larger the probability of committing fraud. For example, among small vendors (< 3 checkout lanes), if risk propensity is greater than 0.9, there is a 95% chance of committing fraud, while if risk propensity is less than 0.3, the vendor has only a 10% chance of being involved in fraud. For larger vendors (> 5 checkout lanes), those with a low-risk propensity (< 0.3) have a 0.01% chance of participating in fraud, while vendors with a high-risk propensity (> 0.9) have a 10% chance of committing fraud. This process will lead to a skewed distribution of vendor risk status by store size over time. In other words, smaller vendors with high-risk propensity will become a high-risk vendor over time because they have a higher chance of being involved in fraud, even when risk propensity was equally distributed among the vendors at the initialization.

Interaction Rules

Two interaction rules were designed for the simulation: (1) a store choice rule and (2) a fraud negotiation rule. During the initialization of the simulation model, each participant is assigned a vendor. This assignment is based on the store choice rule that is adopted from the spatial interaction model developed by Huff (1964), which provides some sense of how participants will choose vendors upon joining the program, as well as in general. In the Huff model, the probability of a consumer visiting a particular store is calculated as a relative measure equal to the ratio of the utility of that store to the sum of utilities of all stores considered by the consumer. More formally, $p_{ij} = U_{ij} / \sum U_{ij}$, where i and j indicate the consumer and store, respectively. The utility (U) consists of two decision factors for store choice, store size of j (S_j) and distance between i and j (D_{ij}). In the original Huff model, store size is measured using store footage. Here, the number of checkout lanes was used as a proxy of store size. Euclidean distance was measured between the locations of participants and vendors. Using this rule, participant agents will show their preference on vendor selection.

Once theoretical store choice is identified using the store choice rule as a base, a fraud negotiation rule is executed. During each iteration, a participant agent visits a selected vendor agent. Then, randomly selected participants are exposed to fraud offer by vendor agent. They negotiate fraud depending upon the result of a coin toss. The result of the coin toss is influenced by their risk propensity. Agents with high-risk propensities will have higher chance to have a decision of involving in fraud. Fraud negotiation between participant and vendor agents results in two possible outcomes depending upon their agreement. If both agents agree to commit or not commit fraud at the initial contact, then participant agents continue to visit the vendor and use their benefits throughout the simulation. Individuals do not make rational choices all of the time, so randomness is introduced for some participants who have high-risk propensity but are not involved in fraud by chance. Participant agents who were not involved in fraud, but have a relatively high risk propensity (> 0.6), will have a 1% of chance of moving to random vendors during each step. The participant agents run the fraud negotiation rule with new vendors until they find a comparable vendor. When one party refuses to be involved, fraud negotiation fails. In this case, participant agents move to the next vendor selected by the store choice rule and run the fraud negotiation rule again.

Voucher Exchange and Fraudulent Behavior

Along with the interaction rules, three voucher exchange and recording behaviors were identified to simulate vendors' sales activities. First, the public agency agent issues vouchers, each with a mean of $45.00 and ranging from $2.00 to $100.00, to participant agents. A participant agent uses approximately 75% of the voucher value, with a range of 4 to 100%, when exchanging the vouchers for WIC foods. Voucher issuance and benefit exchange for participants at vendors are probabilistically decided within the given ranges.

Second, actual dollar amounts used by participant agents will be recorded differently, depending on the result of the fraud negotiation. If a participant agrees to commit fraud, it will be recorded that the participant used 100% of the benefit. For those who are not involved in fraud, the actual amount used by participants will be recorded. Therefore, actual sales amounts are manipulated depending upon the outcome of the fraud negotiation.

Third, the risk propensities of participant and vendor agents will change, depending upon their decisions and behaviors. It is assumed that risk propensity increases or decreases faster for smaller vendors than larger vendors when they are involved in fraud. Based on these basic assumptions, multiple parameters were tested and revised to identify appropriate sets that closely replicate the statistics from the empirical data. The initial parameters for the basic properties are summarized in Table 2.

SIMULATING FRAUD PATTERNS USING FRAUDISM

Here, the focus is placed on simulating the statistical and spatial patterns of fraud in the policy system using FraudSim. Though a simulation does not prove anything, it can be used to produce data for evaluation and investigation. Using the simulated data based on the assumptions above, statistical patterns are examined first. Spatial patterns are discussed later.

Replicating Descriptive Statistics

To make this simulation tractable, the size of the WIC system was reduced to 20 vendors and 1,000 participants. The simulation was repeated 10 times; each time, the properties of the vendors and participants were randomly generated using the probability distributions described in Table 2. The results of FraudSim exhibit similar store size distribution over multiple runs.

Based on our assumptions, small vendors with a high-risk propensity are more actively involved in fraud. This results in a higher sales volume for some small vendors and, ultimately, more vendors with high-risk status among these small vendors at the end of the simulation. The majority of vendors and participants will not be involved in committing fraud, especially at larger vendors.

Table 2. Initial parameters of the basic properties used in the simulation

	Mean	Std.Dev.	Min	Max
Vendor risk propensity (VRP)	0.40	0.40	0.00	1.00
Participant risk propensity (PRP)	0.40	0.30	0.00	1.00
Voucher values ($)	45.0	40.0	2.0	100.0
Voucher usage by a participant (%)	0.75	0.10	0.04	1.00

A dynamic aspect of the WIC program is also considered in the simulation. For example, Ohio WIC has existed for over 30 years. The pattern of risky vendors in one county in April 2004 only provides a snapshot of the long history of the program. Therefore, statistics in the empirical data reflect only a case in a certain point in time. This chapter is interested in replicating the snapshot using the simulation. For this, the simulation stopped at Time 299, and simulated data are examined in order to be compared with the results of April 2004.

Descriptive statistics of the simulation at Time 299 were reported in Table 3. The absolute sales amounts are approximately 1/10 of the original size of the WIC business in the empirical data with similar distributions. In the simulated data, vendors redeemed approximately 82% of the total voucher costs. Given that the average voucher usage of participants is 75% at the initialization (Table 2), the vendor redemption ratio increased throughout the simulation. A major source of this increase is fraudulent vendors' sales manipulation behaviors. This also inflates the value of the other indicator, food costs per participant at each vendor, which measures how much food a participant redeemed at vendors. On average, food costs per participant at vendors were $40, ranging from $11 to $78. Given the fact that average voucher values in the simulation are $45 and the usage by participants is approximately 75% of the value, it is expected that food costs per participant would be approximately $33 where there is no fraud.

Figure 3 presents the distributions of the sales by the three indicators. The distribution of the empirical data in April 2004 is presented on the left, and the distribution of the simulated data at Time 299 is presented on the right for comparison. The largest difference was found from the vendor redemption ratio. However, this figure shows that, overall, the simulation closely replicates the distributions of WIC sales by the three indicators in the empirical data.

While Figure 3 shows the distribution of WIC sales activities by different monitoring indicators, two questions still remain. The first question is whether the simulation replicates the distribution of high-risk vendors in the empirical data when the individual risk indicators are combined. In other words, the state categorizes vendors as high-risk when two of the three indicators are met at the same time. Therefore, it is expected that the simulation needs to generate a similar distribution of high-risk vendors. The other question is who the outliers are. It is expected that small

Table 3. Descriptive statistics in the simulation at Time 299 (number of vendors = 200)

	Mean	Std. Dev.	Min	Max	Note [2]
Checkout lanes (#)	7	6	1	20	
State payment to vendors ($)	1,070	964	0	4,594	
Voucher costs ($)	1,362	1,298	0	6,043	
Participants per vendor (#)	28	26	0	122	
Risk indicators					
Vendor redemption ratio (%)	82.2	8.8	65.2	100.0	11.0%
WIC sales per checkout lane ($)	313	359	0	2,158	10.0%
Food costs per participant at vendors ($)	40	8	11	78	10.5%

[2] *Percentage of vendors who met each risk indicator*

Figure 3. Distributions of sales activities by three risk indicators: vendor redemption ratio, sales per checkout lane, and food package costs per participant

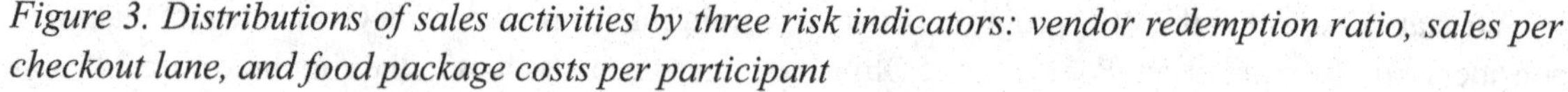

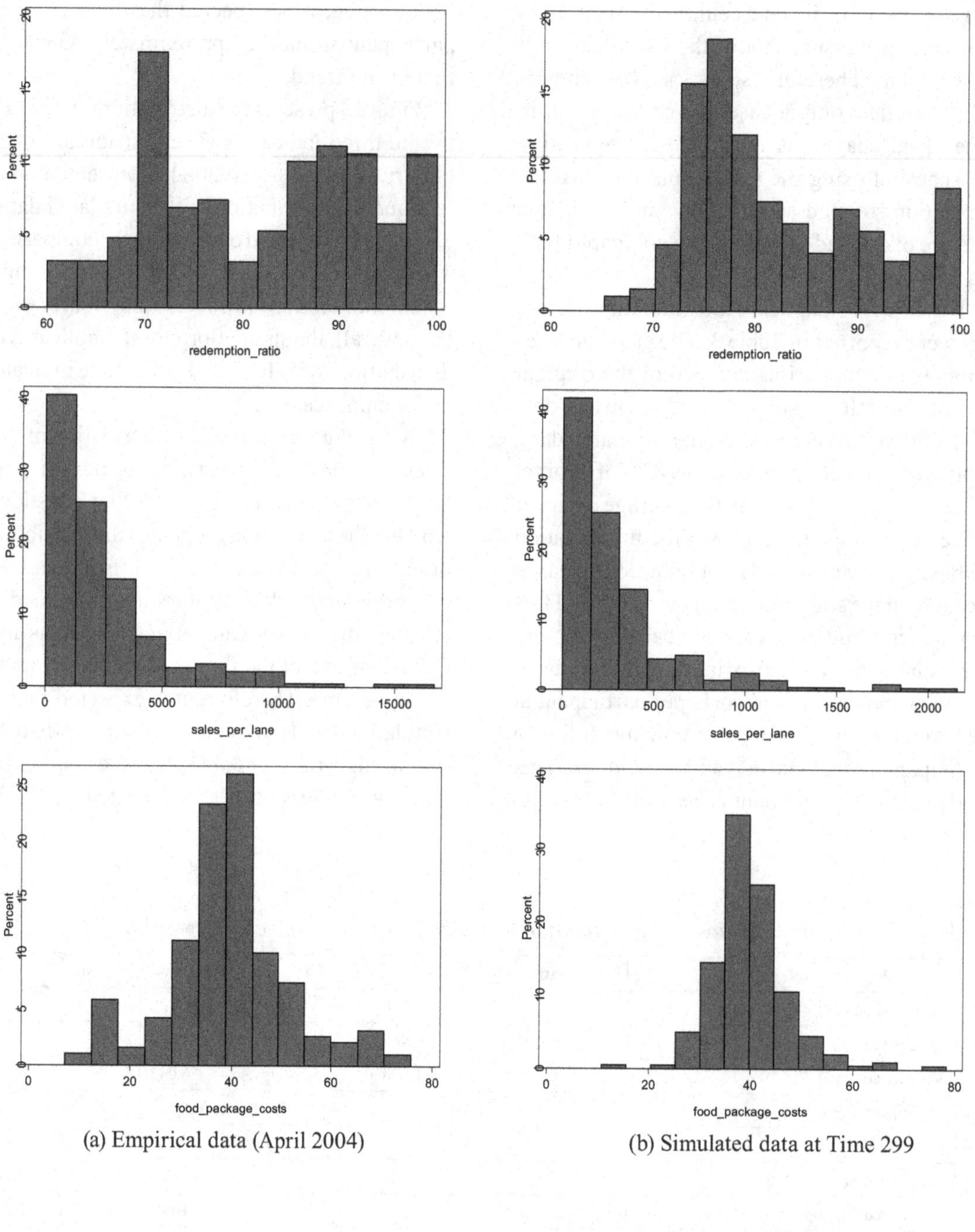

(a) Empirical data (April 2004)

(b) Simulated data at Time 299

vendors are more likely to be identified as having a higher level of risk in both datasets, because the simulation was designed to make small vendors with high-risk propensity were more actively involved in fraud.

Table 4 reports the percentage of vendors at different risk levels in both the empirical and simulated data. Vendors were categorized into four levels based on the risk indicators (from Level 0 to Level 3). For example, when a vendor meets the three risk indicators, the vendor is categorized as Level 3. In the state monitoring system, vendors at Levels 2 and 3 are considered to be high-risk. In the empirical data, approximately 5.3% of vendors

Table 4. Percentage of vendors at different risk levels in the empirical(a), simulated data (b)

Risk level of vendors	Empirical data Percent	Simulated data Percent
Level 0	81.4	75.0
Level 1	13.3	19.5
Level 2	4.8	4.5
Level 3	0.5	1.0

Note: Level 2 and 3 are considered to be high-risk.

Figure 4. Vendor distribution by risk level and store size in the (a) empirical and (b) simulated data

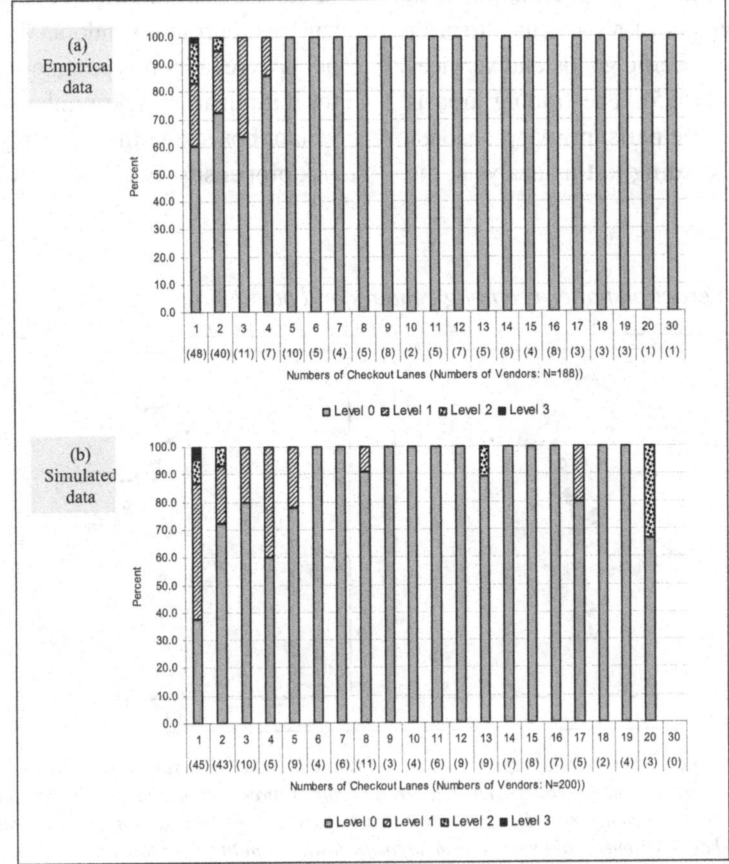

were categorized as high-risk. In the simulated data, approximately 5.5% of vendors were categorized as high-risk. Therefore, this simulation also reasonably replicates the distribution of vendors by risk level in the empirical data.

The distribution of vendors by risk level and store size is presented in Figure 4, and provides information on the outliers. Most vendors at Levels 2 and 3 were one or two checkout lane vendors in both datasets. Numbers in parentheses on the x-axis show the number of vendors that have such a number of checkout lanes in both datasets.

Investigating Spatial Patterns

Along with the descriptive statistics, spatial patterns emerging from the interactions among vendors and participants were examined. In the retailing literature, for example, trading area patterns have been identified. A trading area contains the consumers of a particular firm or groups of firms for specific goods and services (Berman & Evans, 1995). The trading area is broken down into three parts: primary, secondary, and fringe. According to this analysis, the majority of consumers (50 to 80%) come from the primary area, with an additional 15 to 25% of a store's customers in the secondary area. The remaining, most widely dispersed customers come from the fringe area. This implies that proximity to stores is an important criterion for consumer store choices. Store choice or spatial interaction models have conceived and extended this idea as a basic promise (Huff, 1964; McFadden, 1980; Nakanishi & Cooper, 1974, 1982). In Figure 5 (a) and (b), we present two maps that show spatial interaction patterns of normal and high-risk vendors in the empirical data.

To simulate the spatial pattern of vendors and their customers (i.e., WIC participants) using FraudSim, a hypothetical scenario was developed with 10 vendors and 2,000 participants. In the simulation, locations of the vendors and participants were randomly generated within a rectangular landscape. Dots represent participants, while squares represent vendors. Vendors and participants were randomly assigned risk propensities at the initialization. The numbers in decimals in the vendor box shows the randomly assigned vendor risk propensity. Each vendor was also randomly

Figure 5. Spatial interaction patterns among vendors and participants

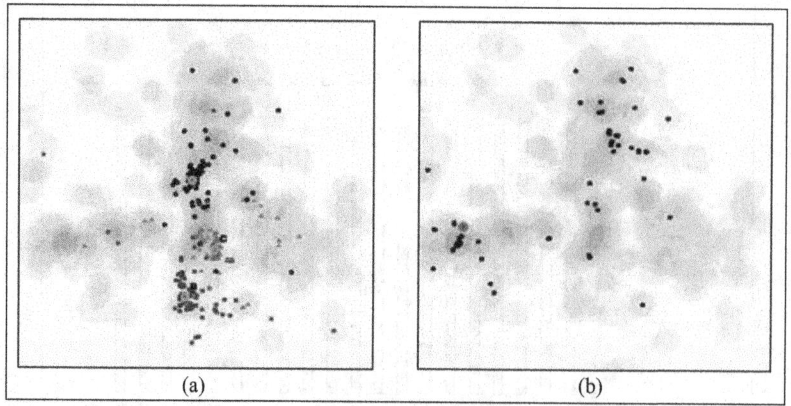

Note: For illustrative purposes, large circles represent selected vendors. Small dots surrounding the vendors present participants who redeemed their benefits at the vendors. The background color represents the density of participants in the county. (a) Presents a normal pattern in which the majority of the store's customers live close to the store; (b) presents the spatial pattern of a high-risk vendor, whose customer mainly come from areas far away from the store location.

assigned to have one to twenty store checkout lanes which are presented in the second number inside each vendor box. The larger the square, the larger the number of checkout lanes.[6]

Figure 6a shows the theoretical spatial pattern that can be expected when the Huff model is based on describing individual choice at the micro level. It is assumed that customers will choose stores based on economic rationality, and will maximize their utility based on certain deterministic factors. It is possible to incorporate other decision factors, such as store quality and availability of parking (summarized in Drezner & Eiselt, 2002), in order to generate different trading area patterns. However, the fundamental logic does not change.

In terms of a high-risk pattern, it is assumed that a vendor with high-risk propensity will lose participants with low risk propensity who are supposed to be served by the vendor, because negotiations to engage in fraud will most likely fail. Instead, these vendors will attract participants with a high-risk propensity. These participants can be those who failed their negotiation with a vendor having low risk propensity at their initial choice. In other words, high-risk vendors lose those who are likely to visit the vendor and attract those who they are not likely to. This is ultimately reflected in the spatial patterns of vendors participating in fraud.

In Figure 6a, two small vendors were identified with relatively high (0.86) and low (0.12) risk propensities. Solid thick circles show the trading area of the vendors. Their interactions with the participant agents they were supposed to serve were watched. Figure 6 b shows the result of fraud negotiations at the initial stage. The vendor with high risk propensity failed to attract participants in the vendor's supposed trading area and started attracting participants who failed in negotiations with their theoretical vendors and were successful in negotiations with the high-risk vendor.

In Figure 6c, at Time 292, the vendor agent with high-risk propensity attracted more participants from hypothetical secondary and fringe areas, while other vendors kept their original patterns at Time 292. It was found that a small vendor next to the high-risk vendor was also developing as high-risk. However, the small vendor with a low risk propensity still maintained its original participants at Time 292. This simulation contrasts the different interactions between vendors and participants based on their risk propensities when the store size is the same.

Figure 6d highlights the distribution of participants visiting the high-risk vendors at Time 308 by whiting out all other vendors from the landscape. The small high-risk vendor lost participants in the primary area and attracted participants from other areas who were not expected to visit from the current theoretical framework. Another developing high-risk vendor (inside dotted circle) also shows similar spatial interaction patterns. The high-risk vendor (inside solid circle) reached to the level of 1.0 (maximum risk propensity) from 0.86, while the low risk vendor remained at the level of 0.15, which is not different from the initial condition (0.12).

In sum, the interactions and interdependency among players in a public delivery system were modeled in our agent-based model, FraudSim, where routine activities of the agents in the policy system were specified. This simulation shows the development of some risky vendors when they opportunistically behave without appropriate guardianship. A possible mechanism underlying the patterns of fraud such as rational choice and fraud negotiation was explored. We assumed that most participants make rational store choice based on certain decision criteria in terms of selecting stores and fraud decisions are made based on their risk propensity and chance. This chapter shows that the agent-based model closely replicates the statistical and spatial patterns of fraud in the policy system at a certain point in time. Therefore, the model can serve as a framework for implementing different theoretical assumptions, modeling other underlying mechanisms, and testing policy options.

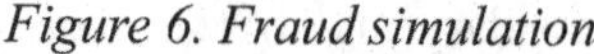

Figure 6. Fraud simulation

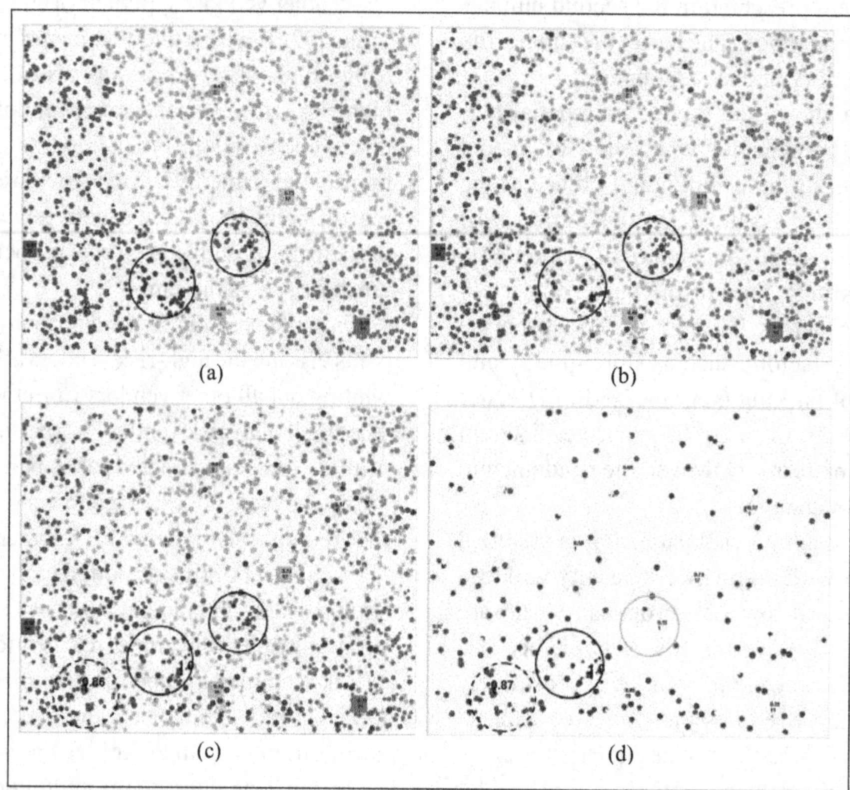

Note: (a) Theoretical vendor choices of participant when the Huff model was deterministically implemented at Time 0. Two small vendors were highlighted: one with relatively high risk propensity (0.86) and the other with relatively low risk propensity (0.12). (b) Fraud negotiations occurred at Time 1. (c) Fraud negotiations continue for those participants who have a relatively high risk propensity (> 0.6) and are not involved in fraud. While the small vendor with low risk propensity remained stable (risk propensity: 0.12 to 0.15), the high-risk vendor was actively attracting participants (risk propensity: 0.86 to 1.0) at Time 292. Another one-lane vendor next to the small high-risk vendor was developing as high-risk (risk propensity: 0.66 to 0.86) at Time 292. Other vendors were maintaining their original trading areas. (d) This highlights the interaction between small vendors with high-risk propensity and participants at Time 308 (black solid and dotted circles). The small vendor with low propensity was faded out (gray solid circle) for the purpose of emphasis. All vendors are small, having one lane. The vendor's risk propensity inside the black solid circle was 0.86 at the beginning and quickly reached to 1.0 at the end of the simulation. The vendor was attracting participants from all areas.

DISCUSSION

This chapter attempts to understand statistical and spatial patterns of fraud in the delivery of public services. Criminologists have intensively explored white-collar crime since Sutherland. Research on white-collar crime has often been focused on the significance of monetary loss or social class. Studies that examine dynamics of white-collar crime within a spatial framework are relatively limited.

This chapter contributes to the body of literature in two different ways. First, we approached white-collar crime using an agent-based model. Fraud in public delivery programs was framed as a complex system, and the underlying mechanisms of such fraud based on rational store choice and fraud negotiation were explored. This allowed us to replicate the distribution of vendors with risk status in the empirical data. Second, in Eck's words (1995), "to examine routine activity theory, simulations could be conducted to determine whether the crime patterns created match those observed in the real world." By comparing the results of the simulation with the observed patterns in the empirical data, we evaluated the legitimacy of the simulation model.

Policy implications can be drawn from this work. First, Kim (2007) identified unusual spatial interaction patterns between participants and vendors from the perspective of traditional store choice models. Her study shows that when fraud occurs in public delivery programs, spatial patterns are different from the prediction of consumer store choice models. The weakness of such approach is that we can only identify those who show abnormal patterns after committing fraud. When the process of developing vendors as high-risk can be understood, public agency may be able to discuss when and where they need to intervene to deter fraud. Second, the simulation can facilitate discussion of policy intervention among policy makers by incorporating their assumptions on the issue into the simulation. Agent-based modeling provides a flexible framework for this activity in practice.

Limitations

A major limitation of this study is that the agent-based model only captures the interaction between vendors and participants at the current stage. In practice, agents act in a more complicated fashion than what has been tested here. Participants can be involved in fraud among themselves, a group of vendors can be assembled to commit organized crimes, or an outside entity can be involved in the WIC business process. In this chapter, one of the main objectives was to develop a foundation on which to build future studies by focusing on the most common fraud mechanisms.

While this simulation stepped forward in terms of introducing dynamics in the choice model, the actual WIC program is much more dynamic than the simulation. For example, in the agent-based model, vendor agents do not exit or get replaced, whereas in the WIC program, vendors are sometimes introduced or withdrawn. Voucher usage by participants was also simplified. Every voucher was used by participant agents each iteration. In reality, some participants may not use their vouchers at all during certain months. It was not tested how these characteristics will change the dynamic of fraud.

The simulation also has limitations in terms of decision-making. In the current simulation, participant and vendor agents make store choices and fraud decisions right away when they meet each other. In reality, both decisions may take longer and both parties may go through the process of trial and error. Other personal characteristics or situations may influence how decisions are made.

In addition to easy decision-making by agents, this simulation is built within the framework of a utility function. One advantage is that some of the well-established models and evidence can be applied in the simulation. A weakness, however, is that the simulation still holds limiting assumptions regarding human behavior. An example of this weakness appears when modeling the situation where a high-risk vendor is replaced by a new vendor. Once the replacement is made by the public agency agent, all participant agents recalculate their store choice probabilities without hesitation. In reality, it may take longer to inform participants and make them visit the new vendor which may alter the dynamics of fraud.

Agent-based models are developing as an alternative tool for studying complex natural and human phenomena. Compared to statistical or optimization procedures, the process of building and testing the models has not been firmly established. Several parts of our model are based on heuristics, rather than on parameters from empirical evidence. This aspect of the current models provides an opportunity, as well as a barrier, for extending this study.

FUTURE RESEARCH DIRECTIONS

When fraud in public delivery programs is approached from a management perspective, traditional criminology literature on criminality adds limited value to understanding the dynamic nature of crime in the real world. Focusing on the nature of criminals and calibrating the causes of crime do not tell us when, how, or why such criminal activities occur in public delivery programs. On the other hand, routine activity theory provides a framework to examine crime events as a convergence of offenders and targets in time and space. However, as Osgood, et al. (1996) suggested, there would not be sharp distinction between offenders and targets in this type of illegal and deviant behavior in the public delivery program. Fraud might be a side effect when players of the program opportunistically behave. This provides us an opportunity to examine the role of place managers or policy interventions in the system.

Crime is difficult to study because the process is not revealed in many cases. Traditional research methods and tools have limitations in studying such hidden processes and understanding the underlying mechanisms. Social simulation models have some promising aspects for studying issues of crime and public health. These models allow us to investigate interactions and interdependency, which is key to understanding the occurrence and diffusion of social issues. Therefore, the applicability of simulation models is more relevant in areas such as crime and public health.

From a policy point of view, simulation models also have advantages, in that policy analysts can test the consequences of certain policy options into the whole system. A current approach to test the effect of policy interventions is to implement pilot studies. This approach has significant weaknesses and is more resource-intensive compared to social simulation techniques. Public managers cannot implement the same pilot project repeatedly for the same people while carefully observing consequences for a long time due to political and administrative constraints. Studying human subjects has ethical and confidential issues. If human and social systems can be studied using agents in a virtual laboratory, research, and practice in the areas of policy and management can be improved.

REFERENCES

Baker, J. S. (2004). The sociological origins of "white-collar crime." *Legal Memorandum, 14.*

Balan, G. C., Cioffi-Revilla, C., Luke, S., Panait, L., & Paus, S. (2003). MASON: A java multi-agent simulation library. In *Proceedings of the Agent 2003 Conference.* Retrieved September 5, 2007, from http://cs.gmu.edu/~eclab/projects/mason/

Bankes, S. C. (2002). Tools and techniques for developing policies for complex and uncertain systems. In *Proceedings of the National Academy of Sciences, 99*(3), 7263-7266.

Barker, T., & Roebuck, J. (1973). *An empirical topology of police corruption: A study in organizational deviance.* Springfield, IL: Charles C. Thomas Publisher.

Benson, M. L., Walker, E. (1988). Sentencing the white-collar offender. *American Sociological Review, 53*(2), 294-302.

Berman, B., & Evans, J. R. (1995). *Retail management: A strategic approach* (6th ed.). New York: Macmillan Publishing Company.

Bolton, R. J., & Hand, D. J. (2002). Statistical fraud detection: A review. *Statistical Science, 17*(3), 235-255.

Braithwaite, J. (1985). White collar crime. *Annual Review of Sociology, 11,* 1-25.

Cohen, L. E., & Felson, M. (1979). Social change and crime rate trends: A routine activity approach. *American Sociological Review, 44*(4), 588-608.

Cooter, R., & Ulen, T. (2000). *Law and economics.* Boston: Addison Wesley Longman, Inc.

Drezner, T., & Eiselt, H. A. (2002). Consumers in competitive location models. In Z. Drezner & H. W. Hamacher (Eds.), *Facility location: Applications and theory* (pp. 151-178). Berlin: Springer.

Eck, J. E. (1995). Examining routine activity theory: A review of two books. *Justice Quarterly, 12*(4), 783-797.

Epstein, J. M., & Axtell, R. (1996). *Growing artificial societies: Social science from the bottom up.* Washington, DC: Brookings Institution Press.

Fawcett, T., & Provost, F. (1997). Adaptive fraud detection. *Data Mining and Knowledge Discovery, 1,* 291-316.

Felson, M. (1987). Routine activities and crime prevention in the developing metropolis. *Criminology, 25*(4), 911-931.

Felson, M. (1994). *Crime and everyday life: Impact and implications for society.* Thousand Oaks, CA: Pine Forge Press.

Friedrichs, D. (2004). Enron et al.: Paradigmatic white collar crime cases for the new century. *Critical Criminology, 12,* 113-132.

General Accountability Office (1998). *Food assistance: Computerized information matching could reduce fraud and abuse in the food stamp program.* GAO/T-RCED-98-254.

General Accountability Office (1999). *Food assistance: Efforts to control fraud and abuse in the WIC program can be strengthened.* Report to Congressional Committee. (GAO/RCED-99-224).

General Accountability Office (2005). *Health care fraud and abuse control program: Results of review of annual reports for fiscal years 2002 and 2003.* GAO-05-134.

Glover, H. D., & Aono, J. Y. (1995). Changing the model for prevention and detection of fraud. *Managerial Auditing Journal, 10*(5), 3-9.

Griffin, S. P. (2002). Actors or activities? On the social construction of "white-collar crime" in the United States. *Crime, Law & Social Change, 37,* 245-276.

Hirschi, T., & Gottfredson, M. (1987). Causes of white-collar crime. *Criminology, 25*(4), 949-974.

Holland, J. H., & Miller, J. H. (1991). Artificial adaptive agents in economic theory. *Learning and Adaptive Economic Behavior, 81*(2).

Huff, D. L. (1964). Defining and estimating a trading area. *Journal of Marketing, 28,* 34-38.

Kim, Y. (2007). Using spatial analysis for monitoring fraud in a public delivery program. *Social Science Computer Review, 25*(3), 287-301.

Levitt, S. D., & Dubner, S. J. (2005). *Freakonomics: A rogue economist explores the hidden side of everything.* New York: William Morrow.

Luke, S., Cioffi-Revilla, C., Panait, L., & Sullivan, K. (2004). MASON: A new multi-agent simulation toolkit. In *Proceedings of the 2004 SwarmFest Workshop.* Retrieved September 5, 2007, from http://cs.gmu.edu/~eclab/projects/mason/.

Lynch, M. J., McGurrin, D., & Fenwick, M. (2004). Disappearing act: The representation of corporate crime research in criminological literature. *Journal of Criminal Justice, 32,* 389-398.

McFadden, D. (1980). Econometric models for probabilistic choice among products. *The Journal of Business, 53*(3), S13-S29.

Miethe, T. D., & Meier, R. F. (1990). Opportunity, choice, and criminal victimization: A test of a theoretical model. *Journal of Research in Crime and Delinquency, 27*(3), 243-266.

Nakanishi, M., & Cooper, L. G. (1974). Parameter estimate for multiplicative interactive choice model: Least squares approach. *Journal of Marketing Research, 11*, 303-311.

Nakanishi, M., & Cooper, L. G. (1982). Simplified estimation procedures for MCI models. *Marketing Science, 1*(3), 314-322.

Osgood, D. W., Wilson, J. K., O'Malley, P. M., Bachman, J. G., & Johnston, L. D. (1996). Routine activities and individual deviant behavior. *American Sociological Review, 61*(4), 635-655.

Provost, F. (2002). Comment on "statistical fraud detection: a review." *Statistical Science, 17*(1), 249-251.

Sutherland, E. H. (1940). White-collar criminality. *American Sociological Review, 5*(1), 1-12.

Sutherland, E. H. (1982). White collar crime is organized crime. In M. D. Ermann & R. J. Lundman. (Eds.). *Corporate and governmental deviance: problems of organizational behavior in contemporary society* (pp. 53-62). New York: Oxford University Press.

United States Department of Agriculture (2001). *WIC vendor management study 1998.* (Report No. WIC-01-WICVM).

Vandenburgh, H. (1999). *Feeding frenzy: organizational deviance in the Texas psychiatric hospital industry.* Lanham, MD: University Press of America, Inc.

Weick, K. E. (1979). *The social psychology of organizing* (2nd ed.). New York, NY: McGraw-Hill, Inc.

Wheeler, S., Weisburd, D., & Bode, N. (1982). Sentencing the white-collar offender: Rhetoric and reality. *American Sociological Review, 47*(5), 641-659.

Wilhelm, W. K. (2004). The fraud management lifecycle theory: A holistic approach to fraud management. *Journal of Economic Crime Management, 2*(2). Retrieved September 5, 2007, from http://www.utica.edu/academic/institutes/ecii/jecm/

Additional Reading

Axelrod, R. (1984). *The evolution of cooperation.* New York: Basic Books.

Axelrod, R. (1997). *The complexity of cooperation: Agent-based models of competition and collaboration.* Princeton, NJ: Princeton Studies in Complexity.

Ayres, I., & Levitt, S. D. (1998). Measuring positive externalities from unobservable victim precaution: An empirical analysis of Lojack. *The Quarterly Journal of Economics, 113*(1), 43-77.

Becker, G. S. (1968). Crime and punishment: An economic approach. In R. Febrero and P. S. Schwartz. (Eds.), *The essence of Becker* (pp. 463-517). Stanford, CA: Hoover Institution Press.

Becker, G. S. (1976). The economic approach to human behavior. In R. Febrero and P. S. Schwartz. (Eds.), *The essence of Becker* (pp. 463-517). Stanford, CA: Hoover Institution Press.

Cornish, D. B., & Clarke, R. V. (Eds.). (1986). *The reasoning criminal: Rational choice perspectives on offending.* New York: Springer-Verlag.

Eck, J. E., & Weisburd, D. (Eds.). (1995). *Crime and place.* Monsey, NY: Criminal Justice Press.

Eck, J. E., & Chainey, S. P., Cameron, J., & Wilson, R. (2006). *Mapping crime: Understanding hotspots.* Washington, DC: United State National Institute of Justice.

Felson, M. (2006). *Crime and nature.* Thousand Oaks, CA: Sage Publications.

Grasmick, H. G., & Green, D. E. (1980). Legal punishment, social disapproval and internationalization as inhibitors of illegal behavior. *The Journal of Criminal Law and Criminology, 71*(3), 325-335.

Grogger, J. (1991). Certainty vs. severity of punishment. *Economic Inquiry, 29*(2), 297-309.

Lattimore, P., & Witte, A. (1986). Models of decision making under uncertainty: The criminal choice. In D. B. Cornish & R. V. Clarke. (Eds.). *The reasoning criminal: Rational choice perspectives on offending* (pp. 129-149). New York: Springer-Verlag.

Levitt, S. D. (1996). The effect of prison population size on crime rates: Evidence from prison overcrowding litigation. *Quarterly Journal of Economics, 111,* 319-352.

Levitt, S. D. (1997). Using electoral cycles in police hiring to estimate the effect of police on crime. *American Economic Review, 87*(3), 270-290.

Liu, L., Wang, X., Eck, J., & Liang, J. (2005). Simulating crime events and crime patterns in a RA/CA model. In F. Wang. (Ed.). *Geographic information systems and crime analysis*. (pp. 197-213). Hershey, PA: Idea Group Publishing.

Vaughan, D. (1998). Rational choice, situated action, and the social control of organizations. *Law and Society Review, 32*(1), 23-61.

Vaughan, D. (1999). The dark side of organizations: Mistake, misconduct, and disaster. *Annual Review of Sociology, 25*, 271-305.

ENDNOTES

1 We are grateful to Anand Desai, Robert Greenbaum, John R. Current, colleagues at the John Glenn School of Public Affairs and Geography, and four anonymous reviewers who provided valuable comments. We are responsible for remaining errors. This chapter was presented at the Ninth Crime Mapping Research Conference at Pittsburgh, PA in March 28 - 31, 2007.

2 Given the nature and characteristics of vendors, participants, and employees in the program, the direct comparison of these numbers is not appropriate.

3 Data analysis was performed in May 2005 and was approved for publication without identifying the county and vendor names.

4 The total number of participants who redeemed their benefits was 28,887 in the month. However, participants usually visit more than a vendor to redeem their benefits each month. In April 2004, each participant visited approximately 1.5 vendors.

5 MASON stands for "Multi-Agent Simulation Of Neighborhoods... or Networks... or something..." http://www.cs.gmu.edu/~eclab/projects/mason/

6 The same size squares are used for vendors with more than 3 checkout lanes for presentation.

Section IV
Crime Justice Operation Simulations

Chapter XVII
Development of an Intelligent Patrol Routing System Using GIS and Computer Simulations

Joseph Szakas
The University of Maine at Augusta, USA

Christian Trefftz
Grand Valley State University, USA

Raul Ramirez
R2 Research and Consulting, USA

Eric Jefferis
Kent State University, USA

ABSTRACT

Patrolling in a nonrandom, but focused manner is an important activity in law enforcement. The use of geographic information systems, the emerging real-time data sets (spatial and nonspatial) and the ability via global positioning systems to identify locations of patrol units provide the environment to discuss the concept and requirements of an intelligent patrol routing system. This intelligent patrol routing system will combine available data utilizing Map Algebra and a data structure known as a Voronoi diagram to create a real-time updatable raster surface over the patrolling area to identify destination locations and routes for all patrol units. This information system will allow all patrol units to function "in concert" under a coordinated plan, and make good use of limited patrolling resources, and provide the means of evaluating current patrol strategies.This chapter discusses the algorithmic foundation, implications, requirements, and simulation of a GIS based intelligent patrol routing system.

INTRODUCTION

Information systems, both spatial and nonspatial, are successfully utilized by law enforcement officials. These systems often perform fundamental data processing techniques such as storage and query (e.g., fingerprint or DNA), whereas information systems that collect vast amounts of data and perform deterministic tasks to assist in decision-making are deemed intelligent systems. The strongest evidence of police effectiveness in reducing crime and disorder is found in the case of geographically focused police practices (Weisburd & Eck 2004). As police patrols constitute an important element in the implementation portion of any geographic-focused crime-fighting plan, this chapter will discuss work in progress in the development and simulation of an intelligent patrol routing system. Such a system will allow all patrol units to function under a coordinated plan, as opposed to N individual patrols locked in predefined wards or patrol areas by determining the destination, routes and spatial dispersion of all patrol units. This approach will allow patrols to be an improved tool within a problem oriented policing or other focused crime fighting approaches. One of the goals of the proposed system is to ensure that individual patrols are working in concert, where the system will allow the big picture to be seen. This routing system will be both probabilistic and deterministic by incorporating existing digital data sets (spatial and nonspatial), which will determine and direct the real-time routes for each unit within a given patrol.

There is a pressing need, when dealing with large volumes of data, to whittle down automatically these vast amounts of data for this type of complex event processing to get VIRT or "Valued Information at the Right Time" (Denning, 2006). With the ever increasing sophistication of GIS, growing amounts of relevant, timely and accessible digital data, increasing power of computer systems to create real-time solutions, and increasing use of GPS, the environment is well suited for the development of an intelligent routing system to facilitate the routing and assignments of patrols.

BACKGROUND

Routine activities and lifestyle theories explain situational opportunities that enabled criminal events to take place (Cohen & Felson 1979; Hindelang, Gottfredson, & Garafalo 1978). These very similar theories are often conceptualized as subsets of a broader *opportunity model* perspective (Cohen, Kluegel, & Land 1981; Cornish & Clarke, 1986). In essence, these opportunity models of crime describe the coming together of motivated offenders and suitable targets in a time and place that is lacking capable guardianship. Therefore, these opportunity perspectives focus attention on facilitators of criminal events rather than causes of criminality. Police have historically been local government's best attempt at providing capable guardianship to its citizens. The traditional method of police patrols often spatially divides the space to protect into "static" or unchanging regions (i.e., patrol wards, or "beats") and then assign units to patrol within each region in the hope that response times will be minimized, and with the additional increase of guardian presence, a reduced opportunity for criminal activity would occur.

The manner in which actual patrols are carried out can increase the effectiveness of patrols. Studies have demonstrated, for example, that focusing police patrols on crime hot spots is more effective than simple random patrol (Sherman & Weisburd 1995; Sherman, Gartin, & Buerger, 1989). Generally, traditional policing practice assumes that standard strategies (e.g., preventative patrol, rapid response, investigations, and increasing numbers of police) can be uniformly applied across geographical space with little concern for variations in crime levels, crime types or other factors (Weisburd & Eck 2004).

Reviews of policing strategies however, have uncovered little systematic evidence to support these traditional policing practices (Skogan & Frydl 2004; Weisburd & Eck 2004). Fortunately, a growing body of literature has demonstrated that geographically focused interventions and problem-solving strategies hold great promise for crime reduction (Skogan & Frydl 2004; Weisburd & Eck 2004). A limitation of traditional police patrols is that when a patrol unit (or subset of patrolling units) is responding to a call, a specific region is no longer being patrolled (or at the very least the patrol manpower is reduced), and thus more vulnerable to crime.

In recent years, academic researchers have begun to interpret their findings in more user-friendly terms, and deliver actionable strategies to police practitioners. Case in point, the U.S. Department of Justice, Office of Community Oriented Policing Services published manuscript—*Crime Analysis for Problem Solvers in 60 Small Steps* (Clarke & Eck 2005) is an excellent resource written by academic researchers in inform police problem solvers about effective strategies. The chapter seeks to follow this promising trend of making research guided applications available to the field by enhancing the existing and (perhaps redefining) the current methodology of patrol.

FUNCTIONAL REQUIREMENTS AND SYSTEM OBJECTIVES GOALS

So what should a patrol routing information system do? And perhaps more importantly, how do you know that the system is performing as designed? The identification of a set of systems objective goals and functional requirements for a patrol routing system (or any information system for that matter) is the starting point to address this question. One can begin identifying requirements by examining the requirements of other relevant systems. For example, the task of patrolling finds overlap with delivery routing services (e.g., UPS, Fed Ex) (Calvete, Gale, Oliveros, & Sanchez-Valverde, 2004). Just as there are "windows of opportunity" to deliver a package, there are "windows of opportunity" to commit a crime, and patrols units should "pay attention to daily and weekly rhythms" (Clarke & Eck 2005) by attempting to be at specific locations at specific times and/or dates (e.g., hot spots, bank openings) when risk of crime is highest. Functional requirements and system objective goals specific to an intelligent patrol routing system, should include but are not limited to the following:

- Balance the spatial position of patrols over the entire patrol area to minimize response time and "to provide improved assistance to citizens in crisis" (Skogan & Frydl 2004), while recognizing that some areas require more patrolling than others.
- Provide the means for the entire set of patrol units to function "intelligently": adjusting routes accordingly when one (or more) patrol units are dispatched to a call or otherwise unable to fulfill the "patrol" function.
- Provide meaningful reports and maps to community groups to show how frequent patrols are happening in specific neighborhoods or reports that assess effectiveness of patrols from within the organization (e.g., analysis of the crime with respect to actual patrol information).
- Address high risk areas (i.e., windows of opportunity), to insure that a guardian/patroller is present during "time sensitive" activities such as: Bank/businesses/bar-opening/closing or un-occupied residences (e.g., seasonal homes).
- Minimize predictability of routes (while still providing regional patrol coverage).
- Provide proper routes taking into consideration other factors such as time of day, traffic, congestion, and repair work.

- Report to the patrolling unit what are the risks for the current patrol at the patrol's destination.
- Provide the possibility of precalculating patrol scenarios.
- Factor in existing crime data (e.g., hot spots), and to incorporate real time crime data and factors to allow the system to be "self adapting" as given conditions unfold.
- Provide a measure to evaluate the completeness of a patrol over the area being patrolled.

The importance of these goals and requirements and systems objectives should not be minimized or trivialized. For any information system it is its functional requirements that will be the measure that all Intelligent Patrol Systems' goals will be graded upon, to determine if the system is performing to acceptable levels.

DATA SETS/LAYERS

Layers are a fundamental concept in geographical information systems (GIS) (Clarke, 2002). A given GIS application will have several layers. Each layer will contain data about a set of features that are of interest for that particular application. A GIS application will allow the selection of layers to visualize at any given time. The layers that can be utilized in an intelligent patrol routing system are both numerous and in terms of the layer's storage size are considerably large. It is the large collection of huge data layers that require any intelligent system to "boil down" that data into a more manageable size for decision-making (VIRT). However, there are two layers that are fundamental to the requirements of patrol, specifically, the road layer, which defines the valid areas a patrol can travel, and second, the parcel layers which will contain the candidates for the destination of individual patrols. The road layer could possibly represent both sides of the road but in this discussion will be represented as a centerline of the roads. The attributes of features in the road layer can aid in the sophistication of the patrol routing system as; elevation, speed limit, repair work/construction, rush hour congestion (time dependent), which allows for a more realistic calculation of the time needed to reach the destination for all patrol units. Utilization of these attributes to create a more complete "friction surface" will be discussed more fully in the section on "GIS Operations". One minor requirement is that in the proposed method, the parcels and road must abut to allow the route destination to be calculated. This can be done by buffering the centerline roads until the roads touch the parcel. If the Parcel Id can be projected upon or assigned to the road segment along (or in front of) the parcel, then other routing methods could be implemented where the requirement of the parcels touching the roads, is removed. Information concerning the parcel type (residential, commercial, seasonal home) is relevant and will be one of the many factors to determine when to actually patrol. For example, if the parcel were of type "commercial" then

Figure 1. Shows the attribute of time since last visit (TSLV) of each parcel in the patrol area

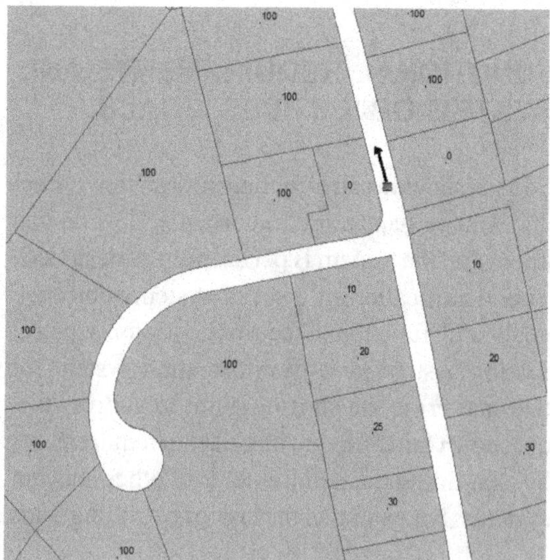

there would normally be people there during the day, but not at night. The situation for residential parcels may be reversed. One specific attribute of the parcel layer that is required by the system is called: "time since last visit", (abbreviated here are TSLV), and seen in Figure 1.

The TSLV (updated for all parcels in real-time) will indicate the last time that a patrolling unit passed by (patrolled) that location. As the patrol unit passes, the value will reset back to zero. The use of the TSLV attribute will be discussed in the next section, but one can envision the use of the values of TSLV in a raster setting similar to an elevation layer (z value or height), where the goal of the patrol will be to minimize (or lower) this "risk" surface. The higher the values of TSLV, the more at risk the parcel is as the longer the parcel has been without a patrol unit passing by the parcel. Other layers will depend on availability, and although this is not an exhaustive list, it should be reminded that this patrol system can and most likely will encompass a vast array of data layers. Data layers such as flood maps (FEMA Q3 Digital flood layers) would help by creating patrols that would avoid certain routes due to flooding. Data layers common to police agencies are crime maps (pin maps or hotspot maps). The robustness and potential of this information system may be seen as even spatial data layers of suspects or parolees (geographic profiles) showing the person's home and work and path to work might be included. Maps showing parcels with existing restraining orders, and more importantly time when risk of a violation of the restraining order might occur. Even layers indicating "coal sack buffers" of those on parole, all could be employed to determine routes and destinations of patrol units.

DATA STRUCTURES: THE VORONOI DIAGRAM

A foundational data structure that is the heart of this routing information system is the Voronoi diagram. The calculation of the Voronoi diagram is a classical problem in computational geometry (Aurenhammer, 1991; Goodman & O'Rourke, 2004; Green & Sibson, 1978). Given a plane and a set of n seed points, one divides the plane into tiles such that all the points in a given tile are closer to a certain seed than to any other seed. Figure 2 shows a Voronoi diagram with five seeds, depicted in this image as the dark points.

In this discussion, each patrol car may be seen as a seed within the city's boundary (the

Figure 2. An example of a Voronoi diagram with 5 seeds using manhattan distances (left) and euclidean distances(right)

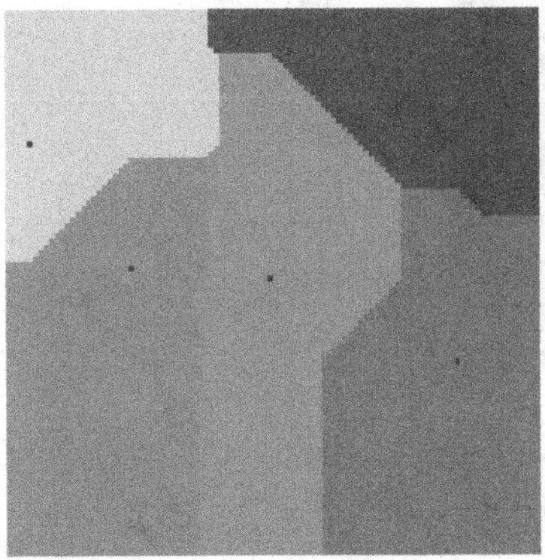

physical two dimensional plane). Using the Voronoi diagram the city is then tiled into zones or regions where parcels in each tile are closest to that patrol car than to any other patrol car. And it is this patrol car (seed) that would be assigned or dispatched to address any incident in that zone. The advantages of a patrol rest on the following characteristic: First the distance factor, makes a simple automatic determination of an assignment as the seed within the tile, is closest than any other seed. The second point is that one knows the seeds of the neighboring (abutting) tiles, and this helps in terms of backups or when the seed within the tile is unavailable, who would among the remaining set would be closest and get the "next" call (Figure 3).

Most of the existing uses of Voronoi diagrams are in the static case (i.e., the seed points do not move, and more importantly the patrol regions/tiles are defined once regardless of the patrol configuration). But, by allowing the change of position of the seeds and hence regenerating the Voronoi diagram, then this dynamic tiling provides continuous updates based specifically on the seeds configurations. It is this dynamic ability of redefining the tiles in real-time that lends itself to improving the patrol systems, in terms of properly assignment destinations to patrol units, balancing the space and minimizing response times. Also two points should be noted. First, is that there are many different distance formulas that could be used to generate the Voronoi diagram (e.g., Euclidean and Manhattan shown in Figure 2 to name just two), there could be distance formulas based upon the other factors such as closeness to seeds based on "time to arrive" that could deal with modern issues of construction, congestion and/or grid lock. Second, is that because the Voronoi is a planar tessellation, it is an approximation tiling in the nonplanar real world, as elevation is not part of the distance calculation. Voronoi diagrams can use other factors besides spatial coordinates (Green & Sibson, 1978) to determine "distance", but that is outside the scope of this discussion. Figure 4 shows the results using a straight Euclidian distance over a region.

Figure 5 shows the result of using the distance layer to calculate a Voronoi diagram on the map of a city with two seeds.

GIS OPERATIONS

From the previous section on "Data Sets/Layers" that are either required or possibly used by an Intelligent Routing system, it should be stated here that there will be a mix of vector and raster datasets, and it should be noted that the calcula-

Figure 3. The results of the Voronoi diagram when one patrol unit becomes unavailable

Figure 4. The results using a straight Euclidean distance on a region. Distances between patrol locations are represented by the radiating circles of different colors.

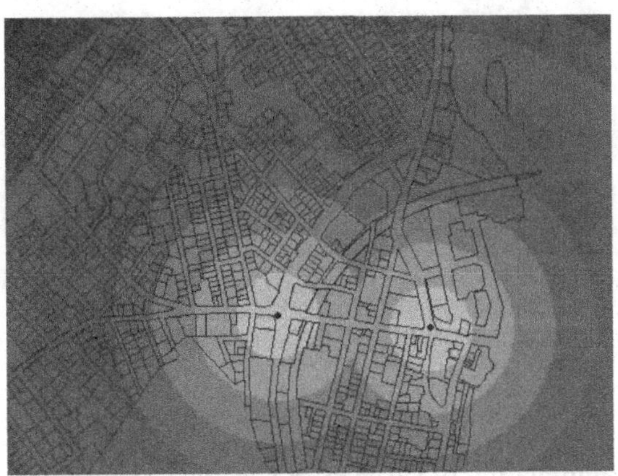

Figure 5. Voronoi diagram calculated from the distance calculation in Figure 4 where the city is patrolled by two patrol cars

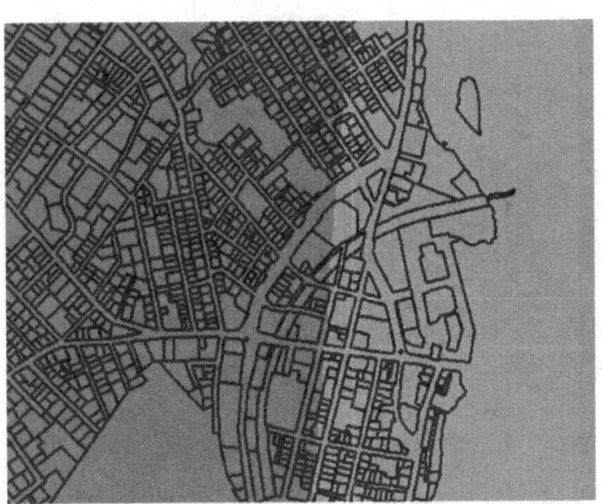

tions could be performed upon raster or vector data. Processing in raster provides us the ability to perform "Map Algebra" which gives users the ability to combine and weigh the importance of each layer in the calculation for determining the strategy for the entire patrol set. Processing in vector would allow the use of Bayesian (or belief) network for the same purpose of Map Algebra. In the following paragraph we describe Map Algebra. A similar description about Bayesian network can be found in Pearl (1985).

Map Algebra can be defined as the "arithmetic of map combination for co-registered layers with raster of identical size and resolution" (Tomlin, 1990), or as "the addition or multiplication of attributed stored in the raster cells" (Clarke, 2002). It is through this Map Algebra process of layer combination that VIRT is achieved (i.e., taking many layers and making one). It is important to note that due to the multiplicative ability of Map Algebra, some layers can have a greater impact (weighted) in determining where to send the patrols, and if weighted high enough, can completely override the system and demand that certain actions happen regardless of the other layers. Also, in the same vein, some layers can have a negative (subtractive), or "frictional" ability to reduce values, in other words, to make certain areas less critical to be patrolled at a given time. For example the need to patrol as often in areas with existing guardians, such as neighborhood crime watch, night watchmen or even houses with alarm systems. Figure 6 is an example of one possible layer that would be converted into raster and included in a Map Algebra calculation which is an identification of two (shaded) neighborhoods, or areas that have has an unusually high level of crime during this patrol period.

The proper weighting of each layer cannot be understated. This is a very difficult task, as different cities have varying crime activities. However, the setting of the weights may be done either subjectively by law enforcement agencies who have heuristics and experience as to the importance of one layer over another, or by perhaps more scientific means where the information system takes past crime data, and "trains" the information system similar to the

Figure 6. An example data layer of hot spots or high crime activity

Figure 7. Three risk surfaces and the summed result (lower right) using map algebra

updates of weights of a neural network systems via backward propagation, but this is still an area of research and future work. It is the arithmetic combination (which can be adjusted for different times, situations and locales) that will create the resulting surface layer in which the identifications, the paths, and destinations for each patrol will be determined.

The following mathematical expression describes the map algebra calculation to identify risk surface showing areas of importance within the patrol region:

$$Risk\_surface = \sum \alpha_1 l_1 t_i + \alpha_2 l_2 t_i + ... + \alpha_i l_i t_i$$

Where l_i is a spatial layer with the same spatial extents as the region being patrolled, containing normalized values. The symbol α_i is the weight (multiplicative) factor as each layer can have varying degrees of importance which can be positive or negative. The symbol t_i is a time mask (one or zero) where some factors are only relevant during specific times (e.g., bank opening or closing). The pixels containing the highest value designate importance and are the ones most likely to be assigned as destinations to the patrols. Figures 7 and 8 show an example of map algebra and the aggregating of surfaces of specific risk together to form a single surface on which to base routing destinations.

One of the functional requirements is to evaluate the completeness of a patrol over the area being patrolled. The TSLV attribute is an aid in both the assessment of the information system and in the route determination. For the parcel layer, as discussed previously, an attribute called "time since last visit" is added. If every parcel that touches the road has this attribute, then at time T0 of the algorithm all parcels TSLV attribute will be initialized to zero. As the algorithm progresses, every parcel will continue to increase in value for every real-time epoch. As a patrol passes, the TSLV will reset to zero for that parcel. Figure 9 shows a region and the TSLV attribute but now converted into a raster layer. This time attribute will be the value for this raster layer contributing to the Map Algebra calculation. It should be restated that The TSLV attribute is just one of potentially many layers that will be available to law enforcement agencies, and the use of just the TSLV attribute for parcels is to provide an example of the concept.

The greater the value of the "time since last visit" attribute for a given parcel, the potentially greater is its map algebra calculation, which should either increase the likelihood that this

Figure 8. Three dimensional representation of aggregated risk surface from Figure 7

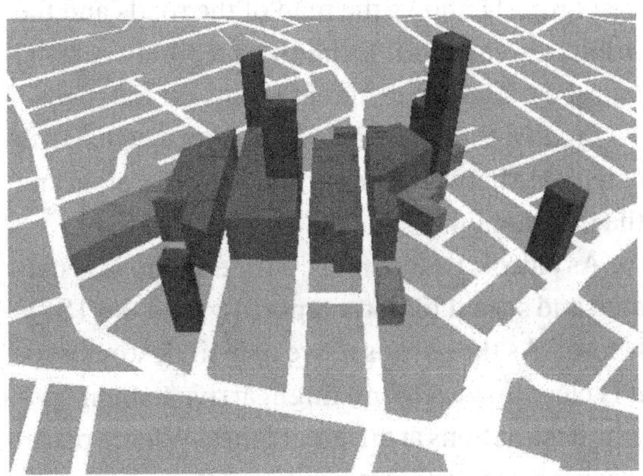

Figure 9. The rasterized parcel layer using Time Since Last Visit attribute as the pixel value

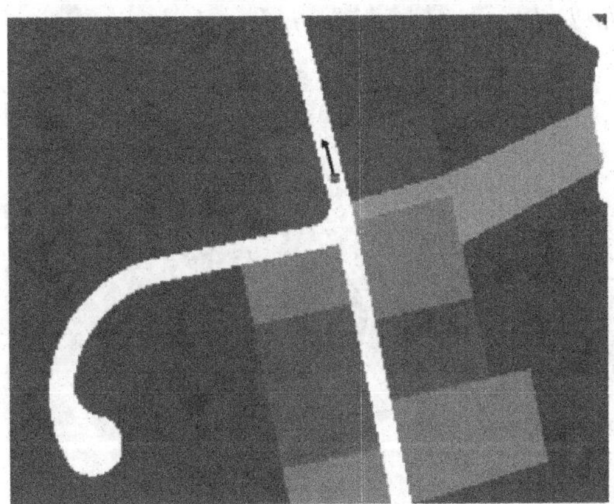

specific parcel will be selected as a destination in the next route calculation, or denote areas that are being unpatrolled.

SIMULATION AND PROPERTIES OF THE ROUTING ALGORITHM

The algorithm to determine the destination of all patrol units is summarized as follows:

Given N patrols, determine N destinations

- FOR each real-time epoch DO
    - Obtain the current spatial extent and active set of patrol units
    - Determine current tiling via a (dynamic) Voronoi diagram
    - Perform map algebra to sum up the relevant layers and determine the max pixel value (i.e., parcel) within each tile
    - Assign the max value to each patrol as its next patrol destination
    - Move patrols
    - Update TSLV attribute accordingly

When one uses raster maps, the route determination is very similar to watershed analysis. In watershed analysis, one addresses the questions of where water will flow given a starting point, and an elevation surface. These elevation values will allow passage or impede the path from source to destination.

Map algebra is performed to create an "elevation" or a risk surface from which the patrol routes will be determined. Relevant layers will be summed up and among these are the parcel layer using TSLV, and a road layer. The road layer will allow the thinning of data, as it will serve as a mask (a raster surface consisting of only zeros and ones; ones for pixels containing a road, and zero otherwise). Once this calculation is completed there will be a raster surface which will have a set of pixels containing a maximum value in each Voronoi tile. This will be the destination. What is different from watershed analysis is that the path to calculate should be the "most beneficial" path, one that would minimize the risk surface calculation, by patrolling high risk areas on the way to selected destinations. The goal of finding the path that contains the maximum sum (max cost) over the shortest path, which is the path where the parcels are in the greatest "need" of being patrolled over the shortest distance path while still reaching the destination at a specific time is a source of future work. So for simplicity, the route determination

Figure 10. Parcels layers, where the dark parcel is where the patrol car is currently located and the light parcel is the patrol car's destination

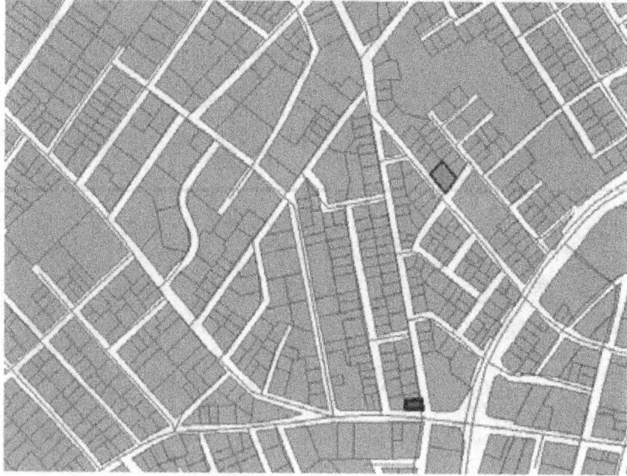

is just the shortest distance via the road network. One interesting point is that the use of the TSLV allows balance and forces pixel (parcels) values to grow in importance overtime and which allow under-patrolled areas to be identified.

Figures 10, 11 and 12 illustrate the procedure described in the previous paragraph. Figure 10 shows the map of a city. The location of the patrol car is depicted next to the dark parcel shaded at the bottom of the image. The destination parcel is lightly shaded just above the patrol parcel.

Figure 11 shows the map of the roads and the results of calculating the distance between the patrol car and the different points on the roads.

Finally, Figure 12 shows the shortest distance calculated between the current patrol location and the destination.

As patrols pass parcels, a time stamp is generated and stored for later reporting, and the TSLV is reset. As the patrols move to their destinations, it is clear that each unit might arrive to their specific destinations at different times. When a patrol reaches a destination, an update of the position and status of all units is received and a recalculation of the Voronoi is made, providing the determination of the next parcel destination for only that particular patrol. The ability to override the system at any time is done by simply weighting a layer in the system to in fact "conclude" the destinations and causing a time epoch update, regardless of the contributions of the other data layers. The need for this kind of action arises when emergencies or higher priority parcels demand action. There is a need to distinguish the difference between the task of patrolling and that of a patrol unit dispatched (a call received). Both are the same in that there is a destination (and a route determination), but

Figure 11. The distance surface utilizing a road mask

Figure 12. The shortest path for the patrol to follow to the destination parcel

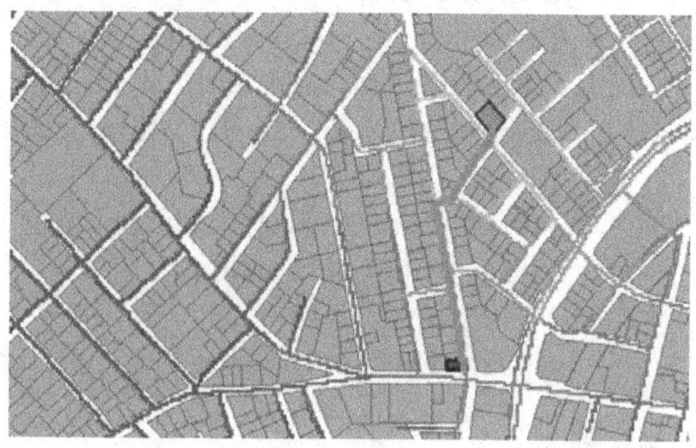

a patrol unit who is dispatched, is no longer officially on patrol, and is no longer considered a seed in the Voronoi diagram calculation, until the unit resumes patrol status (See Figure 3).

Assesment

The assessment of this intelligent patrol routing system, begins with the crime data that is acquired during the actual patrol and the data stored by all parcels during the patrol. So how will we know if this information system is working? Which areas were patrolled the most and least? What was the percentage of parcels that were actually patrolled during a specific period of time (shift/day/week, etc.)? What was the crime rate or activity before and after (during) the period of interest? What was the response time?

It will be possible to look over past days (via data mining) for patterns of missed opportunities. This will be used as feedback to improve the weighting assignments of each data layer used in the Map Algebra calculation. As many law enforcement agencies have limited police resources it is likely that many of the goals and functional requirements listed may not be met. Nevertheless these parameters should still be measured as room for improvement, and also as an argument for additional resources.

FUTURE RESEARCH DIRECTIONS

There are many areas of future research direction. The topics previously discussed are reiterated here. First, the improvement and the selection of the appropriate distance measurement in the determination of the Voronoi diagram. Second, the training and assigning of weighs for each spatial layer utilizing advanced data mining algorithms or perhaps neural networks is open for exploration. Third, improvements to the watershed model to create paths of "greatest need" while still meeting time arrival requirements is an area that potentially could be solved with massive parallelism. Additionally, it should be recognized that one of the advantages of requiring improved response of patrol units appear as effective "first responders". Future work might head towards utilizing expertise of individual patrollers, directing them to risk area where the individual has the best chance for success (e.g., domestic disputes). Work on expanding this intelligent patrol routing system to accommodate and assist in times of disasters, riots, terrorist actions, dragnets, roadblocks, and containment, when the time to set up and implement "command and control" in the repositioning of patrolling resources is most crucial. This information system would have the ability to easily create scenarios for planning purposed (emergency response) both for events where the risk is known (e.g., a levee break, requiring patrol units to be at specific locations) or when one has a predictable event and procedural response, but the location is not known (e.g., a tanker spill). Each of these scenarios can be stored as a layer without any weight (and hence not part of the map algebra calculation) but can be employed at anytime to override the system.

An Intelligent patrol routing system is, essentially, a dynamic system, one that should be able to adjust priorities on the fly and begin to maximize limited resources, and utilize datasets pertinent to law enforcement efforts. One final comment is that this system is very scalable and would to allow regional sharing as patrol units could cross external boundaries. A patrolling entity could request neighbors to migrate towards boundaries. Neighboring towns can be viewed as patrol wards at a different scale.

REFERENCES

Aurenhammer, F. (1991).Voronoi diagrams - A survey of a fundamental geometric data structure. *ACM Computing Surveys, 23*, 345-405.

Calvete H. I., Gale, C., Oliveros, M. J., & Sanchez-Valverde, B. (2004). Vehicle routing problems with soft time windws: An optimization based approach. *Monografias del Seminario Matematico Garcia del Galdeano, 31*, 295-304.

Clarke, K. C. (2002). *Getting started with GIS.* Upper Saddle River, NJ: Prentice Hall.

Clarke, R., & Eck, J. (2005). *Crime analysis for problem solvers in 60 small steps.* Center for Problem Oriented Policing.

Cohen, L. E., & Felson, M. (1979). Social change and crime rate trends: A routine activity approach. *American Sociological Review, 44,* 588-608.

Cohen, L. E., Kluegel, J. R., & Land, K. C. (1981). Social inequality and predatory criminal victimization: An exposition and test of a formal theory. *American Sociological Review, 46,* 505-524.

Cornish, D. B., & Clarke, R.V. (1986). *The reasoning criminal: Rational choice perspectives on offending.* New York: Springer.

Denning, P. J. (2006). Infoglut. *Communications of the ACM, 49*(7), 15-19.

Goodman, J., & O'Rourke, J. (Eds). (2004). *Handbook of discrete and computational geometry* (2nd ed.). Boca Raton, FL: CRC Press.

Green, P. J., & Sibson, R. (1978). Computing Dirichlet Tessellations in the plane. *Computing Journal, 21,* 168-173.

Hindelang, M. J., Gottfredson, M. R., & Garafalo, J. (1978). *Victims of personal crime: An empirical foundation for a theory of personal victimization.* Cambridge: Ballinger.

Pearl, J. (1985). Bayesian Networks: A model of self-activated memory for evidential reasoning. In *Proceedings of the 7th Conference of the Cognitive Science Society, University of California, Irvine,* CA. August 15-17. pp. 329-334.

Sherman, L.W., Gartin, P., & Buerger, M. (1989). Hot spots of predatory crime: Routine activities and the criminology of place. *Criminology, 27,* 27-55.

Sherman, L. W., & Weisburd, D. (1995). General deterrent effects of police patrol in crime "hot spots": A randomized, controlled trial. *Justice Quarterly, 12,* 626-648.

Skogan, W., & Frydl, K. (Eds). (2004). *Fairness and effectiveness in policing: The evidence.* Committee to Review Research on Police Policy and Practices, National Research Council ISBN: 0-309-52559-4,

Szakas, J. S., & Trefftz, C. (2006). Voronoi-diagram based heuristics for the location of mobile and unreliable service providers. In *Proceedings of the Conference on Advances in Computer Science and Technology (ACST).* Puerto Vallarta.

Tomlin, C. D. (1990). *Geographic information systems and cartographic modeling.* Upper Saddle River, NJ: Prentice Hall.

Weisburd, & Eck, J. (2004). What can police do to reduce crime, disorder and fear? *The ANNALS of the American Academy of Political and Social Science, 593*, 42-65

KEY TERMS

We have grouped our recommended readings for the interested reader in three different categories: Policing, Geographical Information Systems and Computational Geometry (which includes Voronoi diagrams).

Policing: A review and discussion about policing and how research has been conducted to evaluate possible improvements to policing can be found in "Fairness and Effectiveness in Policing: The Evidence", in particular in Chapter VI, "The

Effectiveness of Police Activities in Reducing Crime, Disorder, and Fear". The usefulness of geographic information systems to identify hot spots and the effectiveness of patrolling hot spots areas are discussed. An introduction to Community Oriented Policing practices can be found in "Crime Analysis for Problem Solvers in 60 Small Steps" by Ronald V. Clarke and John E. Eck. In particular steps 23, "Diagnose your hot spot", 24, "Know when to use high definition maps", and 25, "Pay attention to daily and weekly rhythms", expand on the premises in this chapter about the importance of using a GIS system to store and integrate information about hot spots and times when patrolling might be especially important.

Geographical Information Systems: "Getting Started with GIS" by K. C. Clarke is a good and recent introductory book to Geographical Information Systems. Another book on the subject is "Geographic Information Systems and Cartographic Modeling" by C. D. Tomlin. The online manual for the ARCGIS (ESRI 2001-2002) Spatial Analyst extension is an excellent introduction to the procedure of performing watershed analysis.

Computational Geometry: An extensive survey of Computational Geometry topics can be found in the "Handbook of Discrete and Computational Geometry" edited by J. Goodman and J O'Rourke (Goodman, & O'Rourke 2004). A classical survey on the Voronoi diagram, in particular, can be found in "Voronoi diagrams—A survey of a fundamental geometric data structure" by F. Aurenhammer. The paper "Voronoi-Diagram based Heuristics for the Location of Mobile and Unreliable Service Providers' by Szakas and Trefftz (2006) discusses heuristics that can be used to relocate mobile service providers when one of them is no longer available. The paper "Vehicle Routing Problems with Soft Time Windows: An Optimization Based Approach", by Calvete, et al., discusses an algorithm to optimize vehicle routes. The approach proposed in this chapter does not guarantee optimality but should be much less expensive to compute. Finally "Quickest Paths, Straight Skeletons, and the City Voronoi Diagram" by Aichholzer, et al. shows another useful way of modifying and applying the Voronoi diagram in a city setting.

Chapter XVIII
Drug Law Enforcement in an Agent-Based Model:
Simulating the Disruption to Street-Level Drug Markets

Anne Dray
Australian National University, Australia

Lorraine Mazerolle
Griffith University, Australia

Pascal Perez
Australian National University, Australia

Alison Ritter
University of New South Wales, Australia

ABSTRACT

This chapter describes an agent-based model called SimDrugPolicing that explores the relative impact of three law enforcement strategies—standard patrol, hotspot policing, and problem-oriented policing—on an archetypal street-based illicit drug market. Using data from Melbourne (Australia), we simulate the relative effectiveness of these different drug law enforcement approaches. We examine the complex interactions between users, dealers, wholesalers, outreach workers and police to examine the relative effectiveness of the three drug law enforcement strategies, analyzing several outcome indicators such as the number of committed crimes, dealers' and users' cash, overdoses and fatal overdoses. Our results show that problem-oriented policing is the most effective approach to disrupting street level drug markets in a simulated urban environment.

INTRODUCTION

Police throughout the world use a variety of street-level enforcement approaches to disrupt street drug market activity. Some aim to reduce the supply of drugs (e.g., crackdowns, raids, and buy-busts), others seek to reduce street-level demand for drugs (e.g., arrest diversion programs with mandated treatment), and other, partnership-oriented strategies (such as problem-oriented policing, third party policing) have been used in conjunction with harm minimization strategies to disrupt the dynamics of street level drug markets. In Australia, drug law enforcement is an essential component of the Australian government's illicit drug control plan. Direct expenditure on drug law enforcement for the year 2003/04 was $740 million and represented 56% of all proactive government spending on illicit drug control (Moore, 2005).

This chapter describes an agent-based model called SimDrugPolicing that explores the relative impact of three types of law enforcement strategies—standard patrol, hotspot policing, and problem-oriented policing—on an archetypal street-based illicit drug market. Using data from Melbourne (Australia), we simulate the relative effectiveness of these different drug law enforcement approaches on the dynamics of street-level drug market activity. We examine the complex interactions between users, dealers, wholesalers, outreach workers and police to examine the effectiveness of each of these drug law enforcement strategies, analyzing several outcome indicators such as the number of committed crimes, dealers' and users' cash, overdoses and fatal overdoses. We also test the advantages and limitations of using agent-based modeling—a technique stemming from complex systems science—in order to support decision-makers and practitioners in implementing illicit drug policies.

The model described in this chapter, named *SimDrugPolicing,* is an extension of *SimDrug* (Perez, Dray, Ritter, Dietze, Moore, & Mazerolle, 2006). *SimDrug* was a prototype agent-based model that assessed the capacity and added value of agent-based modeling as an explorative tool to better understand the dynamics of illicit drug markets. *SimDrug* was initially conceptualized and implemented in order to capture the primary community structures and relationships that support drug use and related outcomes. With *SimDrugPolicing,* we greatly enhance the law enforcement module of *SimDrug* by introducing complexity to the role of police. In *SimDrugPolicing* we draw from a systematic review of street-level drug law enforcement strategies conducted by Mazerolle, Soole, and Rombouts (2006) to model random patrolling, hotspots policing, and problem-oriented policing.

In this chapter we first compare and contrast the three categories of drug law enforcement strategies. The rationale for using agent-based modeling is then discussed, followed by a description of the model itself. Finally, we examine the results of several law enforcement scenarios and discuss the advantages and limitations for using this type of modeling when tackling real policy issues.

DRUG LAW ENFORCEMENT APPROACHES

In a systematic review of street level drug law enforcement approaches, Mazerolle, Soole and Rombouts (2006) adapted Weisburd and Eck's (2004) conceptual model of law enforcement practice to better understand the types of policing strategies that work best to disrupt street-level drug problems. As shown in Figure 1, Weisburd and Eck's model comprises two important dimensions: *diversity of approaches* (ranging from mostly law enforcement to using a wide array of intervention tactics, involving partnerships with other entities) and *focus of approach* (ranging from interventions that lack focus to those interventions that have a high degree of focus either on people or places).

Figure 1. Typology of policing approaches (from Weisburd & Eck, 2004)

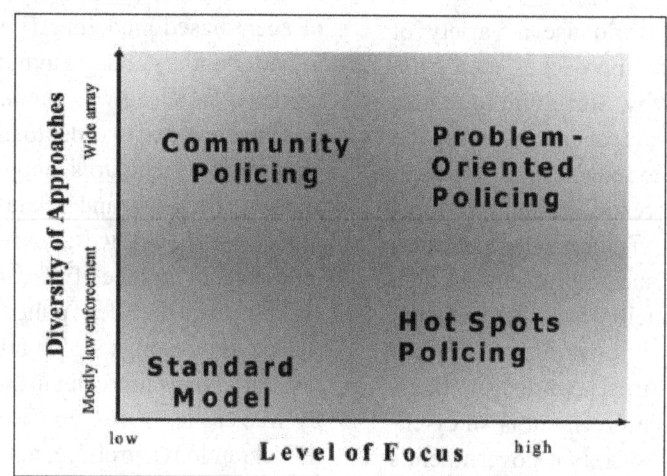

As depicted by this conceptual model, *community policing* typically uses a wide array of tactics, but has a low level of focus, targeting general problems across a community or jurisdiction. *Problem-oriented policing*, by contrast, uses a wide array of tactics, but is generally much more focused either on people or places that repeatedly come to the attention of the police. These two approaches contrast significantly with police strategies that rely principally on law enforcement resources. The *standard model* that includes rapid response, random, preventive patrols and the like has a low level of focus. *Hotspots policing* also relies on law enforcement resources, but, unlike the standard model, the hotspots approach is highly focused on dealing with places or people who generate more than their fair share of crime problems.

The review by Mazerolle, et al. (2006) of drug law enforcement strategies used this conceptual model and found that geographically focused interventions (including problem-oriented policing, third party policing and CPTED initiatives) are more effective than community-wide approaches that use partnerships across wide geographic areas to reduce drug and disorder problems in neighborhoods plagued with drug problems. Importantly, however, the review found that either type of partnership approach (community-wide or geographically focused) is likely to be more effective at reducing drug problems than law enforcement-only efforts (e.g., crackdowns, raids, directed patrols) that target drug hotspots (Mazerolle et al., 2006). That is, police partnerships with a variety of entities (regulators, inspectors, business owners, local councils) that are community-wide *or* geographically focused are more productive in reducing drug problems than law enforcement only approaches focused on hotspots. The standard model of random patrols and rapid response comes a distant last (see Mazerolle et al., 2006; Mazerolle et al., in press; Weisburd & Eck, 2004).

This chapter tests the findings of Mazerolle, et al. (2006) systematic review, simulating the impact of different street-level drug law enforcement approaches. We explore two "specific" approaches—*hot spots* and *problem-oriented policing*—and compare their impact to the outcomes generated by the standard patrol approach (renamed *"random patrol"* in this chapter). We analyze several outcome indicators including the number of committed crimes, dealers' and users' cash, overdoses, and fatal overdoses.

SIMDRUGPOLICING: A NEW AGENT-BASED MODEL

Drawing from the literature on the geography of drug dealing locations (Eck, 1998; Weisburd & Green, 1995; Rengert, Chakravorty, Bole, & Henderson, 2000), we consider the problem of street level drug dealing as based on local, geographic interactions, requiring the creation of adequate models to capture the primary community structures and relationships that support drug use and related outcomes. Using Complexity Theory (Gatrell, 2005) is one approach to exploring drug-dealing systems, enabling analysts to better anticipate implications of drug use for public policy and prevention programming. Street level drug markets tend to behave like complex adaptive systems (Agar & Resinger, 2002; Agar & Wilson, 2002). Illegal drug markets, being highly versatile, alternate between ever changing dynamic equilibriums. They are adaptive to external or internal shocks affecting the system, such as the introduction of new drugs, new cartels and new law enforcement policies (see for example Caulkins & Reuter, 2006; Caulkins, Behrens, Knoll, Tragler, & Zuba, 2004).

Multi-agent systems (Ferber, 1999; Janssen, 2002) are appropriate for exploring illicit drug markets as they focus on the individual components interacting within a given system. This is a purely bottom-up approach where representations of the individual components—the agents—display a large autonomy of action. Hence, system-level behaviors and patterns emerge from a multitude of local interactions.

Model Description

SimDrugPolicing was created using the Cormas© platform (Bousquet, Bakam, Proton, & Le Page, 1998) and developed from VisualWorks© commercial software. *SimDrugPolicing,* while inheriting its main structure from *SimDrug*, emphasizes an exploration of different law enforcement strategies. This section describes the main components of the model (for a more detailed description, see Perez et al., 2006).

SimDrugPolicing was collectively and interactively designed by a group of experts following a participative process (D'Aquino, Le Page, Bousquet, & Bah, 2003; Granath, 1991). The model is thus a mediating object, not a predictive expert system and the final decision-making rests with policy-makers. Engaging with experts at the very early stages of the system development ensures transparency of the model as the entire hypotheses underpinning the system and model rules are jointly created. The expert panel provided the modelers with relevant data sources, helping to build a reliable picture from multiple sources of information. Thus, our final model relies on a variety of data sources, each having its own strengths and weaknesses.

Time Scale

SimDrugPolicing simulates the illegal drug market occurring at the street level in an archetypal environment on a daily basis. One modeling time step is equivalent to a 24-hour day. From a computing perspective, this time scale challenges the computing process but was crucial to capture the daily injecting behaviors amongst regular intravenous drug users. Each simulation is run over an archetypal three-year simulation using real data from 1999 in Melbourne (Dietze, Miller, Clemens, Matthews, Gilmour, & Collins, 2004).

Drug Market

We consider a street market with only two drugs available: "heroin" and "other" (being a generic term for amphetamines, cocaine). The main distinctions between the drugs are their price and related harm (no risk of overdose under "other" drugs). Adapting data from Dietze and his colleagues (2004), heroin and "other" drugs enter the market at the wholesaler level at respectively 150$/g and 125$/g. Prices remain constant throughout the simulation.

Spatial Environment

The spatial grid depicts a 1:10 scale archetypal representation of Melbourne's CBD based on a regular 50x50 square mesh. The size of the grid has been chosen accordingly to the estimated number of users (3,000) and dealers (150) to be modeled and located in the environment (see Dietze et al., 2004. See also next section for details). Each cell in our model—our elementary spatial unit—approximates a *street block* (see Table 1*)*. A *suburb* is defined as an aggregation of neighboring cells (see Figure 2). Five suburbs are created with a different size and shape, regardless of realistic features. Two special cells represent the *Police Station* and the *Treatment Center.* We do not use a real GIS-based representation in this simulated model, given the added complexities of introducing environmental characteristics of the city. We recognize the importance of these environmental factors in shaping street level drug market activity (see Eck & Weisburd, 1995; Eck, 1998) and seek to build micro-level environmental characteristics into later editions of this agent-based model. For this iteration, however, we focus on social behaviors and interactions and merely introduce a cursory attribute ("conductivity") that recognizes, in a rudimentary way, that different street blocks have different levels of drug dealing "attractiveness."

Street Block: The main characteristics of a *street block* are given in the Table 1.

The *wealth* attribute, with an initial value randomly chosen between $100 and $500, is interpreted as a synthetic parameter indicating the social and material capital of the place. Wealth decreases by 5% when a crime is committed and increases by 3% after a 10-day period without crime. These rates of variation are not yet calibrated, instead are solely based on rules-of-thumb.

The concept of risk environment is encapsulated into the *risk* attribute. An empirical linear equation is used to calculate risk values at each time step:

risk = (10 * crimes) + (10 * overdoses) + nb of users on the street block

Risk is used to calculate the *conductivity* of a given street block to drug dealing. The following rule-of-thumb applies:

- One street block becomes *conductive* (1) if there is a dealer or (2) if risk > 20 or (3)

Table 1. Street block attributes, variable type and description

Attribute	Type	Description
overdoses	Integer	Number of daily overdoses on the street block
fatalOverdoses	Integer	Number of daily fatal overdoses on the street block
crimes	Integer	Number of crimes committed by users on the street block
wealth	Integer	Cash value of the street block available for successful crimes
risk	Integer	Global Indicator of environmental risk on the street block
conductivity	Boolean	Attractiveness of the street block for drug dealing

if there are at least four conductive street blocks around.

- One street block becomes *non-conductive* if there is no dealer and (1) if the risk = 0 or (2) if there is at least four non-conducive street blocks around.

Suburb: The spatial environment has been designed to generate heterogeneity in terms of hot-spot locations. The distribution of dealers, users, and conductive street-blocks at the beginning of the simulation favors some suburbs over others. We acknowledge the fact that, in reality, the urban design is a major factor driving illicit-drug markets (Eck & Weisburd, 1995). However, at this stage of the model development, we have simplified the geographic context by only considering street-blocks as the standard unit for dealing locations without incorporating transports hubs, shopping malls or lighting equipment.

Treatment center: We created one treatment center that admits users willing to undergo a treatment program. The overall capacity of the center corresponds to 1000 patients. Three programs are available, differentiated by their duration and estimated success rates. Detoxification and therapeutic community programs are residential while users on methadone maintenance are considered to remain active on the streets and can still inject heroin.

Figure 2. SimDrugPolicing's spatial grid at the beginning of the simulation

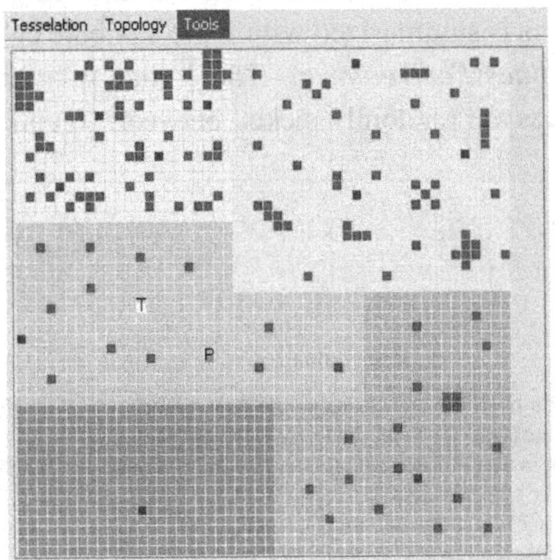

Note: the red grids depict the original conducive cells or hot-spots.

Police station: We created one *police station* for the whole system and 10 "Constables" (patrol officers) linked to it. The police station directs the "constables" to patrol a given area selected according to the rules of the law enforcement strategy (see next section). Arrested users, dealers, and wholesalers are transferred to the police station before being retrieved from the system.

Social Entities

SimDrugPolicing includes different types of social agents: *users*, *dealers*, *wholesalers*, *constables*, and *outreach workers*. Obviously, these computer entities do not accurately mimic individual behaviors of their real life counterparts. Each type represents a minimum set of characteristics and dynamics that allows the whole artificial population to display most of the properties observed in real societies. The inter-disciplinary work of our Expert Panel played a paramount role in defining a consensual set of simplified rules for the corresponding agent to "behave" realistically in our simulated model.

Our Expert Panel also debated whether or not we would create a closed or an open system. In a closed system, the initial set of "agents" remains in the system during the whole simulation, with the exception of individuals that "die" during the simulation. The only way to increase the population is to implement reproduction mechanisms at the level of the agents. An open system allows the entry into and exit from the system of a given number of agents at any point in time. It becomes much more complicated to track any single individual trajectory, yet these types of open systems are better suited to model problems such as bar attendance, airport lounge flows, and market-place encounters. We chose to implement an open system that sustained a constant number of *users*, *dealers*, and *wholesalers*. As such, for each time step, for a given number of users who die from an overdose, overcome their addiction through treatment, or are sentenced to a term in jail, then the equivalent number of new users will enter the system (marketplace) at the next time step. Likewise, a given number of arrested dealers or wholesalers will be automatically replaced. These are strong assumptions. Nonetheless, we adopted this constant population of users, dealers and wholesalers to enable us to clearly see the impact of the three different drug law enforcement approaches.

User: Estimations for the City of Melbourne give a range of 30,000 to 35,000 drug users considered as regular injecting drug users (Dietze, Hickman, & Kimber, 2005). In order to keep computing time into reasonable limits, we created a 1/10th representation of the reality and model only 3,000 *users*. The main characteristics of a user are given in Table 2.

In this model prototype, a user can buy and use only one type of drug at a time from a dealer. Each user is affiliated to one dealer's location and goes to the same hot spot as long as the dealer is selling drugs. As soon as the dealer disappears, all the affiliated users have to find another provider by "walking" around (moving from grid to grid) or contacting friends. Users can become user-dealers if they are wealthy enough to fulfill their own need and buy extra quantities of drug for reselling.

A user will have a 0.5% chance to experience an *overdose* if one of the following conditions is fulfilled (check):

- The previous drug injected was not heroin in.
- The variation in quantity from previous injection > 0.02 g.
- The user exits from an unsuccessful treatment period.

A user experiencing an overdose has a 90% chance of being rescued if there is another user around to call for an ambulance. The two chance parameters are partially calibrated against global figures of fatal and nonfatal overdoses in Melbourne (Dietze et al., 2004). The current stage of model development does not enable changes to individual trajectories nor does it incorporate an algorithm of accrued risk of developing greater dependency. Therefore, users seek to fulfill a given drug need all through their lifetime in the current version of the simulation.

The attitude of users towards treatment programs is summarized within the attribute called *readinessForTreatment*. The initial individual values are randomly picked between 10 and 50.

able 2. User attributes, variable type and description

Attribute	Type	Description
cash	integer	$300/fortnight (welfare) and cash obtained from crimes
drugNeed	integer	Constant value (in g) for light, moderate or severe addiction
myDrug	drug object	Current drug in user's possession (either heroin or 'other')
myDealerLocation	street block	Address of the current dealer
crimeIntention	boolean	True when user is ready to commit a crime
drugShortage	integer	Number of consecutive days without fulfilling drugNeed
overdose	boolean	True when user satisfies one the condition for overdose
readinessForTreatment	integer	Random between 10 and 50, attitude towards treatment program

A decrementing process—borrowed from literature on diffusion of innovation—slowly raises the motivation of the user to enter into treatment each time he/she is targeted by an Outreach Worker (decrement: -1) or each time the user is witnessing or experiencing an overdose (decrement: -1). The value of the attribute is reset at 20 each time a user comes out from an unsuccessful treatment period. The initial range of values is partially calibrated against the observed average chance for a real user to enter a treatment program over a one-year period. When the value of *readinessForTreatment* has reached zero, the corresponding user has 20% chance to enter a Detox program, 10% to enter a TC program, and 70% to enter a Methadone program (Australian Institute of Health and Welfare, 2005). A user under the Methadone program (nonresidential) has a 7% chance at each time step to consume illicit drugs. This percentage is derived from the clinical research literature (2 days /month) (see Teesson, Ross, Darke, Lynsky, Ali, Ritter, & Cooke, 2006).

Dealer: One of the challenges for the expert panel was to estimate a ratio of dealers to users. For *SimDrug* (and *SimDrugPolicing*) we applied a 1/20 ratio, a reflection of the ratios found in the Australian Higher and Magistrate's Courts (ABS, 2004). Thus, 150 *dealers* are initially created. The main characteristics of a dealer are given in Table 3.

At this stage of our model development, dealers can buy only one type of drug at a time from their wholesaler and then sell it to users. The question of the different mark-ups for drugs between wholesaler, dealer, user-dealer, and user is not well understood in the Australian context. Thus, drawing from Moore, Caulkins, Ritter, Dietze, Monagle, and Pruden (2005), we agreed on the following markups:

- Wholesaler's mark-up: x 6.0
- Dealer's mark-up with user: x 2.0
- Dealer's mark-up with user-dealer: x 1.3
- User-Dealer's mark-up with user: x 2.0

Initially dealers are assumed to deal on the street market only. But they are able to assess the risk created by the presence of "constables" in their surroundings. As a consequence, they can choose to freeze temporarily their activities until constables move away.

Wholesaler: Reliable figures from Australian Higher and Magistrate's Courts (ABS, 2004) indicate a ratio of 1/48 between defendants considered as wholesalers or importers, and small dealers. We decided to apply a very conservative ratio of 1/15 in *SimDrugPolicing* in order to take into account the known under-representation of "big fish" in the court's figures. Hence, we created 10 *wholesalers* in the system. In our model, wholesalers are in charge of buying the two types of drugs available on the market (heroin or other) and supply the different dealers with one or the other. Initial *cash* amounts range from $50,000 to $100,000. They can only reset their stocks every 30 "time steps" while dealers come to buy more drugs whenever they need. The availability of

Table 3. Dealer attributes, variable type and description

Attribute	Type	Description
cash	Integer	Randomly initialized between $5000 and $10000
dealType	Symbol	Visible (street market) or Hidden (home based)
myDrug	Drug Object	Current drug type, quantity and quality
myLocation	Street block	Usual dealing place
myWholesaler	Wholesaler agent	Location of current wholesaler

one drug or the other is determined by the ratio between both. This ratio is considered as an externality of the model (depending on successful importation) and it is calculated from an external data file containing monthly values of quantities, market prices, and purities.

Constable: The simulation includes 10 *constables* ("patrol officers") that are initially created and located at the *Police Station*. They can move randomly around the grid or target a specific street block to track down dealers and user-dealers. Regardless of the strategy implemented by the *Police Station*, the constables are given a 10% chance to arrest a dealer and a 40% to arrest a user-dealer when located on the same street-block. These figures are estimated from the raw arrest rates of street level narcotics officers, using random patrolling approaches to the street level drug problem during the pre-intervention phase of the Jersey City Drug Market Analysis Experiment (see Weisburd & Green, 1995). We do not model arrests of users for two reasons: first, police rarely arrest users, unless they are suspected of dealing (hence our rationale for including a user/dealer category of offender) and second, if a user is arrested (e.g., a user/prostitute), they are generally held for a very short period in custody, before being released.

Our simulated model also attempted to model actual police behavior in dealing with wholesalers. We understood that operations against wholesalers are often initiated by special units (i.e., drug squads) and rely on external intelligence or informant information. Hence, we decided that the *police station* has a 0.25% chance to get reliable information, that this information would allow the *police station* to send *constables* to the corresponding address and to execute a search warrant on the wholesalers home. In this scenario, the wholesaler is arrested (exits the system) and the dealers linked to an arrested wholesaler are also exited from the system.

Outreach Worker: 10 *outreach workers* are created and initially located at the *Treatment Center*. Their aim is to encourage users to undertake treatment programs. In our simulation, outreach workers have a purely mechanical effect as they decrease the value of the attribute *readinessForTreatment* for all the users located on the same street block. Although, depending on the law enforcement strategy implemented, the impact on the readiness will vary.

Law Enforcement Strategies

SimDrugPolicing draws from Mazerolle, et al. (2006) systematic review of drug law enforcement approaches to simulate three types of police intervention

Random policing: Under this scenario, the *constables* move randomly across the grid without specifically targeting any given area. They are as likely to patrol wealthy suburbs, as they are to drive around an area with a high concentration of drug hotspots. For each time step, the *police station* randomly selects ten cells and allocates one constable per cell. The police station does not keep track of the past visited cells, thus some cells might be visited several times or not at all within our simulation.

This strategy does not allow for collaboration between *constables* and *outreach workers*. Thus, the *treatment center* acts independently and sends its *outreach workers* to the street blocks displaying the highest overdose rates. This characteristic of our abstraction of random policing is meant to represent the way that random patrols do not partner with other entities nor focus their law enforcement efforts.

Hotspot policing: In this scenario, the *police station* is able to adapt its strategy to changes in the grid environment and direct constables to identified "hotspots". Within our simulation of the hotspots approach, *constables* do not patrol randomly. Rather, constables are directed to target specific grids (i.e., hotspots). The focus remains at the street-block and no suburb is favored over another. A hotspot is defined as a "conducive" street block with a high value of risk. Thus, the *police station* selects the ten street blocks with the highest values of risk (simulating an analytic approach to patrol resource allocation) and sends its *constables* accordingly. As a result of the initial setting of the grid, some suburbs contain more conducive street-blocks than others, thus are more prone to be patrolled by the constables. Under the hotspots drug law enforcement condition, the *police station* keeps track of the past visited cells and a visited cell will always receive three consecutive visits from the constable, reflecting a higher "dose" of attention to the hotspot grid than to other grids.

Problem-oriented policing: This scenario still emphasizes the importance of drug law enforcement at the street-block level but allows for partnership action between *constables* and *outreach workers*. Hence, while acknowledging the diversity of tactics implemented by the police under problem-oriented policing in real life (see Goldstein, 1990; Scott, 2000); our model of problem-oriented policing only examines place-focused partnerships. The constables still target the hotspots with the highest value of risk but this time they are joined by the outreach workers. Thus, the outreach workers move to the same street-blocks as the constables. Our model seeks to simulate the longer-term impact of problem-oriented policing approaches by creating a simulated situation where the police, under this drug law enforcement approach, have a higher impact on the users' readiness to undertake some sort of treatment. Under the hotspot scenario, users in the presence of an outreach worker decrease their readiness by a factor of one. Under the problem-oriented policing scenario, the readiness is decreased by a factor of five. In addition, the joint action of constables and outreach workers triggers a decrease in the risk value of the street-block and ultimately affects the conductivity of the cell.

Community-wide police interventions: At this stage of model development, we have not included a police strategy to simulate "community policing." The community-wide response by the police introduces a number of different complexities into our simulated system that could not be compared to the other three interventions (random patrolling, focusing on hotspots and problem-oriented policing). The three interventions that are compared and contrasted in this chapter are all implemented by the "constables." That is, the constables either patrol the grids randomly, direct their attention to hotspots, or form partnerships with outreach workers. A community-wide drug law enforcement intervention would likely require aggregation of constables and partnerships with other external entities. This type of simulation is doable, but for the purposes of this chapter, we have compared and contrasted the three interventions that can be simulated by individual "constables."

The Modeling Sequence

The Cormas© platform includes sensitivity analysis tools and provides output data directly into Excel format files. Each scenario is run 10 times and Cormas© allows for the recording of output variables such as: the total number of crimes per time step, the cumulative number of non-fatal and fatal overdoses, the number of users injecting heroin or using another drug per time step, the number of users under each type of treatment, the number of successfully treated users, the police station efficiency as measured by the various drug law enforcement interventions, the proportion of users-dealers, and more.

SimDrugPolicing is divided into six successive main stages:

1. Resetting and updating population
2. Updating drug supply on the market
3. Activating users decision-making process
4. Updating treatment center performances
5. Updating street blocks status
6. Activating police station and constable drug law enforcement interventions

The base scenario was set up with the parameters and values described in the previous section. It contains 3,000 Users, 150 Dealers and 10 Wholesalers.

SIMULATIONS AND RESULTS

The results presented in this chapter derive from simulations of the three different policing strategies. The results are presented across a number of outcome variables. First we examine the impact of the three enforcement approaches on the number of arrested dealers, the number of arrested user-dealers and the number of users into treatment. We then examine the impact on crime activity in terms of crimes committed by users and those aborted by users due to risk of constables' apprehension. The influence on the profitability of drug dealing is then studied through the impact of the three policing scenarios on the average and maximum cash at any one time-point (both measures of profitability). We also evaluate the impact of our three drug-law enforcement interventions in terms of overdoses. Finally, we outline the configurations of hotspots at the end of the three-year simulation.

Total Number of Arrested Dealers

In our simulated model, *constables* have the same probability of arrest (10% for dealers and 40% for user-dealers) across the three different drug law enforcement scenarios. However, each simulated strategy creates a specific context in which this individual probability of arrest translates into more or less effective actions. In our simulation, we did not want to model individual officer decisions to arrest (see Klinger, 1994). As such, we opted to hold constant the probability to arrest, and only vary the nature of the police dispatch. Under the *random patrol* strategy we send constables across the grid without specific targets. This minimizes their probability of encountering a dealer or a user.

Figure 3 summarizes the results of the three policing approaches on the total number of arrested dealers. As this figure shows, the *random*

Figure 3. Total number of arrested dealers

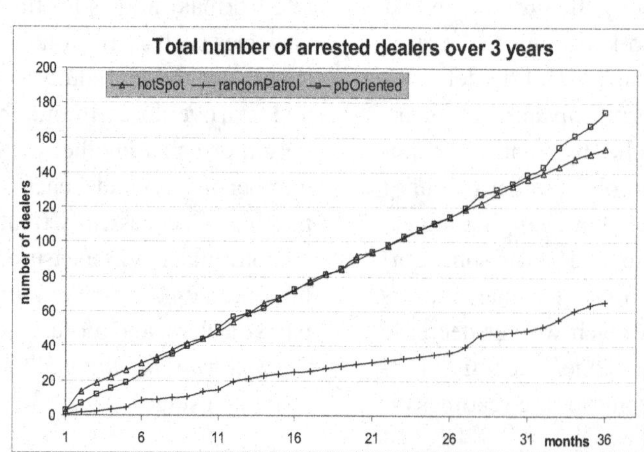

patrol strategy leads to the lowest rate of arrested dealers of the three enforcement approaches. In fact, respectively 42% and 37% less arrests are made, on average, using the random patrol strategy than the *hotspots* and *problem-oriented policing approach*. Interestingly, there are no statistically significant differences between the *hotspots* and *problem-oriented policing* approaches in terms of the average per month of the numbers of arrested dealers throughout the three-year period. These results are replicated when we model the impact of the law enforcement approaches on the numbers of user-dealers. As we would expect to be the case in reality, dealers (and user-dealers) are able to suspend their drug dealing activity during the periods of directed patrols, resulting in a temporary "freezing" of drug dealing activity that resumes at the same level when the constables are no longer present in the grid.

Treatment

Figure 4, shows the impact of the three policing strategies on the total number of users under treatment. Under the problem-oriented policing drug law enforcement intervention scenario, the partnership between constables and outreach workers translates into large numbers of users undertaking treatment in the early stages of the simulation and, conversely, the capacity of 1,000 treatment places is reached earlier in the simulation. In contrast, the random patrol and hotspot strategies take over one and a half years to reach a plateau of 700 users undergoing treatment, far from the total capacity of treatment (1000 places). A drawback of the problem-oriented policing strategy is that they fill the total treatment capacity after six months, an unanticipated side effect that is positive, yet has implications under real life conditions. Later in the simulation period, the effectiveness of the partnership is reduced due to this limited capacity of treatment.

Monthly Crimes Committed by the Users

Figure 5 shows the number of crimes committed by users, on a monthly basis, under the three policing scenarios. The variation between simulations in terms of the chance to arrest a dealer or a user-dealer does not impact on this figure because, in our simulation, crimes are only committed by "users" who need cash. In our model, we assume that user-dealers are wealthy enough to fulfill their

Figure 4. Number of users under treatment

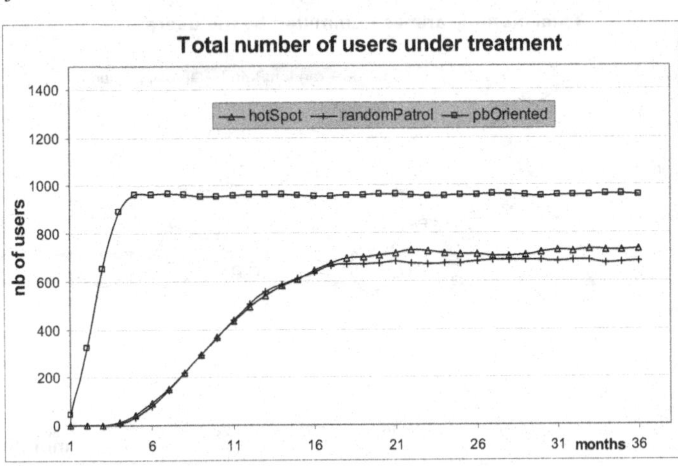

own need and buy extra quantities of drug for reselling. The simulation shows that the *problem-oriented policing* approach led to an average of 3.9 crimes per month per user, compared to 4.2 per month per user under the *hotspots* scenario and 5.1 crimes per month per user under the *random patrol* scenario. This clearly shows the superiority of the *problem-oriented policing* approach. The *problem-oriented policing* approach achieves the best results in terms of the impact on drug-related crime due to the higher rate of diverting users (who we hypothesize commit most of the street crime) into treatment. Indeed, one-third of users are diverted into treatment under the *problem-oriented policing* scenario. The *hotspots* model prevents crimes using a different process. Under the *hotspots* scenario, crimes are prevented through an increased presence of constables in risky suburbs.

The initial observed increase in monthly crime by users under *random patrol* and *hotspot* strategies is due to the fact that initially, most users do not have enough cash to pay for their drug need, hence a large number of users engage in criminal activities. Later on, the average cash situation of the users improves and as a consequence, the number of crimes decreases. The *problem-oriented policing* strategy does not display such a pronounced initial increase because, as shown in Figure 3, users under this scenario are quickly diverted into treatment. The number of crimes plateau's half way through the series for a number of reasons, one being because the treatment center reaches capacity).

Monthly Aborted Crimes

The effectiveness of the drug law enforcement strategies in our model can also be assessed through the analysis of the number of aborted crimes (i.e., intended crimes that aborted because of the presence of the constables in the neighborhood). Obviously, these figures cannot be validated against real observations of "aborted crimes."

Figure 6 shows the total number of aborted crimes per month by users. As this figure shows, the *random patrol* strategy has the most limited impact on user's decision to engage in criminal activities compared to the other two strategies. The *hotspot* approach is shown to be almost four times more effective than the *random patrol* approach and the *problem-oriented policing* strategy

Figure 5. Total monthly crime committed by users

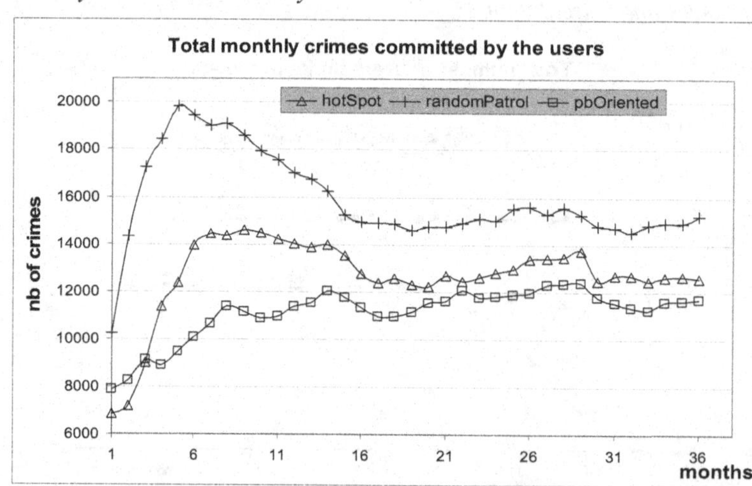

is two times more effective than the *random patrol* approach. Interestingly, the *hotspots* approach is 2.8 times more effective than the *problem-oriented policing* approach in aborting crimes. This result demonstrates how increasing and maintaining police presence in risky areas, from a crime prevention perspective, is more effective than random patrol activities.

Dealer Cash

Another way to assess the impact of the three intervention strategies is to examine, under simulated conditions, differences in the amount of cash available to the dealer. Figure 7 reports the results for the three scenarios on the average monthly amount of cash (in Australian dollars) available to the dealer. As this figure shows, the *problem-oriented policing* approach has the greatest impact on limiting the amount of cash available to dealers. In the simulation, *problem-oriented policing* has two processes operating: one is a direct effect through arresting dealers; the other is an indirect effect on decreasing the demand for drugs by deterring users into treatment. As such, this strategy limits dealers' capacity to accumulate wealth. By contrast, the result for the hotspot strategy is only explained by the direct impact of arrests on the dealer population.

With a limited capacity to arrest dealers (see Figure 3), the *random patrol* strategy offers safer trading conditions to dealers and a longer life span on the market. Hence, on average (see Figure 7), dealers are able to make significant profits from drug dealing under the *random patrol* strategy. At this stage, dealers' economic rationality is very simple: the more they earn from street dealing, the more they buy from their wholesalers. With the mark-up ratio applied in this model, they get a net benefit of $600 per gram of heroin sold to users. In comparison, *hotspot* and *problem-oriented policing* strategies limit dealer profits by 14% and 38% respectively. Both strategies are similarly effective in terms of the number of dealers arrested (see Figure 3), but the latter (*problem-oriented policing*) significantly limits the *amount* of transactions (Figure 7) due to the fact that more users are undergoing treatment (Figure 4).

Monthly User Cash

Another way to examine the impact of policing strategies on the street-level drug market place is to examine the amount of cash available to users as a result of an intervention. The results are presented in Figure 8 and show that the *random patrol* strategy allows users to constantly increase

Figure 6. Number of aborted crimes by users

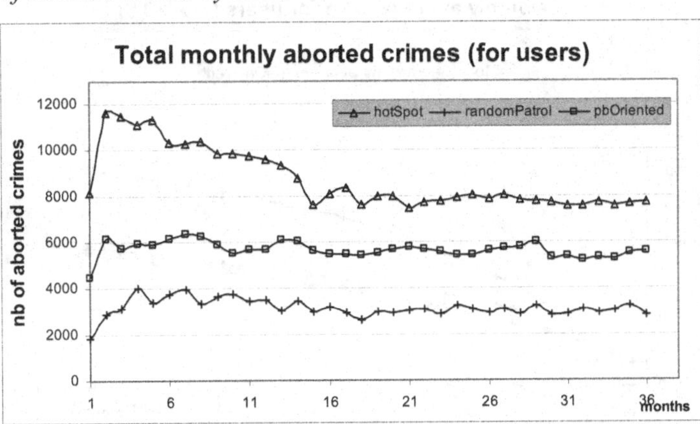

Figure 7. Dealers average cash in Australian dollars ($)

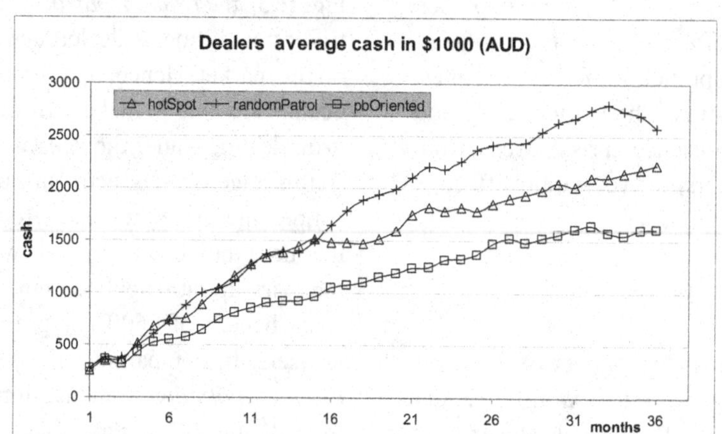

their cash compared with the other two enforcement interventions. This is due to random patrols having a low level of arrests and inferior capacity to prevent crimes committed by users. There is no significant difference between *hotspot* and *problem-oriented policing* strategies, for which the average cash value available to users stabilizes around $980. Importantly, however, the processes that lead to similar outcomes for hotspots and problem-oriented policing strategies are different: the *hotspots* approach limits the number of crimes, whereas *problem-oriented policing* approach puts users into treatment.

Overdoses

Another outcome that is modeled in our simulation is the impact of the intervention strategies on overdoses. Figure 9 presented shows the results of running the simulations against our three drug law enforcement approaches on the moving average of the monthly number of overdoses. As this

Figure 8. Users' cash in Australian dollars ($)

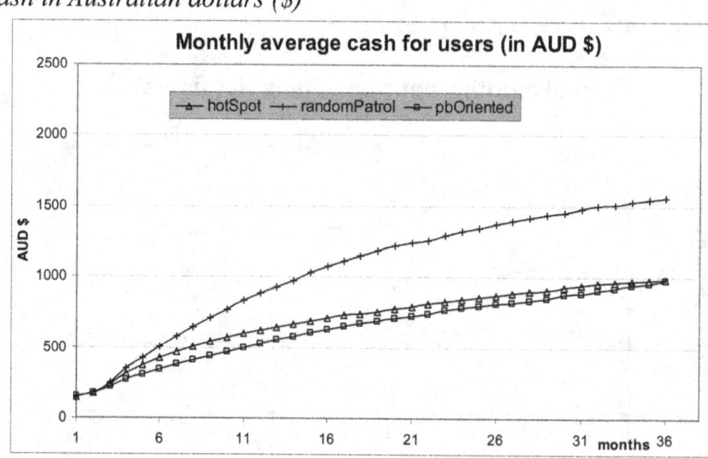

figure shows, there are no significant differences between the three police interventions on patterns of overdoses over time. Although not shown here, no significant differences were detected for fatal overdoses either. This result reflects the cyclical pattern of drug overdoses that are largely the result of external drug supply and likely potency issues, rather than anything that is controllable through drug law enforcement efforts.

Figure 9. Moving average in the number of monthly overdoses

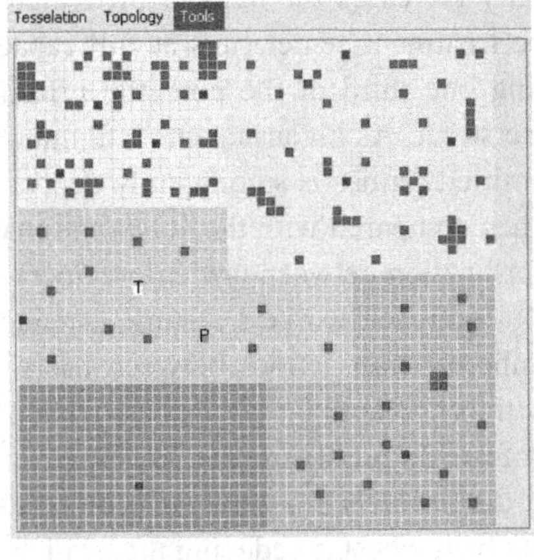

Final Grid

SimDrugPolicing provides an illustration of the impact of contrasted drug law enforcement strategies on the spatial dynamics of street level drug markets. At the end of the simulation described in this chapter, the *random patrol* scenario displays two large hotspots. This result suggests that unfocussed policing patrols across an urban setting limits pressure on dealers and fails to prevent users from committing local crimes. Further, the *random patrol* strategy reinforces the strength and spatial stability of the hot spots by attracting new dealers and more users as time goes by. By contrast, the *hotspot* strategy targets street blocks characterized by high levels of risk (being a function of the number of crimes, overdoses, and users) resulting in four, less intense hotspots than what is created under the random patrol condition. By effectively arresting dealers and preventing crimes, as well as diverting one third of the users to treatment facilities, the *problem-oriented policing* strategy results in a slightly different hotspot configuration both in terms of market intensity and the locales of market operations.

Figure 10. Initial configuration of the grid (same for all scenarios)

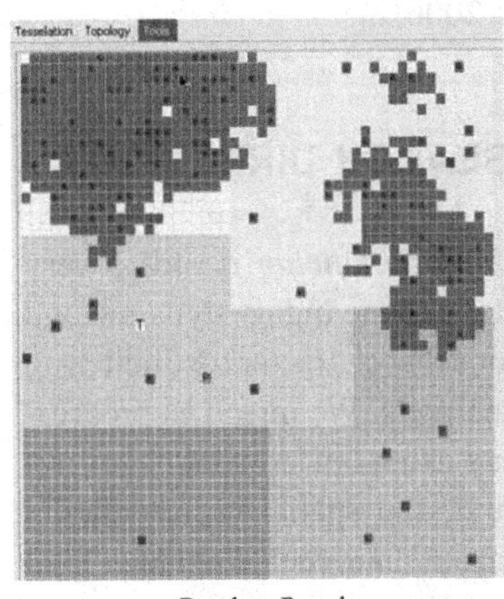

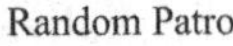

Random Patrol

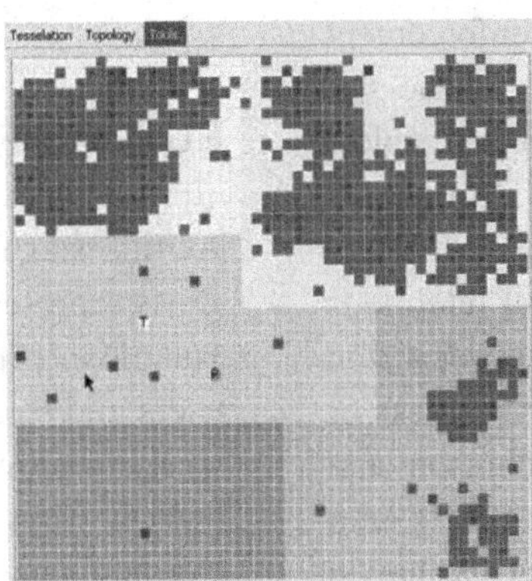

Hotspot

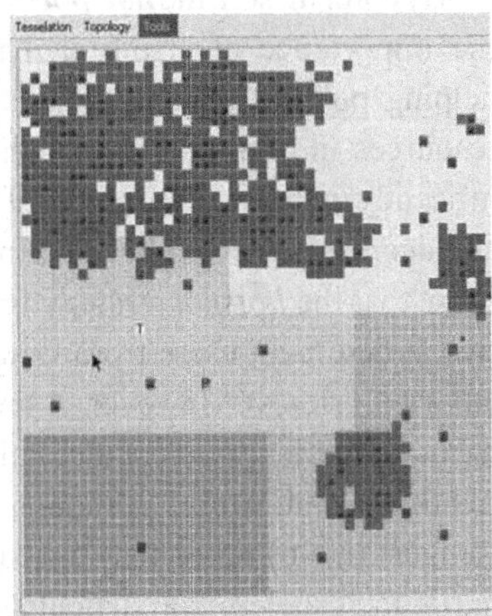

Problem oriented

DISCUSSION AND CONCLUSION

This chapter has explored three different policing strategies implemented in an archetypal urban environment made up of elementary street-blocks belonging to five interconnected suburbs. We opted to simulate a three-year time period, accessing reliable existing data sources and holding constant supply (i.e., price and purity remains constant over the simulation period). Our approach allows us to isolate the effects of the three policing strategies, yet only offers insight under conditions of a stable drug market.

We considered the *random patrol* strategy as a control scenario (nil effect hypothesis) against which the degree of effectiveness of the two other strategies can be compared. This assumption is consistent with conclusions from law enforcement experts who consider random street patrols as highly inefficient to fight drug-related crimes (Mazerolle et al., 2006). The results of our simulation show that the *random patrol* strategy performs very poorly against our evaluation indicators including sustained high level of crimes committed by users, low probabilities of arrest, high profitability for dealers and the creation of two dense drug hotspots. These results support research by Robinson and Rengert (2006) suggesting that variation in random patrol patterns appear to have little effect on crime rates.

By comparison, the *hotspot* strategy simulates the importance of crime analysis in policing, helping police to focus their law enforcement resources in high-risk areas. This scenario significantly increases the number of arrested dealers and decreases the number of crimes. Our results show that the *hotspot* strategy is the most effective at deterring users from criminal intentions (aborted crimes). However, it has no impact on harm reduction (total and fatal overdoses) or treatment indicators. Although Robinson and Rengert (2006) agree that focusing efforts on a particular problem in a particular area may have a deterrent effect, they also argue that crackdowns do not have long-term effects (see also Sherman, 1990). These findings partly support our initial selection of an open system based simulation for *SimDrugPolicing* where the replacement of removed dealers and users at each time step limits the long-term benefits of the hotspot strategy. We acknowledge, however, that reality is much more complex than the mechanistic process presented in our simulated model.

The *problem-oriented policing* strategy relies on concerted efforts between constables and outreach workers. This collaboration considerably increases the impact of police interventions across all selected indicators. As expected, this scenario drastically increases the number of treated users. The treatment center runs at full capacity, retrieving one third of the potential criminals from the street. As a consequence, the number of committed crimes is significantly decreased, even when compared with the *hotspot* scenario. The coordination between law enforcement and treatment outreach workers results in reducing the number of transactions between users and dealers, thus preventing most dealers from making comfortable profits (dealers' average cash). Finally, the *problem-oriented policing* strategy proves to be the best at reducing the availability of drugs in the streets. These results are consistent with a growing body of empirical support for the effectiveness of problem-oriented policing approaches in reducing crime, disorder and fear (Mazerolle et al., 2006).

FUTURE RESEARCH DIRECTIONS

At this stage, *SimDrugPolicing* is still a very gross representation of the highly dynamic and volatile interactions that characterize illicit drug users and street markets. We intend to progressively improve and extend its content in several critical ways. First, the spatial representation can be changed from an archetypal raster grid to a more realistic GIS-based visualization. This would offer an opportunity to include important environmental features like shopping centers, railway stations or town squares that primarily influence street blocks conductivity, and drug-related crimes (Eck & Weisburd, 1995).

Second, we would like to delve deeper into tailoring the alternate law enforcement models by simulating a "community-wide" drug law enforcement approach and creating a greater range of alternative partnerships under the problem-oriented policing model.

Another aspect, missing from the current version of *SimDrugPolicing*, relates to the initiation phase. All users at the commencement of our simulation are regular injectors. We recognize, however, the underlying individual and environmental factors that enhance the initiation phase whereby first time users become regular injectors. In his pioneering work, Agar (2005) explores individual decision-making processes using an agent-based model. Agar's model captures the role played by rumor and peer pressure during different stages of initiation process that could be adapted to tailor an initiation component in *SimDrugPolicing*.

Moreover, the next model development will focus on improving the economical components. Integrating cost-efficiency analysis will provide better insights for policy-makers to compare and evaluate law enforcement strategies.

Finally, we aim to remove the simulated constraints imposed by the open system by introducing dynamic models of prevalence (Dietze et al., 2005). These epidemiological models provide realistic estimates of the proportion of the population choosing between one drug and another over time. Hence, this type of model could be incorporated as a metamodel driving the ratio between removed and created users at each time step.

With these improvements, *SimDrugPolicing* will deliver more reliable and realistic results for policy-makers. They will be able to explore integrated strategies for involving law enforcement, treatment, prevention, and harm reduction aspects. Nonetheless, *SimDrugPolicing* already shows that illicit-drug users and street drug markets do not reach stable-state equilibrium but are characterized by dynamic equilibriums, demonstrating the importance of drug control policies focusing on strategic and adaptive management.

NOTE

This chapter was supported by a grant from the Colonial Foundation Trust to the National Drug and Alcohol Research Centre (with subcontracts to Griffith University, Australian National University and Turning Point Drug and Alcohol Centre). The authors are part of the Drug Policy Modelling Program (DPMP) team (see http://www.dpmp.unsw.edu.au/) and wish to thank Gabriele Bammer, Jonathan Caulkins, Paul Dietze, Tim Moore, and Peter Reuter for their input into the prototype development of *SimDrug*.

REFERENCES

Agar, M. (2005). Agents in living color: Towards emic agent-based models. *Journal of Artificial Societies and Social Simulation, 8*(1).

Agar, M., & Reisinger, H. (2002). A heroin epidemic at the intersection of histories: The 1960's epidemic among African Americans in Baltimore. *Medical Anthropology, 21*(2), 115-56.

Agar, M., & Wilson, D. (2002). DrugMart: Heroin epidemics as complex adaptive systems. *Complexity, 7*(5), 44-52.

Australian Bureau of Statistics (2004). *Criminal courts 2002-03* (Cat No. 5413.0). Canberra: Australian Bureau of Statistics.

Australian Institute of Health and Welfare (2005). Alcohol and other drug treatment services in

Australia 2003–04. *Findings from the National Minimum Data Set.*

Bousquet, F., Bakam, I., Proton, H., & Le Page, C. (1998). CORMAS : Common-pool resources and multi-agent systems. *Lecture Notes in Artificial Intelligence, 1416,* 826-837.

Caulkins, J. P., & Reuter, P. (2006). Illicit drug markets and economic irregularities. *Socio-Economic Planning Sciences, 40,* 1-14.

Caulkins, J. P., Behrens, D. A., Knoll, C., Tragler, G., & Zuba, D. (2004). Modeling dynamic trajectories of initiation and demand: The case of the U.S. cocaine epidemic. *Health Care Management Science, 7*(4), 319-329.

D'Aquino, P., Le Page, C., Bousquet, F., & Bah, A. (2003). Using self-designed role-playing games and a multi-agent system to empower a local decision-making process for land use management: The SelfCormas experiment in Senegal. *Journal of Artificial Societies and Social Simulation, 6*(3).

Dietze, P., Miller, P., Clemens, S., Matthews, S., Gilmour, S., & Collins, L. (2004). The course and consequences of the heroin shortage in Victoria. *NDLERF monograph no. 6.* Adelaide: Australasian Centre for Policing Research.

Dietze, P., Hickman, M., & Kimber, J. (2005). Monograph No. 03: Estimating the prevalence of problematic heroin use in Melbourne. *DPMP monograph series.* Fitzroy: Turning Point Alcohol and Drug Centre.

Eck, J. E., & Weisburd, D. (1995). *Crime and place: Crime prevention studies* (Vol. 4). Monsey, NY: Willow Tree Press.

Eck, J. E. (1998). A general model of the geography of illicit retail market places. In: D. Weisburd & J. Eck (Eds.). *Crime prevention studies* (Vol. 4). Monsey (NY) Criminal Justice Press.

Ferber, J. (1999). *Multi-agent systems: An introduction to distributed artificial intelligence.* New York: Addison-Wesley.

Gatrell, A. C. (2005). Complexity theory and geographies of health: A critical assessment. *Social Science & Medicine, 60,* 2661-2671.

Goldstein, H. (1990). *Problem-oriented policing.* New York: McGraw-Hill Inc.

Granath, J. A. (1991). *Architecture, technology and human Factors: Design in a socio-technical context.* Göteborg: Chalmers University of Technology, Architecture Workspace design.

Janssen, M. A. (Ed.) (2002*). Complexity and ecosystem management: The theory and practice of multi-agent systems.* Cheltenham: Edward Elgar Publishers.

Klinger, D. A. (1994). Demeanor or crime? Why "hostile" citizens are more likely to be arrested. *Criminology, 32*(3), 475.

Mazerolle, L., Soole, D., & Rombouts, S. (2006). Street-level drug law enforcement: A meta-analytic review. *Journal of Experimental Criminology, 2,* 409-435.

Mazerolle, L., Soole, D., & Rombouts, S. (in press). Drug law enforcement: A systematic review. *Police Quarterly.*

Moore, T. J. (2005). Monograph No. 01: What is Australia's "drug budget"? The policy mix of illicit drug-related government spending in Australia. *DPMP monograph series.* Fitzroy: Turning Point Alcohol and Drug Centre.

Moore, T. J., Caulkins, J. P., Ritter, A., Dietze, P., Monagle, S., & Pruden, J. (2005). Monograph No. 09: Heroin markets in Australia: Current understandings and future possibilities. *DPMP monograph series.* Fitzroy: Turning Point Alcohol and Drug Centre.

Perez, P., Dray, A., Ritter, A., Dietze, P., Moore, T., & Mazerolle, L. (2006). SimDrug: Tackling the complexity of illicit drug markets. In D. Batten & P. Perez (Eds.), *Complex science for a complex world, Exploring human ecosystems with agents.* ANU E-Press.

Rengert, G., Chakravorty, S., Bole, T., & Henderson, K. (2000). A geographic analysis of illegal drug markets. In M. Natarajan & M. Hough (Eds.), *Illegal drug markets: From research to prevention policy*. Monsey, NY: Criminal Justice Press.

Robinson, J., & Rengert, G. (2006). Illegal drug markets: The geographic perspective and crime popensity. *Western Criminology Review, 7*(1), 20-32.

Scott, M. S. (2000). *Problem-oriented policing: Reflections on the first 20 years*. Washington, DC: Office of Community-Oriented Policing Services, U.S Department of Justice.

Sherman, L. (1990, March/April). Police crackdowns. *NIL Reports, 2-6*(2).

Teesson, M, Ross, J., Darke, S., Lynsky, M., Ali, R., Ritter, A., & Cooke, R. (2006). One year outcomes for heroin dependence: Findings from the Australian treatment outcome study (ATOS). *Drug and Alcohol Dependence, 83*, 174-180.

Weisburd, D., & Green, L. (1995). Policing drug hotspots: Findings from the Jersey City DMA experiment. *Justice Quarterly, 12* (4), 711-735.

Weisburd, D., & Eck, J. E. (2004). What can police do to reduce crime, disorder and fear? *The ANNALS of the American Academy of Political and Social Science, 593*, 43-65.

ADDITIONAL READING

Agar, M. (2001). Another complex step: A model of heroin experimentation. *Field Methods, 13*(4), 353-369.

Agar, M., & Wilson, D. (2002). Drugmart: Heroin epidemics as complex adaptive systems. *Complexity, 7*(5), 44-52.

Agar, M. (2003). My kingdom for a function: Modeling misadventures of the innumerate. *Journal of Artificial Societies and Social Simulation, 6*(3).

August, G. J., Winters, K. C., Realmuto, G. M., Tarter, R., Perry, C., & Hektner, J. M. (2004). Moving evidence-based drug abuse prevention programs from basic science to practice: Bridging the efficacy effectiveness interface. *Substance Use and Misuse, 39*(10–12), 2017–2053.

Bradbury, R. H., Green, D. G., & Snoad, N. (2000). Are ecosystems complex systems? In T. Bossomaier & D. Green (Eds.),.*Complex systems* (pp 339 – 365). Cambridge: Cambridge University Press.

Caulkins, J., & Reuter, P. (1998). What price data tells us about drug markets. *Journal of Drug Issues, 28*(3), 593-613.

Caulkins, J., & Reuter, P. (2005). Analyzing illicit drug markets when dealers act with limited rationality. In F. Parisi & V. L. Smith (Eds.), *The law and economics of irrational behaviour*. CA: Standford University Press.

Fuqua, J., Stokols, D., Gress, J., Phillips, K., & Harvey, R. (2004). Transdisciplinary collaboration as a basis for enhancing the science and prevention of substance use and abuse. *Substance Use and Misuse, 39*(10–12).

Mazerolle, L., Kadleck, C., & Roehl, J. (2004). Differential police control at drug-dealing places. *Security Journal, 17*(1), 61-69.

Ritter A. (2006). Studying drug markets: Disciplinary contributions. *International Journal of Drug Policy, 17*, 453-463.

Chapter XIX
Using Varieties of Simulation Modeling for Criminal Justice System Analysis

Azadeh Alimadad
Simon Fraser University, Canada

Peter Borwein
Simon Fraser University, Canada

Patricia Brantingham
Simon Fraser University, Canada

Paul Brantingham
Simon Fraser University, Canada

Vahid Dabbaghian-Abdoly
Simon Fraser University, Canada

Ron Ferguson
Simon Fraser University, Canada

Ellen Fowler
Simon Fraser University, Canada

Amir H. Ghaseminejad
Simon Fraser University, Canada

Christopher Giles
Simon Fraser University, Canada

Jenny Li
Simon Fraser University, Canada

Nahanni Pollard
Simon Fraser University, Canada

Alexander Rutherford
Simon Fraser University, Canada

Alexa van der Waall
Simon Fraser University, Canada

ABSTRACT

Criminal justice systems are complex. They are composed of several major subsystems, including the police, courts, and corrections, which are in turn composed of many minor subsystems. Predicting the response of a criminal justice system to change is often difficult. Mathematical modeling and computer simulation can serve as powerful tools for understanding and anticipating the behavior of a criminal justice system when something does change. The focus of this chapter is on three different approaches to modeling and simulating criminal justice systems: process modeling, discrete event simulation, and system dynamics. Recent advances in these modeling techniques combined with recent large increases in computing power make it an ideal time to explore their application to criminal justice systems. This chapter reviews these three approaches to modeling and simulation and presents examples of their application to the British Columbia criminal justice system in order to highlight their usefulness in exploring different types of "what-if" scenarios and policy proposals.

INTRODUCTION

Computational criminology, a new and expanding field driven by the growth in the computational power available to criminological researchers, is opening many exciting avenues of research. The use of simulation modeling to understand, depict, predict, and conduct experiments on the patterns in criminal events is widely illustrated throughout the other chapters in this volume. Simulation modeling can also be used to understand, depict, and conduct policy experiments on the activities and operations of the criminal justice system. This is important because the criminal justice system is the social response through which crime patterns that cannot be prevented must be handled. This chapter explores some contemporary possibilities in the application of computer simulation to criminal justice system issues.

Common law criminal justice systems are composed of complex subsystems, such as police, courts, and corrections, operating in an interconnected yet autonomous fashion. These complex subsystems both contribute to and respond to operational fluctuations amongst their own elements, in other subsystems and across the system as a whole. Social systems structured in this way can be characterized as feedback systems in which system outputs affect the behavior of the system itself over time. Criminological analyses that focus on single components of the justice system are often unable to anticipate or account for the effects of feedbacks from their own operations or from changes in policy or operations in other subsystems. (Brantingham, 1977; Hann, Bailey, & Ross, 1973; McAllister, Atchinson, & Jacobs, 1991). The complexity inherent in the criminal justice system means that policy decisions, such as legislative shifts towards harsher sentences for serious offences, often produce unintended consequences because distal parts of the total system, well-removed from the elements directly effected by the decision, adapt to change in unanticipated ways (Merritt, Fain, & Turner, 2006).

The purpose of this chapter is to show how advances in the application of mathematics in modeling, queuing theory and simulation can help both academic researchers and justice practitioners to emulate and predict the behavior of the justice system more effectively. Modeling and simulation are appropriate tools for analysis of criminal justice system behaviors because they make it possible to handle the uncertainty and variability inherent to complex system interactions with minimum resource expenditure (Harper, 2002; Lowery, 1998).

This chapter examines three different modeling and simulation approaches to the analysis of integrated justice systems: discrete event modeling (Schriber & Brunner, 2004: p142); process modeling (Baquette, 2003); and, system dynamics (Homer & Hirsch, 2006)[1]. Future research may include multi-agent based simulations (MABS) and distributed artificial intelligence models (DAI). In the sections that follow, we discuss the concept of an "Integrated Justice System" as reflected in the law and practice of Canada[2], provide an introduction to mathematical modeling and simulation of complex systems, and provide initial reports of three different simulation models of the British Columbia criminal justice system.

SIMULATION AND MATHEMATICAL MODELING

A model is a simplified representation of a system at some particular point in time or space intended to promote understanding of the real system. Simulation is especially appropriate for the analysis of complexity in systems, such as an integrated justice system, by exposing pertinent feedback structures and relationships between variables to understand system-wide effects (Harrison, Ivatts, & Millard, 2003).

Mathematical modeling is the process of creating a mathematical representation of some phenomenon in order to gain a better understanding of that phenomenon. It is an abstract model that uses mathematical language to describe the behavior of a system. It is a process that attempts to match observations with symbolic statements. During the process of building a mathematical model, the modeler decides what factors are relevant to the problem and what factors can be de-emphasized. Mathematical models are used in the natural sciences, economics, engineering, the social sciences, and at times, in criminology. The mathematical model serves the following purposes:

1. To find an optimal solution to a planning or decision problem.
2. To answer a variety of "what-if" questions.
3. To establish understandings of the relationships among the input data items within a model.
4. To attempt to extrapolate past data to derive meaning (McGraw-Hill Dictionary of Scientific and Technical Terms, 2003).

Process of Model Specification

Prior to building a mathematical model, there are several important considerations in the specification of a system model. First, it is important to develop a conceptual model that visualizes the system in terms of major processes, relationships and variables that form the system. At this stage of the process it is important to consider the level of detail in the specified model. Although there is no clear standard of specific detail to include in a model, a general guideline is that the model must be detailed enough to answer desired questions while being as parsimonious as possible. Too much detail can produce a model that cannot be solved analytically. Second, the modeler must decide whether the processes within the system are best modeled as deterministic or stochastic. Third, the modeler must specify whether the model is dynamic (i.e., includes a time dimension) or static (i.e., time independent). Fourth, models may either represent units of analysis as discrete entities (i.e., distinct units or mutually exclusive categories) or continuous flows (i.e., represented by real numbers like an average rate). These choices are contingent on the purposes of the modeling endeavor (SFU Complex Systems Modelling Group, 2006).

Simulation

Simulation traces the time evolution of a model, enabling one to perceive the interactions that would not otherwise be apparent because of their separation in time or space. Simulation represents time in either discrete units or as a continuous variable, referred to as *discrete time simulation* and *continuous simulation*, respectively. Simulation generally refers to a computerized version of the model, which is run over time to study the implications of the defined interactions. Simulations are generally iterative in their development. One develops a model, simulates it, learns from the simulation, revises the model, and continues the iterations until an adequate level of understanding is developed. Simulation is used in many contexts, including the modeling of natural systems or human systems in order to gain insight into their functioning. Simulation is used to show the effects of interventions in a virtual setting (SFU Complex Systems Modelling Group, 2006).

Once a mathematical model has been developed and simulated, it is critical that the model be subject to calibration, validation, sensitivity testing, and optimization (if possible). Model validation refers in a general sense to a comparison of model output with actual system data. There are numerous methods to validate a mathematical model (see Balci, 1997). Sensitivity analysis involves identifying model parameters that exert the greatest influences on the whole system. Although, a system may have many stages and parameters not all of these are critical to the operation of the system. Last, it is desirable to find the best solutions to questions posed of the system model. This process is termed *optimization*. This is necessary as there may be many possible solutions to particular problems within a system (Balci, 1997).

The formal modeling of systems using a mathematical model attempts to find analytical solutions to problems that enable the prediction of the behavior of the system from a set of parameters and initial conditions. Computer simulation is often used as an adjunct to, or substitution for, modeling systems for which simple analytic solutions are not possible. There are many different types of computer simulations but the common feature they share is the attempt to generate a series of representative scenarios for a model in which a complete enumeration of all possible states of the model is prohibitive or impossible. Several software packages exist for computer-based simulation that facilitates the process of constructing and simulating system models.

VALUE OF MODELING

Criminal justice systems are complex and extremely sensitive to changes in policy, funding and legislation. Therefore, it is imperative to be able to plan for how these changes may affect service delivery for each component, and the system as a whole. Policy makers and others involved in planning need to be fully informed about where bottlenecks may be happening in the system, where external pressures are altering how service is delivered, and how current states of capacity and resources may need to be altered in the future. Modeling provides this information for decision-making, and can inform decisions concerning capacity, resources, and questions relating to impacts of policy and legislative changes.

For those working within or analyzing complex systems such as an integrated justice system, simulation can serve four critical needs (Chung, 2004). The first is that simulation allows the user to gain "insight into the operation of a system" (Chung, 2004, pp. 1-3). A comprehensive view of a complex system, such as an integrated justice system, can be extremely difficult due to the many interdependent and autonomous subcomponents. One valuable aspect of gaining this comprehensive overview of the system is the ability to understand how each subsystem can influence and impact other subsystems. The second is that simulation assists in the development of "operating and resource policies" (Chung, 2004, pp. 1-3) that can help improve the system. In an integrated justice system it is important to know where additional resources are needed and how additional resources may affect other parts of the system. Third, simulation is an ideal environment for "testing new concepts" (Chung, 2004, pp. 1-4) in a complex system, such as the impact of new legislation or changes in parole practices. The fourth benefit of simulation is that this technique allows users to "gain information without disturbing the actual system" (Chung, 2004, pp. 1-4). This means that through the simulation of a complex system, provided that the model is correctly specified with the proper amount of detail, users are able to understand the behavior of the system and subsystems, discover problems in the system, change resourcing practices, and test new policies without directly impacting the current operation or configuration of the justice system.

It is important to note that the form of the questions that emerge from the four benefits of simulation modeling discussed by Chung (2004) depends on several considerations. The first, which is the basis of this chapter and is discussed in detail later in this chapter, is the choice of the modeling technique. The second, is the amount of detail or level of detail of the specified model (Sadowski & Grabau, 2004), termed the "depth" of the model (Carson, 2004). The third consideration is the model boundary and scope, which define the components of a system that are included in the model. This is often referred to as "width" of a model (Carson, 2004). It is these three factors—modeling technique, depth of the model and width of the model—that determine the form and content of any "what if" questions that may be posed of criminal justice systems and answered using simulation modeling.

SIMULATION MODELING IN CRIMINAL JUSTICE LITERATURE

Although mathematical modeling, simulation and queuing theory have a long history dating back to their initial use in the telephone industry prior to World War II (Erlang, 1909; Forrester, 1968), it was not until the 1970's that these techniques were incorporated in criminology to model criminal justice systems. During the 1970's there was a surge of activity using mathematical modeling and simulation, specifically system dynamics modeling, to represent criminal justice systems (Belkin, Blumstein, & Glass, 1971; Blumstein, Cassidy, & Hopkinson, 1975; Blumstein, Cassidy, & Townsend, 1974; Blumstein & Larson, 1972; Cassidy, 1985; Chaiken, Crabill, Holiday, Jaquette, Lawless, & Quade, 1977), with an emphasis on court process models (Brantingham, 1977; Hann et al., 1973; Hann & Salzman, 1976). However, after the 1970's there was a decline in simulation modeling research in criminal justice and criminology[3]. Renewed interest in these techniques in criminology and criminal justice has developed in recent years as expansion in computational capacity and concern with criminal event modeling have made simulation research seem both useful and practicable (Blumstein, 2002; Brantingham & Brantingham, 2004; Harries, 2001; Lind, Chilvers, & Weatherburn, 2001; Livingston, Stewart, & Palk, 2005; Stewart, Spencer, O'Connor, Palk, Livingston, & Allard, 2004).

Mathematical modeling and simulation had originally gained prominence in the study of criminal justice systems under the aegis of the U.S. President's Commission on Law Enforcement and Administration of Justice in the mid-1960's (Blumstein, 1967, 2002; Navarro & Taylor, 1967). Since that Commission, the bulk of the models have been based in the tradition of system analysis and system dynamics (but see Hann et al., 1973; Hann & Salzman, 1976; Larson, Cahn, & Shell, 1993; McAllister et al., 1991). The most elaborate of these early models were JUSSIM (Belkin et al., 1971; Blumstein & Larson, 1972; Chaiken et al., 1977; Cohen, Fields, Lettre, Stafford, & Walker, 1973) in the United States and its Canadian counterpart CANJUS (Blumstein et al., 1975; Blumstein et al., 1974; Cassidy, 1985; Cassidy, Hopkinson, & Mead, 1976). They represent two of the earliest attempts to model "complete" justice systems, and they model flows of offenders through the sequential stages of two North American justice systems.

Many of the early system simulation models were criticized for being deterministic with little consideration of possible system feedback (Blumstein, 2002; Brantingham, 1977; Stewart et al., 2004). This criticism led some researchers to utilize alternative modeling techniques and to improve existing models by incorporating stochastic processes and feedback (see: Blumstein, 2002; Brantingham, 1977; Hann et al., 1973; Hann & Salzman, 1976).

A common thread in most criminal justice simulation modeling efforts is that they have focused the vast majority of their attention on one of the subsystems in an integrated justice system. Much of the simulation modeling focuses on policing and police resources (McGinnis, 1989); on the court system or components of the court system, such as legal aid and pretrial processes (Brantingham, 1977; Comfort, Shapiro, & Volcansek-Clark, 1982; Hann et al., 1973; Hann & Salzman, 1976; Larson et al., 1993; McAllister et al., 1991; Mu, 1996; Nayar & Bleuel, 1973), or corrections, primarily prison systems (Bailey & Hann, 1972; National Council on Crime and Delinquency, 1987; Stollmack, 1973). Furthermore, work that has simulated an entire criminal justice system has tended to focus on either the adult system or the juvenile system (Livingston et al., 2005; Stewart et al., 2004). An integrated justice system must take into account all the justice subsystems which include both the juvenile and adult justice systems.

Another criticism that has been advanced against most simulation models of criminal justice systems is that they do not incorporate queuing theory into the models in a substantive manner (Hann et al., 1973; Hann & Salzman, 1976; Larson et al., 1993; McAllister et al., 1991). This is an important oversight as a substantial body of research has posited system delays as a major factor influencing one or more of the subsystems in the criminal justice system (see: Foschio, 1973; Hann et al., 1973; Haynes, 1973; Law Reform Commission of Canada, 1994). A model that includes queuing processes is able to represent certain stages within a system as queues, where entities in a model (e.g., offenders) wait to be processed in units of time. According to Gross and Harris (1974, p. 2), there are six important aspects of the queuing process that must be defined. These include the arrival pattern of the entities, the service pattern of servers (e.g., police detention, courtroom time), the queue discipline, system capacity (e.g., number of offenders in remand), the number of service channels and the number of service stages.

New interest in the use of integrated justice system simulation models has blossomed among academics and professionals in recent years for at least four separate, but related reasons. First, the continuing expansion of computing power has made it possible to construct and use large-scale simulation models that were simply not possible before. Second, the development of large electronic data archives have made model calibration and validation possible in ways that were not previously feasible. Third, the growing sophistication of criminal justice professionals has led them to ask researchers to explore policy impact questions of increasing complexity. Fourth, the software packages available today that can be used to construct and test discrete event, process and system dynamics models were not readily available to researchers a couple of decades past. For the aid of the reader a review of modeling software packages for each of the three techniques explored in this chapter is included in Appendix A: Modeling Software.

MODELING THE STRUCTURE OF AN INTEGRATED CRIMINAL JUSTICE SYSTEM

The utility of an integrated criminal justice system simulation depends on proper model specification. This specification must include a careful description of the system's structure, that is, the elements of which it is composed and the ways in which those elements are connected by input and output vectors. The structural description must be related to the unit of analysis, such as a particular offender or groups of cases, and to a clear idea of the level of analysis. Specification of the level of analysis is crucial due to the highly complex nature of the system, and the autonomy of each subsystem within it. Generally, the specification of a model is accomplished initially through the

Figure 1. Criminal justice system components and units of analysis

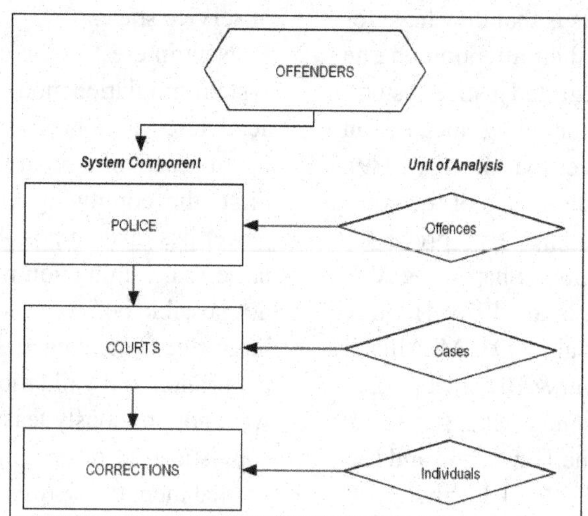

development of a conceptual flow diagram of the system of interest. As shown in Figure 1, the basic composition of a criminal justice system includes police, courts and corrections. Each component may involve, or at least organize information into, a different unit of analysis. For instance, police respond to offences; the court system is concerned with cases that may include groups of offences or groups of offenders or both; and the correctional system deals with individual offenders, rather than cases or offences.

The form and function of criminal justice system components is defined by a national constitution, by legislatures, and, in common law countries, by judicial decisions. In Canada legislative responsibility for criminal justice is divided between the federal government and the provincial governments. The federal government of Canada is responsible for criminal law and criminal procedure, for creation of Superior (jury trial) and Appellate Courts and appointment of their judges, and for creation and operation of a system of prisons and penitentiaries. This has been exercised by Parliament through such Acts as the Criminal Code of Canada, the Judicature Act and the Royal Canadian Mounted Police Act, which created a national police force with powers similar to those of the American FBI, DEA and Secret Service combined. Provincial governments are responsible for the administration of justice within the province. In British Columbia the Legislative Assembly has exercised this power through passage of the BC Police Act; by creation of Provincial Courts that try and dispose 97% of all criminal cases; and by creation of a provincial probation and prison system.

The interconnected nature of the entire Canadian Criminal Justice System as it plays out in British Columbia results in interdependencies and impacts of one agency on another. For instance, changes in police strength and/or policies may result in greater numbers of offenders being charged with offences,thereby increasing the number of offenders awaiting trial. Likewise, a change in judicial operations or policy may result in lengthier sentences, which could impact the capacity of the correctional system. This kind of impact can be compounded by the fact that many offences are defined in the Criminal Code in such a way as to allow the Crown Counsel or the Defence (or sometimes, either) to make elections that can move a criminal trial back and forth

Figure 2a. Offence case flow into court from offence occurrence to laying an information

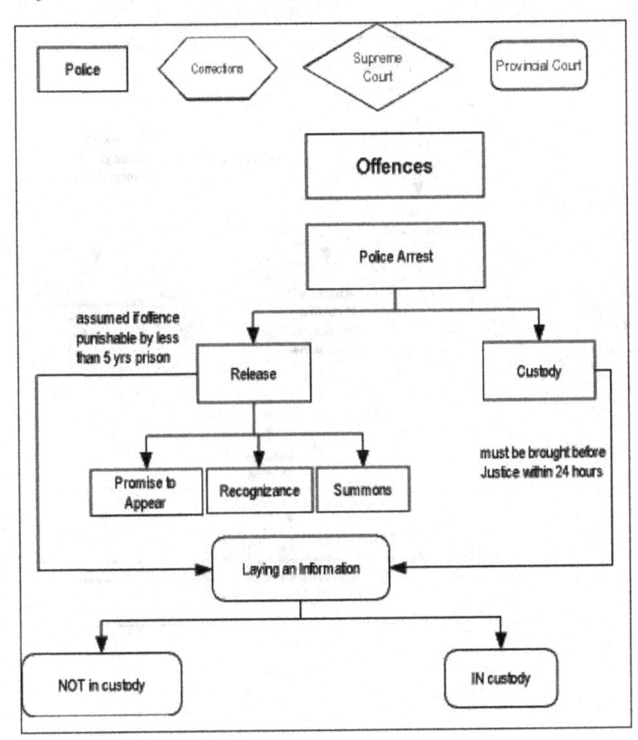

Figure 2b. The police decision to release a suspected offender vs. the decision to hold suspect for a bail hearing

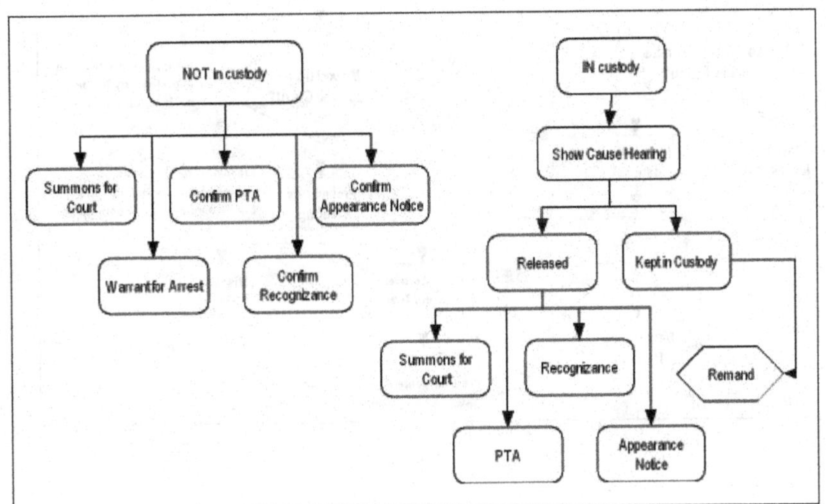

Figure 2c. Prosecutorial decision to approve charges and court election flow (if applicable)

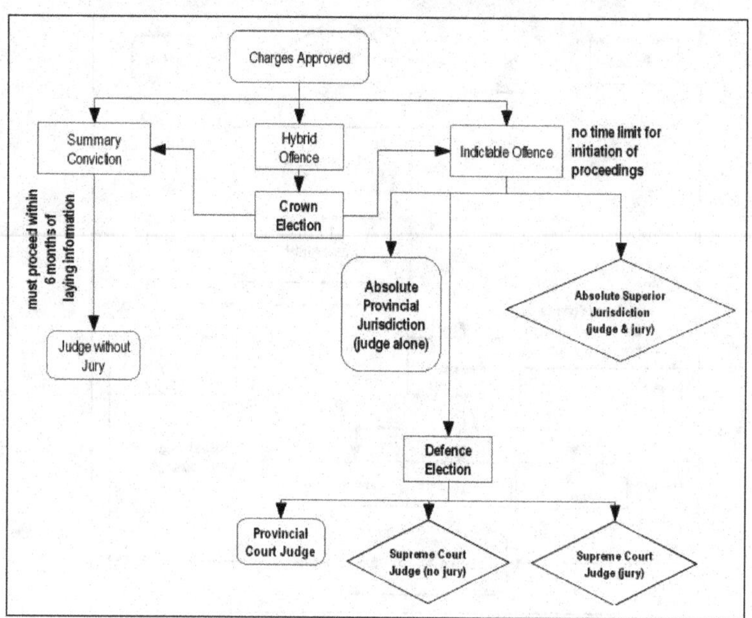

Figure 2d. The first appearance of a defendant and court path of the accused

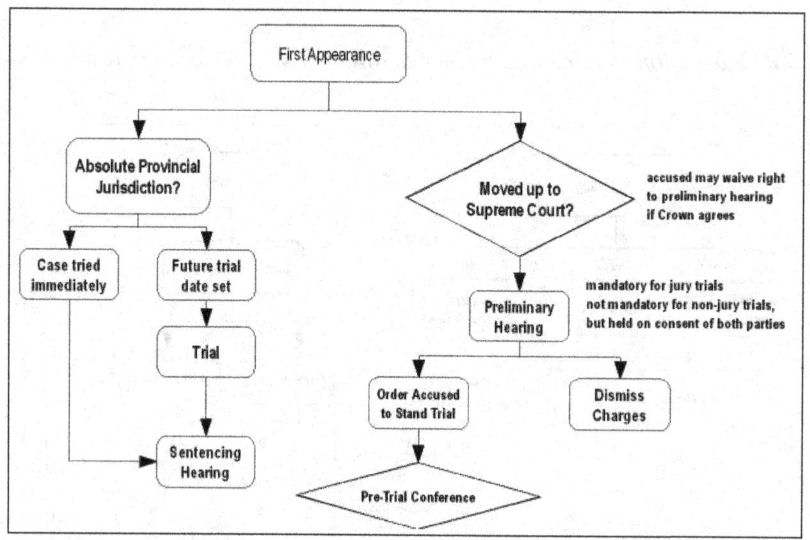

Figure 2e. The outcome of the court process

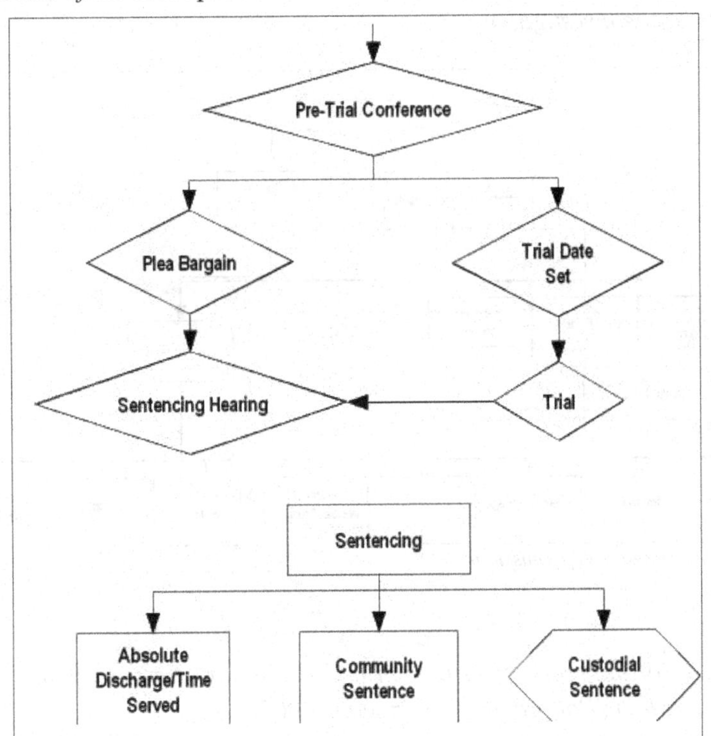

Figure 3a. The investigative steps by the police for a typical break and enter from dispatch to arrival on scene

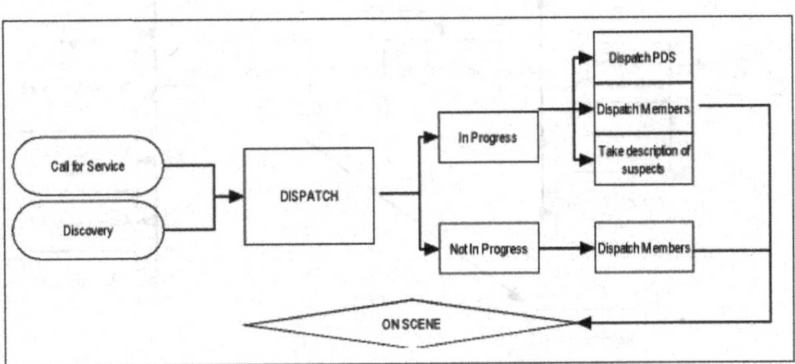

between the Provincial Court and the Superior Court; and by the fact that whether a convicted offender serves a term of imprisonment in the provincial or federal prison system is a function of the length of sentence imposed.

The basic structure of the system can be depicted at a higher level of granularity where each subsystem is further specified. Figure 2 (comprised of Figure 2a to Figure 2e) shows an example of how offences flow into the court

Figure 3b. The investigative steps by the police for a typical break and enter from arrival on scene to the conclusion of the scene investigation

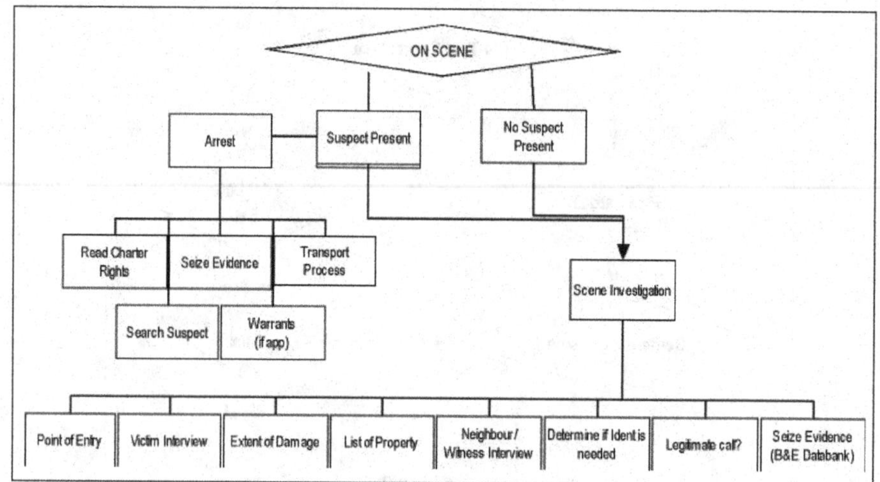

Figure 3c. Conclusion of the scene investigation and investigative process either with an identified suspect or no suspect (Malm, Pollard, & Brantingham, 2005)

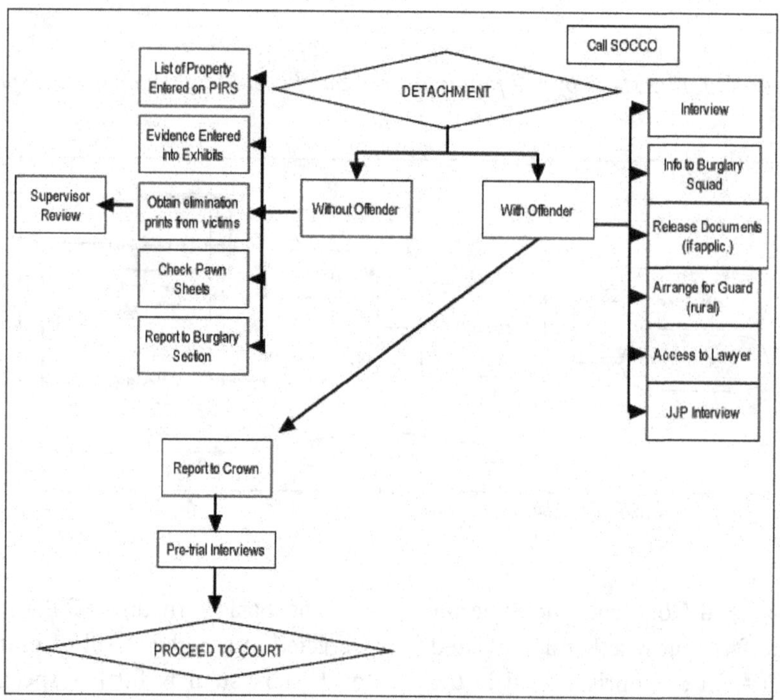

subsystem from the stage of police arrest to the final outcome of the court process. These figures identify the major processes that are involved as offenses and offenders flow into court from the stage of police arrest.

While Figure 2 shows the interconnections in greater detail within the court system, each agency within the system can be viewed through an even finer lens, which would increase the complexity of this model substantially. As an example, to move from known offences to police arrests involves numerous stages on the part of the police and investigation team. For a typical break and enter, the police and other involved agencies would generally need to follow the steps in Figure 3 (comprised of Figure 3a to Figure 3c) in order to prepare a case for trial.

The three simulation approaches described next begin with detailed descriptive models depicting the British Columbia criminal justice system as shown in Figure2. That model is expanded and adjusted in different ways in order to utilize the discrete event, process and dynamic simulation approaches in order to look at criminal justice system operations from slightly different perspective in order to address slightly different operational issues. Queuing theory underpins much of what happens in each of the approaches.

QUEUING THEORY

Queuing theory was developed in the early 1900's to model and optimize telephone networks. Erlang (1909) is generally accepted as the first mathematician to introduce queuing theory. In a seminal paper, Agner Krarup Erlang, an employee of the Danish Telephone Company, addressed the problem of determining the optimal number of telephone operators required to maintain a given service level in a town. Prior to 1950, queuing theory was still largely used in the telephone industry. However, since 1950 it has been applied to computer network design, building design, freeway design, air traffic control, the healthcare system, and many other areas. Within criminal justice, queuing theory has been applied to the arrest to arraignment system in New York City in Larson et al. (1993). A queuing theory approach to modeling criminal justice systems is a natural choice, particularly if the primary quantities of interest are capacity and delays within the system.

The simplest queue is a single server queue (Figure 4), in which "customers" wait to be processed by a "server". In the criminal justice system, depending on the context, customers may refer to offences, cases, or offenders. The servers may be the police, prosecuting attorneys, judges, corrections, or any other aspect of the system which engaged in processing entities within the system.

The simple single server queue is characterized by five basic properties:

1. The **arrival process** describes how customers arrive at the tail of the queue. This process may be either deterministic, in which the customers arrive at predetermined intervals, or stochastic in which the interarrival time is determined by a random process. The interarrival time is defined to be the time between arrivals of successive customers.

Figure 4. Single server queue

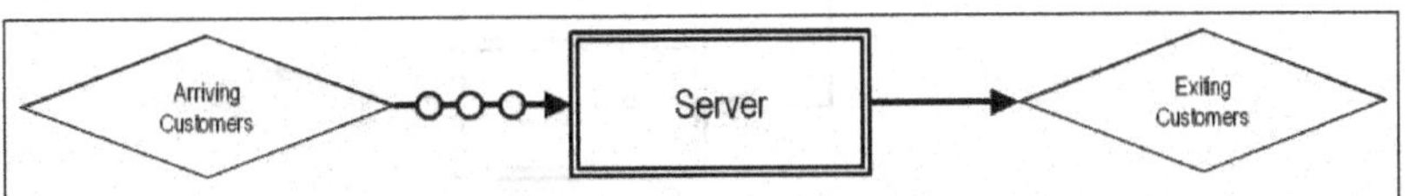

2. The **service process** describes how customers are served by the server. As with the arrival process, this may be either deterministic or stochastic.
3. The **impatience discipline** of a queue specifies rules which determine when customers leave the queue without being served. If the queue has no impatience, then customers always remain in the queue until served. Otherwise, common forms of impatience are reneging and balking. Reneging is when customers leave the queue if their wait time exceeds some value, which may be fixed, deterministically dynamical, or stochastic. Balking is when a customer does not enter the queue, when certain conditions are met. Examples would be customers not entering the queue if it reaches a certain length, or the probability of customers entering the queue being a function of the length of the queue. An example of balking in the criminal justice system occurs when a complainant calls to report an offence, realizes that there is a wait time, and discontinues the call.
4. The **service discipline** refers to the order in which customers are served. Examples include first in first out (FIFO) service, last in first out (LIFO) service, service in random order (SIRO), or through a priority scheme.
5. The **queue capacity** is the maximum number of customers that are allowed in the queue. This may be either fixed or vary over time according to a random process or the state of the system. One way to implement a queue capacity is through a balking rule.

Queuing networks are constructed from single queues by combining them in series, parallel, and with feedback loops. The integrated criminal justice system is a highly complex queuing network. It contains multiserver queues (Figure 5), in which a service discipline determines how more than one server services a single queue.

Additionally, the integrated criminal justice system contains many multistage queues in which customers pass through a succession of servers in a series, as shown in Figure 6.

Another feature of complex queuing networks are feedback loops, which are illustrated in Figure 7.

Figure 5. Multiserver queue

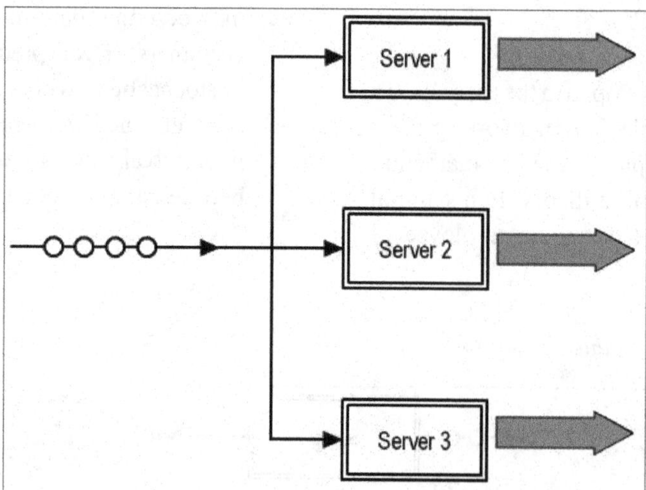

Figure 6. Multistage queue

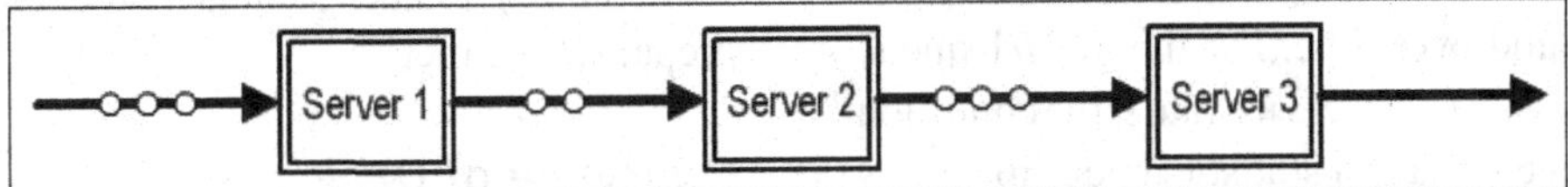

Figure 7. Feedback loop in multistage queue

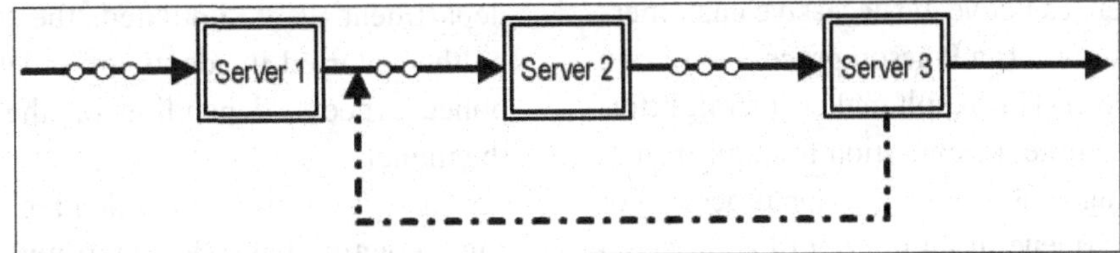

In this network, there would be a rule to define how output from server 3 is split.

To account for fluctuations in the number of offenders, offences, and cases, the criminal justice system may be modeled as a stochastic queuing network. In a stochastic queue, the interarrival times and service times are independent stochastic processes. The most commonly used process is the Poisson process. If the arrival process is a Poisson process with arrival rate *r*, then the probability that the interarrival time between successive customers is less than or equal to *t* is given by an exponential distribution function:

$$\Pr(x \leq t) = 1 - e^{-rt} \quad (1)$$

Likewise, if the service distribution is a Poisson distribution with service rate *s*, then the probability that a service time is less than or equal to *t* is:

$$\Pr(x \leq t) = 1 - e^{-st} \quad (2)$$

The notation used to denote the class of all single server queues with a Poisson distribution for the arrivals and services is *M/M/*1. The first *M* indicates that the arrival process is a Poisson process, the second *M* indicates that the service process is also a Poisson process, and the trailing 1 indicates that the queue has one server.

The importance of the *M/M/*1 class of queues derives from the fact that typically when a queue with general interarrival time and service time distributions is subjected to heavy traffic, it will behave like an *M/M/*1 queue. This guiding principle follows from a number of heavy traffic theorems that hold under different hypotheses. For a review of heavy traffic theorems, see Medhi (1991) and Bramson and Dai (2001).

Under certain conditions, queues may approach an equilibrium or steady state after a long period of time. For a deterministic queue, this means that the length of the queue will approach a constant value in the limit as elapsed time becomes large. However, the concept of equilibrium is more subtle for stochastic queues. A stochastic queue approaches statistical equilibrium if the probability that the queue has any given length approaches a constant value in the limit of large elapsed time. Note that statistical equilibrium is a probabilistic concept. The length of a stochastic queue in statistical equilibrium will vary with time; however, the probability distribution for queue length will be stationary.

In general a queue may not have an equilibrium state. For example, the queue length may grow without bound over time. For the *M/M/*1 queue with arrival rate r and service rate s, the condition for the queue to have a statistical equilibrium is that $r/s < 1$. The ratio $\rho = r/s$ is called the utilization factor of the queue.

For the *M/M/*1 queue in statistical equilibrium, the distribution of interdeparture times (time differences between successive customers exiting the server) is a Poisson process with rate r (Burke, 1956). This result makes it straightforward to determine the condition for equilibrium for a multistage queue with Poisson process. For example, the queue in Figure 8 will approach a statistical equilibrium if r is strictly less than the minimum of s_1, s_2, and s_3.

DISCRETE EVENT SIMULATION (DES)

Discrete event simulation (DES) is a computer-based modeling technique used to mimic the behavior of systems over time. Such systems are characterized by individual units (hence, "discrete") flowing through the systems, each taking a potentially different path based on any number of conditions. DES is used in order to aid understanding of the effect of changes that exogenous and endogenous input factors have on a system (Banks, Carson II, Nelson, & Nicol, 2001; Kelton, Sadowski, & Sturrock, 2007; Pooch & Wall, 1993). If such factors are controllable (endogenous), then using DES in the context of an integrated justice system can lead to better decision-making with regard to the efficient and effective use of resources. If the factors are not controllable (exogenous), then DES can help reveal vulnerability to such changes and contribute to preparing for them.

Overview of DES

The units that flow through a DES-modeled system are called *entities* (Kelton et al., 2007). For example, if the daily operations of a police department were simulated, the entities might be the reported incidents, offenders or perhaps police officers, depending on the objective of the model.

The system through which the entities travel can be pictured as a flowchart with four general types of modules:

1. Entities are generated and start their trips through the system at a *creation module.*
2. They go through many *process modules* at which they undergo transformation, experience changes in status or merely wait. Such processes often involve the consumption of one or more resources.
3. Entities may encounter *points of decision* or uncertainty. At these modules, the path that the entity is about to take is determined randomly or according to a condition.
4. Last, entities depart the system at *disposal modules* (Kelton et al., 2007).

These modules are linked by paths to reflect the logical relationships that are critical to the simulation model. These relationships determine which paths the entities take, and under what conditions, and thus create the interaction among entities. That is, they define the behavior of the system overall.

Figure 8. Multistage M/M/1 in statistical equilibrium

Consider these examples in the context of the integrated justice system:

- A creation module generates incidents of crime (the entities) at time intervals of random length. The incidents have distinguishing characteristics.
- A decision module separates the incidents with a particular characteristic. For example, those with a specific characteristic require several police officers to attend while those without the characteristic require only two officers to attend.
- A process module simulates police attendance at the scene in whatever numbers the decision module specifies. The length of time the officers are occupied with the incident, and otherwise unavailable, may also depend on the characteristics of the incident. The process module "transforms" the entity from a new incident not yet attended to by police to one that has been attended to.

Variables, either discrete or continuous, are used to describe the specific behavior that the entities exhibit at each module. For example, an arrival module could be designated to generate reported incidents with random, exponentially distributed time intervals between them (Banks et al., 2001; Pooch & Wall, 1993). A process module depicting 9-1-1 calls might specify that a specific conversation takes a random length of time that is exactly 5, 10, 15, or 120 seconds.

"Discrete" in "discrete event simulation" refers to the existence of separate and individual entities and the occurrence of separate and individual events. The behavior and interaction of the entities when examined *en masse* and over time reveal the operational characteristics of the system. This can be compared to system dynamics models in which the concepts of individual entities and events are not applicable and certain operating characteristics of the system are defined by the user at the outset (Banks et al., 2001; Kelton et al., 2007; Pooch & Wall, 1993).

Considering an integrated justice system that is similar to a system described above, the entities involved could be offences, citizens (be they law-abiding or not), police officers and others. The stages of the system might include the investigation of the victimization incident, the trial, or the completion of a sentence. The resources consumed by the process steps might include police officers, jail cells, Crown Counsel, police vehicles, or courtrooms. Decision points might include whether the incident is a property crime or a personal crime, whether a guilty plea is obtained or not, or whether the sentence is custodial or not.

The following list of example questions show some of the practical and policy applications of a DES model for criminologists and criminal justice personnel:

- Where are the "bottlenecks" in the integrated justice system? That is, if limited funding were to be added, where would it be most effective?
- In a few years, an unusually large number of officers are scheduled to retire from the police force. If we were not able to recruit adequately, how would our ability to respond to various crimes be affected?
- How much could the case backlog in the courts be reduced if "over-booking" were more widely used?
- Using available research on the relationship between number of past offences committed by a criminal and his or her likelihood of recidivism, how would the crime rate change if custodial sentences were generally lengthened by 10%? Or by 25%?
- If imminent legislation were to require police officers to complete an additional administrative step, ranging from 30 minutes to 2.5 hours, for each offence, how many additional

officers would be needed in order to maintain operating performance? How would our performance suffer if we did not add officers?

An Example of DES and the Integrated Justice System

We now present a DES model of a hypothetical integrated justice system designed with the Arena™ modeling software package (see Appendix A: Modeling Software). We model a miniature and simplified society in which two types of crime (very serious and less serious) occur randomly and four types of resources (police officers, prosecutors, judges, and jail cells) are available for the pursuit, prosecution and punishment of the offenders. An entity is simultaneously the offence and the offender; there is one offence and charge per offender. The scope of the model is from the commission and reporting of the offence to the completion of the trial and, if applicable, the sentencing hearing.

Smooth functioning of the system depends on resources being available; however, the availability of resources fluctuates due to the variability in the demand for them. As a result, backlogs may form, grow and shrink, and excessive waits for certain processes may cause cases to be lost.

Figure 9 shows a section of the Arena™ model from the commission and reporting of the offences to the arrest of the suspects. Arena™ is, effectively, a graphical user interface for the SIMAN programming language (see Appendix A: Modeling Software). Each flowchart shape is associated with a block of programming code in the background. A series of shapes, forming a flowchart, constitutes a whole program. The lines from left to right show the logical paths that entities take.

As mentioned earlier, DES is an effective tool for making sound resource allocation deci-

Figure 9. DES model of an integrated justice system

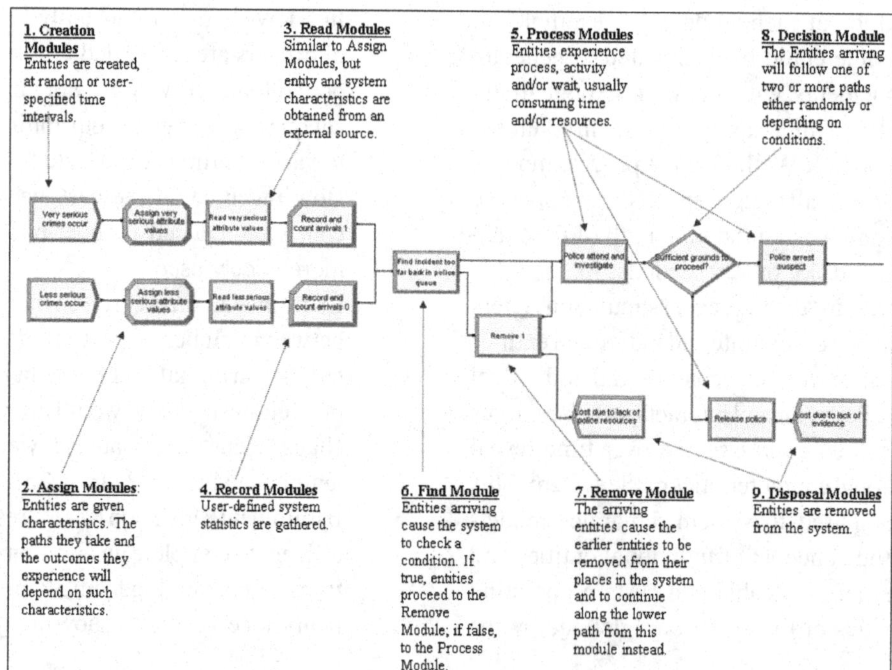

sions. However, before prospective changes are contemplated, the modeler should understand the status quo. Figure 10 and Figure 11 present some sample performance measures over six months of simulated operation using only the resources currently allocated to our hypothetical justice system. There are currently 41 police officers, 32 prosecutors, 15 judges, and an arbitrarily large number of jail cells in place.

Figure 10 shows four plots depicting the utilization of the four resources of the system. The plots reflect zero utilization at time zero because the system is "empty" when the simulation run starts. After a month or so, all of the resources reach their respective general levels of utilization. This initial period is called a "warm-up period" in DES and its output is usually excluded from performance measure calculations.

Figure 11 shows the percentage distribution of outcomes after the same six months of simulation. An entity experiences one of five possible outcomes as it departs the system depending on the characteristics of the offence, the conditions encountered during the flows through the system and randomness. These outcomes may include: (1) The defendant is found guilty and receives a custodial sentence; or, (2) a noncustodial sentence; or, (3) the defendant is acquitted; or, (4) the case is never cleared due to lack of evidence; or, (5) the case is lost from the system due to a shortage of resources.

Next, we present the estimated result of making one resource allocation change. Figure 12 and Figure 13 shows the same performance measures over another six months of simulated operation with an additional 10% (four) of the police officer resource. Notice the effect of increasing the number of police officers by 10% on the operation of the justice system. The utilization rates of prosecutors improve from about 90% to 100%, the utilization rate of judges improves from roughly 65% to 70%. These improvements lead to a reduction in cases lost due to shortages of resources from 6% to 3%.

Figure 10. DES output – resource utilization in an integrated justice system

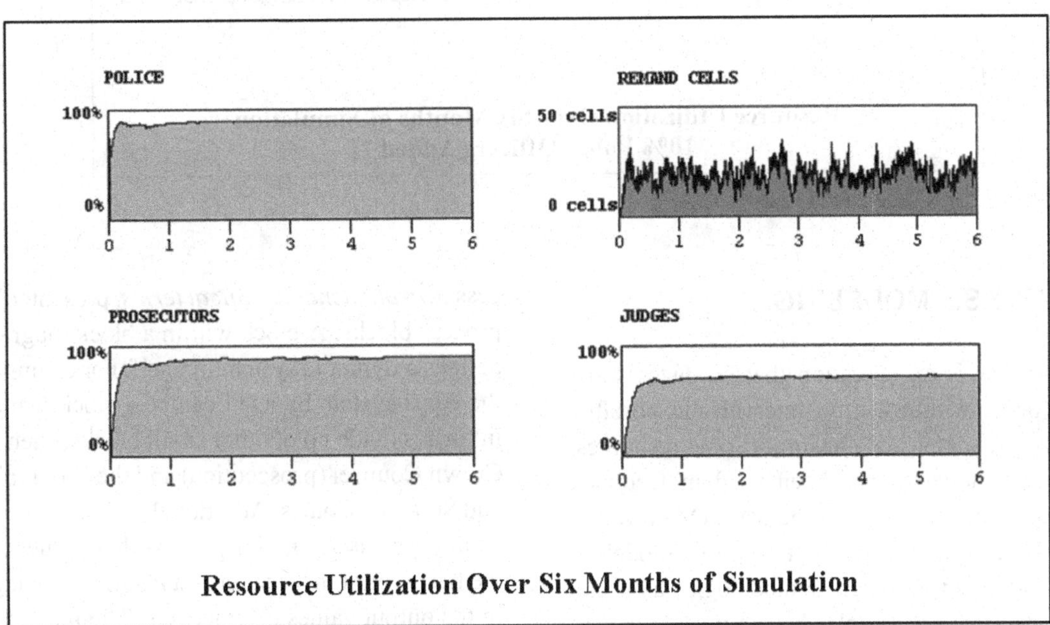

Figure 11. DES output—distribution of outcomes

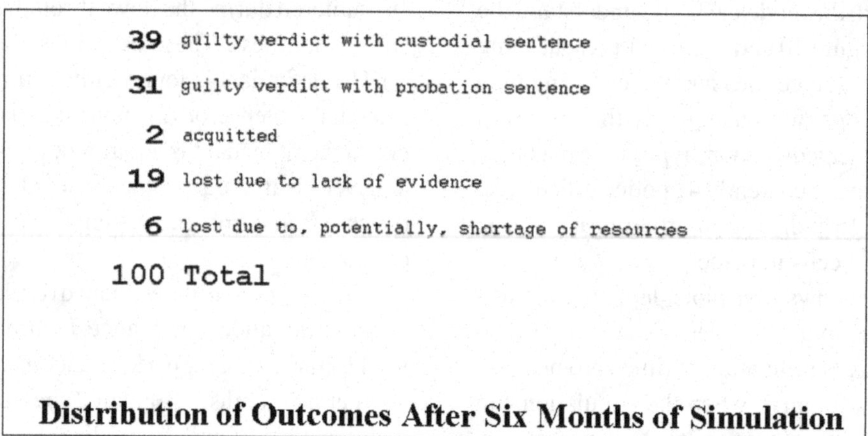

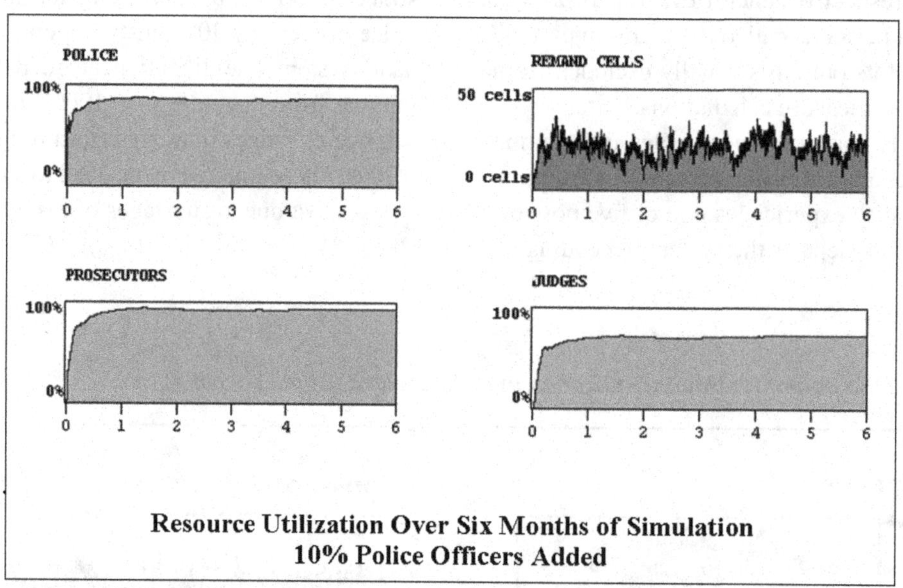

PROCESS MODELING

A process is an operation that produces some outcomes within a time interval and possibly has some inputs and consumes some resources. Process modeling has been used in feedback control theory and signal processing (Mathworks, 2004) for many years. This type of modeling is different from other methodologies as it can encapsulate very complex behaviors of each process in *explicit mathematical terms,* presented as process blocks. A block within a block diagram defines a dynamic system in itself. For example, the court system by itself can be a block, which in turn is made up of other small blocks, such as Crown Counsel (prosecution) and the Provincial and Supreme Courts. Additionally, feedback can be modeled as a complex process that influences the behavior of the system as a result of a change in the output values of processes. The impact of

Figure 12. DES output—resource utilization with a 10% increase to the police officer resource

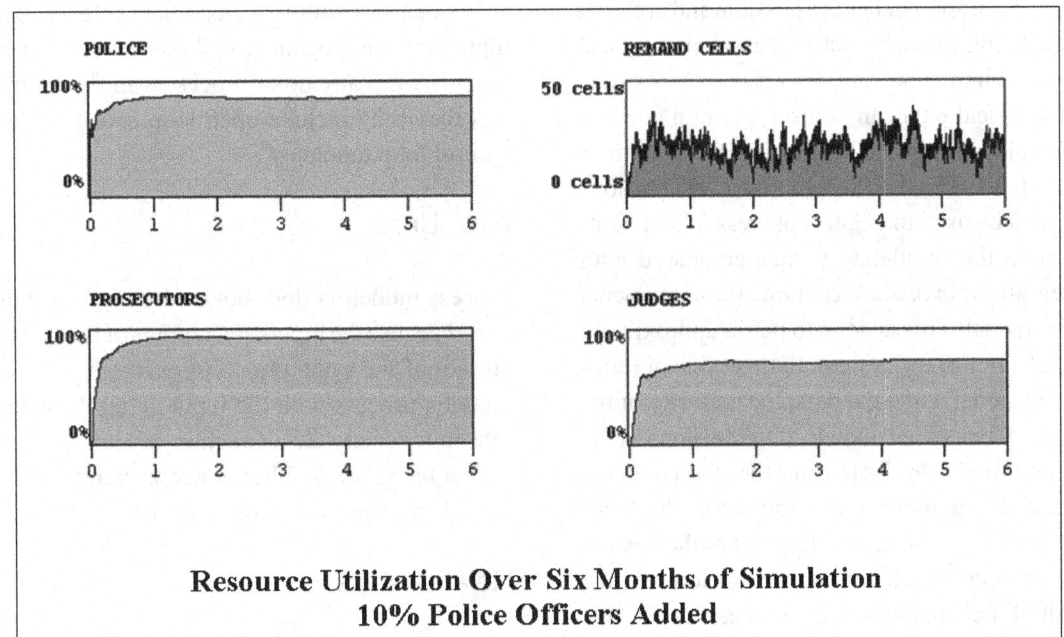

Figure 13. DES output—Distribution of outcomes with a 10% increase to the police officer resource

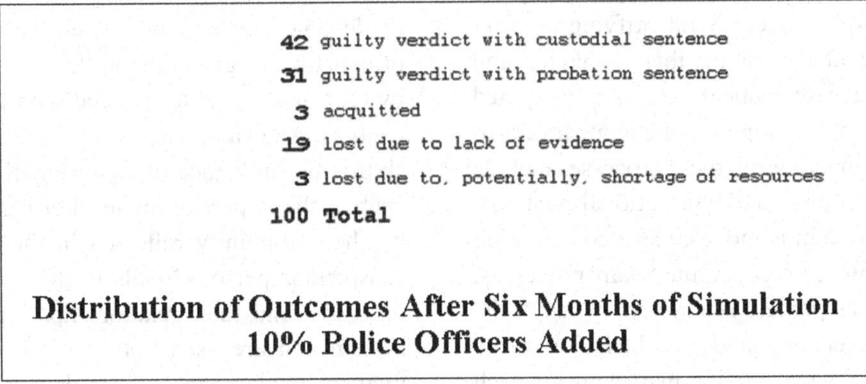

42 guilty verdict with custodial sentence
31 guilty verdict with probation sentence
3 acquitted
19 lost due to lack of evidence
3 lost due to, potentially, shortage of resources
100 Total

Distribution of Outcomes After Six Months of Simulation
10% Police Officers Added

blocks on each other is modeled by connecting lines to blocks in a graphic interface.

Overview of Process Modeling

Process modeling is in fact a *hierarchical modular modeling of systems* using block diagrams to enable the researcher to deal with complex systems that consist of subsystems (Cellier, 1991). *Deductive modeling* is used to model the systems where there is a physical understanding of the process. In contrast, researchers who model complex systems with large uncertainties, as in biology or economics, often try to fit a model to observed data, a method termed *inductive modeling*. Both of the above approaches are possible and are used in modeling the different processes in a hybrid system (Mathworks, 2004).

Statistical data can be used to build a mathematical model of the behavior of the system or subsystems. These conceptualized observations can then be used to create a process model. Output from the simulation is then compared with observations in order to calibrate the coefficients of the model. This is done to better approximate the behavior of the system. In this cycle of refining the model with field data, the maturity of the model increases and may lead to revisions in the original model by increasing the mathematical complexity, number of parameters or the feedback system. Once the model reaches the desired level of accuracy, it can be used to forecast the result of a change in inputs, processes, outputs, or available resources.

Parameters

Process modeling involves building a conceptual abstraction of a system by identifying relevant processes, and describing their behavior and influences in mathematical terms. An Integrated Justice System is composed of a number of processes. At a macro level, these processes include the police, courts, and correctional systems. The entire system is modeled as a combination of subsystems, each containing many processes. Although each process is a system by itself, the decision maker may study the behavior of the system at the macro level or may explicate each process at a finer level of detail. This allows the researcher to model behavior at an abstract level, or to model the subsystems in more detail. Each process has inputs, outputs and a process function describing its behavior. A simplified example can be modeling court as a process; then its input may be the number of cases arriving, its output can be the number of cases sentenced to imprisonment and the function describing its behavior may be (OUT = 0.1 x IN) presenting the fact that on average 10% of cases result in a custodial sentence. The inputs may be exogenous to the system or may be outputs from any other processes in the system and they may include open loop or a feedback control loop topology[4].

Flow Units

Process modeling does not deal with fixed flow units because the inputs and outputs of the system are not of the same type. For example, one can model a process with the input being the crime rate in a society as a function of time and the output being the number of people waiting for a court hearing as a function of time.

Relationships

Process modeling involves relating processes by coupling the output of the processes to input of other processes and recognizing and presenting feedback and feed-forward control relationships between processes. In an integrated justice system, the feedback may be the influence of the growth of court hearing queues on the decisions made by Crown Counsel to proceed with less serious charges. An example of a feed forward relationship is the influence of a preventative process, such as the impact of the level of insecurity felt by the community reflected in the number of "suspicious persons" calls to the police. Block diagrams and their relationships represent the system and are used both for conceptual and mathematical analysis of the dynamic effect of feedback control loops.

Time Units

One of the advantages of process modeling is that each subsystem is described either by a time domain mathematical description of outputs based on inputs or a system transfer function describing its output-input relationship. These transfer

Figure 14. Process modeling—court queue feedback

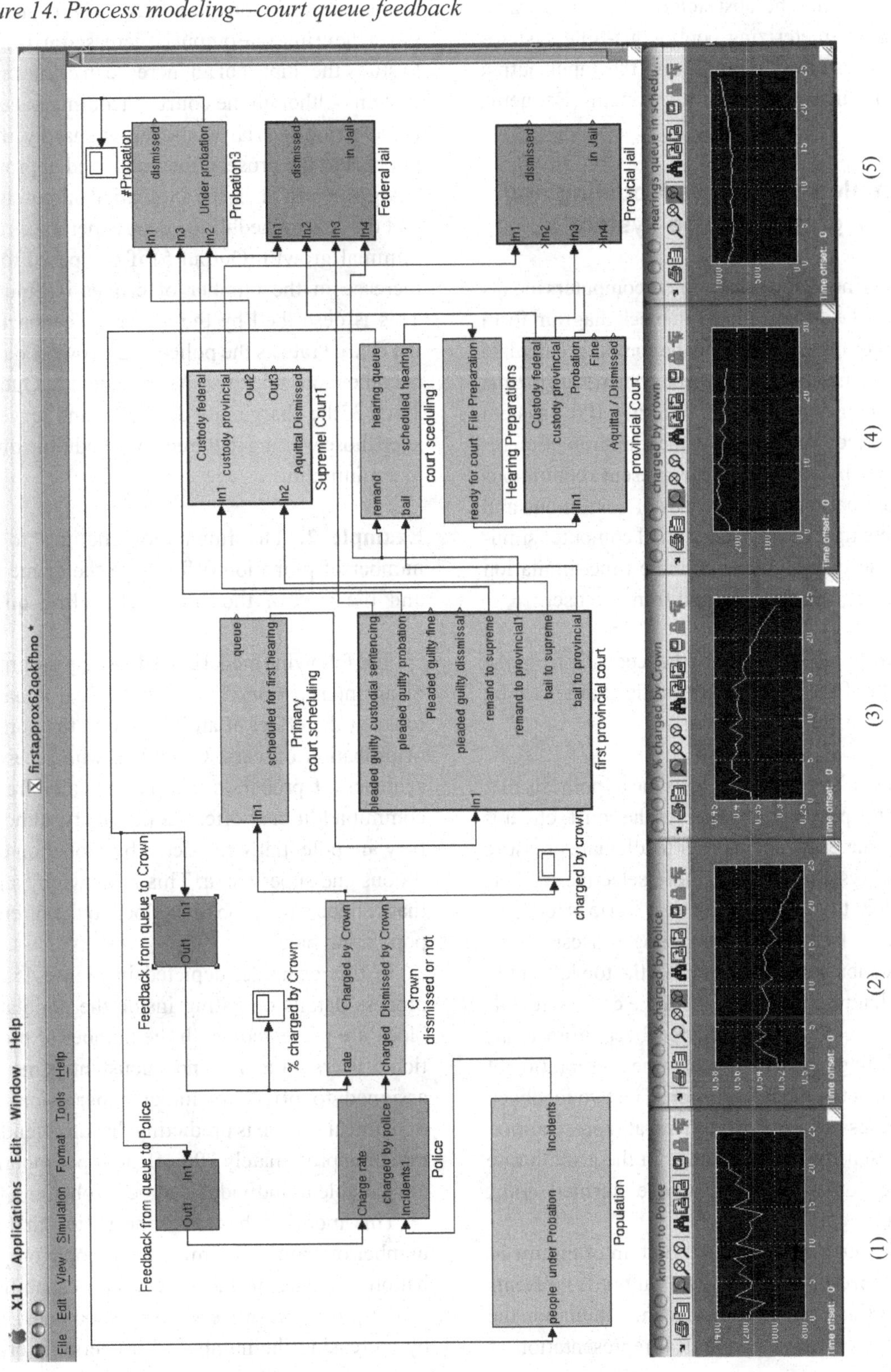

functions may be abstracted as Laplace transforms[5] characterizing continuous-time systems or Z-transforms[6] representing the input-output relationships for discrete-time systems (Baquette, 2003).

Examples of Process Modeling and the Integrated Justice System

Process modeling simulation in computers means storing the process model in block diagram form in the computer and letting the computer calculate the incremental changes in the system state in time steps with controllable granularity. If the system is modeled in continuous time, the simulation results will be interpolated to represent a continuous approximation. In both cases of continuous and discrete time models, the digital computer simulation software will use discrete-time simulation internally, which is masked from the user.

Example 1. The impact of the feedback from the growth of the court queue on the charge rate by the police and prosecution.[7]

The following model tests the hypothesis that when the prosecution observes the court scheduling queue growing, in order to alleviate pressure on the system, they are more selective in their decision to proceed with less serious crimes. The line from court scheduling process to the two feedback blocks located in the top left of the flow diagram (feedback from the court scheduling queue to Crown and feedback from court scheduling queue to police) is the presentation of the impact of the information. The two feedback processes present a mathematical representation of the sensitivity to a change in the growth rate of the court-scheduling queue (termed court scheduling1).

The output charts at the bottom of Figure 14 show the results of simulation. Output 1 represents crimes known to the police. In this simulation the crime data are a hypothetical representation of crime rate variations in society. The right hand tail of the crime rate output is increased artificially to study the impact of an increase in crime on the system. Although the court scheduling queue of those awaiting trial would grow sharply if the police and the prosecution continued approving charges at past rates, the simulation output shows that the court scheduling queue experiences only minimal growth (Output 5) if compared to the increase in the number of crimes (Output 1). This is described by the effect of feedback on the charge rate as the police and Crown Counsel become more selective. As is evident in Outputs 2 and 3, the charge rate decreases and serves to keep those waiting in the court-scheduling queue to a minimum.

Example 2. The impact of changes to the number of probation officers on the crime rate and the size of the court scheduling queue.

The following model is used to study the impact of an intervention. This hypothetical situation looks at the effect of an increase in the number of probation officers. Offenders who receive a sentence of probation are theoretically free to commit additional offences in society, although they are potentially restricted by probation conditions and supervision. This is shown by a line that connects the probation block to the offender population block.

In this example, depicted in Figure 15, the process details operating inside the population block are presented. With the number of probation officers set to 370 and a constant crime rate assigned to offenders under supervision, the dynamical system is predicting that an offending rate of approximately 700 offences per month is attributable to individuals under probation.

This model is based on the notion that the number of crimes committed by people on probation is related to the supervision capabilities of the probation officers, so it is expected that by increasing the number of officers the crime

Figure 15. Process modeling—the impact of probation on the crime rate (current state)

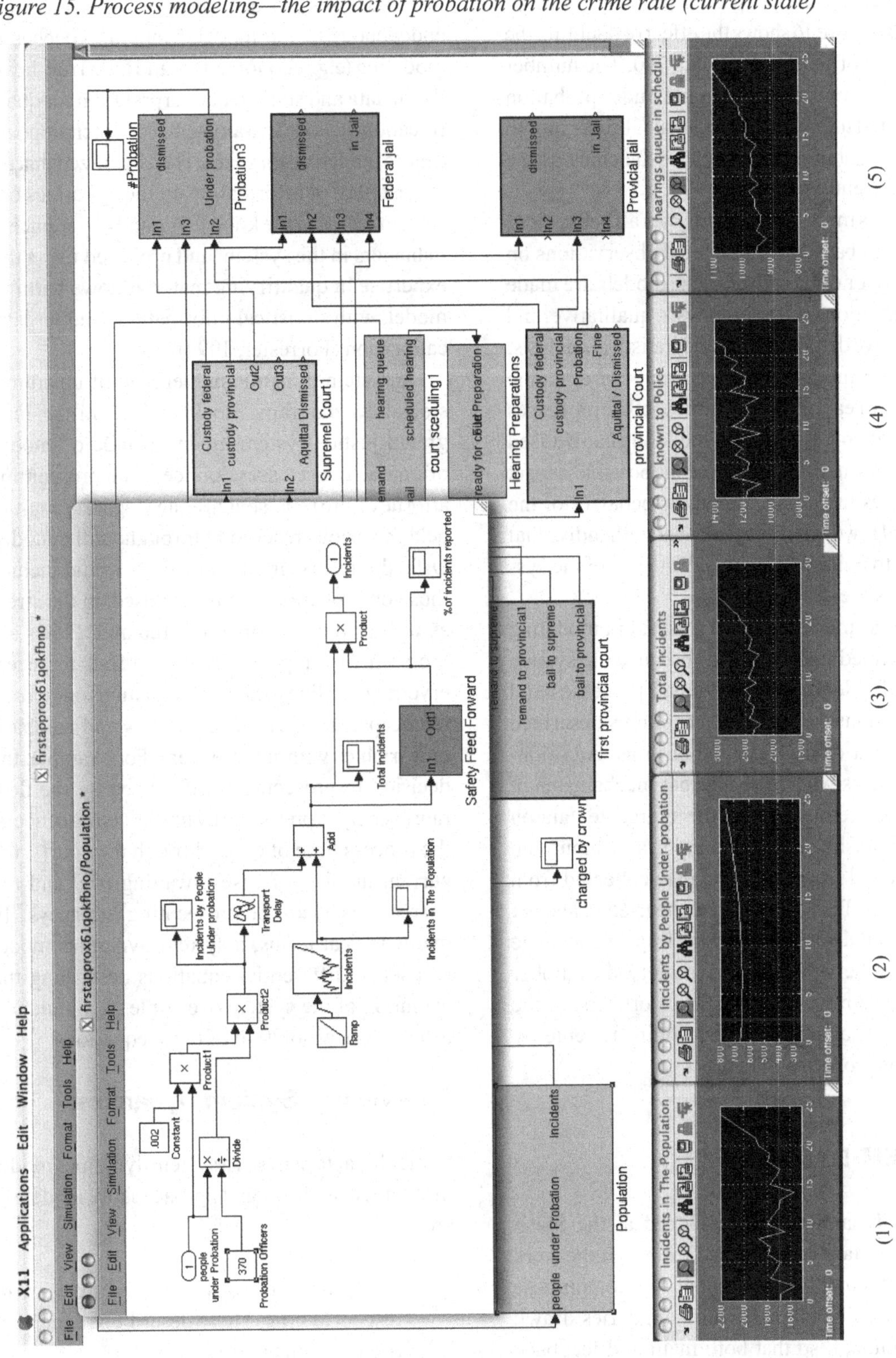

committed by the people on probation will be reduced. Figure 16 shows the effect of doubling the number of officers from 370 to 740. The number of crimes committed by people under probation is expected to be reduced to about 300 per month and the number of the people in the court queue is subsequently reduced.

Process models present the overall behavior of the system based on aggregated observations on the behavior of the system. The models are made by observations, system analysis, qualitative, and quantitative data gathering and statistical analysis, giving the modeler an idea about the dynamic behavior of each process and how other processes affect that process. Process modeling can be used for decision-making regarding the possible impact of changes in parameters on the behavior of the system. However, it does not deal with individual entities to build the dynamic behavior of the system, as is the case in DES.

Process modeling is very useful in modeling an integrated justice system because the system can be divided into well-defined processes and their relationships can be conceptually described in the form of process relationships. Additionally, in cases where the internal mechanisms of processes are not known, the aggregate data on the relationship between output and input can be extracted from statistical data collected from the system. This approach can be used to answer managerial decisions about the impact of change in the number of incidents in society, the number of other resources such as police officers, or the impact of changes in laws pertaining to sentence length or probation policies.

SYSTEM DYNAMICS

System dynamics was developed at the Sloan School of Management at MIT through the work of Jay W. Forrester. His intent was to compose comprehensive models, with boundaries drawn widely enough so that both main and feedback influences on the operation of the system are endogenous to the model. Many approaches to modeling (e.g., econometrics and DES) rely heavily on data and statistical interpretation for quantification of model parameters. Forrester proposed a more inductive approach. He recognized that the largest pool of information on the dynamics of a system rested in the knowledge and experience of managers in the system, and proposed using this expertise in quantifying material flows within a model, with statistical information used for later calibration (Forrester, 1994).

A system dynamic model is built up from a stock-flow diagram. Stocks, which in the integrated justice system model include offenders, offences, court cases, police, and prosecuting attorneys, are represented as aggregate quantities held in various reservoirs throughout the model. Offender reservoirs, for example, would include those on probation or unsupervised on the street as well as those in prison or remand. Flows are represented by pipes which fill and drain these reservoirs according to flow rate equations composed to encapsulate their dependencies and feedback on variables within the system. For example, the decision to prosecute is influenced by the flow rate of charges presented by investigating officers, the process time of cases through the courts, the current number of cases awaiting trial and the current caseloads of prosecuting attorneys. In mathematical terms, a system dynamics model is a set of differential equations describing the evolution of the system over time. A simulation is a numerical solution of these equations.

Overview of System Dynamics

Some characteristics of a system dynamics model in contrast with other approaches to modeling are:

- The flow equations are derivatives with respect to time. These describe a model that is continuous in time.

Figure 16. Process modeling—the effect of increasing the number of probation officers by 100% usage of process modeling in integrated justice systems

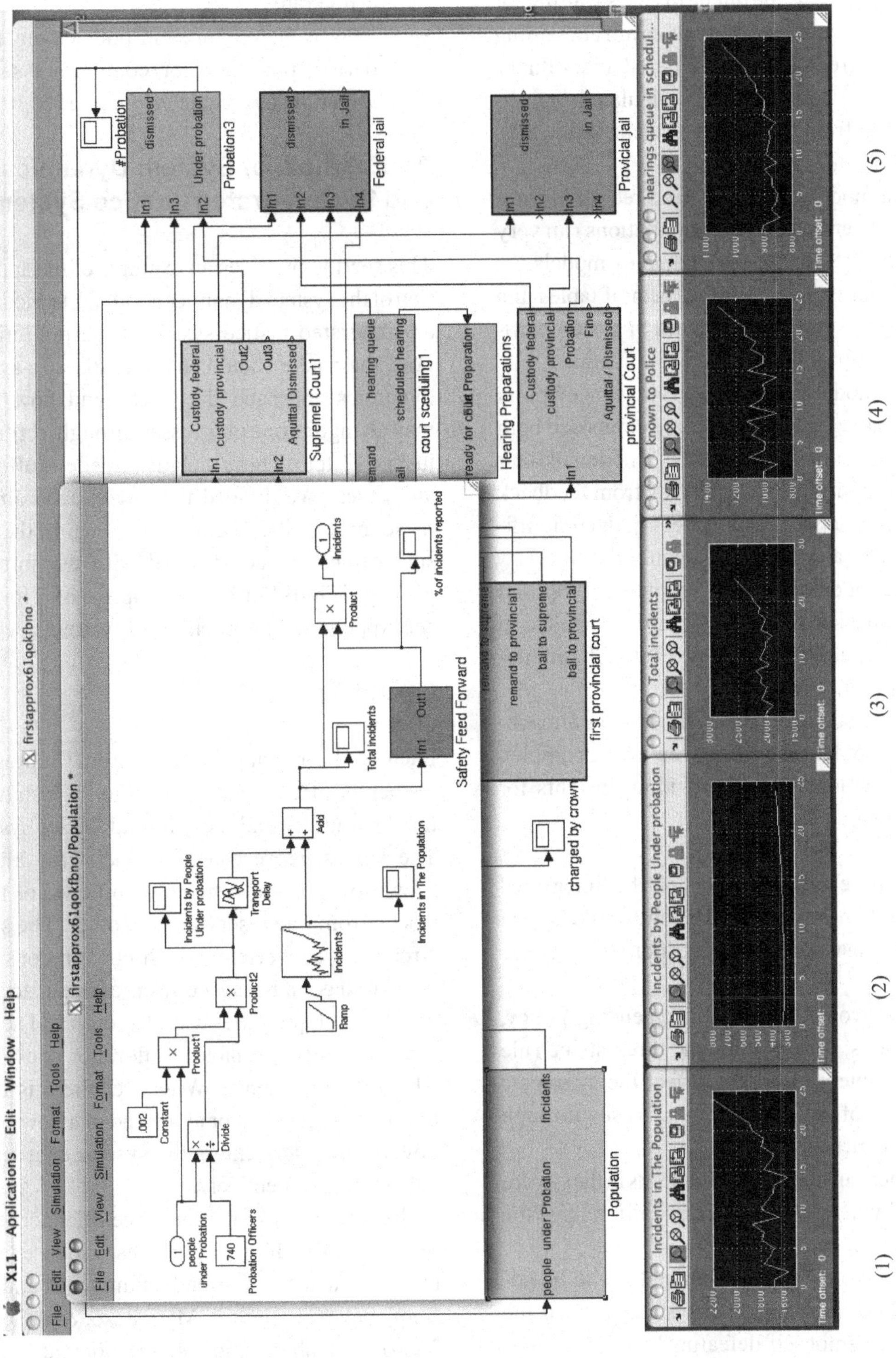

- The model is essentially unconcerned with statistical distributions.
- A queue (e.g., the queue of cases waiting for trial) is represented by a reservoir containing an aggregation of unordered individuals. Waiting times may be calculated or estimated from flow rates of stocks leaving the reservoir.
- The model does not keep a record of individual entities, so that simulations run very quickly, even for very complex models.
- Output is mainly in the form of tables and graphs showing the values of system variables through the time of simulation.
- The model is composed from the viewpoint of managers. Flow rates are composed both from their estimates in the function of their own departments as well as from feedback effects between departments judged significant by a consensus of managers.
- The model is readily adaptable. Proposed feedback effects may be easily included in rate equations and tested through simulation.
- The model may be useful both as a teaching tool for managers in outlining complex interactions and in providing insights for strategic planning.

A comprehensive model of the integrated justice system, as described below, would help in obtaining answers to such questions as:

- How would changes in sentencing policy, such as, for example, the three-strike rule for violent offenders, affect the aggregate flows of different types of cases through the courts?
- Where are the main bottlenecks in the system and where would an intervention have the greatest benefit?
- How would an intervention have to be coordinated between subsystems so that the effect is not self-defeating?
- How would various changes in policies on detention of offenders affect the aggregate crime rate?
- How would changes in policies regarding parole, probation, or community service affect the aggregate crime rate?

An Example of System Dynamics and the Integrated Justice System

This section provides an example of the application of the system dynamics approach to modeling an integrated justice system. As a preliminary note, the reader should be aware that in a system dynamics approach the stocks and flow units may change as one progresses through a criminal justice system. These include offenders, offences and cases. We divided the model according to these three units. The figures shown in the next subsections are constructed with the software package iThink™ (for a description of iThink™, see Appendix A: Modeling Software).

Offenders

Each of the rectangles in Figure 17 represents a stock of offenders according to their status in the community and the criminal justice system. The valves, represented by thick gray arrows show flows, or in some cases biflows, of these stocks from one reservoir to another. The small circles are converters, which contain constants or formulas and may be used as input to flow equations or quantities useful as output. The thin arrows connect variables to flows or converters which they influence. Whenever there is not a box at the beginning or at the end of a flow a new flow of offenders enters the system or it leaves the system, respectively.

Research has shown that free offenders have different offending frequencies which enables the classification of offenders into high and low frequency (Carrington, Matarazzo, & deSouza, 2006). This observation is incorporated into the

Figure 17. System dynamics—offender stock/flow diagram

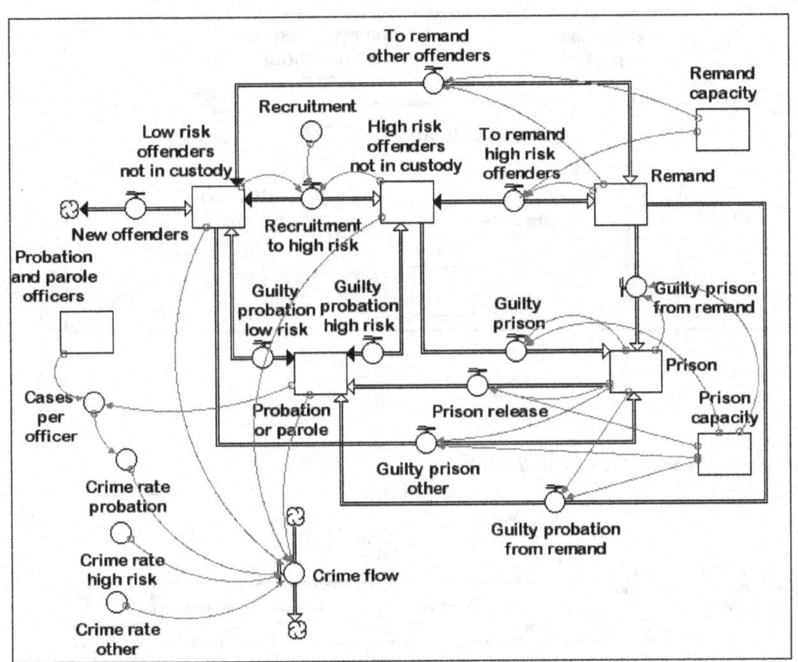

model. There are populations in remand awaiting trial and in prison after sentencing by the court. These are limited by the capacity of detention facilities, which restricts sentencing options. This influence is indicated by the thin arrows from these stocks to the relevant flows. In particular, the flow rate equation is composed using these influence variables acquired through practical knowledge on the operation of the system. There are biflows, flows going both ways, of offenders on the upper left representing both recruitment of new offenders into the justice system and current offenders desisting from crime once released from supervision. Crimes are committed by offenders either free in the community according to respective rates or by those under supervision on parole or probation. This latter rate to a certain degree is affected by the caseloads of the officers involved.

Offences

This section of the model focuses on the policing subsystem. Reported crimes are attended by the police according to the availability of police resources and the seriousness of the offence. For a very small percentage of offences, a suspect is arrested and charged. Depending again on the offence seriousness and available resources, the case is transferred to a stock of offences under further investigation. The size of this stock is limited by police caseloads, with many files becoming inactive on a regular basis. Once a suspect is identified and charges are recommended, the relevant offences are composed into a case file and presented to Crown Counsel.

Cases

This section of the model is concerned with the flow of summary conviction and indictable of-

Figure 18. System dynamics—offenses flow model

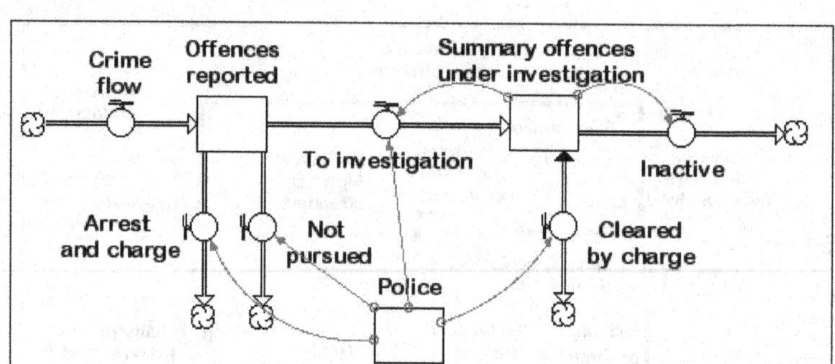

Figure 19. System dynamics—cases flow model

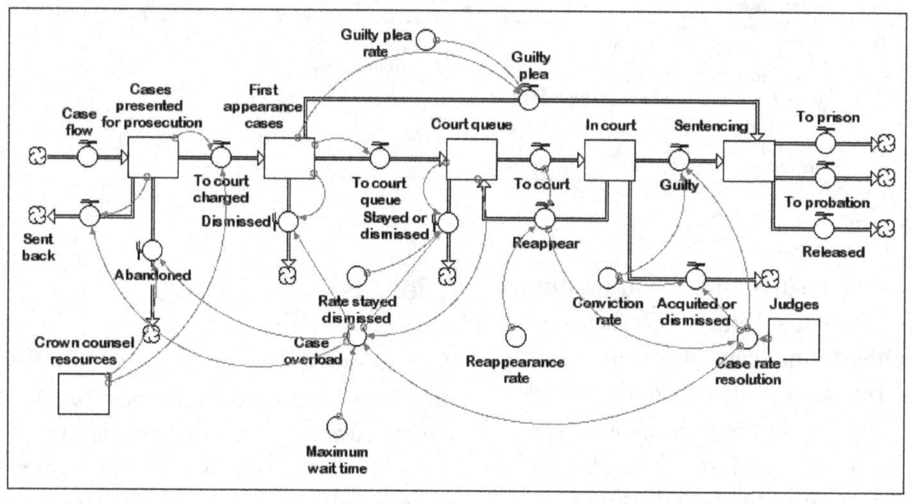

fences through the court system[8]. The important considerations here are court resources and their use. The availability of judges, prosecutors, courtrooms, and possibly other restrictions, determines the rate at which court cases are completed. From this rate and the size of the court queue, an estimate of the time it takes for a case to reach trial can be determined. This is of particular importance when there is a time limit restriction for the commencement of trial. In conjunction with the consideration of the seriousness of the offence and the strength of the case, this influences the decision of prosecutors as to whether a case brought forward by police is prosecuted, abandoned, or sent back for more investigation. The prosecuted cases for which there is no guilty plea may be reassessed, stayed or withdrawn according the same criteria. It has been argued that much of the court delay problem is connected to reappearances that often consume considerable court resources.

The decision to detain a suspect brought to court by denying bail is affected by seriousness of the crime, community security and remand capacity. When a suspect is found guilty, a sentencing decision must be made. The kind of sentence imposed is influenced by prison capacity, the availability of probation officers and by community service resources.

Example 1. The influence of court capacity on the rate of summary offense cases

A simple model of a court system that illustrates the flows of summary offense cases through a court system is depicted in Figure 20. This figure was again created with the software package iThink ™. It shows a simulation of a model that has run over a defined time period. The rectangular boxes in the picture depict the cases at various stages in the court system. The flows (i.e., the thick lines with arrows) transport cases from one stage to the other in a certain time period. It starts with a specific number of charged cases entering the court system during this time period and ends with their verdicts.

Summary conviction cases have a time restriction, dictated by the Criminal Code of Canada, which requires that the commencement of a trial occurs within six months from the laying of an information. The court has a capacity that is related to the number of judges, the number of courtrooms, the number of prosecutors and the amount of ancillary court resources. This capacity gives an upper bound on how many cases can be treated in a certain time period (e.g., per month). A queue of cases waiting to go to court is formed when the court cannot service all of them as they arrive in court. When the queue gets too long, cases are stayed, withdrawn, or dismissed because the trial cannot be initiated within the 6-month time requirement.

In contrast to the conceptual models of "offenders" depicted in Figure 17 and "offences" shown in Figure 18, the model in Figure 20 does not present any of the small influence lines arrows. This is due to the fact that Figure 20 is constructed from several submodels contained within the rectangular boxes (e.g., the Court Queue box). A submodel has a series of stocks, flows and influences; it is a little model inside the larger one. For instance, when one zooms in on the court queue box, Figure 21 appears.

The flows in the submodel are the same as the flows in the bigger model. Hence the same names with a (') sign and with possibly a number added. The small circles compute or contain certain quantities. The boxes are stocks (reservoirs). The only influence we permit is the capacity of the cases that can be treated in court in a month period. The other influences on court capacity can be added later in a similar way.

Output from the model should indicate that the total number of cases dismissed (by a stay

Figure 20. System dynamics—court system output

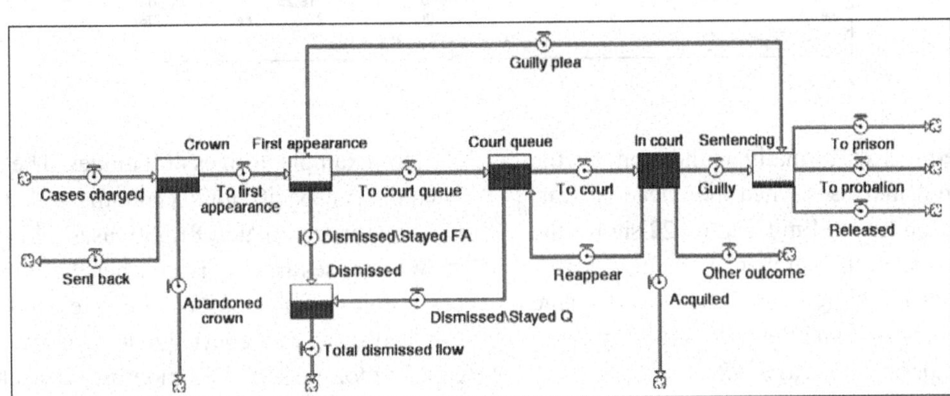

Figure 21. System dynamicsThe effect of court queue length on the number of dismissed cases per month

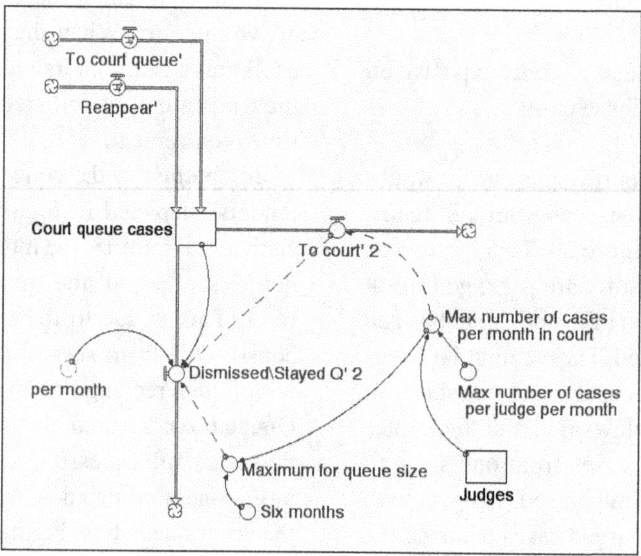

Figure 22. System dynamics—The impact of a 100% increase in the number of judges on the length of the court queue

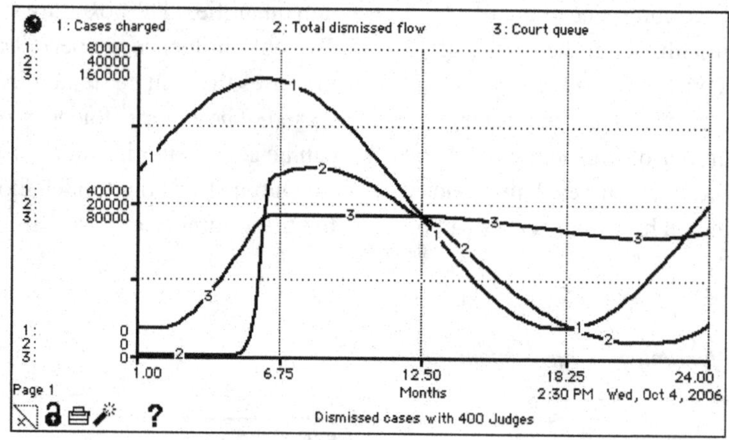

of proceedings or formally withdrawn by the prosecution) increases when the queue is nearing its 6-month time limit. Figure 22 shows the relation between the number of summary cases charged per month (curve #1), the court queue of cases (curve #3) and the total summary cases dismissed per month (curve #2).

This example utilizes 400 judges. The calculated court capacity for six months at that point was set at approximately 81,500 cases. The graphs show that cases are dismissed when the number of cases waiting for a court appearance approaches this capacity. The court queue is close to the capacity for a period of 8 months, illustrated by

Figure 23. System dynamics—The impact of an 100% increase in the number of judges on the length of the court queue

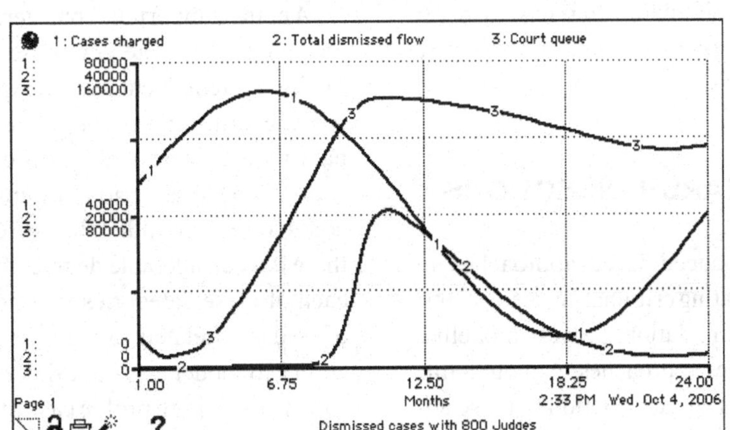

curve #3 between the months 6 and 14. During that time the largest number of cases are dismissed per month. The maximum number of cases dropped in a month is approximately 24,500.

When the court capacity increases, possibly by increasing the number of judges, one could expect fewer cases to be dismissed as a result of the sixth-month constraint for summary offences. Figure 23 depicts the output of the model when the number of judges increases.

The court queue is able to be about twice the size of the previous scenario. Curve #3 in Figure 23 illustrates this calculation. The court capacity is not challenged by the queue for a long period, and cases start to be dismissed later in time than in the previous simulation. The number of cases dismissed does not stay high for a long period, as was the case in the previous scenario. In addition the maximum number of cases dropped in a month is approximately 20,000. Over the whole 24 month period the number of the cases dismissed or stayed is 45% less than in the previous scenario.

CHAPTER SUMMARY AND CONCLUSION

This chapter focuses on a comparison of three types of modeling and simulation applied to criminal justice systems—discrete event models, process models and system dynamics, and the utility of combining information from all three approaches. Discrete event simulation is most appropriate when the distribution of the occurrence of entities and events are known and the system behavior is studied with a limited understanding of the dynamics of the system. Process modeling is best used when the overall behavior of each subsystem is known and the effect of them on each other is studied because the overall impact of a change is not known initially. System dynamics is used to present the aggregate effect of parameter change on the intensity values in a topological form. These contrasting local-global approaches should be viewed as complementary rather than competing as they all present a slightly different understanding of system functioning. Preferably, a comprehensive policy studies tool for use by criminal justice system managers should include all three types of simulation models in order to provide a comprehensive look at alternative management choices.

FUTURE RESEARCH DIRECTIONS

This chapter introduced three approaches to modeling and simulating criminal justice systems; the discrete event simulation, process modeling and system dynamics approaches. Although this chapter is written as an introduction to these approaches for audiences interested in modeling and simulation of criminal justice systems there are several directions of future research that we are undertaking in the context of the criminal justice system in British Columbia.

The first area of future research is focused on expanding the models to accurately represent the concept of an integrated justice system. It requires a detailed consideration of the offending population to incorporate known attributes of the offending population. This information is available from the extensive body of criminal career research. Additionally, a much more detailed consideration of several of the closed subsystems is required. In Canada, offenders aged 12 to 18 (at the time of offence commission) are dealt with under the provisions of the Youth Criminal Justice Act, which has at its basis a separate court system for youth. A significant proportion of reported offenses are committed by youth and this should be modeled in an integrated justice system. An additional subsystem that requires further expansion is the corrections subsystem. The models presented in this chapter to varying degrees included a limited consideration of corrections, including remand, provincial and federal incarceration capacities and the parole process. Moreover, other noncustodial sentencing outcomes require consideration, including the conditional sentence, absolute and conditional discharges, fines, probation, restitution, and compensation and community work service orders.

Another important consideration in building models to accurately represent an integrated justice system includes an expanded focus on specific crime types of interest. The preliminary models presented in this chapter discussed serious and less serious offenses or summary conviction and indictable offenses. However, there is a considerable degree of variation within each of these categories depending on the type of offense. Related to the type of offense is the ability to model a system shock, such as the occurrence of a high profile case in police and court subsystems. Although, these occur infrequently, they have a dramatic impact on the availability of resources in both the court and police subsystem for lengthy time periods. The last direction that we are planning to incorporate to successfully model an integrated justice system in British Columbia is geography. It is well known that justice is not without some degree of regional variation, in terms of offense type importance and the degree of services available in more remote regions of British Columbia.

As this research progresses, depending on the issues being addressed, we may find that we need to explore more complex or hybrid approaches to simulating the criminal justice system. In addition to the three modeling approaches covered in this chapter, these expanded approaches might incorporate multi-agent implementations, network theory, or artificial intelligence.

REFERENCES

Bailey, J., & Hann, R. (1972). *Systems analysis and the corrections system in Ontario*. Toronto: Centre of Criminology, University of Toronto.

Balci, O. (1997). *Verification, validation and accreditation of simulation models*. In S. Andradottir, K. J. Healy, D. H. Withers, & B. L. Nelson (Eds), *Proceedings of the 1997 Winter Simulation Conference* Atlanta, Georgia.

Banks, J., Carson, J., II, Nelson, B., & Nicol, D. (2001). *Discrete event system simulation* (3rd ed.). Saddle River: Prentice Hall.

Baquette, B. W. (2003). *Process control, modeling, design, and simulation.* Upper Saddle River, New Jersey: Prentice Hall.

Belkin, J., Blumstein, A., & Glass, W. (1971). *JUSSIM, an interactive computer program for analysis of criminal justice systems* (Working Paper). Carnegie-Mellon University: Urban Systems Institute, School of Urban and Public Affairs.

Blumstein, A. (1967). Systems analysis and the criminal justice system. *Annals of the American Academy of Political and Social Science, 374*(November), 91-100.

Blumstein, A. (2002). Crime modeling. *Operations Research, 50*(1), 16-24.

Blumstein, A., Cassidy, G., & Hopkinson, G. (1975). *Systems analysis and the Canadian justice system* (CANJUS Project Report No. 14). Ottawa, Canada:, Ministry of the Solicitor General.

Blumstein, A., Cassidy, G., & Townsend, J. (1974). *Implementation of a systems approach to the Canadian criminal justice system* (Statistics Division Report No. 3). Ottawa, Canada: Ministry of the Solicitor General.

Blumstein, A., & Larson, R. (1972). Analysis of a total criminal justice system. In A. Drake, R. Keeney, & P. Morse (Eds.), *Analysis of public systems.* Boston: Massachusetts Institute of Technology.

Bramson, M., & Dai, J. G. (2001). Heavy traffic limits for some queuing networks. *Annals of Applied Probability, 11*, 49-90.

Brantingham, P. (1977). *Dynamic modeling of the felony court system.* Unpublished doctoral dissertation, Florida State University.

Brantingham, P., & Brantingham, P. (2004). Computer simulation as a tool for environmental criminologists. *Security Journal, 17*(1), 21-30.

Burke, P. J. (1956). The output of queuing system. *Operations Research, 4*, 699-704.

Carrington, P. J., Matarazzo, A., & deSouza, P. (2006). *Court careers of a Canadian birth cohort.* Ottawa, Canada: Canadian Centre for Justice Statistics, Statistics Canada.

Carson, J. (2004). *Introduction to modeling and simulation.* In R. Ingalls, M. Rosetti, J. Smith, & B. Peters (Eds), *Proceedings of the 2004 Winter Simulation Conference*, Monterey, California.

Cassidy, G. (1985). Modelling a criminal justice system. In D. Farrington & R. Tarling (Eds.), *Prediction in criminology.* Albany, New York: State University of New York Press.

Cassidy, G., Hopkinson, G., & Mead, D. (1976). *Use of systems models in planning and evaluation* (CANJUS Project Report No. 25). Ottawa, Canada: Ministry of the Solicitor General.

Cellier, F. E. (1991). *Continuous system modeling.* New York: Springer-Verlag.

Chaiken, J., Crabill, T., Holiday, L., Jaquette, D., Lawless, M., & Quade, E. (1977). Summary of operational criminal justice models. In S. Nagel (Ed.), *Modeling the criminal justice system.* Beverly Hills, CA: Sage Publications.

Chung, C. (2004). *Simulation modeling handbook: A practical approach.* New York: CRC Press.

Cohen, J., Fields, K., Lettre, M., Stafford, R., & Walker, C. (1973). Implementation of the JUSSIM model in a criminal justice planning agency. *Journal of Research in Crime and Delinquency, 10*(2), 117-131.

Comfort, J., Shapiro, S., & Volcansek-Clark, M. (1982). *Development of a simulation model of criminal caseflow activities, Decision and policy variables*. Miami, FL: Florida International University.

Erlang, A. K. (1909). The theory of probabilities and telephone conversations. *Nyt Tidsskrift Matematik, 20*, 33-39.

Forrester, J. (1968). *Principles of systems*. Cambridge: Wright-Allen Press, Inc.

Forrester, J. W. (1994). System dynamics, Systems thinking and soft OR. *System Dynamics Review, 10*(2-3), 245-256.

Foschio, L. (1973). Empirical research and the problem of court delay. In Law Enforcement Assistance Administration (Ed.), *Reducing court delay*. Washington: U.S. Department of Justice.

Gross, D., & Harris, C. (1974). *Fundamentals in queuing theory*. New York: Wiley & Sons.

Hann, R., Bailey, L., & Ross, M. (1973). *Decision making in the Canadian criminal court system: A systems analysis Volume I & II*. Toronto: Centre of Criminology, University of Toronto.

Hann, R., & Salzman, L. (1976). *CANCOURT - I: A computerized system simulation model to support planning in court systems*. Toronto: Decision Dynamics Corporation.

Harper, P. (2002). A Framework for operational modelling of hospital resources. *Health Care Management Science, 5*, 165-173.

Harries, R. (2001). *Criminal justice modeling*. London: Home Office Strategic Policy Team.

Harrison, G., Ivatts, S., & Millard, P. (2003). Mathematical modelling: How and why. *British Journal of Health Care Management, 9*, 144-150.

Haynes, P. (1973). Reducing court delay. In Law Enforcement Assistance Administration (Ed.), *Reducing Court Delay*. Washington: U.S. Department of Justice.

Homer, J., & Hirsch, G. (2006). Systems dynamics modeling for public health: Background and opportunities. *American Journal of Public Health, 96*(3), 452-458.

Kelton, W., Sadowski, R., & Sturrock, D. (2007). *Simulation with arena* (4th ed.). New York: McGraw-Hill, Inc.

Larson, R., Cahn, M., & Shell, M. (1993). Improving the New York City arrest-to-arraignment system. *Interfaces, 23*(2), 76-96.

Law Reform Commission of Canada. (1994). *Trial within a reasonable time*. Ottawa, Canada: Public Works and Government Services Canada.

Lind, B., Chilvers, M., & Weatherburn, D. (2001). *Simulating the New South Wales criminal justice system: A stock and flow approach*. Sydney, Australia: New South Wales Bureau of Crime Statistics and Research.

Livingston, M., Stewart, A., & Palk, G. (2005). *A micro-simulation model of the juvenile justice system in queensland*. In A. Zerger & R. M. Argent (Eds). In *Proceedings of the MODSIM 2005 International Congress on Modelling and Simulation*.

Lowery, J. (1998). *Getting started in simulation in healthcare*. In D. Medeiros, E. Watson, J. Carson & M. Manivannan (Eds), *Proceedings of the 1998 Winter Simulation Conference*, Washington, D.C.

Malm, A., Pollard, N., Brantingham, P. J., Tinsley, P., Plecas, D., Brantingham, P. L., et al. (2005). *A 30 year analysis of police service delivery and costing in British Columbia*. Ottawa, Canada: "E" Division, Royal Canadian Mounted Police.

Mathworks (2004). *Simulink: Simulation and model based design* (Version 6).

McAllister, W., Atchinson, J., & Jacobs, N. (1991). A simulation model of pretrial felony case processing: A queuing system analysis. *Journal of Quantitative Criminology, 7*(3), 291-314.

McGinnis, J. (1989). Predicting police force attrition, promotion and demographic change: A computer simulation model. *Canadian Police College Journal, 13*(2), 87-127.

McGraw-Hill Dictionary of Scientific and Technical Terms (2003). McGraw-Hill Companies, Inc.

Medhi, J. (1991). *Stochastic models in queuing theory.* San Diego, CA: Academic Press.

Merritt, N., Fain, T., & Turner, S. (2006). Oregon's get tough sentencing reform: A lesson in justice system adaptation. *Criminology & Public Policy, 5*(1), 5-36.

Mu, S. (1996). *Forecasting the need and cost: An exploration of the system dynamics of legal aid.* Unpublished doctoral dissertation, Simon Fraser University, Burnaby.

National Council on Crime and Delinquency (1987). *Correctional population simulation model: Model description.* San Francisco: The National Council on Crime and Delinquency.

Navarro, J., & Taylor, J. (1967). An application of systems analysis to aid in the efficient administration of justice. *Judicature, 51*(2), 47-52.

Nayar, R., & Bleuel, W. (1973). Simulation of a criminal court case processing system. In Law Enforcement Assistance Administration (Ed.), *Reducing court delay.* Washington: U.S. Department of Justice.

Pooch, U., & Wall, J. (1993). *Discrete event simulation: A practical approach.* Boca Raton: CRC Press, Inc.

Sadowski, D., & Grabau, M. (2004). *Tips for successful practice of simulation.* In R. Ingalls, M. Rosetti, J. Smith & B. Peters (Eds), *Proceedings of the 2004 Winter Simulation Conference*, Monterey, California.

Schriber, T., & Brunner, D. (2004). *Inside discrete-event simulation software: How it works and why it matters.* In R. Ingalls, M. Rosetti, J. Smith & B. Peters (Eds), *Proceedings of the 2004 Winter Simulation Conference*, Monterey, California.

SFU Complex Systems Modelling Group. (2006). *Modelling the demand for healthcare.* Burnaby: British Columbia Ministry of Health.

Stewart, A., Spencer, N., O'Connor, I., Palk, G., Livingston, M., & Allard, T. (2004). Juvenile justice simulation model. In *Australian Research Council Strategic Partnerships with Industry Research and Training* (Vol. August). Brisbane, Australia: Australian Research Council Strategic Partnerships with Industry Research and Training.

Stollmack, S. (1973). Predicting inmate populations from arrest, Court disposition and recidivism rates. *Journal of Research in Crime and Delinquency, 10*(2), 141-162.

ADDITIONAL READING

Ahmed, N. (2006). *Dynamic systems and control with applications.* Hackensack, NJ: World Scientific Publishing Company

Antsaklis, P. (1997). *Linear systems.* New York, NY: McGraw-Hill.

Banks, J., Carson II, J., Nelson, B., & Nicol, D. (2001). *Discrete event system simulation* (3rd ed.). Saddle River, NJ: Prentice Hall.

Belkin, J., Blumstein, A., & Glass, W. (1971). *JUSSIM, An interactive computer program for analysis of criminal justice systems* (Working Paper). Carnegie-Mellon University: Urban Systems Institute, School of Urban and Public Affairs.

Blumstein, A. (2002). Crime modeling. *Operations Research, 50*(1), 16-24.

Boxma, O., Koole, G., & Lui, Z. (1994). Queuing-theoretic solution methods for models of distributed and parallel systems. In O. Boxma, & G. Koole, (Eds.), *Performance evaluation of parallel and distributed systems—solution methods* (pp. 1-24). Amsterdam: CWI.

Brantingham, P. (1977). *Dynamic modeling of the felony court system.* Unpublished doctoral dissertation, Florida State University.

Cassandra, C., & Lafortune, S. (1999). *Introduction to discrete event systems.* New York: Springer.

Cellier, F. E. (1991). *Continuous system modeling.* New York: Springer-Verlag.

Chen, H., & Yao, D. (2001). *Fundamentals of queuing networks.* New York: Springer.

Chung, C. (2004). *Simulation modeling handbook: A practical approach.* New York: CRC Press.

Cohen, J. (1982). *The single server.* Amsterdam: North-Holland.

Fishman, G. (2001). *Discrete-event simulation: Modeling, programming and analysis.* New York: Springer.

Fishman, G. (1978). *Principles of discrete event simulation.* New York: John Wiley & Sons, Inc.

Forrester, J. (1968). *Principles of systems.* Cambridge: Wright-Allen Press, Inc.

Forrester, J. W. (1994). System dynamics, Systems thinking and soft OR. *System Dynamics Review, 10*(2-3), 245-256.

Gross, D., & Harris, C. (1974). *Fundamentals in queuing theory.* New York: Wiley & Sons.

Kailath, T. (1980). *Linear systems.* Englewood Cliffs, NJ: Prentice Hall.

Kelton, W., Sadowski, R., & Sturrock, D. (2007). *Simulation with arena* (4th ed.). New York: McGraw-Hill, Inc.

Larson, R., Cahn, M., & Shell, M. (1993). Improving the New York City arrest-to-arraignment system. *Interfaces, 23*(2), 76-96.

Maltz, M. (1994). From Poisson to present: Applying operations research to problems of crime and justice. *Journal of Quantitative Criminology,* 12(1), 3-61.

Medhi, J. (1991). *Stochastic models in queuing theory.* San Diego, CA: Academic Press.

Mistra, J. (1986). Distributed discrete-event simulation. *ACM Computing Surveys,* 18(1), 39-65.

Morgan, P. (1985). *Modeling the criminal justice system.* London: Home Office.

Oppenheim, A., Willsky, A., & Nawab, S. (1997). *Signals & systems* (2nd ed.). Upper Saddle River, NJ: Prentice Hall.

Pooch, U., & Wall, J. (1993). *Discrete event simulation: A practical approach.* Boca Raton, FL: CRC Press.

Poularikas, A., & Seely, S. (1991). *Signals and systems* (2nd ed.). Boston: PWS-Kent Publishing Company.

Pullinger, H. (1985). *The criminal justice system model: The flow model.* London: Home Office.

Sloan School of Management (2007). *MIT system dynamics in education project.* Retrieved September 4, 2007, from http://sysdyn.clexchange.org

Stidham, S., Jr. (2002). Analysis, design and control of queuing systems. *Operations Research,* 50, 197-216.

Van Dijk, N. (1997). Why queuing never vanishes. *European Journal of Operations Research,* 99, 463-476.

Zeigler, B. (1991). Object-oriented modeling and discrete-event simulation. In M. Yovits (Ed.), *Advances in computers* (Volume 33, pp. 67-114). San Diego, CA: Academic Press Professional.

ENDNOTES

1 The theoretical foundations of these modeling techniques can be explored in much more detail through the additional readings section at the end of this chapter.

2 Most common-law-based systems are broadly similar although all differ in detail. For instance in Canadian terminology prosecutors are usually referred to as "Crown Counsel" or just "Crown" while the equivalent term in the United States would typically be "District Attorney" or "State's Attorney"; "summary offences" in Canada are similar to but not exactly the same as "misdemeanors" in the United States; "parole" describes a form of post-imprisonment supervision in Canada, England and the United States, but there are specific differences in parole operation in the three countries.

3 (For some exceptions see: Comfort, Shapiro, & Volcansek-Clark, 1982; Larson, Cahn, & Shell, 1993; McAllister et al., 1991; Morgan, 1985; Mu, 1996; Pullinger, 1985)

4 A system has feedback if the output of a process directly or indirectly effects at least one of its inputs. For example, if process A has an output that effects process B we have an open loop system; however, if the output of A or the output of B directly or indirectly effects one of the inputs of A we have a feedback loop.

5 Many systems are modeled by linear ordinary differential equations and Laplace transforms which significantly reduce the effort required to solve these equations by converting them to algebraic equations. For example, instead of dealing with $dN/dT=-aN$ one can deal with the algebraic equation $sN(s)-N(0)+aN(s)=0$

6 If the equations describing the behavior of the system are explained in discrete time one can use z-transformation, instead of using Laplace transformation, to simplify and study the process.

7 It is important to note that the results of the simulations shown here are hypothetical and are used for the purpose of demonstration.

8 In the context of the United States, an indictable offense is a felony and a summary conviction offense is a misdemeanor.

9 http://www.scicos.org/

APPENDIX A. MODELING SOFTWARE

Discrete Event Simulation Software

Arena™

Arena™ is based on the SIMAN simulation language, with a graphical user interface. Building an Arena™ model is similar to building a flowchart in which each shape (called a "module") that is placed in the flowchart comes with a block of SIMAN code behind it. Modules define the system logic and the physical components such as machines, operators, storage areas and traffic routes. Arena™ has several templates into which dozens of standard modules are organized.

In addition to the core modeling elements just described, that are graphics capabilities and the Input Analyzer of Arena™. Arena™ animation enables the modeler to show the flow of entities, the growing and shrinking of queues, the status of resources and the changing values of performance statistics over the course of the simulation run. This animation is valuable for two reasons in particular: First, it helps the modeler to validate his or her model—to verify that the system is behaving as intended. Second, it is an excellent means of demonstrating the operation of a system to lay audiences. The Input Analyzer is a tool that automatically selects the probability distribution and parameters that best reflect pre-existing sample data that is to be used as input to the Arena model. This would apply to random arrival processes, services times, etc.

Arena™ was developed and is supported by Rockwell Automation, Inc. It is available for Microsoft Windows 98™, Windows ME™, Windows 2000™, Windows Server 2003™, and Windows XP™. Rockwell Automation also offers OptQuest, an optimization suite for Arena.

Process Modeling Software Tools

Packages like Simulink™ and Scicos[9] provide facilities for describing processes in block diagrams and can simulate the behavior of the system with discrete or continuous changes in system state. These simulation tools run on a digital computer so they use discrete time solution with programmable resolution to simulate the behavior.

Matlab™

Matlab™ is a package by Mathworks which is useful for numerical computation, data visualization and linear systems analysis (Baquette, 2003).

Simulink™

Simulink™ is an extension to Matlab™ that is far more useful for control system simulation. It uses block diagrams as graphical presentation of a mathematical model of a dynamic system. A block within a block diagram defines a dynamic system in itself (Mathworks, 2004). Simulink™ block diagrams define time-based relationships between signals and state variables. The solution of a block diagram is obtained by evaluating these relationships over time, where time starts at a user specified "start time" and ends at a user specified "stop time." Each evaluation of these relationships is referred to as a time step. Signals represent quantities that change over time and are defined for all points in time between the block diagram's start and stop time. The relationships between signals and state variables are defined by a set of equations represented by blocks. Each block consists of a set of equations. These equations define a relationship between the input signals, output signals and the state variables. The behavior of the system can be modeled by a number of blocks presenting fundamental mathematical operations including differentiation and integration or a Laplace transform transfer function (Mathworks, 2004).

System Dynamics Software

iThink™ and STELLA™

The software packages iThink™ and STELLA™ are distributed by the company isee™ systems (http://www.iseesystems.com). These packages are comparable. iThink™ is intended to be for a business environment, while STELLA™ is more for educational and research purposes. They both offer a practical way to construct and visualize complex systems. They can provide a whole model or big picture view of the entire system needed to be modeled.

iThink™ and STELLA™ have an icon-based graphical interface. Relationships and feed-back are visible via causal loop diagrams. By using the graphical interface, the model's (differential) equations are generated automatically. There are various built-in stock types, such as reservoirs, queues and ovens. It is possible to construct submodels. Data can be imported from and exported to a Microsoft® Excel file.

With a mathematical view in mind, discrete and continuous processes are both possible. Some mathematical functions are built-in and sensitivity analysis is available. The results of a simulation can be represented as graphs, tables, animations, QuickTime® movies, or files.

Section V
Conclusion

Chapter XX
Varieties of Artificial Crime Analysis:
Purpose, Structure, and Evidence in Crime Simulations

John Eck
University of Cincinnati, USA

Lin Liu
University of Cincinnati, USA

ABSTRACT

Since the beginnings of this millennium, there has been a burgeoning interest in the use of simulation methods for the study of crime. In a remarkably short period, crime researchers using simulations have applied the method in a wide variety of ways. Let us look at some of the first simulations—four simulations developed by three different teams working independently—to describe this diversity.

INTRODUCTION

Liang (2001) constructed the first crime pattern simulation for his dissertation, supervised by Liu and Eck, and publicly presented his analysis at the UCGIS Summer Assembly in 2001 (Liang, Liu, & Eck, 2001). His simulation implemented aspects of routine activity theory with two types of agents: store robbers and store managers. Managers were immobile, but updated their protection based on "news" of robberies transmitted using cellular automata. Robbers moved randomly around a street grid, copied from a small area of Cincinnati, and decided to rob a store they encountered based on a comparison of their capabilities with the store's protection level. The resulting pattern of robberies looked surprisingly similar to the actual pattern of robberies in the same geographic area (Liu, Wang, Eck, & Liang , 2005).

Following this simulation Wang (2005) developed a simulation of street robberies, also under Liu and Eck's supervision. In Wang's simulation both the targets of crimes (pedestrians) and the offenders were mobile and both types of agents learned their routes. Pedestrian agents assessed the costs of distance and crime risk in choosing their routes. Offender agents choose their routes by assessing the availability of pedestrians. Routine activity theory, crime pattern theory, and rational choice perspectives informed the construction of this simulation. Wang used agent based modeling to orchestrate agent mobility and used cellular automata to communicate crime risk.

Pieter van Baal (2004) was interested in examining the social structure of deterrence theory. In his simulation, developed for his doctoral dissertation under the supervision of Henk Elffers, van Baal created a virtual world where nonmobile agents made choices about whether to commit crimes based on their perceived chances of being "audited" by authorities and the rewards for committing crime. Agents formed their risk perceptions based on their experiences, and the experience of their neighbors, of being audited. Van Baals' simulation was only weakly spatial—a cellular automata model was used to describe agents' social networks. Though his cellular automata model had a two-dimensional arrangement, it was meant to mimic a social network rather than a real geographical arrangement.

These three simulations were constructed to explore theoretical problems in crime. Batty, Desyllas, and Duxbury (2003) were interested in a very practical problem. They simulated pedestrian movement patterns at London's Notting Hill Carnival to find ways to reduce crowding and threats to public safety at this festival. Their goal was to mimic a real event and provide policy guidance to planners of future events. The researchers had detailed information on the street patterns, obstructions to movement, destination points, and crowd size at these points. They used swarm intelligence to model pedestrian flow among these points, thus producing a picture of when and where crowding became problematic. The simulation allowed planners to examine how crowding responded to closing streets and erecting barriers.

Since 2001 a number of other individuals and teams have begun working on crime simulations, and many of these efforts are represented in this volume. Let us look at some of the differences among simulations, using the four examples to illustrate the differences. Some simulations are heavily information intensive (Batty, Desyllas, & Duxbury, 2003) while other simulations are data-sparse (Liang, 2001; Wang, 2005; van Baal, 2004): relying on deductive logic from a set of basic assumptions. Some simulations involve strong spatial arrangements (Batty, Desyllas, & Duxbury, 2003; Liang, 2001; Wang, 2005), while others do not (van Baal, 2004). Agent mobility varies from no mobility (van Baal, 2004), to limited mobility (Liang, 2001), to high mobility with search capability (Batty, Desyllas, & Duxbury, 2003; Wang, 2005). Some simulations are designed for policy planning (Batty, Desyllas, & Duxbury, 2003) while others are designed to examine theory (Liang, 2001; Wang, 2005; van Baal, 2004). In all cases, the researchers who create them believe that their simulations of artificial crime patterns provide information useful for understanding how actual crimes are committed.

In this chapter we organize this diversity of approaches, contrast simulation methods to other research methods, and look at the process and prospects of simulation methods for the study of crime and related phenomena. This chapter addresses six questions:

1. What are the purposes of artificial crime analysis?
2. What are the characteristics of crime simulations?
3. How does artificial crime analysis compare to other research methods?
4. When should simulations be used?

5. Who should construct simulations?
6. What is the future of artificial crime analysis?

We begin by looking at the purposes of artificial crime analysis. We describe four purposes. We next turn to seven important features of simulations, and we show how these characteristics are related to each other. Then we show how the purpose of a simulation influences its characteristics. This leads to a comparison of simulation methods to five other commonly used crime research methods. We will describe how simulations combine strengths of methods for theorizing and methods for testing theories, but have some important limitations. Following this discussion, we look at the circumstances in which simulations are useful and the situations in which they are not. In the penultimate section we examine the characteristics of the people who need to be involved in producing crime and justice simulations. Finally, we speculate on how crime and justice simulations might develop and offer some cautions about their future.

WHAT ARE THE PURPOSES OF ARTIFICIAL CRIME ANALYSIS?

Simulations serve several of purposes and a simulation developed for one purpose may be unsuitable for other purposes. So any discussion of the value of simulating crime needs to begin with the specific goals that the researchers are trying to achieve. There are four major reasons for using simulations: theorizing, estimating, testing, and planning.

First, simulations can be an extremely useful part of the process of theorizing. This volume contains several examples of simulations constructed for this purpose (Brantingham & Tita; Elffers & van Baal; Furtado, et. al.; Groff; Kim, & Xiao; Wang, Liu, & Eck). In each case, the researchers are interested in determining whether commonly observed crime patterns could arise from simple processes. If the simulations can mimic real world phenomena by using a limited set of simple processes, this suggests that the theories encapsulated in the software may be sufficient to explain the phenomena. Experimenting with these artificial crime production systems can help formulate hypotheses that can be tested using real data. Wang (2005) and Wang, Liu, and Eck (in this volume) experimentally vary the cognitive processes of agents. Groff (in this volume) conducts a different type of experiment. She varies the content of the theory to show that a theory with specific constructs produces more realistic crime patterns than a simulation without these constructs. If altering settings changes the simulated pattern from one that is recognizable in the real world to one that is not, then we have discovered something potentially important about how crime is produced. If we produce patterns that are far from reality we might hypothesize that the processes being simulated are unlikely to be operating in the real world.

Second, simulations can be used to test policies. Szakas, et al. (in this volume) propose the use of simulations to test various police patrol methods. They suggest that police simulations might be particularly useful for planning police reactions to rare and catastrophic events (e.g., natural disasters, terrorist attacks, and mass accidents). Similarly, Brantingham, et al. (in this volume) propose that simulations can be used to test the impact of programs prior to implementation. Dray, et al. (in this volume) look at the effects of forms of policing on heroin related harms and discover that one form of policing is probably more effective than other forms. Their simulation has the characteristics of an experiment, but an experiment that would be impossible to conduct in the real world. In reality it is impossible to run three types of policing strategies simultaneously throughout the same city. As is the case with theorizing, simulated policy experiments can examine situations that are impossible using empirical research methods.

Third, simulations can be used for planning and administrative purposes. Alimadad, et al. (in this volume) describe a criminal justice system simulation. The simulation allows policy makers to examine what would happen to downstream parts of the system if they make changes to earlier parts of the system. Szakas, et al. (in this volume) suggest that simulations can be used to create planning scenarios for emergency situations. Planning simulations are very similar to the use of simulations to test policies, but they are less specific about the changes being implemented. A planning simulation might ask what would happen to court backlogs if arrests were increased, but would not specify how arrests are increased. A policy testing simulation might ask whether changing a particular policing practice result in more arrests.

Fourth, simulations can be used to estimate the magnitude of hidden phenomena so that these estimates can be used in other forms of research. Chainey and Desyllas (in this volume) provide an example in their paper showing how pedestrian movement was estimated. The numbers of pedestrians on specific blocks at different times of day are important as denominators for other research, but these figures are not available from existing data sources and special purpose data collection would be prohibitively expensive. Simulating the pedestrian movement based on known information provides a useful alternative. Liu (2007) and Liu and Eck (2007) used a simulation of traffic flow to estimate the numbers of black and white drivers in small areas of Cincinnati over the course of a 24 hour period. These data were needed to address concerns about racial profiling. The simulation was necessary because the resident population was only part of the population who could be stopped by the police and the number of drivers of either race varied by time of day and area of the city. Three other chapters in this volume (Li, Meenar, & Wei) describe methods for simulating important variables that might drive crime, or create the substrates upon which crime patterns form.

All simulations ask the same basic question, "If this process is a reasonable reflection of reality, then what is the expected outcome?" In this sense, simulations are a form of theorizing. This idea is captured by Daniel Dennett (2003, p. 218), "... computer simulations are actually philosophical thought experiments, intuition pumps, not empirical experiments. They systematically explore the implications of sets of assumptions." Later, we will look at this point in greater detail.

Simulations are not the only way to accomplish these goals, and they are certainly not the dominant approach. Behind these four specific purposes are two general reasons for using simulations. First, it is well known that data on crime and justice are bad. Nonreporting of crimes, faulty memories, lapses in official record keeping, and intentional distortions introduced by the actions of offenders and other agents all contribute to this state of affairs. Sometimes there is no data at all. For example, we do not know how many offenders are operating at any given moment. Even everyday phenomena, like the number of pedestrians or vehicles, are often unknown. Conclusions from empirical research are severely limited by these errors and missing information.

Simulations allow us to temporarily side step these problems. Theories can be manipulated without data errors confounding our thinking. Bench testing programs with simulations allows us to look at mechanisms that are often hidden by lack of data. Planning can be conducted using what-if scenarios. But simulations depend on valid representations of agents, their backcloth, and their interactions. And the simulator may get this wrong. *Simulations trade the risks of being misled by errors in the data for the risks of misunderstanding of the processes.* Other forms of research, such as qualitative research, make the other type of trade; accepting the errors in empirical observation to avoid errors based on misunderstanding of the underlying processes. Much research attempts a compromise—accepting errors in the conceptual processes and in the empirical observations.

Even if there were no errors in crime and justice data, and all relevant data were available, we would still find simulations useful. Theories are summaries of the phenomena being examined. They highlight the particular features of the phenomena that are thought to be useful, and ignore the many details that are much less important. In this way, theories are like maps and political cartoons. A map only displays a particular set of geographic features and ignores many other features that could be displayed. A political cartoon highlights a few prominent features of a well-known politician and ignores many other details. Simulations of crime and justice are useful for cutting through the huge amount of available detail to focus on a few very salient features. In the language of information theory, simulations suppress noise and enhance signals. Of course, the simulator chooses the features of the process that are signal and those which are noise, and the simulator could be wrong.

Later we will contrast simulation methods and other research methods. For now we should simply point out that the limitations on simulation research are very similar to other research methods. A researcher is always betting that she is measuring theoretical constructs appropriately, collecting the relevant data, and specifying her statistical models correctly. The question we should ask of any method, including simulations, is how its limitations compare to alternatives that could be used to answer the same questions under the same circumstances. Method selection, like crime prevention, is highly situational.

WHAT ARE THE CHARACTERISTICS OF CRIME SIMULATIONS?

We have discussed four purposes for creating simulations. We turn now to their internal features. There are seven decisions we must make when building a simulation. We have listed them in the first column of Table 1. The second and third columns name the alternatives we can select. The order of this list is arbitrary. As we will show in a moment, a researcher must consider all of these characteristics.

Continuity. The researcher must decide whether to describe a continuous or discrete process. Alimadad, et al. (in this volume) compare discrete and continuous simulations of criminal justice systems. Most continuous processes require the use of differential equations. These require a mathematical translation of the theory. At

Table 1. Classifying simulations by characteristics

Characteristic	Alternatives	
Continuity*	Continuous	Discrete
Environment*	Artificial	Real
Foundation*	Data	Theory
Substrate*	Spatial	Aspatial
Movement*	Stationary	Mobile
Probabilistic*	Deterministic	Stochastic
Scale	Micro	Macro
* Adapted from Liu (2007).		

this time, for most interesting questions, crime theory is not sufficiently developed to support such mathematical models. Additionally, there are many processes that cannot be reduced to a set of differential equations. That is why most recent simulations of crime patterns use computer algorithms, rather than mathematical equations, to create discrete simulations.

Environment. The researcher has the choice between modeling a real environment or an artificial environment. Groff (in this volume) uses Seattle's street grid while Brantingham and Tita (in this volume) and Furtado, et al. (in this volume) use abstract artificial environments. A real environment seems to offer the advantage of greater fit to reality (see Hayslett-McCall et al., in this volume), but as Elffers and van Baal (in this volume) point out, the increased detail comes at the price of a decrease in comprehension. As we will discuss, the choice of real vs. artificial is bound up with the purposes of a simulation.

Foundation. The source of information for writing the program code is another decision. The simulator can base the code on empirical data derived from physical and social measurement. A simulation using information describing the actual population of an area, the actual street patterns, and building characteristics is an example of a simulation founded on data (see, i.e., Batty, Desyllas, & Duxbury, 2003). A theory-based simulation relies on processes described by theories. These theories may be informed by empirical evidence, but they are far more abstract than a simulation grounded in real world details (see Birks, Donkin, & Wellsmith, in this volume). The simulators can combine data and theory, as suggested by Hayslett-McCall, et al. (in this volume) and applied by Groff (in this volume).

Substrate. A substrate is a network that connects agents, allows them to communicate or move, and upon which patterns form.[1] A substrate can be spatial, in which case principles of geography are applicable, or it can be aspatial, in which case other theoretical perspectives apply. If agents move, then they move on a spatial substrate. If they do not move, but only communicate, then either a spatial or aspatial substrate is involved. A simulation built on an aspatial substrate will not take into account, for example, physical distances or compass directions among agents. A social network is an example of an aspatial substrate (see Furtado et al., in this volume). The justice system simulation of Alimadad, et al. (in this volume) is also aspatial. Here the criminal justice system is the substrate. In contrast, Wang, Liu, and Eck; Brantingham, et al.; and Groff (all in this volume) use spatial geographies as substrates. It is possible to build a simulation with both aspatial and spatial substrates (e.g., a social network linked to a street pattern showing where agents in the network live). In this case, the simulation could show both spatial and aspatial patterns.

Movement. A simulation can include several types of agents. Do these agents move? If none of the agents move, then the simulation uses stationary agents. If some or all types of agents move, then the simulation uses mobile agents. Mobile agents move on a spatial substrate. They are a necessary element of any simulation that attempts to describe how spatial crime patterns emerge from micro-level processes. Some agents may move randomly, while others may move with intelligence gained through an adaptive learning process such as swarm intelligence (see Furtado et al.; Wang, Liu, & Eck, in this volume).

Probabilistic. The simulation can be written so that the outcomes of any process are determined only by their inputs. Then, if the processes were started over and given the same inputs, the same outcomes would result. However, if instead of writing the simulation deterministically, one describes the process so that outcomes are created by inputs and a random element, then each time the process is run with the same input, different outcomes will result. The simulation is then stochastic. A deterministic simulation of offender decision would show the decision as, "If E is present in the environment near the offender then the offender will pick action A, always." A stochastic simulation would show the decision as, "If E is present near the offender then the offender will pick action A with probability p." The offender movement models examined by Brantingham and Tita (in this volume) are stochastic.

Scale. Finally, the researcher needs to choose between modeling crime at the person and place level (micro) or at some aggregate level, such as population or neighborhood. Micro level simulations will have individual agents acting on a substrate (spatial or aspatial) that structures how the agents interact. The environment, artificial or real, constrains or enhances various types of interactions. The outcome of these interactions will be a pattern of crimes that emerges at a level higher than the agents. That is, the pattern cannot be reduced to a summary measure of the individual agents. A macro level simulation begins with aggregate characteristics of people and places (e.g., average time spent away from home, mean number of crimes committed per year, or average distance between buildings). The results describe crime for a population or area, but without the variation and detail that micro level simulations can produce. Environmental criminology theory provides a better description of micro-level interactions than macro-level interactions, so recent developments in theory-driven simulations have been at the micro-level. The development of macro-theory simulations requires better macro-theories. However, when theory is weak but summary data is strong, macro-simulations underpinned by data are useful.

The choice of one characteristic is likely to influence the choice of other characteristics. Table 2 asks the question, "Are some decisions dependent

Table 2. Dependence among characteristics of simulations

Is Column dependent on Row? →	**1 continuity**	**2 environment**	**3 foundation**	**4 substrate**	**5 movement**	**6 probability**	**7 scale**
1 Continuity (continuous/ discrete)		If continuous then artificial	If continuous then theory	If continuous then aspatial	If continuous then stationary	no	If continuous then macro
2 Environment (artificial/real)	If real then discrete		If artificial then theory	If either then spatial	no	If real then stochastic	no
3 Foundation (data/theory)	If data then discrete	If data then real		no	no	If data then stochastic	no
4 Substrate (spatial/aspatial)	If spatial then discrete	If aspatial no environment	no		If aspatial then stationary	no	no
5 Movement (mobile/stationary)	If mobile then discrete	no	no	If mobile then spatial		no	If mobile then micro
6 Probabilistic (deterministic/ stochastic)	no	If deterministic then artificial	If deterministic then theory	no	no		no
7 Scale (micro/macro)	If micro then discrete	no	no	no	If macro then stationary	no	

on other decisions." If one picked, for example, a spatial substrate (row 4) would this influence the other decisions (columns 1 through 7)? Yes, it does influence the choice of environment as well as two other choices (continuity and movement). The choice of substrate does not influence three choices (foundation, probability, or scale). Ignoring the diagonal cells, we see that there are 22 dependencies out of possible 42 pairs (52%). Clearly, someone building a simulation cannot mix simulation characteristics at will. Planning a simulation is not a linear process of stepping through a series of independent decisions. Rather multiple criteria have to be considered iteratively.

Links between a simulation's purpose and its characteristics further constrain a researcher's choices (Table 3). Simulations for theory elaboration have maximum flexibility and simulations to estimate hidden phenomena have the least. Simulations for policy planning and program testing are in between, but much more constrained than theory simulations. Fewer constraints make simulations easier to construct. And fewer constraints allow greater diversity of simulations. For these reasons we can expect most simulations to be developed for exploring theoretical questions rather than for estimating hidden phenomena, planning, or program testing.

HOW DOES ARTIFICIAL CRIME ANALYSIS COMPARE TO OTHER RESEARCH METHODS?

Of the four reasons for artificial crime analysis, three involve examining causes of crime patterns or justice system outcomes. Estimation of hidden phenomena is the exception so we will drop it from the discussions that follow. How do simulation methods compare to alternative methods for assessing causal processes? We will contrast simulations to five other commonly used research methods used to study causal relationships. We divide the six methods into two categories: theorizing and testing (Table 4). Theorizing involves creating explanations, so the three methods in this category help formulate conjectures. Testing involves determining whether or not the theories are valid. These methods are used to refute conjectures (Popper, 1992).

Standard theorizing is our first method. Here the researcher proposing a set of relationships

Table 3. Classifying simulation by purpose and characteristics

CHARACTERISTICS	PURPOSES			
	Theory elaboration	**Estimation of hidden phenomena**	**Policy Planning**	**Program Testing**
Continuity	Continuous or Discrete	Discrete	Discrete	Discrete
Environment	None or Artificial	Real	Real	Artificial or Real
Foundation	Theory	Data	Theory or Data	Theory or Data
Substrate	Aspatial or Spatial	Spatial	Spatial	Spatial
Movement	Stationary or Mobile	Stationary or Mobile	Stationary or Mobile	Stationary or Mobile
Probabilistic	Deterministic or Stochastic	Stochastic	Stochastic	Stochastic
Scale	Micro or Macro	Micro or Macro	Micro or Macro	Micro or Macro

among a group of independent variables to explain some outcome, a dependent variable. The researcher must define the outcome to be explained, the nature of the variables involved, the functional relationships among all the variables, and the conditions under which the proposed theory is expected to work. The researcher attempts to show why the conjecture explains the outcome better than extant explanations. The principle reason for using data is to demonstrate the plausibility of the theory—why others should take it seriously enough to undertake further scientific enquiry, including testing; but there is no scientific requirement to present data to bolster a new theory. This means that there are no requirements for statistical analysis or research design. Of far greater importance is that the theory explains the outcome using clearly stated logical processes that are consistent with know facts about the phenomena.

Simulations are another form of theorizing. Like standard theorizing, simulations do not have to use data or statistical analysis, though they can. Simulations require considerable use of logical processes because these form the basis for writing the simulation program. Translating a verbal theory into a simulation formalizes the theory and can reveal logical inconsistencies and gaps (see, Birks, Donkin, & Wellsmith, in this volume). Simulations make considerable use of designs to compare the results of alternative parameter settings. In this sense, simulations import features from experiments into the theorizing process (see Townsley & Johnson, in this volume).

Qualitative observational studies are the third method theorizing. In these studies the researcher is immersed in the phenomena of interest and tries to gain a textured understanding of the processes involved. Our placement of this form of research in the category of theorizing rather than testing may be considered somewhat controversial. We defend this choice on the grounds that qualitative studies seldom employ designs that can eliminate rival explanations. Their strength is in revealing relationships and variables that might be overlooked by quantitative research, suggesting new ideas for how these variables might produce the outcome, and show why the new ideas are plausible. Qualitative observation studies do not require much statistical analysis or design. They do however require moderate to high levels of process description and are very data intensive.

Nonexperimental studies are the first of three methods for testing theories. The researcher collects quantitative data and subjects them to analysis to tease out statistical evidence that variations in the proposed independent variable are actually associated with variations in the dependent variable, after controlling for possible confounding variables and relationships. Generally these studies do not examine process information, but only examine the correlation between two variables, with varying numbers and forms of controls. That is, they do not show how X causes Y, but only that X and Y are associated after controlling for other possible causes. Nonexperimental research is data and analysis intensive, but makes limited use of design to explore causal relations.

Quasi-experiments are design intensive. Though researchers use statistical analysis of data to eliminate rival explanations, their principle method for testing whether there is a causal connection between two variables is to manipulate the values of the independent variable of interest and see what happens to the dependent variable. Though there are many types of quasi-experimental designs, in a standard design the values of the outcome before a treatment are compared to the values of the same outcome after treatment, and this is compared to changes in the outcome (from before to after treatment) for a control group.

Randomized experiments almost completely substitute design for statistical manipulation of data. Randomly assigning values of the independent variable to participants in the study assures that those getting the treatment are, on average, like those not getting the treatment. Therefore, any differences in the outcome can be due only to the treatment and cannot be due to rival explanations. Like the other two testing methods, experimental designs do not require information on processes. After a well constructed randomized experiment with a positive outcome we can be virtually certain X causes Y, though we might not know how X causes Y.

The top panel of Table 4 summarizes this discussion. In the bottom panel we look at the types of evidence that these methods can provide. The rows are the conditions necessary to demonstrate a causal connection between two variables.

It is necessary to show how X could cause Y, if one is to establish that X does cause Y. If the causal mechanism is not well understood the theory is incomplete. Even with strong evidence that X causes Y (say from randomized experiments) there is doubt as to whether this is a valid conclusion, unless there is a clear explanation of the process linking changes in X to changes in Y. An instructive example comes from medicine. Despite strong experimental evidence that a type of bacteria (*Helicobacter pylori*) caused a common form of stomach ulcer (including a randomized trial showing success at treating ulcer patients with antibiotics), many in the medical community did not find these results convincing. One of the difficulties was that gastroenterologists (physicians specializing in digestive disorders) were convinced that the highly acidic conditions in the stomach were inhospitable to bacteria. When scientists showed that *H. pylori* could live in the human stomach and proposed a mechanism that showed how these bacteria created ulcers (by increasing the acidity of the stomach), the theory gained acceptance (Thagard, 1999).

Theorizing methods score higher than testing methods on their ability to demonstrate

Table 4. Comparions of methods

	Theorizing			Testing		
	Standard Theorizing	**Simulation for Elaboration**	**Qualitative observation**	**Nonexperimental**	**Quasi-Experimental**	**Randomized Experiments**
INPUTS: Makes use of						
Processes[1]	moderate-high	high	moderate-high	low	low	low
Data[2]	low	low	high	high	high	high
Stat. Analysis[3]	none	low	low	high	moderate-high	moderate
Design[4]	none	high	low	low	high	high
OUTPUTS: Evidence of						
Mechanism[5]	moderate-high	high	moderate-high	low	low	low
Association[6]	none	high	low	high	high	high
Temporal Order[7]	none	high	low	low-moderate	high	high
Nonspuriousness[8]	none	low-moderate	low	low-moderate	moderate-high	high

1 Degree to which the method describes how processes produce intermediate and final results.
2 Degree to which the method relies on collection of empirical observations.
3 Degree to which the method relies upon statistical manipulation of data.
4 Degree to which designs are used to assign values to independent variables prior to data collection.
5 Degree to which the method provides a detailed description of the causal processes that link pairs of variables.
6 Degree to which the method can provide valid evidence of a statistical association among two or more variables.
7 Degree to which the method can determine the temporal sequence of changes in variables' values.
8 Degree to which the method can eliminate alternative hypotheses that could explain the study findings.

mechanism. This is because the testing methods commonly used in crime research focus on establishing a correlation between variables rather than on showing how two variables influence each other. A mechanism is a theoretical construct – a conjecture about how X could create Y. Though it requires testing, it originates in the scientific imagination.

Testing methods are much stronger with regard to establishing *association* but qualitative studies and standard theorizing are particularly weak in this regard. Simulations, on the other hand, can establish association among artificial variables. That is, a simulation can show that changes in Xa (the simulated version of X) are associated with changes in Ya (the simulated versions of Y). The question is whether the artificial variables have a strong connection to their real counterparts: is Xa reasonably equivalent to X and is Ya reasonably equivalent to Y?[2] At the conclusion of a simulation we can say with confidence that if these equivalences are great enough, X and Y are associated.

Temporal order refers to evidence that the proposed cause comes before the proposed outcome: that changes in X precede changes in Y. Quasi-experiments and randomized experiments fare well by this criterion. Nonexperimental studies vary; time series analysis can provide strong evidence, but cross-sectional studies provide little or no evidence of temporal order. Standard theorizing provides no evidence and observational studies provide weak evidence of temporal order, in general. Simulations do provide evidence here, providing we assume the simulation captures the salient features of the real processes. This is because the program code imbeds the temporal sequence in its "if-then" statements. Further, simulations allow experimental manipulation so we know precisely which variable changed first. Nevertheless, this evidence is contingent on the validity of the assumption that the simulation is a reasonable reflection of reality.

The final criteria for establishing a causal connection among variables is that all rival explanations for the cause of Y are eliminated. That is, the proposed causal relationship between X and Y is *nonspurious*. Randomized experiments excel on this criterion. Quasi-experiments and nonexperiments vary considerably, but generally quasi-experiments do better than nonexperiments, particularly cross-sectional nonexperimental designs. Standard theorizing can only propose a hypothetical causal connection, and offer logical arguments in its favor so they are weak on these criteria. Qualitative studies are also relatively weak, though case studies using process tracing might provide high confidence in particular circumstances (George & Bennett, 2005).

As we have argued for association and temporal order, if simulations are to provide evidence of nonspuriousness, it is necessary that the simulation imbed a valid reflection of the underlying processes. Though this is a necessary condition, it is not a sufficient condition for nonspuriousness. That it because there could be other processes, not in the simulation, that could give rise to the same outcomes. In fact, we can imagine two or more simulations, based on very different processes that appear to fit reality, that produce the same outcome. In such a circumstance we could not determine which simulation is the best representation of reality without additional information from empirical research. In this respect, simulations are like nonexperimental designs; they cannot completely eliminate all rivals.

We have seen that artificial crime analysis fares well with respect to other methods commonly used to study crime and justice. No single method is strong on all criteria. This suggests that we would want to tackle any important question with multiple methods. Simulations appear to have high potential when combined with other methods. In theorizing, simulations can augment either standard theorizing or qualitative observations to formalize processes and establish mechanism. The ability to experiment in simulations could help theorists understand the logical consequences of their verbal theory statements and improve the plausibility of theories. In testing, simulations can provide evidence of mechanism. Simulations can provide information about experimental outcomes that cannot be examined empirically; when it is physically impossible to manipulate settings or ethically reprehensible to do so. And empirical studies can provide evidence of the validity of the simulations. In short, the question is not which method is best, but how to use the methods in concert.

WHEN SHOULD SIMULATIONS BE USED?

Though simulations are an important part of a research portfolio, are there circumstances in which simulations are particular appropriate and other circumstances in which they are to be avoided? This is the question we explore next.

Simulations are particularly useful when one or more of the following four criteria are met:

1. **There is a theory that can describe a mechanism.** If the theory is very detailed and there a set of well understood mechanisms then a simulation can be very useful. These conditions are usually met when applying theories from environmental criminology. Crime pattern theory describes the movement of offenders (Brantingham & Brantingham, 1993). Routine activity theory describes the immediate situation surrounding potential crime events (Felson, 2002). Eck and Clarke (2003) show how this theory can be extended to explain crimes on other substrates. Rational choice and situational crime prevention describe how offenders make choices that convert these potential events into actual events (Clarke, 1995).
2. **Data describing the mechanisms are unavailable or the data contain high levels of error and are of uncertain quality.** This is often the case in the study of crime: much crime is unreported, and the recording practices for reported crime have high levels of error.
3. **The events in question are rare but very harmful, so it is critical to develop policy guidance, even in the absence of strong empirical support.** Terrorist attacks in North America or Great Britain might be a good example of this. If terrorist decision making can be articulated by experts and imbedded in computer code, then terrorist simulations might be useful for prevention planning.
4. **It is important to answer "what if" questions.** If these questions are numerous, have many interactions, or cannot be answered empirically, then simulations provide the only method for using experiments to answer them. Many of the questions about crime and justice we are interested in answering do not allow empirical experimentation: for example, What if we changed the street pattern? Or, what if offenders are rapid learners but potential victims are not (see Wang, 2005).

There are also four circumstances when simulations may not be useful. If one or more of the following criteria are met, then artificial crime analysis probably should be avoided.

1. **Little is known of the process or the theories are ambiguous.** A good example of this is community policing. The concept is too vague to give guidance to programmers to write the necessary software (Eck, 2007). We would not expect simulation to become an important part of traditional criminology because the theories about how individuals

move into and out of crime are too vague to guide the writing of the software.

2. **Mechanism is unimportant to answering the question.** Simulations will not be helpful if a statistical association is sufficient; one does not need to know how the association rises. Short term crime forecasting fits this condition; we may not be interested in what causes tomorrow's crime but we do want to know how much there will be.
3. **Strong evidence is required to answer the question and it is feasible to collect the evidence.** If empirical evidence is mandatory, then simulations can only provide a supporting role. This might involve using a simulation to help plan an experiment or using it to conduct sensitivity analysis of experimental findings. We might use a simulation to help develop a strong empirical study of a police program, but we will need the empirical results of an actual experiment to make sound policy choices.
4. **Computation is expensive, inflexible, and difficult.** If a very large scale simulation is needed to answer a simple question, then it's doubtful it is worth undertaking the endeavor. Though it is technically feasible to build a street level crime simulation of a metropolitan area—including building placement, size, and footprints, commuter schedules, and transport networks—this is a very expensive undertaking and would require significant training for the simulation users, and constant updating.

Artificial crime analysis can be very useful in specific circumstances, but is unlikely to be helpful in other circumstances. Many of the topics in criminology are not suitable to simulations because the theories are not specified in sufficient detail to operationalize them within a computer. Ecological theories of neighborhood crime are a good example. Despite their lengthy pedigree, the mechanisms by which neighborhood (or individual) characteristics change over time have not been articulated sufficiently to allow simulations. On the other hand, the thought processes required to build a simulation might serve as an engine for specifying the mechanisms that could explain variations in neighborhood crime levels. So it is possible that simulation methods could provoke better theories which then could be empirically tested. The challenge is that theories are most often created by individuals, but simulation construction may be the quintessential team enterprise.

WHO SHOULD CONSTRUCT SIMULATIONS?

Artificial crime analysis requires a set skills and knowledge that few individuals possess.[3] If the simulation is to examine crime events, then knowledge of the theories of environmental criminology are required.[4] If the simulation is to examine the operations of criminal justice institutions—police, courts, and corrections—then the researchers will need to know about these organizations. If the simulation is heavily reliant on data from criminal justice agencies, including crime data, then the researcher will need to know a great deal about how these data are produced, the under reporting of crime, how recording errors occur, and other limitations of these data. Experts in these areas can be found in criminology and criminal justice departments of universities. However, simulations require other types of expertise that is scarce in these departments.

Spatial simulations, particularly if using real environments, require researchers with expertise in geographic information systems. Though there are some important exceptions, most criminology and criminal justice researchers have only a shallow understanding of this area, at best. Most of the experts will be found in geography departments, among researchers who usually know little about crime and justice theories or data.

All simulations require computer programming skills, though very simple simulations of basic theoretical concepts might not require great expertise in this area. However, many interesting questions cannot be answered without more complex simulations that requiring a level of programming skill seldom found in criminology, criminal justice, or even geography departments. Consequently, computer scientists may be required and these experts are unlikely to be familiar with crime or geographical theories and data.

Crime overlaps all human endeavors. There is also a multiplicity of models for portraying crime patterns. Consequently, we should expect the involvement of experts in many other areas such as anthropology, biology, economics, mathematics, physics, psychology, political science, sociology and other fields as researchers explore the various ways crime forms patterns in different contexts.

Artificial crime analysis is an inherently multidisciplinary field. This is well illustrated by the many coauthored chapters in this volume involving researchers from a variety of disciplines. We expect that progress in this area will depend on the ability to create teams of researchers with backgrounds in crime, geography, computer science and other fields.

WHAT IS THE FUTURE OF ARTIFICIAL CRIME ANALYSIS?

In a very short time, there has developed a body of simulations of spatial crime patterns. The chapters of this volume show the variety of approaches and their connections to the far longer and richer simulation tradition within geography. This growth has been spurred by three interrelated developments. First, researchers involved in environmental criminology—based on a synergy of routine activity theory (Felson, 2002), crime pattern theory (Brantingham & Brantingham, 1993), rational choice perspectives (Clarke & Cornish, 2000), situational crime prevention (Clarke, 1995), and problem-oriented policing (Goldstein, 1990)—developed an international network semi-independent of traditional criminology. Their work focused on how crimes are committed and the patterns they form (rather than on how offenders develop and are treated by government programs). These theories consolidated into the field of Crime Science.

Second, environmental criminologists' interests in spatial patterns made them interested in collaborating with geographers, and entice more geographers into crime research. Geographers brought with them their expertise in geographic information systems and a connection to a modeling tradition richer than the "multivariate statistical" tradition of criminologists.

Third, the outsider perspective of crime scientists freed them to pursue techniques and methods outside the mainstream criminological traditions.

Artificial crime analysis is likely to continue to grow. Even at these very early stages it already has shown promise in helping to pursue a wide variety of crime questions, spatial and nonspatial, theoretical and applied. It is clear that simulations of crime fill a useful niche that was not being filled by standard methods in criminology or crime sciences. Simulations have become important parts of the research method portfolio in the natural sciences—physics, astronomy, chemistry, geology, biology, and environmental studies—and are increasingly used to answer questions in other sciences, such as geography, economics, political science, sociology, psychology, and anthropology. These developments provide a context that is highly supportive of adapting simulation methods to the study of crime and justice.

Some Problems

The long-term success of simulations will require more than initial successes and the fact that other disciplines make profitable use of simulations.

Though there are many factors that need to be addressed to assure the long-term success of artificial crime analysis, six stand out: teams, theory, specificity, replication, competition, and validation. Let's look briefly at each of these problems.

Teams. As we have discussed, most simulations require teams. Despite the fact that criminology and criminal justice is a hybrid of various disciplines, it has struggled over the last two decades to create an independent discipline. Simulation modeling goes against this trend. Multidisciplinary teams are easier to establish when there is a common practical problem that needs to be addressed, than when one is trying to study a class of phenomena, such as the development of crime patterns. At this stage academics involved in crime and justice research are unprepared to create simulations and their graduate schools neither attract students with these capabilities nor prepare them for use of these methods. While other disciplines can build simulations of crime, experts in these areas are unfamiliar with the theories and research on crime and criminal justice institutions. In the absence of multidisciplinary teams simulations are likely to be either computationally primitive or substantively naïve.

Theory. Theories used by environmental criminology and crime sciences are particularly amenable to simulation. Consequently, they are likely to become the platform for simulating processes where crime patterns are either an input or an output. A simulation of police directed patrol activities, for example, could use a crime pattern simulation as an input, and could output police deployment back to the crime simulation (Eck, 2007). However, theories of crime patterns will have to be more crime specific if they are to guide useful simulations. For example, a simulation of store robberies has only one type of moving agent, the robbers, but a simulation of street robbery must account for movement of both robbers and potential victims. Some crimes might not require spatial environments—many white-collar crimes, for example see Kim and Xiao (in this volume). To date, environmental criminological theories have focused on offender behavior. If simulations are to be helpful, these theories need to account for decision making by nonoffenders: potential victims, people who control places, and police, for example. In short, simulations cannot develop unless theory also develops. Fortunately, the process of building simulations can lead to better theories by forcing theorists to write algorithms that spell out mechanisms.

Specificity. Though we use the term "crime" as if it referred to a singular class of processes, the fact is that it encompasses a very diverse array of processes. Should artificial crime analysis be crime specific? The importance of crime specificity is central to two important and well-tested crime reduction theories: problem-oriented policing (Goldstein, 1990) and situational crime prevention (Clarke, 1995). Crime simulations will have to be as diverse as the processes they describe. Nevertheless, there are important global phenomena simulations can investigate (for three examples, see Brantingham & Tita, Elffers; van Baal; Furtado, et al., in this volume). But some processes contributing to crime patterns are not global. So it is also necessary for simulations to be crime specific. In this volume we has simulations of burglary (Hayslett-McCall, et al.), street robbery (Chainey & Desyllas; Groff; Wang, Liu, & Eck), drug dealing and use (Dray et al.), fraud in public delivery programs (Kim & Xiao). In our work, we found that even seemingly related crimes like store robbery and street robbery required different simulations (Liu et al., 2005; Wang, Liu, & Eck, in this volume). We would expect that this is true of many other apparently similar crimes. However, once we have a large body of crime specific simulations, comparisons of these simulations may reveal commonalities that might not now be apparent. Building crime general simulations out of these common features could reveal deeper insights into crime. Progress in artificial crime analysis is likely to be enhanced by this give and take between crime general and crime specific simulations.

Replication. Simulation efforts, like all studies, need to be replicated. There are two levels of replication. First, given a simulation program, can the results of a study based on this simulation be repeated on the same simulation? That is, if others used the same parameter setting would the same results arise? If the simulation is deterministic, the failure to replicate the findings suggests that there are problems in the programming. If the simulation is stochastic, the failure to replicate the findings may be due to random influences. To demonstrate a replication failure one must eliminate the hypothesis that random influences account for the differences. Averages of many simulation runs need to be compared.

The second level involves building multiple simulations, using the same theories, of the same phenomenon. If the theory is sound, then we would expect alternative operationalizations of the same theory to yield similar results. Failure of convergence suggests the phenomenon is highly sensitive to subtle differences in the interpretation of the theory. This could lead to refinements in the theory.

Competition. While replication seeks convergence, competition seeks differences. Given a particular phenomenon, can it be explained by two different theories? If so, which does better? Competitions among two or more simulations, each based on a different theory can be used to test theories. This suggests a weakness in environmental criminology and crime science: the theories are cooperative rather than competitive. However, there are competing explanations within this field. Here are three examples of questions that environmental criminology cannot answer because the theories can be used to support both answers. Is repeat victimization due to the behavior of victims (same victim, different offenders) or the behavior of offenders (same victim, same offenders)? Do crowds protect against victimization by adding guardianship, or do the conditions necessary for crowds provide access to offenders? Does firearm ownership increase guardianship or does it increase the capability of offenders? Simulations might help sort out the answers to questions like these by pointing to conditions that favor one answer and alternative conditions that favor the other answer.

Validity. How does one know if the simulation is a reasonably accurate reflection of reality? By definition it cannot be an exact duplicate, but must be a "cartoon" version, just as a map must capture important geographical features but ignores other features and distorts the features it does show. Theories do the same thing—summarize complex processes in a few statements that ignore many details. With cartoons, maps, and theories we judge accuracy by how well it serves our purposes. Does the cartoon allow us to immediately recognize the elected official being parodied? Does the map allow me to drive from Beaconsfield to Basingstoke? Does the theory imply an effective intervention? These all involve a comparison between the abstraction and some real world phenomena. And in each case, we presume that we can perceive the real world phenomena without significant distortion; the cartoon resembles the elected official's picture on television, that following the map directions does not need supplemental instructions from strangers, and that program results can be measured accurately.

But we cannot assume we perceive crime without distortion. Observed crime patterns are filtered by the ways with which crimes are reported and the methods the police use to classify and record them. A perfectly accurate simulation could provide a "god's eye view" of the true crime pattern, but not show the "human eye view" of the pattern (as reflected in reported crime data). In such a circumstance we are likely to mistakenly reject the simulation, despite its (unknown) accuracy. Validation will require modeling the methods by which we produce crime data, so that the simulation provides two outputs: the "god's eye view" and the "human eye view". We could validate such simulations by comparing the simulated human eye view to the reported crime data, and then take the "God's eye view" as a reasonable approximation of the real underlying crime pattern (Eck, 2007).

These are all difficult problems that can be addressed, but probably not completely solved. A measure of the success in artificial crime analysis will be the development of debates around attempts to make progress in these areas.

Two Risks

We will close with a discussion of two risks that will result if artificial crime analysis proves to be successful. Calling them risks probably underestimates the probability of their occurrences, as experience in the study of crime and other fields suggest that these might be inevitable downside consequences.

The first consequence of success is that a group of researchers may arise who only study crime simulations and have no contact with the phenomena their simulations are designed to investigate. They will debate amongst themselves the utility of various modeling techniques and algorithms. Researchers who have practical problems that simulations might help resolve are likely to left out of these technical discussions. The development of a corps of simulation methods experts can improve the quality of simulations and increase the number of questions that simulations can address. However, if this group becomes divorced from the practical questions that motivate the development of crime simulations, then much their simulation work will have little utility.

The second negative consequence of success maybe that the enthusiasm for artificial crime analysis will lead to some making outrageously confident predictions and policy recommendations based on technically sound simulations that have not been thoroughly tested. Simulations have all the trappings of "science" so the results may appear more credible than is warranted. Some criminologists already enjoy speculating in public on topics that are barely understood. We have great difficulty understanding, for example, what led to the drop in homicides in the 1990's, but that has not prevented some social scientists from dogmatically promoting their pet explanations. Further, criminology has a history of embracing useful methods and exaggerating the utility of these methods. Every new method from the use of linear regression, to hierarchical linear models, to randomized experiments, to geographic information systems, to meta-analysis, and to systematic reviews have been oversold by their proponents. This is an inevitable minor annoyance. But simulations carry bigger risk if oversold. As policy makers learn of simulations, they will demand answers that simulationists cannot reliably answer. Some simulationists will aggressively provide answers to maintain public interest in and funding for their works. The overselling of the benefits of simulations will undermine confidence in the approach. Much can be learned by reviewing the public use of simulations in other fields—such as the environmental sciences (for example, see Pilkey & Pilkey-Jarvis, 2007)—that have a long history of using simulations to address important policy concerns.

CONCLUSION

In this final chapter, we have reviewed the status of artificial crime analysis. We have shown that there are several purposes for creating simulations and the characteristics of simulations are bound up with these purposes. We have seen that simulation methods share some of the strengths of other methods commonly used to study crime, but also have some distinguishing features; primarily the combination of theoretical experimentation. We have seen that there are circumstances where simulations appear to be quite useful, but there are other circumstances in which simulations are probably not appropriate. We have noted that the creation of complex simulations will require multi-disciplinary teams. And we described a number of problems that simulationists will have to confront as the use of artificial crime analysis increases. Even though crime pattern simulations have a very short history, they have produced a diverse array of approaches to the study of crime, and these initial efforts have made substantial contributions to our understanding of crime. The next steps will be to learn from these initial experiences and integrate artificial crime analysis into the portfolio of crime research methods that we teach and use everyday.

REFERENCES

Batty, M., Jake, D., & Elspeth, D. (2003). Safety in numbers? Modelling crowds and designing control for the Notting Hill Carnival. *Urban Studies, 40*(8), 1573-1590.

Brantingham, P. L., & Brantingham, P. J. (1993). Environment, routine, and situation: Toward a pattern theory of crime. In R. V. Clarke & M. Felson (Eds.), *Routine activity and rational choice* (pp. 259-294). New Brunswick, NJ: Transaction.

Clarke, R. V. (1995). Situational crime prevention. In M. Tonry & D. Farrington (Eds.), *Building a safer society: Strategic approaches to crime prevention* (pp. 91-150). Chicago: University of Chicago Press.

Clarke, R. V., & Cornish, D. B. (2000). Rational choice. In R. Paternoster & R. Bachman (Eds.). *Explaining crime and criminals: Essays in contemporary Criminological Theory.* Los Angeles, CA: Roxbury.

Dennett, D. (2003). *Freedom evolves.* New York: Viking.

Eck, J. (2007). Simulating police outcomes: A framework for understanding policing strategies. In *Proceedings of the meeting on Crime Hot Spots: Behavioral, Computational and Mathematical Models.* Los Angeles, CA: Institute for Pure and Applied Mathematics, University of California, Los Angeles.

Eck, J., & Clarke, R. V. (2003). Classifying common police problems: A routine activity approach. In M. J. Smith & D. B. Cornish (Eds.), *Theory for practice in situational crime prevention: Vol. 16. Crime prevention studies* (pp. 7-40). Monsey, NY: Criminal Justice Press.

Felson, M. (2002). *Crime and everyday life* (3rd ed.). Thousand Oaks, CA: Sage.

George, A. L., & Bennett, A. (2005). *Case studies and theory development in the social sciences.* Cambridge: MIT Press.

Goldstein, H. (1990). *Problem-oriented policing.* New York: McGraw-Hill.

Liang, J. (2001). *Simulating crimes and crime patterns using cellular automata and GIS.* Unpublished doctoral Dissertation, Department of Geography, University of Cincinnati.

Liang, J., Liu, L., & Eck, J. (2001, June 22). Simulating crimes and crime patterns using cellular automata and GIS. In *Proceedings of the 2001 UCGIS Summer Assembly.* Buffalo, New York. Retrieved September 3, 2007, from http://www.ucgis.org/f2oppor.html

Liu, L. (2007, January 29 - February 2). The role of street network in crime analysis and simulation. In *Proceedings of the meeting on Crime Hot Spots: Behavioral, Computational and Mathematical Models.* Los Angeles, CA: Institute for Pure and

Applied Mathematics, University of California, Los Angeles.

Liu, L., & Eck, J. E. (2007). Analysis of police vehicle stops in Cincinnati: A geographic perspective. *Geography Research Forum, 27,* 29-51,

Liu, L., Wang, X. , Eck, J., & Liang, J. (2005). Simulating crime events and crime patterns in a RA/CA model. In F. Wang (Ed.), *Geographic information systems and crime analysis* (pp. 198-213). Hershey, PA: Idea Group Publishing.

Pilkey, O. H., & Pilkey-Jarvis, L. (2007). *Useless arithmetic: Why environmental scientists can't predict the future.* New York: Columbia University Press.

Popper, K. R. (1992). *Conjectures and refutations: The growth of scientific knowledge.* New York: Routledge.

Thagard, P. (1999). *How scientists study diseases.* Princeton, NJ: Princeton University Press.

van Baal, P. (2004). *Computer simulations of criminal deterrence.* Hoofddorp, Netherlands: Boom Juridische Uitgevers.

Wang, X. (2005). *Spatial adaptive crime event simulation with the RA/CA/ABM computational laboratory.* Unpublished doctoral dissertation. Department of Geography, University of Cincinnati.

ADDITIONAL READINGS

Batty, M. (2005). *Cities and complexity: Understanding cities with cellular automata, agent-based models, and fractals.* Cambridge: MIT Press.

Beavon, D. J. K., Brantingham, P. L., & Brantingham P. J. (1994). The influence of street networks on the patterning of property offenses. In R. V. Clarke (Ed.), *Crime prevention studies* (Vol. 2, pp. 115-148). Monsey, NY: Criminal Justice Press.

Benenson, I., & Torrens, P. (2004). *Geosimulation: Automata-based modeling of urban phenomena.* New York: Wiley.

Benoit, K. (2001). Simulation methodologies for political scientists. *Political Methodologist, 12*(1), 10-15.

Bernasco, W. (2007). The usefulness of measuring spatial opportunity structures for tracking down offenders: A theoretical analysis of geographic offender profiling using simulation studies. *Psychology, Crime & Law, 13*(2), 155-171.

Berry, B. J. L., Kiel, L. D., & Elliott, E. (2002). Adaptive agents, intelligence, and emergent human organization: Capturing complexity through Agent-based modeling. In *Proceedings of the National Academy of Sciences,* (Supplement 3, pp. 7187-7188).

Brantingham, P.L., & Brantingham, P. J. (2004). Computer simulation as a tool for environmental criminologists. *Security Journal, 17*(1), 21-30.

Cioffi-Revilla, C. (2002). Invariance and universality in social agent-based simulations. In *Proceedings of the National Academy of Sciences,* (Supplement 3., pp. 7314-7316).

Epstein, J. M. (2007). *Generative social science: Studies in agent-based computational modeling.* Princeton, NJ: Princeton University Press.

Epstein, J. M., & Axtell, R. (1996). *Growing artificial societies: Social science from the bottom up.* Cambridge: MIT Press.

Gimblett, H. R. (2002). *Integrating geographic information systems and agent-based modeling techinques for simulating social and ecological processes.* New York: Oxford University Press.

Gilbert, N., & Troitzsch, K. G. (2005). *Simulation for the social scientist.* Open University Press.

Hillier, B., & Hanson, J. (2005). *The social logic of space.* Cambridge: Cambridge University Press.

Holland, J. H. (1998). *Emergence: From chaos to order.* Reading, MA: Perseus Books.

Langton, C. G. (Ed.). (2000). *Artificial life: An overview.* Cambridge: MIT Press.

Miller, J. H., & Page, S. E. (2007). *Complex adaptive systems: An introduction to computational models of social life.* Princeton, NJ: Princeton University Press.

Prietula, M. J., Carley, K. M., & Gasser, L. (Eds.). (1998). *Simulating organizations: Computational models of institutions and groups.* Menlo Park, CA: AAAI Press/MIT Press.

Sawyer, R. K. (2005). *Social emergence: Societies as complex systems.* Cambridge University Press.

Shadish, W. R., Cook, T. D., & Campbell, D. T. (2002). *Experimentation and quasi-experimental designs for general causal inference.* New York: Houghton Mifflin.

ENDNOTES

1 Though the term "backcloth" is often used to describe the background, we choose the term "substrate" to reinforce the idea that more than spatial geography is included in the meaning of the term. According to the Webster's College Dictionary (Random House, 1997) a substrate is, "(1) The surface or medium on which an organism lives or grows. (2) The substance acted upon by an enzyme. (3) The foundation on which an integrated electronic circuit is formed or fabricated." Another useful term that would accurately describe the background is "media". However, this term is likely to be confused with the news media so discussions of how information is communicated among agents could become difficult to interpret.

2 Note that this is the flipside of the coin of construct validity: do our measurements capture the theoretical meaning of X? In short, we take the theory as the standard and ask whether our observational processes produce results that fit the theoretical construct. In simulations we do the opposite; we use the observations as the standard to determine the validity of the simulation.

3 For a notable counter example, see Groff, in this volume.

4 Criminological theories that describe how people become offenders, but not how they offend, are not helpful in understanding patterns of crime events.

Compilation of References

Abler, R., Adams, J. S., & Gould, P. (1971). *Spatial organization: The geographers' view of the world.* Englewood Cliffs, New Jersey: Prentice-Hall.

Adams, T. M. (2001). *Historical homicide hot spots: The case of three cities.* Ann Arbor, MI: UMI.

Agar, M. (2005). Agents in living color: Towards emic agent-based models. *Journal of Artificial Societies and Social Simulation, 8*(1).

Agar, M., & Reisinger, H. (2002). A heroin epidemic at the intersection of histories: The 1960's epidemic among African Americans in Baltimore. *Medical Anthropology, 21*(2), 115-56.

Agar, M., & Wilson, D. (2002). DrugMart: Heroin epidemics as complex adaptive systems. *Complexity, 7*(5), 44-52.

Aguirre, B. E., Quarantelli, E. L., & Mendoza, J. L. (1998). The collective behavior of fads: The characteristics, effects, and career of streaking. *American Sociological Review, 53*, 569-584.

Aitken, S. C., Cutter, S. L., Foote, K. E., & Sell, J. L. (1989). Environmental perception and behavioral geography. In Wilmott & Gaile (Eds.), *Geography in america* (pp. 218-238).

Akers, R., Krohn, M., Lanza-Kaduce, L., & Radosevich, M. (1979). Social learning and deviant behavior: A specific test of a general theory. *American Sociological Review, 44*,(4), 636-655.

Albrecht, J. (2005). A new age for geosimulation. *Transactions in GIS, 9*(4), 451-454.

Al-Kodmany, K. (2002). Visualization tools and methods in community planning: From freehand sketches to virtual reality. *Journal of Planning Literature, 17*(2), 189-211.

Allen, E. (2001). INDEX: Software for community indicators. In R. Brail & R. Klosterman (Eds.), *Planning support systems: Integrating geographic information systems, models, and visualization tools* (pp. 229-261). Redlands, CA: ESRI Press.

Alonso, J., Fernandez, A., & Fort, H. (2006). Prisoner's dilemma cellular automata revisited: Evolution of cooperation under environmental pressure. *Journal of Statistical Mechanics: Theory and Experiment, P06013*, 1-15.

Altman, S. A. (1998). *Foraging for survival: Yearling baboons in africa.* Chicago: University of Chicago Press.

American Planning Association. (2002). *Policy guide on smart growth.* Retrieved August 26, 2007, from http://www.planning.org/policyguides/pdf/SmartGrowth.pdf

An, L., Linderman, M., Qi, J., Shortridge, A., & Liu, J. (2005). Exploring complexity in a human-environment system: An agent-based spatial model for multidisciplinary and multiscale integration. *Annals of the Association of American Geographers, 95*(1), 54-79.

Anselin, L. (1995). Local indicators of spatial association -LISA. *Geographical Analysis, 27*(2), 93-115.

Anselin, L., & Florax, R. (1995). Small sample properties of tests for spatial dependence in regression models: Some further results. *New directions in spatial econometrics* (pp. 21-74). Berlin: Springer-Verlag.

Arapaki, E., Argyrakis, P., & Bunde, A. (2004). Diffusion-driven spreading phenomena: The structure of the hull of the visited territory. *Physical Review E, 69*(3).

Arentze, T. A., & Timmermans, H. J. P. (2003). Modeling learning and adaptation processes in activity travel choice: A framework and numerical experiments. *Transportation, 30*, 37-62.

Atlas, R., & LeBlanc, W. (1994). The impact on crime of street closures and barricades: A Florida case study. *Security Journal, 5*, 140-145.

Attoui, A. (2000). *Real-time and multi-agent systems.* Berlin: Springer-Verlag.

Aurenhammer, F. (1991).Voronoi diagrams - A survey of a fundamental geometric data structure. *ACM Computing Surveys, 23*, 345-405.

Australian Bureau of Statistics (2004). *Criminal courts 2002-03* (Cat No. 5413.0). Canberra: Australian Bureau of Statistics.

Australian Institute of Health and Welfare (2005). Alcohol and other drug treatment services in Australia 2003–04. *Findings from the National Minimum Data Set.*

Axelrod, R. (1997). *Advancing the art of simulation in the social sciences.* In R. Conte, R. Hegselmann, & P. Terna (Eds.), *Simulating social phenomena.* Lecture Notes in Economics and Mathematical Systems. Berlin: Springer-Verlag.

Axtell, R., Axelrod, R., Epstein, J. M., & Cohen, M. D. (1996). Aligning simulation models: A case study and results. *Computational and Mathematical Organization Theory, 1*(2), 123-141.

Bailey, J., & Hann, R. (1972). *Systems analysis and the corrections system in Ontario.* Toronto: Centre of Criminology, University of Toronto.

Bailey, T. C., & Gatrell, A. C. (1995). *Interactive spatial data analysis.* Essex: Longman Group Limited.

Baker, J. S. (2004). The sociological origins of "white-collar crime." *Legal Memorandum, 14.*

Balan, G. C., Cioffi-Revilla, C., Luke, S., Panait, L., & Paus, S. (2003). MASON: A java multi-agent simulation library. In *Proceedings of the Agent 2003 Conference.* Retrieved September 5, 2007, from http://cs.gmu.edu/~eclab/projects/mason/

Balci, O. (1997). *Verification, validation and accreditation of simulation models.* In S. Andradottir, K. J. Healy, D. H. Withers, & B. L. Nelson (Eds). In *Proceedings of the 1997 Winter Simulation Conference* Atlanta, Georgia.

Baller, R. D., Anselin, L., Messner, S. F., Deane, G., & Hawkins, D. F. (2001). Structural covariates of U.S. county homicide rates: Incorporating spatial effects. *Criminology, 39*(3), 561-590.

Balshaw, M. (2003). Digital cities: Multimedia research and American urban studies. *Journal of Urban History, 29*(4), 421-436.

Bankes, S. C. (2002). Tools and techniques for developing policies for complex and uncertain systems. In *Proceedings of the National Academy of Sciences, 99*(3), 7263-7266.

Banks, J., Carson, J., II, Nelson, B., & Nicol, D. (2001). *Discrete event system simulation* (3rd ed.). Saddle River: Prentice Hall.

Baquette, B. W. (2003). *Process control, modeling, design, and simulation.* Upper Saddle River, New Jersey: Prentice Hall.

Barabási, A. (2002). *Linked: The new science of networks.* Cambridge: Perseus Pulishing.

Barcelól, J., & Michalopoulos, P. G. (2000). *Implementation of microscopic modeling to traffic simulation for ITS applications.* Presented at the Intelligent Transportation Systems Conference in Torino, Italy.

Barker, T., & Roebuck, J. (1973). *An empirical topology of police corruption: A study in organizational deviance.* Springfield, IL: Charles C. Thomas Publisher.

Barr, R., & Pease, K. (1990). Crime placement, displacement and deflection. In M. Tonry & N. Morris (Eds.), *Crime and justice: A review of research* (Vol. 12). Chicago: University of Chicago Press.

Barra, T. D. (2001). Integrated landuse and transport modeling: The Tranus experience. In R. Brail & R. Klosterman (Eds.), *Planning support systems: Integrating geographic information systems, models, and visualization tools* (pp. 129-156). Redlands, CA: ESRI Press.

Barredo, J. I., Kasanko, M., McCormick, N., & Lavalle, C. (2003). Modelling dynamic spatial processes: Simulation of urban future scenarios through cellular automata. *Landscape and Urban Planning, 64*, 145-160.

Bartumeus, F., Peters, F., Pueyo, S., Marrase, C., & Catalan, J. (2003). Helical levy walks: Adjusting searching statistics to resource availability in microzooplankton. *Proceedings Of The National Academy Of Sciences Of The United States Of America, 100*(22), 12771-12775.

Batty, M. (1997). Cellular automata and urban form: A primer. *Journal of the American Planning Association, 63*(2), 266-274.

Batty, M. (2005). Agents, cells, and cities: New representational models for simulating multiscale urban dynamics. *Environment and Planning A, 37*, 1373-1394.

Batty, M. (2005a). Approaches to modeling in GIS: Spatial representation and temporal dynamics. In D. J. Maguire, M. Batty, & M. Goodchild (Eds.), *GIS, Spatial analysis, and modeling* (pp. 41-65). Redlands, CA: ESRI Press.

Batty, M. (2005b). Introduction to Chapter 3: Socioeconomic applications. In D. J. Maguire, M. Batty, & M. Goodchild (Eds.), *GIS, Spatial analysis, and modeling* (pp. 147-149). Redlands, CA: ESRI Press.

Batty, M. et al. (2001). Visualizing the city: Communicating urban design to planners and decision makers. In R. Brail, & R. Klosterman (Eds.), *Planning support systems: Integrating geographic information systems, models, and visualization tools* (pp. 405-443). Redlands, CA: ESRI Press.

Batty, M., & Torrens, P. M. (2005). Modelling and prediction in a complex world. *Futures, 37*, 745-766.

Batty, M., & Xie, Y. (1994). From cells to cities. *Environment and Planning B: Planning and Design, 21*, 531-548.

Batty, M., & Xie, Y. (1997). Possible urban automata. *Environment and Planning B: Planning and Design, 24*, 175-192.

Batty, M., & Xie, Y. (2005). Urban growth using cellular automata models. In D. J. Maguire, M. Batty, & M. Goodchild (Eds.), *GIS, Spatial analysis, and modeling* (pp. 151-172). Redlands, CA: ESRI Press.

Batty, M., Desyllas, J., & Duxbury, E. (2003). Safety in numbers? Modelling crowds and designing control for the Notting Hill carnival. *Urban Studies, 40*, 1573-1590.

Batty, M., Jake, D., & Elspeth, D. (2003). Safety in numbers? Modelling crowds and designing control for the Notting Hill Carnival. *Urban Studies, 40*(8), 1573-1590.

Batty, M., Longley, P., & Fotheringham, S. (1989). Urban growth and form: Scaling, fractal geometry, and diffusion-limited aggregation. *Environment and Planning A: Environment and Planning, 21*, 1447-1472.

Batty, M., Xie, Y., & Sun, Y. (1999). Modeling urban dynamics through GIS-based cellular automata. *Computers, Environment and Urban Systems, 23*, 205-233.

Batty, M., Xie, Y., & Sun, Z. L. (1999). Modeling urban dynamics through GIS-based cellular automata. *Computers, Environment and Urban Systems, 23*, 205-233.

Baumgartner, K. C., Ferrari, S., & Salfati, C. G. (2005). Bayesian network modeling of offender behavior for criminal profiling. In *Proceedings of 44th IEEE Conference on decision and control and 2005 European Control Conference* (pp. 2702- 2709).

Beavon, D. J. K., Brantingham, P. J., & Brantingham, P. L. (1994). The influence of street networks on the pattterning of property offenses. In R. V. Clarke (Ed.), *Crime prevention studies* (Vol. 2, pp. 115-148). Monsey, NY: Criminal Justice Press.

Bederson, B. B. (2000). Fisheye menus. In *Proceedings of the 13th Annual ACM Symposium on User interface Software and Technology*, San Diego, California (pp. 217-225) ACM Press. Retrieved August 24, 2007, from http://doi.acm.org/10.1145/354401.354782

Belkin, J., Blumstein, A., & Glass, W. (1971). *JUSSIM, an interactive computer program for analysis of criminal justice systems* (Working Paper). Carnegie-Mellon University: Urban Systems Institute, School of Urban and Public Affairs.

Ben-Akiva, M. E., Ramming, M. S., & Bkhor, S. (2004). Route choice model. *Human behaviour and traffic networks.* Berlin: Springer-Verlag.

Ben-Akiva, M., & Bierlaire, M. (1999). Discrete choice methods and their applications to short term travel decision. In R. W. Hall (Ed.), *Handbook of transportation science.*

Benenson, I. & Torrens, P.M. (2005). *Geosimulation: Automata-based modeling of urban phenomena.* London: John Wiley & Sons.

Benham, J., Patel, B. (1976). A method for estimating pedestrian volume in a central business district. *Transportation Research Record, 629*, 22-26.

Benson, M. L., Walker, E. (1988). Sentencing the white-collar offender. *American Sociological Review, 53*(2), 294-302.

Berke, P. R., Godschalk, D. R., Kaiser, E. J., & Rodriguez, D. A. (2006). *Urban landuse planning.* Chicago: University of Illinois Press.

Berman, B., & Evans, J. R. (1995). *Retail management: A strategic approach* (6th ed.). New York: Macmillan Publishing Company.

Bernasco, W., & Luykx, F. (2003). Effects of attractiveness, opportunity and accessibility to burglars on residential burglary rates of urban neighborhoods. *Criminology, 41*(3), 981-1001.

Bernasco, W., & Nieuwbeerta, P. (2005). How do residential burglars select target areas? A new approach to the analysis of criminal location choice. *British Journal Of Criminology, 45*(3), 296-315.

Berry, B. J. L. (1972). Hierarchical diffusion: The basis of developmental filtering and spread in a system of growth centers. In N. Hansen (Ed.), *Growth centers in regional economic development.* New York: Free Press.

Bettini, C., Wang, X. S., & Jajodia, S. (1998). Temporal semantic assumptions and their use in databases. *IEEE transactions on knowledge and data engineering, 10*(2), 277-296.

Biderman, A. D., & Reiss, A. J., Jr. (1967). On exploring the "Dark Figure" of crime. *Annals of the American Academy of Political and Social Science, 374*, 1-15.

Blass, A., & Gurevich, Y. (2003). Abstract state machines capture parallel algorithms. *ACM transactions on computation logic, 4*(4), 578-651.

Block, C. R., Dabdoub, M., & Fregly, S. (1995). *Crime analysis through computer mapping.* Washington, DC: Police Executive Research Forum.

Block, C. R., Dabdoub, M., & Fregly, S. (Eds.) (1995). *Crime analysis through computer mapping* (pp. 15-32). Washington, D.C.: Police Executive Research Forum..

Block, R. L., & Block, C. R. (1995). Space, place, and crime: Hot spot areas and hot places of liquor-related crime. In J. Eck & D. Weisburd (Eds.), *Crime and place.* Monsey, NY: Willow Tree.

Blue, V. J., & Adler, J. L. (2001). Cellular automata microsimulation for modeling bi-directional pedestrian walkways. *Transportation Research Part B, 35*, 293-312.

Blumstein, A. (1967). Systems analysis and the criminal justice system. *Annals of the American Academy of Political and Social Science, 374*(November), 91-100.

Blumstein, A. (2002). Crime modeling. *Operations Research, 50*(1), 16-24.

Blumstein, A., & Larson, R. (1972). Analysis of a total criminal justice system. In A. Drake, R. Keeney, & P. Morse (Eds.), *Analysis of public systems.* Boston: Massachusetts Institute of Technology.

Blumstein, A., Cassidy, G., & Hopkinson, G. (1975). *Systems analysis and the Canadian justice system* (CANJUS Project Report No. 14). Ottawa, Canada:, Ministry of the Solicitor General.

Blumstein, A., Cassidy, G., & Townsend, J. (1974). *Implementation of a systems approach to the Canadian criminal justice system* (Statistics Division Report No. 3). Ottawa, Canada: Ministry of the Solicitor General.

Boggs, S. L. (1965). Urban crime patterns. *American Sociological Review, 30*, 899-908.

Bolton, R. J., & Hand, D. J. (2002). Statistical fraud detection: A review. *Statistical Science, 17*(3), 235-255.

Bonabeau, E. (2002). Agent-based modeling: Methods and techniques for simulating human systems. In *Proceedings of the National Academy of Sciences of the United States of America (PNAS)*, 99(3), 7280-7287.

Bonabeau, E., Dorigo, M., & Theraulaz, G. (1999). *Swarm intelligence: From natural to artificial systems.* Santa Fe Institute Studies in the Sciences of Complexity Series: Oxford Press.

Bonneau, G-P., Ertl, T., & Nielson, G. M. (Eds.) (2006). *Scientific visualization: The visual extraction of knowledge from data.* Berlin: Springer.

Boots, B. N., & Tiefelsdorf, M. (2000). Global and local spatial autocorrelation in bounded regular tessellations. *Journal of Geographical Systems, 2*, 319-348.

Börger, E. (2004). *The ASM ground model method as a foundation of requirements engineering.* In N. Dershowitz (Ed.), *Verification: Theory and practice: LNCS 2772* (pp. 146-161). Springer.

Börger, E., & Stärk, R. (2003). *Abstract state machines: A method for high-level system design and analysis.* Springer-Verlag.

Borne, P., Fayech, B., Hammadi, S., & Maouche, S. (2003). Decision support system for urban transportation networks. *IEEE transaction on systems, man and cybernetics, Part C, 33*(1), 67-77.

Bottoms, A. E., & Wale, P. (2002). Environmental criminology. In M. Maguire, R. Morgan & R. Reiner (Eds.), *The Oxford handbook of criminology* (3rd ed., pp.620-656). Oxford: Oxford University Press.

Bottoms, A. E., & Wiles, P. (2002). Environmental criminology. In M. Maguire, R. Morgan, & R. Reiner (Eds.), *The Oxford handbook of criminology* (3rd ed.) (pp. 620-656). Oxford: Oxford University Press.

Bottoms, A. E., Claytor, A., & Wiles, P. (1992). Housing markets and residential community crime careers: A case study from Sheffield. In D. J. Evans, N. R. Fyfe & D. T. Herbert (Eds.), *Crime, policing and place: Essays in environmental criminology* (pp. 118-144). London: Routledge.

Bousquet, F., Bakam, I., Proton, H., & Le Page, C. (1998). CORMAS : Common-pool resources and multi-agent systems. *Lecture Notes in Artificial Intelligence, 1416,* 826-837.

Bowers, K. (2007) Crime risk models: Specifying boundaries and environmental backcloths. In *Proceedings of the Crime Hot Spots: Behavioral, Computational and Mathematical Models, IPAM, UCLA.*

Bowers, K. J., & Johnson, S. D. (2005). Domestic burglary repeats and space-time clusters: The dimensions of risk. *European Journal of Criminology, 2*(1), 67-92.

Brahan, J. W., Lam, K. P., Chan, H., & Leung, W. (1998). AICAMS: artificial intelligence crime analysis and management system. *Knowledge-Based Systems, 11*, 355-361.

Braithwaite, J. (1985). White collar crime. *Annual Review of Sociology, 11,* 1-25.

Bramson, M., & Dai, J. G. (2001). Heavy traffic limits for some queuing networks. *Annals of Applied Probability, 11*, 49-90.

Brantingham, & Brantingham (1995). Criminality and place: Crime generators and crime attractors. *European Journal on Criminal Policy and Research, 3*, 3.

Brantingham, P. (1977). *Dynamic modeling of the felony court system.* Unpublished doctoral dissertation, Florida State University.

Brantingham, P. J. (2003). A neutral model of stone raw material procurement. *American Antiquity, 68*(3), 487-509.

Brantingham, P. J. (2006). Measuring forager mobility. *Current Anthropology, 47*, 435-459.

Brantingham, P. J., & Brantingham P. L. (1993b). Nodes, paths and edges: Considerations on the complexity of crime and the physical environment. *Journal of Environmental Psychology, 13*, 3-28.

Brantingham, P. J., & Brantingham P. L. (2004). Computer simulation as a tool for environmental criminologists. *Security Journal, 17*, 21-30.

Brantingham, P. J., & Brantingham, P. L. (1978). A theoretical model of crime site selection. In M. Krohn, & R. L. Akers (Eds.), *Crime, law and sanctions*. Beverly Hills, CA: Sage Publications.

Brantingham, P. J., & Brantingham, P. L. (1981). *Environmental criminology.* Beverley Hills, CA: Sage.

Brantingham, P. J., & Brantingham, P. L. (1981). Notes on the geometry of crime. In P. Brantingham & P. Brantingham (Eds.), *Environmental criminology* (pp. 27-54). Prospect Heights, IL: Waveland Press, Inc.

Brantingham, P. J., & Brantingham, P. L. (1984). *Patterns in crime*. New York: Macmillan.

Brantingham, P. J., & Brantingham, P. L. (1991). Introduction: The dimensions of crime. In P. J. Brantingham, & P. L. Brantingham (Eds.), *Environmental criminology* (pp.7-26). Waveland Press.

Brantingham, P. J., & Brantingham, P. L. (1993a). Environment, routine and situation: Toward a pattern theory of crime. In R. V. Clarke, & M. Felson (Eds.), *Routine activity and rational choice: Advances in criminological theory* (Vol. 5., pp. 259-294). New Brunswick, NJ: Transaction Publication.

Brantingham, P. J., Bertozzi, A., Tita, G., & Chayes, L. (2006.). *UC mathematical and simulation modeling of crime project.* Retrieved September 5, 2007, from http://paleo.sscnet.ucla.edu/ucmasc.htm

Brantingham, P. J., Brantingham P. L., & Glässer, U. (2005a). Computer simulation as a research tool in criminology and criminal justice. *Criminal Justice Matters, 58*, 18-19.

Brantingham, P. J., Brantingham, P. L., & Wong, P. S. (1991). How public transit feeds private crime: Notes on the Vancouver sky train experience. *Security Journal, 2*, 91-95.

Brantingham, P. L., & Brantingham, P. J. (1993). Environment, routine, and situation: Toward a pattern theory of crime. In R.V. Clarke & M. Felson (Eds.), *Routine activity and rational choice, Advances in Criminological Theory* (Vol. 5). New Brunswick, NJ: Transaction Publishers.

Brantingham, P. L., & Brantingham, P. J. (1993). Nodes, paths and edges—Considerations on the complexity of crime and the physical-environment. *Journal Of Environmental Psychology, 13*(1), 3-28.

Brantingham, P. L., & Brantingham, P. J. (1995). Criminality of place: Crime generators and crime attractors. *European Journal on Criminal Policy and Research, 3*(3), 5-26.

Brantingham, P. L., & Brantingham, P. J. (2003). *Computer simulation as a tool for environmental criminologists.* Paper presented at the presented at 11th International Symposium on Environmental Criminology and Crime Analysis, University of Cincinnati.

Brantingham, P. L., & Brantingham, P. J. (2004). Computer simulation as a tool for environmental criminologists. *Security Journal, 17*(1), 21-30.

Brantingham, P. L., & Groff, E. R. (2004). *The future of agent-based simulation in environmental criminology.* Paper presented at the American Society of Criminology, Nashville, TN.

Brantingham, P. L., Brantingham, P. J., & Glässer, U. (2005). Computer simulation as a research tool in criminlology and criminal justice. *Criminal Justice Matters, 58.*

Brantingham, P. L., Glässer, U., Kinney, B., Singh, K., & Vajihollahi, A. (2005b). Modelling urban crime patterns: Viewing multi-agent systems as abstract state machines. In D. Beauquier, E. Börger, & A. Slissenko, (Eds.), In *Proceedings of the 12th International Workshop on Abstract State Machines* (pp. 101-117). Paris: Universite de Paris.

Brantingham, P. L., Glässer, U., Kinney, B., Singh, K., & Vajihollahi, M. (2005b). A computational model for simulating spatial aspects of crime in urban environments. In *Proceedings of 2005 IEEE International Conference on Systems, Man, and Cybernetics, Hawaii, USA* (pp. 3667- 3674).

Brantingham, P. L., Glässer, U., Singh, K., & Vajihollahi, M. (2005c). *Mastermind: Modeling and simulation of criminal activity in urban environments* (Tech. Rep. SFU-CMPT-TR-2005-14). Burnaby, Canada, Simon Fraser University. Revised version of SFU-CMPT-TR-2005-01.

Brantingham, P., & Brantingham, P. (1979). Environment, routine, and situation: Toward a pattern theory of crime. In R. Clark & M. Felson (Eds.), *Routine activity and rational choice* (Vol. 5) (pp. 259 – 294).Transaction Books

Brantingham, P., & Brantingham, P. (2004). Computer simulation as a tool for environmental criminologists. *Security Journal, 17*(1), 21-30.

Brantingham, P.J. & Brantingham P. L. (1991). *Environmental Criminology.* (2nd Ed.) Prospect Heights, IL: Waveland Press.

Bratman, M. E., Israel, D., & Pollack, M. E. (1988). Plans and resource-bounded practical reasoning. *Computational Intelligence, 4*, 349-355.

Brimicombe, A. J., Ralphs, M. P., & Sampson, A. (2001). An analysis of the role of neighborhood ethnic composition in the geographical distribution of racially motivated incidents. *British Journal of Criminology, 41*(2), 293-308.

Brooks, R. A. (1996, May). From earwigs to humans. In *Proceedings IIAS The Third Brain and Mind International Symposium Concept Formation, Thinking and Their Development*, Kyoto, Japan (pp.59-66).

Brown, D. E. (1998). The regional crime analysis program (ReCAP): A framework for mining data to catch criminals. In *Proceedings of 1998 IEEE International Conference on Systems, Man, and Cybernetics, San Diego, California* (pp. 2848-2853).

Brown, D. G., Riolo, R., Robinson, D. T., North, M., & Rand, W. (2005). Spatial process and data models: Toward integration of agent-based models and GIS. *Journal of Geographic Systems, 7*, 25-47.

Brown, M. A. (1982). Modelling the spatial distribution of suburban crime. *Economic Geography, 58*(3), 247-261.

Brunswik, E. (1952). The conceptual framework of psychology. *International Encyclopedia of Unified Science, 1*(10).

Buchanan, M. (2002). Nexus: Small worlds and the groundbreaking science of networks. New York: W. W. Norton.

Bureau of Labor Statistics. (2003). *Metropolitan area employment and unemployment: January 2003*. Bureau of Labor Statistics, United States Department of Labor. Retrieved September 2, 2007, from the World Wide Web: www.bls.gov/news.release/archives/metro_03262003.pdf

Burke, P. J. (1956). The output of queuing system. *Operations Research, 4*, 699-704.

Bursik, R. (1988). Social disorganization and theories of crime and delinquency: Problems and prospects. *Criminology, 26*, 519-551.

Bursik, R. J., & Grasmick, H. G. (1993). *Neighborhoods and crime*. San Francisco: Lexington Books.

Byrne, J. (1986). Cities, citizens, and crime: The ecological/nonecological debate reconsidered. In J. Byrne, & R. J. Sampson (Eds.), *The social ecology of crime* (pp. 77-101). New York: Springer-Verlag.

Byrne, J. M., & Sampson, R. J. (1986). *The social ecology of crime*. New York: Srpinger-Verlag.

Calvete H. I., Gale, C., Oliveros, M. J., & Sanchez-Valverde, B. (2004). Vehicle routing problems with soft time windws: An optimization based approach. *Monografias del Seminario Matematico Garcia del Galdeano, 31*, 295-304.

Calvó-Armengol, A., & Zenou, Y. (2004). Social networks and crime decisions: The role of social structure in facilitating delinquent behavior. *International Economic Review, 45*(3), 939–58.

Camazine, S., Deneubourg, J.-L., Franks, N. R., Sneyd, J., Theraulaz, G., & Bonabeau, E. (2001). *Self-organization in biological systems*. Princeton: Princeton University Press.

Camerer, C. F. (2000). Prospect theory in the wild: Evidence from the field. In D. Kahneman, & A. Tversky (Eds.), *Choices, values and frames*. Cambridge: Cambridge University Press.

Campbell, D. T. (1957). Factors relevant to the validity of experiments in social settings. *Psychological Bulletin, 54*, 297-312

Campbell, D. T., & Stanley, J. C. (1963). *Experimental and quasi-experimental designs for research*. Chicago: Rand-McNally.

Cansado, T. M. L. (2005). Alocação e despacho de recursos para combate à criminalidade. Master dissertation, UFMG, Belo Horizonte.

Canter, & Gregory. (1994). Identifying the residential location of rapists. *Journal of Forensic Science, 34*, 169-175.

Canter, & Larkin. (1993). The environmental range of serial rapists. *Journal of Environmental Psychology, 13*, 64-70.

Canter, D., & Larkin, P. (1993). The environmental range of serial rapists. *Journal Of Environmental Psychology, 13*(1), 63-69.

Card, S. (2006). *Using vision to think*. Paper presented at Symposium on the Future of Visualization. Charlotte Visualization Center, Charlotte, NC. Retrieved August 24, 2007, from http://www.viscenter.uncc.edu/symposium06/

Carrington, P. J., Matarazzo, A., & deSouza, P. (2006). *Court careers of a Canadian birth cohort*. Ottawa, Canada: Canadian Centre for Justice Statistics, Statistics Canada.

Carson, J. (2004). *Introduction to modeling and simulation*. In R. Ingalls, M. Rosetti, J. Smith, & B. Peters (Eds). In *Proceedings of the 2004 Winter Simulation Conference*, Monterey, California.

Carter, R. L. (1979). *The criminal's image of the city*. New York: Pergamon Press.

Cascetta, E., & Papola, A. (2001). Implicit availability/perception logit models for route choice in transportatoin network. In *Proceedings of the 8th World Conference on Transport Research*, Antwerp.

Cascetta, E., Nuzzolo, A., Russo, F., & Vitetta, A. (1996). A modified logit route choice results for interurban networks. Transportation and traffic theory. In *Proceedings from the Theirteenth International Symposium on Transportation and Traffic Theory*, Lyon, France.

Cassidy, G. (1985). Modelling a criminal justice system. In D. Farrington & R. Tarling (Eds.), *Prediction in criminology*. Albany, New York: State University of New York Press.

Cassidy, G., Hopkinson, G., & Mead, D. (1976). *Use of systems models in planning and evaluation* (CANJUS Project Report No. 25). Ottawa, Canada: Ministry of the Solicitor General.

Caulkins, J. P., & Reuter, P. (2006). Illicit drug markets and economic irregularities. *Socio-Economic Planning Sciences, 40*, 1-14.

Caulkins, J. P., Behrens, D. A., Knoll, C., Tragler, G., & Zuba, D. (2004). Modeling dynamic trajectories of initiation and demand: The case of the U.S. cocaine epidemic. *Health Care Management Science, 7*(4), 319-329.

Ceccato, V., Haining, R., & Signoretta, P. (2002). Exploring offence statistics in Stockholm city using spatial analysis tools. *Annals of the Association of American Geographers, 92*(1), 29-51.

Cellier, F. E. (1991). *Continuous system modeling.* New York: Springer-Verlag.

Cervero, R. (2003). Road expansion, urban growth, and induced travel. *Journal of American Planning Association, 69*(2), 145-163.

Chaiken, J., Crabill, T., Holiday, L., Jaquette, D., Lawless, M., & Quade, E. (1977). Summary of operational criminal justice models. In S. Nagel (Ed.), *Modeling the criminal justice system.* Beverly Hills, CA: Sage Publications.

Chainey, S. P., & Desyllas, J. (2004). Measuring, identifying and analysing street crime risk. In *Proceedings at the 2004 UK National Crime Mapping Conference, University of London, London.* Retrieved August 28, 2007, from www.jdi.ucl.ac.uk/news_events/conferences/index.php

Chainey, S. P., & Ratcliffe, J. H (2005). *GIS and crime mapping.* London: Wiley.

Chaitin, G. (1990). *Information, randomness and incompleteness* (2nd ed.). Singapore: World Scientific.

Chalmers, A. F. (1999). *What is this thing called Science?* (3rd ed). Maidenhead, UK: Open University Press.

Chattoe, E., & Hamill, H. (2005). It's not who you know—It's what you know about people you don't know that counts: Extending the analysis of crime groups as social networks. *British Journal of Criminology, 45*(6), 860-876.

Chen, H., Miranda, R., & Zeng, D. D. (2003). *Intelligence and security informatics: First NSF/NIJ Symposium*, ISI 2003 (Vol. 2665) Tucson, AZ.

Chenery, S., Henshaw, C., & Pease, K. (1999). *Illegal parking in disabled bays: A means of offender targeting.* Briefing Note 1/99. London: Home Office Policing and Reducing Crime Unit.

Chorley, R. J., & Haggett, P. (Eds.). (1967). *Models in geography.* London: Methuen & Co.

Chu, L. Y., Liu, H. X., Oh, J.-S., & Recker, W. (2004). A calibration procedure for microscopic traffic simulation. In *Proceedings of the 83th Transportation Research Board Annual Meeting in Washington, D.C.*

Chung, C. (2004). *Simulation modeling handbook: A practical approach.* New York: CRC Press.

Clarke, K. C. (2002). *Getting started with GIS.* Upper Saddle River, NJ: Prentice Hall.

Clarke, K. C., & Gaydos, L. (1998). Loose-coupling a cellular automaton model and GIS: Long-term urban growth prediction for San Francisco and Washington/Baltimore. *International Journal of Geographical Information Science, 12*, 699-714.

Clarke, K. C., & Gaydos, L. J. (1998). Loose-coupling a cellular automata model and GIS: long-term urban growth prediction for San Francisco and Washington/Baltimore. *International Journal of Geographical Information Science, 12*(7), 699-714.

Clarke, K. C., Brass, J. A., & Riggan, P. J. (1994). A cellular automata model of wildfire propagation and extinction. *Photogrammetric Engineering & Remote Sensing, 60*, 1355-1367.

Clarke, K. C., Brass, J. A., & Riggan, P. J. (1994). A cellular automata model of wildfire propagation and extinction. *Photogrammetric Engineering & Remote Sensing, 60*, 1355-1367.

Clarke, K. C., Gaydos, L., & Hoppen, S. (1997). A self-modifying cellular automaton model of historical urbanization in the San Francisco Bay area. *Environment and Planning B: Planning and Design, 24*, 247-261.

Clarke, R. (1995). Situational crime prevention. In M. Tonry & D. Farrington (Eds.), *Building a safer society: Strategic approaches to crime prevention* (Vol. 19, pp. 91-150). Chicago: University of Chicago Press.

Clarke, R. V. (1983). Situational crime prevention: Its theoretical basis and practical scope. In M. Tony & N. Morris (Eds.), *Crime andjustice: An annual review ofresearch* (Vol. 4) (pp. 225-256). Chicago: University of Chicago Press.

Clarke, R. V. (1993). *Crime prevention studies.* Monsey: NY: Criminal Justice Press.

Clarke, R. V. (1995). Situational crime prevention. In M. Tonry & D.P. Farrington (Eds.), *Crime andjustice* (Vol. 19). *Building a safer society – Strategic approaches to crime prevention.* Chicago: The University of Chicago Press.

Clarke, R. V. (1999). Hot products: Understanding, anticipating and reducing demand for stolen goods. *Police research series, Paper 112.* London: Home Office.

Clarke, R. V. (2004). Closing streets and alleys to reduce crime: Should you go down this road. *Problem-oriented guides for police, Response guides series No. 2.* US Department of Justice, Washington, DC: Office of Community Oriented Policing Services.

Clarke, R. V. (2004). Crime proofing of products: The idea and the substance. *IEEE Technology and Society Magazine, 23*(3), 21-27.

Clarke, R. V. (Ed.). (1997). *Situational crime prevention: Successful case studies* (2nd ed.). Guilderland, NY: Harrow & Heston.

Clarke, R. V., & Cornish, D. B. (2000). Rational choice. In R. Paternoster & R. Bachman (Eds.). *Explaining crime and criminals: Essays in contemporary Criminological Theory.* Los Angeles, CA: Roxbury.

Clarke, R. V., & Cornish, D. B. (1985). Modeling offender's decisions: A framework for Research and policy. In M. Tonry & N. Morris (Eds.), *Crime andjustice: An Annual Review of Research* (Vol. 6). Chicago: University of Chicago Press.

Clarke, R. V., & Eck, J. (2003). *Become a problem-solving crime analyst in 55 small steps.* London: Jill Dando Institute, University College. Retrieved August 28, 2007, from http://www.jdi.ucl.ac.uk/publications/other_publications/55steps

Clarke, R. V., & Eck, J. (2003). *Become a problem-solving crime analyst.* London: Jill Dando Institute of Crime Science, University College London. Retrieved September 1. 2007, from http://www.jdi.ucl.ac.uk/publications/other_publications/55steps, last accessed October 14, 2006.

Clarke, R. V., & Eck, J. E. (2005). *Crime analysis for problem solvers in 660 small steps.* Washington, DC: Office of Community Oriented Policing Services, U.S. Department of Justice.

Clarke, R. V., & Felson, M. (1993). Criminology, routine activity, and rational choice. In R.V. Clarke and M. Felson (Eds.), *Routine activity and rational choice, Advances in criminological theories* (Vol. 5). New Brunswick: Transaction.

Clarke, R. V., & Felson, M. (1993). Introduction: Criminology, routine activity and rational choice. In R. V. Clarke & M. Felson (Eds.), *Routine activity and rational choice: Vol. 5. Advances in criminological theory.* New Brunswick, NJ: Transaction Publishers.

Clarke, R. V., & Mayhew, P. (1998). Preventing crime in parking lots: What we know and what we need to know. In M. Felson, & R. B. Peiser (Eds.), *Reducing crime through real estate development and management.* Urban Land Institute.

Cliff, A. D., & Ord, J. K. (1975). Space time modelling with an application to regional forecasting. *Transaction of the Institute of British Geographers, 64,* 119-128.

Cliff, A. D., Haggett, P., Ord, J. K., & Versey, G. R. (1981). *Spatial diffusion: An historical geography of epidemics in an island community.* Cambridge: Cambridge University Press.

Cohen, B. (1980). *Deviant street networks.* Lexigton, MA: Lexington Books.

Cohen, G. (1996). *Memory in the real world.* (2nd ed). Hove: Psychology Press.

Cohen, J., & Tita, G. (1999a). Diffusion in homicide: Exploring a general method for detecting spatial diffusion processes. *Journal of Quantitative Criminology, 15*(4), 451-493.

Cohen, J., & Tita, G. (1999b). Editors' introduction. *Journal of Quantitative Criminology, 15*(4), 373-378.

Cohen, J., Fields, K., Lettre, M., Stafford, R., & Walker, C. (1973). Implementation of the JUSSIM model in a criminal justice planning agency. *Journal of Research in Crime and Delinquency, 10*(2), 117-131.

Cohen, L. E., & Felson, M. (1979). Social change and crime rate trends: A routine activity approach. *American Sociological Review, 44*, 588-608.

Cohen, L. E., Kluegel, J. R., & Land, K. C. (1981). Social inequality and predatory criminal victimization: An exposition and test of a formal theory. *American Sociological Review, 46*, 505-524.

Comfort, J., Shapiro, S., & Volcansek-Clark, M. (1982). *Development of a simulation model of criminal caseflow activities, Decision and policy variables.* Miami, FL: Florida International University.

CommunityViz Web site. (2006). *Community viz products.* Retrieved August 26, 2007, from http://www.communityviz.com

Conclelis, H. (1988). Of mice and men: What rodent populations can teach us about complex spatial dynamics. *Environment and Planning A: Environment and Planning, 20*, 99-109.

Conclelis, H. (1989). Macrostructure and micro-behaviour in a metropolitan area. *Environment and Planning B: Planning and Design, 16*, 141-54.

Cook, G. (2006). *Near match of DNA could lead police to more suspects.* Globe.

Cook, T. D., & Campbell, D. T. (1979). *Quasi-experimentation: Design and analysis issues for field settings.* Chicago: Rand-McNally.

Coornhert, D.Vzn. (1587). *Boeventucht* [*Disciplining villains*]. Amsterdam: Harmen Muller.

Cooter, R., & Ulen, T. (2000). *Law and economics.* Boston: Addison Wesley Longman, Inc.

Cork, D. (1999). Examining space-time interaction in city-level homicide data: Crack markets and the diffusion of guns among youth. *Journal of Quantitative Criminology, 15*(4), 379-406.

Cornish, D. B. (1994). The procedural analysis of offending and its relevance for situational prevention. In R.V. Clarke (Ed.), *Crime prevention studies* (Vol.3). Monsey, N.Y.: Criminal Justice Press.

Cornish, D. B., & Clarke, R. V. (Eds.) (1986). *The reasoning criminal: Rational choice perspectives on offending.* New York: Springer.

Cornish, D. B., & Clarke, R.V. (1986). *The reasoning criminal: Rational choice perspectives on offending.* New York: Springer.

Cornish, D., & Clarke, R. V. (1986). Introduction. In D. Cornish & R. V. Clarke (Eds.), *The reasoning criminal* (pp. 1-16). New York: Springer-Verlag.

Costello, A. & Wiles, P. (2001). GIS and the journey to crime: An analysis of patterns in South Yorkshire. In A. Hirschfield & K. Bowers (Eds.), *Mapping and analysing crime data: Lessons from research and practice* (pp. 27-60). London: Taylor and Francis.

Couclelis, H. (1985). Cellular worlds: A framework for modeling micro-macro dynamics. *Environment and Planning A, 17*, 585-596.

Couclelis, H. (1988). Of mice and men: What rodent populations can teach us about complex spatial dynamics. *Environment and Planning A, 20*, 99-109.

Couclelis, H. (1989). Macrostructure and microbehavior in a metropolitan area. *Environment and Planning B, 16*, 141-154.

Couclelis, H. (1997). From cellular automata to urban models: New principles for model development and implementation, *Environment and Planning B: Planning and Design, 24*, 165-174.

Craglia, M., Haining, R., & Signoretta, P. (2001). Modelling high-intensity crime areas in english cities. *Urban Studies, 38*(11), 1921-1941.

Craglia, M., Haining, R., & Wiles, P. (2000). A comparative evaluation of approaches to urban crime pattern analysis. *Urban Studies, 37*(4), 711-729.

Craig, W., Harris, T., & Weiner, D. (2002). *Community participation and geographical information systems.* London: Taylor and Francis.

Criterion planners Web site. (2006). Retrieved August 26, 2007, from http://www.crit.com

Cronbach, L. J. (1982). *Designing evaluations of educational and social program.* San Francisco: Jossey-Bass.

Cronbach, L. J., Ambron, S. R., Dornbusch, S. M., Hess, R. D., Hornik, R. C., Phillips, D. C., Walker, D. F., & Weiner, S. S. (1980). *Toward reform of program evaluation.* San Francisco: Jossey-Bass.

Cullingworth, B., & Caves, R. W. (2003). *Planning in the USA: Policies, issues and processes.* London: Routledge (Taylor & Francis Group).

Cusson, M. (2002). *Prévenir la délinquance.* Paris: Presses Universitaires de France.

D'Aquino, P., Le Page, C., Bousquet, F., & Bah, A. (2003). Using self-designed role-playing games and a multi-agent system to empower a local decision-making process for land use management: The SelfCormas experiment in Senegal. *Journal of Artificial Societies and Social Simulation, 6*(3).

Davidsson, P. (2002). Agent based social simulation: A computer science view. *Journal of Artificial Societies and Social Simulation, 5*(1).

Deadman, P. D., Brown, R. D., & Gimblett, H. R. (1993). Modelling rural residential settlement patterns with cellular automata. *Journal of Environmental Management, 37,* 147-160.

Deane, G., Beck, E. M., & Tolnay, S. E. (1998). Incorporating space into social histories: How spatial processes operate and how we observe them. *International Review of Social history, 43,* 57-80.

DeFrances, C. J., & Smith, S. K. (1994). *Crime and neighborhoods.*

Dennett, D. (2003). *Freedom evolves.* New York: Viking.

Denning, P. J. (2006). Infoglut. *Communications of the ACM, 49*(7), 15-19.

Dibble, C. (2001). *Theory in a complex world: GeoGraph computational laboratories.* Unpublished doctoral dissertation, University of California Santa Barbara, Santa Barbara.

Dietze, P., Hickman, M., & Kimber, J. (2005). Monograph No. 03: Estimating the prevalence of problematic heroin use in Melbourne. *DPMP monograph series.* Fitzroy: Turning Point Alcohol and Drug Centre.

Dietze, P., Miller, P., Clemens, S., Matthews, S., Gilmour, S., & Collins, L. (2004). The course and consequences of the heroin shortage in Victoria. *NDLERF monograph no. 6.* Adelaide: Australasian Centre for Policing Research.

Dijkstra, E. (1959). A note on two problems in connexion with graphs. *Numerische Mathematik, 1,* 269-271.

Donkin, S., & Wellsmith, M. (2006). Cars stolen in burglaries: The Sandwell experience. *Security Journal, 19*(1), 22-32.

Doran, J., Palmer, M., Gilbert, N., & Mellars, P. (1994). The EOS project: Modelling upper paleolithic social change. In N. Gilbert & J. Doran (Eds.), *Simulating society: The computer simulation of social phenomena* (pp. 195-221). London: UCL Press.

Dowling, D. (1999). Experimenting on theories. *Science in Context, 12*(2), 261-273.

Drezner, T., & Eiselt, H. A. (2002). Consumers in competitive location models. In Z. Drezner & H. W. Hamacher (Eds.), *Facility location: Applications and theory* (pp. 151-178). Berlin: Springer.

Driver's License Examining Bureau (1996, July). *Kansas driving handbook.* Topeka, Kansas.

Drogoul, A., & Ferber, J. (1992). Multi-agent simulation as a tool for modeling societies: Application to social differentiation in ant colonies. In *Proceedings of 4th European Workshop on on Modelling Autonomous Agents in a Multi-Agent World, Artificial Social Systems* (MAAMAW), Lecture Notes in Computer Science (Vol. 830, pp. 3-23).

Drogoul, A., & Ferber, J. (1994). Multi-agent simulation as a tool for studying emergent processes in societies. In N. Gilbert & J. Doran (Eds.), *Simulating society: The computer simulation of social phenomena* (pp. 127-142). London: UCL Press.

Durkheim, E. (1897). *Le suicide.* Paris: F. Alcan.

Duxbury, E., & Desyllas, J. (2000). *St. Giles circus: Report on current patterns of pedestrian movement and accidents.* London: Intelligent Space Partnership.

Duxbury, E., & Desyllas, J. (2001). *Shoreditch triangle pedestrian movement and safety report.* London: Intelligent Space Partnership.

Eck, J. (2007). Simulating police outcomes: A framework for understanding policing strategies. In *Proceedings of the meeting on Crime Hot Spots: Behavioral, Computational and Mathematical Models.* Los Angeles, CA: Institute for Pure and Applied Mathematics, University of California, Los Angeles.

Eck, J. E. (1994). Examining routine activites theory: A review of two books. *Justice Quarterly, 12,* 783-797.

Eck, J. E. (1998). A general model of the geography of illicit retail market places. In: D. Weisburd & J. Eck (Eds.). *Crime prevention studies* (Vol. 4). Monsey (NY) Criminal Justice Press.

Eck, J. E. (2001). Policing and crime event concentration. In R. F. Meier, L. W. Kennedy, & V. F. Sacco (Eds.), *The process and structure of crime: Criminal event and crime analysis: Vol. 9. Advances in criminological theory,* (pp. 249-276). New Brunswick, NJ: Transaction Publishers.

Eck, J. E. (2003). Police problems: The complexity of problem theory, research and evaluation. In J. Knutsson (Ed.), *Problem-oriented policing: From innovation to mainstream: Vol. 15. Crime prevention studies,* (pp. 67-102). Monsey, NY: Criminal Justice Press.

Eck, J. E. (2005). *Using crime pattern simulations to elaborate theory.* Paper presented at the American Society of Criminology, Toronto.

Eck, J. E., & Liu, L. (2004). *Routine activity theory in a RA/CA crime simulation.* Paper presented at the American Society of Criminology, Nashville, TN.

Eck, J. E., & Weisburd, D. (1995). *Crime and place: Crime prevention studies* (Vol. 4). Monsey, NY: Willow Tree Press.

Eck, J. E., & Weisburd, D. (1995). Crime places in crime theory. In J. E Eck & D. Weisburd (Eds.), *Crime and place: Vol. 4. Crime prevention studies* (pp. 1-33). Monsey, NY: Criminal Justice Press.

Eck, J. E., & Weisburd, D. (1995). Crime places in crime theory. In J. E. Eck & D. Weisburd (Eds.), *Crime and place.* Monsey, NY: Criminal Justice Press.

Eck, J. E., & Weisburd, D. L. (1995). *Crime and place.* Monsey, NY: Willow Tree Press.

Eck, J. E., Chainey, S. P., Cameron, J. G., Leitner, M., & Wilson, R. E. (2005). *Mapping crime: Understanding hot spots.* USA: National Institute of Justice. Retrieved August 28, 2007, from www.ojp.usdoj.gov/nij

Eck, J. E., Clarke, R. V, & Guerette, R. (2007). Risky facilities: Crime concentration in homogeneous sets of establishments and facilities. In G. Farrell, K. J. Bowers, S. D. Johnson, & M. Townsley (Eds.), *Imagination for crime prevention: Vol. 19. Crime prevention studies* (pp. 225-264). Monsey, NY: Criminal Justice Press.

Eck, J., & Clarke, R. V. (2003). Classifying common police problems: A routine activity approach. In M. J. Smith & D. B. Cornish (Eds.), *Theory for practice in situational crime prevention: Vol. 16. Crime prevention studies* (pp. 7–40). Monsey, NY: Criminal Justice Press.

Edmonds, B., & Hales, D. (2003). Replication, replication and replication: Some hard lessons from model alignment. *Journal of Artificial Societies and Social Simulation,* 6(4). Retrieved August 22, 2007, from http://jasss.soc.surrey.ac.uk/6/4/11.html

Ekblom, P., & Tilley, N. (2000). Going equipped: Criminology, situational crime prevention and the resourceful offender. *British journal of criminology,* 40(3), 376-398.

Engel-Frisch, G. (1943). Some neglected temporal aspects of human ecology. *Social Forces, 22*(1/4), 43-47.

Epstein, J. M., & Axtell, R. (1996). *Growing artificial societies.* Washington. D.C.: Brookings Institution Press.

Epstein, J. M., & Axtell, R. (1996). *Growing artificial societies: Social science from the bottom up.* Washington, DC: Brookings Institution Press.

Erlang, A. K. (1909). The theory of probabilities and telephone conversations. *Nyt Tidsskrift Matematik, 20,* 33-39.

ESRI (2003). *Business location data.* Redlands, CA: Environmental Systems Research Institute.

ESRI (2005). *ArcGIS 9.1.* Redlands, CA: Environmental Systems Research Institute.

ESRI Web site. (2007). Retrieved August 26, 2007, from http://www.esri.com

Ettema, D., Tamminga, G. & Timmermans, H. (2003, August). A micro-simulation model system of departure time and route choice under travel time uncertainty. In *Proceedings of the 10th International Conference on Travel Behaviour Research Lucerne*, (pp. 10-15).

Evans, S., & Steadman, P. (2003). Interfacing land-use transport models with GIS: The Inverness model. In P. Longley, & M. Batty (Eds.), *Advanced spatial analysis: The CASA book of GIS* (pp. 289-307). Redlands, CA: ESRI Press.

Fang, L., Hipel, K. W., Kilgour, D. M., & Peng, X. (2003). A decision support system for interactive decision making-Part I: Model formulation. *IEEE Transactions on Systems, Man and Cybernetics, Part C, 33*(1), 42-55.

Farahbod, R. (2004). *Extending and refining an abstract operational semantics of the web services architecture for the business process execution language*. Unpublished master's thesis, Simon Fraser University, Burnaby, Canada.

Farahbod, R., & Glässer, U. (2006). Semantic blueprints of discrete dynamic systems: Challenges and needs in computational modeling of complex behavior. In *Proceedings of the 6th Int'l Heinz Nixdorf Symposium*, Paderborn, Germany.

Farrell, G., & Pease, K. (Eds.). (2001). Repeat victimization. *Crime prevention studies* (Vol. 12). Monsey, NY: Criminal Justice Press.

Farrington, D. P. (1986). Age and crime. In M. Tonry & N. Norris (Eds.), *Crime and justice—An annual review of research*. Chicago: The University of Chicago Press.

Farrington, D. P., & Langan, P. (1998). *Crime and justice in the United States and in England and Wales 1981-96*. Washington, D.C.: Bureau of Justice.

Fawcett, T., & Provost, F. (1997). Adaptive fraud detection. *Data Mining and Knowledge Discovery, 1*, 291-316.

Felson, M. (1987). Routine activities and crime prevention in the developing metropolis. *Criminology, 25*(4), 911-931.

Felson, M. (1994). *Crime and everyday life: Impact and implications for society*. Thousand Oaks, CA: Pine Forge Press.

Felson, M. (1995). Those who discourage crime. In J. E. Eck & D. Weisburd (Eds.), *Crime and place: Vol. 4. Crime prevention Studies* (pp. 53-66). Monsey, NY: Criminal Justice Press.

Felson, M. (2006). *Crime and nature*. Thousand Oaks: Sage.

Felson, M., & Poulson, E. (2003). Simple indicators of crime by time of day. *International Journal of Forecasting, 19*, 595-601.

Ferber, J. (1999). *Multi-agent systems: An introduction to distributed artificial* intelligence. Harlow: Addison Wesley Longman.

Flemming, Z., Brantingham, P. L., & Brantingham, P. J. (1994). Exploring auto theft in British Columbia. In R. V. Clarke (Ed.), *Crime prevention studies* (Vol. 3, pp. 47-90). Monsey, NY: Criminal Justice Press.

Florax, R., & Vlist, A. V. D. (2003). Spatial econometric data analysis: Moving beyond traditional models. *International Regional Science Review, 26*(3), 223-243.

Forrester, J. (1968). *Principles of systems*. Cambridge: Wright-Allen Press, Inc.

Forrester, J. W. (1994). System dynamics, Systems thinking and soft OR. *System Dynamics Review, 10*(2-3), 245-256.

Foschio, L. (1973). Empirical research and the problem of court delay. In Law Enforcement Assistance Administration (Ed.), *Reducing court delay*. Washington: U.S. Department of Justice.

Franklin, S., & Graesser, A. (1996) Is it an agent, or just a program?: A taxonomy of autonomous agents. Intelligent Agents III: In *Proceedings of the Third International Workshop on Agent Theories, Architectures, and Languages*, (ATAL'96), Lecture Notes in AI, Third International Workshop on Agent Theories, Architectures, and Languages, (ATAL'96), Springer-Verlag.

Franklin, S., & Graesser, A. (1997). Is it an agent, or just a program? A taxonomy for autonomous agents. In *Proceedings of the workshop on intelligent agents III, agent theories, architectures, and languages ECAI '96* (pp. 21-35). London: Springer-Verlag.

Friedrichs, D. (2004). Enron et al.: Paradigmatic white collar crime cases for the new century. *Critical Criminology, 12*, 113-132.

Frischer, M., Anderson, S., Hickman, M., & Heatlie, H. (2002). Diffusion of drug misuse in Scotland: Findings from the 1993 and 1996 Scottish crime surveys. *Addiction Research & Theory, 10*(1), 83-95.

Fruin, J. (1971.) *Pedestrian and planning design.* Alabama: Elevator World Inc.

Fry, B., & Reas, C. *Processing* 1.0 (BETA). Retrieved August 24, 2007, from http://processing.org/

Galster, G., Hanson, R., Ratcliffe, M. R., Wolman, H., Coleman, S., & Freihage, J. (2001). Wrestling sprawl to the ground: Defining and measuring an elusive concept. *Housing Policy Debate, 12*(4), 681-717.

Gatrell, A. C. (2005). Complexity theory and geographies of health: A critical assessment. *Social Science & Medicine, 60*, 2661-2671.

General Accountability Office (1998). *Food assistance: Computerized information matching could reduce fraud and abuse in the food stamp program.* GAO/T-RCED-98-254.

General Accountability Office (1999). *Food assistance: Efforts to control fraud and abuse in the WIC program can be strengthened.* Report to Congressional Committee. (GAO/RCED-99-224).

General Accountability Office (2005). *Health care fraud and abuse control program: Results of review of annual reports for fiscal years 2002 and 2003.* GAO-05-134.

George, A. L., & Bennett, A. (2005). *Case studies and theory development in the social sciences.* Cambridge: MIT Press.

Getis, A., & Ord, J. K. (1996). Local spatial statistics: and overview. In P. Longley & M. Batty (Eds.), *Spatial analysis: Modelling in a GIS environment* (pp. 261-277). Cambridge: Geoinformation International.

Gilbert, N., & Conte, R. (1995). *Artificial societies: The computer simulation of social life.* London: UCL Press.

Gilbert, N., & Doran, J. (1994). *Simulating societies.* UCL Press.

Gilbert, N., & Terna, P. (1999). *How to build and use agent-based models in social science.* Discussion Paper. Retrieved September 2, 2007, from http://web.econ.unito.it/terna/deposito/gil_ter.pdf

Gilbert, N., & Troitzsch, K. G. (1999). *Simulation for the social scientist.* Buckingham: Open University Press.

Gimblett, H. R. (Ed.). (2002). *Integrating geographic information systems and agent-based modeling techniques for simulating social and ecological processes.* Oxford: Oxford University Press.

Gipps, P. G. (2001). A model for the structure of lane changing decisions. *Transportation Research, 20B*, 403-414.

Glaeser, E., Sacerdote, B., & Scheinkman, J. (1996, May). Crime and social interactions. *Quarterly Journal of Economics, 111*(2), 507-48.

Glässer, U., Rastkar, S., & Vajihollahi, M. (2006). Computational modeling and experimental validation of aviation security procedures. In S. Mehrotra, D. D. Zeng, & H. Chen (Eds.), *Intelligence and security informatics: Vol. 3975 of LNCS* (pp. 420-431). Berlin: Springer-Verlag.

Glover, H. D., & Aono, J. Y. (1995). Changing the model for prevention and detection of fraud. *Managerial Auditing Journal, 10*(5), 3-9.

Goldstein, H. (1990). *Problem-oriented policing.* New York: McGraw-Hill Inc.

Goldstein, H. (1990). *Problem-oriented policing.* New York: McGraw-Hill.

Golledge, R. G., & Stimson, R. J. (1997). *Spatial behavior: A geographical perspective.* New York: Guilford Press.

Golledge, R. G., & Timmermans, H. (1990). Applications of behavioural research on spatial problems I: cognition. *Progress in Human Geography, 14*, 57-99.

Goodchild, M. (2005). GIS, spatial analysis, and modeling overview. In D. J. Maguire, M. Batty, & M. Goodchild (Eds.), *GIS, Spatial analysis, and modeling* (pp. 1-17). Redlands, CA: ESRI Press.

Goodchild, M. F. (2003) Geographic information science and systems for environmental management. *Annual Review of Environmental Resources, 28*, 493-519.

Goodman, J., & O'Rourke, J. (Eds). (2004). *Handbook of discrete and computational geometry* (2nd ed.). Boca Raton, FL: CRC Press.

Gottfredson, M. R., & Hirschi, T. (1990). *A general theory of crime.* Stanford: Stanford University Press.

Gottheil, E., & Gabor, T. (1984). Offender characteristics and spatial mobility. *Canadian Journal of Criminology, 26*, 267-281.

Granath, J. A. (1991). *Architecture, technology and human Factors: Design in a socio-technical context*. Göteborg: Chalmers University of Technology, Architecture Workspace design.

Grasmick, H. G., Tittle, C. R., Bursik, R. J., & Arneklev, B. J. (1993). Testing the core empirical implications of Gottfredson and Hirschi's general theory of crime. *Journal of Research in Crime and Delinquency, 30*(1), 5-29.

Green, D., Tridgell, A., & Malcom, G. A. (1990) Interactive simulation of bushfires in heterogeneous fuels. *Mathematical Computation and Modelling, 13*, 57-66.

Green, P. J., & Sibson, R. (1978). Computing Dirichlet Tessellations in the plane. *Computing Journal, 21*, 168-173.

Greenberg, S. (1986). Fear and its relationship to crime, neighborhood deterioration, and informal social control. In J. Byrne, & R. J. Sampson (Eds.), *The social ecology of crime* (pp. 47-62). New York: Springer-Verlag.

Griffin, S. P. (2002). Actors or activities? On the social construction of "white-collar crime" in the United States. *Crime, Law & Social Change, 37*, 245-276.

Griffith, D. A. (1996). Some guidelines for specifying the geographic weights matrix contained in spatial statistical models. In S. L. Arlinghaus (Ed.), *Practical handbook of spatial statistics*. Boca Raton: CRC.

Groff, E. R. (2006). *Exploring the geography of routine activity theory: A spatio-temporal test using street robbery*. Unpublished doctoral dissertation, University of Maryland. Retrieved September 1, 2007, from

Groff, E. R. (in press-a). Simulation for theory testing and experimentation: An example using routine activity theory and street robbery. *Journal of Quantitative Criminology*.

Groff, E. R. (in press-b). "Situating" simulation to model human spatio-temporal interactions: An example using crime events. *Transactions in GIS*.

Groff, E., & McEwen, T. (2006). *Exploring the spatial configuration of places related to homicide events*. Washington, D.C.

Gross, D., & Harris, C. (1974). *Fundamentals in queuing theory*. New York: Wiley & Sons.

Guerlain S., Brown D. E., & Mastrangelo, C. (2000). Intelligent decision support systems. *IEEE International Conference on Systems, Man, and Cybernetics, 3*, 1934 – 1938.

Gunderson, L., & Brown, D. (2000). Using a multi-agent model to predict both physical and cyber criminal activity. In *Proceedings of the IEEE International Conference on Systems, Man, and Cybernetics, 4*, 2338-2343.

Gupta, J. N. D., Forgionne, G. A., & Mora, T. M. (Eds). (2006). Intelligent decision-making support systems: Foundations, applications and challenges. *Decision engineering*, Springer.

Gurevich, Y. (1995). Evolving algebras 1993: Lipari guide. In E. Börger (Ed.), *Specification and validation methods* (pp. 9-36). Oxford University Press.

Gurevich, Y. (2000). Sequential abstract state machines capture sequential algorithms. *ACM Transactions on Computational Logic, 1*, 77-111.

Hagerstrand, T. (1967). *Innovation diffusion as a spatial process*. Chicago: University of Chicago Press.

Hägerstrand, T. (1970). What about people in regional science? *Papers of the Regional Science Association, 24*, 7-21.

Hägerstrand, T. (1973). The domain of human geography. In R. J. Chorley (Ed.), *Directions in geography* (pp. 67-87). London: Methuen.

Hägerstrand, T. (1975). Space, time, and human conditions. In A. Karlqvist, L. Lundqvist, & F. Snickars (Eds.), *Dynamic allocation of urban space* (pp. 3-14). Farnborough: Saxon House.

Haggett, P., Cliff, A. D., & Frey, A. (1977). *Locational analysis in human geography*. London: Edard Arnold.

Haining, R. (1983). Spatial and spatial-temporal interaction models and the analysis of patterns of diffusion. *Transactions (Institute of British Geographers), 8*, 158-186.

Hakim, S., & Buck, A. (1991). *Residential burglary: The Hakim-Buck study on suburban alarm effectiveness*. Philadelphia, PA: Temple University, Department of Economics.

Hamill, L. (2000). The introduction of new technology into the household. *Personal Technologies, 4*, 1-16.

Hann, R., & Salzman, L. (1976). *CANCOURT - I: A computerized system simulation model to support planning in court systems.* Toronto: Decision Dynamics Corporation.

Hann, R., Bailey, L., & Ross, M. (1973). *Decision making in the Canadian criminal court system: A systems analysis Volume I & II.* Toronto: Centre of Criminology, University of Toronto.

Hanson, C. E., & Wieczorek, W. F. (2002). Alcohol mortality: A comparison of spatial clustering methods. *Social Science & Medicine, 55*, 791-802.

Harper, P. (2002). A Framework for operational modelling of hospital resources. *Health Care Management Science, 5*, 165-173.

Harries, K. (1999). *Mapping crime: Principle and practice.* United States National Institute of Justice. Retrieved August 28, 2007, from http://www.ojp.usdoj.gov/nij/maps/pubs.html

Harries, R. (2001). *Criminal justice modeling.* London: Home Office Strategic Policy Team.

Harris, B. (1989). Beyond geographic information systems: Computers and the planning professional. *Journal of American Planning Association, 55*, 85-92.

Harris, B., & Batty, M. (1993). Locational models, geographic information and planning support systems. *Journal of Planning Education and Research, 12*, 184-198.

Harrison, G., Ivatts, S., & Millard, P. (2003). Mathematical modelling: How and why. *British Journal of Health Care Management, 9*, 144-150.

Harvey, D. (1969). *Explanation in geography.* London: Edward Arnold Publishers.

Hasse, J. (2004). A geospatial approach to measuring new development tracts for characteristics of sprawl. *Landscape Journal: Design, Planning and Management of the Land, 23*(1), 52-67.

Hawley, A. (1950). *Human ecology.* New York: Ronald Press Co.

Haynes, P. (1973). Reducing court delay. In Law Enforcement Assistance Administration (Ed.), *Reducing Court Delay.* Washington: U.S. Department of Justice.

Hearnden, I., & Magill, C. (2004). Decision-making by house burglars: Offenders perspectives. *Home office findings* 249. London: Home Office.

Hendrick, J. S., Howell, T. J., London, D. M., Luehrs, E. M., Saliba, M., Brown, D., et al. (2004). Webcat: The design and implementation of the web-based crime analysis toolkit. In *Proceedings of the 2004 IEEE systems and information engineering design symposium* (pp. 95-103).

Hermann, C., & Maroko, A. (2006). Crime pattern analysis: Exploring Bronx auto thefts using GIS. In J. Maantay, & J. Ziegler (Eds.), *GIS for the urban environment* (pp. 408-413). Redlands, CA: ESRI Press.

Hesseling, R. B. P. (1992). Using data on offender mobility in ecological research. *Journal of Quantitative Criminology, 8*, 95-112.

Hillier, B. (1996). *Space is the machine.* Cambridge University Press.

Hillier, B., Penn, A., Hanson, J., Grajewski, T., & Xu, J. (1993). Natural movement: Or configuration and attraction in urban pedestrian movement. *Environment and Planning B: Planning and Design, 20*, 29-66.

Hindelang, M. J., Gottfredson, M. R., & Garafalo, J. (1978). *Victims of personal crime: An empirical foundation for a theory of personal victimization.* Cambridge: Ballinger.

Hindelang, M. J., Gottfredson, M. R., & Garofalo, J. (1978). *Victims of personal crime.* Cambridge: Ballinger.

Hirschfield, A., & Bowers, K. J. (2001). The development of a social, demographic and land use profiler for areas of high crime. *British Journal of Criminology, 37*(1), 103-120.

Hirschi, T., & Gottfredson, M. (1987). Causes of white-collar crime. *Criminology, 25*(4), 949-974.

Hochmair, H. H., & Karlsson, V. (2004). Investigation of preference between the least-angle strategy and the initial segment strategy for route selection in unknown environments. In C. Freksa, M. Knauff, B. Krieg-Brückner, B. Nebel, & T. Barkowsky (Eds.), *Spatial cognition IV: LNCS 3343* (pp. 79-97). Berlin: Springer-Verlag.

Hogeweg, P., (1988) Cellular automata as a paradigm for ecological modeling. *Applied Mathematics and Computation, 27*, 81-100.

Holland, J. H., & Miller, J. H. (1991). Artificial adaptive agents in economic theory. *Learning and Adaptive Economic Behavior, 81*(2).

Hollinger, P. C., Offer, D., & Ostrov, E. (1987). An epidemiologic study of violent death, population changes, and the potential for prediction. *American Journal of Psychiatry, 144*, 215-219.

Home Office (2001a). *Crime reduction toolkit: Focus area and hotspots. Crime reduction unit.* Retrieved August 28, 2007, from www.crimereduction.gov.uk/toolkits/fa00.htm

Home Office (2003). *Crime in England and Wales: April 2002 to March 2003.* London: Home Office. Retrieved August 28, 2007, from www.homeoffice.gov.uk

Home Office (2005). *Crime mapping: Improving performance, a good practice guide for front line officers.* London: Home Office. Retrieved August 28, 2007, from http://www.jdi.ucl.ac.uk/downloads/publications/other_publications/crime_mapping_guide.pdf

Homer, J., & Hirsch, G. (2006). Systems dynamics modeling for public health: Background and opportunities. *American Journal of Public Health, 96*(3), 452-458.

Hooimeijer, P., & Oskamp, A. (1999) Advances in the microsimulation of demographic behavior. In Van Wissen L. J. G., & Dykstra P. A. (Eds.), *Population issues: An interdisciplinary focus* (The Plenum series on demographic methods and population analysis) (pp. 229-263). New York: Plenum Press.

Hopkins, L. D. (1999). Structure of a planning support system for urban development. *Environment and Planning B: Planning and Design, 26*, 81-98.

Hopkins, L. D., Kaza, N., & Pallathucheril, V. G. (2005). A data model to represent plans and regulations in urban simulation models. In D. J. Maguire, M. Batty, & M. Goodchild (Eds.), *GIS, Spatial analysis, and modeling* (pp. 173-201). Redlands, CA: ESRI Press.

Horton, F. E., & Reynolds, D. R. (1971). Action space differentials in cities. In H. McConnell & D. Yaseen (Eds.), *Perspectives in geography: Models of spatial interaction* (pp. 83-102). Dekab, IL: Northern Illinois University Press.

Houtzager, B., & Baerveldt, C. (1999). Just like normal: A social network study of the relation between petty crime and the intimacy of adolescent friendships. *Social Behavior and Personality, 27*(2), 117–192.

Howarth, P. J., (1986). Landsat digital enhancements for change detection in urban environment. *Remote Sensing of Environment, 13*, 149-160.

Hua, L., & Brown, D. E. (1998). Spatial-temporal event prediction: A new model. In *Proceedings of 1998 IEEE International Conference on Systems, Man, and Cybernetics, San Diego, California,* (pp. 2933-2937).

Hubbell, S. P. (2001). *The unified neutral theory of biodiversity and biogeography.* Princeton: Princeton University Press.

Huberman, B.A., & Glance, N. (1993). Evolutionary games and computer simulation. *Proceedings of the National Academy of Sciences, 90*, 7716-7718.

Hudson-Smith, A., & Evans, S. (2003). Virtual cities: From CAD to 3-D GIS. In P. Longley, & M. Batty (Eds.), *Advanced spatial analysis: The CASA book of GIS* (pp. 41-60). Redlands, CA: ESRI Press.

Huff, D. L. (1964). Defining and estimating a trading area. *Journal of Marketing, 28*, 34-38.

Hunter, A. J. (1985). Private, parochial, and public social orders: The problem of crime and incivility in urban communities. In G. D. Suttles & M. N. Zald (Eds.), *The challenge of social control: Citizenship and institution building in modern society* (pp. 230-242). Norwood, NJ: Ablex Publishing.

Institute for transport studies, Leeds University, United Kingdom. Micro-Simulation Tools. Retrieved August 30, 2007, from http://www.its.leeds.ac.uk/projects/smartest/links.html

Ioannidis, J. P. A. (2005). Why most published research findings are false. *PLoS Medicine, 2*(8), 696-701.

Janssen, M. A. (Ed.) (2002). *Complexity and ecosystem management: The theory and practice of multi-agent systems.* Cheltenham: Edward Elgar Publishers.

Java Universal Network/Graph Framework. Retrieved September 6, 2007, from http://jung.sourceforge.net/

Jennings, N. R., & Wooldridge, M. (Eds.). (1998). *Agent technology: Foundations, applications, and markets*. New York: Springer-Verlag.

Jensen, J. R., Rutchey, K., Koch, M. S., & Narumalani, S. (1995). Inland wetland change detection in the Everglades Water Conservation Area 2A using a time series of normalized remotely sensed data. *Photogrammetric Engineering and Remote Sensing, 61*, 199-209.

Jepson, W. H., Liggett, R. S., & Friedman, S. (2001). An integrated environment for urban simulation. In R. Brail, & R. Klosterman (Eds.), *Planning support systems: Integrating geographic information systems, models, and visualization tools* (pp. 387-404). Redlands, CA: ESRI Press.

Johnson, S. D., & Bowers, K. J. (2004). The burglary as clue to the future: The beginnings of prospective hot-spotting. *European Journal of Criminology, 1*(2), 237-255.

Johnson, S. D., & Bowers, K. J. (2004). The stability of space-time clusters of burglary. *The British Journal of Criminology, 44*(1), 55-65.

Johnson, S. D., Bernasco, W., Bowers, K. J., Elffers, H., Ratcliffe, J., Rengert, G., & Townsley, M. T. (in press). Space-time patterns of risk: A cross national assessment of residential burglary victimization. *Journal of Quantitative Criminology*.

Johnson, S. D., Bernasco, W., Bowers, K. J., Elffers, H., Ratcliffe, J., Rengert, G., & Townsley, M. T. (in press). *Near repeats: A crossnational assessment of residential burglary*.

Jung, J. (1971). *The experimenters dilemma*. New York: Harper Row.

Kahneman, D., & Tversky, A. (1979). Prospect theory: An analysis of decision under risk. *Econometrica, 47*, 263-291.

Kaysi, I., Ben-Akiva, M., & Palma, A. D. (1995). Design aspects of advanced traveler information system. *Urban traffic networks: Dynamic flow modeling and control*. Springer-Verlag.

Kaza, S., Xu, J., Marshall, B., & Chen, H. (2005). Topological analysis of criminal activity networks in multiple jurisdictions.

Kellerman, A. (1966). *Understanding and preventing violence: A public health perspective*. Washington: U.S. Government Printing Offices.

Kelling, G. L., Pate, T., Dieckman, D., & Brown, C. (1974). *The Kansas City preventive patrol experiment: A summary report*. Washington, DC: Police Foundation.

Kelly, E. D., & Becker, B. (2000). *Community planning: An introduction to the comprehensive plan*. Washington, D.C.: Island Press.

Kelton, W., Sadowski, R., & Sturrock, D. (2007). *Simulation with arena* (4th ed.). New York: McGraw-Hill, Inc.

Kennedy, L. W., & Forde, D. R. (1990). Risky lifestyles and dangerous results: Routine activities and exposure to crime. *Sociology and Social Research, 74*(4), 208-211.

Kent, J., Leitner, M., & Curtis, A. (2006). Evaluating the usefulness of functional distance measures when calibrating jouney-to-crime distance decay functions. *Computers, Environment and Urban Systems, 30*, 181-200.

Kianmehr, K., & Alhajj, R. (2006). Crime hot-spots prediction using support vector machine. In *Proceedings of 2006 IEEE International Conference on Computer Systems and Applications* (pp. 952- 959).

Kim, Y. (in press). Using spatial analysis for monitoring fraud in a public delivery program. *Social Science Computer Review*.

Klinger, D. A. (1994). Demeanor or crime? Why "hostile" citizens are more likely to be arrested. *Criminology, 32*(3), 475.

Klosterman, R. E. (1999). The what-if? Collaborative planning support system. *Environment and Planning B: Planning and Design, 26*, 393-408.

Klüver, J., & Stoica, C. (2003). Simulations of group dynamics with different models. *Journal of Artificial Societies and Social Simulation, 6*(4). Retrieved August 22, 2007, from http://jasss.soc.surrey.ac.uk/6/4/8.html

Knippenberg, C. V., & Knippenberg, A. V. (1986). Discussion on measurement of indifference band. *Transportation Research Record, 1085*, 47-49.

Knox, E. G., & Bartlett, M. S. (1964). The detection of space-time interactions. *Applied Statistics, 13*(1), 25-30.

Koch, A. J., & Meinhardt, H. (1994). Biological pattern-formation—From basic mechanisms to complex structures. *Reviews Of Modern Physics, 66*(4), 1481-1507.

Kocsis, R. N., Rayw.Cooksey, Irwin, H. J., & Allen, G. (2002). A further assessment of "circle theory" for geographic psychological profiling. *Australian and New Zealand Journal of Criminology, 35*, 43.

Koffka, K. (1967). *Principles of gestalt psychology*. Harcourt.

Kolodner, J., & Leake, D. (1996). A tutorial introduction to case-based reasoning. In D. Leake (Ed.), *Case-based reasoning: Experiences, lessons, and future directions* (pp. 31-65). AAAI Press.

Kovvali, V., Alexiadis, V., & Zhang, L. (2006). Video-based vehicle trajectory data collection. In *Proceedings of the 86th Transportation Research Board Annual Meeting in Washington, D.C.*

Kwan, M.-P. (1998). Space-time and intregral measures of individual accessibility: A comparative analysis using a point-based framework. *Geographical Analysis, 30*, 191-216.

Land, K. C., & Deane, G. (1992). On the large-sample estimation of regression models with spatial effects terms: A two-stage least squares approach. *Sociological Methodology, 22*, 221-248.

Landis, J. D. (1995). Imagining land use futures: Applying the California urban futures model. *Journal of American Planning Association, 61*(4), 438-457.

Landis, J. D. (2001). CUF, CUR II, and CURBA: A family of spatially explicit urban growth and land-use policy simulation models. In R. Brail, & R. Klosterman (Eds.), *Planning support systems: Integrating geographic information systems, models, and visualization tools* (pp. 157-200). Redlands, CA: ESRI Press.

Langendorf, R. (2001). Computer-aided visualization: possibilities for urban design, planning, and management. In R. Brail, & R. Klosterman (Eds.), *Planning support systems: Integrating geographic information systems, models, and visualization tools* (pp. 309-359). Redlands, CA: ESRI Press.

Larralde, H., Trunfio, P., Havlin, S., Stanley, H. E., & Weiss, G. H. (1992). Territory covered by n diffusing particles. *Nature, 355*(6359), 423-426.

Larson, R., Cahn, M., & Shell, M. (1993). Improving the New York City arrest-to-arraignment system. *Interfaces, 23*(2), 76-96.

LaVigne, N. G., Wartell, J. (1998). *Crime mapping case studies: Successes in the field*. Washington, D.C.: Police Executive Research Forum.

Law Reform Commission of Canada. (1994). *Trial within a reasonable time*. Ottawa, Canada: Public Works and Government Services Canada.

Law, J., & Haining, R. (2004). A Bayesian approach to modeling binary data: The case of high-intensity crime areas. *Geographical Analysis, 36*(3), 187-216.

Lee, D. B. (1973). Requiem for large-scale models. *Journal of the American Institute of Planners, 39*, 163-178.

Lenntorp, B. (1978). A time-geographic simulation model of individual activity programmes. In T. Carlstein, D. Parkes, & N. J. Thrift (Eds.), *Human geography and time geography* (pp. 162-199). New York: Halsted Press.

Levine, J., Inam, A., & Torng, G. (2005). A choice-based rationale for land use and transportation alternatives: Evidence from Boston and Atlanta. *Journal of Planning Education and Research, 24*, 317-330.

Levine, N. (2005). *CrimeStat: A spatial statistics program for the analysis of crime incident locations (v 3.0)*. Washington, D.C.: Ned Levine & Associates, Houston, TX, and the National Institute of Justice.

Levitt, S. D., & Dubner, S. J. (2005). *Freakonomics: A rogue economist explores the hidden side of everything*. New York: William Morrow.

Li, X., & Yeh, A. G. O. (1998). Principal component analysis of stacked multi-temporal images for monitoring of rapid urban expansion in the Pearl River Delta. *International Journal of Remote Sensing, 19*(8), 1501-1518.

Li, X., & Yeh, A. G. O. (2000). Modelling sustainable urban development by the integration of constrained cellular automata and GIS. *International Journal of Geographical Information Science, 14*(2), 131-152.

Li, X., & Yeh, A. G. O. (2001). Calibration of cellular automata by using neural networks for the simulation of complex urban systems. *Environment and Planning A: Environment and Planning*, 33, 1445-1462.

Lieberman, E., & Rathi, A. K. (2000). Traffic simulation. *Revised monograph on traffic flow theory*. Update and expansion of the transportation research board (TRB) (Special Report No. 165). Retrieved August 30, 2007, from http://www.tfhrc.gov/its/tft/tft.htm

Lind, B., Chilvers, M., & Weatherburn, D. (2001). *Simulating the New South Wales criminal justice system: A stock and flow approach*. Sydney, Australia: New South Wales Bureau of Crime Statistics and Research.

Liu, L. (2007, January 29 - February 2). The role of street network in crime analysis and simulation. In *Proceedings of the meeting on Crime Hot Spots: Behavioral, Computational and Mathematical Models*. Los Angeles, CA: Institute for Pure and Applied Mathematics, University of California, Los Angeles.

Liu, L., & Eck, J. E. (in press). Analyzing traffic stops in Cincinnati: A geographic perspective. *Geography Research Forum*.

Liu, L., Wang, X. , Eck, J., & Liang, J. (2005). Simulating crime events and crime patterns in a RA/CA model. In F. Wang (Ed.), *Geographic information systems and crime analysis* (pp. 198-213). Reading, PA: Idea Publishing.

Livingston, M., Stewart, A., & Palk, G. (2005). *A microsimulation model of the juvenile justice system in queensland*. In A. Zerger & R. M. Argent (Eds). In *Proceedings of the MODSIM 2005 International Congress on Modelling and Simulation*.

Lloyd, D., Haklay, M., Thurstain-Goodwin, M., & Tobon, C. (2003). Visualizing spatial structure in urban data. In P. Longley, & M. Batty (Eds.), *Advanced spatial analysis: The CASA book of GIS* (pp. 267-288). Redlands, CA: ESRI Press.

Lodha, S., & Verma, A. (1999). Animations of crime map using virtual reality modeling language. *Western Criminology Review*. Retrieved August 24, 2007, from http://wcr.sonoma.edu/v1n2/lodha.html

Loftin, C. (1986). Assaultive violence as a contagious social process. *Bulletin of the New York Academy of Medicine, 62*, 550-555.

Longley, P. A., & Batty, M. (Eds.) (2003). Advances spatial analysis: Extending GIS. *Advanced spatial analysis: The CASA book of GIS* (pp. 1-17). Redlands, CA: ESRI Press.

Longshore, D., Turner, S., & Stein, J. A. (1996). Self-control in a criminal sample: An examination of construct validity. *Criminology, 34*(2), 209-228.

Loukaitou-Sideris, A., Liggett, R., & Iseki, H. (2002). The geography of transit crime: Documentation and evaluation of crime incidence on and around the green line stations in Los Angeles. *Journal of Planning Education and Research, 22*,135-151.

Løvås, G. G. (1998). Models of wayfinding in emergency evacuations. *EuropeanJjournal of Operational Research, 105* (3), 371-389.

Lowery, J. (1998). *Getting started in simulation in healthcare*. In D. Medeiros, E. Watson, J. Carson & M. Manivannan (Eds). In *Proceedings of the 1998 Winter Simulation Conference*, Washington, D.C.

Luck, M., & d'Inverno, M. (1995). A formal framework for agency and autonomy. In V. Lesser & L. Gasser (Eds.), In *Proceedings of the first international conference on multi-agent systems (ICMAS-95), San Francisco, California*, (pp. 254-260). AAAI Press.

Luke, S., Cioffi-Revilla, C., Panait, L., & Sullivan, K. (2004). MASON: A new multi-agent simulation toolkit. In *Proceedings of the 2004 SwarmFest Workshop*. Retrieved September 5, 2007, from http://cs.gmu.edu/~eclab/projects/mason/.

Lynch, K. (1960). *The image of the city*. Cambridge: M.I.T. Press.

Lynch, M. J., McGurrin, D., & Fenwick, M. (2004). Disappearing act: The representation of corporate crime research in criminological literature. *Journal of Criminal Justice, 32*, 389-398.

Macy, M. W., & Willer, R. (2002). From factors to actors: Computational sociology and agent-based modeling. *Annual Review of Sociology, 28*, 143-166.

Maguire, D. J. (2005). Towards a GIS platform for spatial analysis and modeling. In D. J. Maguire, M. Batty, & M.

Goodchild, (Eds.), *GIS, Spatial analysis, and modeling* (pp. 19-39). Redlands, CA: ESRI Press.

Maguire, D. J., Batty, M., & Goodchild, M. F. (Eds.) (2005). GIS, spatial analysis and modeling: Current status and future prospects. *GIS, Spatial analysis, and modeling* (pp. 445-455). Redlands, CA: ESRI Press.

Maguire, M. (2002). Crime statistics: The "data explosion" and its implications. In M. Maguire, R. Morgan, & R. Reiner (Eds.), *The Oxford handbook of criminology* (3rd ed.) (pp. 322-375). Oxford: Oxford University Press.

Mahmassani, H. M., & Chang, G. L. (1985). Dynamic aspects of departure-time choice behavior in a commuting system: Theoretical framework and experimental analysis. *Transportation Research Record, 1037,* 88-101.

Mahmassani, H. S., & Tong, C. C. (1986). Availability of information and dynamics of departure time choice: Experimental investigation. *Transportation Research Record, 1085*, 33-47.

Mahmassani, H. S., & Weimann, J. (2004). Experiments with route and departure time choices of commuters under real-time information: Heuristics and adjustment processes. *Human behaviour and traffic networks.* Berlin: Springer-Verlag.

Malm, A., Pollard, N., Brantingham, P. J., Tinsley, P., Plecas, D., Brantingham, P. L., et al. (2005). *A 30 year analysis of police service delivery and costing in British Columbia.* Ottawa, Canada: "E" Division, Royal Canadian Mounted Police.

Manson, S. M. (2001). Calibration, verification, and validation (Section 2.4). In D. C. Parker, T. Berger, S. M. Manson, & W. J. M. (mng. ed. (Eds.), *Agent-based models of land-use and land-cover change.*

Marthaler, D., Bertozzi, A. L., & Schwartz, I. B. (2004). *Searches based on a priori information: The biased levy walk.* Los Angeles: UCLA Center for Applied Mathematics Report 04-50.

Martin, G. (1970). The fantastic combinations of John Conway's new solitaire game "Life." *Scientific American, 223*, 120-123.

Mataric, M. J. (1992). Integration of representation into goal-driven behavior-based robots. *IEEE Transactions on Robotics and Automation, 8*(3), 304-312.

Mataric, M. J. (1995). Issues and approaches in the design of collective autonomous agents. *Robotics and Autonomous Systems, 16*(2-4), 321-331.

Mathworks (2004). *Simulink: Simulation and model based design* (Version 6).

May, A. D. (1990). *Traffic flow fundamentals.* Englewood Cliffs, New Jersey: Prentice Hall.

Mazerolle, L., Soole, D., & Rombouts, S. (2006). Street-level drug law enforcement: A meta-analytic review. *Journal of Experimental Criminology, 2*, 409-435.

Mazerolle, L., Soole, D., & Rombouts, S. (in press). Drug law enforcement: A systematic review. *Police Quarterly.*

McAllister, W., Atchinson, J., & Jacobs, N. (1991). A simulation model of pretrial felony case processing: A queuing system analysis. *Journal of Quantitative Criminology, 7*(3), 291-314.

McFadden, D. (1980). Econometric models for probabilistic choice among products. *The Journal of Business, 53*(3), S13-S29.

McGinnis, J. (1989). Predicting police force attrition, Promotion and demographic change: A computer simulation model. *Canadian Police College Journal, 13*(2), 87-127.

McGraw-Hill Dictionary of Scientific and Technical Terms (2003). McGraw-Hill Companies, Inc.

Medhi, J. (1991). *Stochastic models in queuing theory.* San Diego, CA: Academic Press.

Meenar, M., Bari, A., & Sherry, J. (2004, August). *Growth management plan for Milford Township, PA: Suitability analysis and buildout scenarios.* Paper presented at the meeting of the ESRI International User Conference, San Diego, CA.

Mencken, F. C., & Barnett, C. (1999). Murder, nonnegligent manslaughter, and spatial autocorrelation in mid-south counties. *Journal of Quantitative Criminology, 15*(4), 407-422.

Merritt, N., Fain, T., & Turner, S. (2006). Oregon's get tough sentencing reform: A lesson in justice system adaptation. *Criminology & Public Policy, 5*(1), 5-36.

Messner, S. F., & Anselin, L. (2004). Spatial analyses of homicide with areal data. In M. F. Goodchild & D. G. Janelle

(Eds.), *Best practices in spatially integrated social science* (pp. 127-144). New York: Oxford University Press.

Messner, S. F., & Tardiff, K. (1986). *The social ecology of urban homicide: An application of the 'Routine activities approach. Criminology, 22*, 241-67.

Messner, S. F., Anselin, L., Baller, R. D., Hawkins, D. F., Deane, G., & Tolnay, S. E. (1999). The spatial patterning of county homicide rates: An application of exploratory spatial data analysis. *Journal of Quantitative Criminology, 15*(4), 423-450.

Meyer, B. (1997). *Object-orientated software construction* (2nd ed.). New York: Prentice Hall.

Miethe, T. D., & Meier, R. F. (1990). Opportunity, choice, and criminal victimization: A test of a theoretical model. *Journal of Research in Crime and Delinquency, 27*(3), 243-266.

Mikhailov, L., & Singh, M. G. (2003). Fuzzy analytic network process and its application to the development of decision support systems. *IEEE Transactions on Systems, Man and Cybernetics, Part C, 33*(1), 33-41.

Miller, E. J., Hunt, J. D., Abraham, J. E., & Salvini, P. A. (2004). Microsimulating urban systems. *Computers, Environment and Urban Systems, 28*(2004), 9-44.

Miller, E. J., Roorda, M. J., & Carrasoc, J. A. (2005). A tour-based model of travel mode choice. *Transportation, 32*, 399-422.

Miller, H. J. (1991). Modelling accessibility using space-time prism concepts within geographical information systems. *International Journal Geographical Information Systems, 5*(3), 287-301.

Miller, H. J. (2005). A measurement theory for time geography. *Geographical Analysis, 37*, 17-45.

Minderhoud, M. M., & Bovy, H. L. (2001). Extended time-to-collision measures for road traffic safety assessment. *Accident Analysis and Prevention, 33*(1), 89-97.

Minor, W., & Harry, J. (1982). Deterrent and experimental effects in perceptual deterrence research: A replication and extension. *Journal of Research in Crime and Delinquency, 19*, 190-203.

Mitchell, A. (1999). *The ESRI guide to GIS analysis: Vol. 1. Geographic patterns & relationships*. Redlands, CA: Environmental Systems Research Institute Press.

Moonesinghe, R., Khoury, M. J., & Janssens, A. C. J. W. (2007). Most published research findings are false—But a little replication goes a long way. *PLoS Medicine, 4*(2), 218-221.

Moore, T. J. (2005). Monograph No. 01: What is Australia's "drug budget"? The policy mix of illicit drug-related government spending in Australia. *DPMP monograph series*. Fitzroy: Turning Point Alcohol and Drug Centre.

Moore, T. J., Caulkins, J. P., Ritter, A., Dietze, P., Monagle, S., & Pruden, J. (2005). Monograph No. 09: Heroin markets in Australia: Current understandings and future possibilities. *DPMP monograph series*. Fitzroy: Turning Point Alcohol and Drug Centre.

Morenoff, J. D., & Sampson, R. J. (1997). Violent crime and the spatial dynamics of neighborhood transition: Chicago, 1970-1990. *Social Forces, 76*, 31-64.

Morrill, R., Gaile, G. L., & Thrall, G. I. (1988). *Spatial diffusion* (Vol. 10). Beverly Hills, CA: Sage.

Moss, S., & Edmonds, B. (2005). Sociology and simulation: Statistical and qualitative cross-validation. *The American Journal of Sociology, 110*(4), 1095-1131.

Moss, S., & Edmonds, B. (2005). Towards good social science. *Journal of Artificial Societies and Social Simulation, 8*(4). Retrieved August 22, 2007, from <http://jasss.soc.surrey.ac.uk/8/4/13.html

Mu, S. (1996). *Forecasting the need and cost: An exploration of the system dynamics of legal aid*. Unpublished doctoral dissertation, Simon Fraser University, Burnaby.

MVA (2000). *Profiling the populations available for stops and searches*. Police Research Series Paper 131. London: Home Office.

Nagin, D. S. (1998). Criminal deterrence research at the outset of the twenty-first century. In M. Tonry (Ed.), *Crime and justice: A review of research* (Vol. 23). Chicago: University of Chicago Press.

Nakanishi, M., & Cooper, L. G. (1974). Parameter estimate for multiplicative interactive choice model: Least squares approach. *Journal of Marketing Research, 11*, 303-311.

Nakanishi, M., & Cooper, L. G. (1982). Simplified estimation procedures for MCI models. *Marketing Science, 1*(3), 314-322.

Nakao, H. (2000). Multi-scaling properties of truncated levy flights. *Physics Letters A, 266*(4-6), 282-289.

Narasimha, M. A. S. (2005). Application of traffic simulation models in transportation planning. *Design and operations*. White Paper. Korve Engineering, Inc.

National Council on Crime and Delinquency (1987). *Correctional population simulation model: Model description.* San Francisco: The National Council on Crime and Delinquency.

Navarro, J., & Taylor, J. (1967). An application of systems analysis to aid in the efficient administration of justice. *Judicature, 51*(2), 47-52.

Nayar, R., & Bleuel, W. (1973). Simulation of a criminal court case processing system. In Law Enforcement Assistance Administration (Ed.), *Reducing court delay.* Washington: U.S. Department of Justice.

Neisser, U. (1978). Memory: What are the important questions? In M. M. Gruneberg, P. E., Morris, & R. N. Sykes (Eds.), *Practical aspects of memory.* London: Academic Press.

Newman, M. E. J. (2005). Power laws, Pareto distributions and Zipf's law. *Contemporary Physics, 46*(5), 323-351.

Newman, P., & Kenworthy, J. (1999). *Sustainability and cities, Overcoming automobile dependance.* Island Press.

Nijkamp, P., & Reggiani, A. (1996). Space-time synergetics in innovation diffusion: A nested network simulation approach. *Geographical Analysis, 28,* 18-37.

North, M. J., Collier, N. T., & Vos, J. R. (2006). Experiences creating three implementations of the repast agent modeling toolkit. *ACM Transactions on Modeling and Computer Simulation, 16*(1), 1-25.

Nowak, M. A., & May, R. (1992). Evolutionary games and spatial chaos. *Nature, 359,* 826-829.

O'Kane, J. B., Fisher, R. M., & Green, L. (1994). Mapping campus crime. *Security Journal, 5*(3), 172-180.

O'Sullivan, D. (2004a). Complexity science and human geography. *Transactions of the Institute of British Geographers, 29,* 282-295.

O'Sullivan, D. (2004b). Too much of the wrong kind of data: Implications for the practice of micro-scale modeling. In M. F. Goodchild & D. G. Janelle (Eds.), *Spatially integrated social science* (pp. 95-107). New York: Oxford University Press.

Oatley, G. C., & Ewart, B. W. (2003). Crimes analysis software: "Pins in maps," clustering and Bayes net prediction. *Expert Systems with Applications, 25*(4), 569-588.

Okabe, A., Boots, B., & Sugihara, K. (1992). *Spatial tessellations: Concepts and applications of Voronoi diagrams.* New York: Wiley & Sons.

OpenGL Architecture Review Board & Shreiner, D. (2004), *OpenGL(R) reference manual: The official reference document to OpenGL, Version 1.4* (4th Edition). Addison-Wesley Professional.

Ord, J. K., & Getis, A. (1995). Local spatial autocorrelation statistics: Distributional issues and an application. *Geographical Analysis, 27*(4), 286-306.

Oreskes, N., Shrader-Frechette, K., & Belitz, K. (1994). Verification, validation, and confirmation of numerical models in the earth sciences. *Science, 263*(5147), 641-646.

Osgood, D. W., Wilson, J. K., O'Malley, P. M., Bachman, J. G., & Johnston, L. D. (1996). Routine activities and individual deviant behavior. *American Sociological Review, 61*(4), 635-655.

Ostrom, T. M. (1988). Computer simulation: The third symbol system. *Journal of Experimental Psychology, 24,* 381-392.

Parker, J., & Grasmick, H. G. (1979). Linking actual and perceived certainty of punishment. *Criminology, 17,* 366-379.

Paternoster R., Saltzman, L. E., Waldo, G. P. & Chiricos, G. (1983b). Perceived risk and social control: Do sanctions really deter? *Law & Society Review 17,* 457-479.

Paternoster, R., Saltzman, L. E., Waldo, G. P. & Chiricos, G. (1983a). Estimating perceptual stability and deterrent effects: The role of perceived legal punishment in the inhibition of criminal involvement. *Journal of Criminal Law and Criminology, 74,* 270-297.

Pawson, R., & Tilley, N. (1997). *Realistic evaluation.* London: Sage.

Pease, K. (1998). *Repeat victimisation: Taking stock.* Crime Detection and Prevention Series Paper 90. London: Home Office.

Pease, K. (1998). Repeat victimisation: Taking stock. *Crime detection and prevention series, Paper 90.* London: Home Office.

Pederson, P. (1970). Innovation diffusion within and between national urban systems. *Geographical Analysis, 2,* 203-254.

Perez, P., Dray, A., Ritter, A., Dietze, P., Moore, T., & Mazerolle, L. (2003). Simdrug: A multi-agent system tackling the complexity of illicit drug markets in Australia. In N. Gilbert, N. Ferrand, D. Batten, & P. Perez (Eds.), *Complex science for a complex world. Exploring human ecosystems with agents* (pp. 193-223). Canberra Australia: ANU E Press.

Perez, P., Dray, A., Ritter, A., Dietze, P., Moore, T., & Mazerolle, L. (2006). SimDrug: Tackling the complexity of illicit drug markets. In D. Batten & P. Perez (Eds.), *Complex science for a complex world, Exploring human ecosystems with agents.* ANU E-Press.

Perkins, D., Meeks, J., & Taylor, R. (1992). The physical environment of street blocks and resident perceptions of crime and disorder: Implications for theory and measurement. *Journal of Environmental Psychology, 12,* 21-34.

Perlman, D. (2006, March 29). Scientists recreate action of '06 quake: Detailed depiction of temblor's severity. *San Francisco Chronicle.*

Pfeiffer, R., & Scheier, C. (1999). *Understanding intelligence.* Cambridge: MIT Press.

Phillips, P. D. (1980). Characteristics and typology of the journey to crime. In D. E. Georges-Abeyie & K. D. Harries (Eds.), *Crime: A spatial perspective* (pp. 167-180). New York: Columbia University Press.

Phipps, M. (1989). Dynamical behavior of cellular automata under constraints of neighborhood coherence. *Geographical Analysis, 21,* 197-215.

Piliavin, I., Gartner, R., Thornton, G., & Matsueda, L. M. (1986). Crime, deterrence and rational choice. *American Sociological Review, 51,* 101-119.

Pilkey, O. H., & Pilkey-Jarvis, L. (2007). *Useless arithmetic: Why environmental scientists can't predict the future.* New York: Columbia University Press.

Planet9 Studios Web site. (2006). Retrieved August 26, 2007, from http://www.planet9.com

Polvi, N., Looman, T., Humphries, C., & Pease, K. (1990). Repeat break-and-enter victimization: Time course and crime prevention opportunity. *Journal of Police Science and Administration, 17*(1), 8-11.

Polydoroulou, A., Ben-Akiva, M., and Kaysi, I. (1994). Influence of traffic information on drivers' route choice behavior. *Transportation Research Record, 1453,* 56-65.

Pontius, G. R., & Malanson, J. (2005). Comparison of the structure and accuracy of two land change models. *International Journal of Geographical Information Science, 19*(2), 243-265.

Pooch, U., & Wall, J. (1993). *Discrete event simulation: A practical approach.* Boca Raton: CRC Press, Inc.

Popper, K. (1959). *The logic of scientific discovery.* Hutchinson & Co.

Popper, K. R. (1972). *The logic of scientific discovery.* London: Hutchinson.

Popper, K. R. (1992). *Conjectures and refutations: The growth of scientific knowledge.* New York: Routledge.

Poyner, B., & Webb, B. (1993). What works in crime prevention: An overview of evaluations. In R. Clarke (Ed.), *Crime prevention studies* (Vol. 1). Monsey, NY: Criminal Justice Press.

Pred, A. (1967). *Behavior and location: Foundations for a geographic and dynamic location theory, Part I.* Gleerup: Lund.

Pred, A. (1996). The choreography of existence: Comments on Hagerstrand's time-geography and its usefulness. *Economic Geography, 53,* 207-221.

Provost, F. (2002). Comment on "statistical fraud detection: a review." *Statistical Science, 17*(1), 249-251.

Pushkarev, B., & Zupan, J. (1975). Urban space for pedestrians. Cambridge: MIT Press.

Putman, S., & Chan, S. (2001). The METROPILUS planning support system: Urban models and GIS. In R. Brail, & R. Klosterman (Eds.), *Planning support systems: Integrating geographic information systems, models, and visualization tools* (pp. 99-128). Redlands, CA: ESRI Press.

Pyle, G. F. (1976). Spatial and temporal aspects of crime in Cleveland, Ohio. *American Behavioral Scientist, 20*, 175-198.

Ramos-Fernandez, G., Mateos, J. L., Miramontes, O., Cocho, G., Larralde, H., & Ayala-Orozco, B. (2004). Levy walk patterns in the foraging movements of spider monkeys (ateles geoffroyi). *Behavioral Ecology And Sociobiology, 55*(3), 223-230.

Rand, A. (1986). Mobility triangles. In R. M. Figlio, S. Hakim, & G. F. Rengert (Eds.), *Metropolitan crime patterns*. Monsey, NY: Criminal Justice Press.

Ratcliffe, J. (2004). *HotSpot detective for mapInfo Helpfile* (Version 2.0).

Ratcliffe, J. H. (2001). Policing urban burglary. *Trends and issues in crime and criminal justice (No. 213).* Canberra: Australian Institute of Criminology.

Ratcliffe, J. H. (2002). Aoristic signatures and the spatio-temporal analysis of high volume crime patterns. *Journal of Quantitive Criminology, 18*(1), 23-43.

Ratcliffe, J. H. (2006). A temporal constrain theory to explain opportunity-based spatial offending. *Journal of Research in Crime and Delinquency, 43*(3), 261-291.

Ratcliffe, J. H., & McCullagh, M. J. (1998). Identifying repeat victimization with GIS. *British Journal of Criminology, 38*(4), 651-662.

Ratcliffe, J. H., & McCullagh, M. J. (1999). Hotbeds of crime and the search for spatial accuracy. *Journal of Geographical Systems,* 1, 385-398.

Ratcliffe, J., & McCullagh, M. (1998). The perception of crime hot spots: A spatial study in nottingham, U.K. In N. LaVigne, & J. Wartell (Eds.), *Crime mapping case studies: Successes in the field.* Washington, DC: Police Executive Research Forum.

Reis, D., Melo, A., Coelho, A. L. V., & Furtado, V. (2006). *GAPatrol: An evolutionary multi-agent approach for the automatic definition of hotspots and patrol routes. In* J. S. Sichman, H. Coelho, & S. Oliveira (Eds.). In *Proceedings of IBERAMIA/SBIA 2006*, Lecture Notes in Artificial Intelligence (LNAI) 4140, pp. 118-127.

Reiss, A. J., & Roth, J. (1993). *Understanding and preventing violence* (Vol. 1). Washington, D.C.: National Academy Press.

Rengert, G. (1988). The locations of facilities and crime. *Journal of Security of Administration, 11*(2), 12-16.

Rengert, G. F. (1981). Burglary in Philadelphia: A critique of opportunity structure model. In P. Brantingham & P. Brantingham (Eds.), *Environmental criminology* (pp.167-188). Beverly Hills, CA: Sage Publications.

Rengert, G. F. (1991). Burglary in Philadelphia: A critique of an opportunity structure model. In P. J. Brantingham & P. L. Brandtingham (Eds.), *Environmental criminology* (pp. 189-201). Prospect Heights, IL: Waveland Press Inc.

Rengert, G. F. (1992). The journey to crime: Conceptual foundations and policy implications. In D. J. Evans, N. R. Fyfe, & D. T. Herbert (Eds.), *Crime, policing and place: Essays in environmental criminology* (pp.109-117). London: Routlede.

Rengert, G. F., & Wasilchick, J. (2000). *Suburban burglary: A tale of two suburbs*. Springfield, IL: Charles Thomas Publishers.

Rengert, G. F., Piquero, A. R., & Jones, P. R. (1999). Distance decay reexamined. *Criminology, 37*(2), 427-445.

Rengert, G., Chakravorty, S., Bole, T., & Henderson, K. (2000). A geographic analysis of illegal drug markets. In M. Natarajan & M. Hough (Eds.), *Illegal drug markets: From research to prevention policy.* Monsey, NY: Criminal Justice Press.

Rengert, G., Piquero, A. R., & Jones, P. R. (1999). Distance decay reexamined. *Criminology, 37*, 427-445.

Reppetto, T. A. (1974). *Residential crime.* Cambridge: Ballinger.

Rhodes, W. M., & Conley, C. (1981). Crime and mobility: An empirical study. In P. J. Brantingham & P. L. Brantingham

(Eds.), *Environmental criminology*. Beverley Hills, CA: Sage Publications.

Ribarsky, W. (2006). *Symposium on the future of visualization.*, Charlotte, NC: Charlotte Visualization Center. Retrieved August 24, 2007, from http://www.viscenter.uncc.edu/symposium06/

Rice, K., & Smith, W. (2002). Socioecological models of automotive theft: Integrating routine activity and social disorganization approaches. *The Journal of Research in Crime and Delinquency, 39*(3), 304-336.

Richiardi, M., Leombruni, R., Sonnessa, M., & Saam, N. (2006). A common protocol for agent-based social simulation. *Journal of Artificial Societies and Social Simulation, 9*(1). Retrieved August 22, 2007, from http://jasss.soc.surrey.ac.uk/9/1/15.html

Riolo, R. L., Cohen, M. D., & Axelrod, R (2001). Evolution of cooperation without reciprocity. *Nature, 411*, 441-443.

Roach, J. (2006, August). Those who do big bad things also usually do little bad things: Identifying active serious offenders using offender self-selection. In *Proceedings of the 6th Annual Conference of the European Society of Criminology*, Tübingen, Germany.

Robben, H. S. J. (1991). *A behavioral simulation and documented behavior approach to income tax evasion.* Deventer: Kluwer.

Robinson, J., & Rengert, G. (2006). Illegal drug markets: The geographic perspective and crime popensity. *Western Criminology Review, 7*(1), 20-32.

Robinson, W. S. (1950). Ecological correlations and the behavior of individuals. *American Sociological Review, 15*(3), 351-357.

Robinson, W. S. (1950). Ecological correlations and the behavior of individuals. *American Sociological Review, 15*, 351-357.

Rogers, E. M. (1993). The diffusion of innovation model. In I. Masser & H. J. Onsrud (Eds.), *Diffusion and use of geographic information technologies* (pp. 9-24). Dordrecht: Kluwer.

Roncek, D. W. (1981). Dangerous places: Crime and residential environment. *Social forces*, 60(1), 74-96.

Roncek, D., & Maier, P. A. (1991). Bars, blocks and crime revisited: Linking theory of routine activities to the empiricism of hot spots. *Criminology, 29*, 725-753.

Ropella, G. E., Railsback, S. F., & Jackson, S. K. (2002). Software engineering considerations for individual-based models. *Natural Resource Modeling, 15*(1), 5-22.

Rossmo, D. K. (2000). *Geographic profiling.* Boca Raton, FL: CRC Press.

Rossmo, K. (1995). *Geographic profiling: Target patterns of serial murderers.* Unpublished doctoral thesis. Burnaby: Simon Fraser University

Rothery, R. W. (2000). Car following models. *Revised monograph on traffic flow theory.* Update and expansion of the transportation research board (TRB) (Special Report No. 165). Retrieved August 31, 2007, from http://www.tfhrc.gov/its/tft/tft.htm

Russel, S. J., & Norvig, P. (2003). *Artificial intelligence: A modern approach* (2nd ed.). Prentice Hall.

Sadowski, D., & Grabau, M. (2004). *Tips for successful practice of simulation.* In R. Ingalls, M. Rosetti, J. Smith & B. Peters (Eds). In *Proceedings of the 2004 Winter Simulation Conference*, Monterey, California.

Sagovsky, A., & Johnson, S. D. (in press). When does repeat victimisation occur? *Australian and New Zealand Journal of Criminology.*

Sampson, R. J. (1985). Neighborhood and crime: The structural determinants of personal victimization. *Journal of Research in Crime and Delinquency, 22*, 7-40.

Sampson, R. J. (1986). Crime in cities: The effects of formal and informal social control. In A. J. Reiss & M. Tonry (Eds.), *Communities and crime.* Chicago: University of Chicago Press.

Sampson, R. J. (1987). Does an intact family reduce burglary risk for its neighbors? *Sociology and Social Research, 71*, 204-207.

Sampson, R. J. (1993). Linking time and place: Dynamic contextualism and the future of criminological inquiry. *Journal of Research in Crime and Delinquency, 30*(4), 426-444.

Sampson, R. J., & Groves, W. B. (1989). Community structure and crime: Testing social-disorganization theory. *American Journal of Sociology, 94*(4).

Sampson, R. J., & Morenoff, J. D. (2004). Spatial (dis)advantage and homicide in chicago neighborhoods. In M. F. Goodchild & D. G. Janelle (Eds.), *Spatially integrated social science*. New York: Oxford University Press Inc.

Sampson, R. J., & Wilson, W. J. (1995). Race, crime and urban inequality. In J. Hagan & R.D. Peterson (Eds.), *Crime and inequlity* (pp. 37-54), Stanford University Press.

Schreckenberg, M., & Selten, R. (Eds.). (2004). Route choice model. *Human behaviour and traffic networks*. Berlin: Springer-Verlag .

Schriber, T., & Brunner, D. (2004). *Inside discrete-event simulation software: How it works and why it matters*. In R. Ingalls, M. Rosetti, J. Smith & B. Peters (Eds). In *Proceedings of the 2004 Winter Simulation Conference*, Monterey, California.

Scott, J. P (2000). *Social network analysis: A handbook*. Sage Publications.

Scott, M. S. (2000). *Problem-oriented policing: Reflections on the first 20 years*. Washington, DC: Office of Community-Oriented Policing Services, U.S Department of Justice.

Semboloni, F. (1997). An urban and regional model based on cellular automata. *Environment and Planning B: Planning and Design, 24*, 589-612.

SFU Complex Systems Modelling Group. (2006). *Modelling the demand for healthcare*. Burnaby: British Columbia Ministry of Health.

Shadish, W. R., Cook, T. D., & Campbell, D. T. (2002). *Experimental and quasi-experimental designs for generalised causal inference*. New York: Houghton Mifflin Company.

Shaw, C. R., & McKay, H. D. (1942). *Juvenile delinquency and urban areas, a study of rates of delinquents in relation to differential characteristics of local communities in American cities*. Chicago: The University of Chicago Press.

Shaw, C. R., & McKay, H. D. (1942). Juvenile Delinquency and Urban Areas. Chicago, IL: University of Chicago Press.

Sherman, L. (1990, March/April). Police crackdowns. *NIL Reports, 2-6*(2).

Sherman, L. (1992). *Policing domestic violence*. New York: Free Press.

Sherman, L. W. (1995). Hot spots of crime and criminal careers of places. In J. E. Eck & D. Weisburd (Eds.), *Crime and place, Crime Prevention Studies* (Vol. 4) (pp. 35-52). Monsey, NY: Criminal Justice Press.

Sherman, L. W., & Berk, R. A (1984). The specific deterrent effects of arrest for domestic assault. *American Sociological Review, 49*(2), 261-272.

Sherman, L. W., & Weisburd, D. (1995). General deterrent effects of police patrol in crime "hot spots": A randomized, controlled trial. *Justice Quarterly, 12*, 626-648.

Sherman, L. W., Gartin, P. R., & Buerger, M. E. (1989). Hot spots of predatory crime: Routine activities and the criminology of place. *Criminology, 27*(1), 27-55.

Shlesinger, M. F., Zaslavsky, G. M., & Klafter, J. (1993). Strange kinetics. *Nature, 363*(6424), 31-37.

Shneiderman, B. (1992, January). Tree visualization with tree-maps: 2-d space-filling approach. *ACM Transactions on Graphics, 11*(1), 92-99. Retrieved August 24, 2007, from http://doi.acm.org/10.1145/102377.115768

Silva, E. A., & Clarke, K. C. (2002). Calibration of the SLEUTH urban growth model for Lisbon and Porto, Portugal. *Computers, Environment and Urban Systems, 26*, 525-552.

Simon, H. (1982). *Models of bounded rationality*. Cambridge: MIT Press.

Simpson, D. M. (2001). Virtual reality and urban simulation in planning: A literature review and topical bibliography. *Journal of Planning Literature, 15*(3), 359-376.

Singh, K. (2005). *An abstract mathematical framework for semantic modeling and simulation of urban crime patterns*. Unpublished master's thesis, Simon Fraser University, Burnaby, Canada.

Skogan, W. (1986). Fear of crime and neighborhood change. In J. Albert, J. Reiss, & M. Tonry (Eds.), *Communities and crime* (Vol. 8, pp. 216). Chicago: University of Chicago Press.

Skogan, W. (1990). *Disorder and Decline: Crime and the Spiral of Decay in American Neighborhoods*. New York: The Free Press.

Skogan, W., & Frydl, K. (Eds). (2004). *Fairness and effectiveness in policing: The evidence*. Committee to Review Research on Police Policy and Practices, National Research Council ISBN: 0-309-52559-4,

Small, K. A. (1982). The scheduling of consumer activities: Work trips. *The American Economic Review, 72*, 467-479.

Smith, R., 1991, The application of cellular automata to the erosion of landscapes. *Earth Surface Processes and Landforms, 16*, 273-281.

Smith, S. K., & DeFrances, C. J. (1994). *Crime and Neighborhoods*.

Smith, W. R., Frazee, S. G., & Davison, E. L. (2000). Furthering the integration of routine activity and social disorganization theories: Small units of analysis and the study of street robbery as a diffusion process. *Criminology, 38*(2), 489-523.

Smith, W., Bond, J. W., & Townsley, M. (in press). Determining how journeys-to-crime vary: Measuring inter- and intra-offender crime trip distributions. In D. Weisburd, W. Bernasco & G. Bruinsma (Eds.), *Putting crime in its place: Units of analysis in spatial crime research*. New York: Springer.

Snook, B. (2004). Individual differences in distance traveled by serial burglars. *Journal of Investigative Psychology and Offender Profiling, 1*, 53-66.

Sole, R. V., & Bascompte, J. (2006). *Self-organization in complex ecosystems*. Princeton: Princeton University Press.

Sole, R. V., Bartumeus, F., & Gamarra, J. G. P. (2005). Gap percolation in rainforests. *Oikos, 110*(1), 177-185.

Sonnenfeld, J. (1972). Geography, perception and the behavioral environment. In P. W. English & R. C. Mayfield (Eds.), *Man, space and the environment* (pp. 244-251). New York: Oxford University Press.

Spelman, W. (1995). Criminal careers of public places. In J. E Eck, & D. Weisburd (Eds.), *Crime and Place. Crime Prevention Studies, Vol. 4* (pp. 1-33). Monsey, NY: Criminal Justice Press.

Stephens, D. W., & Krebs, J. R. (1986). *Foraging theory*. Princeton: Princeton University Press.

Stewart, A., Spencer, N., O'Connor, I., Palk, G., Livingston, M., & Allard, T. (2004). Juvenile justice simulation model. In *Australian Research Council Strategic Partnerships with Industry Research and Training* (Vol. August). Brisbane, Australia: Australian Research Council Strategic Partnerships with Industry Research and Training.

Stollmack, S. (1973). Predicting inmate populations from arrest, Court disposition and recidivism rates. *Journal of Research in Crime and Delinquency, 10*(2), 141-162.
Sun Microsystems (2006). *Java platform, standard edition*. Retrieved September 5, 2007, from http://java.sun.com

Sutherland, E. (1974). *Principles of criminology* (4th ed.). Philadelphia: J. B. Lippincott Company.
Zipf, G. K. (1949). Human behaviour and the principle of least-effort. Cambridge: Addison-Wesley
Sutherland, E. H. (1940). White-collar criminality. *American Sociological Review, 5*(1), 1-12.

Sutherland, E. H. (1982). White collar crime is organized crime. In M. D. Ermann & R. J. Lundman. (Eds.). *Corporate and governmental deviance: problems of organizational behavior in contemporary society* (pp. 53-62). New York: Oxford University Press.

Sutton, R. S., & Barto, A. G. (1998). *Reinforcement learning: An introduction*. Cambridge: MIT Press.

Sycara, K. P. (1998, Fall). Multiagent systems. *AI magazine*, 79-92.

Szakas, J. S., & Trefftz, C. (2006). Voronoi-diagram based heuristics for the location of mobile and unreliable service providers. In *Proceedings of the Conference on Advances in Computer Science and Technology (ACST)*. Puerto Vallarta.

Takeyama, M., & Couclelis, H. (1997). Map dynamics: Integrating cellular automata and GIS through Geo-Algebra. *International Journal of Geographical Information Science, 11*, 73-91.

Tao, R. H. (2002). Impact analysis of work zone merging behaviors on upstream traffic. In *Proceedings at the Institute of Transportation Engineers 2002 Annual Meeting.*

Tao, R. H., Wei, H., Wang, Y. H., & Sisiopiku, V. P. (2005). Modeling speed disturbance absorption following SAS chains: Integrated car-following and lane-changing scenarios. *Transportation Research Record, 1934*, 83-93.

Taylor, H. H. (2001). *The health status of the near east side community and neighborhood conditions.* Buffalo, NY: State University of New York at Buffalo, Center for Urban Studies.

Taylor, R. B. (1997). Social order and disorder of street blocks and neighborhoods: Ecology, microecology, and the systemic model of social disorganization. *Journal of Research in Crime and Delinquency, 34*(1), 113-155.

Teesson, M, Ross, J., Darke, S., Lynsky, M., Ali, R., Ritter, A., & Cooke, R. (2006). One year outcomes for heroin dependence: Findings from the Australian treatment outcome study (ATOS). *Drug and Alcohol Dependence, 83*, 174-180.

Terna, P. (1998) Simulation tools for social scientists: Building agent based models with SWARM. *Journal of Artificial Societies and Social Simulation.*

Thagard, P. (1999). *How scientists study diseases.* Princeton, NJ: Princeton University Press.

Thaler, R. (1985). Mental accounting and consumer choice. *Marketing Science, 4*, 199-214.

Thrift, N. J., & Bennett, R. R. (Eds.). (1978). *Towards the dynamic analysis of spatial systems.* London: Pion Limited.

Thrift, N. J., & Pred, A. (1981). Time-geography: A new beginning. *Progress in Human Geography, 5*(2), 277-286.

Tilley, N. (2000). Experimentation and criminal justice policies in the united kingdom. *Crime & Delinquency, 46*(2), 194-213.

Tita & Griffiths. (2005). Traveling to violence: The case for a mobility-based spatial typology of homicide. *Journal of Research in Crime and Delinquency, 42*, 275-308.

Tita, G., & Cohen, J. (2004). Measuring spatial diffusion of shots fired activity across city neighborhoods. In M. F. Goodchild, & D. G. Janelle (Eds.), *Spatially integrated social science* (pp. 171-204). New York: Oxford.

Tobler, W. R. (1979). Cellular geography. In S. Gale. & G. Olsson. (Eds.), *Philosophy in geography* (pp. 279-386). D Reidel, Dordrecht.

Tobon, C., & Haklay, M. (2003). Human-computer interaction and usability evaluation in GIScience. In P. Longley, & M. Batty (Eds.), *Advanced spatial analysis: The CASA book of GIS* (pp. 391-406). Redlands, CA: ESRI Press.

Toledo, T. Choudhry, C. F., & Ben-Akiva, M. E. (2005). Lane-changing model with explicit target lane choice. *Transportation Research Record, 1934*, 157-165.

Tomlin, C. D. (1990). *Geographic information systems and cartographic modeling.* Upper Saddle River, NJ: Prentice Hall.

Topaz, C. M., & Bertozzi, A. L. (2004). Swarming patterns in a two-dimensional kinematic model for biological groups. *Siam Journal On Applied Mathematics, 65*(1), 152-174.

Torrens, P. (2006). Simulating sprawl. *Annals of the Association of American Geographers, 96*, 248-275.

Torrens, P. M. (2003). Automata-based models of urban systems. In P. Longley, & M. Batty (Eds.), *Advanced spatial analysis: The CASA book of GIS* (pp. 61-79). Redlands, CA: ESRI Press.

Townsley, M. T., & Pease, K. (2002). How efficiently can we target prolific offenders? *International Journal of Police Science & Management, 4*(4), 323-331.

Townsley, M., Homel, R. & Chaseling, J. (2003). Infectious burglaries: A test of the near repeat hypothesis. *British Journal of Criminology, 43*, 615-633.

Townsley, M., Homel, R., & Chaseling, J. (2000). Repeat burglary victimisation: Spatial and temporal patterns. *Australian and New Zealand Journal of Criminology, 33*(1), 37-63.

Transport for London (2003). *Analysis of the transport programme to support the draft London plan.* Technical Report. Transport for London.

Treemap Project. *HCIL*, University of Maryland. Retrieved August 24, 2007, from http://www.cs.umd.edu/hcil/treemap/

Tseloni, A., & Pease, K. (2003). Repeat personal victimization: "Boosts" or "Flags"?. *British Journal of Criminology, 43*(1), 196-212.

Tufte, E. R. (1997). *Visual explanations: Images and quantities, evidence and narrative*. Cheshire, UK: Graphic Press.

Turchin, P. (1996). Fractal analyses of animal movement: A critique. *Ecology, 77*(7), 2086-2090.

Turchin, P. (1998). *Quantitative analysis of movement: Measuring and modeling population redistribution in animals and plants*. Sunderland: Sinauer Associates.

Turchin, P. (2003). *Complex population dynamics: A theoretical/empirical synthesis*. Princeton: Princeton University Press.

Turner, B. L., & Meyer, W. B. (1994). *Changes in land use and land cover: A global perspective*. New York: Cambridge University Press.

Turner, S. (1969). Delinquency and distance. In J. T. Sellin & M. E. Wolfgang (Eds.), *Delinquency: selected studies*. New York: Wiley.

U.S. Census Bureau (2002). *County business patterns*. U.S. Census Bureau. Retrieved, September 2, 2007, from http://censtats.census.gov/cbpnaic/cbpnaic.shtml

U.S. Census Bureau (Cartographer) (2000). *Census 2000: Summary tape file 1 (SF1)*

United States Department of Agriculture (2001). *WIC vendor management study 1998*. (Report No. WIC-01-WICVM).

UTMC (2000). *Review of current and future data requirements and detector technologies and the implications for UTMC*. Urban Traffic Management and Contol, Deliverable 2. Retrieved August 28, 2007, from http://www.utmc.gov.uk/research/index.htm

Van Baal, P. (2004) *Computer simulations of criminal deterrence. From public policy to local interaction to individual behaviour*. Den Haag: Boom Juridische uitgevers.

van Baal, P. (2004). *Computer simulations of criminal deterrence*. Hoofddorp, Netherlands: Boom Juridische Uitgevers.

van Baal, P. (2004). *Computer simulations of criminal deterrence: From public policy to local interaction to individual behavior*. Den Haag, Netherlands: BJU Boom Juridische uitgevers.

Vandenburgh, H. (1999). *Feeding frenzy: organizational deviance in the Texas psychiatric hospital industry*. Lanham, MD: University Press of America, Inc.

Vaugh, K., Kitamura, R., & Jovanis, P. P. (1995). Experimental analysis and modeling of advice compliance: Results from advanced traveler information system simulation experiments. *Transportation Research Record, 1485*, 18-26.

Vigne, N. G. L., & Groff, E. R. (2001). The evolution of crime mapping in the United States: from the descriptive to the analytic. In A. Hirschfield, & K. Bowers (Eds.), *Mapping and analysing crime data*. New York: Taylor & Francis.

Visher, C. A., & Roth, J. A. (1986). Participation in criminal careers. In A. Blumstein, J. Cohen, J. A. Roth, & C. A. Visher (Eds.), *Criminal careers and "Career Criminals"* (Vol. I, pp. 211-291). Washington, D.C.: National Academy Press.

Viswanathan, G. M., Afanasyev, V., Buldyrev, S. V., Murphy, E. J., Prince, P. A., & Stanley, H. E. (1996). Levy flight search patterns of wandering albatrosses. *Nature, 381*(6581), 413-415.

Viswanathan, G. M., Bartumeus, F., Buldyrev, S. V., Catalan, J., Fulco, U. L., Havlin, S., et al. (2002). Levy flight random searches in biological phenomena. *Physica A-Statistical Mechanics And Its Applications, 314*(1-4), 208-213.

Viswanathan, G. M., Buldyrev, S. V., Havlin, S., da Luz, M. G. E., Raposo, E. P., & Stanley, H. E. (1999). Optimizing the success of random searches. *Nature, 401*(6756), 911-914.

Vold, G. B., Bernard, T. J., & Snipes, J. B. (1998). *Theoretical criminology* (4th ed.). New York: Oxford University Press.

Voltz, D. (1999). *Mapping illicit drug markets*. Brisbane, Australia: Queensland Police Service.

von Neumann, J. (1949) Theory and organization of complicated automata. In A. W. Burks (Ed.), *Theory of self-reproducing automata (Part One)* (pp. 29-87). Urbana: University of Illinois Press.

Vovsha, P. (1997). The cross-nested logit model: Application to mode choice in the Tel-Aviv Metropolitan Area. *Transportation Research Record, 1607*, 6-15.

Waddell, P. (2001). Between politics and planning: UrbanSim as a decision-support system for metropolitan planning. In R. Brail, & R. Klosterman (Eds.), *Planning support systems: Integrating geographic information systems, models, and visualization tools* (pp. 201-228). Redlands, CA: ESRI Press.

Wahle, J., Neubert, L., Esser, J., & Schreckenberg, M. (2001) A cellular automaton traffic flow model for online simulation of traffic. *Parallel Computing, 27*, 719-735.

Walker, A., Kershaw, C., & Nicholas, S. (2006). Crime in England and Wales 2005/06. *Home Office Statistical Bulletin 12/06*. London: Home Office.

Walker, R. (2004). Theorizing land-cover and land-use change: The case of tropical deforestation. *International Regional Science Review, 27*(3), 247–270.

Waller, I. (1982). What reduces residential burglary – Action and research in Seattle and Toronto. In H. J. Schneider (Ed.). *Victim in international perspective*. Berlin: Walter de Gruyter.

Walmsley, D. J., & Lewis, G. J. (1993). *People and environment: Behavioral approaches in human geography*. Essex: Longman Scientific & Technical.

Walsh, W. F., & Vito, G. F. (2004). The meaning of COMSTAT: Meaning and response. *Journal of Contemporary Criminal Justice, 20*(1), 51-69.

Wang, X. (2005). *Spatial adaptive crime event simulation using the RA/CA/ABM computational laboratory*. Unpublished doctoral dissertation, University of Cincinnati, Cincinnati.

Wang, X. (2005). Spatial adaptive crime event simulation with the RA/CA/ABM computational laboratory. Unpublished doctoral dissertation. Department of Geography, University of Cincinnati.

Wang, X. (2005). Spatial adaptive crime event simulation with the RA/CA/ABM computational laboratory. Unpublished doctoral dissertation. Department of Geography, University of Cincinnati.

Wang, X., Liu, L., & Eck, J. (2004). *A spatial dynamic simulation of crime using Agent-based modeling*. Paper presented at the Association of American Geographers, Philadelphia, PA.

Ward, D. P., Murray, A. T., & Phinn, S. R. (2000). A stochastically constrained cellular model of urban growth. *Computers, Environment and Urban Systems, 24*, 539-558.

Warner, B. D., & Pierce, G. L. (1993). Reexamining social disorganization theory using calls to the police as a measure of crime. *Criminology, 31*(4), 493-517.

Warren, J., Reboussin, R., Hazelwood, R. R., Cummings, A., Gibbs, N., & Trumbetta, S. (1998). Crime scene and distance correlates of serial rape. *Journal of Quantitative Criminology, 14*, 35-59.

Webber, M. (1972). *The impact of uncertainty on location*. Cambridge: MIT Press.

Weber, J., & Kwan, M.-P. (2002). Bringing time back in: A study on the influence of travel time variations and facility opening hours on individual accessibility. *The Professional Geographer, 54*, 226-240.

Weber, J., & Kwan, M.-P. (2003). Evaluating the effects of geographic contexts on individual accessibility: A multilevel approach. *Urban Geography, 24*(8), 647-671.

Webley, P., Robben, H. S. J., Elffers, H., & Hessing, D. J. (1991) *Tax evasion: An experimental approach*. European Monographs on Social Psychology, Cambridge: Cambridge University Press.

Webster, C. J., & Wu, F. (1999a). Regulation, land use mix and urban performance. Part 1: Theory. *Environment and Planning A: Environment and Planning, 31*, 1433-1442.

Webster, C. J., & Wu, F. (1999b). Regulation, land use mix and urban performance. Part 2: Simulation. *Environment and Planning A: Environment and Planning, 31*, 1529-1545.

Wegener, M. (2005). Urban land-use transportation models. In R. Brail, & R. Klosterman (Eds.), *Planning support systems: Integrating geographic information systems, models, and visualization tools* (pp. 203-220). Redlands, CA: ESRI Press.

Wei, H, Lee, J., Li, Q., & Li, C. (2000). Observation-based lane-vehicle-assignment hierarchy: Microscopic simulation on an urban street network. *Transportation Research Record, 1710*, 96-103.

Wei, H. (1999). Observed lane-choice and lane-changing behaviors on an urban street network using video-capture-based approach and suggested structures of their models. Unpublsihed doctoral dissertation, University of Kansas.

Wei, H., Meyer, E., & Lee, J. (2001). Models for route-choice reflecting the use of travel information in a vehicle-based microscopic simulation system. In *Proceedings of the 80th Transportation Research Board Annual Meeting in Washington, D.C.*

Wei, H., Meyer, E., Feng, C., & Lee, J. (2002). Characterizing lane-choice behavior to build rules as part of lane-based traffic micro-simulation hierarchy. In *Proceedings of the 81st Transportation Research Board Annual Meeting,* Washington, D.C.

Wei, H., Meyer, E., Lee, J., & Feng, C. E. (2000). Characterizing and modeling observed lane-changing behavior for lane-vehicle-based microscopic simulation on an urban street network. *Transportation Research Record, 1710* , 104-113.

Wei, H., Meyer, E., Lee, J., & Feng, C. E. (2005). Video-capture-based approach to extract multiple vehicular trajectory data for traffic modeling. *ASCE Journal of Transportation Engineering, 131*(7), 496-505.

Weick, K. E. (1979*). The social psychology of organizing* (2nd ed.). New York, NY: McGraw-Hill, Inc.

Weisburd, & Eck, J. (2004). What can police do to reduce crime, disorder and fear? *The ANNALS of the American Academy of Political and Social Science, 593*, 42-65

Weisburd, D. L. (2002). From criminals to criminal contexts: Reorienting crime prevention. In E. Waring & D. Weisburd (Eds.), *Crime & social organization* (Vol. 10, pp. 197-216). New Brunswick, NJ: Transactions Publishers.

Weisburd, D. L., Lum, C., & Yang, S.-M. (2004). *The criminal careers of places: A longitudinal study.* Washington, D.C.: US Department of Justice, National Institute of Justice.

Weisburd, D., & Eck, J. E. (2004). What can police do to reduce crime, disorder and fear? *The ANNALS of the American Academy of Political and Social Science, 593,* 43-65.

Weisburd, D., & Green, L. (1995). Policing drug hotspots: Findings from the Jersey City DMA experiment. *Justice Quarterly, 12* (4), 711-735.

Weisburd, D., & McEwen, T. (Eds.) (1997). *Crime mapping and crime prevention.* Monsey, NY: Criminal Justice Press.

Weiss, G. (Ed.) (1999). *Multiagent systems – A modern approach to distributed artificial intelligence.* Cambridge: MIT Press.

Wellsmith, M., & Guille, H. (2005). Fixed penalty notices as a means of offender selection. *International Journal of Police Science and Management, 7*(1).

Werker, C., & Brenner, T. (2004). Empirical calibration of simulation models (Papers on economics and evolution No. 0410). Jena: Max Planck Institute of Economics.

What If Web site. (2006). Retrieved August 26, 2007, from http://www.what-if-pss.com

Wheeler, S., Weisburd, D., & Bode, N. (1982). Sentencing the white-collar offender: Rhetoric and reality. *American Sociological Review, 47*(5), 641-659.

White, C. R. (1932). The relation of felonies to environmental factors in Indianapolis. *Social Forces, 10,* 498-509.

White, R., & Engelen, G. (1992). *Cellular dynamics and GIS: Modelling spatial complexity.* Working Paper 9264, Research Institute for Knowledge Systems, Maastricht, The Netherlands.

White, R., & Engelen, G. (1993). Cellular automata and fractal urban form: A cellular modelling approach to the evolution of urban land-use patterns. *Environment and Planning A: Environment and Planning, 25,* 1175-1199.

White, R., & Engelen, G. (1993). Cellular automata and fractal urban form: a cellular modelling approach to the evolution of urban land-use patterns. *Environment and Planning A, 25,* 1175-1199.

White, R., & Engelen, G. (1997). Cellular automata as the basis of integrated dynamic regional modelling. *Environment and Planning B: Planning and Design, 24,* 235-246.

White, R., Engelen, G., & Uijee, I. (1997). The use of constrained cellular automata for high-resolution modeling of urban land-use dynamics. *Environment and Planning B: Planning and Design, 24,* 323-343.

Wiles, P., & Costello, A. (2000). *The 'road to nowhere': The evidence for travelling criminals.* London: Home Office.

Wiles, P., & Costello, A. (2000). The "Road to Nowhere": The evidence for traveling criminals. *Home Office research study No. 207.* London: Home Office Research.

Wilhelm, W. K. (2004). The fraud management lifecycle theory: A holistic approach to fraud management. *Journal ofEconomic Crime Management, 2*(2). Retrieved September 5, 2007, from http://www.utica.edu/academic/institutes/ecii/jecm/

Williamson, D., Mclafferty, S., McGuire Philip, G., Ross, T. A., Mollenkopf, J. H., Goldsmith, V., & Quinn, S. (2001). Tools in the spatial analysis of crime. In A. Hirschfield & K. Bowers (Eds.), *Mapping and analysing crime data: Lessons from research and rractice* (pp. 187-203). London: Taylor & Francis.

Willumsen, L. G., & Ortúzar, J. de D. (1994). *Modeling transport.* Sussex, England: John Wiley and Sons Ltd.

Wilson, J. Q., & Herrnstein, R. J. (1985). *Crime and human nature.* New York: Simon and Schuster.

Wilson, W. J. (1987). *The truly disadvantaged: The inner city, the underclass, and public policy.* Chicago: University of Chicago Press.

Winoto, P. (2002). *A simulation of the market for offenses in multiagent systems: Is zero crime rates attainable?* In *Proceedings of the Multi-Agent-Based Simulation, Third International Workshop*, Bologna, Italy.

Wolfram, S. (1984). Cellular automata as models of complexity. *Nature, 31*(4), 419-424.

Wolfram, S. (1986). *Theory and applications of cellular automata.* Singapore: World Scientific.

Wolman, M. G., & Fournier, F. G. A. (Eds.) (1987). *Land transformation in agriculture.* Chichester, UK: John Wiley and Sons.

Wooldridge, M. (2002a). Intelligent agents: The key concepts. In M. Luck, V. Marik, O. Stepankova, & R. Trappl (Eds.), *Multi-agent systems and applications II* (pp.3-43). Springer.

Wooldridge, M. (2002b). *An introduction to multiagent systems.* John Wiley and Sons Ltd.

Wooldridge, M., & Jennings, N. R. (1995). Intelligent agents: Theory and practice. *The Knowledge Engineering Review, 10*(2), 115-152.

Wortley, R. (2001). A classification of techniques for controlling situational precipitators of crime. *Security Journal, 14*, 63-82.

Wright R. T., & Decker S. H. (1997). *Armed robbers in action: Stickups and street culture.* Boston: Northeastern University Press.

Wright, R., & Decker, S. H. (1994). Choosing the target. *Burglars on the job: Streetlife and residential break-ins.* Boston: Northeastern University Press.

Wu, F. (1998). An experiment on the general poly-centricity of urban growth in a cellular automatic city. *Environment and Planning B: Planning and Design, 25*, 103-126.

Wu, F. (1999). GIS-based simulation as an exploratory analysis for space-time processes. *Journal of Geographical Systems, 1*, 199-218.

Wu, F. (2000). A parameterized urban cellular model combining spontaneous and self-organizing growth. In P. Atkinson & D. Martin. (Eds.), *GIS and geo-computation* (pp. 73-85). New York: Taylor and Francis.

Wu, F. (2002). Calibration of stochastic cellular automata: the application to rural-urban land conversions. *International Journal of Geographical Information Sciences, 16*(8), 795-818.

Wu, F., & Webster, C. J. (1998). Simulation of land development through the integration of cellular automata and multi-criteria evaluation. *Environment and Planning B: Planning and Design, 25*,103-126.

Xue, Y., & Brown, D. E. (2003). A decision model for spatial site selection by criminals: A foundation for law enforcement decision support. *IEEE Transactions on Systems, Man and Cybernetics, Part C, 33*(1), 78-85.

Yeh, A. G. (2005). The integration of case-based reasoning and GIS in a planning support system. In D. J. Maguire, M. Batty, & M. Goodchild (Eds.), *GIS, Spatial analysis, and modeling* (pp. 289-314). Redlands, CA: ESRI Press.

Yeh, A. G. O., & Li, X. (2006). Errors and uncertainties in urban cellular automata. *Computers, Environment and Urban Systems, 30*(1), 10-28.

Yeh, A. G. O., & X. Li. (2001). A constrained CA model for the simulation and planning of sustainable urban forms using GIS. *Environment and Planning B: Planning and Design, 28*, 733-753.

York, D. (2007). *Sandia computer simulation monitors traffic in contraband nuclear material.* Retrieved August 24, 2007, from http://www.sciencedaily.com/releases/2007/01/070117134034.htm

Yuste, S. B., & Acedo, L. (2000). Number of distinct sites visited by n random walkers on a euclidean lattice. *Physical Review E, 61*(3), 2340-2347.

Zhang, Y. L., Owen, L. E., & Clark, J. (1998). A multi-regime approach for microscopic traffic simulation. In *Proceedings of the 77th Transportation Research Board Annual Meeting in Washington, D.C.*

About the Contributors

Lin Liu is professor of geography at the University of Cincinnati. His main area of expertise is geographic information science (GIS) and its applications to urban-economic problems. He became interested in crime analysis and simulation in year 2000. Dr. Liu is a former president of the Association of the Chinese Professionals in GIS—Abroad. He currently serves in the advisory panel of the Geography and Regional Science program at the National Science Foundation. Dr. Liu received his BS and MS degrees from Peking University and his PhD in Geography from the Ohio State University.

John Eck is professor of criminal justice at the University of Cincinnati. He has written extensively on police effectiveness, drug markets, crime patterns, and crime prevention. He is an individual affiliate of the Center for Problem-Oriented Policing and was a member of the National Academy of Sciences Committee to Review Research on Police Policy and Practices. Dr. Eck received his BS and MS degrees from the University of Michigan and his PhD in Criminology from the University of Maryland. Before earning his PhD, Eck directed research for the Police Executive Research Forum, a police research organization in Washington, D.C.

* * * * *

Azadeh Alimadad completed her BS in Mathematics in Iran and holds a MS in Biostatistics from Carleton University. She is a PhD student in health modeling at SFU and is a member of the Complex Systems Modelling Group in the Center for Interdisciplinary Research in the Mathematical and Computational Sciences (IRMACS) at Simon Fraser University. She is focused on applying epidemiological compartmental models to problems both in epidemiology and other fields.

Mairon Belchior is an undergraduate student studying Computer Science at the University of Fortaleza. His research interests include Artificial Intelligence, Multi-Agents Systems, Genetic Algorithms and Swarm Intelligence. He had a scholarship from CNPQ (National Council for Scientific and Technological Development) in 2005 and 2006. Currently, he is an exchange student at Ball State University.

Daniel Birks is a Research Fellow at the UCL Jill Dando Institute of Crime Science. He has worked on numerous crime prevention research projects in conjunction with the Home Office and several police forces in the UK. His research interests include the development of innovative crime analysis and decision support techniques and tools. In particular, prospective models of crime, the application of simulation techniques within criminology, the study of offender predation patterns, and the use of data-mining in crime analysis.

Peter Borwein holds a Burnaby Mountain Chair in Mathematics at SFU and is the Executive Director of the Center for Interdisciplinary Research in the Mathematical and Computational Sciences (IRMACS). He is the author of 6 books and over 150 research articles. His research interests span Diophantine and computational number theory, classical analysis, and symbolic computation. An award-winning mathematician, he leads three major initiatives within the national mathematics groups, including MITACS, PIMS and IRMACS. He has been involved in a number of large-scale computational number theory and combinatorial problems. The highly successful CFI-funded IRMACS Centre is based on a unique model for interdisciplinary research. It builds on a core cluster of mathematical and computational expertise to forge multidisciplinary collaborations within the sciences.

P. Jeffrey Brantingham is a Professor of Anthropology at the University of California, Los Angeles. He studies the evolution of human foraging adaptations and conducts fieldwork in China, Mongolia, and Tibet. Mathematical and simulation modeling have become an increasingly important part of Brantingham's work on understanding human foraging adaptations. His work on crime is based on the premise that criminal offenders are modern day hunter-gatherers and that many of the mathematical and simulation techniques that he uses for studying the archaeological record are equally applicable to the study of crime pattern formation.

Patricia Brantingham is RCMP University Professor of Computational Criminology, Director of the Institute for Canadian Urban Research Studies (ICURS) and Co-Director of the ICURS Laboratory at Simon Fraser University. A mathematician and urban planner by training, she is the author or editor of two-dozen books and scientific monographs and more than 100 articles and scientific papers. Dr. Brantingham is the leader of an international collaboration in computational criminology that links together a dozen university research laboratories around the world in the study of crime patterns using modern computational power. Recent research has looked at the patterns of crime at shopping malls and on transit systems, the distribution of crimes on road networks, and the location of crime in complex urban ecologies. She has been particularly interested in the use of intensive simulation techniques in modeling crime patterns and criminal justice system behavior.

Paul Brantingham is RCMP University Professor of Crime Analysis and Co-Director of the ICURS Laboratory at Simon Fraser University. A lawyer and criminologist by training, he is author or editor of more than 20 books and scientific monographs, and more than 100 articles and scientific papers. Professor Brantingham has been involved in crime analysis and crime prevention research for more than 20 years. He is one of the co-developers of the primary/secondary/tertiary model of crime prevention now commonly used by criminologists and crime prevention specialists. He is well known for work on offender decision making and on the ways in which the physical environment shapes both the incidence and the fear of crime. Recent research has included study of the geography of persistent offending and of displacement phenomena and study of the complexity and diversity of crime patterns.

Alex Breuer is a graduate student in Computer Science at Indiana University, where he works at the Open Systems Lab. He received his B.S. in Computer and Information Science from the University of Delaware in 2002, and M.S. from Indiana University in 2007. His research interests focus on scientific computing and visualization.

Virginia Carver is a PhD candidate in Criminology and undergraduate lecturer at the University of Texas at Dallas (USA). Currently she is researching the relationship between drug use, drug arrest, and employment. Her professional presentations include the annual meetings of the American Society of Criminology and the Academy of Criminal Justice Sciences.

Spencer Chainey is Director of Geographical Information Science at the Jill Dando Institute of Crime Science, University College London. Much of his work is focused towards developing the utility of crime mapping to aid intelligence development and information sharing, including the development of techniques and approaches that are utilized by police forces and community safety partnerships. His work has influenced national policy, and has contributed to policing and crime reduction developments in the USA, Canada, Brazil, Australia, and New Zealand.

Bryan Chastain is a PhD candidate in Geospatial Information Sciences at the University of Texas at Dallas. Bryan has a background in computer science, with a BS from Baylor University in Waco, Texas, as well as in geography, with a M.A. from The Ohio State University in Columbus, Ohio. His current research focuses on applying agent-based modeling as a tool for spatial analysis and simulation within GIS. He has presented research at the annual meeting of the Association of American Geographers.

André L. V. Coelho was born on June 11, 1974, in Fortaleza, Ceará, Brazil. He received the BS degree in Computer Engineering in 1996, and earned the MS, and PhD degrees in Electrical Engineering (specialization in Computer Engineering) in 1998 and 2004, respectively, all from the State University of Campinas (Unicamp), Brazil. Currently, he is an adjunct professor affiliated with the Graduate Program in Applied Informatics at the University of Fortaleza (Unifor), Brazil, conducting research in computational intelligence, metaheuristics, multiagent systems, machine learning, and data mining. He has a record of published papers on these themes. He is a member of IEEE.

Kevin M. Curtin is an Assistant Professor of Geographic Information Science (GIS) at the University of Texas at Dallas. He specializes in network GIS, optimal location science, and transportation data modeling, and teaches courses in world regional geography, introductory GIS, network GIS, GIS theories, and transportation and logistics. He is the author of book chapters and peer reviewed journal articles in the fields of geography, location science, and transportation science. He works extensively with academic researchers, government agencies, and private businesses to provide geographically informed data analyses.

Vahid Dabbaghian-Abdoly received his PhD from Carleton University in computational algebra. His research interests include computational mathematics and mathematical modeling. He has developed a package for the computational algebra system GAP and worked on a number of joint projects with Maplesoft. He is currently a member of the Complex Systems Modelling Group in the Center for Interdisciplinary Research in the Mathematical and Computational Sciences (IRMACS) at Simon Fraser University.

Jake Desyllas is Director and a founding partner of Intelligent Space and directs the urban and public space division of the practice. He is responsible for the development of Intelligent Space's pioneering software for modeling pedestrian flows. He was an independent cross-party expert advisor to the 2002

UK parliamentary debate on Walking in Towns and Cities, and has led consulting and research projects on pedestrian movement and space use in the UK, Germany, Australia, and Chile.

Susan Donkin is a Research Fellow at the UCL Jill Dando Institute of Crime Science. After graduating from the University of Toronto, she worked in crime prevention and legal psychiatry, acquiring substantial experience in the development and delivery of both academic criminological research and practical crime prevention programs. Her research interests include the application of computer simulation in criminology, offender adaptation, political violence and terrorism, as well as alternative forms of justice.

Anne Dray is a Research Fellow at the Australian National University. An agronomist by training, her current research focuses on exploring complex systems using agent-based modeling. Relevant stakeholders and policy makers are involved in the early stages of models development through participatory modeling. She has applied this approach in diverse contexts including equitable water allocation in Tarawa (Republic of Kiribati), coral reef conservation in Mexico and groundwater salinity control in Western Australia. In the field of illicit drugs, she has developed SimDrug, an agent-based model dedicated to explore illicit drug markets in Australia.

Henk Elffers graduated in mathematical statistics at the University of Amsterdam and got his Ph.D. in psychology of law at Erasmus University Rotterdam, on a thesis on income tax evasion. He held various research appointments in Amsterdam (mathematics), Utrecht (geography), Rotterdam (law and psychology) and is presently senior-researcher at the Netherlands Institute for the Study of Crime and Law Enforcement NSCR (Leiden, the Netherlands), and professor of Psychology and Law at Antwerp University (Belgium). His research interest comprise spatial aspects of crime, rational choice theory of rule compliance, simulation methods in criminology, statistics in the courtroom, relationship between judges and the general public, and measurement in criminology.

Ron Ferguson completed a PhD in Mathematics at the University of British Columbia in the field of computational algebra. Dr. Ferguson has a broad research background in mathematics, including pure and computational problems. For the last two years he has been a member of the Complex Systems Modelling Group in the Center for Interdisciplinary Research in the Mathematical and Computational Sciences (IRMACS) at Simon Fraser University where he has focused on system dynamics and analytic methods.

Ellen Fowler holds a Master of Science in Operations Research from the University of British Columbia and a Bachelor of Arts in Economics from Simon Fraser University. In addition, she is a lecturer at the Business Schools of both alma maters and an O.R. consultant. Her main interests lie in mathematical programming, discrete event simulation and optimization. Currently, she is a member of the Complex Systems Modelling Group in the Center for Interdisciplinary Research in the Mathematical and Computational Sciences (IRMACS) at Simon Fraser University.

Vasco Furtado is professor of computer science at University of Fortaleza (UNIFOR), Brazil, where he also leads a team of researchers in the Knowledge Engineering group that studies agent-based simulation and agent's explanation on the Web. He has coordinated and developed research and development projects on the law enforcement domain. Furtado holds a PhD in Informatique from the University of Aix-Marseille III, France. He has just finished his sabbatical year in the Knowledge Systems Laboratory at Stanford University in 2006–07. Further information about publications and projects is available at http://www.mentores.com.br/vasco/index.html.

Amir Ghaseminejad, a faculty member of School of Business at Capilano College and Computer Science and Information Systems Department at Langara College, holds a MS in Computer Hardware Engineering from Sharif University. His research interests include technology and society interrelationships, systems analysis, databases and information management. He has many years of experience in design, development and management of Software Projects and is an expert in Internet technologies, operating systems and databases. His current research is focused on the application of hybrid models combining process control and discrete event simulation in modeling complex systems and the effect of modern technologies on democratic decision-making. Currently, he is a member of the Complex Systems Modelling Group in the Center for Interdisciplinary Research in the Mathematical and Computational Sciences (IRMACS) at Simon Fraser University.

Christopher Giles completed a BA in criminology from the University of Manitoba and holds a Master of Arts degree in criminology from Simon Fraser University. At present, Mr. Giles is completing his Doctor of Philosophy degree in Criminology at Simon Fraser University. He is a researcher in the Institute for Canadian Urban Research Studies, where he is involved in modeling and simulation of criminal justice systems. His areas of interest include criminal careers, research methodology in criminology and mathematical modeling and simulation of criminal justice systems.

Uwe Glässer is Associate Professor and Director of Computing Science and Director of the Software Technology Laboratory at Simon Fraser University. He is Co-Director of the ASM Research Center, a virtual research center with research groups all over Europe and North America. In his research on formal aspects of software technology and applications of formal methods, he regularly collaborates with industry and public agencies. He is a coauthor of a widely used ITU-T industry standard and known for his work on semantic foundations of system design languages. More recent work focuses on intelligent decision support and computational models of security processes.

Elizabeth Groff has spent the last 15 years applying spatial analysis to the study of crime-related issues at both the local and national levels. As GIS Coordinator, she institutionalized the use of geographic information systems (GIS) at the Charlotte-Mecklenburg Police Department. As a Social Science Analyst at the National Institute of Justice's Crime Mapping Research Center she promoted the analytic use of mapping in criminal justice agencies. As a Senior Research Associate at the Institute for Law and Justice she began a micro level longitudinal study of crime in Seattle, Washington; started testing the use of simulation models for understanding street robbery; and completed an examination of the impacts of technology acquisitions in law enforcement agencies. She is currently an Assistant Professor in the Department of Criminal Justice at Temple University. Her research interests include: crime and place; modeling geographical influences on human activity; crime prevention; and policing.

Karen L. Hayslett-McCall is currently an Assistant Professor of Criminology and GIS at the University of Texas at Dallas. She received her PhD from The Pennsylvania State University in 2002. While at Penn State, she worked as a GIS Analyst in the Population Research Institute. Dr. Hayslett-McCall's research interests include neighborhood effects on crime, the journey to crime, policing, criminological theory, the refinement of contextual definitions through the application of neighborhood infrastructure data, and the integration of multilevel models and spatial statistics with GIS. She has presented research at the annual meetings of the American Society of Criminology, Academy of Criminal Justice Sciences, and she has been an invited speaker on several occasions at the Crime Mapping Research Conference, and is an invited speaker at the American Sociological Meetings (Fall 2007).

Josh Hursey is a PhD bound graduate student at Indiana University. He received his BA in Computer Science from Earlham College in the spring of 2003. He received his MS degree in Computer Science from Indiana University in the spring of 2006. He is currently working in the Open Systems Laboratory on the Open MPI project under the direction of Dr. Andrew Lumsdaine. His primary research interests focus on parallel and distributed systems, scalable fault tolerance techniques, and scientific computing.

Piper Jackson is a MS candidate in Computing Science at Simon Fraser University. He previously completed a degree in Asian Studies and Communications at McGill University. He has spent several years living in Japan, and can speak Japanese fluently. Academically, he is interested in software design: in particular, the topics of simulation and abstraction. His research focuses on modeling and simulation of criminal target selection behavior.

Eric Jefferis is an Assistant Professor in the Department of Justice Studies at Kent State University. He is also a Research Fellow at Kent State University's Institute for the Study and Prevention of Violence (ISPV). Dr. Jefferis' research interests include the spatio-temporal analysis of crime; hot spotting methods; factors that influence citizens' perceptions of the police; and the effectiveness of new policing strategies and technologies. Prior to joining the ISPV, he was a Social Science Analyst at the National Institute of Justice. He received his Ph.D. in Criminal Justice from the University of Cincinnati.

Shane D. Johnson is currently a senior lecturer (Associate Professor) at the UCL Jill Dando Institute of Crime Science. He has a particular interest in the spatial and temporal distribution of crime, crime forecasting and design against crime. He has conducted work for a variety of sponsors including the Arts and Humanities Research Council (AHRC) and the Home Office, and currently coordinates an international research network funded by the British Academy. He has published over 40 original research papers within the fields of criminology and forensic psychology in journals including the Journal of Quantitative Criminology and Criminology and Public Policy.

Youngho Kim is a geographer who is interested in space-time surveillance, spatial statistics, econometrics, and GIS with applications to criminology and epidemiology modeling. Kim, as a PhD student in the OSU geography department, has taught several courses such as World Regional Geography, GIS, Cartography, and Spatial Statistics as an instructor or TA. He received a research development award by the Criminal Justice Research Center in the Ohio State University in 2003. Currently, Kim has been an active member of the Association of American Geographer since 2002 and has participated in the SAM (Spatial Analysis and Modeling) paper competition in 2007.

Yushim Kim is a postPhD researcher at the John Glenn School of Public Affairs at the Ohio State University. Her research interests include decision-making and policy analysis focusing on health/welfare programs and public management. She has utilized spatial analysis and social simulation techniques for crime in a public service delivery program. Email: kim.1031@osu.edu.

Bryan Kinney is Assistant Professor of Criminology and Co-Director of the Institute for Canadian Urban Research Studies (ICURS) Laboratory at Simon Fraser University. His recent publications include collaborative projects with researchers from computing and geographic information sciences in the development of computational methods for criminology. Dr. Kinney's primary research area focuses on understanding the distribution of crime and the movement of agents within the criminal justice system. He is currently overseeing the development of an interoperable crime information warehouse for criminal justice data in the province of British Columbia.

Jenny Li holds a BS in Mathematics from Simon Fraser University. Currently, she is a student in the applied mathematics program at Simon Fraser University. Ms. Li is a member of the Complex Systems Modelling Group in the Center for Interdisciplinary Research in the Mathematical and Computational Sciences (IRMACS) at Simon Fraser University where she works on discrete event simulation models in various applied fields.

Xia Li is professor of the School of Geography and planning, Sun Yat-sen University. His major research interests include remote sensing, geographical information systems, land use changes, and urban simulation. His papers have been widely published in known international journals, such as International Journal of Geographical Information Science, Remote Sensing of Environment, Photogrammetric Engineering & Remote Sensing, International Journal of Remote Sensing, Environment and Planning A, Environment and Planning B, Journal of Environmental Management, Landscape and Urban Planning.

Lorraine Mazerolle is a Professor in the School of Criminology and Criminal Justice at Griffith University and the Deputy Director of the Key Centre for Ethics, Law, Governance and Justice. She received her Ph.D. from Rutgers University, New Jersey in 1993 and spent an additional seven years as an academic in the USA (at Northeastern University and the University of Cincinnati). She is the recipient of numerous US and Australian national competitive research grants on topics such as problem-oriented policing, police technologies (e.g., crime mapping, gunshot detection systems, 3-1-1 call systems), community crime control, civil remedies, street-level drug enforcement, and policing public housing sites. In 2003, Professor Mazerolle was admitted as a Fellow of the Academy of Experimental Criminologists and now serves as the Vice President of the Academy. She also serves on the Board of Studies for the Australian Institute for Police Management, on the Capital Cities Lord Mayors Drug Advisory Board and as an Associate Editor of the Journal of Experimental Criminology. Professor Mazerolle is the lead author (with Janet Ransley) of Third Party Policing (Cambridge University Press), sole author of Policing Places with Drug Problems (Sage Publications) and a co-editor, with Jan Roehl, of Civil Remedies and Crime Prevention (Criminal Justice Press). She has written many scholarly articles on policing, drug law enforcement, displacement of crime, and crime prevention.

Mahbubur R. Meenar is the Senior GIS Design Specialist of the Center for Sustainable Communities and Adjunct Assistant Professor of the Community and Regional Planning Department at Temple University. Mr. Meenar received his MS degree in Urban Planning from the State University of New York at Buffalo and a BS degree in Architecture from Bangladesh University of Engineering and Technology. His research interests include environmental modeling, 3-D GIS visualization, sustainable development, and GIS applications in disaster management and environmental planning.

Adriano Melo is a MS student at the Master of Applied Informatics at the University of Fortaleza (UNIFOR/MIA). His research interests include Multi-Agents Systems, Genetic Algorithms and Swarm Intelligence. He majored Computer Science at the University of Fortaleza in 2003 and received a diploma of Specialist in Information Technology from the Federal University of Ceará in 2005.

Ronaldo Menezes is associate professor in computer science at Florida Institute of Technology. He received his BS in computer science in 1992 from the University of Fortaleza, Brazil. He was awarded MS (by research) in Computer Science in the field of Parallel Computing Models in 1995 from the State University of Campinas, Brazil. In 2000 he was awarded his PhD in computer science at the University of York, UK. He is a member of many organizations such as IEEE, ACM, SBC and AWC. He is currently member of the elected group of officials of the ACM SIGAPP (Special Interest Group in Applied Computing). He has published more than 40 papers in international events and journals. He is a program committee member of many conferences and workshops in Swarm Intelligence and Coordination. His research interests are in the field of Swarm Intelligence and Coordination in Multi-agent Systems.

Pascal Perez, associate professor, is presently developing an international research network called "Human Ecosystems Modelling with Agents (HEMA)". Multi-agent system approaches are used to implement companion modeling with local communities in the Asia-Pacific region. Field research is used to nurture a postgraduate course based on these innovative methodologies. Associate Professor Perez's research interests include water management, cropping systems and evaluation of irrigation efficiency, crop water balance modeling, and simulation of social/environmental interactions through a Multi Agent Systems approach. He has worked extensively in Western Africa, Middle East, South East Asia (Indonesia, Thailand). His published papers have appeared in Environmental Modelling & Software, Agronomie, and Agri, Ecos & Env.

Nahanni Pollard is a third-year PhD student in the School of Criminology at Simon Fraser University, and currently works as a Research Advisor for the Vancouver Police Department. Her research background focuses on criminal justice system analysis, chronic offenders, sentencing practices, police studies, advanced statistical techniques, and spatial analysis of crime patterns. Her BA and MA are both from Simon Fraser University, where she has studied primarily with Patricia and Paul Brantingham.

Fang Qiu is currently an Associate Professor of GIS and Remote Sensing at the University of Texas at Dallas. He received his PhD from the University of South Carolina in 2000. Dr. Qiu's research and instructional areas are remote sensing, neural network and fuzzy logic, GIS application software development, spatial analysis, modeling and simulation, and their application in public health and crime related problems. His research work at the University of Texas at Dallas is being funded by major federal government agencies, such as NSF, NASA, EPA, CDC, and so forth.

J. Raul Ramirez is the president of R2 Research and Consulting, a Mapping and GIS consulting company in Columbus, Ohio. Before that, he worked at The Ohio State University Center for Mapping and retired in 2005. Doctor Ramirez has more than 30 years of research experience in mapping and GIS and has published more than 60 technical papers describing his research.

Alison Ritter is an Associate Professor at the National Drug and Alcohol Research Centre, with adjunct appointments with the Regulatory Institutions Network, The Australian National University and the Key Centre for Ethics, Law, Justice and Governance, Griffith University. After completing her MS in Clinical Psychology, she worked full-time as a clinical psychologist. During this time, she commenced her PhD in treatment outcomes associated with acquired brain injury. A subsequent move to a policy position with the Victorian Department of Human Services led to a secondment to establish the Turning Point Alcohol and Drug Centre on behalf of Government in 1994. As Deputy Director of Turning Point Alcohol and Drug Centre from 1995 to 2005, Alison completed numerous clinical research projects, including trials of new medications for the treatment of heroin dependence and managed epidemiological, health services research and evaluation. With an NHMRC Research Fellowship and a significant philanthropic grant, Alison is currently director of a major illicit drug policy research program, the Drug Policy Modelling Program in collaboration with scholars from The ANU, Turning Point Alcohol and Drug Centre and Griffith University School of Criminology. The goal of the work is to advance illicit drug policy through improving the evidence-base, developing new policy decision-making tools and understanding the best mix of policy options (law enforcement, prevention, treatment, and harm reduction) and the ways in which these different policy options dynamically interact. Associate Professor Ritter is Executive Editor of the Drug and Alcohol Review, Vice President of the Australian Professional Society on Alcohol & Drugs, and a member of the College of Problems on Drug Dependence (CPDD). A/Prof Ritter reviews for a range of competitive funding bodies and international addictions journals.

Alexander Rutherford is the Leader of the Complex Systems Modelling Group at IRMACS and an Adjunct Professor in the Department of Mathematics. Prior to joining IRMACS, he was the Scientific Executive Officer at the Pacific Institute for the Mathematical Sciences (PIMS). He holds a PhD in Mathematical Physics from the University of British Columbia and held post PhD fellowships at the Swiss Federal Institute of Technology (ETH) in Zurich, Switzerland, and the International School for Advanced Studies (SISSA) in Trieste, Italy. His research spans a wide range of fields within the mathematical sciences. In mathematical physics his main focus has been on quantum many-body problems. In health research, he worked on the design and evaluation of protocols for electronic health records, surgical waitlists and queuing theory and epidemiological compartmental models. His current interests include applying first principles from theoretical physics to problems in the health and social sciences.

Janis L. Schubert is a PhD candidate in Geospatial Information Sciences at the University of Texas at Dallas and a National Defense Science and Engineering Graduate (NDSEG) Fellow. Janis has a background in psychology, with a BA from Rice University in Houston, Texas (USA), as well as over 10 years of professional experience in computer software and database design and implementation. Her current research focuses on the analysis of space-time issues and the development of GIS applications to facilitate this analysis. She has presented research at the annual meetings of the American Society of Criminology and the Association of American Geographers.

Tonya Stroman is a second year MS student in Human Computer Interaction at the School of Informatics at Indiana University. Her main area of interest is user-experience in living and learning spaces. More specifically, she is interested in research involving virtual technology as a research and solution tool in these domains. Currently she is exploring these questions through her research in increasing habitability of space structures intended for long-term space missions.

Joseph Szakas is an Associate Professor in the Computer Information Systems Department at The University of Maine at Augusta. He obtained MS Degrees in both Computer Science and Geodetic Sciences, and received his PhD in Geodetic Science from The Ohio State University, where he worked at the OSU Center for Mapping. Dr. Szakas also worked at the Crime Mapping Research Center at the National Institute of Justice in Washington, DC. His research interests are in computational geometric algorithms for massively parallel machines and applying that research to the field of crime mapping.

George Tita is a Professor of Criminology at the University of California, Irvine. His interests include the study of interpersonal violence with a focus of homicide, urban street gangs, and the community context of crime. His methodological toolkit includes both qualitative and quantitative approaches, with a strong interest in mapping and spatial analysis. Tita is involved with an interdisciplinary group of scholars working to promote the use of spatial statistics and analysis throughout the social sciences. Additionally, Tita is continuing his work on modeling the epidemics/spatial diffusion of violence over space and time.

Michael Townsley is currently a Senior Research Fellow at the UCL Jill Dando Institute of Crime Science, University College London. Trained as a statistician, his research has focussed on crime analysis, problem-oriented policing and quantitative methods in a criminal justice setting, all with a view to preventing crime. His current research projects include the spatial and temporal modeling of crime and the analysis of large novel data sets.

Christian Trefftz received a BS in Computer Science from Universidad EAFIT, a MS in Computer Science from Western Michigan University and a PhD in Computer Science from Michigan State University. His research interest is parallel processing and its applications. He is currently an Associate Professor at the School of Computing at Grand Valley State University in Allendale, Michigan.

Mona Vajihollahi is currently a PhD candidate of computing science at Simon Fraser University (SFU). She is Project Manager and Research Assistant at the Institute for Canadian Urban Research Studies (ICURS) and the Software Technology Laboratories at SFU. Her research focuses on novel applications of formal methods, and computational modeling, and simulation of public safety and security systems. Her work includes developing intelligent decision support systems in Computational Criminology and new tools for analyzing civil aviation security procedures.

Pieter van Baal graduated in economics at Erasmus University Rotterdam and got his Ph.D. in criminology at the same university, on a thesis on computer simulations of criminal deterrence. He is presently a researcher at the National Institute for Public Health and the Environment RIVM in Bilthoven, The Netherlands. His research activity is focusing on ex ante evaluation of health policy measures, by studying effects on life expectancy, quality of life and health, using simulation methods in the framework of the RIVM Chronic Disease Model, of which he is one of the co-authors.

Alexa van der Waall received her PhD in Mathematics at the Universiteit Utrecht in the Netherlands. Her mathematical fields of expertise include differential Galois theory, number theory, and computer algebra. She developed and implemented specialized software code on the topic of differential Galois theory for the computer algebra system MAGMA at the University of Sydney, Australia. She is and has been involved in various scientific projects at Simon Fraser University (SFU) in British Columbia. Currently, she is a member of the Complex Systems Modelling Group in the Center for Interdisciplinary Research in the Mathematical and Computational Sciences (IRMACS) at Simon Fraser University where she develops systems dynamics models for various applied fields.

Arvind Verma has served in the Indian police for 17 years in the State of Bihar, holding several senior level positions such as Superintendent and Assistant Inspector General in the organization. His first degree was in Engineering Mathematics from the Indian Institute of Technology- Kanpur and he earned his PhD degree in Criminology from Simon Fraser University- Canada. His PhD work was concerned with analysis of criminal justice data using a variety of mathematical techniques such as Fuzzy Logic, Topology and Fractals. He has served as the Managing Editor of Police Practice and Research: An International Journal and continue to be its Continental Editor. He is an advisor to the Bureau of Police Research and Development in India. His current research interests are in Data Analysis and Visualization, Criminal Justice in India and Comparative Policing. He is the author of three books and numerous articles.

Xuguang Wang received his PhD in Geography from the University of Cincinnati. He is currently a GIS software engineer in the Environmental Systems Research Institute (ESRI), Inc. He specializes in developing raster-based spatial analysis functionalities. He has been involved in developing cellular automata and agent-based models for crime simulation purposes. His research interest also includes map animation and temporal GIS.

Heng Wei is an Assistant Professor of Transportation Systems Engineering at The University of Cincinnati. His research is on microscopic traffic simulation modeling, advanced technology and quantitative methods for highway safety, and traffic flow theory and characteristics. Dr. Wei is internationally recognized for his over 75 published papers and book chapters, and recipient of 10 national and international professional awards. Dr. Wei received M.S. and Ph.D. degrees from The University of Kansas, B.S. and MS degrees from Beijing University of Technology, China, all in Civil Engineering.

Melanie Wellsmith is employed as a Senior Lecturer in criminology at the University of Huddersfield. Prior to this she spent four years as a research fellow with the UCL Jill Dando Institute of Crime Science. During this time she was involved in numerous research projects, primarily using secondary analysis of police crime data. She has published in the areas of offender self-selection, stolen property and emerging methods of car theft. Her current research is focused on the locations of crime events; most notably the concepts of crime attractors, crime generators and risky facilities. In addition to her academic career, Melanie has worked as a special constable (volunteer police officer) and a crime analyst.

Ningchuan Xiao is an assistant professor at Department of Geography in The Ohio State University. His research interests include geographical information science, spatial analysis, and spatial decision support systems.

Index

D

E

F

G

H

I

J

L

M

N

O

P

Q

R

S